Introduction to
Systems
Analysis
and
Design

Fourth Edition

Igor Hawryszkiewycz

PRENTICE HALL

Sydney New York Toronto Mexico New Delhi
London Tokyo Singapore Rio de Janeiro

Acquisitions Editor: Matthew Coxhill
Production Editor: Andrew Brock
Cover and text design: Range Left Design
Typeset by Keyboard Wizards Pty Ltd, Allambie Heights, NSW

Printed in Australia by Star Printery, Erskineville, NSW

2 3 4 5 02 01 00 99 98

ISBN 013 896887 X

**National Library of Australia
Cataloguing-in-Publication Data**

Hawryszkiewycz, I.T. (Igor Titus).

    4th ed.
    Includes bibliographical references and index.
    ISBN 013 896887 X.

    1. System analysis. 2. System design. I. Title.

004.21

**Library of Congress
Cataloging-in-Publication Data**

Hawryszkiewycz, I.T. (Igor Titus).
    Introduction to systems analysis and design
    Igor Hawryszkiewycz—4th ed.

    p.   cm.
    Includes bibliographical references and index.
    ISBN 013 896887 X. (paperback)

    1. System analysis. 2. System design. I. Title.

| T57.6.H39 | 1997 | 97–35090 |
| 004.2'1–dc21 | | CIP |

Prentice Hall of Australia Pty Ltd, *Sydney*
Prentice Hall, Inc., *Upper Saddle River, New Jersey*
Prentice Hall Canada, Inc., *Toronto*
Prentice Hall Hispanoamericana, *SA, Mexico*
Prentice Hall of India Private Ltd. *New Delhi*
Prentice Hall International, Inc., *London*
Prentice Hall of Japan, Inc., *Tokyo*
Simon & Schuster (Asia) Pte Ltd
Editora Prentice Hall do Brasil Ltda, *Rio de Janeiro*

PRENTICE HALL

A division of Simon & Schuster

Contents

5   Requirements analysis   81

6   Interviewing   99

Preface

The fourth edition of the book consolidates many of the new topics introduced in the third edition. In particular, it describes system development by making a distinction between the development process, the management process and supporting processes in line with evolving standards, while placing greater emphasis on quality. It also emphasises the importance of communication by making distinctions between the kinds of communication needed in different phases of the development process, and stressing the importance of using suitable terms at different development phases. The fourth edition also introduces new material, especially on the object-oriented approach to provide a better balance with conventionally structured systems analysis. It also provides an introduction to open systems methods, especially the use of rich pictures, as well as introducing the trend to electronic commerce and data warehousing.

The book begins by describing the increasing variety of systems that are now being supported. It continues with a distinction between transaction systems that support business applications, and those systems that support the coordination that is essential in fostering teamwork.

The book then discusses the importance of good communication, especially during requirements analysis, and outlines different analysis approaches. It then describes the use of models to precisely define systems and describes both the structured analysis and the object-oriented approach. It continues its comprehensive coverage of dataflow modeling as well as entity-relationship modeling and various ways of describing processes. Object orientation, however, now has an additional chapter to describe its role in the development process, including emphasis on the use of cases and additional sections throughout the book describing the use of object-oriented techniques at different development phases.

This increased variety of systems leads to an increased variety of development processes. Thus apart from the linear cycle there are other development processes, each suitable for a different kind of problem. For this reason, the book introduces design in a more abstract way—it looks at what it is that we do when we design systems, such as generating ideas, evaluating them or choosing among alternatives.

Then the methods are introduced as a way of organizing these activities. The way of organizing itself depends on the kind of problem and there is some discussion on finding the best development process for a given problem. The book thus has a discussion on prototyping as well as considering approaches used in designing group support systems.

Systems analysis and design techniques continue to be introduced in the sequence in which they would be needed during systems analysis and design. The book first outlines the steps followed in analysis and design and then describes each step in detail, introducing the techniques to be used at that point. It then discusses how techniques for describing data, processes and flows can be integrated and how models developed during analysis can be converted to working systems during design.

The fourth edition of the book continues to be one for beginners. It does not assume any knowledge of systems analysis or design. However, it does assume that readers have some basic knowledge about computers. For example, readers should know that data is stored on computer disks and that these disks are controlled by a processor. Readers should also know that data can be input into a computer through devices such as cards or through terminals and that outputs can then be obtained on the terminal screen or from an output printer. Readers should also know that computers can communicate between themselves or remote devices via communications links. Some knowledge of programming and algorithms is also useful but not essential.

To assist students' understanding, additional examples have been provided. Each chapter is followed by discussion questions and problems to illustrate the techniques described. Four text cases are used throughout the book to illustrate the various methods described in the book.

Igor Hawryszkiewycz

The system design environment

1

CONTENTS

KEY LEARNING OBJECTIVES

Development, management and support processes

The importance of specifying systems

The role played by users, analysts and designers in an information system

The relationship between the various people in building information systems

The role of computers in information systems

The structure of computer-based information systems

◇ INTRODUCTION

Computers are now becoming part of virtually every activity in organizations. The earliest applications that used computers were business applications, such as keeping records of transactions, airline reservations, or the amount of goods that are available in a warehouse. There were also early applications in design problems, such as designing a building or setting up a project schedule. Their use has gradually expanded and now computers are increasingly used for everyday activities, such as sending messages and arranging appointments or meetings.

There are not only a variety of uses of computers in systems, but there are also many different ways to build systems. Sometimes a system just evolves. It may start with a very simple program to which more and more functionality is gradually added. Sometimes systems are built experimentally, trying out new ideas as the system is built. On the other hand, the development of an information system for a large business application must be carefully planned and monitored. Many information systems now use computer systems for manipulating information and are sometimes called computer-based information systems. This book is about building such computer-based information systems. It describes the different approaches for building them and the use to which each different approach is put.

PROCESSES IN BUILDING INFORMATION SYSTEMS

System
A collection of components that work together to realise an objective.

Information system
A system that provides information to people in an organization.

Management process
The tasks required to manage a development process.

Supporting process
A process to provide facilities needed by development teams.

System specification
A precise description of what the system must do.

User requirements
What users expect the system to do for them.

There are a number of activities or processes that are associated with building **information systems**. Foremost in this book is the **development process**, which is what we actually do to build a system. But there are other things that go on as well. For example, there is the **management process**, which is mainly concerned with organizing the work, ensuring that adequate resources are made available, and monitoring the progress of the work. There are also **supporting processes**, which provide developers with computers, manage documentation, and facilitate communications between people working in teams on projects.

ORGANIZATION OF THE BOOK

This book covers all of the processes identified above, but concentrates on system development. It begins by describing some typical systems in Chapters 2 and 3. It then describes how to choose what systems to build, and the importance of identifying what people require from the system and of developing a **system specification** that correctly specifies these **user requirements**. Chapter 7 then describes alternative development processes for building computer-based information systems. The book continues by describing modeling methods that can be used during system development. These models are used to gain precision and to avoid ambiguities that are often found in natural language system descriptions. Modeling techniques achieve precision by using precise modeling constructs and process descriptions, and by precisely defining system requirements. Many different modeling methods are used in practice; some to describe processes, others to describe data, and still others to describe information flows in systems. The book describes the methods used in structured systems analysis, as well as those used in object modeling.

The book then examines how to construct the specified systems. Chapter 14 begins by developing a top-level model of a new system and continues by describing the detailed techniques used in system design. Chapter 15 discusses the importance of interfaces to computers and explains how to design them. Subsequent chapters describe how system specifications are converted to a working system. Chapters 16 and 17 describe how data models are converted to a database, and Chapter 18 describes the conversion of process descriptions to programs. Precision is again emphasized in design. We need to convert the proposed model to a working system and not go through a process of interpretation, thus losing some precision. Chapter 19 outlines some practical methodologies that integrate analysis and design.

The book then describes project management processes in Chapter 20. It covers issues such as project planning, resource allocation, and monitoring project progress. Chapter 21 discusses strategic planning and its role in determining the sequence in which applications are developed in an organization. Chapter 22 describes some techniques used to assure system quality.

The book uses several text cases to illustrate the modeling techniques and design ideas. These cases are used in a number of chapters to illustrate how systems evolve during information system design. The cases emphasize two important design issues. One is integration of one or more existing or **legacy systems** to meet some new requirement; the other issue is distribution of processing across a variety of distributed locations. From this you will see how complex some of these systems are and what must be done to build them. You will also see why a book about analyzing, designing and building systems is needed.

Legacy system
An existing working computer system that is to be used in a new business process.

DEVELOPMENT PROCESSES

Methods of building **computer-based information systems** vary from *ad hoc* to highly structured. *Ad hoc* approaches are often used to build simple personal support systems—for example, a spreadsheet to keep the budget for a manager, or a personal system to keep addresses. A more formal approach is needed to develop larger systems, which are becoming increasingly complex. At the same time, there is an increasing demand to build systems that are in a sense *correct* and do what is expected of them. A formal, rather than *ad hoc*, approach is required to achieve correctness. It requires that system requirements must be exactly defined before actual construction begins. Otherwise, how can we say that the system is correct? As a result, there is a lot of similarity between building computer systems and building other kinds of systems. For example, if you look at Figure 1.1 you will see that there are a number of important activities in building a house. First, there is the concept, the dream house, which is generally reduced to a more concrete specification by taking into consideration the needs of the owners, their available funds, the rules that govern building, and any other constraints. This is often done by discussion with an architect with a knowledge of the building trade. The result is a plan that specifies the requirements of a system, and this plan must be followed by the builder to produce the required house.

The same thing happens when building a computer system. First, there is the concept of a dream system to solve a business problem. This is discussed and analyzed

Computer-based information system
An information system that uses computers.

to clearly identify the user requirements, while taking into account various needs and constraints. The requirements are then used to produce a system specification, which has the same purpose as a house plan, to specify how the future information system will satisfy user requirements. It is important here to distinguish between the initial concept and the resulting system specification. Both play an important role in the **development process**. The first comes up with an idea, whereas the second is the practical realization of that idea. In between there are other activities, such as carrying out a detailed analysis of the system and identifying detailed user requirements. All these detailed development activities will be described in Chapters 8 to 18.

There are other ways of building systems—for example, we may have a grand plan but build it piece by piece, just as we may build part of a house, but leave scope for later extensions. There are also experimental ways of building systems. We may build an initial prototype, experiment with it, discover new requirements, amend the system, and so on. This process, often used in engineering, enables new features to be added to the system at each step and to be tested before proceeding to the next step.

There are, however, some differences that distinguish the building of information systems from other systems. One important difference is that there are no universal

Development process
A set of steps used to build a system.

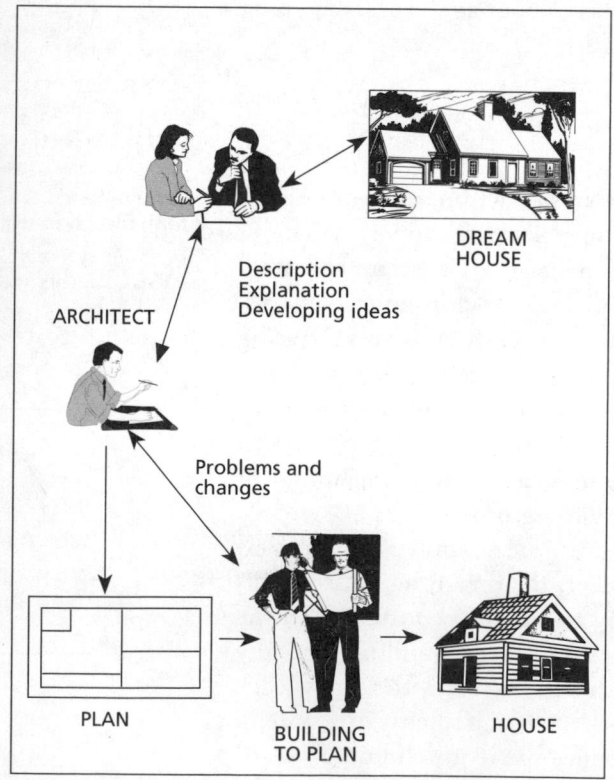
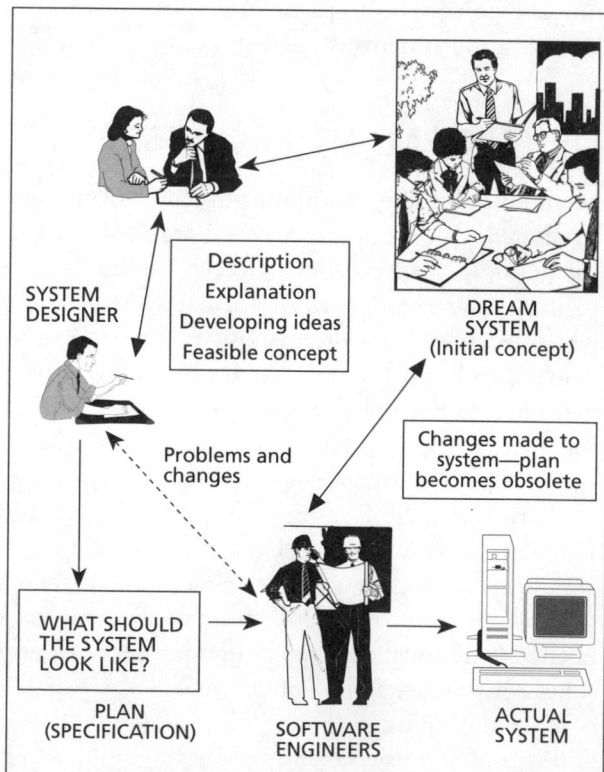

Figure 1.1 *The building process*

standards for information systems. Thus, for example, house plans are often checked by local councils and must adhere to building codes. There are no such codes for information systems. Information systems' requirements also tend to change as development proceeds. Such change, because of deadlines, can often bypass the original plan, which can lead to the eventual breakdown of the whole process. In contrast, when building houses any change must be approved by the relevant authorities, again ensuring that standards are met. There is, however, increasing emphasis on developing universal standards and managing the process of change when building computer systems.

METHODS AND TOOLS

An engineering approach to building systems requires certain methods and tools to be used to ensure that systems are built in the most effective way. One term often found here is **system development methodology**. The methodology defines the set of steps followed to build the system. It also provides a variety of supporting methods and tools. **Modeling methods**, for example produce models which help us to understand the system and its requirements and then to develop system specifications. These models are primarily used in analysis. There are also **productivity tools** to help people develop the models and convert them to working systems.

A large number of system development methodologies and productivity tools are available for building computer-based information systems. Different methodologies use different sets of steps or processes to build systems, as well as different productivity tools. Good methodologies must include a way to determine system requirements. The methodologies must also provide supporting methods and tools which ensure that a system is built in the quickest and cheapest way, and they must pay special attention to simplifying user interaction with computers. The term *quality* is often used to describe systems that work well and satisfy all these criteria. We must thus choose the right method if we are to build a quality system. We will come back to this term many times in this book.

The usual sequence of steps in methodologies is to propose the solution, develop a system specification, and then design and build the system. Analysis is used during these activities to gain an understanding of an existing system and what is required of it. Usually analysis produces a system description and a set of user requirements for a new system. These requirements lead to the specification for the new system. Design, which follows, proposes the new system that meets these requirements. Once the design is approved, the system is built. A new system may be built afresh or by changing the existing system. There is some advantage when building a system to look for suitable existing modules and then put them together in a way that satisfies user requirements. This reduces the cost of building a system and the time needed to put it into place.

MANAGEMENT PROCESSES

Creating a new system requires many activities and involves many people. One of the most important activities is choosing the right problem to solve, proposing a feasible way to solve it, and describing this solution in a system specification. The

System development methodology
A predefined set of steps, together with a collection of tools used to design a system.

Productivity tools
Software systems that assist analysts and designers to build computer-based information systems.

Modeling method
A method used to construct a model of a system.

chosen system must also fit into the existing environment and must be very easy to use. It is often necessary to spend considerable time gaining a thorough understanding of the system and its problems. It is only after developing a good understanding that it becomes possible to propose changes that will produce a better system without causing unforeseen effects.

Once changes are proposed, it becomes necessary to ensure that the system is built in the most effective way. A myriad of things need to be done to create a system from its requirements. Equipment must be chosen and new programs written to support these processes on the equipment. The systems must be tested, and users must be shown how to use them. All of these activities must be properly organized and people assigned responsibilities to carry them out.

WHO IS INVOLVED IN BUILDING INFORMATION SYSTEMS?

There are a large number of different people involved in building an information system. Most people are aware of some of the more technical roles—in particular, the **programmers**, systems analysts, **business analysts** and **computer operators**. Perhaps the most important people, however, are the users.   *Users* are people who have a stake in the information system because they need the system to carry out their responsibilities within the organization. Such users are called system users or end users. The term *end user* is often reserved for users who not only use the system but also develop some of the computer parts of the system. Users play a very important role in systems analysis. They define the user requirements for the new system in the ways described in Chapter 5.

The organization's **management** is also involved in system development. Management is concerned with system efficiency and effectiveness. Managers want to know what is going on and whether it can be done better. Hence, they are interested in what is to be built and how it can improve the whole system. They are also interested in what resources are required to make any system improvements and whether these resources could be deployed better elsewhere.

To do its job, management requires reports of project progress in order to know what is being achieved. Management also requires clear statements of project goals, as well as estimates of resource use and completion times. Many systems analysts find management reporting demands a nuisance. However, it must be remembered that building an information system is only one of the activities of the organization. The organization could use the funds expended on a new system to expand its sales force instead. Thus, management must at all times be aware of what is going on to ensure that it utilizes the organization's resources in the best possible way. It is important to remember that management may also be making decisions at a number of levels. They may, for example, be deciding whether to open a new store and thus increase sales outlets, or to install a new computer to increase efficiency. New computer developments in that context will have to be justified in terms of overall organizational strategy, rather than simply choosing a computer system for a particular activity.

Programmer
A person who writes computer programs.

Business analyst
A person analyzing a business at the subject level.

Computer operator
A person who operates computers.

Management
People responsible for organizing and allocating resources.

ORGANIZING THE PEOPLE

In most organizations, people are allocated to departments which carry out the routine work of the organization, such as hiring people, and producing and selling the organization's products. Most organizations also have a department known as the Information Systems (IS) department, whose prime responsibility is to build and run computer-based information systems in the organization.

In the early days of computing, all computer systems were developed by the people in the IS department. The IS department was responsible for all computing equipment and was the only department with people who possessed the skills necessary to build computer-based systems. The IS department was important because it controlled a scarce resource—namely, computers and the people who develop systems for them.

Although the IS department was responsible for building and maintaining information systems, many other people were involved in deciding what was actually built; most importantly, users and management. This required liaison between the IS department and users to ensure that the equipment necessary for the new system was available and that the system would fit in with the computer development plan of the organization.

Many organizations have now distributed some of their computer equipment and personnel to other departments. The distribution of systems, and the ease of building them, has meant that it has become possible to shift the responsibility for building systems from the IS department to people in the organization's **business units**, who in many cases now have responsibility for building their own systems. They may either do it themselves, in the case of a simple system, or hire external experts or even get the IS department to do it. The role of the IS department has thus changed from being responsible for deciding what systems will be built, to being a service department that must compete with external organizations in meeting the needs of the business units.

Business unit
A part of a business responsible for a well-defined business operation.

In this environment, the IS department is often responsible for developing systems that are used throughout the organization, while end users develop systems specific to their local tasks. IS departments, rather than being responsible for all the computing work, are now required to coordinate the work of such end users and to manage the increasingly complex computer network. They also provide specialized consulting services and advice to end users.

In fact, many organizations have adopted the policy of **outsourcing**. This means that they create a separate organization out of their IS department. The IS department must run as an independent entity, providing service to the operating department in competition with other possible sources of this service.

Outsourcing
Arranging for computer processing to be done outside the organization.

WHAT DOES A SYSTEMS ANALYST DO?

Systems analysis is an important activity that takes place when new information systems are being built or existing ones are changed. Its most crucial role is in defining user requirements. But why are special activities, such as systems analysis, needed to build good information systems? Why don't these things happen as a matter of course in an organization?

Systems analysis
Finding out what a system does and what its needs are.

Systems analysis, often now called business systems analysis to emphasize its business emphasis, is needed in the first instance to clearly identify what is possible and how a new system will work. This includes gathering the necessary data and developing models for new systems. This is not an easy task because, in large systems, many people need to be satisfied and many conflicts resolved. In that context a systems analyst must play many roles. Primarily, **systems analysts** help people solve their problems by defining what new systems must do. In that role they must understand the problems, and suggest solutions and ways of implementing them. Often they must help resolve conflicts as different people in the organization may have different needs. Analysts have to justify their solutions to different classes of users, often in terms of the whole organization, and thus they are expected to see their work as being relevant to the whole organization. It is not always an easy job, as the analyst is often an agent of change where some people may not want change.

Thus, as a rule, systems analysis is difficult but rewarding work. There are many constraints imposed on the analyst and many people to satisfy. But there is the reward of successfully implementing a new system. A systems analyst must spend a lot of time talking to users and finding out how they use the system, any problems they may have with the system and what they expect from it. As a result, such work calls for good *analytical* and *communication skills.* Systems analysts must learn about the system and understand users' expectations of it. They should be receptive to new ideas but still have concern for users of the existing system and their needs. It is the systems analyst's job to satisfy the requirements of all these users within the constraints imposed by management.

The systems analyst must be able to find out details about the system itself. To do this, the analyst will have to look at such things as forms used in the system, data used by the organization's personnel, contents of computer files, and computer outputs and inputs. Systems analysts must also be able to work in environments that have considerable ambiguity and uncertainty. In such environments there are often conflicting accounts of what is happening and what is needed, and different users perceive different system problems. The systems analyst must be able to resolve these kinds of conflict and produce an agreed-upon statement of the system operation and problems.

Systems analysts must also be **creative** and imaginative in producing new solutions to meet user requirements. They must have knowledge of techniques and devices that exist outside the organization, as well as a good understanding of what is needed inside. They must then put all the pieces together in a creative way to satisfy these requirements. This, of course, may require more than one try. The analyst usually starts with more than one possible solution. Some of these solutions may be totally unsuitable, whereas others may be acceptable after some changes have been made. Such solutions may then be amended and then justified again. Often this is done in an **interactive** way and at all times systems analysts must be responsive and creative, using all their knowledge to work toward an effective and acceptable solution.

Systems analysis has become more difficult over the last decade or so. Early systems analysts worked on relatively simple systems which did only one thing or had only one function. Now systems tend to be more complex, using data from a large number of sources and a larger variety of equipment than was available with early systems.

System analyst
A person who analyses the way the system works and its problems.

Creativity
Coming up with new and innovative ideas.

Interaction
The way people work together to achieve a goal.

Consequently, systems analysts need better tools to assist them in their analytical work. A major objective of this book is to describe such tools and how analysts would use them to analyze systems.

SUPPORTING PROCESSES

There are also a number of supporting activities that are part of information systems development. One of the most obvious is to ensure that the necessary equipment is provided for building the systems. But there are other needs here—in particular, providing support for people to work together on teams and for documenting the work.

THE IMPORTANCE OF TEAMWORK AND COMMUNICATION

Information systems are built by teams of people. These teams must include people with the expertise needed to build the system and to organize the teams in ways that suit the development process. In Chapter 7 we will outline different development processes and the best team structures to support them. Team structures must be chosen to ensure that the system is built in the minimum time. It is necessary to ensure that tasks are assigned to team members with the expertise needed by the tasks. It is also necessary to provide the **communication** paths that ensure that all team members are aware of each others' activity so as to avoid overlap and unnecessary delays and to ensure that everyone is working toward the same goal.

Communication
Interchange of information between people and/or machines.

KEEPING TRACK OF DESIGN DOCUMENTS

Documentation plays a major role in communication processes. Documents describe the status of tasks and must be distributed quickly to those team members that are affected by these tasks. Documents include the system specifications themselves, as well as designs of specific parts, test specifications and the actual programs. All these documents are related, but they can also change during the development process. They are used by different people to build different parts that eventually make up the whole system. In large systems these documents may well number in the hundreds. Special care must be taken to prevent errors arising because team members do not have the latest documents. The term **configuration management** is used to describe systems that manage documents.

Configuration management
Managing a configuration.

SYSTEM STRUCTURES

One question that people often ask when discussing system analysis and design is: what is a system? What is it that we are generally analyzing and designing? There are a number of ways of answering this question, depending on the general approach that is being used in design.

One view of the system is that shown in Figure 1.2. It simply shows the system as a computer system and the components that make up a computer system. The system in Figure 1.2 is made up of three components: a computer, a file for data

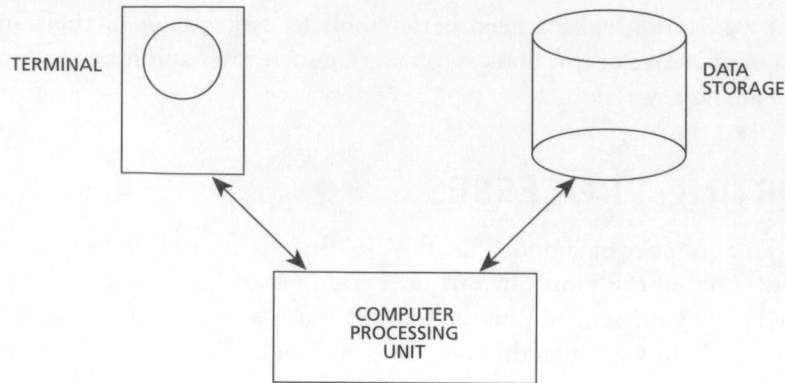

Figure 1.2 *The computer as a system*

storage and a terminal that provides an interface to the user. The figure also shows the connections between these three components.

The view of the system shown in Figure 1.2 is too constrained for the purposes of this book. It simply describes computers and not how they are used. Our aim here is to study systems that use computers to solve problems for users. We will not use the view in Figure 1.2 in this book because we are considering systems with a wider scope than simply computers. We will study systems that include computers to solve some wider problem.

Another way to view systems is shown in Figure 1.3. This is a more theoretical or abstract view that concerns the fundamental systems issues. Theoretical approaches to systems have introduced many generalized principles. *Goal setting* is one such principle. It defines exactly what the system is supposed to do. Then there are principles concerned with system structure and behavior. One such principle is the **system boundary**. This defines the components that make up the system. Anything outside the system boundary

System boundary
The set of system components that can be changed during system design.

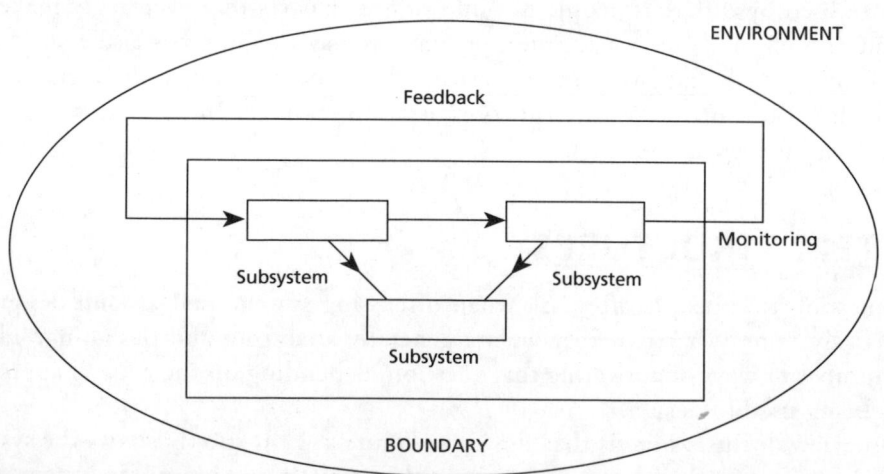

Figure 1.3 *A theoretical view of systems*

is known as the **system environment**. A system can be made up of any number of **subsystems**. Each subsystem carries out part of the system function. Subsystems are important because they can help to handle systems complexity and thus improve the understanding of a system. Each subsystem carries out some part of the system objective. The subsystems communicate by passing messages between themselves. A good system will be made up of highly independent subsystems with minimal flows between them. Minimizing flows in turn minimizes complexity and simplifies the system.

There are also a number of principles concerned with system behavior. One such important principle is feedback. **Feedback** is the idea of **monitoring** the current system output and comparing it to the system goal. Any variations from the goal are then fed back into the system and used to adjust it to ensure that it meets its goal. To do this it is necessary to monitor the system to see if it is meeting its goal.

We will not emphasize the theoretical approach in this book but will nevertheless use many principles from it. For example, the idea of subsystems is very important. Any information system contains many subsystems. Some may use computers; others may be manual processes. Goals are also important in information systems. Each such system has a purpose and must work toward that purpose. Feedback also arises in information systems. It provides the outputs that are used to monitor system performance and possibly to change some activities in the system.

In this book we place greater emphasis on the components that make up a computer-based information system, but at the same time we use the general ideas about systems. Our approach, however, goes beyond the simple system shown in Figure 1.2 and includes people as well as processes.

Thus the general view of the system used in this book is shown in Figure 1.4. Figure 1.4 views systems as collections of *people, computer networks* and *processes* that define the **formal interactions** between people such as one person sending a form that requests some action from another person. In addition, there are the more **informal interactions** that take place in any organization, which are now increasingly supported by computers through systems such as electronic mail. Processes themselves are now receiving more attention in organizations. They define how systems work and they must be properly designed to ensure that systems work well.

PEOPLE, PROCESSES AND DATA

People, of course, are an important component of any information system. Information is produced and used by people in an organization. People use this information in their everyday activities to make decisions on what is to be done. Such decisions may be routine; for example, a bank teller may use the computer to check the account balance before allowing a withdrawal. There may also be more complex decisions; for example, what shares to include in a share portfolio or what supplier to select for a given mix of parts and prices.

Information systems must support all of these kinds of user activities. To do this they must establish **processes** that ensure that the right people receive the right information at the right time. These processes determine what is to be done with data as it enters and passes through the system. For example, what do we do when

System environment
Things outside the system study that can effect system behaviour.

Subsystem
A part of a system.

Feedback
Using variations from a system goal to change system behavior.

Monitoring a system
Checks made to see if a system is meeting its goals.

Formal interaction
A set of rules that define how people must interact.

Informal interaction
Working together without a set of prearranged rules.

Process
A set of steps that define how things are done.

Figure 1.4 *The basic components of a computer-based information system*

a customer order arrives? There must be a process that defines how the order is to pass through the system and the people that will deal with the order. The process will tell us who to send the order to and what that person will do with it. Thus processes must support the tasks carried out by each person, as well as the *interaction* between people. Interaction between people is being given more attention in computer systems, because good systems should make it easy for people working toward the same goal to communicate with each other. We will return to the subject of interaction in Chapter 2.

Finally, there is the *equipment* that is used to store the data, move it around the organization and carry out any computation in data. The equipment includes the computers themselves, their disk drives, input devices, interfaces to computer users, and any communication devices that may send data to computers from remote places or send data between two computers. There are, of course, other kinds of equipment used in information systems, such as filing cabinets and drawers or microfiche, but, in this book, these are of secondary interest only. A system like that shown in Figure 1.4 has many of the characteristics of the system in Figure 1.3. It has a boundary and interacts with its environment. It has many components, including equipment and people. It also has flows between these components. There is also feedback, because outputs from the system can influence its operation.

Our goal is to build computer-based information systems that support people in the organization. This goal may be to improve an organization's accounting system in order to produce new reports. It may be to speed up the processing of orders. It may also be to improve the way that people work and *interact* in the organization and to inform them of any actions they must take. Interaction between people may be both very *formal and structured,* as in many business systems where everyone has a prearranged responsibility. Or it may be *informal*, where people simply interchange messages to inform others about what they are doing or to ask questions. Interaction may also support **collaboration**, where people decide on a common goal, such as developing a report or arranging a meeting. Thus, more and more importance is being placed on using computers to support *communication* within organizatons' business processes in order to improve interaction and teamwork.

Collaboration
Two or more people deciding together on their future activities.

DATABASES—A VARIETY OF ARTIFACTS

Information systems also include data. The term **database** is often used to refer to the data stored on a computer. The database in its broadest form is all the data in the organization. It not only includes the structured records, but can also include forms, letters and notes that people may keep. Commonly, however, the term *database* refers to only that part of the information stored on computers. In the past, this used to be mainly the structured records, such as accounts or orders; now it increasingly includes text documents, images and other kinds of artifacts.

Database
An organized store of data.

Until recently, most data processed by computers were numeric or alphanumeric data concerning the system. An example is inventory databases containing records of the quantity of items held in a warehouse. Similarly, financial data may contain account names and the balance against each account. Recent developments allow the extension of the kinds of data in information systems to include data other than records. It is now possible, for example, to store graphs or even pictures on computers and to combine these in the same document. The term **multimedia** is frequently used to define the storage of data other than records. These media include record data, graphs, pictures, or even voice and movies. There are now systems available that can process these media, display them on workstations, and allow users to combine information in various media into one document.

Multimedia
Integrated storage of information in different media such as graphs, voice, video or alphanumeric data.

As a consequence, the terms *database* and *file* sometimes imply a very restrictive viewpoint on information processed on computers, as they are usually closely associated with record-based information. Furthermore, the types of structures used on computers are more than just collections of records. We can now store reports made up of components of different media, records that include graphs and so on, or messages that contain voice. We thus use the term **artifacts** to refer to the various objects that can now be processed on computers.

Artifact
An object processed by a computer.

PERSONAL SYSTEMS

Computer-based information systems may be very simple systems like that shown in Figure 1.5. Here the system supports one person only to keep track of their records. In this system a person has a small computer, sometimes a laptop, and enters data into that computer. The data may be simple records such as daily sales. One entry is made for each sale. The entry states the item sold (e.g. a hammer), the quantity of items sold (e.g. 30) and the sale price (e.g. $95). Each entry is stored as a record on a file on the computer disk. At the end of the day, the computer can generate reports from the stored file showing total sales and sales trends. The user can use this information to make decisions about what items to stock or to plan future advertising

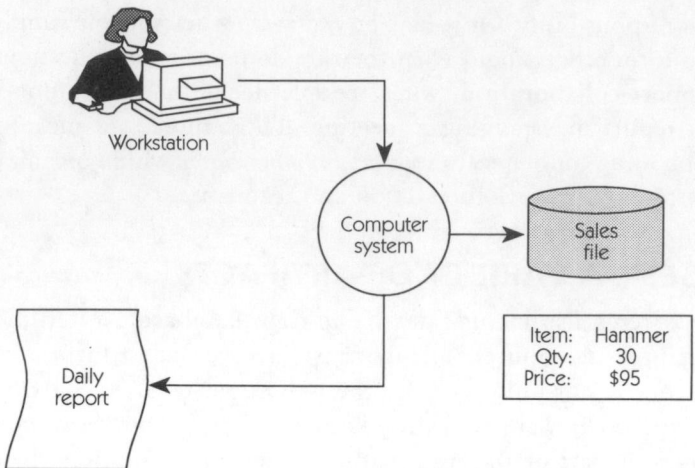

Figure 1.5 *A small computer-based information system*

campaigns. Designers of such systems must decide how to store the needed data in the computer and then design the software that will allow users to use this data.

Most systems, however, are more complex than the one shown in Figure 1.5. They typically support interaction between a number of people and use more than one computer system. They allow personal systems to be interconnected as a **computer network**, with individual systems centralized or distributed.

CENTRALIZED SYSTEMS

In a centralized system like that shown in Figure 1.6, a number of users are connected to a computer system through terminals, or what are now more commonly known as workstations. The computer system supports a number of databases, with two, the inventory and financial databases, shown in Figure 1.6. The computer system contains the program that allows users to access the database. Many centralized computer systems support structured processes made up of a *predefined sequence* of steps, where the completion of a step by one user initiates a predefined action by another user.

Data warehousing and data mining

Most centralized systems, in many organizations, are used to maintain a central repository of records. For example, banks, insurance companies and airlines need to maintain records of their customers. A popular term used for this kind of system is **data warehousing**. Here all company-wide information is stored on one large database, which is made available to users throughout the whole organization. Most data warehousing is going beyond simply storing current data. It now provides better access to historical information to allow anslysts to study patterns in past activities. Such historical data can contain a large amount of undiscovered information. This information may be in the form of patterns of events that, on their own, have little significance but when combined yield interesting insights. Analysis of such information, because

Computer network
A set of computers connected by communication lines.

Data warehousing
The storage of large volumes of data for organizational use.

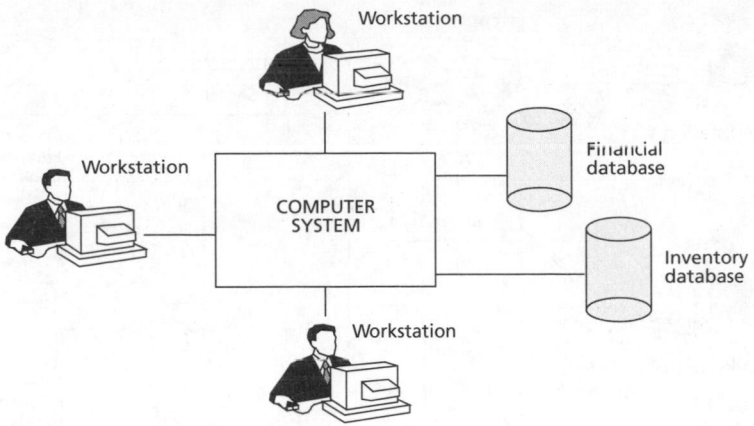

Figure 1.6 *A centralized system supporting a number of users*

it tries to unearth what may not be obvious, is known as **data mining**. Such analysis may look at areas such as examining insurance claim patterns, investment decisions, and so on, to give the organization an idea of what people do and how to react to it. For example, it may be possible to find a correlation between purchasing habits and economic factors. Similarly, emerging patterns of insurance claims may be detected, which would have an obvious impact on premiums.

Data mining
Looking for patterns in databases.

DISTRIBUTED SYSTEMS

Typically, however, computer systems are now becoming more distributed, and most organizations have more than one computer system connected together to form the computer network. Furthermore, as workstations become more and more powerful, it is becoming more common to carry out a significant amount of computation on the workstation itself. One common configuration is known as the client-server configuration.

Client-server systems

In a **client-server** network, the workstation is known as the client, while the computer system is known as the server. The server stores the data commonly used by its connected clients, as well as common programs for the users. When a computation is needed, both the data and the program can be sent from the server to the client workstation; the computation is then completed on the workstation and the data returned to the server. Alternatively, the client can request the server to carry out some computation and return the result.

Client-server process
A process that describes how a server provides a service to a client.

A network can be made up of many servers and each server can support a different database. One such system is shown in Figure 1.7. Here Server 2 supports the financial database and Server 3 the inventory database. There is also Server 1, which provides some local services to the workstations, such as printer services.

People in the network can access any of the servers through their workstations. Links between the computer systems allow workstations connected to one system to access data in other systems and reports to be generated using data from all systems.

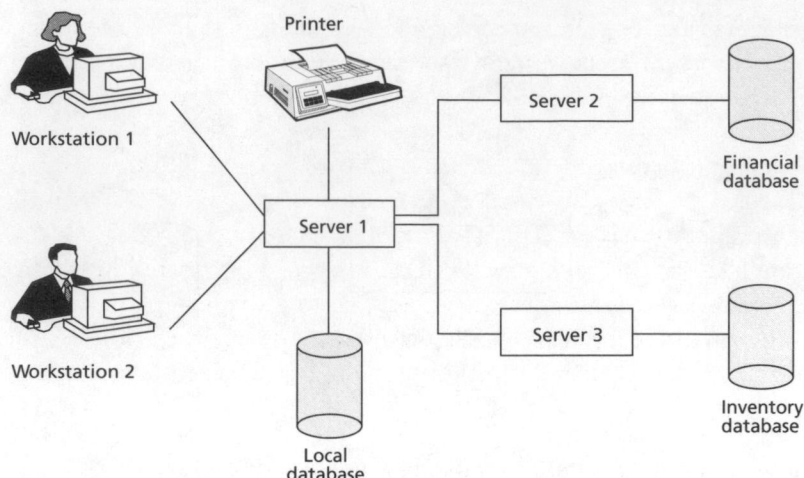

Figure 1.7 *A computer network*

Computer networks introduce their own design issues. One, for example, is how to distribute the database. Another is that it is important for any distribution to be **transparent** to a user. In a transparent system all the user has to do is request an action in the system and obtain a response, but not be concerned with the machine which carries out the action. Or the user accesses data as if it were on one machine, with the system itself taking care of the distribution.

In most organizations, computer networks now support virtually all of the organization's functions. Thus many organizations have their financial data, production outputs and plans, current inventory, sales and personnel records stored on their computer systems. These systems have many users, many kinds of inputs and many kinds of output reports. It is still common for large, structured, corporate-wide functions to be supported by large computers that store the corporate database. Individual support is mostly provided by personal computers, whereas groups are supported by local area networks or by access to the large computer.

Connecting systems

Many organizations, however, have computers built by different manufacturers with programs written using different software. Such systems were often developed in different parts of the organization. Special care is needed to connect systems into networks. Such networks are known as **heterogeneous** networks, as compared to **homogeneous** networks where all computer systems use the same equipment and software. A problem arises when organizations wish to develop business processes that can span a number of different systems and must thus construct heterogeneous networks. They must decide whether to totally redesign their systems using homogeneous software and hardware, or to come up with structures that support connection of heterogeneous systems.

An important aspect of using heterogeneous systems is how to gain access to data at these systems in a way where location is transparent to the user. There are two options in **integrating** databases at more than one system. One is to integrate

Transparent access
Accessing data from a network independently of its location in the network.

Heterogeneous network
A computer network made up of different computers and software.

Homogeneous network
A computer network made up of the same computers and network.

Integrated databases
A set of databases managed by a single controlling system.

them by placing them under one controller. The other is to have a **federated** system where databases at different systems are individually managed but can be accessed in a unified way to solve a particular problem. Figure 1.8 shows one way of federating databases.

The nodes in a heterogeneous network, shown in Figure 1.8, are accessed through correcting software that can exchange messages between heterogeneous systems. Application programs that use data from more than one node must access the network nodes through this software. Such integration is becoming more important, because new business procedures are increasingly required to use information from more than one existing system. Such correcting software can be specially written, although the World Wide Web is increasingly seen as providing the needed connectivity through Intranets.

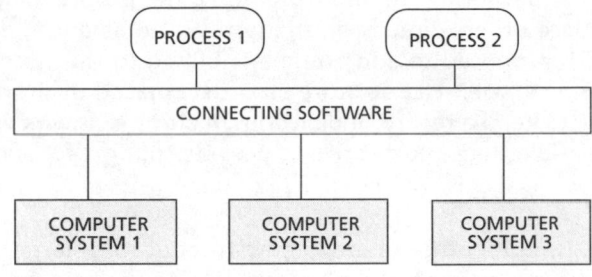

Figure 1.8 *Connecting heterogeneous systems*

Issues in network design

There are a number of other issues introduced by networking. One important issue is **privacy** or **security**. Security must be provided to prevent information being lost or destroyed. Privacy is needed to ensure that users connected to such systems do not either deliberately or inadvertently access—or, what is worse, change—information that does not belong to them. Thus a system like an interactive marketing system must be built in such a way that producers cannot gain access to orders placed with other producers and consumers cannot gain access to orders placed by other consumers.

TEXT CASE A: Interactive Marketing

SITUATION
A cooperative organization for producers of perishable goods has been formed to assist the producers to sell their products. The producers are all located close to one another, and the cooperative's objectives are to advise producers on the products they should sell and assist them to sell their products. The cooperative includes a large number of producers of perishable goods, as well as a large number of consumers or sales outlets. Each consumer usually buys a small proportion of the goods. For this reason the producers, or the cooperative on their behalf, must advertise available products widely as soon as they are available, almost on a daily basis. A distribution network is also needed to get the goods to their consumers as quickly as possible to prevent loss through wastage. The problem is further complicated by the fact that there is a range of goods and a large number of consumers

Federated database system
A set of databases managed independently but accessible in a unified way.

Privacy
Ensuring that information remains accessible to one or a selected number of people.

Security
Ensuring that computer system faults do not destroy the information stored about a system.

each with a different preference. For example, the goods may be different kinds of fish, such as tuna, shark and so on. Each kind of fish or catch can be of a given size or quality, and catches can vary over time. Consumers may be restaurants, supermarkets or small shops. Each may have specialized needs for some of the products.

The cooperative has proposed that an interactive marketing system be developed to connect the producers and consumers. The proposed system would look like that shown in Figure 1.9. The proposed system would support a number of activities that are needed to get the product to the consumer. First, consumers must be informed about the availability of the product. To do this, the system would allow producers to record their available products and provide an enquiry system to look up these products. These are illustrated by functions 1 and 2 in Figure 1.9. The information about products is stored in a file, named MARKET-DATA. Then subsystems must be provided to allow product orders to be placed and deliveries of the products arranged. Finally, an invoicing subsystem is needed to arrange payments.

To ensure that deliveries are made promptly, the proposed system also allows consumers to place orders directly on the system and arranges deliveries of these orders. Later it is proposed to add automatic billing to the system. The proposed system includes an ORDER-FILE to store all orders placed in the system, as well as a DELIVERY-FILE to keep a record of deliveries. A study is now needed to determine whether it is feasible to use computers to provide support for such a system.

ISSUES

One important issue identified here is how to educate a large number of users, most of whom have little contact with computers, to use computer systems in their everyday work. Another issue is who will maintain the proposed system, which will be utilized in a manner similar to that shown in Figure 1.6. The producers and consumers will have a terminal connected to a central computer with access to data on the computer database, but there is an option of actually distributing the processing

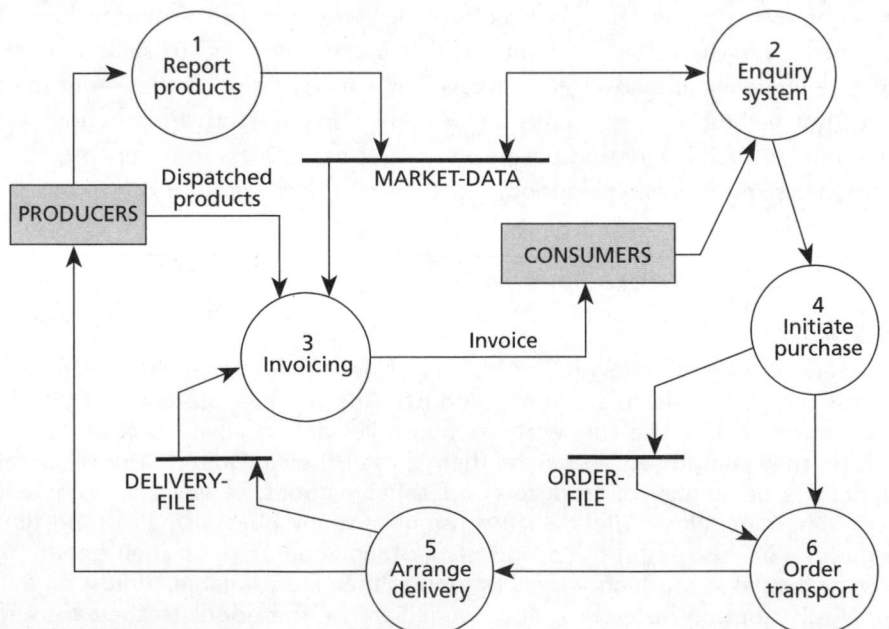

Figure 1.9 *An interactive marketing system*

across a number of computers. There has also been a suggestion that the computer store and display pictures of the products offered for sale.

There are some shortfalls in the system described so far. It does not support direct contact between producers and consumers but only allows them to access data on the same database. Thus an important human element is removed, preventing activities such as negotiating a price. It is also difficult to keep track of the progress of an order and to answer questions on expected delivery times. We will deal with some of these issues in Chapter 2.

 ## SUMMARY

This chapter defined what is meant by computer-based information systems and systems analysis, and discussed what is involved in designing such systems. It described trends to integrate processing across a number of distributed sites. Computer-based information systems are made up of people, procedures and equipment. Systems analysts design computer-based information systems that help the organization's personnel in their work.

We saw that a wide variety of people are involved in a system and that systems analysts must work with all the people involved. Hence, analysts are required to have good communication skills. It is also necessary to provide systems analysts with good tools to assist them in their work.

 ## DISCUSSION QUESTIONS

1.1 What are the main components of a computer-based information system?

1.2 What are the main processes in systems development?

1.3 Why is systems analysis necessary?

1.4 Who are the main personnel involved in systems analysis?

1.5 What qualities should a systems analyst have? How would you acquire these qualities?

1.6 What is the role of users during systems analysis and design?

1.7 How does the IS department get involved in systems analysis and design?

1.8 What conflicts are likely to occur in systems analysis and design?

1.9 What is meant by the outsourcing of the IS department?

1.10 What are some important system principles?

1.11 What are the three main components of a computer-based information system and how do they relate to each other?

1.12 What are the characteristics of personal computer systems?

1.13 How has distribution changed the way in which systems work?

1.14 What are client-server systems?

1.15 Why is security and privacy important on distributed systems?

1.16 Why is it important to be able to integrate existing systems?

1.17 How has system distribution affected the way systems are built?

 EXERCISES

1.1 Consider the interactive marketing system. Can you propose some alternative structures for such systems? For example, what would the structure look like if:

(a) the producers were distributed across the country rather than within close proximity of each other?

(b) some of the functions—for example ordering and delivery—were carried out on different computers?

1.2 Is negotiation between producers and suppliers important? What facilities would have to be included in the system to support negotiation?

BIBLIOGRAPHY

Alter, S. (1992), *Information Systems: A Management Perspective*, Addison-Wesley, Reading, Massachusetts.

Elmagarmid, A.K. and Pu, C. (eds) (September 1990), *ACM Computing Surveys*, Special Issue on Heterogeneous Databases, Vol. 22, No. 3.

Heimberger, D. and McLeod, D. (July 1985), 'A federated architecture for information management', *ACM Transactions on Office Information Systems*, Vol. 3, No. 3, pp. 253–78.

Lucas, H.C. Jr (1986), *Information Systems Concepts for Management* (3rd edn), McGraw-Hill, New York.

Parker, C.S. (1992), *Understanding Computers and Information Processing: Today and Tomorrow* (4th edn), The Dryden Press, A Harcourt Brace Jovanovich College Publisher.

Schultheis, R. and Sumner, M. (1992), *Management Information Systems: The Manager's View* (2nd edn), Irwin, Homewood, Illinois.

Senn, J.A., *Information Systems in Management* (4th edn), Wadsworth Publishers, Belmont, California.

Whitten, J.L., Bentley, C.D. and Berlow, V.M. (1994), *System Analysis and Design* (3rd edn), Irwin, Burr Ridge, Illinois.

Systems for coordination

2

CONTENTS

KEY LEARNING OBJECTIVES

The importance of analyzing work practices
How people communicate in organizations
The importance of processes
The difference between working as individuals and working in groups
The different kinds of group activities
Alternative ways to build group support systems

INTRODUCTION

We can view analysis from two perspectives. One perspective is that of the system and what it is supposed to do. The other perspective is that of the work practices followed by people. These work practices include those followed by the people who use the information systems and by the people who build those systems. Work practice can be divided into what people do individually and what they do in teams. Because of increased emphasis on teamwork, analysis must ensure that systems meet objectives while also supporting teamwork within the system. This chapter will describe the ways in which people work together and outline how computers can be used to support these different ways. The next chapter will describe some specific business systems.

It is now common to make a distinction between planned work *and* situated work. *In planned work it is possible to predefine the tasks to be done and the sequence of doing them. Everyone can then be assigned a task and know ahead of time what is expected of them. Situated work is to some extent the opposite—here work cannot be predefined, but people carry out tasks as the need arises. People are now expected to be able to adapt to particular work situations using the knowledge about the situation that is available to them.*

There are, of course, other classifications of work. One other obvious classification is by the complexity of the problem itself. The problem may be a routine task, such as updating a record, or it may require a complex decision, such as how to make a large investment. This leads to a distinction between creative and routine tasks and raises the question of how to support these two kinds of tasks.

The kinds of teamwork supported by computers also depend on the organizational structure itself. There is a strong relationship between computers and organizations, because computer systems can influence the way people work and interact within the organization. This in turn can influence the organizational structure. We begin by describing the changing nature of organizations and then describe the kinds of interactions found in most organizations.

THE CHANGING ORGANIZATION

There are two ways of viewing the organization. One is as a traditional hierarchical structure. The other is a flatter structure with people working in task-oriented teams. Most organizations are usually a mix of the two with a trend toward the flatter structures. This trend places more emphasis on teamwork, with people working in task teams toward well-defined objectives. People in teams may include those employed by the organization and those outside the organization. Another emphasis is on the processes actually followed by people in organizations.

A HIERARCHICAL VIEW

An early accepted view of organizations, first proposed by Anthony (1965), sees organizations in the three levels shown in Figure 2.1—the *strategic* level, the *management* level and the *operational* level. The management structure is hierarchical and elaborates strategic objectives in a top-down way until tasks, which define the work needed to realize the objectives, are identified for the operational level. Thus people at each

Figure 2.1 *Organizational levels*

management level determine the tasks needed to be carried out at the next level and delegate these tasks to lower levels. The people at the strategic or top-management level decide on the broad objectives for an organization. The management level must acquire and arrange the resources to meet the goals, and define the detailed tasks to be carried out at the operational level. These resources are the people, machines, buildings and computers needed to accomplish the goals. The detailed tasks are then carried out by people at the operational level.

As an example, consider an organization that may be producing a class of product, say, perfumes. People at the strategic level may make a decision on the particular kind of product, the marketing strategy, including the target consumer group, and the funds to be invested. Management level personnel must then arrange resources to implement this strategy. This may include hiring staff, making promotion arrangements and even arranging production, if necessary. The operations level people then carry out the operational tasks such as preparing brochures, distributing perfume bottles or sending out invoices.

In such hierarchical organizations, coordination between people at the operational levels is through the hierarchy. Communications paths are such that any requests or difficulties at one operational group are reported to management, who then may coordinate with management of other operational groups to resolve any problems. Such coordination through the management structure is necessary to ensure that management is informed of any changes in resource requirements and that all levels of management are aware of changes at any point of the operational structure. This kind of structure has always assumed a relatively stable environment simply because a change to such hierarchical structures often requires major organizational changes.

TOWARDS FLATTER STRUCTURES

However, many organizations now exist in environments where customer preferences, as well as economic factors, are continually changing. As a consequence, organizations must continually change to meet rapidly changing demands in these more volatile environments. In addition, products often require inputs of many skills and must often be customized to particular customer needs. This requires organizations that can quickly bring together people who have such skills and that can make changes quickly at the operational level by rearranging both resources and the tasks that people do. We are thus looking for more adaptive structures that make it easier to bring people from different parts of the organization together and to rearrange their activities as customer needs change. Such rearrangement is often difficult if it is to proceed through a number of hierarchical organizational levels, each with its own priorities. As a result, there has been a tendency to reduce the number of levels and to encourage change by supporting coordination at the operational levels. Computers also make fewer levels possible because they make it easier to reduce information from objective to operational levels.

Workgroup
A group of people working to a common goal.

Empowerment
Giving people additional authority within an organization.

The result is what is sometimes known as the formation of **workgroups** concerned with specific and often limited tasks. Such workgroups are usually **empowered** to make decisions on the use of resources without reference to management, whose main goal in this kind of organization is to provide support to the groups rather than to direct them. Workgroups are focused, with specialists from various functions contributing to the task. Close collaboration in workgroups requires individuals to have a wide knowledge of the organization. In hierarchical organizations, each individual is concerned with their individual function, be it inventory control or financial management. In flatter structures, each individual must also have some understanding of the functions carried out by other groups with which the individual coordinates, as well as knowing how to coordinate with these groups. We thus make a distinction here between the organization's functions, often the responsibility of business units, and processes. **Functions** are tasks that must be done for an organization to operate—for example, purchasing parts, hiring personnel, and so on. **Processes**, on the other hand, define the coordination that is needed to ensure that these tasks are done in a way that accomplishes the organization's goals.

Function
A part that produces well defined outputs from given inputs.

Process
A component of a DFD that describes how input data is converted to output data.

A task team can be made up of people from a number of organizational units. Figure 2.2, for example, shows a team of people from the Personnel, Inventory, Marketing and Accounting departments. Such workgroups do things like jointly preparing a document—for example, a marketing plan as in Figure 2.2. Each workgroup may require people with different skills to match the objective of the workgroup.

Thus in computer system design there may be a group of analysts and a group of designers. They will meet quite often for discussions and make decisions on their next activity and what is to be done about designing the system. Then there are various engineering designs where one may, for example, be designing a building or a bridge.

This view of organizations has been elaborated by Drucker (1988), in what is now a famous paper which suggests that flatter structures are needed because organizations are becoming information-rich. This implies that most information resides at the operational level of the enterprise and work must be organized to make best use of this information. Flatter structures thus enable information that exists at these levels to be coordinated, which leads to better decisions. The flattening of organizational structures changes the way in which people work. It adds responsibilities at the operational level, placing more emphasis on control through coordination at that level rather than on direction from the management level. The way in which individuals work and interact with each other is also different. One individual may now interact with

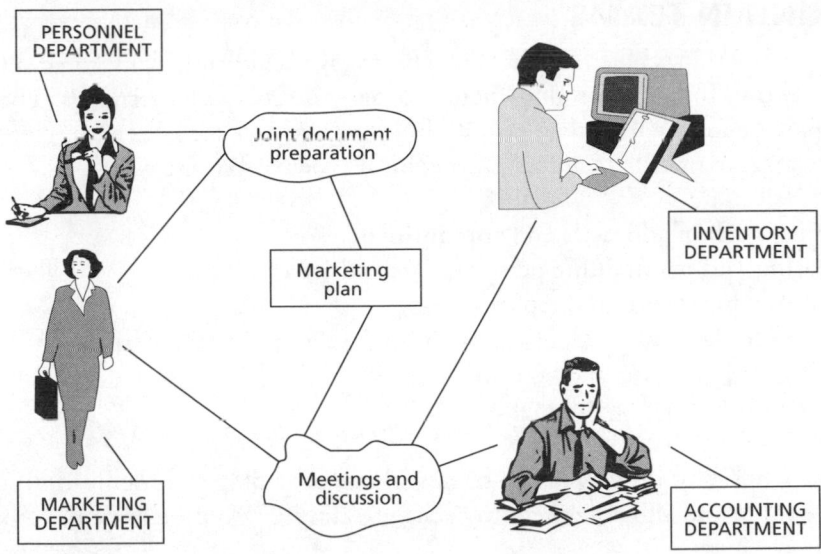

Figure 2.2 *Flat task-oriented structures*

individuals in many other groups. In hierarchical structures, interaction usually takes place only between individuals at adjacent hierarchical levels. Management in the flatter structures facilitates rather than directs activities.

Types of groups

Groups can be characterized in many ways—for example they may be *open* or *closed*. Open groups allow members to be freely added or deleted from the group. Groups may also be loosely or tightly *coupled*. Loosely coupled groups allow members to act independently of each other, whereas tightly coupled groups impose restrictions on such interactions. Many groups can also contain people from outside the organization, as for example, consultants.

There are thus many different kinds of groups and different kinds of computer support needed. There is also some advantage in drawing out the common characteristics of such groups to simplify the design of support systems. Sprague and McNurin (1993), for example, has attempted to classify different kinds of groups. These range in their degree of openness and coupling. They include:

- authority groups that support hierarchical relationships;
- meetings and committees;
- project teams and task groups;
- information exchange networks;
- business relationship groups;
- clerical processing groups; and
- social networks.

WORKING IN TEAMS

People do many things together in teams. These may include totally informal activities, such as meeting in a lunch room where they may discuss their activities. They may also prepare reports with other people, hold meetings, or do even simpler things like share a database. There are also mechanical types of activities such as:

- keeping track of addresses and appointments;
- preparing and maintaining personal files and letters;
- preparing documents and reports;
- finding and keeping track of information needed to carry out tasks;
- sending and receiving messages and files; and
- holding discussions with other people.

The important factors in supporting teamwork are providing communication support between people and allowing them to exchange and work on the same documents.

THE IMPORTANCE OF PROCESS

There is now considerable emphasis placed on processes in organizations. The term *processes* fundamentally describes the way we do things. It also defines the steps we follow in doing things. It is important that processes work well. If we do things in a sloppy and inaccurate manner, then we will not have a good outcome. The term *quality* is often used to describe how we want our processes to work. This word does not have a precise definition. It can mean having no errors in the system, or serving a customer in a minimum time, or reducing our routine work. It is often up to the organization to define what it means by quality and to set up processes to achieve it. Many people are now looking at the processes in their business and rearranging them to meet quality requirements; the term **business process re-engineering** is often used in this context. It means rearranging the way we do our business. Such rearrangement is not centered on increasing the use of computers. It simply asks how we want things done and whether computers will support us in doing these things better.

Business process re-engineering
Changing an existing business process.

Processes often require people to work together to reach some goal. This may be to increase sales, reduce delivery times or improve some other business operation. The type of support needed differs for each kind of group, depending on what they are doing. It will also depend on whether team members are at the same or different locations, and on whether they work at the same or different times. The term **asynchronous** is used where people refer to shared information at different times. **Synchronous** interaction is where people are in communication at the same time.

Asynchronous cooperation
Cooperation where the participants refer to shared information at different times.

A rough division may be made as follows:

- support for informal networking simply to interchange information between people;
- support for personal relationships that require a sequence of interchanges with records kept about them, as, for example, found in decision making;
- support for planned work where structured procedures are set up to follow a predefined process; and

Synchronous cooperation
Cooperation where the participants refer to shared information at the same time.

- support for design teams who must create new artifacts and whose work is situated rather than planned work.

Software known as **groupware** or **CSCW (Computer Supported Cooperative Work)** is now increasingly used to support teams. Such software must be able to support a variety of working environments. For example, if group members are at different locations, then group support through an electronic meeting may be needed. Another example of a group support system is where an appointments system is needed to make arrangements for meetings.

Groupware
Software that assists workgroups.

CSCW (Computer Supported Cooperative Work)
Systems that support groups of people working towards a common goal.

INFORMATION EXCHANGE AND PERSONAL RELATIONSHIPS

One of the most fundamental support tools for people is to exchange messages and information. This kind of interaction happens in any organization and includes telephone calls, meeting in corridors, messages scratched on pieces of paper, and so on. It can also be more formal and includes meetings, committees, and so on. It is important because it allows people to develop a perception of what is going on and what possible problems can influence their decisions. Perhaps the best known set of electronic support systems for this purpose are electronic mail and the Internet.

SUPPORTING INFORMATION EXCHANGE

There is now an increasing tendency to use computer networks to exchange information. The simplest support for message exchange is known as electronic mail, or **e-mail**, where users simply send messages to each other. Electronic mail systems are supported by computer networks. Such networks can be local to an organization or they can be interorganizational networks, such as the **Internet**. The Internet has now become almost a household name, with millions of people connected to its services as well as storing a myriad of information either as files on FTP (File Transfer Protocol) sites or as part of the World Wide Web. This includes the ability to send electronic mail, a variety of news groups on specialist topics, as well as search engines to find information based on specified keywords.

Networks within organizations are known as local area networks, where they support one organizational unit. Alternatively, **Intranets** are being set up to support communication across the whole organization. Intranets use the same technology as the Internet, but access is restricted to people within the organization.

Each user on such networks has their own unique electronic address, and all messages with that address are directed to the user. Most networks support information exchange that goes beyond simply electronic messages. This can include:

- attaching files to messages;
- broadcasting a message to a whole group or collecting information from a group;
- setting up bulletin boards and news services; and
- setting up file libraries.

E-mail
A way of using computers to exchange messages between people

Internet
A world wide public network allowing global exchange of information.

Intranet
A network supporting information exchange within an organization.

There is no particular protocol followed in sending messages using e-mail, nor is there any requirement for the receiver to respond to messages. Message interchange can become more structured by identifying special groups to whom messages are sent. For example, a message may be sent to all managers, or all salespersons, and so on. Facilities are now often provided for users to sort and store received messages, redirect them or respond to them.

The danger with e-mail is that people may suddenly find themselves flooded with messages, in much the same way as letterboxes are often flooded with advertising brochures. The next step is to provide a filter, where a receiver can specify the characteristics of received messages. An alternative is to use **bulletin boards**. Members direct all their messages to a bulletin board where they are posted and other members can look up their bulletin board at their convenience. Most of the early electronic messaging systems involved the exchange of textual information. Since the early 1990s the World Wide Web has become part of the Internet and can be used to store and distribute information in any medium.

Bulletin board
A space that stores messages accessible to all members by a cooperating group.

The World Wide Web and intranets

World Wide Web
A service supported on the Internet for the exchange of multimedia information.

The **World Wide Web** (WWW) uses a standard format to store and transmit information from one site to another using the Internet. It was rapidly accepted following its introduction in the early 1990s because it could be used to store multimedia data and provided the means to easily search through this data. Information on the WWW is stored as pages, with each page having a unique address, known as the URL address. An organization develops a WWW site, which has any number of pages, with one page, known as the home page, as the major entry into the site. This home page has links to other pages on the site which can easily be reached from the home page. Thus, all that is needed is to know an organization's home page address. Once this is found, all other pages at the site can then be traced from the home page. The most common pages on most sites include:

- a brief description of the organization's mission;
- news items about recent events and successes in the organization;
- frequently asked questions (FAQs) about the organization;
- descriptions of the organization's products and services;
- contact points and addresses; and
- in an increasing number of cases, the ability to place orders directly with the organization.

WWW sites can be used for many purposes. Perhaps the most common use is to publicize an organization's activities. Here the home page includes a brief description of the organization's mission, usually in the form of a description of the products and services it provides. Some sites now provide information like product catalogs, as well as help facilities to assist customers having problems with the organization's products.

A typical WWW home page (http://WWW.qantas.com.au) is shown in Figure 2.3. It shows the home page for the Australian airline QANTAS. The site provides information on its services to any Internet user. Thus there is a page on destinations and leisure holidays, and advice on business travel, including information for frequent fliers, how to make reservations and any specials currently on offer. There is also a news service that contains news releases about recent activities, interesting articles and even the in-flight entertainment guide for the current month. In addition, there are airline schedules for future dates that give the best route for a given start and end location, and there is arrivals and departures information for the current day.

Figure 2.3 is typical of sites that primarily provide information about their products and contact points. There is also an increase in the number of sites that allow direct ordering of services, although these have to take special precautions to ensure the security of financial transactions.

SUPPORTING PERSONAL RELATIONSHIPS

Support for personal relationships provides people with the services needed to communicate effectively and to maintain productive and satisfying relationships. Here we are concerned with things like groups forming opinions on and agreements for further action. Such group support systems introduce a new dimension into computing, as they must emulate the behavior of people in organizations. Thus not only is it necessary to solve the technical problem of allowing groups to interact using computers, but also to cater for the variety of social situations that occur in groups.

Formal meetings

Formal meetings or committees are perhaps the most common group interactions found in organizations. They are most often face-to-face at the same location. Computer support raises the possibility of holding a synchronous meeting with people at different locations. As a matter of interest, let us see what is needed to support such meetings. These are illustrated in Figure 2.4. First, each member would need a screen and the same information perhaps even the faces of the other members would appear on each screen. There must also be protocol control to define the process to be followed in the meeting. This is where there is a big difference between meetings where participants are face-to-face and those where they are at different locations. In a face-to-face meeting, the tone of voice, gestures, raised voices, all have some meaning and can influence the meeting. This is not the case where members are at different locations. Here we can only input messages into the system, and a process must be devised to control the flow of messages and display them to participants at either location. Such control can also make it difficult for individuals to gain unwarranted priority by raising their voices or because of their position. This leads to considerable debate about the conduct of such a meeting and whether the outcome is better or worse than a face-to-face meeting. It is generally agreed that further research is needed to determine whether electronic meetings produce effective results.

Figure 2.4 illustrates one advantage of electronic meetings where members are all at the same place. There is the link to the corporate database. Participants can easily gain access to information in the database and bring it forward for discussion at the meeting. This leads, of course, to the possibility of mixed electronic and face-

Figure 2.3 *QANTAS Airways' home page*

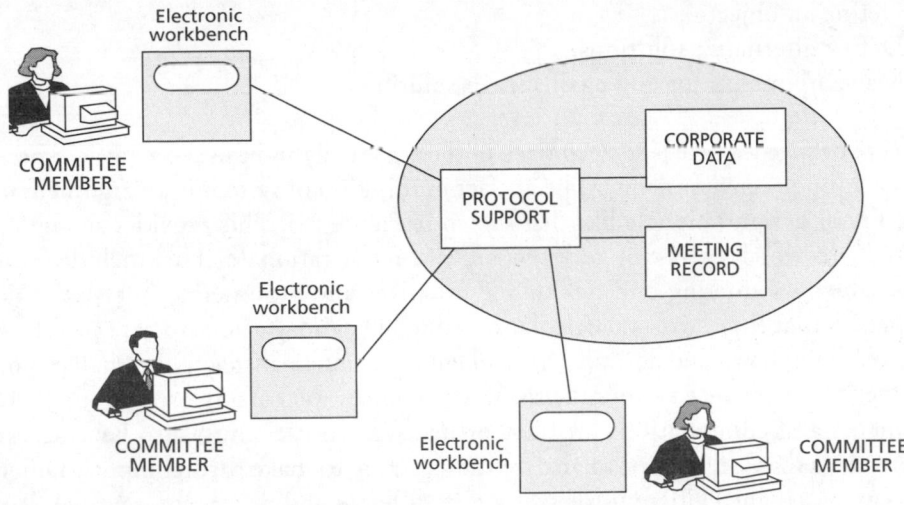

Figure 2.4 *An electronic meeting*

to-face components to the meeting. Information can be collected and displayed with participants at a distance, whereas actual discussion takes place face-to-face. Other tools can be also brought into the meeting—for example, support for decision making and argumentation.

Decision support systems

Decision support systems assist groups to make complex decisions. There are many ways to make decisions. Some decisions require an optimization algorithm—for example, scheduling of deliveries. Its goal is to reduce costs by scheduling deliveries in order to minimize travel expenses. You cannot simply choose the best delivery routes by entering a number of independent transactions. You would need to set up a number of trial routes, estimate their costs and gradually improve on them. You may also solve this problem by using a mathematical algorithm.

Many decision support systems are experimental in nature, where the user tries different inputs to see their effects. The response is used to try new inputs, and the process continues until a satisfactory result is obtained. Most decision support systems are based on a model that is continually refined. The user inputs some possibilities into the model and evaluates them. Then other possibilities may be tried. For example, different price trends may be input into a portfolio management system and their effect on a given portfolio examined. More sophisticated systems may try different price variations to find one that satisfies desired performance criteria. Share portfolio management is a typical decision support system, the question here being what shares to buy to get a balance of capital growth and income return. The user must enter expected trends and then try different portfolios to see how they perform against these trends.

A third kind of decision is one of a policy nature where one develops alternate positions and then justifies them by argumentation. The steps taken are:

Decision support system
A system that supports decision making.

1. Define an objective.
2. Define alternative solutions.
3. Make arguments for and against each solution.

The support needed here is to keep track of the arguments and the alternatives, especially in asynchronous environments. The artifact in this kind of system is an **argumentation structure** or **design rationale** like that shown in Figure 2.5. This provides an argument structure to which users can add new arguments or rationale. This includes simple actions such as entering and deleting alternatives and arguments, but also making summaries that may favor a particular decision. They may also associate people with particular arguments and activate them whenever a statement related to that argument is made. More advanced support provides references to artifacts used to support the arguments and computations on these artifacts. Each user must also have access to various tools that can be used to analyze the structure to make further inputs. Different users can be assigned different roles, and give different abilities, as for example, setting up a new alternative.

Decision support usually assumes asynchronous interaction, although there can be some advantage in synchronous discussion to resolve conflicts.

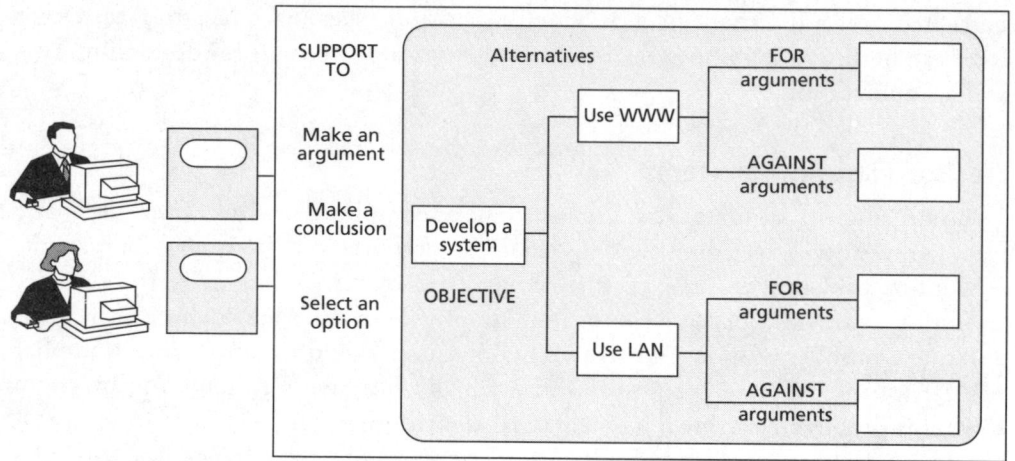

Figure 2.5 *Argumentation structure*

SUPPORTING PLANNED WORK

Prespecified or structured interactions are usually defined as workflows made up of a set of steps called **planned work**. The process is predefined as a sequence of steps, and each step is usually carried out by one person. For example, Figure 2.6 shows a process used to buy a part. This starts with a request for a part. The request is approved, purchases are arranged and a delivery is made. There will be one or more, often different, persons involved at each step. A further important property of interaction here is that each person may be at a different location. Furthermore, each person may carry out their tasks at different times. Thus a person enters a request at some particular time, whereas the approver can look at this request much later.

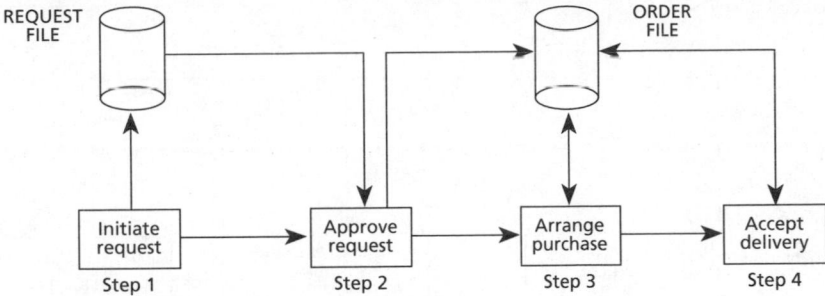

Figure 2.6 *Structured workflows*

One way is for them to simply pass messages between themselves. Thus a requestor will pass the request either as a form or by word of mouth to the approver. Another way is for coordination to be achieved through shared files. Each action is recorded by a person on a file. Such records are then used to inform others to carry out some action. In Figure 2.6 there are two files. One is a file of requests and the other a file of orders. A recorded request can activate an approver. Once the request is approved, it becomes an order and activates other people to begin to arrange a purchase. The next step is to accept a delivery when the parts are ready. Each step has some particular task, and each task may be carried out by a different person. Each task may update a file.

Systems like that shown in Figure 2.6 are often called **workflow processes**. The term *workflow* is used because there is a defined flow of information and defined actions to be taken at different points of this flow. This kind of process can be easily supported by computers. To do this we often use **transaction processing systems**. LOTUS Notes has become one of the more popular systems used to support such planned work.

TRANSACTION PROCESSING SYSTEMS

The term **transaction** is used here because it often implies an interaction with the database. Such interactions occur continually in a workflow, as people have to manipulate data at defined workflow stages. Computer programs can be used to allow people to access the database, make any necessary changes to the database and use them to initiate a further transaction. Thus if an order is approved, it becomes the completion of an approve transaction. This may then activate the arrange transaction, and so on.

Most computer systems provide software for transaction processing. These often include a standard computer procedure for making a transaction. One example of this kind of procedure is shown in Figure 2.7. The transaction system first checks the transaction to ensure that no erroneous data are input into the computer. The transaction must then pass through a number of checks. The first check is usually called an edit, which ensures that all the needed data are included in the transaction in a correct format. Thus, for example, we may check to see if an account number has been entered in a bank withdrawal transaction and if this is in the correct format.

Workflow process
A process made up of a predefined set of steps.

Transaction processing system
A computer system that manages transactions.

Transaction
A simple interaction with a computer database.

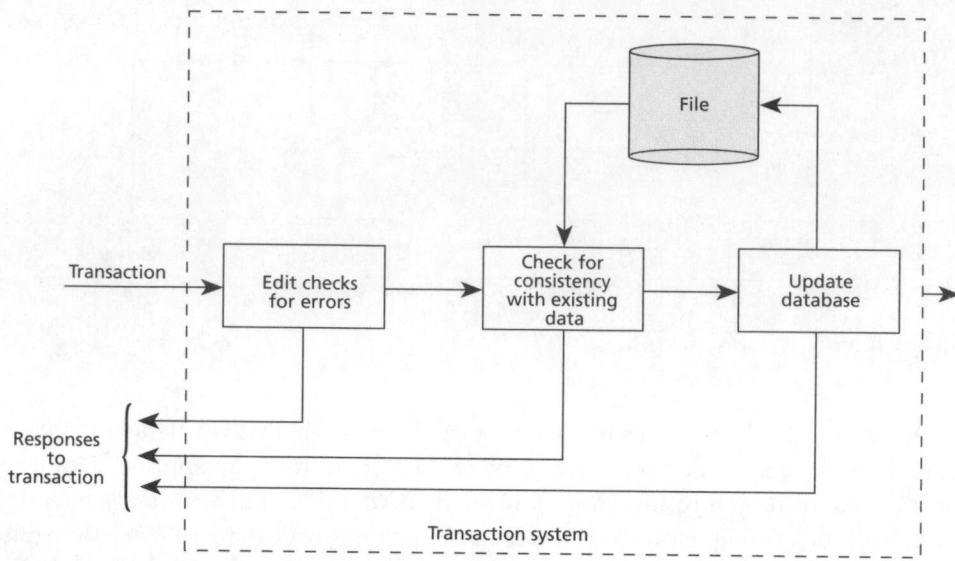

Figure 2.7 *Transaction processing*

This means that numeric data appear in numeric fields and alphanumeric data appear in alphanumeric fields. The edit also makes sure that there are no fields where information is missing. This is followed by checks which ensure that the input data are consistent with existing data in the database. A typical check here is to see if the account number in a bank withdrawal transaction actually exists in the database or whether there are sufficient funds to cover the withdrawal request. Once all the checks are made, the transaction is used to update the database.

The transaction system provides responses to the user as the transaction progresses through the system. Any errors and inconsistencies, as well as the result of the final updated database, are reported. Responses can be provided in a number of ways, depending on the transaction system mode.

Transactions may be input in *on-line* or in *batch* mode. In the **on-line** mode, transactions are input into the system as soon as they arise. In the **batch** mode, transactions are collected into batches which may be held for a while and input into the computer later, often overnight when computers are not busy processing on-line transactions. A common example of on-line systems is bank transactions. A bank withdrawal is entered directly into the computer system at the time the withdrawal is made. The person who entered the transaction receives an immediate response from the computer. Thus the system will immediately inform the operator if there are sufficient funds to meet the withdrawal.

Batched transaction systems do not provide such immediate responses. In a batch system, a number of transactions are collected before entry into a computer system. For example, a number of hourly work slips may be collected during the day and gathered into a batch. This batch will be input into the computer system at the end of the day, processed overnight, and the user will obtain any responses on the following day. It should perhaps be noted that batched transaction systems are not

On-line transactions
A transaction made through a terminal.

Batch system
A system that groups a number of transactions for later processing.

commonly used now, as there has been a trend to distributed on-line systems over the last few years.

SUPPORTING SITUATED WORK

Situated work is often unstructured. It often requires closer coordination than structured or preplanned work in a number of ways. First, the situation tends to change more rapidly, requiring team members to quickly adapt to the change and to coordinate their activities at a much more detailed level. Second, this closer coordination requires more face-to-face interaction. Planned work, on the other hand, can be carried out with less face-to-face interaction.

> **Situated work**
> Work where the next task is determined from the current situation.

Perhaps the most common example of situated work is **design** of an artifact, where different people work on different parts of the artifact. This artifact may be a joint report, an engineering design, a budget or a project proposal. Each part of the design must fit precisely with the other parts, but the final detailed artifact structure cannot be precisely prespecified. The design process also cannot be precisely defined because an outcome at one point of the design may require new and unpredicted work at other points. However, we know that the process is made up of a variety of tasks, some totally creative while others are more routine.

> **Design**
> Creation of an artifact.

The design process often starts by **brainstorming** for ideas for the design. This is a highly creative task where new ideas are proposed. It is often performed with close and spontaneous interaction between a number of designers. Most people suggest that coordination for this interaction must be synchronous or face-to-face to get this spontaneous interaction. We may then evaluate some of the ideas using fairly routine processes. This can often be done by individuals operating independently of the group, with the results brought together for further consultation. Then we may try other ideas until an agreement is reached. The interesting thing about design is that both the nature of the tasks and the interactions can change at different stages of the design process. We may go from highly creative interaction to more routine evaluations that require less interaction. We may also move between synchronous and asynchronous interaction. Correspondingly, interfaces for collaborative design should support random swapping between these different kinds of tasks and interactions.

> **Brainstorming**
> Coming up with new ideas.

A possible set of design tasks and processes is shown in Figure 2.8. The goal is to produce an artifact. The design proceeds in an environment of constant negotiation and division of work by the team members. This negotiation and sharing occurs during the creative phases as well as during evaluations and construction. The process can be as follows:

1. The artifact (report) structure is defined, proceeding through suggestions and evaluations.
2. A decision is made on who is to write each part.
3. Team members each develop a part of the report.
4. The parts are evaluated by all team members to see how they fit together.
5. When everyone is happy with each part, the report is put together.

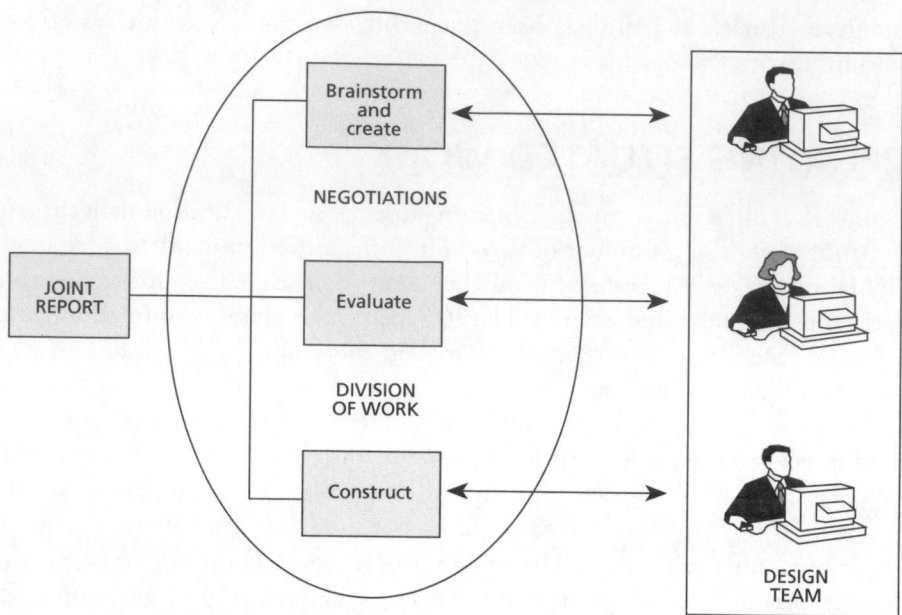

Figure 2.8 *Collaborative design activities*

Each of these activities may be subject to negotiations between team members as they decide on the goals of their work. The components of the design environment may use the kind of support used in other activities. For example, the negotiation may be supported by a decision support system that uses an argumentation structure like that shown in Figure 2.5.

Cooperative design
Creating new artifacts by joint agreements between a number of participants.

Research is now in progress on how to support such **cooperative design** activities using computers. Much of this work concerns finding the best ways for people separated by distance to work together. This often centers on face-to-face interaction using video conferencing with the goal of providing the same kind of rapport as exists with face-to-face discussion at the same location. Computer support for this work requires informal processes that allow designers to easily change modes. Thus someone may make some informal sketches and ask for a second opinion. The response may include another alternative. Following a response, the first person may make further changes and ask for other changes. This kind of discussion may continue for a while. Questions arise on how much of this discussion must be synchronous and what, if any, can take place through asynchronous interchange of messages. Research is concentrating on supporting such synchronous discussion, determining what delays can be tolerated between requests for comments and their response and how to manage the artifacts that are generated.

CHOOSING THE SUPPORT SYSTEM

We have defined group processes that may contain many tasks and activities. There are things like getting ideas that appear in decision support and design situations. There is the necessity to meet and form an opinion. There is also the need to evaluate opinions and decide what to do. The other dimension is the process needed to do all these things. Again, we have identified processes that are well defined, such as workflows found in many business processes. There are also processes that almost create themselves as the problem evolves. One question asked is: how can we support all these processes? How do we choose the computer tools to provide the support? We discuss such support in the remainder of this chapter.

IDENTIFYING THE GROUP ACTIVITIES

The first step when providing support for groups is to analyze the kind of work they do.

TEXT CASE B: Managing an Agency

SITUATION

The agency manager is required to prepare a feasibility study on building a freeway between two locations. This requires some preliminary designs to be completed and financial estimates to be made, as well as consideration given to external policy issues such as the environment and the position of the freeway. The project must therefore consider both the strategic and social issues centered around building freeways and the more operational and managerial tasks of designing the freeway and estimating its cost.

The manager must form a committee to work on the policy issues and establish a number of task-oriented workgroups to propose preliminary designs and make financial estimates on the cost of building the freeway. The two major operational workgroups are a design team making preliminary design decisions and a smaller financial planning workgroup. A structure must be established to support coordination between these groups. There must be coordination between the design and economic workgroups to ensure that estimates use the correct design data. There must also be coordination to ensure that the results produced by the workgroups are available to the committee. Alternatively, the committee may require the design groups to evaluate a particular option.

The manager consults the organization's directory, as well as accessing other directories or individuals to obtain people with the right background for the committee. Often it is necessary to get external members or consultants to serve on the committee. The manager also sets up the workgroups using internal agency staff, as well as a number of external consultants where necessary. The committee and workgroups must be given adequate support to carry out their work. The manager is required by the organization's quality policy to ensure that support is provided to these workgroups, including computer support where needed. In particular, it must include support for joint report preparation, easy consultations and coordination, and support for making decisions and disseminating information to community groups. Support for formal and informal interchange of messages between workgroup members is also important.

Provision has to be made to easily assign and redistribute tasks among workgroup members and to keep each workgroup participant aware of the progress of the workgroup, as well as of related work in other groups. It should also be possible to change the workgroup structure itself. Examples of the kind of change supported may be:

- changes to the composition of the committee and redistribution of tasks between other members;
- movement of committee members between different locations; and
- changes to the composition of the workgroups.

ISSUES

One important issue is how much of this support is to be provided by computer networks. One problem here is that two different kinds of support are needed. One is the support needed for the strategic considerations, and the other is the support for the workgroups to make their design computations and financial estimates. The support needed for strategic consideration tends to be more unstructured and dynamic, whereas the workgroups require access to more structured data and tools. Still another kind of support is for coordination between the various groups. This includes support for committee members to hold their meetings and relate policy issues to any information produced by the workgroups.

The workgroup members require access to the necessary databases and reports, both financial and design, to do their work. These databases may be distributed and heterogeneous and some may use a variety of media as well as design tools needed for computations. Sometimes, data from more than one database must be presented to designers as a single screen, requiring integration of databases.

The committee members must keep track of their meetings and organize the paperwork involved in these meetings. They also need access to the latest information on policy development and the ability to relate information generated by the workgroups to policy issues.

PROVIDING SYSTEMS FOR UNSTRUCTURED WORK

Most people suggest that the best way to provide support to teams is by using commercial software rather than building new systems. There are a growing number of software products for typical group activities such as holding meetings, making appointments, and so on. What we can thus do is identify the group activities and select a software component for each such activity. We then tailor the different components to specific group needs and then integrate them into a single system. This idea is illustrated in Figure 2.9. It shows a **platform** made up of a number of different technologies or **networking services**, as for example, electronic mail, artifact management or decision support. Users should be able to select and integrate these services into a system that supports their work practice. Thus, for example, it should be possible to quickly put together the discussion, brainstorming, artifact management and decision support systems to define the structure of an artifact. Then it should be possible to easily add electronic mail to extend the work to asynchronous collaboration. Furthermore, the combination should be **seamless**. This means that to the user the combined services should be seen in an integrated way, with information moved between each service with ease and without unnecessary conversions or recourse to operating systems for support.

The approach shown in Figure 2.9 assumes that it is always possible to connect together software produced by different manufacturers into a seamless platform. This is not always the case. The kind of problem that often arises is that the software does not do exactly what is needed or that it is difficult to match two software systems

Platform
A collection of computer services.

Network service
A technical system to support interaction between people.

Seamless platform
A platform whose services are closely integrated.

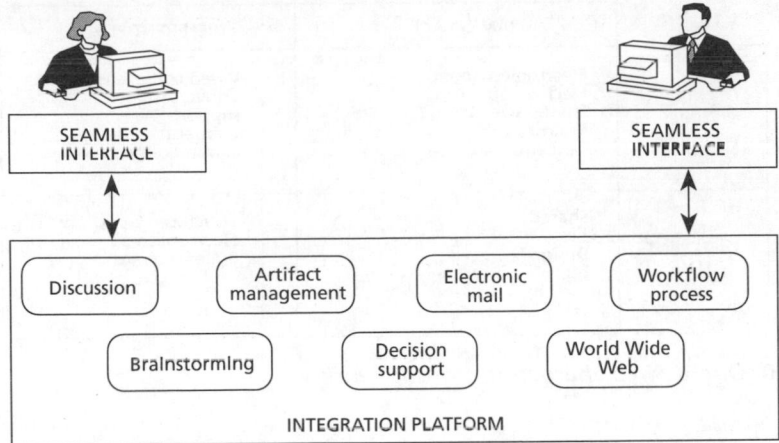

Figure 2.9 *Integrating software*

intended for related activities within the group. One approach here is to use a core technology that seamlessly supports a large variety of services and allows new services to be added. An alternate approach is to develop **middleware** that connects different services.

Middleware
Software that connects network services.

SELECTING FOR TIME AND SPACE

The specific software selected will depend on the relationship of team members in time and space. Figure 2.10 shows the different kinds of situations that must be supported by groupware. One, for example, is interaction that takes place at the same time but at different locations. The important point about Figure 2.10 is its indication of the technology needed in each of the partitions. The most obvious, for example, is a video conference meeting with participants at different locations. Another combination is the same place but different times and is exemplified by sharing a database.

The different time, different place situation indicates a mail system with storage, such as e-mail, or a structured transaction system. And support of the same time and same place is exemplified by electronic meetings. Electronic meetings need a technology where two computers are connected so that an input at one end appears immediately at the other end. Such technology is not needed where interaction takes place with users at different times. Now we need some way to store inputs from one user for later use by another user, as for example, occurs with e-mail.

It is also possible to introduce new modes of activity—for example, an extended meeting that carries on over a number of days with members in different places interacting at different times. What is needed to make this idea work is generic software that can be customized for particular group needs. What we have, for example, is a module (or system) designed to hold meetings. We take this module and tailor it to our particular group by selecting the people for the meeting and the tools they need for the meeting. We may also select an artifact management module and tailor it to the needs of the

	SAME PLACE	DIFFERENT PLACE
SAME TIME	Electronic meeting Electronic board Shared screen Brainstorming Audience response	Video conferencing Conversation support Cooperative design Group editors
DIFFERENT TIME	Shared files Design tools	Structured workflow Electronic mail Bulletin board

Figure 2.10 *One way to characterize group work*

group. Then we must integrate these modules so that we can pass information between them at the interface. The generic activities may be any of those that we discussed in this chapter. They may include decision-making modules, brainstorming modules and procedural modules, as well as support for social communication. A particular support environment may include any subset of these. The challenge in group support work is to identify a useful set of generic modules and to build these modules in a way that allows them to be easily put together. There is considerable research in progress to meet this challenge. The research centers around identifying what is generally done in group activities. The next challenge is to build the modules and allow them to be easily customized and connected to meet particular needs.

The only alternative to customization is to write each group support system. This is usually not economical because of the complexity of the systems. Thus you can be sure that with a trend to group work, there will be more and more emphasis on building tools that can be customized to particular needs. This kind of support tool formation raises the question of **reuse**. Reuse is important in group situations which are naturally dynamic. We often do not have the time (or the resources) to write a new program to support new group dynamics. A system that is already available, but perhaps needs some tailoring, is much more preferable in these environments.

One example of a general purpose system is LOTUS Notes. It is a system built for supporting such integration. It is supported on IBM PCs and allows users to integrate e-mail, bulletin boards, meeting scheduling, document sharing and other activities.

Reuse
Using an existing system or module for a new task.

TEXT CASE B: Managing an Agency—Selecting the Tools

The problem facing the agency manager is to choose the most appropriate options for providing support. First, it is relatively simple to provide the various members with personal support tools such as word processing and so on. It is also relatively straightforward to provide tools needed in design and estimates. The various task teams are more closely located and their computations relatively well defined. The most important tasks will be to ensure good contact between the two workgroups and to ensure that their computations are made available in committee deliberations.

Such coordination support is more difficult. The agency manager has the problem of deciding what amount of coordination can be supported by computers and what is to be done using the conventional means of committee meetings, fax communication, and so on. The manager must therefore consider whether electronic meeting facilities are to be provided. Some of the people can be placed on e-mail. Or perhaps there should be a computer-based bulletin board. Much of the choice here is determined by costs and the local availability of group members.

In this particular case, the committee members are often at different places and there would be some benefit in providing electronic facilities to get the benefit of the members' knowledge. Again, much of the committee work concerns the formulation of positions that can be used to keep track of committee deliberations. They would be even more useful if design or estimates made by teams could be integrated with the argumentation.

On the other hand, we can emphasize the use of the fax, but this will make it more difficult to keep track of records. It is also difficult to use faxes when the group members are mobile and fax numbers can rapidly change. It is better to have the member register regularly for information interchange. This makes it possible to provide access to the latest versions of documents to all concerned members and also to register any replies.

SUMMARY

This chapter described changing workplace environments and the different kinds of support that need to be provided for each kind of environment. It particularly differentiated between computer systems that support individuals and those that support groups. It then outlined the different kinds of interaction between group members and defined different classes of group work. This included social networks, clerical procedures, decision support systems and design groups. The chapter described some characteristics of these different kinds of groups and identified how to put together computer systems to support them.

DISCUSSION QUESTIONS

2.1   What is the difference between planned and situated work?

2.2   What are the disadvantages of hierarchical organization structures?

2.3   How does an individual's work change in a flatter organizational structure?

2.4   Why is group work becoming more important?

2.5   Describe some activities commonly found in group work.

2.6   What are the different kinds of communication found in organizations?

2.7   Describe what you understand by workflows.

2.8   Describe the characteristics of some different group support systems.

2.9   Why is it preferable to synthesize group support systems from existing components rather than building them from scratch?

◇ **EXERCISE**

2.1 Consider the interactive marketing organization. Do you think any of the kinds of support facilities described in this chapter could be usefully employed in interactive marketing?

BIBLIOGRAPHY

Anthony, R.N. (1965), *Planning and Control Systems: A Framework for Analysis*, Harvard Graduate School of Business Administration, Boston.

Berners-Lee, T., Cailliau, R., Luotonen, A., Nielsen, H. and Secret, A. (1994), 'The World Wide Web' *Communications of the ACM*, Vol. 37, No. 8, pp. 76–82.

December, J. and Randall, N. (1995), *The World Wide Web Unleashed* (2nd edn), Sams.net Publishing, Indianapolis.

Dern, D. (1994), *The Internet Guide to New Users*, McGraw-Hill, New York.

Drucker, P.F. (January–February 1988), 'The coming of the new organizations', *Harvard Business Review*, pp. 45–53.

Ellis, C.A., Gibbs, S.J. and Rein, G.L. (January 1991), 'Groupware: some issues and experiences', *Communications of the ACM*, Vol. 34, No. 1, pp. 38–58.

Grudin, J. (January 1991), 'Special section on computer supported cooperative work', *Communications of the ACM*, Vol. 34, No. 12.

Hawryszkiewycz, I.T. (1997), *Designing the networked enterprize*, Artech House, Boston.

Kling, R. (December 1991), 'Cooperation, coordination and control in computer supported work', *Communications of the ACM*, Vol. 34, No. 12, pp. 83–8.

Neuwirth, C.M., Kaufer, D.S., Chandhok, R. and Morris, J.H. (1990), 'Issues in the design of computer support for co-authoring and commenting', *Proceedings of the CSCW90 Conference*, pp. 183–93.

Sprague, R.H. and McNurin, B.C. (1993), *Information Systems Management and Practice* (3rd edn), Prentice-Hall International, Englewood Cliffs, New Jersey.

Suchman, L. (1987), *Plans and Situated Action: The Problem of Human-Machine Communication*, Cambridge University Press, Cambridge.

———(September 1995), 'Making work visible', *Communications of the ACM*, Vol. 38, No. 9.

Winograd, T. (1987–88), 'A language/action perspective on the design of cooperative work', *Human-Computer Interaction*, Vol. 3, pp. 3–30.

Winograd, T. and Flores, F. (1986), *Understanding Computers and Cognition: A New Foundation for Design*, Ablex Publishing Corporation, Norwood, New Jersey.

Some business information systems

3

CONTENTS

KEY LEARNING OBJECTIVES

The kinds of business units often found in organizations

The difference between a business unit's static and dynamic structure

The relationship between a business unit and a business process

Some common information systems

The nature of business processes

Why there is a need to re-engineer business processes

Why quality is important

The advantages of system integration

INTRODUCTION

The previous chapter described many ways of working found in information systems. Some of this work is carried out in groups, while some is done by individuals. Chapter 2, however, did not describe any specific systems. This chapter will describe some typical computer-based information systems that support the more common business units found in organizations. The business units described in this chapter are the common units that are needed to keep most organizations functioning—for example, accounting or human resources. There are also many industry-specific units—for example, portfolio management for an investment firm or a reservation system for an airline or bus company.

An organization's business unit has its static and dynamic components. The static component describes the structure and function of the unit, whereas the dynamic component describes the processes in the unit. In this chapter we will describe some of the more common business units and their processes.

Although the business units described here deal with a specific function, they nevertheless have one important common requirement—they must work well and accurately and help the business to grow and achieve its objectives. They must also be integrated so that they can work together to fulfill the organization's mission rather than working toward their own ends. Working well and accurately is sometimes hard to define. The term quality is often used to describe systems that work well. It can mean many things to many people. Quality is a general term that is used to define our or our client's expectation of a good system. This usually means that there are few errors in the system, the users are happy with it, and everybody knows what is going on. We will continue to expand on the term quality as we describe systems in more detail.

INTRODUCTION TO TYPICAL INFORMATION SYSTEMS

Organization chart
A chart that shows the business units of the organization.

Human resources subsystem
The part of a business that maintains personnel policy.

Personnel development subsystem
A business system for maintaining peoples skills.

Personnel subsystem
A business system for keeping information about people.

Many of the static and dynamic components of a business unit are realized by a computer-based information system. If you look at typical organizations you will find that they have many common business units. Consequently, they will have similar information systems. The structure chart of business units in a typical **organization chart** is illustrated in Figure 3.1. Many of the business units in the structure chart will be supported by computer-based information systems. The information system can therefore be divided into a number of subsystems where there is a separate subsystem for each business unit. Each subsystem may be further subdivided if necessary.

Some important information subsystems found in most organizations include:

- The **human resources subsystem**, which maintains information concerning the organization's personnel. This subsystem is made up of the personnel subsystem and often the payroll subsystem, although the trend now is for payroll to become part of the accounting subsystem, while the human resources subsystem concentrates on **personnel development**. The **personnel subsystem** keeps track of personal data such as date of birth, address, marital status, and so on. It can also contain information on a person's employment record, their start date and appointments in the organization, their personal skills, and vacation records and entitlements.

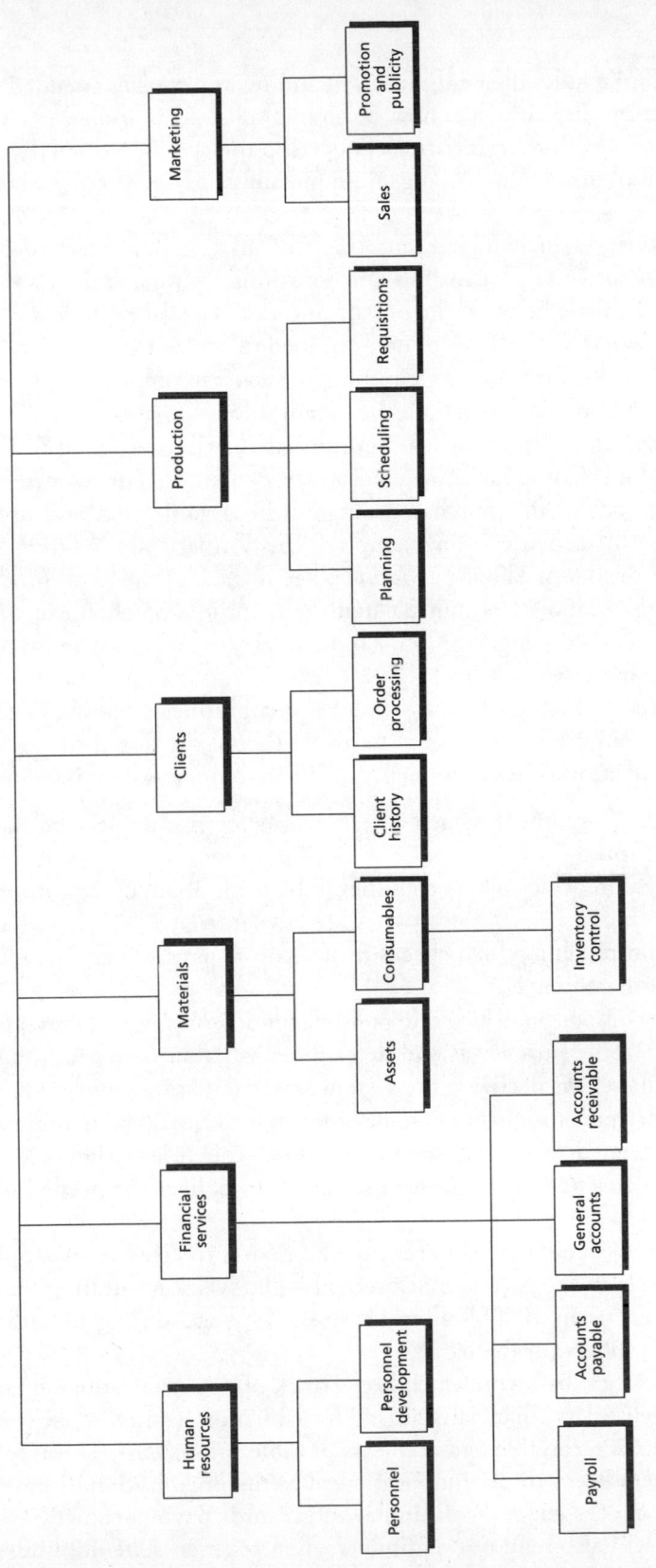

Figure 3.1 *Typical information systems—static structure*

Other information includes their education, including any courses attended while with the organization. In many cases now, personnel subsystems arrange or provide courses for personnel within organizations to develop their skills. System dynamics include movement of people between organizational units, paying people or changes to their skills.

Materials subsystem
The part of the business that keeps track of its material resources.

- The **materials subsystem**, which keeps track of all the items owned by an organization. It records item quantities and locations, as well as their value. A distinction is often made between the organization's *assets* and *consumable items*. Assets are characterized by the kinds of items needed to carry out an organization's activities. They can be furniture, or equipment such as computer equipment. Assets are usually distributed throughout the organization. Organizations therefore need an asset register to keep track of equipment distributed for use in their day-to-day operations. Consumable materials are of two kinds. The *parts inventory* keeps track of material items purchased outside the organization and used by the organization in its activities—for example, paper, or parts needed to produce the organization's products. The *stock inventory* keeps track of the items produced and sold by the organization. Consumable items are kept in a warehouse or various storage locations within the organization. An organization maintains an inventory of its consumable materials.

A typical parts inventory system includes the components shown in Figure 3.2. Its goal is to purchase parts and issue these parts as required to the other units of the organization. The components of the inventory system include:

— the parts issues component, which is responsible for issuing parts to the rest of the organization;
— the enquiry system, which allows enquiries to be made about current inventory levels;
— a stocktake component, which checks for any discrepancies between records and actual store contents;
— the reordering component, which is responsible for ordering parts from suppliers. It monitors current store levels and determines whether new parts must be ordered. To make this decision, the system keeps statistics about item usage in order to determine the quantities to be ordered. It must also keep information about times needed to deliver items, sometimes called lead times, so as to ensure that sufficient time is given to suppliers to deliver the needed items; and
— the parts delivery system, which keeps track of parts received from suppliers. It adds the parts to the current stock record and advises accounting that the parts have been received. This advice is needed by accounting to authorize payment to suppliers for the parts.

Financial services system
A system that keeps track of an organization's financial resources.

Accounts receivable
A subsystem that keeps track of moneys owed to the organization.

- The **financial services subsystem**, which keeps track of an organization's financial transactions as well as its financial status. The two most common subsystems here are the accounts receivable and accounts payable subsystems. The **accounts receivable** subsystem keeps track of moneys owed to the organization. It produces invoices for sales, checks client credit limits, and records payments made against these invoices. It will also send out reminders when payments are overdue. This

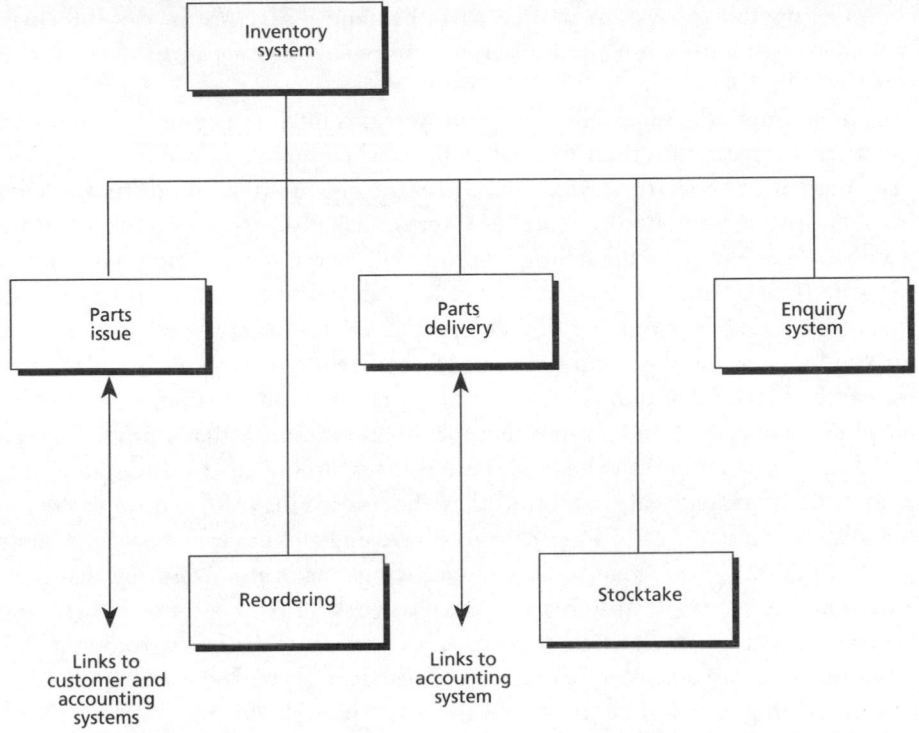

Figure 3.2 *Inventory control system*

subsystem has an account for every one of the organization's customers. It is then responsible for keeping track of customer payments. It checks that the payment for each invoice is made and checks the payment against the invoice. Any differences between the payment and the invoice must be resolved. The system also keeps track of the time taken by customers to make payments. Some systems can identify customers who are always late in making payments and bar them from receiving further credit.

The **accounts payable** subsystem is the reverse of the accounts receivable subsystem and keeps track of the moneys owed by the organization. It keeps track of purchases made by the organization by recording outgoing orders. Invoices received from suppliers are then checked against the orders to ensure that the invoice only lists goods that have actually been received. When the invoices are verified, payments are made to suppliers.

Most organizations also have a **general accounts** subsystem to keep track of funds used by internal departments. This subsystem produces reports about the organization's assets and its use of resources. This includes setting up budgets for the organization's departments and projects, and monitoring spending against these budgets. It also produces end of year reports about the organization's assets and liabilities, and a statement showing the organization's income and expenses for the year.

Accounts payable
The subsystem that keeps track of the money owed by the organization.

General accounts
A system that keeps track of funds within an organization.

Payroll subsystem
A business system for paying the organization's personnel.

Marketing subsystem.
A system that determines what an organization is to produce and then publicizes its products.

Market research
Determining how to make products acceptable to customers.

Client relations subsystem
That part of the system that interacts directly with the organization's clients.

Clients
People from outside an organization that deal with an organization.

Production subsystem
An organizational function that produces physical goods.

The **payroll subsystem** is often part of financial services. It uses information about entitlements from the human resources subsystem to produce paychecks on a regular basis.

In addition, the financial services subsystem is often responsible for developing plans and forecasts on the financial status of the organization.

• The **marketing subsystem**, which publicizes the organization's products and services to its clients or potential clients. Marketing usually has two functions. One is to determine a strategy for selling its products or even for deciding what products to sell. It often includes market surveys to determine what is needed outside the organization. The number of potential clients may be estimated and the services or products needed by them determined. Sometimes this work is called **market research**. Market research is important for many reasons. Primarily it establishes what customers need and ensures that the organization is actually producing useful products. It will establish the most desirable features of its products and services and build a market strategy around these features. This information is then used to create a marketing campaign through advertising and other forms of information dissemination, which may include advertising, mailouts or simply visiting the customer. Of course, much preliminary work must be done before actual dissemination begins. The likes and preferences of potential customers must be determined, as well as their location. This data is needed to ensure that the information gets to the right people and is of the right form.

The other function of marketing is to sell the products and services. This often requires calls to be made to potential clients, display of goods and selling the product. Sales units are often closely related to marketing. They are responsible for selling the marketed products. Each sale results in an order, which is sent to stock inventory to supply the items and accounting to issue an invoice. The sales unit may also predict future sales or keep track of sales by customers.

• The **client relations subsystem**, which maintains contact with the organization's **clients**. Organizations can differ in the kinds of external clients they have and the kind of information kept about them. Some organizations have customers who order goods from the organization. The organization keeps track of orders made by these customers and of deliveries made to them. Other organizations, in particular public agencies, have clients who get assistance from the organization. These organizations must keep personal records about their clients, such as their address or their financial and employment status. In all cases, privacy and security are important issues, as people do not like information about them to be widely distributed. The provision of what are commonly known as 'help desk' facilities is now common. These assist clients who have problems to quickly get any expert assistance they need.

• The **production subsystem**, which is found in organizations that produce physical goods. Such organizations may have one or more factories that use consumable items to produce products which are later sold to customers. They need to maintain an information system about their production facilities, as well as schedules for these facilities. A production system includes a planning subsystem to determine what goods are to be produced, and a scheduling subsystem to schedule machines in order to produce these goods. It may also include a subsystem to requisition consumable items needed to produce these goods and to deliver produced items into inventory.

Each of the business units in Figure 3.1 satisfies some organizational need. Most organizations now provide computer support for most of their business units. The trend in most organizations is to increasingly computerize their information systems but to do so in a way that meets broad organizational goals. This often requires existing systems to be changed to support new business processes.

SYSTEM INTEGRATION

Figure 3.1 is a static representation of information systems. It illustrates each information subsystem as self-contained and does not show the information flows between the subsystems. When you look at the dynamics of business operation you will find that there are many information flows between the subsystems. For example, orders from clients are sent from sales to the accounting subsystem to generate invoices, and to production subsystems to generate requisitions for parts that go to the materials subsystem. Scheduling systems in production usually interact with payroll to establish the amount of time worked by employees during production.

Thus the trend now is to integrate these units to support organization-wide business processes. Many of these business processes involve more than one information subsystem and, as a consequence, such subsystems cannot often be built independently of each other. If this were done there could be duplication of data, as each organization-wide business process could include its own subsystem for the same business unit. Alternatively, if there were a policy to maintain separation of information subsystems, then there would be considerable message flow between them. There are two ways of integrating subsystems so as to avoid these problems.

One way to support integration is shown in Figure 3.3. Here there is a layer of software between the business process and the information subsystems to assist integration. This layer of software takes service requests from the business process and sends them to the business unit, which then transmits the response back to the business process. The term **client-server** is often used to describe this kind of operation. Here the business process is the client, and the information system for the business unit provides services to that process. The client-server approach is now supported by the client-server architectures described in Chapter 1. The World Wide Web technology can also be used to achieve such integration though Intranets. Again, the pressure is on the business units to provide a quality service to the process.

Client-server process
A process that describes how a server provides a service to a client.

Another approach to integration is to have a centralized database management unit, or a data warehouse. This does not mean that all the data would be in the one location, or that one section would be responsible for it. Each subsystem can still be responsible for its own data, with the centralized database management unit providing the services needed to maintain this data. Business processes are able to obtain information easily from any subsystem through the integrated database management unit.

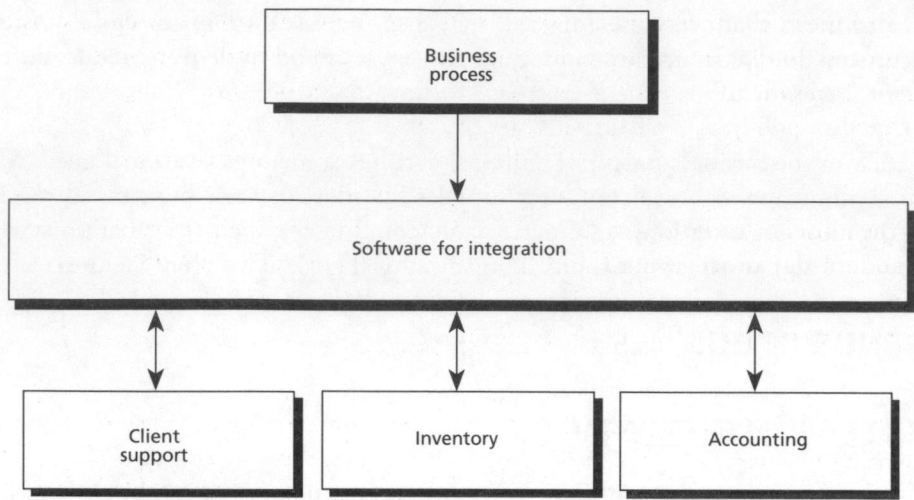

Figure 3.3 *Structure of a business process*

 # BUSINESS PROCESSES

To obtain an accurate understanding of what information systems look like, it is also necessary to show the dynamics of the subsystems or the business processes in which they participate.

Business process
A set of steps used to achieve a business goal.

Business processes define the way the business or organization works and the way it does business. They define the way the organization achieves its goals, interacts with its clients and carries out its internal operations. An organization carries out a variety of business processes. There can be business processes within a business unit that are used to carry out the unit's function. There can also be organization-wide processes that include a number of business units. The trend to organization-wide processes is growing along with the trend to the flat organizational structures described in Chapter 2. It is also now common to identify **critical business processes**, which are those organization-wide processes that are crucial to the survival of the business. They are usually processes concerned with providing service to the business's clients. It may be the process used to install a telephone in a telephone company, the process used to provide the items ordered by a customer or the way a hospital treats its patients. Such processes use information from more than one business unit.

Critical business process
A business process that is crucial to the survival of a business and supports the core business of the organization.

Processes can often be defined at a number of levels. There may be a business-wide process that activates subsidiary processes in a business unit. For example, an organization-wide process to satisfy a client order may activate an invoicing process in the accounting unit, as well as a requisition process to obtain a part from a warehouse. Again, we raise the issue of quality, as business process designers must now emphasize process quality. The word *quality* is widely used but has no universal definition. It simply means doing the best one can. Generally, in the context of a process, it means that the number of process errors and unpredictable events are reduced, the process goals are achieved at minimum cost, and both the customers and people within the organization who participate in the process are satisfied with the process. Satisfaction can also mean that everyone is aware at all times of what is happening to objects in the process so that information about any activity can be readily obtained. How this is done is specific to a system. What we often do is define our own quality requirements, or a quality policy, and ensure that the processes meet these requirements.

A word of caution. Simply installing a computer to automate a process does not necessarily improve the process. We should first define what the process must do and then install a computer to support the process. We now describe some characteristics of modern-day processes and some processes found in business units.

TRENDS IN BUSINESS PROCESSES

Computer technology has had and will continue to have a considerable impact on the way in which business is carried out. Furthermore, computer systems are now providing new ways of working, rather than just automating existing processes. They are also providing new ways of doing business with the outside world.

New ways of working are supported by the kinds of systems that were described in Chapter 2. They support teams and make it possible for people to see the wider context of their work through networking technologies. Thus, although people often work on local data on their personal computer, they can now make their work readily accessible to others on a network. Within the organization, ways can be devised for members who initiated actions to be kept aware of the outcomes of their actions, as well as the outcomes of other people's work. They can then respond more quickly to developments within the organization. People can also interact with others using the network, thus improving teamwork in the ways described in Chapter 2. This particularly applies to task-oriented workgroups that may initiate actions with a number of functional units and need to coordinate their work.

At the other end of the scale are the large corporate systems, such as banking accounts, insurance policies, reservation systems, and so on. In most cases, these systems use the idea of data warehousing to store their large volumes of data. Here people often work on part of the database. They can make copies of database records on their personal computer, work on them and seek the advice of others while doing so.

New technologies have also made new ways of working with clients possible both to provide a better service to the organization's clients and to extend the client base. It is now possible to deal more easily with clients' more specialized needs and to provide quick responses to their requests. In either case there is a tendency to develop closer relationships with clients; this is sometimes called extending the organization to include clients.

Extending the organization

Many organizations are developing closer relationships with their clients in a bid to maintain their support. To do this, they must provide a better interface between the client and the organization. Two approaches are possible. One is an internal World Wide Web network that stores information about products and provides access to experts who can be contacted for advice. Another is to provide a better level of contact with the client, usually through an electronic help desk which the client can contact with a query or request. The person receiving the query or request has easy access to the organization's data and experts, thus enabling them to handle the request or resolve the query and then reply to the client.

Electronic commerce

The World Wide Web is expected to have an increasing impact on trade. Although many of the early sites were mainly concerned with publicizing an organization's products and providing contacts, there is now more emphasis on supporting trade. This requires two issues to be solved. The first is the technical one of providing the interfaces through which potential clients can place orders. Many organizations are now developing interfaces for searches for required products, followed by direct placement of orders for those products. Potential clients browsing the Web can read this information and, if they wish, either make an enquiry or directly place a request for service, or order a product, through the site. This request is processed against a database and people who can fulfill the service or order notified about any actions that are needed. Another kind of site here are electronic shopping malls, which can provide access to a variety of businesses through the one site.

The other problem is to manage the actual financial transactions, or what is often referred to as electronic commerce. An important problem to be solved in managing financial transactions is that of security to prevent people making fraudulent entries, getting unauthorized access to accounts, or altering transactions either to get benefits or simply to interfere in the process. More and more techniques are evolving to provide the needed security, ranging from authentication using passwords or smart cards, to more complex crytographic techniques.

HUMAN RESOURCE UNIT PROCESSES

The majority of processes in the human resources system are internal, although there are times when a process includes external participants. One example of the latter is the way organizations hire people. This may include steps such as:

- advertising a position;
- selecting applicants for interview;
- interviewing applicants;
- making an offer; and
- placing a successful applicant.

The process must be complete, and responsibility for each step should be assigned to someone in the organization. Confidentiality must also be maintained throughout the process.

Most other human resource processes are internal to the organization. They monitor changes to personnel status, such as a promotion, and update records about these changes. Most personnel systems are now interactive, where personal records can be displayed on the terminal for either enquiry purposes or for amendment and updating. Security and privacy are very important in personnel systems, and care must be taken to ensure that personal details are not freely available throughout the organization but are restricted to those personnel directly concerned with personal records maintenance.

There are usually interfaces between the human resources system and other business units. Such interfaces usually center around providing support to business unit managers in managing their employees, including providing training support and defining employment conditions and standards. The human resources function also interfaces to the financial services unit to provide information used to develop the personnel budget within a business unit and to provide advice on personnel levels for future planning.

Almost all organizations have now automated their payroll processes. Payroll systems usually differ from personnel systems because they concern regular processing rather than being required to support a large volume of *ad hoc* enquiries. Many are therefore transaction-oriented, with transactions processed in batches. A batch run is made on each payday to generate paychecks or payslips. All the data needed for the payroll run are collected prior to the run. This data may be obtained from other systems or input directly for payroll use. Once the information is available, a payroll run is made.

The payroll run will look at the employee's current level and determine the salary for that level. It will then deduct the employee's commitments such as medical, insurance or union deductions and do any computations on overtime payments or special duties undertaken by the employee. All these adjustments will generate the employee's net pay. Finally, the system will refer to tax tables and subtract the tax payable to obtain the employee's net income.

CLIENT SERVICES PROCESSES

Client services processes are almost always defined to be critical processes. They provide the interface to the organization's clients and must ensure that clients continue to do business with the organization. Most clients nowadays demand better and better services, with a consequent emphasis in organizations on providing what is now commonly known as a **quality service**. *Service* is now a generic term that can include selling an item to a customer, providing entertainment, or providing assistance or social security payments.

Quality service
A service that meets all client needs in a mutually satisfactory way.

Figure 3.4 illustrates a broad and generic view of the customer service process together with two examples. The process usually begins with the client approaching the organization with a specific request—for example, placing an order or making a request for a social security payment. This request is recorded and checked to see if the requested service can be provided and whether the order specifies its requirements completely and accurately. This may involve a check to see whether a part is available or a client is eligible for a security benefit. If so, arrangements are then made within the organization to provide the service. This may be arranging for goods to be delivered or payments to be made to clients. Any problems found at this stage are clarified with the customer. There is usually a follow-up on the service. It may involve a payment, in which case the accounting system will become involved in the process, or finding out whether the customer was satisfied with the service.

Usually, the client system should follow up such requests to ensure that the service is carried out and also answer any customer queries about the service. This is now usually the function of a help desk system. Emphasis on quality usually means that

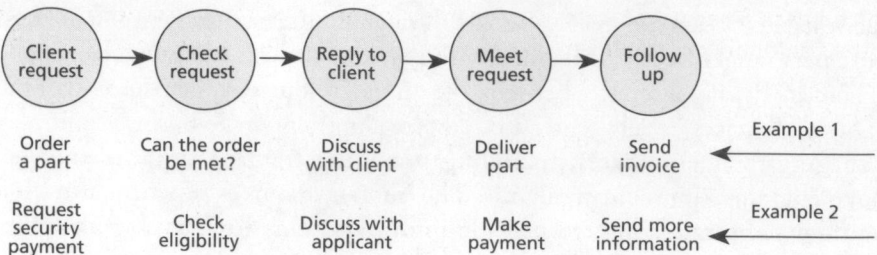

Figure 3.4 *Providing a client service*

a client can always be kept informed of what the organization can do for them, as well as being able to quickly answer questions on the progress of any requested service.

The process must also deal with exceptional conditions and client enquiries. Thus there may be changes to the order or the order may be totally cancelled. An alternative is to place a back-order for the unavailable items. A back-order means that the order is placed on 'hold'. It waits until all the ordered items are obtained and is then filled. Alternatively, some of the ordered items may be supplied immediately, while only the unavailable items are back-ordered. The information system must be designed in such a way that it is able to cope with all these possibilities.

Client systems are often integrated with other systems. Ordering systems are therefore often integrated with the inventory and accounting systems. Checking a client request and delivering a service may involve the inventory system, whereas the accounting unit would be involved in any financial transactions associated with the service.

Customer service processes can be, and often are, automated through a help desk. They are usually interactive to allow client queries to be easily resolved. For example, in an on-line ordering system, an order clerk will enter the order into the computer. The computer will then respond by describing the status of the ordered items. If all the ordered items are available, the computer will simply verify the order and generate a requisition to the warehouse. If, however, some of the ordered goods are not in the warehouse, the order clerk will be informed immediately. The order clerk will then probably contact the customer for advice about the action to be taken.

There is also a trend to provide better services for regular clients. This may be to provide direct access to an organization's products and to allow clients to keep track of their business with an organization. Typical examples are banks, which allow clients themselves to initiate transactions and to move funds between their accounts.

Let us look at a typical company and see if we can identify some of the kinds of systems that are typically found in organizations.

TEXT CASE C: Universal Electronics

SITUATION

A nationwide organization, here called Universal Electronics, manufactures and delivers consumable electronic items to its customers. It has three production facilities, each specializing in a range of items. Manufactured items are sent to any of its 20 regional centers where they are stored. Each regional center has access to a central computer which keeps a record of items stored at each center. Customer orders are received at the regional center, which arranges deliveries of items ordered at the center to customers.

The organization must meet a number of objectives that are forced on it by competition in the field. The most important of these is to maintain prompt and reliable service. Its goal is to deliver on the day following the order in order to reduce the likelihood of cancelled sales. To achieve this goal, it is important to maintain adequate inventories at each regional center and to properly schedule deliveries.

Figures 3.5 and 3.6 describe how orders are processed by the organization. The figures also introduce some modeling techniques that are described in more detail in later chapters. Figure 3.5 is a data flow diagram which outlines what happens in a system. The system functions are represented by circles. The inputs to the system consist of customer orders, which are first received (function 1) by a regional center, and verified to see if they are complete (function 2). Incomplete orders are returned to the customer.

A decision (function 3) is then made on how to satisfy a verified order. If all the items in an order are locally available at the regional center that received the order, then a customer delivery advice and an invoice are generated for the order (functions 5 and 6). If the items are not available at the receiving center but are available at another center, a transfer request is generated (function 4). The transfer request requires another regional center to transfer the needed items to the center that received the order and the regional center must keep track of the transfer request. If the items are not available at any regional center then the customer is informed that the order cannot be quickly met.

Both the customer delivery advice and the transfer request are used to prepare delivery dockets at the appropriate regional center (function 7). These delivery dockets are sent to vehicle schedulers at each regional center to arrange vehicles to deliver the ordered items (function 8).

You should note that Figure 3.5 only tells us what is being done, not how it is done. For example, it is not clear whether a computer is used at all and, if so, for what purpose. This kind of diagram is called a logical diagram.

To show how the functions in a logical diagram are carried out, we need a physical diagram of the system. Figure 3.6 is such a diagram. This figure uses a large variety of symbols. It shows that order clerks, who are located at each of the organization's regional centers, receive and verify customer orders. Once verified, the orders are entered into a computer via a terminal. A check is made to see if the items are at the regional center using the centralized inventory system. If items are not found in this inventory, a transfer request is generated to another regional center to arrange the transfer.

A SHIPPING program is run centrally on a regular basis. The SHIPPING program generates the customer delivery advices, invoices and transfer requests. The computer system produces two lists at 2 p.m. each day. One list, which goes to the regional center and is printed out on a local printer, is used by the center's personnel to prepare the deliveries. The other list goes to the vehicle schedulers who use it to develop vehicle routes to make the necessary deliveries the next day.

Apart from the delivery system shown in Figures 3.5 and 3.6, there are also other systems in the organization. One of these is the production system, which deals with item production. A variety of items are manufactured, and each kind of item requires a different set of machines. The machines must be carefully scheduled to maximize their use and to produce the maximum number of items. These items

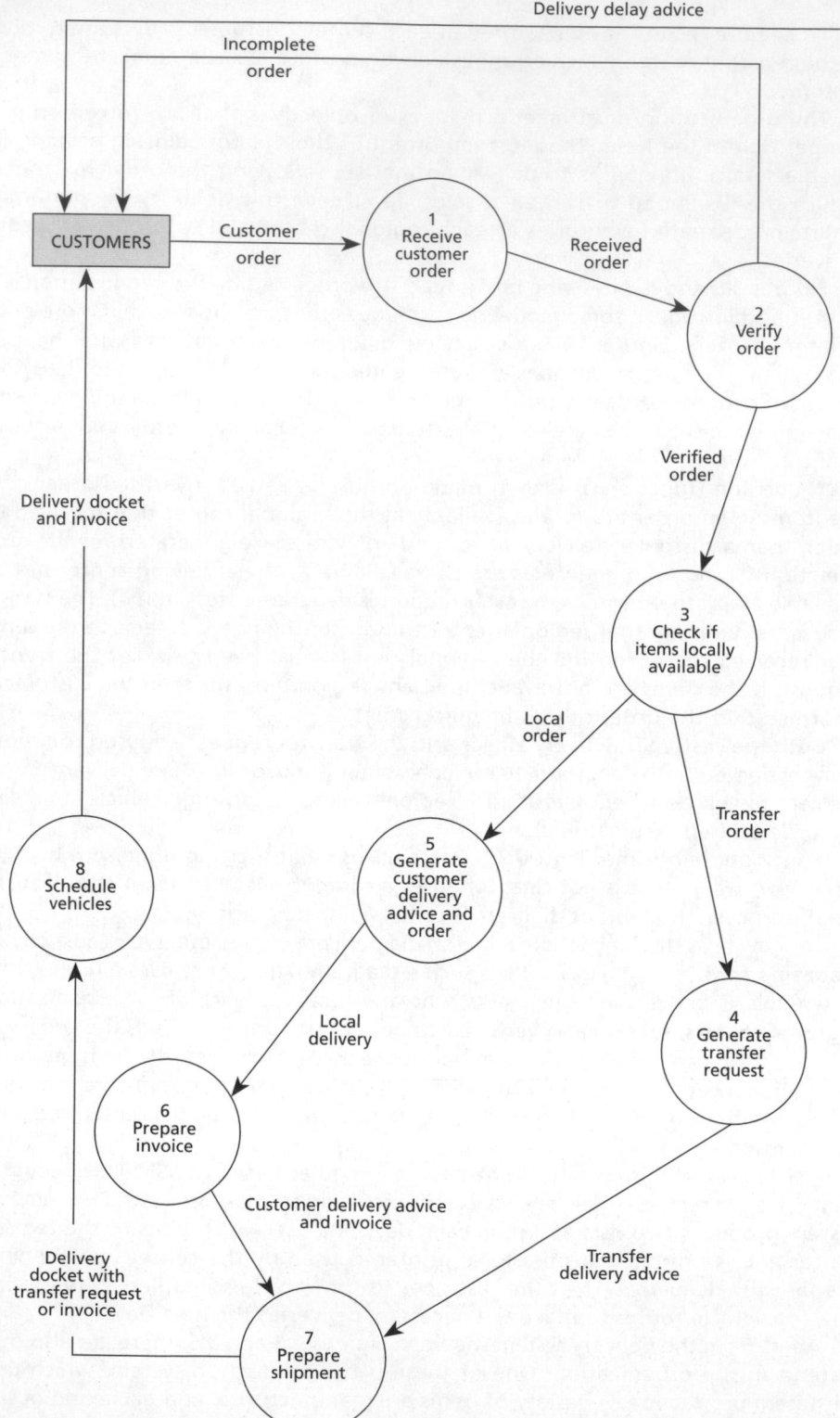

Figure 3.5 *Data flows in Universal Electronics*

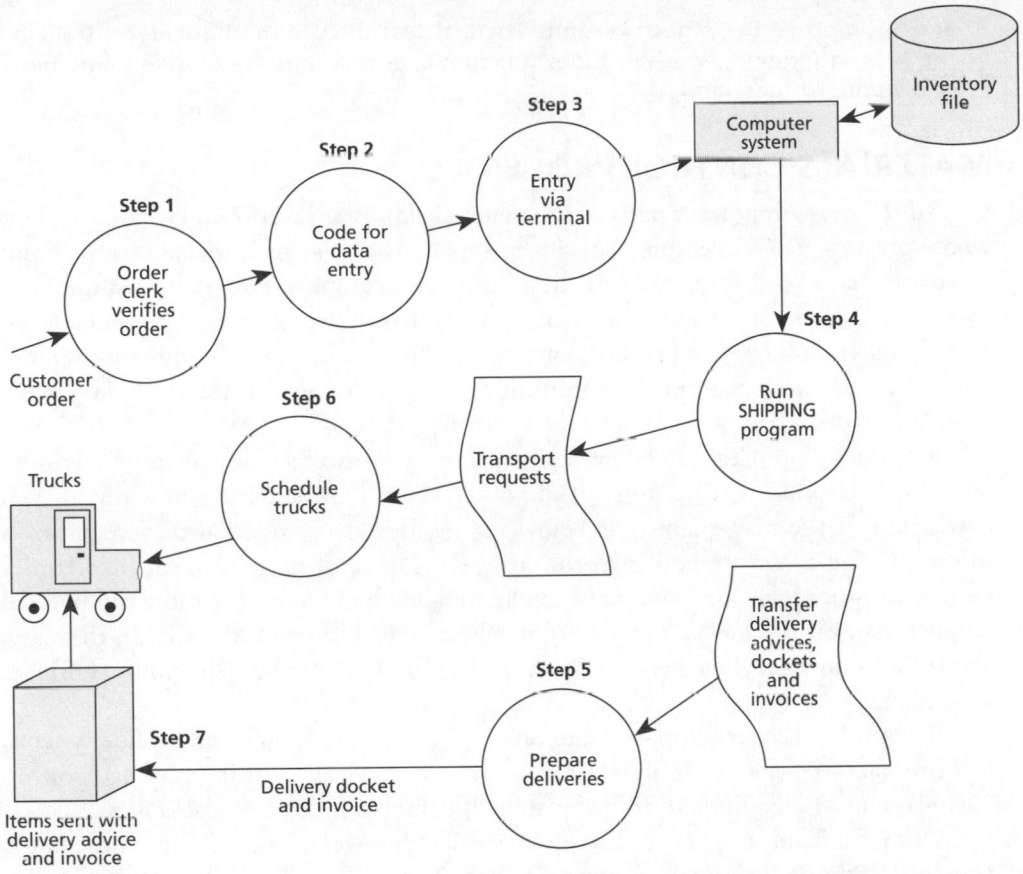

Figure 3.6 *Physical implementation*

are then shipped to the depots and the shipments are added to the inventory file for each regional center. The organization also has a payroll system already computerized and a computerized accounts receivable system.

ISSUES

On examining the system, it is found that the criterion of 'delivery next day' places considerable pressure on the regional centers. Priorities are often given to filling orders that require transfers from other centers, with the result that local deliveries get little attention. Because of this, it is suspected that regional centers carry inventories larger than necessary to ensure that all orders can be locally met and little attention can be given to follow-up activities. Questions have been raised about the possibility of decentralizing responsibilities for inventories to enable better control and of having a central store at the production facilities to provide parts unavailable locally. The possibility of using computers to interactively schedule vehicles has often been raised.

Similar questions have been raised about other subsystems. For example, functions 1 and 2, which are part of the customer service unit, are candidates for distribution again because of local conditions and to support follow-up activities. Decentralizing stock inventory (functions 3, 4, 5, 7 and 8) could also result in better inventory control through the ability to check items directly through the inventory system and to improve the stocktake unit. There is less discussion about decentralizing the accounting unit, which includes function 6, as accounts are seen as being more of a standard function.

MATERIALS CONTROL PROCESSES

Inventory
The business function that manages an organization's parts.

One of the more important parts of the material subsystem is **inventory** management, whose primary goal is to ensure that all necessary parts can be made available throughout the organization or products easily distributed to customers. However, this does not mean that as many items as possible should be stored in the organization's warehouses. Stored items cost money and do not generate any returns while stored. Thus an inventory control system must maintain the minimum possible number of items in store while ensuring that needed items are always available.

A reordering process can be implemented in two ways. One way is to set a reorder level for each kind of part. Every time a withdrawal is made, the new quantity is computed. If the new quantity is below the reorder level, then reordering action is initiated. The other method is to run a regular check of part levels and to reorder parts when stock levels are found to be too low. Reordering can become more complicated where organizations have a number of warehouses at different locations. In this case, action can sometimes be taken to transfer parts from one warehouse to cover shortages in another.

Inventory processes are mostly supported by a mixture of batch and on-line systems. On-line facilities are necessary to improve client services by being able to look up current item availability and to make any adjustments following stocktakes.

Ordering from suppliers is usually by the batch system. There is a periodic batch run to determine whether any items are beginning to run low. The batch run also generates quantities of parts to be ordered. Orders are then sent to suppliers to obtain these parts. Sophisticated processes can produce these orders by computer, but to do this they have to keep information about suppliers and the prices they charge for parts. Ordering is often a mix of computer and manual operation, which takes over in areas like negotiating discounts for large purchases or expediting urgent requirements.

PRODUCTION AND OTHER PROCESSES

In this chapter we have outlined only some of the business processes. There are many others. Production processes, for example, are often critical processes within an organization. A badly designed production process can mean that equipment lies idle waiting for parts to arrive or that produced parts are late, causing customers to cancel their orders and place them with other organizations.

RE-ENGINEERING THE BUSINESS PROCESS

A typical business information system at the present time consists of many systems that were written in the past and still use old methods and technologies. They often support only one business unit. These systems are generally called *legacy systems*. On the other hand, most organizations are now demanding support for organization-wide processes that support new ways of working. Organization-wide business processes have tended to depend on the type of facilities provided by individual business units. Systems built for business units did not usually have the business process as an important priority. There is now considerable pressure on businesses to improve their processes and thus create a better way of doing business. The term *business process re-engineering* often appears in this context. It refers to the identification of organization-wide business processes and changing existing systems to support the business process. This often also requires some changes to be made to the information systems in business units.

Re-engineering the business process must begin by identifying what the process must do. It must often start with existing systems. We then identify the business process needs and choose the best way to support the process, changing the legacy systems if needed. The important thing to remember in re-engineering the business process is that such re-engineering must be process- and not technology-driven. Thus, as shown in Figure 3.7, we must first define how the business process is to work. The criteria here are factors like improving client service, removing unnecessary duplication, ensuring that everyone is aware of what is going on, and reducing system errors. The main purpose of the business unit, then, is to set the standard that satisfies quality service requirements. We then need to look at how to use computers to make it work in this way.

Re-engineering
Changing an existing system.

There are many aspects to re-engineering. One is the trend toward using newer technologies to support the new ways of working. Another is the closer integration of business units. Each requires a different approach. Integration of business units can sometimes be achieved by building a higher-level system that provides interfaces to access existing business units. This requires the development of the higher-level

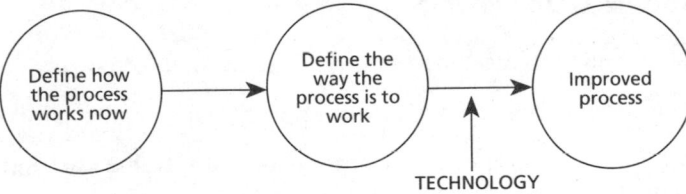

Figure 3.7 *Re-engineering*

system, together with changes to interfaces at each of the business units. Another approach is to change the way the business unit itself works. This may require a change in the way it is set up—perhaps by adopting a data warehouse approach or a technology, such as object orientation, that can support better distribution.

> ### TEXT CASE C: Universal Electronics—Problems with Business Processes
>
> Within the context of the business process, Universal Electronics must see the client service process as critical to its business, with a goal to assure just-in-time delivery while minimizing inventory holdings. If it cannot deliver on time, customers will go elsewhere. This process closely follows Example 1 shown in Figure 3.4. On examination, the most obvious parts for re-engineering are those functions concerned with meeting the request—that is, the delivery of ordered parts. Here we must search for parts across a number of regional centers and follow up with a complex scheduling system. There is also no requirement to follow up with customers apart from sending them an invoice. What is needed is better integration of these subsystems, together with better follow-up.

 **SUMMARY**

This chapter described some computer-based information systems as being made up of subsystems that support business units and their processes. It then described some common business units and their features, and followed this with a description of their processes. The business process is now becoming paramount, and many systems are being redesigned to meet business process needs. Most business processes involve more than one business unit, and systems are now being redesigned to allow easy integration of processes in individual business units into organization-wide business processes. The chapter outlined some broad strategies for such integration.

 DISCUSSION QUESTIONS

3.1   What are some typical information systems in an organization?

3.2   Why is it necessary to have information systems in an organization?

3.3   What is the purpose of an inventory control system? Can an inventory control system also be a decision support system?

3.4   Why are financial service systems important in an organization?

3.5   What kind of information is stored in a personnel system?

3.6   Name some different kinds of clients.

3.7   What do you understand by the term *electronic commerce*?

3.8   Why is it desirable to extend an organization to include its clients?

3.9   What do you understand by a quality service?

3.10   What do you understand by the term *business process*?

3.11   What is the relationship between a business process and a business function?

3.12   What kind of information flows between a customer and an inventory control system?

3.13   What properties do client systems have in common?

3.14   Why is marketing important?

3.15   What flows would you expect between marketing and other subsystems?

3.16   How can functions be integrated to support a business process?

3.17   When would you carry out a technical redesign without a corresponding business process redesign?

 ## EXERCISES

3.1   Look at our text case on Universal Electronics and consider integration of subsystems. Where would such integration be most effective? How would you change the system to handle enquiries from customers about the progress of their orders?

3.2   Identify the critical processes in the interactive marketing system in Text Case A.

3.3   What process do you use to learn about systems analysis and design?

BIBLIOGRAPHY

Davenport, R.A. (1993), *Innovation Processes in Business,* Harvard University Press, Boston.

Jacobson, I. and Lindstrom, F. (1991), 'Re-enginerring of old systems to an object-oriented architecture', *Proceedings of the OOPSLA'91* conference, pp. 340–350.

O'Brien, J.A. (1994), *Introduction to Information Systems in Business Management* (7th edn), Irwin, Homewood, Illinois.

Pyle, R. (June 1996), 'Electronic commerce and the Internet', *Communications of the ACM, Special Issue on Electronic Commerce,* Vol. 39, No. 6.

Concept formation

4

CONTENTS

KEY LEARNING OBJECTIVES

How to identify problems in a system
The importance of finding the right problem to solve
Defining conceptual solutions
How to justify solutions to a problem
Defining economic, operational and technical feasibilities
Preparing project proposals

INTRODUCTION

*Perhaps one of the most important and first questions to ask in systems work is: what problem are we going to tackle? Or, what system should we analyze and how might we improve it? It is important to realize that it is necessary first to identify the problem to be solved. We must then justify that solving the problem is worthwhile in terms useful to the business and not just interesting because it is innovative in its use of computers. This justification is made to ourselves, to our peers and, more importantly, to users and management. Finding the right problem to solve is perhaps the most important thing we do. If we solve the wrong problem, we will be wasting our time and resources, as our solution is of no value to anyone. This chapter describes how to find problems to solve, and how to propose and justify any solutions. Solutions at this stage are broad in concept and are sometimes known as the **conceptual solution**.*

Conceptual solution
A broad description of how a system will work.

Agreeing on a conceptual solution is often seen as the first phase of any development process. The conceptual solution is then used later in the development process to define detailed user requirements and create precise system specifications. This chapter describes ways of arriving at conceptual solutions, while Chapter 5 describes ways of determining user requirements.

FINDING THE PROBLEM

Problems can be identified in many different ways, some of which are informal. For example, we might gain the impression that improvements can be made simply by listening to what people are saying, or there might be something we want to do that someone else is doing, or something might be said at a conference or meeting. In any case, we often compare what is happening now to what we think should be happening. We get ideas about what should be happening both internally and externally. Internally, it might become obvious that something is not being done the way it should, simply by examining problem reports or listening to people's viewpoints. Externally, we can compare our operations against some accepted benchmark or by looking at what our competitors are doing. External factors might also include changes in government policy, client preferences or simply new ideas that are reported in the literature.

FINDING PROBLEMS USING EXTERNAL CONSIDERATIONS

Some of the ways of finding problems externally are:

- using normative models, which describe an accepted or conventional way of doing something;
- using historical models of the ways in which organizations develop. This is particularly useful in information systems design because of the development of technology;
- comparing our activities against a competitor's activities; and
- analyzing changes to government policy and community attitudes.

These external conditions can be used to identify differences between the way things are done in our organization and the accepted way of doing things outside. One obvious observation here is to note the areas where computers are used effectively by others and then look into using them for that purpose as well. Changes to government rules are also important. Changes to tax policy, for example, will often require changes to accounting systems.

FINDING PROBLEMS USING INTERNAL CONSIDERATIONS

Goals must be developed within the practical bounds of the organization. One way to ensure this is to break down the project goal into more detailed subgoals that consider organizational constraints. These subgoals are used in later stages to guide detailed analysis and design. One way to set goals is to identify deficiencies in the existing system. The project goal will then be to remove such deficiencies. Deficiencies are often found in the course of interviews or by examining documents about system performance. During initial analysis, therefore, interviewers should search for deficiencies such as:

- missing functions;
- unsatisfactory performance; or
- excessively costly operations.

One question that often arises here, is when to judge an operation as deficient. For example, is a two-day delivery cycle for a product acceptable or not? Unfortunately, there is no such thing as a universal acceptability measure—for example, that a three-day delivery is the universally acceptable delivery time. Obviously, delivery times will depend on the type of product and the industry. What one often has to do is look at similar systems or at competitor operations to make judgments on whether a particular operation is deficient. Competitor performance is often an important factor in setting goals, so analysts should always examine the methods of similar organizations to see whether some of these can be used in the proposed system. Technical developments outside an organization are also an important source of information, especially for systems that use computers. New external technical developments must be evaluated to see if they can be used to improve internal system operation.

As an example of defining conceptual solutions, let us look at the following organization.

TEXT CASE D: Construction Company

SITUATION
Two departments in a construction company have independently set up their own computer systems. The function of one department, the purchasing department, is to issue purchase orders (PO) to suppliers for project parts. The function of the second department, the dispatch department, is to receive parts from suppliers and forward them to project sites.

The two systems developed by these departments are shown in Figure 4.1. The project ordering system (POS) was developed by the purchasing department, and the goods received system (GRS) was developed by the dispatch department. Figure

4.1 shows these two systems, the files kept by them and the system inputs and outputs.

The POS system was developed on a small computer system to order parts required by projects. Projects teams put in PROJECT-REQUISITIONS for parts and the purchasing department selects firms to supply them. Over time the purchasing department has developed a SUPPLIER-FILE that contains information such as supplier address, items available from suppliers and item prices. It also contains more subjective information such as comments about supplier reliability and expected delivery time.

The SUPPLIER-FILE is used by personnel in the purchasing department to negotiate purchases with suppliers. Once a purchase is negotiated, a purchase order is issued to the selected supplier. A copy of the purchase order is also stored in the PURCHASE-ORDERS-FILE. It is identified by a unique purchase order number (PO-NO). A project request may be split up between a number of suppliers, although all items with the same ITEM-NO in a PROJECT-REQUISITION are always purchased from the same supplier. A purchase order may also contain items requested by more than one project team. You should note that a purchase order sent to a supplier does not contain

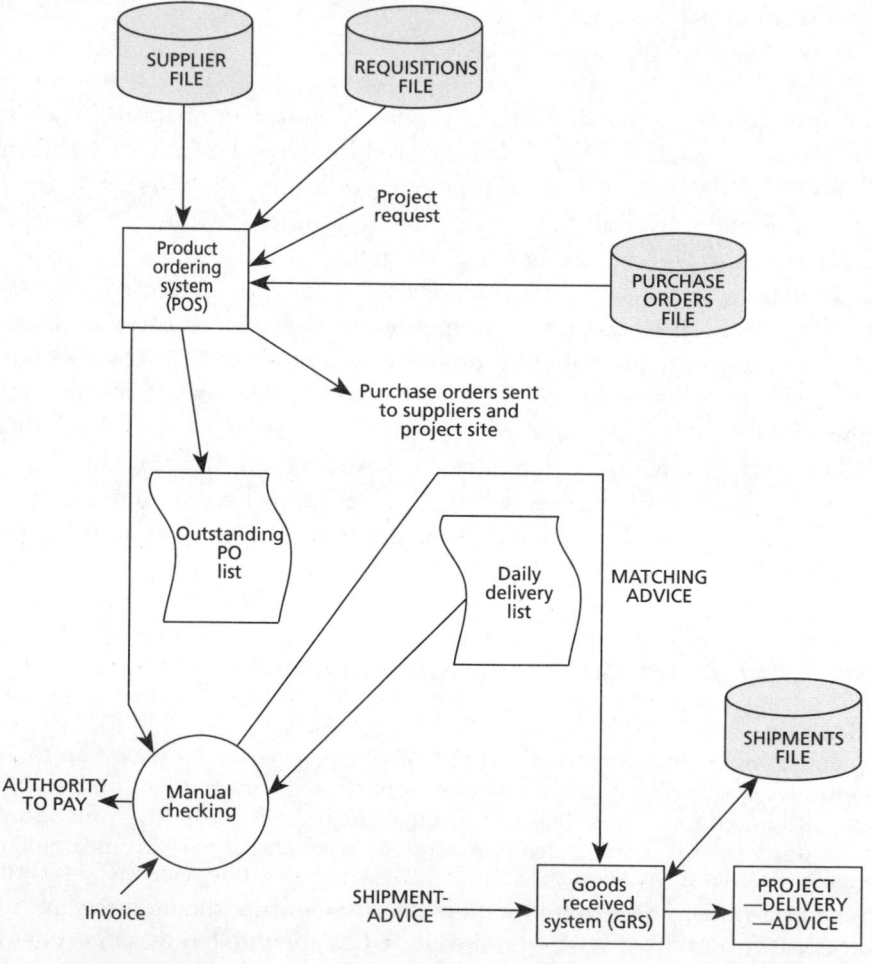

Figure 4.1 *Project ordering and goods received systems*

any reference to projects. The reference to purchase orders for items in a PROJECT-REQUISITION are stored in the REQUISITIONS-FILE, which contains all project requests with references to their purchase orders. These references appear as PO-NO for each ITEM-NO in the REQUISITIONS-FILE.

The GRS system has been developed to keep track of goods after they arrive in store. It also uses another small computer system to record shipments received from suppliers and to record the store where these shipments are held. A SHIPMENT-ADVICE is received with each shipment. The shipment is stored somewhere in the organization and the information in SHIPMENT-ADVICE together with its LOCATION is stored in the SHIPMENT-FILE. You should remember that the shipment advices from suppliers do not include any information about projects but only include PO-NOs. This means that the PO-NO in the shipment must be matched against PO-NOs in the REQUISITIONS-FILE to locate the project that needs the parts, and to track whether all ordered parts have been received. This is further complicated by the fact that each shipment advice can contain items ordered from the supplier in more than one purchase order.

Such matching must refer to the POS system, as this system contains cross-references in the REQUISITIONS-FILE between project team requests and purchase orders. Invoice processing is currently a manual process.

ISSUES

There has been some concern about the elapsed time between project requisitions and project deliveries. A number of causes have been mooted for this, including the complicated nature of manual matching and the fact that no inventory is held and each requisition requires a purchase to be made from suppliers. It has been decided to analyze this system to see if any improvements can be made and how they can be achieved.

One perceived issue is that the incompatible computers used in the two systems make it too difficult to transfer data between computers. As a result, shipments are matched manually against purchase orders to determine the project that needs the received parts. This is done by creating an outstanding purchase order list generated by POS and matching this list against lines on a daily delivery list generated by GRS. Manual checking matches PO-NOs, which appear in both lists. Once a match is found, the GRS system is informed (using a MATCHING-ADVICE sent via a terminal) of the project to which the items in a shipment are to be dispatched. The GRS system uses this advice to generate a PROJECT-DELIVERY-ADVICE, which is sent to the project site with the parts. Once a delivery for a project request is made, the corresponding purchase order must be cleared from the POS system.

The whole matching process is complicated by partial shipments of purchase orders and part deliveries of project shipments, and by the need to match invoices received from suppliers to shipments and thus ensure that payments are not made prior to the arrival of the invoiced items. The process is not of a high quality because manual matching often results in delayed deliveries or deliveries made to the wrong places.

Usually, problems are identified against backgrounds like that discussed for the Construction Company. The impression throughout the organization is that the system should be improved. What has to be done is to define problems in the system and propose ways to overcome them.

TEXT CASE D: Construction Company—Defining the Problems

We can identify deficiencies in all these three categories for the Construction Company. It does not maintain an inventory of frequently used parts, which could satisfy many part requests by withdrawing parts from the store. The lack of an inventory would probably emerge in the course of interviews. Project personnel would no doubt complain about delays caused by waiting for suppliers to deliver and they might say, 'Why can't some of these parts be held in store?'

An example of unsatisfactory performance is delays in obtaining needed parts. This is caused by many factors, one of which is not having an inventory control system. Other examples of poor performance are supplier delivery delays, the time taken to place a purchase order, and the manual checking of shipments against project requests.

Manual checking is an example of an excessively costly operation because automated checks would be both quicker and cheaper than current manual methods.

The specified goals must be to remove these deficiencies. For instance, if it takes too long to process an order, the goal would be to speed up order processing. The statement of the goal should, in the first instance, be concise and specific. It should not be the detailed specification, which is developed as a next step. If it is a new system, all that is needed is a broad and overriding objective stating what is to be done and its effect on the information system. For example, a broad goal statement may take the following form:

- *Project goal*: Reduce the time between the project requisitions and goods delivery.
- *Project goal*: Eliminate errors and delays in order processing.

Broad goals are often expanded into more detailed subgoals. Subgoals are obtained by asking the question: 'How can we reduce the elapsed time between project request and part delivery?' There are a number of possibilities here. For example, we could:

- create an inventory to hold frequently used parts in local stores;
- improve the method for determining project delivery sites for a particular supplier shipment;
- improve the procedures for verifying invoices and shipments;
- create a help desk environment where requisitions are allocated to one person who pursues it through to completion; and
- re-engineer the process to integrate the goods received system (GRS) and the project ordering system (POS) to reduce the manual effort needed to maintain information flows between these two computer systems.

These subgoals will be used later to propose alternative solutions.

So far we have identified a problem and suggested some solutions. Let us now look at how to justify whether the problem is worth solving and proposing a project to solve it.

JUSTIFYING A SOLUTION

One important guideline for defining conceptual solutions is to remember that such solutions should not be unrealizable ideals that are subsequently ignored. They must be developed within the practical bounds of the organization. Having found a problem or come up with an idea and identified conceptual solutions, we now have to justify these solutions. To do this, it is necessary to determine whether the solutions are feasible. **Feasibility analysis** usually considers a number of alternative solutions, one of which is chosen as the most satisfactory solution. It is advisable to investigate as many alternatives as possible to ensure that the best solution is chosen. Just using the first idea that comes to mind is not the best approach. A certain amount of skill is needed to propose good alternatives and choose the right direction.

Figure 4.2 shows the activities involved in finding suitable solutions. One activity in problem definition is to clearly state what problems are being addressed or ideas investigated. These define any system deficiencies that must be addressed in the solution, and in turn define the project goals. The other is feasibility analysis, which determines whether solutions are achievable.

Feasibility analysis commences once the project goal is set. The first feasibility analysis step proposes a set of solutions that can realize the project goal. These solutions are usually descriptions of what the new system should look like. The next step evaluates the feasibility of such solutions. Such evaluation often indicates shortcomings in the initial goals—for instance, people may be asking for too much. Alternatively, new

Feasibility analysis
An evaluation of whether it is worthwhile to proceed with a project.

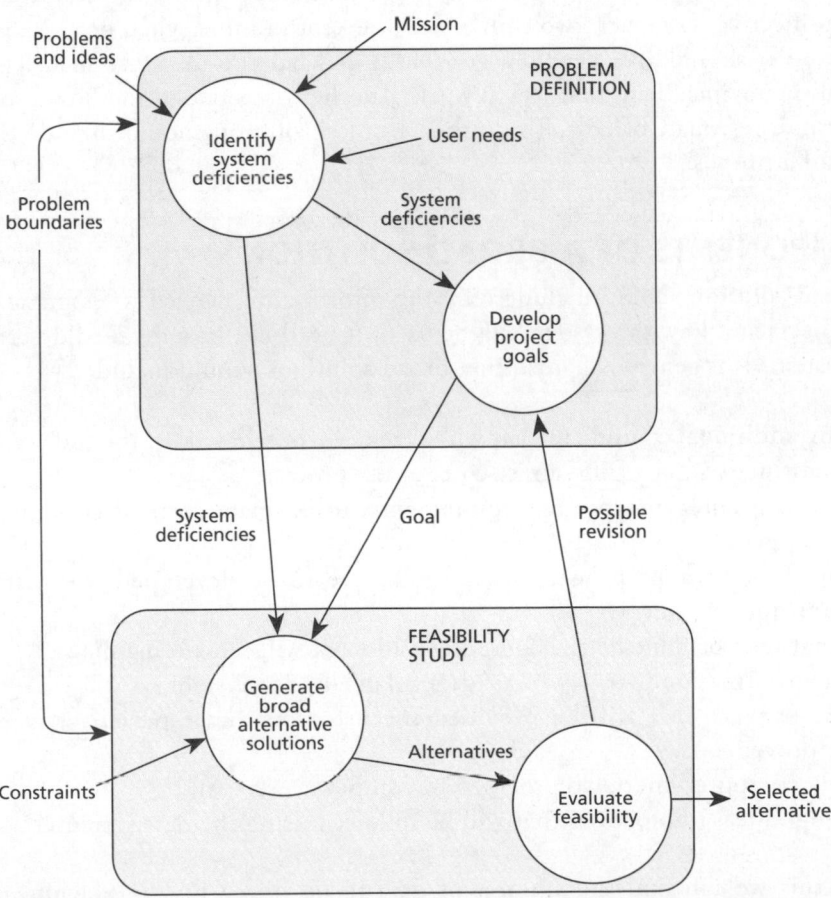

Figure 4.2 *Activities in problem definition and feasibility analysis*

insights gained through broad evaluations can identify new opportunities which can, in turn, lead to goal modifications. This process can go on for a while as goals are adjusted and alternative solutions evaluated. These steps are now described in more detail.

 # GENERATING BROAD ALTERNATIVE SOLUTIONS

Feasibility analysis begins once the goals are defined and agreed upon. It starts by generating broad possible solutions, which are used to give an indication of what the new system should look like. This is where creativity and imagination are used. Analysts must think up new ways of doing things—generate new ideas. There is no need to go into the detailed system operation yet. The solution should provide enough information to make reasonable estimates about project cost and give users an indication of how the new system will fit into the organization. It is important not to exert considerable effort at this stage only to find out that the project is not worthwhile or that there is a need to significantly change the original goal.

For a novice it is often difficult to say what a broad solution is and how it differs from a detailed one. The judgment of what to include in a broad solution is often very subjective. However, two things must be kept in mind when proposing a broad solution: it should give people a good idea of what the new system will look like and also convince them that it will work. Another objective of the broad solution is to form an estimate of cost. To do this, a broad solution should include the major parts of a proposed system.

COMPONENTS OF A BROAD SOLUTION

A broad solution should include only the information needed to estimate the cost of projects and how the system will be used. It need not be a detailed description of the system. It is generally agreed that broad solutions should include:

- any additional equipment that will have to be purchased for the project, in order to estimate some of the direct costs of the project;
- any computer networking requirements, to estimate costs of communications equipment;
- any new computer systems that will have to be developed, to estimate the development cost;
- what is to be done by the computer and what will remain manual;
- the information that will be made available by the system;
- the services that will be provided to customers and especially any expected improvements;
- any computer interfaces provided to computer users; and
- rough ideas of processes that will be followed using the new system.

From this we can find the amount of data to be stored on the machine and any transmission costs of getting data to and from the machine.

Only broad descriptions need be given here. As an example, at this stage we may suggest a report, give it a name and state what its contents are to be. However, detailed report layouts, interfaces or handling error conditions should not be specified. All that needs to be specified is the information provided in reports and interfaces. Details of these will be covered in later phases of the development process. What is needed now is a broad statement of the kind of information that will be made available to users and its effect on user operations.

One should not, however, become extreme here and propose alternatives that obviously cannot be supported in the organization. The organization has certain constraints on the amounts of available funds and personnel skills, and on working and accepted standards. Proposed solutions should obviously not exceed such funding limits or ignore some critical system operation or data need.

TEXT CASE D: Construction Company—Broad Alternative Solutions

Some broad solutions for the Construction Company are illustrated and a number of alternative solutions proposed. There are, of course, totally manual solutions which could improve matching and information flows. However, we will concentrate only on computer-based solutions, which are illustrated in Figure 4.3.

Solution 1 is a totally technical solution—to install network connections between the two systems so that they can exchange information between themselves; in fact, going to a client-server architecture. However, this may be rejected on technical grounds because there is no vendor software for easily creating a client-server environment that include clients based on the different software systems used in POS and GRS. Development of software in-house to set up a client-server environment may not be considered feasible because of lack of expertise.

Solution 2 is to move one of the systems from one computer to the other. Thus we can move the GRS system on to the POS system and develop the inventory system and the matching program on the POS computer. Of course, the reverse is also possible—that is, to move the POS system on to the GRS computer. Hence, there are two solutions here:

* *Solution 2A*—move the GRS system to the POS computer; or
* *Solution 2B*—move the POS system to the GRS computer.

Both these solutions will require an entire rewrite of either the GRS or the POS system.

Solution 3 is a new approach. It is to convert the entire system on to the organization's centralized installation. This may have some support, particularly if some of the data generated by the GRS or POS applications are used by other applications already on, or planned for, the central installation.

Solution 4 is to leave the GRS and POS systems as they are and develop yet another system for the checking and inventory functions. This solution may be rejected on operational grounds, as there will still be too much manual work needed to move information between the systems. In fact, the amount of such manual work may be increased because there are now three and not two systems.

Finally, Solution 5 is proposed as a compromise solution. In this solution a part of the POS system is moved to the GRS system so that GRS now receives project requests. An inventory subsystem is also proposed for the GRS system, and invoice checking is added to the POS system. When a project request arrives, a check is

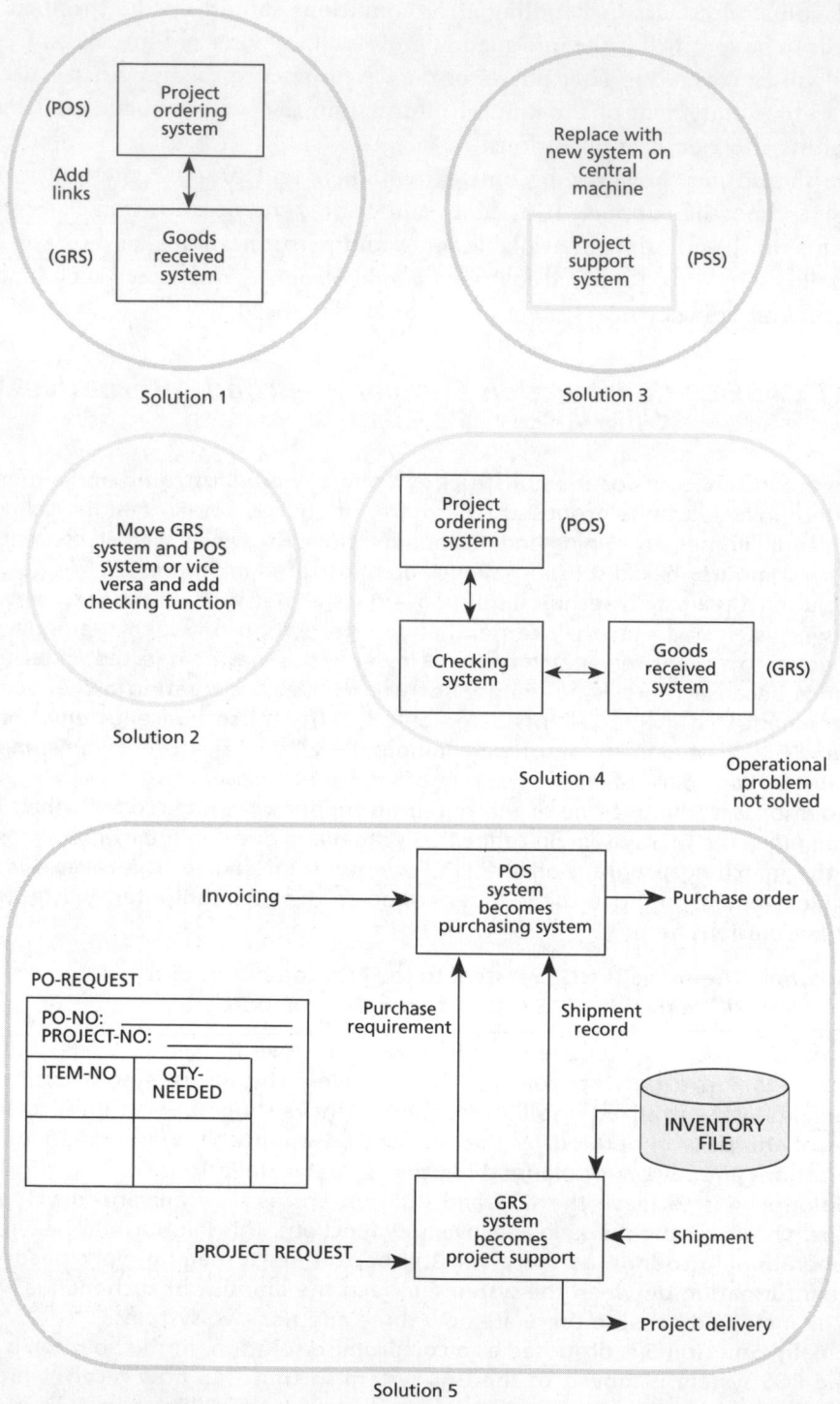

Figure 4.3 *Broad solutions of Text Case D*

made in the GRS system to see if it can be met from inventory. If it cannot, then a purchase requirement together with a purchase order number is generated and sent to the POS system, which selects a supplier and issues a purchase order. Note, however, that a reference to the purchase order is kept in the new PO-REQUEST in the GRS system. This reference is used to match the project request to the shipment when it arrives at the GRS system. The shipment record is sent to the POS system where it is checked against the invoice.

Solution 5 was proposed as an alternative to Solution 2. It requires less redevelopment because only part of the existing system is redeveloped. However, in comparison to Solution 2, which is totally automated, this proposal still requires some manual work to transfer shipment records and purchase requisitions from the GRS system to the POS system. Such a transfer can be achieved without manual transcription either by copying information on disks that are moved between machines, or using a local area network. In this way, all checking is now automated.

EVALUATING THE PROPOSAL

Once proposals are generated, they are evaluated. Three things must be done to establish feasibility. First, it is necessary to check that the project is technically feasible. Does the organization have the technology and skills necessary to carry out the project and, if not, how should the required technology and skills be obtained? Second, operational feasibility must be established. To do this, it is necessary to consult the system users to see if the proposed solution satisfies user objectives and can be fitted into current system operation. Third, project economic feasibility needs to be checked. The study must determine whether the project's goals can be achieved within the resource limits allocated to it. It must also determine whether it is worthwhile to proceed with the project at all, or whether the benefits obtained from the new system are not worth the costs (in which case, the project will be terminated).

Technical feasibility. This evaluation determines whether the technology needed for the proposed system is available and how it can be integrated within the organization. Technical evaluation must also assess whether the existing systems can be upgraded to use the new technology and whether the organization has the expertise to use it.

Operational feasibility. Operational feasibility covers two aspects. One is a technical performance aspect and the other is acceptance within the organization. Technical performance includes issues such as determining whether the system can provide the right information for the organization's personnel, and whether the system can be organized so that it always delivers this information at the right place and on time. Acceptance revolves around the current system and its personnel. Operational feasibility must determine how the proposed system will fit in with the current operations and what, if any, job restructuring and retraining may be needed to implement the system. The evaluation must then determine the general attitudes and skills of existing personnel and whether any such restructuring of jobs will be acceptable to the current users.

Economic feasibility. This evaluation looks at the financial aspects of the project. It determines whether the investment needed to implement the system will be recovered.

Technical feasibility
An evaluation to determine whether a system can be technically built.

Operational feasibility
An evaluation to determine whether a system is operationally acceptable.

Economic feasibility
An evaluation to determine whether a system is economically acceptable.

RISK ANALYSIS

The idea of risk analysis centers on identifying those aspects of a project where there is the largest uncertainty about getting a successful outcome. Once areas of high risk are identified they are given special attention. This may be to either take an alternative course of action or to manage it in special ways. For example, suppose there is a proposal to use a new technical method or product, which is new on the market and offers many advantages, but the organization does not have people with skills to use. If there is a perceived high risk of large project delays resulting from building familiarity with the method, then a decision may be made to use existing products. Alternatively a prototyping approach may be adopted, where the new product is gradually introduced in less critical parts of the project and its use expanded with experience in its use.

 # ECONOMIC FEASIBILITY

Economic feasibility concerns returns from investments in a project. It determines whether it is worthwhile to invest the money in the proposed project or whether something else should be done with it. Some organizations, especially those with large projects, place great emphasis on economic analysis. It is not worthwhile spending a lot of money on a project for no returns, especially if there are many other things which could be done with that money.

To carry out an economic feasibility study, it is necessary to place actual money values against any purchases or activities needed to implement the project. It is also necessary to place money values against any benefits that will accrue from a new system created by the project. Such calculations are often described as cost-benefit analysis.

COST-BENEFIT ANALYSIS

Cost-benefit analysis usually includes two steps: producing the estimates of costs and benefits, and determining whether the project is worthwhile once these costs are ascertained.

Producing costs and benefits

The goal is to produce a list of what is required to implement the system and a list of the new system's benefits.

Cost-benefit analysis is always clouded by both tangible and intangible items. Tangible items are those to which direct values can be attached (e.g. the purchase of equipment, time spent by people writing programs, or items such as insurance costs or the cost of borrowing money). Some tangible costs often associated with computer system development are:

- *Equipment costs for the new system.* Various items of computing equipment, as well as items such as accommodation costs and furniture, are included here.

- *Personnel costs.* These include personnel needed to develop the new system and those who will subsequently run the system when it is established. Analysts, designers and programmers will be needed to build the system. Also included are any costs incurred to train system users.
- *Material costs.* These include stationery, manual production and other documentation costs.
- *Conversion costs.* The costs of designing new forms and procedures and of the possible parallel running of the existing and new systems are included here.
- *Training costs.* These include the cost of training users of the new system, as well as developers who may be required to use new technologies.
- *Other costs.* Sometimes consultants' costs are included here, together with management overheads, secretarial support, travel budgets, and so on.

Intangible items, on the other hand, are those whose values cannot be precisely determined and are the result of subjective judgment. For example, how much is saved by completing a project earlier or providing new information to decision makers? Considerable argument can take place before agreement is reached on such intangible costs.

The sum value of costs of items needed to implement the system is known as the cost of the system. The sum value of the savings made is known as the benefit of the new system. Once we agree on the costs and benefits, we can evaluate whether the project is economically viable.

The cost estimates are usually used to set the project budget. Often it is convenient to divide these costs into project phases to give management an idea of when funds and personnel will be needed. The cost estimates need to be worked out very carefully. One should avoid omitting anything from the estimates, as this will necessitate requests for more funds because something was forgotten.

On the other side of the evaluation are the benefits of the project, which may also be tangible or intangible. Tangible benefits include those benefits that can be measured in actual dollar terms. Such benefits can include reduced production costs through the introduction of new technologies or reduced processing costs through the use of computers. Less tangible benefits include the possibility of increased sales through improvments to the ordering system, or the possibility of a wider market through better distribution of marketing data. Measurements of these benefits are not direct but are based on estimates of what can happen when a new ordering or marketing system is introduced. Management must be convinced that the estimates are accurate if they are to accept the evaluation.

Still less tangible, or perhaps intangible, benefits are those benefits that cannot be measured. For example, what is the benefit of better decision making through computer support or the benefit of maintaining a good business image?

Determining whether a project is worthwhile

The costs and benefits are used to determine whether a project is economically feasible. There are two ways to do this: the payback method and the present value method.

The payback method. The payback method defines the time required to recover the money spent on a project. The concept is quite simple. We know how much a project will cost to start. We also know the costs and benefits for each succeeding year. The difference between the cost and the benefit for each year will be the saving or net benefit for the year. The computation to determine the number of years needed to recover the costs is quite simple. As an example, consider Table 4.1, which shows the cost of implementing a project in the Year 0 to be $110,000. Benefits from the project are obtained over the next five years, and the net benefits are also shown in Table 4.1. If you add the values in the benefit column, you will note that the original $110,000 invested is returned some time towards the end of Year 3. Hence the payback period is about 2.9 years.

The present value method. The payback method is not always the best way to determine economic feasibility. It does not seem to make much sense to put, say, $10,000 into a project and recover $12,000 in Year 5. You might as well put the $10,000 into an investment account at 10 percent and get $16,105 in that time. Given an investment rate of 10 percent, one would have to recover more than $16,105 in Year 5 (assuming no returns in Years 1 to 4) to make the project worthwhile. This is where the present x«˙ue method comes in.

Table 4.1 *A present value evaluation*

Year	Cost	Benefit	Present value of benefit	Discount factor (10%)	Discount factor (15%)
0	$110,000				
1	—	$20,000	$18,180	.909	.866
2	—	$40,000	$33,040	.826	.756
3	—	$60,000	$45,060	.751	.658
4	—	$30,000	$20,490	.683	.571
5	—	$10,000	$ 6,210	.621	.497
		Total amount	$122,980		

The idea of the present value method is to determine how much money it is worthwhile investing now in order to receive a given return in some years' time. The answer obviously depends on the interest rate used in the evaluation. Thus, the present value of $16,105 in Year 5 is $10,000 today at 10 percent interest. If a project that pays back $16,105 in Year 5 costs $11,000 today, that project is not worthwhile. On the other hand, it is worthwhile if it only costs $9000 today.

To some extent the present value method works backwards. First, the project benefits are estimated for each year from today. Then, we compute the present value of these savings. If the project cost exceeds the present value, then it is not worthwhile.

Let us look again at Table 4.1 to see whether the project is worthwhile at a discount rate of 10 percent. To do this, we find the present value of the benefit at each year. The formula is:

Present value $\times (1 + r/100)^n$ = Benefit at Year n
We call $1/(1 + r/100)^n$ the discount factor in Table 4.1.

Thus, for example, the present value of the $40,000 benefit at Year 2 is computed as:

$$\text{Present value} = 40{,}000/(1 + 10/100)^2$$
$$= 33{,}057$$

Note that the sum of the present values in Table 4.1 is $122,980. As this exceeds $110,000, the project is worthwhile.

You may wish to compute the present value of the benefits in Table 4.1 at 15 percent interest. The result is $109,140.

TEXT CASE D: Construction Company—Evaluating Feasibilities

Of the alternatives proposed in Figure 4.3, Solution 1 can be eliminated on technical feasibility grounds and Solution 4 on operational feasibility grounds. This leaves Solutions 2, 3 and 5 for further consideration, using economic feasibility.

The costs relevant to the broad solutions outlined for the Construction Company are illustrated in Table 4.2, which shows the costs of converting existing systems to new systems and the costs of developing new systems. You will note that it costs more to convert the POS system to the GRS computer than to convert the GRS system to the POS computer. This is because of the more complex interface used in supplier selection and the conversion of the supplier database.

Table 4.2 *Initial development cost estimates*

Tasks		Cost
A	Convert POS system to the GRS computer	$90,000
B	Convert GRS system to the PO computer	$60,000
C	Develop delivery checking systems (DCS) to replace manual checking	$30,000
D	Develop inventory control system (INV)	$50,000
E	Develop invoice input interface (INIT)	$20,000
F	Move project order interface from POS system to GRS system (Solution 5)	$20,000

Table 4.3 applies the costs in Table 4.2 to the alternative broad solutions. Each broad solution includes more than one activity. Thus, Solution 2A converts the POS system to the GRS computer (cost of Task A), develops a delivery checking system (cost of Task C), an inventory control system (cost of Task D) and an invoice input interface (cost of Task E). These four costs make up the total cost of Solution 2A. The component costs of all the other solutions are shown in Table 4.3.

We have costed Solution 4 here for illustration. The cost includes $15,000 for some additional hardware to implement checking on a separate computer.

Table 4.3 *Initial alternative cost estimates*

Solution	Tasks in solution	Cost
2A	A($90,000) + C($30,000) + D($50,000) + E($20,000)	$190,000
2B	B($60 000) + C($30,000) + D($50,000) + E($20,000)	$160,000
3	G($150,000) + C($30,000) + D($50,000) + E($20,000)	$250,000
4	Hardware cost ($15,000) + C($30,000) + D($50,000) + E($20,000)	$115,000
5	F($20,000) + C($30,000) + E($20,000) + D($50,000)	$120,000

SELECTING AN ALTERNATIVE

Ideally, a detailed cost analysis should be made for each alternative, but this is seldom possible. We would not choose one alternative simply because it is slightly cheaper than another. There are other considerations. Some alternatives are quickly ruled out on technical or operational grounds, or because of other internal organizational considerations. These may be things like selecting an alternative that matches skills with the organization or, perhaps, choosing a site for expansion that has been ignored for some time.

TEXT CASE D: Construction Company—Selecting the Alternative

In Text Case D, Solution 1 has already been ruled out on technical grounds and Solution 4 on operational grounds. Usually only two or three alternatives are evaluated in detail. Once the evaluation is complete, selection begins.

An economic comparison such as that shown in Table 4.3 is usually a good start for selection. Some solutions, such as 2A, can be eliminated straight away. Obviously, 2B would be preferable to 2A because it is cheaper. Now we must choose between Solutions 2B, 3 and 5. Because of its cost, Solution 3 could also be quickly eliminated unless there were some intangible reasons for going to the centralized system. Assuming that none exist, we are reduced to choosing between 2B and 5. This is resolved by determining the value of doing invoice checking automatically (something done in 2B and not 5). Is the value of such a check worth the extra $40,000?

The final determination of the value of the project is shown by the present value computations in Table 4.4. These computations use a discount factor of 10 percent. They use only direct benefits, and no intangible benefits are included. The direct benefits are the savings in staff who previously did the checking. The saving per annum for Solution 5 is $40,000 and for Solution 2B is $50,000. The difference is the extra manual work to transfer shipment notices between the two systems in Solution 5. The present value for Solution 2B is $155,350 compared to the cost of $160,000. This solution would not be economically acceptable on direct economic costs. The present value for Solution 5 is $124,280 compared to the cost of $120,000. Thus, on direct economic costs, this solution is acceptable but, as you will note, not much is gained by the project on direct costs alone. However, if intangible savings or quicker project completions because of quicker part deliveries were to be added, the returns would be more substantial. Thus, in all probability, the project would go ahead using Solution 5, because it requires less initial investment than solution 2B.

Table 4.4 *Present value analysis for Text Case D (using a discount rate of 10%)*

(a) Savings (Solution 5)

Year	Amount	Present value
1	40,000	$36,360
2	40,000	$33,040
3	40,000	$30,040
4	40,000	$24,840

Total present value: $124,280

(b) Savings (Solution 2B)

Year	Amount	Present value
1	50,000	$45,450
2	50,000	$41,300
3	50,000	$37,550
4	50,000	$31,050

Total present value: $155,350

PREPARING A STATEMENT OF USER REQUIREMENTS

Once our analysis is complete, it is necessary to prepare a proposal. The proposal itself may be long and detailed or relatively short, depending on the size and importance of the project. The proposal will include the kind of information described in this chapter, but it must be presented in a form that clearly specifies the advantages of the project to the organization and its users. It must be clear and precise and specify the goals. It must also present the arguments, using the kind of information produced in this chapter. Above all, it must stress the advantages it will bring to the organization and the improvements that will be made once the new system is in place.

The proposal must instill in the readers—who are usually the ones who will contribute the funds for the project—confidence that the proposer has clearly thought out the goals, the risks and the alternatives, and that it provides the best course of action. The proposal should include all the issues covered in this chapter and present them in such a way that they convince management and users to proceed with the project. Suggested sections include:

- a statement that defines the business problem being solved;
- the chosen solution, explaining why it was chosen and briefly indicating the other alternatives;
- a description of how the new system will work and its impact on external clients and internal users;
- justification for choosing the preferred alternative and its economic, technical and operational advantages;
- what various people in the organization will have to do to implement the solution; and
- the effect of the solution on the way people work, including any new skills needed by people and the way these skills can be learnt.

The proposal usually goes to management, so it must be written in a language that is understood by them. It must be precise and concentrate on identifying the problem and convincing management that the proposed solution will be beneficial to the organization. Rejected solutions may also be briefly listed and discussed.

 # SUMMARY

This chapter described how a project is started. The first step is to define the project goal, and the next is to evaluate the feasibility of achieving this goal.

The chapter outlined methods used to define the goal and evaluate its feasibility, together with the necessity of proposing a number of broad solutions and then evaluating the technical, operational and economic feasibility of these solutions. The most satisfactory of these solutions is then selected for implementation and a statement of requirements prepared.

DISCUSSION QUESTIONS

4.1 Why is identifying a problem important?

4.2 How would you go about identifying problems?

4.3 'Maximizing benefits for given costs' is one possible criterion for comparing alternative proposals. In what environment would this criterion be most appropriate? Name some other criteria with which you are familiar and the environments to which they apply.

4.4 Why are constraints important when alternative solutions to a problem are proposed?

4.5 Why is a system proposal needed?

 ## EXERCISES

4.1 Propose alternative broad solutions for the truck-scheduling system described in Text Case C.

4.2 Suppose you have done a cost-benefit analysis and found that the estimated cost of a proposed project is $230,000. The benefits of the project over an estimated life of six years are:

- Year 1—$50,000
- Year 2—$80,000
- Year 3—$65,000
- Year 4—$50,000
- Year 5—$40,000
- Year 6—$20,000

Would you proceed with the project, given a 10 percent discount rate?

4.3 Have another look at proposed Solution 1, the client-server approach, for the Construction Company. Describe ways of implementing the solution.

BIBLIOGRAPHY

Bentley, R., Hughes, J.A., Randall, D., Rodden, T., Sawyer, P., Shapiro, D. and Sommerville, I. (1992), 'Ethnographically-informed systems design for air traffic control', *Proceedings of the CSCW92 Conference*, Toronto, pp. 123–29.

Goldberg, R. and Lorin, M. (eds) (1982), *The Economics of Information Processing*, Wiley-Interscience, New York.

Jordan, B. (June 1993), 'Ethnographic workplace studies and CSCW', *Proceedings of the 12th Interdisciplinary Workshop on Informatics and Psychology*, Shaerding, Australia, North-Holland Publishing Co., Amsterdam.

King, J.L. and Schrems, E.L. (March 1978), 'Cost-benefit analysis in information systems development and operation', *ACM Computing Surveys*, Vol. 13 No. 1, pp. 19–34.

Requirements analysis

5

CONTENTS

KEY LEARNING OBJECTIVES

The importance of defining requirements
Solving problems in system development
Analysis and requirements models
Translation from usage terms to system terms
Understanding the system through observation
Prototyping
Storyboard prototyping

INTRODUCTION

Much has been said about building correct systems that work according to user needs. However, correct systems can only be built if it is known exactly what the user needs and what the system must do. One of the most important factors in building correct systems, therefore, is to first clearly define what the system must do. There are two major steps. The first step, which was described in Chapter 4, is to agree on a broad conceptual solution. The next step is a detailed analysis of user requirements, followed by a system specification. This step is needed to develop a good understanding of the system and its problems. Usually it produces an analysis model which clearly describes how a system works now, as well as a requirements model of what the new system must do. Identifying detailed user requirements is becoming even more important in the complex systems that are now being developed. It has also been extremely important in what are known as critical systems, *where malfunctions can lead to severe system failures or even catastrophes.*

There are many ways to develop system requirements. One of these, however, is not simply sitting down and drawing a model of the system or setting user requirements in the privacy of an office. It can only be done by going out and discussing with users what they require of the system and then building systems that satisfy these requirements. The requirements-gathering methods may themselves depend on the kind of system being studied. There may be differences in searching for information in highly structured systems, or in systems that contain highly volatile group environments, or in unstructured systems such as those often found in decision support. Thus, in summary, it is necessary to determine the best way to identify requirements and then to spend some time studying and observing the system, talking to its users, and obtaining information in many other ways about how the system works and what is needed of the new system.

In the engineering sense, described in Chapter 1, requirements are used to produce a specification—as happens when building a bridge or a house. For example, how much traffic should the bridge carry? How long will it be? Or how many rooms will there be in the house? It is only when these specifications are clearly specified that we can say whether the finished product, the bridge or the house, is correct—that is, it is what we wanted. The goal, which is still proving to be elusive, is to develop such precise specifications for computer system requirements, so that we can precisely say what we want and then say whether the produced system is correct or not.

THE IMPORTANCE OF COMMUNICATION

Requirements analysis must ultimately result in a specification which unambiguously describes what has to be built. The engineering discipline has now developed many ways of specifying requirements. There are plans, models, prototypes and simulations. Ways to define computer system requirements are also emerging. A common computer view of requirements analysis is shown in Figure 5.1. Here there is the business process, like running a bank or making a decision about share purchases, which the new system will support. Then there is the final implementation of the system. In the middle is system specification, which defines how the new system is to look. A system specification is preceded by defining a broad conceptual solution, which was described in

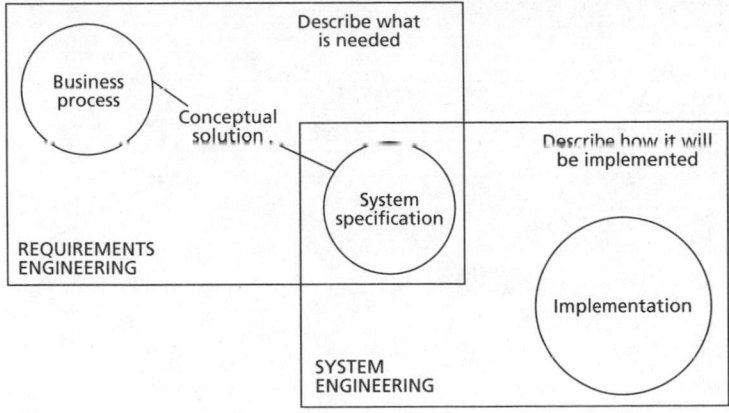

Figure 5.1 *The role of requirements analysis*

Chapter 4. Ultimately, however, the conceptual solution must be expanded into the system specification, which clearly defines what the implemented system will look like, what it must do and how it fits into the business process. The question then is what are the best tools to use to develop the specification? The answer is that precision is achieved by building models, which leads to the next question: what form should these models take? To answer this question, it is perhaps best to look at what people actually do during system development.

WHAT DO WE DO IN SYSTEM DEVELOPMENT?

Figure 5.2 shows the main activities in system development. To begin with, analysts discuss the system with users to familiarize themselves with it and to get a better idea of what the new system will be required to do. New ideas are also discussed and evaluated, with arguments and positions about the new system developed. Previous knowledge, or experience with similar systems, is used when developing new ideas. There may also be some experimentation to find out if some of the various proposed ideas can be put into practice; opinions are formed and often used in design. During this time we maintain a record of what was discussed and what conclusions were reached about the system. This record becomes part of our general experience, or group memory, which can be used in this or other projects. Many of the activities in Figure 5.2, such as design and decision making or simple explanations, are carried out in the ways described in Chapter 2.

There are two other important aspects here. One aspect is communication. In all of these processes it is necessary to reach agreement, to specify what we are to do and to represent it in an unambiguous way. The second aspect is organization of this work into a process that must eventually produce a new system. This chapter will describe the ways in which we can communicate or negotiate to reach agreements and develop system specifications. Organizing activities into a development process is described in Chapter 7. Perhaps the most important aspect of all these activities is to ensure that no ambiguities arise in discussions between the various people involved in analysis. Such ambiguities can easily arise because of the different jargon used by

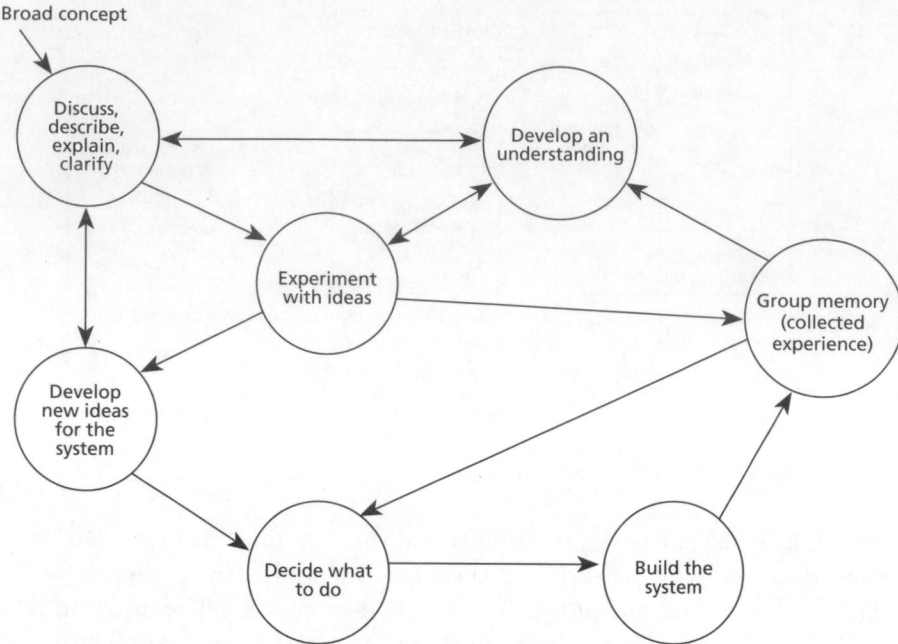

Figure 5.2 *Some activities in problem solving*

different people—in particular, the users, who often speak in terms common to their domain, and computer analysts, who may use computer terms. The goal of any analysis must be to ensure that all of these people eventually 'speak the same language' so that the correct requirements are identified.

DIFFERENT 'LANGUAGES'

Another way of looking at communication involves recognizing that people use a language that suits their **world**. For example, users talk about their problem domain, such as how to manage bank transactions and make decisions—this is the **usage world**. They like to use **terms** common to their work and to describe their work in terms of **scenarios**—that is, by giving examples of things that happen in their world. Computer system developers, on the other hand, prefer to talk about computer systems, using terms particular to this **development world**, such as operating systems, databases and so on. We need to find a way to bring these two worlds together. To do this, it is necessary to translate from the language in one world to that of another in an unambiguous way. This might involve using a number of interim steps or other languages, as shown in Figure 5.3.

The first step is the usage world, where the language commonly describes the way the user works, usually in terms of examples. The next step is the **subject world**. Here we try to make sense of the usage world in clear, unambiguous, but now well-defined, terms rather than in terms of specific scenarios. In this way we discover the essence of the system. Some of the user terms will now be unambiguously defined to eliminate any jargon that is common in the usage world. Thus the precise meanings of terms like *quote* or *premium* in a given organization are defined, and are not what analysts think they mean

System world
A system seen and defined using general system terms.

Usage world
A system seen and described using everyday terms.

Terms
Words with specific meaning used to describe systems.

Scenario
A description of a process in the usage world.

Development world
The context in which technical development takes place.

Subject world
A system seen and described in well-defined business terms.

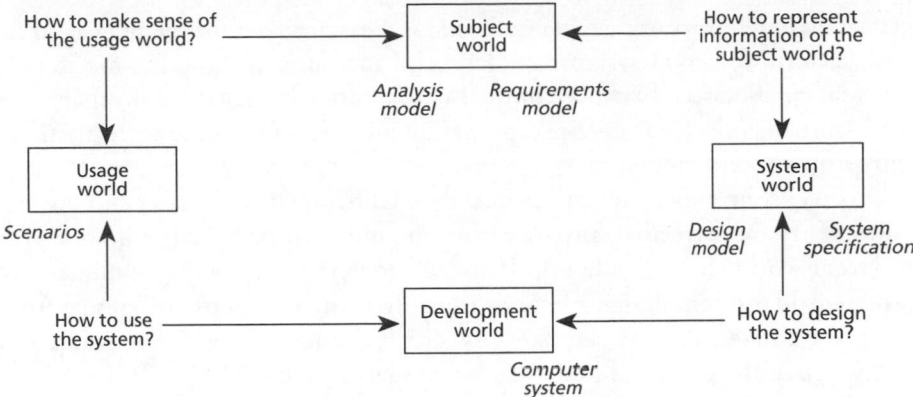

Figure 5.3 *The worlds in system development*

using their common knowledge. In fact, there is an increasing demand for subject specialists who can deal with the complexities found in specific subject worlds, such as insurance or banking. A clear picture begins to emerge of how the usage world works in terms that describe general processes rather than individual scenarios. The most essential characteristics also begin to emerge at this stage. These terms are used in the statement of requirements, which should include as one of its components a precise glossary of terms.

The next step is to represent the subject terms in abstract system terms that are later useful to the developers but can still be understood by the users. Such system terms are used to build the **analysis models** which become part of the system specification and are easily converted to computer systems. These system models are described in detail in Chapters 8 to 12.

Analysis models
A description of the way in which a system works.

REPRESENTING SYSTEMS

An important activity in systems development is to build representations or models in the different worlds. These models are built using the terms identified for each world and thus become precise system representations in that world. The models are used to keep track of what has been done to date and what else needs to be done to complete information gathering.

A number of different models may be created as one proceeds through the development process. The development process centers around converting an initial usage world model, through subject and system models, to a computer system. In fact, development processes are often characterized by the models they support at each step with different processes using different models. Examples of models include:

- the *analysis model*, which describes how the system works now in terms of the subject world;
- the *requirements model*, which describes what users need in terms of the subject world; and
- the *design model*, which describes the required computer system in terms of the system world.

Models and conversion play an important role in quality assurance. In the first instance, models themselves must satisfy some criteria related to good practice. Thus, there are accepted ways of carrying on business, best practices for the usage and subject world, criteria for good systems models, and measures for good computer system performance. The second aspect of quality assurance is that the conversion process must ensure that all characteristics captured in one world model are correctly translated into the next world model.

Quality is an important aspect in the conversion. It is necessary to ensure that requirements are correctly translated from the usage world to the subject world and the system world. It is equally important to judge the quality of the models created in each world. System design methods thus often include steps and guidelines to be used in the conversion, and standards by which to judge models. For example, there are now what are known as best practice models in particular subject worlds, such as banking or insurance, which can be used to guide designers to produce good models. Standards are also being created for system world models.

Many development processes are supported by computer tools, known as CASE (Computer Assisted Software Engineering) tools which help designers to develop and maintain their models.

 ## IDENTIFYING REQUIREMENTS

An important aspect of modeling is its role as a communications tool in determining requirements. Usually the following approach is used. An analyst will develop a model following an initial discussion with a user. A repeat visit may then validate the model with the user. Once agreement is reached on the model, further detailed data may be gathered to elaborate the model. This iterative approach serves a number of purposes. First, it ensures that there is always a record of the information gathered to date. Second, it serves to ensure the correctness of the information by continually verifying with the user the results. This ensures that an analyst does not get too far ahead using erroneous assumptions.

Requirements must in the first instance be identified from information collected in the usage world. Analysts must concentrate on the ways in which the new system can improve this world and express their improvements in usage world terms by explaining the proposed scenarios for the new system. However, the requirements must also be defined in general terms, more common to the subject world, which can then be converted to specifications in the system world. One important aspect here is to use general terms so that systems can support a large range of scenarios rather than just one. Thus in the subject world we try to identify general terms in the subject world, whereas in the system world we define general system terms. These terms must be chosen in ways that make it easy to translate them from one world to another.

Rich picture
A pictorial representation of a system.

Soft system methodology
A development process centering on the user and subject worlds.

DESCRIBING THE USAGE WORLD

One way to describe the usage world is to use **rich pictures**. This is the premise of what are known as **soft systems methodologies**, where the usage world is described in terms as close as possible to what people see happening in their world—by pictures and scenarios. Examples from the usage world are then used to develop a subject world model by defining the terms that will be used to describe this world. The choice of concepts is left open to the designers.

TEXT CASE B: Managing an Agency—Analyzing Broad Level Interactions

The manager of an agency decided that one of the first steps in supporting the committee would be to define the activities between the people involved and how they interact with each other. These interactions are illustrated in Figure 5.4, which is a simple diagram identifying the roles involved in the project and joining those roles that are likely to interact. The interactions are shown in the clouded shapes. The rich picture also shows the main artifacts used in the system. These are shown in rectangular boxes. Thus there are early discussions to decide on report contents and assignment of part of it to different workgroups. Then draft sections are exchanged between the different groups, whereas a draft report is considered by the committee meeting. Part of the analysis is to write a scenario for each such interaction. For example, the script for the committee chairperson–committee member interaction may include headings such as 'Arrange meeting', 'Discussion' and 'Minute verification'.

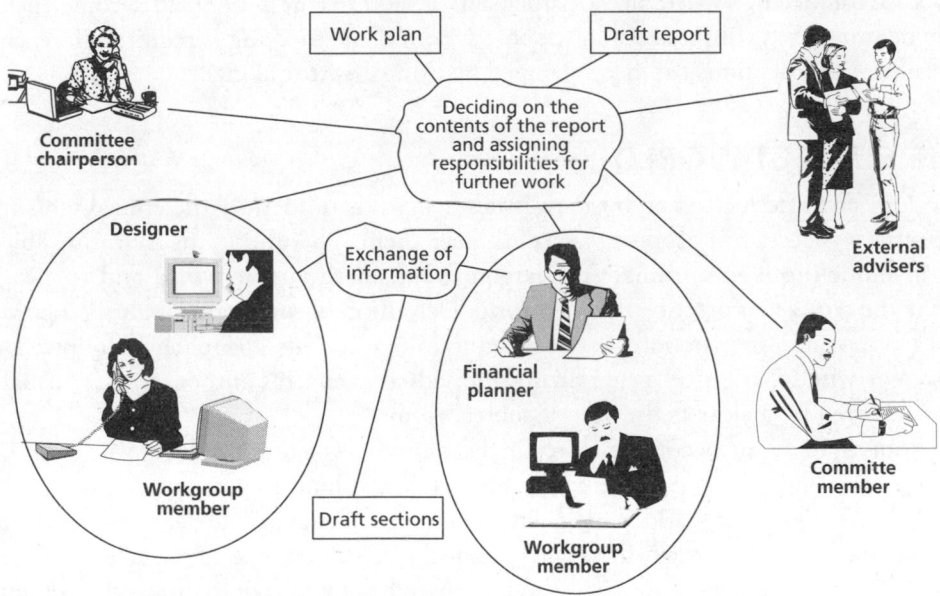

Figure 5.4 *A rich picture showing interactions between people*

Scenarios

Scenarios support models such as the rich picture by illustrating system dynamics using typical sequences of actions in the user world. For example, one scenario for the system in Figure 5.4 may be that given below.

1. The committee chairperson writes a project brief and assigns it to different workgroups.

2. Workgroup leaders coordinate their workgroups by discussing the brief and then creating an initial draft which is passed between the workgroup members.
3. Workgroup leaders meet occasionally with the chairperson and external advisers and other nominated committee members to resolve any conflicts.

Scenarios may take different forms. There may be a specific instance that describes a particular time when a group leader handed a brief to individual people, saying: 'Develop a marketing proposal for a new perfume.' This scenario may describe not only the process followed, but also the problems found and the ways in which they were overcome. A number of such instances may then be used to develop a more general scenario which can cover these specific instances. It may also identify a variety of exception cases that may arise in the scenario. Ways of defining scenarios are now becoming more formalized. For example, scenarios have become a very popular way of describing requirements in object-oriented design, where general scenarios are known as *use cases*. We will discuss use cases in the chapter on object-oriented analysis (Chapter 11).

Scenarios can be expanded to indicate the kind of support to be provided for the interactions. Expansion includes identifying interaction characteristics and choosing appropriate software for them. Thus, for example, a teleconferencing system may be proposed for meetings where all the participants are at different locations. Teleconferencing may be integrated with a decision support system if the meeting is required to reach a decision. Draft sections can be exchanged by using electronic mail. .

THE SUBJECT WORLD

The subject world focuses on business issues. Its goal is to identify the crucial measures of business success and propose ways to achieve them. The important factor in subject world modeling is to eliminate the jargon found in the usage world and to clearly define the terms that describe the user world. Definition of such terms is also recognized as an important step in soft systems methodologies. This approach is followed in object-oriented design by generalizing individual scenarios into use cases, usually accompanied by a clear definition of subject terms.

Many systems are becoming increasingly complex. As a result, subject world models are one of the least known in the conversion process. There are few criteria that can be used to evaluate subject world models, although there is a tendency to define best practices in many industries. Eventually these will become the guidelines used to evaluate the subject world. There is also a trend for people to become subject world specialists—for example, the bank analysis specialist, whose main activity may be to develop models of the subject world and to express them as conceptual schema in the system world.

Soft systems methodologies approach the subject world by defining standard subject terms once the initial analysis is completed. These terms are then used to create a subject world model.

THE SYSTEM WORLD

In the system world we begin to talk more in general system ways which can be applied to any problem. This area is often termed *conceptual modeling* in computer system design. It describes the system in terms that are useful to computer systems designers in developing a computer system specification. One set of terms comes under the general heading of *structured systems analysis*. They include models such as data flow diagrams, entities and relationships, and process descriptions. Another set of terms comes from object-oriented design. These two approaches for defining systems are described in subsequent chapters in this book. In this chapter, we concentrate on collecting the data needed to identify requirements.

COLLECTION METHODS

Remember that defining user requirements requires an understanding of how the system works and what its problems are. We now examine methods for collecting information in order to develop such an understanding. There are many important issues to consider in getting a clear picture of a system. One is to look at the current business processes in the system and identify the tasks in those processes. Or one can begin by examining particular system functions and their tasks. The tasks can then be examined in detail. Such examination can identify the users, who carry out the tasks, the interactions between the users, the tools they use and the artifacts on which they operate. Thus an analyst must always consider the users and what they do. How do they use the artifacts? With whom do they interact? Where do they find information? This has an important bearing on the way the system works. Remember also that there is no such thing as a standard system. It is not useful, therefore, to have preconceived ideas about a system and analysts must approach any study with an open mind. There are four main ways of doing this—namely, by:

- *asking questions* by interviewing people in the system, through surveys and questionnaires, or by electronic means using e-mail or a discussion database;
- *observational studies*, including ethnography, or by participating within the user environment;
- *prototyping* either the requirements or the interface; and
- *formal sessions*, including structured workshops, group discussions and facilitated teams.

Another important consideration is the methods used for maintaining records of the information found and for documenting and analyzing this information—that is, translating from the subject world to the usage world. The kind of activities carried out by analysts in this sequence range from simply keeping notes to building models of the system. Computer systems themselves may often support an analyst in storing information. Some of these productivity tools will be described in a later chapter.

GATHERING INFORMATION BY ASKING QUESTIONS

Interviewing is perhaps the most commonly used technique in analysis. There is no real way to avoid interviews as they must precede any other method for gathering information about system requirements. It is always necessary first to approach someone and ask them what their problems and priorities are, and later to discuss with them the results of your analysis. Interviewing is discussed at length in the next chapter.

QUESTIONNAIRES

Questionnaires provide an alternative to interviews for finding out information about a system. Questionnaires are made up of questions about information sought by the analyst. The questionnaire is then sent to the user, and replies are analyzed by the analyst.

There are a number of disadvantages in using questionnaires. First, they are mostly suited to closed questions and are not effective for open questions such as 'Describe your general duties' or 'What are the most important system components?' Second, questionnaire questions are usually not answered completely and will often express some current concern rather than long-term concerns. Thus, the response to 'Describe your general duties' will often include the things the user did in the last day or so. A set of follow-up questions is usually necessary to establish activities over a longer period of time and this is best done by an interview rather than a long questionnaire.

Questionnaires, however, are useful when the same kind of information is sought from a number of users. This is especially so if that information is of a quantitative nature—for example, finding out how many calls salespeople make each day. A questionnaire which asks that question is simply sent out to all the salespeople in the organization.

It is also possible to use questionnaires to get an idea about the quality and performance of systems. This can be done by using structured questions that include a range of replies and require the responder to tick one of them. For example, a question to customers on the quality of service may read as follows:

Do you feel that our deliveries to you are:

> Always prompt?
> As good as can be expected?
> Sometimes late?
> Often late?

Questionnaires, of course, often include many questions designed to find out information about a system component. For example, we might have a questionnaire like that shown in Figure 5.5. Here we are trying to establish the usefulness of a program developed to support a large number of insurance brokers in preparing insurance quotations. The first question establishes the user's familiarity with the program. This is followed by a question that indicates the user's general experience. Then questions are asked about whether the user finds the program useful, and finally suggestions are asked for regarding a possible improvement. A collection of responses can then be used to establish the general acceptability of the program and to determine whether it should continue to be used and whether any changes are needed.

In summary, questionnaires are used to supplement other techniques. They are useful for gathering numerical data or getting relatively simple opinions from a number

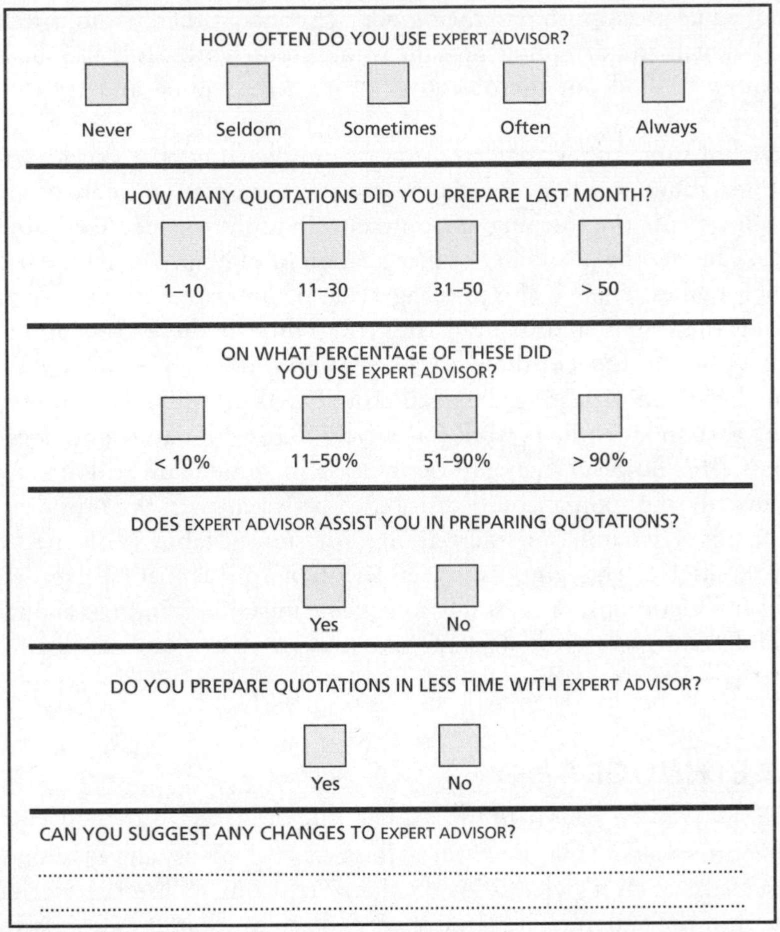

HOW OFTEN DO YOU USE EXPERT ADVISOR?

Never | Seldom | Sometimes | Often | Always

HOW MANY QUOTATIONS DID YOU PREPARE LAST MONTH?

1–10 | 11–30 | 31–50 | > 50

ON WHAT PERCENTAGE OF THESE DID YOU USE EXPERT ADVISOR?

< 10% | 11–50% | 51–90% | > 90%

DOES EXPERT ADVISOR ASSIST YOU IN PREPARING QUOTATIONS?

Yes | No

DO YOU PREPARE QUOTATIONS IN LESS TIME WITH EXPERT ADVISOR?

Yes | No

CAN YOU SUGGEST ANY CHANGES TO EXPERT ADVISOR?

Figure 5.5 *A questionnaire*

of people, but they are not very effective for in-depth searches or for identifying system problems or solutions. Interviews tend to be more successful for this purpose.

ELECTRONIC DATA GATHERING

Electronic communication systems are increasingly being used to gather information. Thus it is possible to use electronic mail to broadcast a question to a number of users in an organization to obtain their viewpoint on a particular issue. Alternatively, an electronic bulletin board can be used to allow potential users to record their requirements.

GATHERING INFORMATION BY OBSERVATION

Interviewing and other ways of asking questions are characterized by having analysts learn about the system without themselves getting involved in the system. Interviews often emphasize what an individual does and how to support them, rather than looking at the individual's relationship to their group. The analyst then has to correlate findings about individuals and determine how the whole group works. It is also the interviewer's responsibility to find out the objectives of each individual and try to make them cohesive.

There are some other characteristics of interviewing that can lead to incorrect assumptions about a system. One is the danger that because the interview is usually carried out outside the working environment, the interviewee may distort replies to questions. There is the possibility of exaggeration or of emphasizing the less important aspects of activities. There is also the danger that the interviewer may have preconceived ideas about the system and its needs and try to impose these ideas into the study or interpret replies in terms of these preconceived notions.

A further disadvantage of data gathering based on individual interviews is that it assumes that an individual's work is relatively routine in nature and does not change over time. This, however, may not be the case in some team situations where tasks are dynamically and spontaneously distributed between users. We thus have a situation where there is a dynamic, or time varying, division of labor, with the rules for this division themselves changing. Interviewees often find it difficult to describe these situations in exact terms, thus leading to possible misunderstandings about the system. Ethnography aims to overcome some of these problems. It does this by observing the usage world and recording activities within it.

USING ETHNOGRAPHY

Ethnography
Gathering information
by observation.

Ethnography is not a new field but, rather, a new approach to analyzing computer system requirements. One of its most important goals is not to superimpose the interviewer's or analyst's viewpoint on the system but to use the viewpoint of the people within the system. The terms *emic* and *etic* are sometimes used to stress this distinction. An **etic** view of the system is the 'outside view' or what the analyst sees, whereas the **emic** view is the 'inside view' or what the system users see. The goal is not to superimpose the outside view on to a system and consequently identify the wrong problems, but to actually see what goes on from the insider's viewpoint. The main characteristics of ethnographic studies are:

Etic
An outside view of a
system.

Emic
An inside view of a
system.

- analysts observe or possibly even participate in such activities;
- any interviews are conducted *in situ*, possibly as informal discussion rather than formal interview;
- there is emphasis on examining the interaction between users;
- there is emphasis on tracing communication links; and
- there is detailed analysis of artifacts.

Ethnographic studies therefore place a different orientation on information gathering. The emphasis is on observation of system activities, and perhaps even active participation in these activities by analysts, and on observing the system from within rather than from the outside. The ethnographic approach has a number of advantages. First, because interviewing is carried out *in situ*, the system is directly observed as it actually works.

The users are not disturbed in their activities, and information is gathered directly and not from an informal description obtained through interviews.

Analysis by participation

Ethnographic studies, because of their emphasis on interaction, are particularly important in studying the way that groups of people work. Their goal is to study the dynamic social situations that occur in such environments. It is usual here to identify communities or workers and to analyze their interactions. One way to gather information is by actually participating in group activities. The analyst becomes a member of a team, perhaps in an indirect capacity, assisting other team members. Successful studies, for example, have been undertaken on the way air traffic controllers work (Bentley et al., 1992).

Analysis by observation

The goal here is to observe what people do in an unobtrusive way. The best way to do this is by video recording. It is important in video recording to ensure that the presence of the video camera itself does not alter behavior while at the same time collecting sufficient in-depth information to make useful observations. This requires considerable skill both in the placement of video recording equipment and the setting of the video camera itself. Once a video is complete, analysis commences. Analysis is usually carried out in conjunction with participants of the work setting. The result of the review session is a script of user activities and their interaction with each other.

Some analysis techniques

Ethnography itself includes a number of techniques. Some of these (Jordan, 1993) are:

* *Analyzing people's roles*: This identifies how a particular person feels about their work and the kinds of problems they encounter. The goal is to gather information on the practices followed by people carrying out a particular task.
* *Analyzing interaction*: Interaction analysis defines how users work together in groups. A simple diagram may be produced, showing the various system roles and their relationships. Then scripts may be developed to describe such relationships in more detail. This often leads to the identification of communities of practice that are spontaneously formed around a particular task.
* *Analyzing location*: A study is made of what happens at a particular place over a period of time. Often the study produces a set of snapshots of activities during that period.
* *Analyzing artifacts*: The emphasis on artifact analysis is how it fits into the flow of work rather than on artifact structure in its own right. Important aspects are:
  — how an artifact flows through the system;
  — use of artifacts by teams rather than individuals;
  — considering the artifact as a work space in its own right.
* *Task analysis*: The analyst studies the processes within a system and the role of individual users. Emphasis is on the information needed by the user and what the user does with the information and where it is obtained.

Although ethnography has been mainly applied in the study of detailed interactions within dynamic group environments, we can learn from it in its more general application to analysis. For example, we may identify the interactions at a broad rather than detailed level and then use them as a guideline in our further analysis.

FROM OBSERVATION TO DESIGN

Another characteristic of the ethnographic approach is that objectives are developed with user participation. Considerable time, for example, may be spent on the design of workspaces through experimentation. Such workspaces not only include the computer screen but also the physical space used for any manual work on associated documentation or paperwork.

Ethnography can, of course, be made to fit in with other methods of information gathering. It can, for example, be used to bring the social issues into analysis, because it emphasizes interaction. There is also a clear link between ethnography and prototyping. It should be possible to take some of the information found in analysis and gradually use it to build systems.

GATHERING INFORMATION BY PROTOTYPING

Prototyping
A method used to test or illustrate an idea and build a system in an explorative way.

Prototyping is a term that is often used to mean different things. We can build prototypes for many reasons: to test a new idea, or as a first step in development, or as a tool for requirements analysis.

Historically, most prototypes were used to test a new idea or design. You often hear of prototypes being used in engineering. These were based on models that were used to illustrate a system. For example, we could have a model of a plane in a wind tunnel to test a design. The model would be 'flown' in the wind tunnel, measurements made on performance and then used, if necessary, to modify the design. Once the designers are satisfied with the results of the model, the real plane would be built. In this case, the prototype is built to illustrate the feasibility of the new system and is then virtually discarded.

The main role of prototyping in information systems design is to improve requirements definition by involving potential system users. Prototyping is primarily an experimental method. A rough system is built, and users can experiment with it and make comments in usage model terms about its suitability for the workplace. Their reactions are obtained and used to define requirements in an iterative way.

Prototyping has the added advantage that it serves to create a culture of democracy by involving users in its development, rather than a culture where only the analyst and designer play the leading role. It can thus ensure user commitment to the developed system by involving users early in the decision-making process. It removes the rigid boundaries that exist between analysts and users and can lead to better elicitation of user requirements and, eventually, better systems. It is now commonly used in design, especially where systems cannot be easily prespecified. We shall describe how prototyping is used in system development in Chapter 7.

In many cases prototypes can be used in the final system and hence not all parts of a system prototype are discarded. There are, of course, different kinds of prototyping. One way may be to actually build the system while designing it. Another just illustrates some components of the system, which are eventually discarded. Still a third and very common approach is to simulate interactive processes to see whether they satisfy user needs.

INTERFACE PROTOTYPING

Perhaps the most common way of prototyping is to develop screens that illustrate what users will have to do in the new system. This can then be used to describe to users the kind of information that would be made available to them from the system and how they can work with this information. For example, we may construct an interface to illustrate to a user the kind of inputs and possible outputs that a proposed system would require. However, the actual system would not be written. Instead, stored example screens could be illustrated to a user. Thus, in our interactive marketing system, we could build an interface that illustrates the availability of a product to potential customers and then get their reaction. We could also propose input screens to gauge their acceptability. Of course, one could argue that this can be done simply by drawing the screens on paper. However, it is found that the actual illustration of screens is a better approach, particularly if the potential user can experiment with some sample inputs and outputs and suggest changes to them.

PROTOTYPING PROCESSES

Prototypes can also be used to describe a process that involves a number of users. The term **storyboarding** is often used to describe this approach. In storyboarding, a series of small prototypes are tied together, so that the user can see how the whole system works.

Storyboarding
A sequence of computer screens to describe how a system will be used.

A storyboard is often developed as a sequence of screens, almost like developing a film script. Thus, there may be a screen that displays what a requisition may look like. The user can experiment with this screen and change its layout to adapt it to a particular method of working. Then we may develop an approval screen. The storyboard then becomes two steps. We can show the kind of input on the requisition screen and illustrate how it results in the approve screen. Then we can develop an order screen, and so on. Thus a storyboard evolves, and users as well as designers can begin to see how the system will work. It should be noted that, initially, screen inputs need not result in any actual computations. All that the underlying program does is move data from one screen to another without storing it in a database or checking input for correctness. As the prototype develops, we may add to these programs a database or some checking. Thus the prototype may gradually evolve into a working system.

TEXT CASE A: Interactive Marketing—A Storyboard

ISSUES

Our interactive marketing must be accepted by producers if it is to be successfully implemented. Most of the producers have little familiarity with computers and consequently cannot easily express their requirements. However, the requirements, particularly the user interface, must be known prior to building the system.

SOLUTION

The proposed solution here is to use prototyping to elicit user requirements. It is proposed to set up a series of screens to explain to producers all the steps they would have to follow to use the system. We start with the three screens shown in Figure 5.6, one to show the initial input, the second an offer received and a third the delivery advice. We can now use the screens as a basis for discussion with the producers.

The screens are developed to follow the sequence of the process used by the producers. In that sense we can use a discussion framework. For example, we could say: 'The first thing that you do is enter the following on the screen.' At that stage you may enquire if something else is needed from the producer, or discuss screen layout in more detail. Then you can discuss the offer screen and how to respond to it. The menu here allows the initial offer to be retrieved or buyer details found. The screens for these have not yet been devised, but it is possible to discuss with producers what they would like to have on these screens. Other questions can be asked related to issues like screen layout or, indeed, whether this screen is needed at all or whether offers should be automatically accepted. In this way you can find out what offers can be automatically accepted or what else is needed to make a decision. You may then discuss reporting procedures for automatically accepted offers. The discussion will lead on to deliveries and so on.

One particular issue for discussion is the numbering scheme used for offers and purchases.

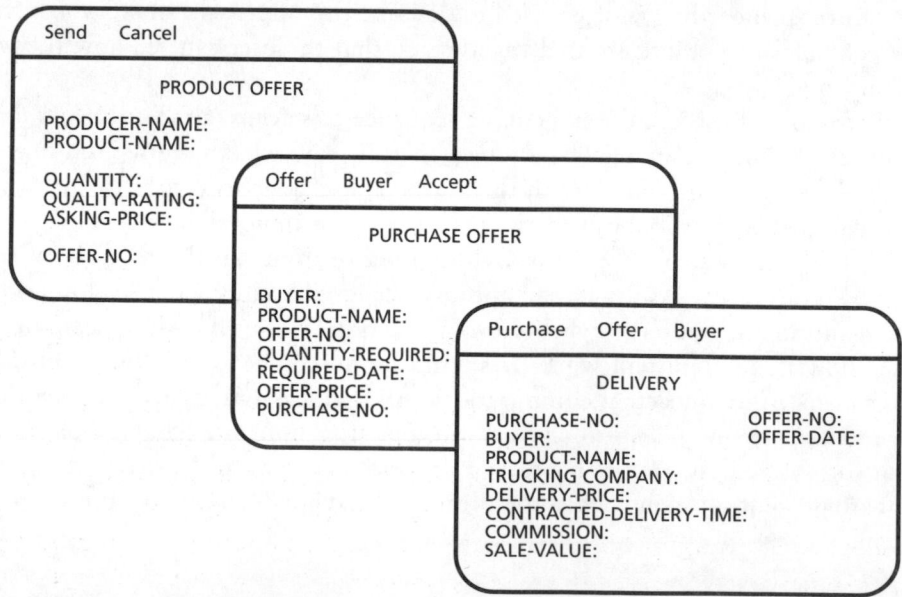

Figure 5.6 An initial storyboard

PROTOTYPING TO TEST A NEW IDEA

Prototyping is used when a totally novel system is proposed. No early experience exists with a similar system, and so a model is needed to gain experience with the kind of problems that can be expected when developing the full-blown system.

A typical example of prototyping is testing a new algorithm. We may have heard of an algorithm that may be useful for a given problem. We could test the algorithm on some sample data to determine whether it does what we want and to measure its performance. If this turns out to be satisfactory, then the algorithm will be used to develop the system.

An Example—Winning at Horse Races

Suppose someone has an idea about how to predict the winners of horse races. This requires considerable amounts of information about horse characteristics and history, as well as track and weather conditions during races. The algorithm proposed is quite experimental. Obviously most people would be sceptical about any such proposal, but suppose you want to try it anyway. It would be unwise to start by collecting information about all horses and races. This could be quite expensive and nothing may come of it.

A better way to proceed would be to gather information about a small subset of horses and races and perhaps try a modified algorithm on this data. Once such a system is implemented, we can experiment with it to see if we can indeed predict winners. If so, the system is then extended to include all races and horses.

WORKSHOPS AND BRAINSTORMING SESSIONS

Workshops are increasingly being used to elicit new ideas for systems. The idea behind them is to get people who are familiar with the issues together to spontaneously explore ways of improving a system. They are often asked to raise issues and comment on them. Usually this discussion is facilitated to ensure that it is focused and does not drift away from the main design issues and methods are provided to continually record issues and subsequent discussions.

SUMMARY

This chapter began by describing the importance of defining the requirements for the new system. It stressed that communication is one of the most important issues in eliciting requirements and described the different levels, or worlds, at which such information can be gathered. Whatever the level, it is important to define unambiguous terms that are used in communication. The advantages of building models and of converting from one model to another during the development process were also outlined.

The chapter then described ways of collecting information about the system, through asking questions, participation in user teams, ethnography and prototyping.

In general, gathering of information by asking questions is used in most transaction systems with well-defined flows. Prototyping is better suited to experimental systems, and as decision support. Participation and ethnography have been susggested for group work, which requires close study in a social setting.

DISCUSSION QUESTIONS

5.1 Why is it necessary to go through a number of 'worlds' in modeling systems?

5.2 Why are unambiguous terms needed in the different worlds?

5.3 Why is modeling important?

5.4 What do you understand by the term *subject world*?

5.5 What is the difference between the subject and usage worlds?

5.6 Why are scenarios important?

5.7 Where would participation be the best way of gathering requirements?

5.8 Describe how the use of modeling can improve 'system quality'.

5.9 Are you familiar with any systems where a prototype problem-solving approach would be useful?

5.10 What do you understand by the term *storyboard*?

EXERCISE

5.1 Develop a rich picture for the interactive marketing case (Text Case A).

BIBLIOGRAPHY

Anriole, S.J. (1992), *Storyboard Prototyping: A New Approach to User Requirements Analysis* (2nd edn), QED Information Sciences, Inc., Wellesley, Massachusetts.

Brittan, J.N.G. (February 1980), 'Design for a changing environment', *The Computer Journal*, Vol. 23 No. 1, pp. 13–19.

Jeffrey, H.J. and Putman, A.O. (March 1994), 'Relationship definition and management: tools for requirements analysis', *Journal of Systems Software*, Vol. 24, No. 3, pp. 277—94.

Keil, M. and Carmel, E. (May 1995), 'Customer–developer links in software development', *Communications of the ACM*, Vol. 38, No. 5, pp. 33–44.

King, D. (1984), *Current Practices in Software Development*, Yourdon Press, New York.

Madsen, K.H. and Aiken, P.H. (June 1993), 'Experiences using cooperative interactive storyboard prototyping' *Communications of the ACM*, Vol. 36, No. 4, pp. 57–66.

Mason, R.E.A. and Carey, T.T. (May 1983), 'Prototyping interactive information systems', *Communications of the ACM*, Vol. 26, No. 5, pp. 347–54.

Tamai, T. (June 1993), 'Current practices in software processes for system planning and requirements analysis', *Information and Software Technology*, Vol. 35, No. 6, pp. 339–44.

6

Interviewing

 **CONTENTS**

 KEY LEARNING OBJECTIVES

The information sources in an organization
Developing an interview strategy
How to carry out an interview

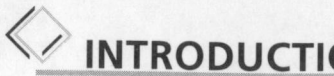

INTRODUCTION

The previous chapter described a number of ways of determining user requirements. Whatever the method, however, some time must be spent in talking to or interviewing people in the organization. Such interviews may only be in the initial stages to identify the major issues, or they can proceed throughout the entire life of a project, perhaps mixed with other methods to supplement discussion.

Apart from the methods used in determining requirements, it is important to identify the information sources and to determine what, in the broad sense, must be analyzed. This chapter describes some alternative methods used to gather information. It starts by describing the sources of such information. It is often said that systems can only be correct if they are correctly specified at the beginning.

INFORMATION SOURCES

There are a variety of sources of information about a system. Each source usually yields a different kind of information and requires a different search method to get that information.

SYSTEM USERS

System users are the most important information source. From them it is possible to find out the existing system activities and to determine the user objectives and requirements. There are a number of ways of gathering information from users. One way is through interviews. Another is to use questionnaires. A third is through observation of user activities and behavior. Interviews are one of the main methods used to gather information. (Interview techniques are described later in this chapter.) The interview approach may depend on the kind of user. For example, an overview is often sought with management, whereas detailed task information is sought from the users who carry out the tasks. There are also users who may cooperate more readily than others. There may be users who are in favor of change and will provide considerable support, whereas others, who may have their positions to preserve, may not readily volunteer information. You might get someone who repeatedly exaggerates or who may even deliberately mislead you because they are not in favor of a study or any change. Later we will describe some interviewing methods that can be used with different kinds of users.

FORMS AND DOCUMENTS

Forms and documents are useful sources of information about system data flows and transactions. There are many different kinds of such documents in any large system. They may include management information such as budgets or they may be detailed records of transactions within a business. It is important for the analyst to identify the complete list of such documents. Such a list is usually obtained from the system users. Analysts then go through the documents and analyze their contents. At this time it is usual to check for duplication of data and for naming consistency to ensure the same data item does not appear under two names. It should again be noted that analysis should not begin by doing a detailed analysis of forms without first contacting users. You might just be unlucky and start with a form that is either out of date or no longer used. You should start by interviewing users and from them get the most recent and relevant forms.

COMPUTER PROGRAMS

Computer programs can be used to determine the details of data structures or processes. The search methods are often laborious and involve reading the program or its documentation, sometimes running the program with test data to see what it does, and examining the current user interface. Examination of existing programs is becoming an important part of analysis because many systems now use computers and an analyst must determine what exactly the current system does. The outcome of the design may be a proposal to redesign the existing computer system to meet new user requirements.

Of particular importance are the interactions with an existing computer system. The kind of information presented to users must also be examined during analysis. This information is often particularly useful, because it can identify specific shortfalls in the current system.

PROCEDURE MANUALS

Procedure manuals specify user activities in a business process. They can be used by analysts to determine detailed user activities, which is important in detailed system design. The search method is again a detailed examination of the contents of the manual. However, just as with forms and documents, it is necessary to make sure that the latest procedures are examined in a study. Many organizations are notorious for not updating their procedure manuals, so you should always check with a user any information obtained from a procedure manual.

REPORTS

This source indicates the kinds of outputs needed by users. It can be used as a basis for user interviews to determine any new output requirements that users may have.

It is very unlikely that one of these sources on its own will provide all the information that an analyst needs. If you start with an existing system, it is almost certain that you will have to obtain information about the organization from most, if not all, of these sources. The search procedure determines how to proceed through a search of these sources.

GATHERING INFORMATION THROUGH INTERVIEWING

Interviewing is the main approach used to analyze large structured systems. It is used by analysts to gradually build a subject world model and to understand any system problems. There are many important factors in successful interviewing. The

Interviewing
Gathering information by asking questions.

first is to choose people to interview. This is important, as the analyst must ensure that all key people within the study boundary are considered. The next important factor is finding the right way to conduct an individual interview. Here, good interpersonal relationships must be considered and the interviewer must establish some rapport with the interviewee to ensure the cooperation necessary to get all the relevant facts.

Information gathering through interviewing for a large and complex system can be an onerous task. Information must be gathered in an organized way to ensure that nothing is overlooked and that all system detail is eventually captured. All users must be consulted to ensure that every system problem and each user requirement is identified and that useful objectives are proposed. The search must avoid situations where different analysts seek the same information from the same user.

Before beginning such a system study, an analyst or team of analysts must establish a **search strategy** for gathering the information needed to develop a model of a system. As illustrated in Figure 6.1, this search strategy is established by selecting the sources from which information is to be obtained and determining the methods to obtain the information from each source. These sources and methods are combined into a **search procedure**. The search procedure defines where to begin the search and how to continue. It also identifies the sequence in which sources will be searched and what information is to be gathered at each step.

INTERVIEW SEARCH PROCEDURES

Information gathering in large systems with many information sources must proceed in an organized way to ensure that all the relevant information needed to build the system is obtained. Analysts must determine what information needs to be gathered

Search strategy
A selection of sources and methods to be used to gather information about a system.

Search procedure
The process followed to gather information about a system.

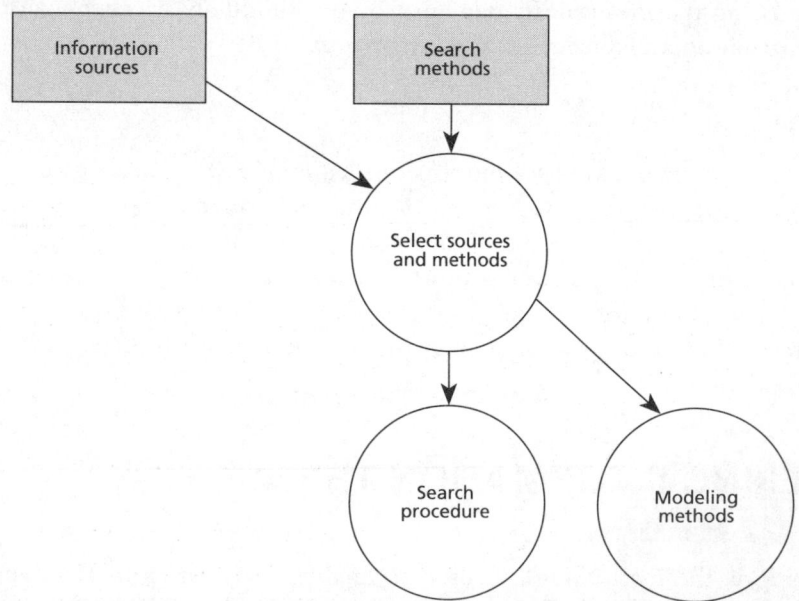

Figure 6.1 *Developing a search strategy*

and the users who are to supply this information. They must then seek this information in an orderly way so that vital information is not neglected and people are not repeatedly bothered by being asked the same questions. To avoid such problems, it is necessary to develop a search procedure for gathering information. This procedure will define the steps to be followed in gathering information and the information to be obtained at each step. Such steps usually require the search to proceed in a top-down manner, objectives to be set for each step, and an appropriate search method to be chosen for each step.

The search procedure suggests what order is to be used to search information sources and what methods are to be used as the search proceeds. Thus the search procedure becomes a plan stating what information is to be obtained from each source and what sequence is to be used to search the sources.

Proceeding in a top-down way

Most interview search procedures require all information sources to be examined to ensure that all information about the system is gathered. They suggest that this information be sought in a top-down way to gradually build up the system model. One should not proceed sequentially by first collecting all information about the system and then building the system model. Such an approach would be difficult to manage and may lead to errors. There would also be a large volume of seemingly unrelated information, which the analyst would have to sift through to try to reconcile inconsistencies and fill in missing pieces. In these circumstances it is easy to overlook vital data, create incomplete models, or find that analysts are repeating interviews with disgruntled users

A more orderly approach is therefore needed. The search procedures should specify the organizational level at which interviews should start, the personnel to be interviewed and any other information sources to be used. They should also include an interview plan for users and allow time for examining detailed information. Such a plan must ensure that all users are considered in the study. Leaving out an important user may lead to later problems, as that user may feel that their work has not been considered and they will then have less commitment to any new proposals or follow-up work. Many procedures follow a top-down approach, as shown in Figure 6.2. They begin with a set of initial interviews to find out what the system is about, usually by interviewing the higher levels of management, to get an overall picture.

Starting with management. The objective of interviewing management is to clearly identify the major components within the system and tasks within these components. These initial interviews identify functions within or sometimes even outside the problem boundary. Often analysts will look at some of the more important reports or documents at this stage. They will then draw a top-level system model and verify this model during the following set of interviews.

There are also other reasons for commencing interviews with management. First, management is aware of what goes on in the system and can give you leads as to how to go about getting information. They will suggest good sources of information, the people to interview to get this information, and they will introduce you to these

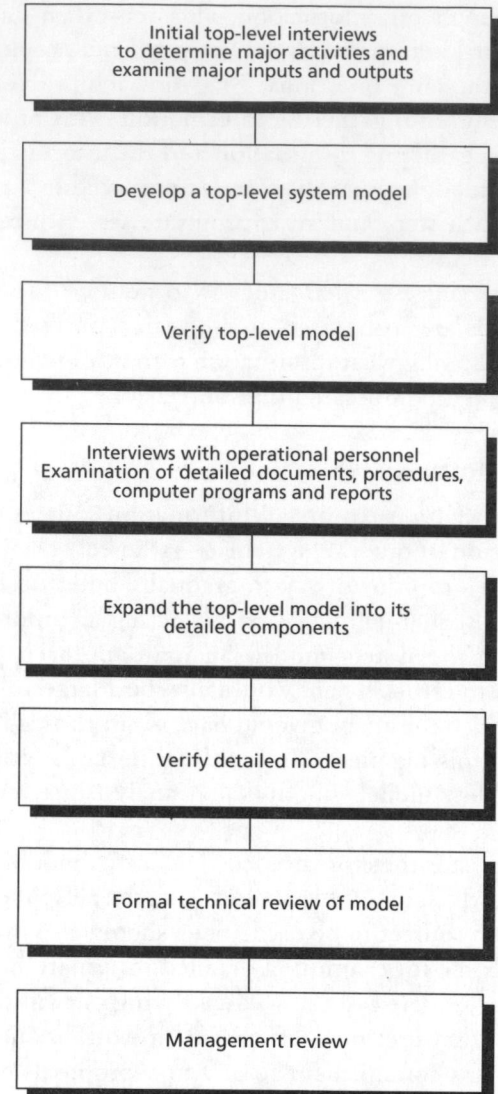

Figure 6.2 *Search procedure for an existing system*

people. It also ensures that management is on your side and will encourage cooperation from their section. Simply turning up and interviewing people in a section can have many undesirable effects. Management may feel that an investigation is in place about their activities without their knowledge, or they might feel that you are distracting their workers from important duties in their section. You must therefore make management aware of your goals early in the study and of how your work will affect their section. It is important to establish confidence in management about your abilities. This can often be done by showing interest in their problems and describing how you can solve them in a systematic way. For example, a start may be to introduce yourself, state the reason you are there, what you expect to get from the study, how long it will take, what steps you propose to follow and what you will produce. You must ensure that management feels you are there to help them solve problems, not to find blame, and that you do not unduly disturb the operation of their section.

Considering detailed operations. Once the top-level model is validated, the next phase of the study may be to look at each of the major system components in turn. The objective now will be to find the operation of the major business processes or functions of the system. These in turn will identify further detailed components and so on. As you go into detail, there may be less emphasis on interviewing and more time spent on looking at things such as forms, computer programs or system reports. Analysts use this new, detailed information to expand the top-level model, which is then verified with the users. This should be done in an iterative manner.

The search for more detailed information usually begins by interviewing operational personnel. These interviews establish detailed sources of information including computer programs, reports and manuals. This procedure may be repeated a number of times as increasingly detailed information is sought. These subsequent interviews and searches become more important as the analyst learns more and more about the system. The analyst begins to identify problems in the system and, together with the users, to establish the objectives for the new system.

An analysis model is built during the interviews. This model is updated following each interview and checked in a follow-up interview. The analyst then searches for more detailed information and makes further updates to the model. Interviews at the detailed levels can thus be structured to fill in identified gaps or to obtain information that is needed to complete previously incompletely defined functions. These gaps will be identified as the analyst is developing the model. The iterations go on until the analyst is happy with the model. The iterations can be seen as part of the model validation process. Each iteration checks that model changes made in the previous iteration correctly describe the system. The model then proceeds through a more formal validation by being submitted for a number of formal reviews, starting with technical reviews to formally establish model correctness. Finally, it is submitted to a management review for agreement on system objectives and to obtain resources to develop the new system.

The kind of data sought at the lower levels depends on the system. If a computer system is to be improved, the analyst would look at existing computer systems and programs. If manual procedures are to be improved, the analyst would make a detailed examination of current procedures. In most cases, both the computer system and user procedure would be examined.

WHAT IF THERE IS NO EXISTING SYSTEM?

So far we have assumed that there is an existing system, parts of which are to be automated. But what if this is not the case, and there is no existing system? In that case we cannot examine what is currently happening nor identify current user activities. In a sense, the search procedures are now simpler because there are fewer sources of information. The procedures now emphasize user requirements and place less emphasis on the study of existing components. There are no reports or computer programs to go through and no manuals to examine. The whole procedure centers around interviews, but the thrust of these interviews is now different. The interviews do not need to search out how a system works but must determine users' expectations of the new system. They must then define the business processes and users' roles in these processes. Prototyping is often useful here. We can build up typical interfaces and outputs to get reactions from users on the kind of system behavior they would like.

Where totally new systems are proposed, analysts often look at sources outside the system for information. Often the new system is being suggested because someone has seen it somewhere else. Analysts can examine these external systems to see whether any of their features are applicable to the proposed new system.

 ## THE INTERVIEW PLAN

The interview plan specifies:

- the users to be interviewed;
- the sequence in which the users are interviewed; and
- the interview plan for each user.

The first step in developing an interview plan is to identify the users to be interviewed. Often an organization chart can be used to identify such users. This chart describes the organization's units, the positions in these units and each position's occupant. The analyst uses the project's terms of reference to select the organizational units that fall within the boundary of the system study and are likely to be affected by any new system. Persons in these units then become candidates for interviewing. It is usually wise to begin interviewing at the top levels of the organizational areas, in order to get support and cooperation from management before beginning to look into particular organizational activities or suggesting new solutions. Management may then often suggest other users that should be interviewed and is more likely to support any proposed changes.

There are also some common goals in each interview. Preparation for the interview is always essential. The analyst should have an idea of what information is needed from the interview and ask direct questions to get this information. The analyst should always endeavor to obtain leads as to where to get more information. If the current interviewee cannot answer, the analyst should ask for advice about where to go next.

The interview process thus follows a fairly structured path. You gain an appreciation of the overall system operation from management, then you go into detailed operations by interviewing system users at various levels of system operation.

You should not expect to obtain all of the information required from one user in the course of one interview. There is usually a series of two, three or even more interviews with a given user. Usually the analyst begins with an initial interview to meet the users. This first interview is then followed by a number of fact-gathering interviews to gather all the major facts known to the user. Then there may be one or more follow-up interviews to verify these facts and any models developed by the analyst and to gain additional information to complete the analyst's study.

Let us now consider the interview itself.

THE INTERVIEW

It is important to establish a good relationship with interviewees and this should start right at the beginning. Even some simple things are important here. For example, you should call and arrange an interview time and not simply barge in and expect the interviewee to drop everything to talk to you. You should also limit interviews to about 45 or 60 minutes and not expect people to give large amounts of their valuable time to you. If you are taking notes or recording the interview, ask for permission.

The interview should proceed in an organized and friendly manner. The interviewer should always be courteous and respect the user's needs and position. You should give the interviewee time to answer your questions, seek clarification if necessary and occasionally summarize what you have learnt from them. You must give users confidence in your abilities and reassure them that you are there to help them solve some of their problems.

There are some basic premises that you should always be aware of when conducting interviews. First, you must gain the confidence of your interviewees. To do this you must convince the interviewee of your own abilities and show that you are proceeding in an organized way and will not waste their time. You must also be sympathetic to their problems and not become aggressive and create the impression that you are there to apportion blame. It is not a good idea, for example, to begin by saying:

'I hear that there is something terribly wrong with the system and I am here to fix it.'

A better approach may be to begin by saying:

'You might have heard that a study into your system has been started to see how we can provide you with better support for your work. As a first step in this study, I am here to see exactly what you do and how we can better support you in your work.'

It is important not to force solutions upon users but rather to play the role of an advisor. Computer jargon should not be used to impress the user, though interviewers should explain the limitations of the computer in user terms and describe how it can assist users in their work. You should not try to elicit the response you want by asking leading questions, such as:

'You agree that the best solution is a computer solution?'

It is better to ask users for suggestions about what might be done to improve the system and then follow up these suggestions.

Interviewers should also take care to ensure that they obtain all the needed information from interviews. It helps to let the user know what information is required from the interview. The interviewer should then seek this information gradually and be precise and direct in their questioning. You should not get to a stage where you keep saying:

'I forget, did I ask you last time whether . . . ?'

It is better to obtain information gradually, and at a follow-up interview begin with:

'From last time, I understand that the following happens.'

You might then show the user a model you have developed and say:

'I have developed the following model from our last meeting. Can you verify whether this is correct?'

Then go through the model, explain it and check it. The model may also be amended if it has any inaccuracies. The analyst is then ready to further elaborate on the model. The next step may be to say something like:

'Today I would like to follow up some of these points.'

The follow-up questions then find out more about the system. In this way progress is apparent to both the analyst and the interviewee. The model and information about it grows at each interview. Analysts will be satisfied because their knowledge about the system is continually growing. The interviewees will be more cooperative because they can see that their time is being used productively.

THE INTERVIEW STRUCTURE

It is necessary to proceed in an orderly manner to get the best out of interviews. Figure 6.3 illustrates a procedure that has been found effective over time. It begins with some preliminaries. For example, analysts will have to introduce themselves at the first interview.

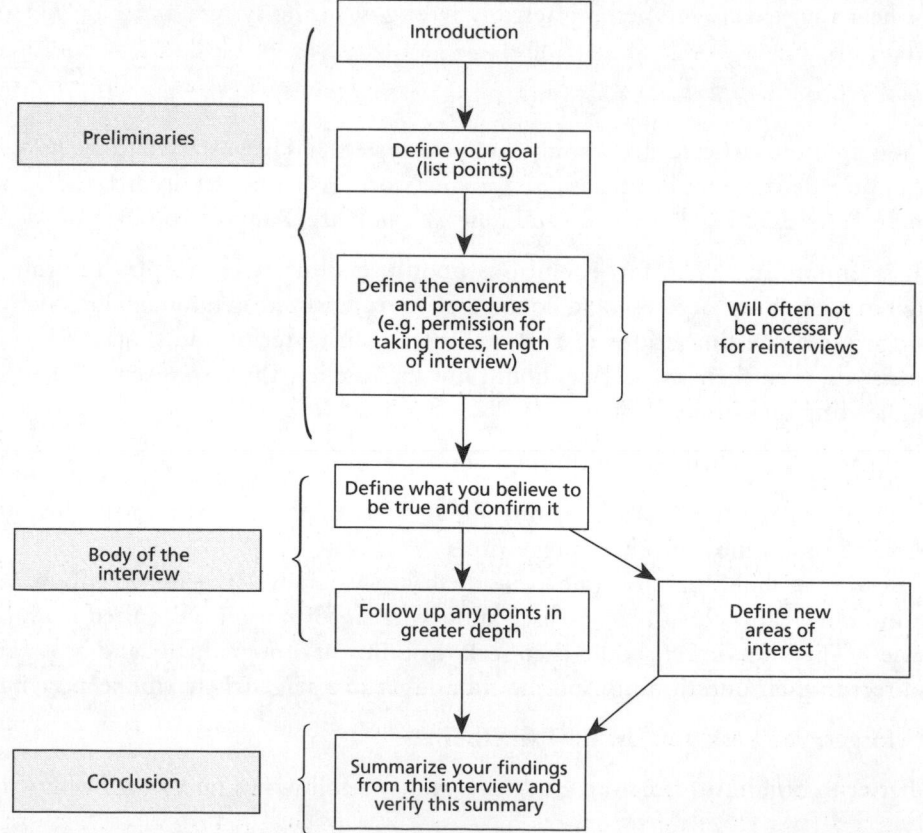

Figure 6.3 *A typical interview*

Then some interview criteria may be identified. These include the length of the interview and what you expect to get from it, as well as obtaining permission to take any notes or make recordings. It is a good idea to do this so that the interviewee will know what is expected from the interview and hence feel more able to contribute to it constructively.

Once the preliminaries are over, the main part of the interview can begin. It is usually a good idea to start by confirming any information you obtained from an earlier interview or any intervening investigation. At this stage you might show any models you have developed or confirm some of your beliefs about the system. This serves to put the interviewee in the picture and also helps you to find any errors in your data. Once you reach agreement, follow up any relevant points in more detail.

The interview should be concluded by summarizing what you have found out in the interview and confirming it. Finally, it is usually a good idea to arrange a time for the next interview if this is considered necessary.

HOW TO GET INFORMATION FROM INTERVIEWS

One of the most important points about interviewing is what questions you need to ask. It is important to ask the right questions in the correct order to get the most out of interviews. Questions can be characterized by their subject content and type. Obviously, the subject content of a question will depend on the specific system study. However, the type of question can be generalized and there are general guidelines to help you choose the most appropriate questioning method for the interview in question.

It is often convenient to make a distinction between three kinds of questions. There are *open questions*, the *closed questions* and *probes*. **Open questions** are general questions that establish a person's viewpoint on a particular subject. Thus there might be a question such as:

Open question
A question that requires the responder to express a viewpoint.

'What do you think of personal computers in your type of work?', or

'How relevant is the sales forecast to your activity?'

Closed questions are more specific and usually require a specific answer. For example, you might have questions such as:

Closed question
A question that requires a direct answer.

'Where do you send your summary of orders?', or

'How often do you need to get information about inventory levels from the warehouse?'

A closed question often restricts an interviewee to some specific answer. This may be a number, an explanation of a report, or a reason for doing something. The answer to a closed question can then be followed with a probe to get more detail. **Probes** are questions that follow up an earlier answer. For example:

Probe
A question that follows an earlier question.

'Why do you send the summary of order to account?', or

'Why do you need this information so often?'

Interviewers must often select a particular questioning method for an interview. This method will use alternate sequences of closed and open questions. Some possible sequences are described.

Open then closed

It is often suggested that the first interview with a user should emphasize open questions. This enables analysts to identify the values a user places on the system and helps in gaining an impression about the user's likes and dislikes. This may then shape future interviews. Open questions also prompt the user to volunteer more detailed information so that closed questions may be unnecessary. Variations on this sequence are of course possible. An analyst, for example, may spend all the interview time on open questions. Alternatively, for a small system it may be possible to get into closed questions very quickly.

Open, closed and then open again

It is possible to start with open questions, follow them with closed questions and then finish up with some more open questions. This approach is used mostly in follow-up interviews. It is an easy way to gradually lead a user into detailed questioning. Some people, when answering an open question, may provide enough information to make future detailed questions unnecessary. It is also possible to start with detailed questions and finish with open questions. This can be useful when searching for user requirements. You might spend some time following up points about, say, placing orders, and then at the conclusion you might ask:

'What do you think would be a better way to place orders?'

Such a follow-up question will be very useful in getting an idea of what the user requires from the system. The user has expressed some ideas, then described some details and possibly problems with the system, and is probably now in the mood to state what is really needed.

Closed then open

Interviews that start with closed questions are often used when interviewees, for one reason or another, are not ready to volunteer information. They may be shy and find it difficult to get into a discussion, or they may simply be uncooperative and not in favor of a study. Asking an open question makes it difficult for the interviewee to avoid giving an answer. In this case it is usual to start with closed questions, follow up with some open questions and then often to conclude with some closed questions. For example, one might start with a closed question such as:

'How do you choose a supplier?'

Following some further probes to find the detailed process, the interviewer may then ask:

'What other ways are there for choosing suppliers?'

There might be a discussion of the alternatives and you might settle on one. The interviewer might then ask:

'Suppose we had a computer system for choosing suppliers. Would you use their latest price for a given part, or would you consider the trend over the past few months?'

This might then be followed by a discussion of the requirements the user has for making a decision.

Choosing the alternative

The type of approach you choose will often depend on the type of interviewee. It is often wise for a first interview to start with a series of open questions to develop rapport between the interviewer and a user. Detailed closed questions can follow later. With an uncooperative, reticent or shy user who finds it difficult to offer opinions, it may be better to start an interview with closed questions. They are usually easier to answer and harder to avoid. Having answered the initial questions, these users may feel more at ease about giving their opinions.

FOLLOWING UP FOR DETAILED INFORMATION

Information can also be obtained from documents, forms or other media. There are two aspects of examining detailed documents. One is simply to look at their content to determine what makes up the flows and stores in a system. The other is to analyze the content of such reports in detail to find out what in-depth relationships the system contains. Determining the contents of sources such as documents, reports or computer programs tends to be relatively informal. Analysts must go through these sources, look at their content and note it down on the system model. Often the search is guided by the modeling techniques provided by the design methodology. Thus, when we examine programs, reports, procedures or documents, we compare them to the current system model. As we do this, we add any new information to the model and check for any inconsistencies. Alternatively, we could use the current model to determine if there is any missing information and then go to the appropriate source to find it.

In-depth analysis may be more formal. For example, one might examine advertising budgets and compare them against sale variations to determine the effectiveness of advertising. Excessive inventory maintenance costs may also call for an analysis of inventory records and levels of holdings. Financial data are often used in such detailed analysis. For example, there may be a problem where the cost of providing items is too great. This will probably call for a detailed cost analysis to find out where the greatest cost overruns occur.

One aspect of in-depth analysis is that it is not possible to examine all relevant data. We cannot look at the cost of every item produced, or at all the items held in a warehouse. Analysts must choose samples of information for such analysis, and use the correct sample selection technique to select the sample.

SUMMARY

This chapter mainly concentrated on one important method of gathering information, the interview. It described a number of important points to remember when organizing a search for information about the system using interviewing. It considered how to plan a search strategy, and examined the differences between search strategies where there is an existing system and those where there is no existing system.

DISCUSSION QUESTIONS

6.1 What are the sources of information about a system?

6.2 What is meant by the term *search method*?

6.3 Why is interviewing one of the most frequently used search methods?

6.4 What are the important factors for devising a search strategy?

6.5 Would a search strategy for an existing system differ from a search strategy for a new system? How would it differ?

6.6 Why is an interview plan important?

6.7 Who are the important users that must be interviewed? How would you find them?

6.8 Describe how you would carry out an interview.

6.9 How would you go about establishing a good relationship with a user?

6.10 What is the difference between closed and open questions?

6.11 Describe some ways of questioning during an interview. Describe some typical users and the most appropriate questioning method for them.

6.12 What are some of the disadvantages of interviewing?

6.13 Describe some situations where division of labor occurs dynamically.

BIBLIOGRAPHY

Cash, C.J. and Stewart, W.B. Jr (1986), *Interviewing Principles and Practices* (4th edn), Brown Company Publishers, Dubuque, Iowa.

Dwyer, J. (1993), *The Business Communication Handbook* (3rd edn), Prentice-Hall, New York.

The development process

7

CONTENTS

KEY LEARNING OBJECTIVES

Work practices in development
Choosing teams to match work practices
The importance of quality in system development
The linear cycle
Evolutionary design and prototyping

◇ INTRODUCTION

Chapter 1 outlined the three major processes used to build systems—the development, support and management processes. This chapter concentrates on the development process, while describing its relationship to the other processes. It sees the development process in the way shown in Figure 7.1. This follows the ideas of earlier chapters, which divide the development process into four process steps—defining the broad solution, finding the detailed user requirements including developing the system specification, and designing and constructing the system. In addition, support must be provided to organize the people into effective teams and to provide them with documentation tools that enable them to keep track of the information. Such documentation must ensure that they always have the latest correct information to work with. The term configuration management *is often used to describe the way in which documentation is managed. Support is also provided through CASE tools, which allow designers to maintain the models that are built during the development process.*

When one looks at the activities in detail, one sees that there are many ways to develop systems, each suited to different kinds of problems. Thus the development process used to design an organization-wide transaction system is different from that used to design a system to support decisions on what assets to buy. The former is usually built in a number of steps and centers around planned work, whereas the latter tends to be more experimental and centers around situated work. Furthermore, different models may be used to represent systems at different development steps.

Different development methods often need different kinds of work practices to be followed. Thus in some cases work can be easily subdivided and allocated to people who work independently; in others, people may have to work closely together. This in turn affects the way they exchange information, calling for different support processes and team structures. A good system will provide the right match of team to process, support it with proper tools and documentation, and provide the correct level of management. Guidelines are now becoming available through standards that suggest both what must be done in the

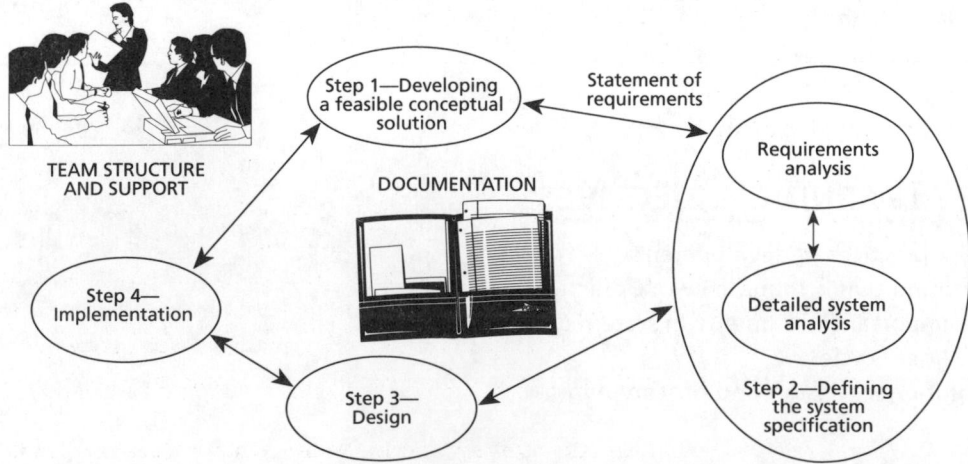

Figure 7.1 *The development environment*

development process and the process steps themselves. The Institute of Electrical and Electronic Engineers (IEEE) has proposed a number of standards for this purpose. This chapter will describe a number of development processes that closely follow these standards. It begins by describing different team structures and support tools, and then examines the kind of team structure needed by the different processes.

TEAMS AND THEIR WORK

It is now increasingly recognized that teamwork is important in system development. A good environment will provide a match between the team structures and work practices needed by a development process. It is common to distinguish between two ways of doing work—planned work and situated work. In planned work, steps and tasks are predefined and assigned to people. Planned work is often suited to large projects where different tasks are carried out by different people who must closely coordinate their activities. Teams must be organized in a way that complements the design steps. This includes clearly defining the **role** and responsibilities of team members, organizing ways for them to coordinate their activities and providing them with the supporting documentation.

Role
The responsibility undertaken by a person.

In situated work, tasks cannot be predefined as they depend on the outcomes of previous tasks. People in teams, however, have the knowledge needed to quickly evaluate the outcome of tasks and decide on subsequent action. Team structures can be different and require communication that keeps each team member aware of what the other team members are doing.

Team structures can also change in different project phases. The initial phases require considerable user involvement to set system objectives and to help develop the model of the existing system. The role of computer professionals in these phases may be minimal, but it increases in subsequent phases where technical system design becomes important.

Different projects may also call for team members with different backgrounds. For example, people with database expertise should be available for database design, and communications specialists should be consulted about any computer system distribution problems. Obviously, the right mix of people and resources can go a long way to ensure that problems are solved in the most effective manner.

TYPES OF TEAM STRUCTURE

There is no optimum team structure that can be used for all projects. The question is whether to formally structure the teams or to let them evolve as the project develops. Different system development environments need different team structures. The chosen team structure will depend on the variety, complexity and size of the system. The structure of the team can depend on the type of problem and the stage of development.

A useful framework for distinguishing between kinds of teams, based on the word of Constantine (1993), is to make a distinction between the following team structures:

- *Structured or closed* teams, usually working toward well-defined requirements and where the work can be subdivided into well-defined tasks. People are assigned specific tasks and are required to carry them out in a predefined sequence. Here communication requires the smooth flow of information from one task to the next.

- *Open* structures, where requirements are well-defined but there can be continual negotiation on how to achieve them. Here team members must be able easily to move between roles, and new roles are created as the development process changes.

- *Random* team structures, where the requirements are very broad and can change rapidly, often depending on earlier outcomes, and team members have a wide scope in which to contribute. This type of structure is usually found where there is a large component of situated work such as in research environments or highly innovative projects. Here all the team members can make *ad hoc* contributions to the work, and communication requires everyone to know what everyone else is doing.

- *Synchronous or mission-oriented* teams, usually working toward a relatively stable goal but where the specific requirements can change. The team is characterized by continual planning and agreement on requirements changes. Planning in this sense is continuous, but there is a common mission. Team members, guided by the mission, are aware of what must be done in particular circumstances.

STRUCTURED TEAMS

Structured teams are most common in planned work, where everyone is assigned a task and the tasks must be carried out in a predefined sequence. This type of team can be effective in projects that include many repetitive and similar tasks, such as an environment where:

- the technology is stable;
- the problem is well defined; and
- the project is large in size.

One example may be a system that requires the development of a large number of relatively straightforward screens. Or it may be a batch system made up of many program modules each requiring considerable editing. Resource control is often considered of paramount importance in these environments. Many of the project tasks, although not identical, are similar, and hence many practitioners feel that the tasks can be effectively standardized and coordinated using highly structured project management techniques. Most team members have very similar roles—that is, as programmers developing code for some system part. The major project problem here is to coordinate the activities of these programmers. Structured teams require a structured documentation system, with team members required to produce specific documents at the completion of their tasks.

Chief programmer teams

A chief programmer team (Baker, 1972) is a particular form of structured team with well-defined but different roles for all team members. The number of team members can depend on the size of the project—a typical team structure is shown in Figure 7.2. The core of the team consists of the chief programmer, the assistant chief programmer and the program librarian. Briefly, the chief programmer is responsible for the functional structure of the programming system and writes the most difficult system programs. In small projects, the chief programmer may be the only programmer in the team, with the remainder of the team acting in a supportive role. In most cases, the chief programmer has an assistant to take over if necessary. The program librarian is there to maintain up-to-date program documentation.

Bigger projects require many more members. For example, the team may include additional programmers and, if the project size is large, there may be a manager to do the administrative tasks and an editor to prepare documents. Each of them may have a secretary and there may also be someone to devise system tests. The team may have a number of specialists—for example, a language specialist or someone who has a very good understanding of system editors and utilities.

SYNCHRONOUS AND OPEN TEAM STRUCTURES

Synchronous and open structures are also found in planned work, where goals are also generally fixed but where the way the work is carried out can change. However, in this case tasks may not be all predefined or assigned to particular users. Instead, when particular circumstances arise, everyone knows what task is affected or if a new task is needed and quick agreement is reached on who will carry out this task.

RANDOM TEAMS

These teams are best suited to projects such as decision support systems, or complex systems whose goals evolve as the project proceeds. Projects are no longer made up of predefined tasks, and new tasks must be defined as new, and often unpredictable,

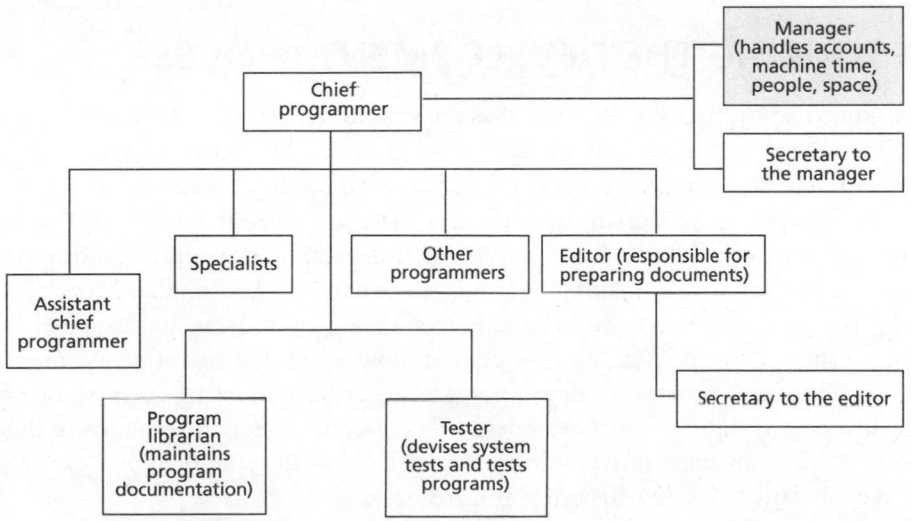

Figure 7.2 *Chief programmer team*

circumstances arise. Teams in such projects are made up of members with a variety of skills, with no person being an expert in all computer specialties, nor one person or a small group of people completely understanding all the details of the system. Instead, individuals with particular skills may be called to contribute to the project as the need for these skills arises. Different people contribute at different times as their knowledge is required.

Furthermore, continuous adjustment of goals also calls for continuous reassignment of tasks. This is done in a random manner in random team structures, where someone will pick up a task when it becomes apparent. Random teams require agreement and negotiation to assign such tasks.

Often people assume roles in these team structures. Rettic (1993) describes a number of roles and how they evolve for different projects. Usually, a team begins with a team leader role, with the rest being team members. The team leader in such teams does not usually assign tasks to other members, but is someone who facilitates the work of the rest of the team by arranging meetings, removing obstacles to progress and recording progress toward achieving a goal. Then as work evolves, new roles may develop. Particular roles can include an implementer, who develops the programs, or a technical reviewer, who validates outputs against requirements, or a scribe, who keeps records of meetings, or a specialist consultant. Some of these roles, such as a scribe, may rotate between team members.

Many such teams can include users, and in fact this is common where there is a high degree of end-user development. End-user teams are usually composed of functional specialists whose main concern is the effective operation of their business system. Members of such teams often do not have the time to keep up with all computer developments and need specialist support on computing tools and techniques. Such support is often provided through specialist end-user consultants who can either be seconded to end-user teams from the information systems department or provide general consultative advice as needed.

System life cycle
Another term for the problem-solving cycle.

DESCRIBING THE DEVELOPMENT PROCESS

Problem-solving cycle
A set of steps that start with a set of user requirements and produces a system that satisfies these requirements.

System development cycle
Another term for the problem-solving cycle.

Software process
Another term for the system life cycle but concentrating on software development.

Development processes are also known as the **system life cycle**, or the **problem-solving cycle** or sometimes as the **system development cycle**. The term **software process** is now also used to define the process used in system development.

A development process must include all the activities described in Chapter 5 and summarized in Figure 5.2. They include developing an understanding of the system, creating models, making decisions on what is to be done and planning the work. The question is whether the activities in Figure 5.2 can be arranged into a formal process. Should system developers follow a defined set of steps, much the same as a business process, to develop a system, or have more free rein to bring out their utmost creativity? But if designers have a free rein, how do we ensure that the system is built on time and at minimum cost? Good development life cycles must achieve a balance between structure and freedom.

A development process must balance all of these needs to ensure completion while supporting the freedom needed to ensure creativity. System designers should therefore not just continue to create new ideas without ever putting them into practice. At the same time, they should not simply implement the first design they think of using a set of strict process rules. How this balance is reached between structure and freedom often depends on the kind of system being designed.

The development process must satisfy a number of other criteria. Perhaps the overriding criterion is to ensure that the system meets the original user requirements and that it works without error. Formerly, requirements were defined, the system was built, and then the whole system was tested to see if it met the requirements without error. Any errors found were corrected. The approach of leaving error detection to the end, however, is no longer used. It was usually found that a large number of errors appeared in systems built in this way, and considerable time and effort was needed to clear them up. For this reason the trend has been to introduce various checks during the process to ensure that the number of errors on completion is minimized.

The word *quality* is sometimes used to define our goal of producing error-free systems that meet user requirements with minimum effort. Consequently, **quality assurance** mechanisms are introduced into the development process to assure that there are no deviations from the requirements as development proceeds. Quality assurance mechanisms check the process at its various stages to ensure that requirements are not lost or changed during the process and that errors are minimized. Quality assurance mechanisms include **validation** of outputs from various activities against original requirements. They also include **verification** of individual activities to ensure that each activity correctly converts its output to an input. Finally, they include the **testing** of working components. Validation and verification are applied progressively during system development to ensure that the final system meets its requirements.

DEFINING THE DEVELOPMENT STEPS

Perhaps the simplest view of the development process is a sequence of tasks, an approach that was used in the early days of developing computer-based information systems. Usually, a large number of detailed activities are needed to build an information system. Typical activities include writing a program, designing a form, finding out what a user needs, or selecting a piece of equipment. The first step in creating a life cycle is to list these activities. In addition to listing activities, we should specify the sequence for these activities. This can be shown on a chart similar to that in Figure 7.3. This chart shows an initial set of activities, in this case, 'Analyze accounts', 'Analyze sales' and 'Examine existing computer system'. The arrows in the diagram show the activities that can be completed before another activity can start. For example, in Figure 7.3 the existing computer system must be examined before the computer data model can be drawn. Similarly, both 'Analyze accounts' and 'Analyze sales' must be completed before 'Redesign forms' and 'Construct data structure for sales accounts' can start.

The kind of chart shown in Figure 7.3 was used in the early days of system development but is seldom used now because most projects consist of a large number of activities linked by complex interdependencies. Plotting all these activities and dependencies on one chart becomes far too complex. In addition, later project activities

Quality assurance
A process to ensure the development of quality products.

Validation
Checking whether a particular product satisfies user requirements.

Verification
Checks to ensure that a particular input has been converted correctly to an output.

Testing
Checking to see if a system does what it is supposed to do.

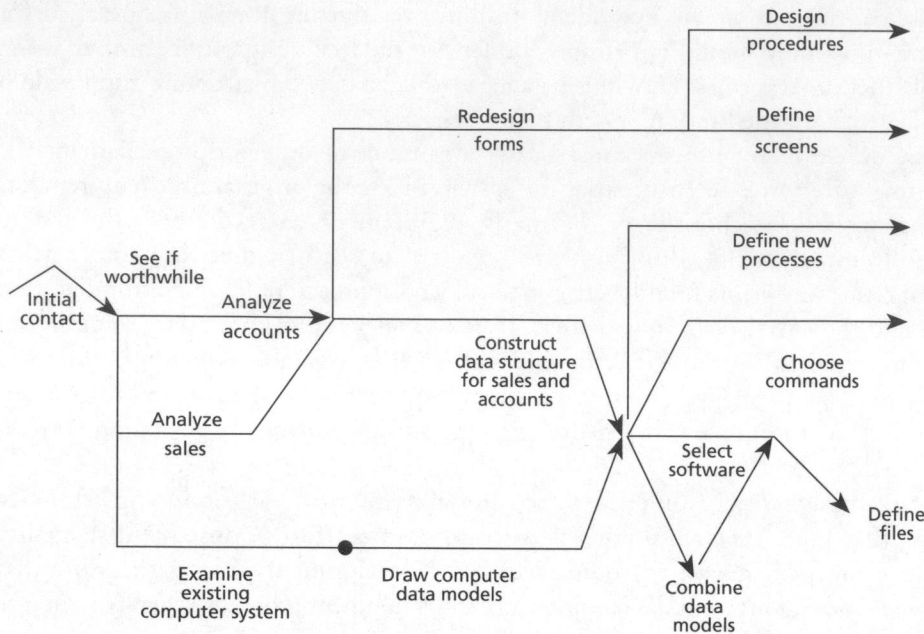

Figure 7.3 *Listing the requisite activities*

often depend on the outcomes of earlier project activities, so the planner is required to predict some of these outcomes. If the predictions are wrong, as is often the case, the chart must be changed during the course of the project—sometimes frequently. These changes can become such a problem that they detract from the project work. The last thing we want to do is to introduce another problem into the design of a new system.

For this reason it is now more common to define development processes in a more abstract way, usually as a set of higher-level phases. Each phase is made up of more detailed activities, and each has a specific goal and produces a well-defined output, usually including a model. However, the detailed activities for each phase are not defined at the start of the project. Usually, each phase is reviewed when it is completed. The review produces a report on the outcome of the phase; it also defines the goal, as well as a detailed plan for the next phase. It is therefore unnecessary to make a detailed plan for the whole project before it is started; only a plan for the first phase is needed at the start.

THE LINEAR OR WATERFALL CYCLE

Linear cycle
A set of predefined steps for building a system.

Waterfall cycle
The same as linear cycle.

The **linear** or **waterfall cycle** is a development process that centers around planned work and is best suited for projects where the requirements can be clearly defined. The linear cycle groups development activities into a sequence of consecutive phases, as shown in Figure 7.4, which depicts the major phases—concept formation, system requirements definition, system design and development. It also includes installation and post-installation activities that usually follow the completion of development. Each phase itself is made up of more detailed activities. Testing proceeds in parallel with the major phases. A broad test strategy is defined at the time the system requirements are identified. Detailed test design takes place during system design, and testing is part of the development phase. Each phase in the sequence can only commence after the previous phase has been completed. Each **phase** usually produces one or more models, or products in later phases. These models and products are shown in Figure 7.4 as the rounded boxes with underlined headings. The models become part of a phase report, which describes what has been achieved in this phase and outlines a plan for the next phase. The report also includes any models, new or expanded user requirements, design decisions and problems encountered. This information is used at the next phase. Phase reports are also used to keep management informed of project progress, so that management can use the reports to change project direction and to allocate resources to the project.

Phase
A step in the development process.

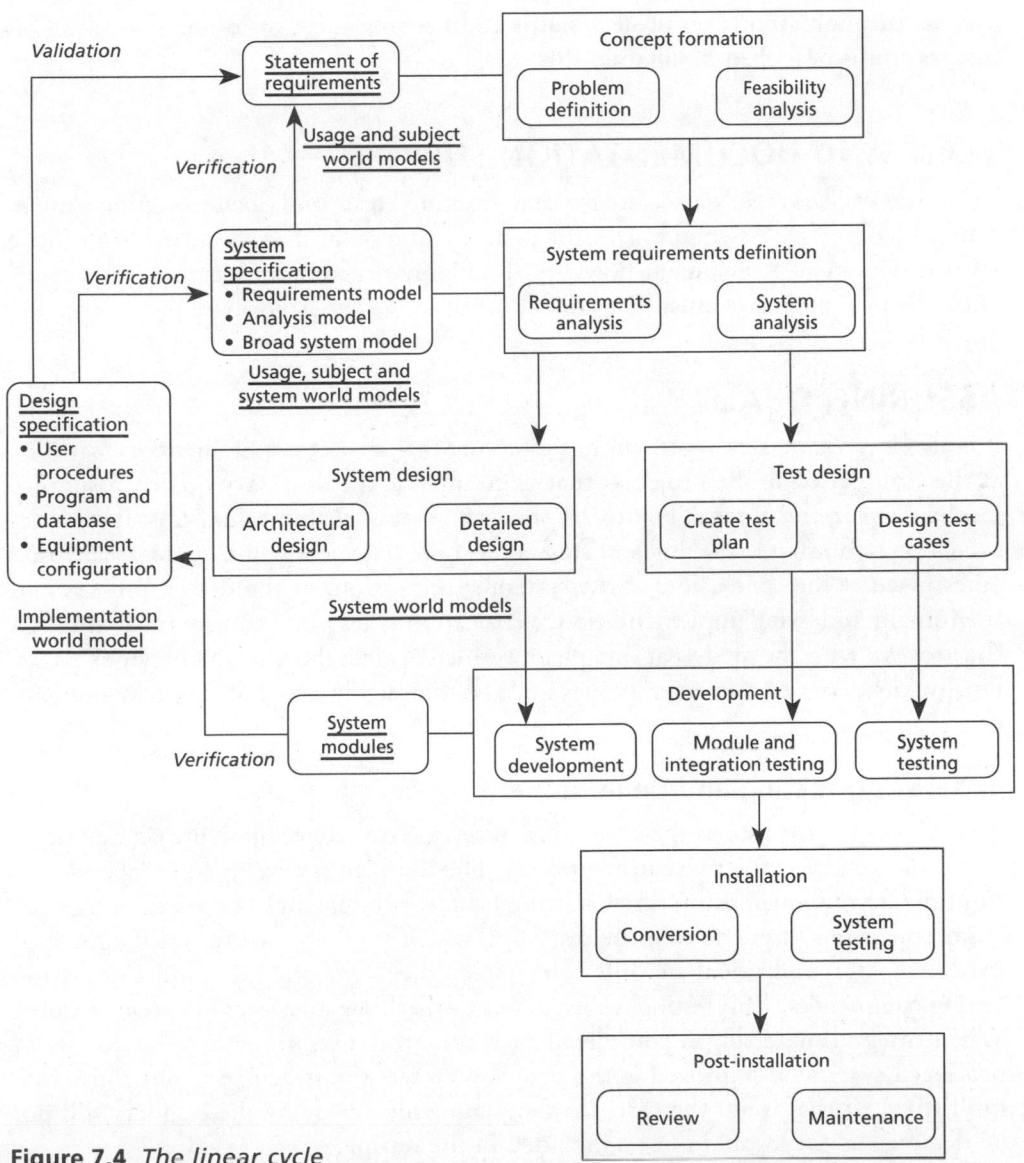

Figure 7.4 *The linear cycle*

The models produced in the different phases serve as important communication tools in the way described in Chapter 5, with communication progressing from the usage to implementation worlds. Thus, as described in Chapter 4, concept formation produces a statement of requirements predominantly in user world terms. The system specification definition produces a system specification that is usually made up of three models: a requirements model in user terms, a subject world model of the system, and a broad system-level specification. Design produces a design specification in system world terms, whereas development produces the implemented system modules.

Linear cycle phases are chosen to encourage top-down problem solving. Designers must first define the problem to be solved and then use an ordered set of steps to reach a solution. The linear cycle gives the project direction, and provides guidance on what should be done as the project proceeds. It is integrated with the management process through reports on project status and keeping track of resource needs. This integration is described in Chapter 20.

TEAM AND DOCUMENTATION SUPPORT

The linear cycle is usually associated with a structured team and documentation system. Team members are assigned to specific phases and tasks and are required to produce specific documents. Document flows are also highly structured. Documents produced at the end of one phase must be available as inputs to the next phase.

ASSURING QUALITY

It is also important to take precautions to ensure that all user requirements are satisfied at the completion of the project—that is, to include the necessary quality assurance mechanisms in the process. Figure 7.4 shows one set of such mechanisms. It includes validation of outputs at the different steps against the statement requirements. Validation takes place at the conclusion of the system specification, of the design process and then finally following implementation. Verification takes place continuously through the process, with the models at one phase verified against those of the previous phase. Finally, any designed software modules must be thoroughly tested during development.

Separating testing and development

Another important issue is the separation of testing from development, where testing is shown as a separate activity in Figure 7.4. The test plan is developed independently from the development team, often starting from the statement of requirements. Each requirement produces one or more test cases, which are then used to test the finished modules. After individual modules are tested, they are combined and integration testing commences. This testing is carried out to check the interfaces between modules. When integration testing is completed then system tests commence. The quality of produced systems is improved if the people who test the systems are not those that built them. If that is not the case, then any omissions made by the builders will not be detected as they would not be included in the testing.

LINEAR CYCLE PHASES

The linear cycle begins with concept definition. As described in Chapter 4, concept definition is made up of two parts. The first is problem definition, which leads to the project goal. The second, feasibility analysis, determines a feasible way to achieve this goal. Feasibility analysis usually considers a number of project alternatives, one of which is chosen as the most satisfactory solution. It is advisable to investigate as many alternatives as possible to ensure that the best project direction is chosen. Just using the first idea that comes to mind is not the best approach. A certain amount of skill is needed to propose good alternatives and choose the right direction. The linear cycle attempts to structure this process by providing guidelines for generating alternatives.

This phase is important because it sets the direction for the remainder of the project and must be completed before the project can continue. Furthermore, the project direction in the linear cycle is set without going into detailed design. There is no point in virtually building a new system to see whether it satisfies the goal. Instead, a number of alternatives should be evaluated first to find the best way to satisfy the project goal.

Phase 1—Problem definition

Many people consider problem definition to be the most important phase. It provides a broad **statement of user requirements**, in user world terms—or what the users expect the system to do—and thus sets the direction for the whole project. This phase also sets the project bounds, which define what parts of the system can be changed by the project and what parts are to remain the same. The resources to be made available to the project are also often specified in this phase. These three important factors—the project goal, project bounds and resource limits—are sometimes called the project's terms of reference. Because of their importance, they are set by the organization's management.

Statement of user requirements
A formal definition of what the new system must do.

TEXT CASE A: Interactive Marketing—Defining a Problem

As an example, let us consider Text Case A—the interactive marketing of perishable goods. The overriding goal here is to ensure that perishable products are sold and distributed as quickly as possible. This goal may be stated quite explicitly, such as *80 percent of all products must be distributed within three days*, or some similar figures. When one looks at the whole system one can see a number of activities that can be directly related to the goal, as well as those that are not directly related. Those that are directly related include:

- the dissemination of information about available products to consumers;
- arrangements for transportation; and
- placing of orders for the products.

Activities not directly related to the goal may include:

- invoicing the consumers; and
- payment for the product.

This subdivision indicates the bounds of the project, or at least the project priorities. The directly related activities would initially be within the bounds, whereas the others would be outside the project bounds. Or we should at least initially give priority to activities directly related to the goal. Now we might consider all the directly related activities. Perhaps, after some discussion with the users, we may decide that the biggest problem in meeting the goal is letting consumers know what products are available. Transport may contribute to the problem. However, it may be felt at this stage that advertising products is the bigger problem. Furthermore, there may not be enough funds to study the entire system and we may confine our study initially to the communication links between producers and consumers. These become our problem bounds, and our terms of reference become how to improve communications between producers and consumers in order to improve sales. A statement of requirements will then center on improving communication between producers and consumers to ensure that consumers become aware of product availability and can order and obtain them in the minimum time. Thus the concept becomes one of an easy-to-access product availability register or a database with facilities to easily order products.

Part of the concept formation phase is the feasibility study, which proposes one or more conceptual solutions to the problem set for the project. Each conceptual solution gives an idea of what the new system will look like. The solutions define what will be done on the computer and will remain manual. They also indicate what input will be needed by the systems and what outputs will be produced. These solutions must be proven feasible, and a preferred solution must be accepted using the methods described in Chapter 4.

Many beginners find the idea of a conceptual solution hard to understand. All that is needed at this stage is a very broad idea of the solution, enough to give potential users an estimate of whether it can work and how much it is likely to cost. It is usually a good idea to consider a number of possible solutions at this stage. For example, consider Text Case A.

TEXT CASE A: Interactive Marketing—Feasibility

There are a number of possibilities for meeting the goal determined in Phase 1. Not all of them must use computers. For example, we may suggest the following:

- run an advertising campaign;
- employ a larger sales force to inform customers of available products;
- call potential customers whenever a product is available;
- employ a group of telephonists to relay messages between producers and consumers; and
- have a DIAL-UP service with messages about the latest products.

There is also, of course, a computer solution, especially that of using the World Wide Web. Here we might have a computer with a database that contains details of available products accessible through the Internet. Producers can enter information about their available products into the database as soon as the product is available. Consumers can browse through this database at any time to enquire about products and place their orders directly through the computer. A more sophisticated approach would be to allow consumers to place agents into the system stating their product requirements. They would be notified automatically by these agents whenever products needed by them become available.

Once we have these possibilities, we may consider them in turn. Often the first step is to eliminate alternatives that are obviously impractical or not operational. For example, groups of telephonists may not be a good idea. The problem of each telephonist not knowing what messages other telephonists have received probably cannot be overcome. DIAL-UP services may not be very useful either. If 100 producers each leave a 30-second message, consumers must spend 50 minutes to listen to them all. Again, this is not a very practical solution. Advertising may also prove not very effective because of the lead times in placing advertisements in newspapers. A visiting sales force also may not work because of the frequency of visits. This leaves us with the computer solution. We may propose that the marketing database be stored on a computer, and then consider ways of storing such a database.

It is often necessary to gather supporting data for such arguments. For example, estimates of numbers of transactions may be needed to estimate the feasibility of using groups of telephonists. The amount of data needed may be used to estimate the usefulness of DIAL-UP services. The volumes of data and transactions are needed to estimate the costs of the computer solution. Often, initial conceptual solutions may be modified in view of the supporting data. This additional information will lead to more detailed knowledge about the system. It will produce more information about the data needed by consumers and the communication patterns between consumers and producers. It will also define, in more detail, any difficulties in distributing product data to consumers.

The decision is made, in this case, to develop a Web site for the system. The concept is then elaborated into a broad statement of user requirements, which is to support on-demand contact between suppliers and consumers. In detail, it requires:

- direct entry into the WWW database by producers of products for sale;
- consumers to be able to browse the database using prespecified keywords;
- direct ordering through the Web site; and
- contact addresses, and links where possible, to potential transport companies.

Phase output. The output from Phase 1 principally defines the user requirements of the new system. It defines the proposed business solution and any new or changed business processes, usually with some sample scenarios. It consists of the project goal, its bounds, and the terms of reference for the project. Furthermore, it may include any restrictions on the project, such as the parts of the existing system which cannot be changed, as well as those which can. Resource limitations are also often specified at this time to indicate the funds and personnel available for the project. This will include a rough idea of the resource requirements of each of the subsequent project phases. It will contain tentative start and completion dates for each phase and the number of persons expected to be involved in each phase.

The statement of what the new system will do becomes a statement of requirements for further work and sets the guidelines for the next phase, which elaborates these requirements in detail.

Phase 2—Developing the system specification

During the development of the system specification it is necessary to find out more about the system problems and what users require of any new or changed system. This whole process is usually characterized by the following activities:

- producing a detailed analysis model describing how the current system works and what it does, usually in subject world terms;
- using the statement of requirements, together with the more detailed systems analysis, to state what is needed from the new system by a **requirements model** in user terms;
- producing a detailed model in subject terms of what the new system will do and how it will work—here called the **design model**; and
- producing a high-level description of computer system requirements using system terms.

Requirements model
A description of what users require the system to do.

Design model
A description of the required system using system terms.

The analyst must search for information about the system by conducting interviews with system users and using questionnaires and other means of data gathering to produce the analysis model. The actual processes used in requirements analysis were described in Chapters 5 and 6. This involves spending considerable time examining components, such as the various forms used in the system, as well as the operation of existing computer systems. The goal is to produce a set of clear statements about the way the new system is to work. These statements must define how the users use the system now and how they want to use it in the future, preferably in usage world terms and with supporting models. Modeling methods used to create the analysis model are described in the next few chapters. They include the methods known as structured systems analysis, described in Chapters 8 to 10, and object modeling, described in Chapters 11 and 12. The design model is usually a revised version of the analysis model that now includes the requirements.

In a large system, such analysis can produce a large volume of information. This information must be maintained, updated when necessary, and made available to designers and users. **CASE (Computer Assisted Software Engineering) tools** are often used to maintain these models.

CASE tools
Computer Assisted Software Engineering tools used to keep track of system models.

TEXT CASE A: Interactive Marketing—System Specification

In the interactive marketing case, the first step would be to find out what information is actually sent between producers and consumers. Furthermore, we would carry out a precise analysis of the kind of information that is available about products, where this information is available and how it is presently distributed, how long the distribution takes, and so on. The analysis in this case would be relatively minimal as no system exists, with products traded through wholesalers. The analysis would concentrate on what is actually needed. Thus, consumers may be asked to look at the current situation and to suggest what information they need, when they need it and how it should be presented. A design model and broad architecture would then be developed. The idea behind these latter components of the specification is shown in Figure 7.5. The design model in figure 7.5(a) shows the processes that would be supported by the circles and how data flows between them. The two main files, AVAILABLE-PRODUCTS and SALES, are also illustrated. The specification would also contain a list of items that appear in the files as well as a description of the functions.

The other important activity here is to produce the broad system specification that describes the main system components. This is shown in Figure 7.5(b). The format of inputs and outputs will be defined at this point, and the data to be stored identified.

(a) The design model

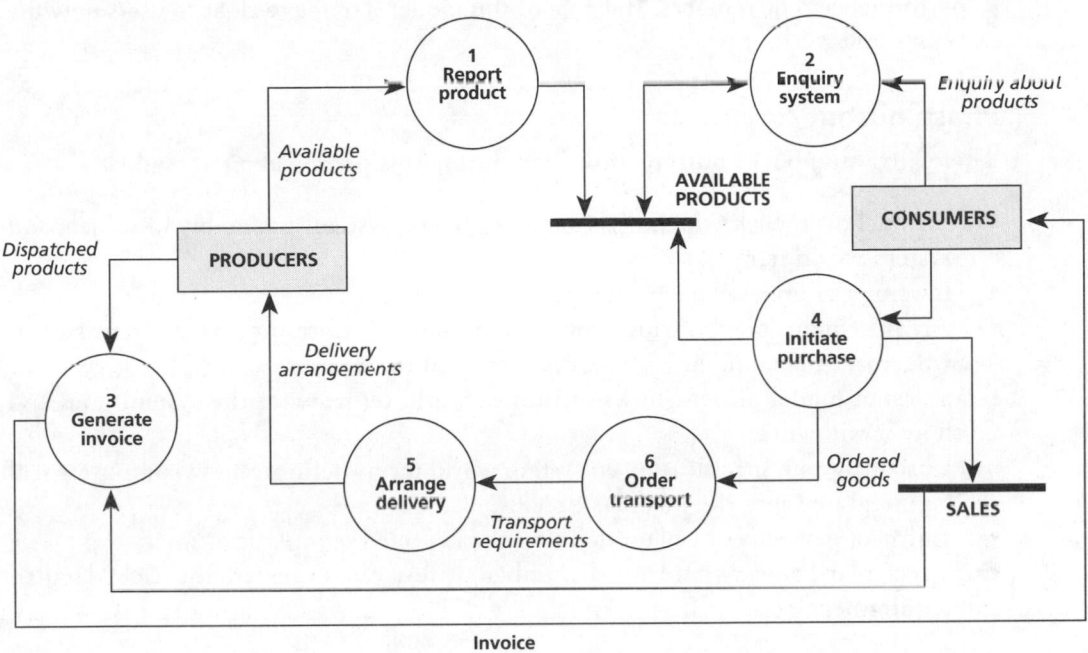

(b) The broad system model

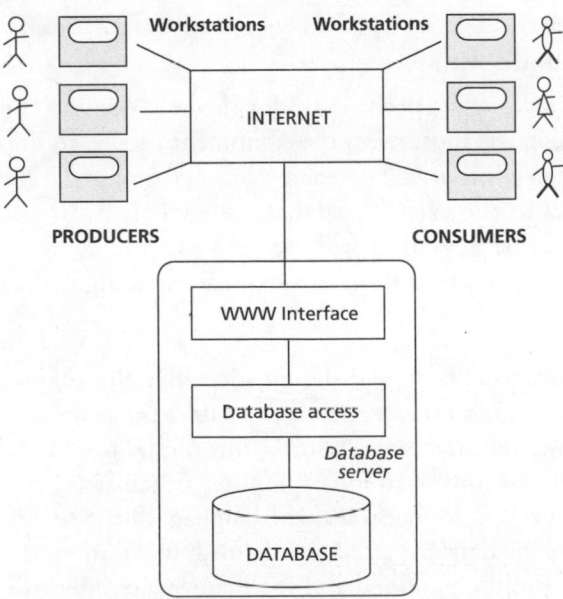

Figure 7.5 *System components*

> The third component is the requirements model, which is defined in terms of scenarios that describe how the system works from the user's perspective, together with performance requirements. The goal of this model is to make clear to users how the system will work.

Phase output

There are a number of outputs produced during this phase. These include:

- the analysis model, which describes the existing system, preferably in subject and system world terms;
- revisions to project goals and cost-benefit estimates;
- a requirements model, which specifies in usage world terms how the new system will work, including any interfaces presented to the user;
- a design model, which shows in subject world terms what the system does and how it will work;
- a broad system specification in system world terms defining how computers will be integrated into the business process;
- a project development plan, defining the expected completion times; and
- a test plan, where there are a number of test cases created for each detailed requirement.

Part of the management review of this phase is to reach an agreement on the detailed requirements and the system specification. Once agreement is reached, design can commence. The system specification is also validated against requirements and the existing system. Validation in this case often incorporates the ideas of structured walkthroughs, which are described in Chapter 21.

Phase 3—System design

This phase produces a design specification for the new system. There are many things to be done here. Designers must select the equipment needed to implement the system. They must specify new programs or changes to existing programs, as well as a new database or changes to the existing database. Designers must also produce detailed procedures that describe how users will use the system.

System design usually proceeds in two steps: broad design (Phase 3A) and detailed design (Phase 3B).

Phase 3A—broad design. The broad design identifies the main architecture of the proposed system. This architecture is verified against the proposed system model and validated against user requirements. During this phase, the models produced in the system specification are converted into computer systems.

For the interactive marketing stage, the languages used to develop the databases would be chosen and the database structures defined. In addition, the directory structure for the Web pages would be defined and the major pages identified.

At the conclusion of broad design the network configuration, including the size of the computer and the software needed to put the system together, is defined. It will also state which software can be purchased off-the-shelf and which requires new programs to be developed. The design may also suggest whether the computer should be rented or purchased, and whether programs are to be developed using internal programmers or external contractors.

Phase 3B—detailed design. It is only when a broad solution is chosen that detailed design starts. During the detailed design phase, the database and program modules are designed and detailed user procedures are documented. The interactions between the system users and computers are also defined. These interfaces define exactly what the user will be expected to do to use the system. The methods used to do this are described in Chapters 15 to 18.

Phase output. The output of the design phase includes an implementation model for the new system. This includes the proposed equipment configuration together with specifications for the database and computer programs. Detailed user procedures are also provided. These include any input forms and computer interaction between users and the computer. The user manual is also ready at the end of this phase. This output, particularly the proposed interactions between the computer and the system users, is validated against user requirements.

Phase 4—System development

Like the design phase, this phase is often broken up into two smaller phases: development and implementation. The individual system components are built during the development period. Programs are written and tested, and user interfaces are developed and tried by users. The database is initialized with data.

During implementation, the components built during development are put into operational use. Usually this means that the new and old systems are run in parallel for some time. To complete the changeover, users must be trained in system operation and any existing procedures converted to the new system.

One important part of construction is testing. It is necessary to test all modules to make sure they are error-free once they are put into operation. Testing can be a process on its own. We first test individual modules, then we test their interfaces and see how they work together.

Phase output. At the end of this phase, users are provided with a working system. This includes the set of working programs and an initialized database. Any system documentation describing the programs is also completed. All users have by now been trained and can use the new system.

SYSTEM TESTING

System testing is recognized as an important part of quality assurance. Testing, as shown in Figure 7.4, proceeds in parallel with system development. This idea is illustrated in Figure 7.6. Here a test plan is developed in parallel with system design. The test plan is then used to develop test cases that are used in system testing. Testing proceeds through

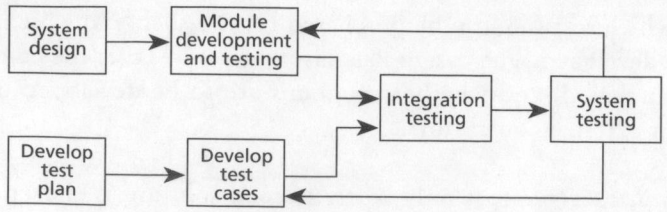

Figure 7.6 *Testing*

a number of steps. First, individual program modules are tested by their developers. Once individual modules are tested, the next step is to test whether they can be combined. This is known as integration testing. During integration testing, groups of modules are combined into test modules and tested together. The goal is to determine whether the interfaces between modules work. Then the entire system is tested. It is important to design test cases that test all the conditions that can arise in system inputs, while at the same time ensuring that the tests do not take too long.

WHAT HAPPENS AFTER PROJECT COMPLETION?

The system is considered to be working when Phase 4 has been completed. However, there are still a number of activities that take place after a system is completed. The two main activities are the post-implementation review and maintenance.

Post-implementation review

The post-implementation review usually takes place about a year after the system is implemented. It evaluates the new system to see if it has indeed satisfied the goals set for it and realized the expected benefits. If they have not, a study is made to see why not. Part of this study is the project life cycle itself. It is important at this stage to go back to the original goals of the project. Thus in the case of the interactive marketing system, the question would be whether sales of products have increased, not whether the computer system is working. Decisions made during the project are evaluated to see if they could have been better in the light of the experience gained from the project. This evaluation then sets guidelines for decision making in future projects. In addition, post-evaluation may suggest minor changes to be made to the system. In exceptional circumstances, where the system is performing badly, post-evaluation may suggest a total redesign.

Maintenance

Maintenance is necessary to eliminate errors in the system during its working life and to tune the system to any variations in its working environment. There are always some errors detected that must be corrected. Often small system deficiencies are found as a system is brought into operation, and changes are made to remove these deficiencies. Information system planners must always plan for resource availability to carry out these maintenance functions.

If a major change to a system is needed, a new project may have to be set up to carry out the change. This new project will then proceed through all the above life-cycle phases.

SOME PROBLEMS WITH THE LINEAR CYCLE

The linear cycle has one important property: it has definite sign-off points where some activities terminate. All of its activities are performed in a strict sequence. One phase must be completed before the next phase starts, and no phase can be repeated.

The cycle assumes that one can develop and specify precisely a system in a top-down manner. Successive phases elaborate the system in increasing detail, with each phase defining a partial solution and then calling for a more detailed evaluation in the next phase.

In practice, however, one often finds that assumptions made in the early phases no longer hold, that some of the early work was incomplete, or (even more likely) that something was overlooked or not completely understood. As a result, it may be necessary to return to an earlier phase and redefine an objective or redo some of the earlier work. What happens in this situation is shown in Figure 7.7. During system design we may discover that an objective defined in the feasibility study cannot be realized as easily as at first thought. Hence a return to the feasibility study may be necessary to redefine the objective. A worse scenario is when problems arise during

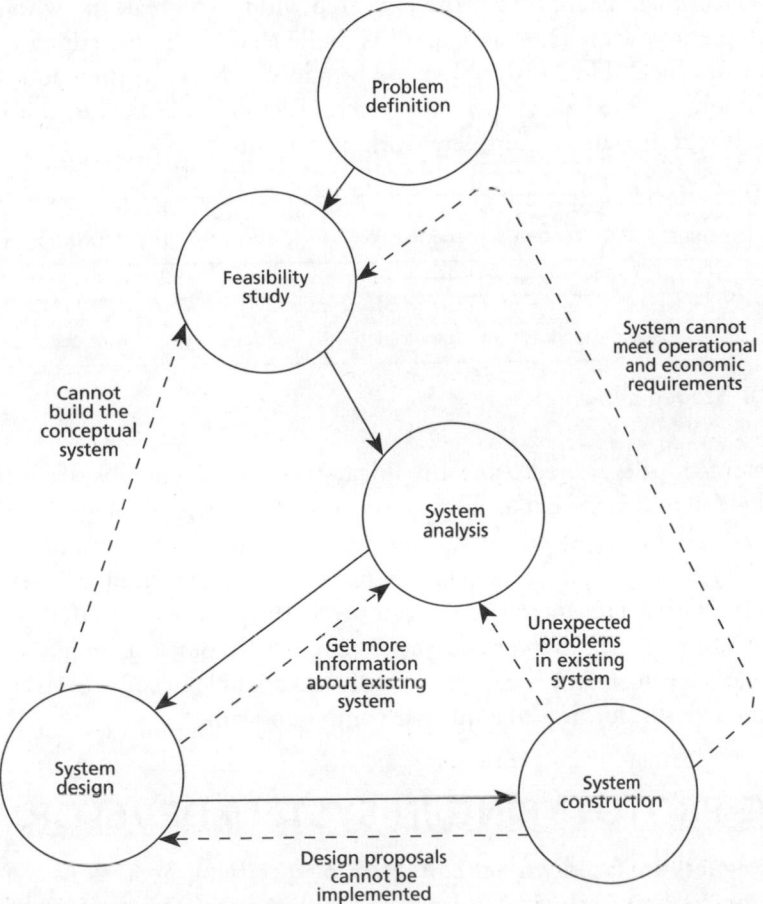

Figure 7.7 *Possible problems in a linear cycle*

implementation and these require a system redesign or a return to the feasibility study. Often, implementation detects some previously undiscovered problem in the system, calling for more systems analysis.

Problem-solving cycles like the one shown in Figure 7.7 are often called *loopy linear*. They arise by default because something was overlooked in the original plan. Iteration, or 'loopiness', is seen as being costly and is to be avoided. It generally requires wasteful rework of earlier phases.

One reason for project errors and consequent loopiness is that the problem being solved is too large or too uncertain. If it is too large, it is advisable to break it up into smaller stages and build the system a stage at a time.

STAGED DEVELOPMENT

Staged development
Building a system by parts.

Staged development is illustrated in Figure 7.8. It can only be used where it is possible to break a problem up into a number of distinct subsystems. Thus the first step may be a global concept phase that determines the size of the project. The study may suggest that the project is very large and that it should be developed in stages. If staged development is approved, the next step will be to break the whole project up into a number of stages. Thus we could first build a system to disseminate information about our products. Then ordering could be added. We could then add details about transportation, followed by an invoicing system. Each of these can be built up separately and then integrated into a complete working system.

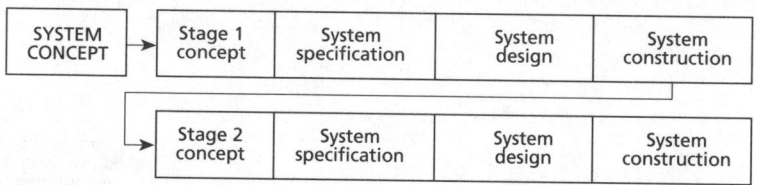

Figure 7.8 *Staged design*

Each stage is developed using the linear cycle and each subsystem is developed separately. You will note that each stage starts with its own problem definition phase. This is necessary to get a detailed evaluation and plan for each stage, and also to evaluate the feasibility of integrating the system produced in each stage with the systems developed in previous stages. The stage then continues with specification, design and system implementation. Figure 7.8 shows the stages being carried out sequentially—that is, Stage 2 commences when Stage 1 is completed. It is also possible in some cases to develop the stages concurrently, leading to a quicker completion time.

USING PROTOTYPING IN SYSTEM DEVELOPMENT

Often designers are faced with the problem of specifying operations that cannot be specified precisely using a model. Imprecise systems occur when it is not possible to develop a precise system specification. This often occurs in organizations that are just starting to use computers or in novel applications where there is no previous experience. Instead, it is more appropriate to develop the system gradually, learning about system capabilities as one goes along.

One example of imprecise systems is the interactive system with a lot of user dialog. Designers do not wish to risk users' rejection by prespecifying all the dialogs and screens. A set of trial screens and dialogs is developed and handed over to users for experimentation, after which changes may be proposed. Then a further experimentation follows until a satisfactory set of screens and dialogs is obtained.

Another type of imprecise problem involves workgroup computing. Here again it is not possible to precisely define all the interactions needed to effectively support group work and it is better to allow the system to be designed in an experimental way.

Prototyping is often used in system development to clarify user requirements in imprecise systems. A decision to use prototyping is usually made in the feasibility phase. Within the context of Figure 7.9, prototyping is used to gain a better understanding of possible solutions and the prototype then becomes the requirements model in the system specification phase. The dotted line indicates that some parts of the prototype may eventually become parts of the new system.

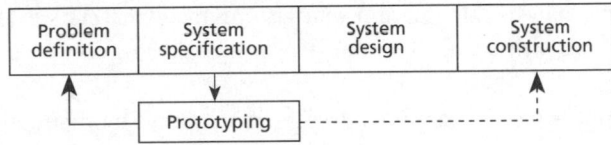

Figure 7.9 *Prototyping in systems development*

◇ EVOLUTIONARY DEVELOPMENT

Evolutionary design is yet another way of designing systems that cannot be precisely specified. It combines elements of staged design and prototyping. It develops the whole project as a number of stages, with the outcomes of one stage serving to identify the conceptual solutions for the next stage.

Evolutionary design
An experimental way of gradually building a system.

Evolutionary design, therefore, is often experimental in nature. Development starts with some small part of the system. For example, a new payroll system may be tried on one project or one department only, or the system may be developed to cater for some of the data only. Take a goods ordering system where ordering procedures differ for different kinds of goods: one way to start would be to develop a system for the subset of goods which are ordered in a straightforward manner. Once this is done and understood, we can go on to the next set of goods.

Evolutionary design does not assume that we can subdivide the problem into distinct and loosely coupled stages and design the system in one pass through these phases, as is the case with staged development. Instead, the system is developed gradually. We develop a system part and learn more about the problem from the operation of that part. We then use knowledge gained from this operation to define the next part to be developed. This part is then developed and the process continues.

In evolutionary design, each step adds a new capability to the system, and experience gained with a system is used to define the requirements for the next step. The next step extends system capability a little bit further and the process continues until no further improvement appears possible or worthwhile.

One kind of problem that is particularly susceptible to the evolutionary approach is decision support systems where the interactions used to support the decision making cannot be accurately predicted and an experimental approach is needed.

DECISION SUPPORT SYSTEMS

The problem here differs from that found in imprecise systems. In imprecise systems, it is clear that the system will eventually do what is expected of it, even though it is not clear how the system is to work. Decision support systems have a further degree of uncertainty because it is not clear whether a computer can actually be used to solve the problem. Alter (1984), for example, describes a taxonomy of decision systems and suggests that any decision system evolves through a number of stages. The stages mentioned by Alter are:

- A data analysis system that provides data useful to decision making. The decision maker must still decide on what is relevant in the data.
- Presentation of analysis information that automatically extracts information needed for a decision but still leaves it to the decision maker to compare the data against expectations.
- A decision support system based on a representation model that defines the expected system behavior and compares this to the actual behavior. Accounting models are frequently used here.
- A decision support system using an optimization model that uses the variations to decide on actions that can optimize future behavior.

Vehicle scheduling in Universal Electronics (Text Case C) is one such example.

TEXT CASE C: Universal Electronics—Decisions on Schedules

SITUATION—TRUCK SCHEDULING

A closer examination of this system was undertaken to study the ways used to schedule deliveries. Schedulers must ensure that most, if not all, outstanding deliveries are made on the next day at minimum cost. This calls for scheduling of vehicles to ensure that fewer vehicles are used in fewer miles while ensuring next-day delivery for the ordered items. Although one of the main objectives of scheduling is to minimize the number of vehicles and the distance traveled, other factors should also be taken into consideration. These include order priorities and a fair distribution of workload between drivers. Scheduling must also take into account varying road conditions due to road repairs, unusual traffic or inclement weather.

The scheduler takes each individual order in the daily list and places it in a pigeonhole that corresponds to the area of the customer. After all the orders are pigeonholed, the scheduler examines the order pattern and develops a routine plan based on experience with similar order patterns. There is no specific way in which such routes are chosen, and the final route is the outcome of the scheduler's experience with this work.

ISSUES

Our goal here is to choose the best allocation of truck routes. It is not clear whether the current method achieves this goal, and how, if at all, the computer can assist the scheduling. To find a better way, it is necessary to experiment with different approaches. The idea of evolutionary design is to control such experimentation so that we gradually learn how a particular decision is made and structure this decision in small steps. The question, then, is how to proceed in such experimentation.

SOLUTION

A solution based on Alter's steps can be followed here. A possible first step is to develop a system that organizes truck scheduling data in a way that is convenient for selecting routes. It may, for example, do the posting by sorting deliveries into their zones and producing a listing of such postings. This will save the scheduler some time in manual posting.

The next step may be to provide some analytical data together with the listing. This may include presentation of the total loads to be sent into each area and the number of trucks needed to carry these loads. It may also suggest an initial solution and compare it with yesterday's solution.

The next phase is to develop a representation model of the system which includes information not included in the earlier phases. Things like time needed to load the vehicles or times needed to travel between locations are now stored in the computer. The system asks the scheduler for a trial solution and computes factors like total distance traveled by trucks and the delivery times. The scheduler may then modify the initial solution and see how the changes affect these factors. This may continue until a satisfactory schedule is found.

Finally, the optimization model searches for the best solution without any help from the scheduler.

IMPLEMENTING EVOLUTIONARY PROBLEM SOLVING

Evolutionary cycles differ from linear cycles in the way that systems are brought into operation. In linear problem solving, the whole system is brought into service after the implementation phase. Thus, users do not take responsibility for the system until the implementation plan is complete. In evolutionary design, transfer of ownership and conversion usually becomes a gradual process.

A method for such gradual transfer has been suggested by Lucas (1978) and is shown in Figure 7.10. Development commences with a pilot system which may be part of our goods ordering process, a computer interface or the first part of a decision support system. The pilot system will include some key reports and provide users with an initial appreciation of the proposed system capability. These will be discussed with the users to gauge their satisfaction. The goal of the process, called *initial groping*, is to ensure that the user has sufficient knowledge of the project to constructively contribute to its development. It is also to ensure that the user is actively involved in the review of system specifications. As agreement is reached, the system is developed and parts of the system are gradually transferred to the user.

Major functions are defined in conjunction with the user during the initial groping, as a result of which the user slowly assumes the responsibility for the functions and puts them to use. Eventually the system evolves to a stage where all the major functions have been transferred to the user area and put into use. The operation is then in its

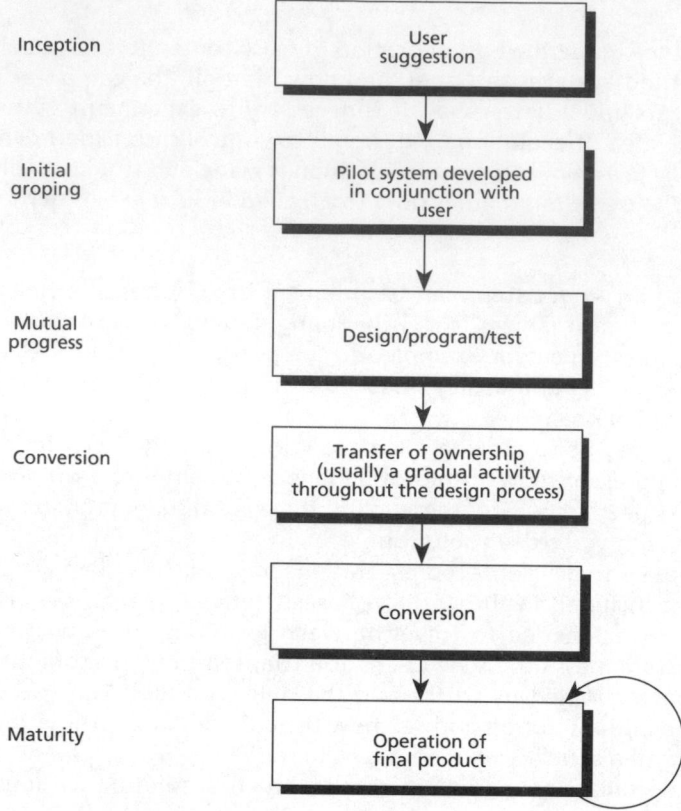

Figure 7.10 *An evolutionary design method*

mature stage. Changes can still be made to the mature system, although these are less frequent than in the initial stages.

THE SPIRAL MODEL

One formal approach to evolutionary development is the spiral model (Boehm, 1988). The idea of the spiral model is shown in Figure 7.11. It shows system development proceeding by the development of successive prototypes, with each new prototype adding additional functionality and being integrated with the previous prototype. Each of the cycles follows the linear cycle, with the first part being to define requirements for the new prototype. The evaluation at this stage can consider the risks and concentrate on reducing risk in parts at each prototype rather than as a whole. The system is thus developed gradually by successive developments of prototypes, followed by risk analysis to determine the most likely path to successful development.

CHOOSING A PROBLEM-SOLVING CYCLE

Different kinds of problems usually call for different problem-solving cycles and it is important to choose the most suitable cycle for a given problem. The choice is influenced by the nature of the problem, in particular:

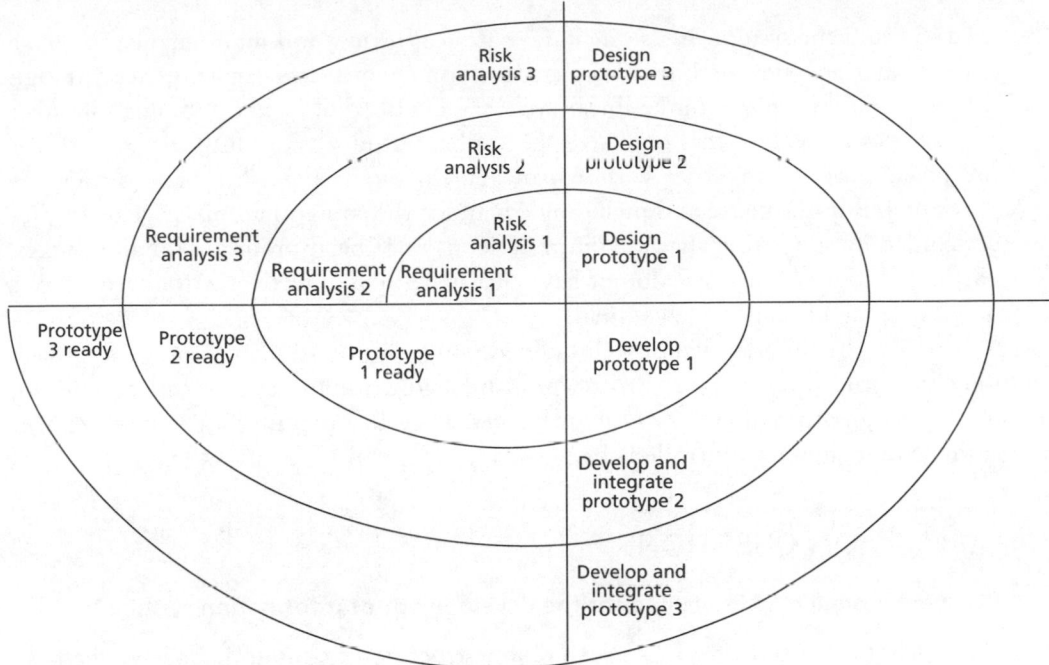

Figure 7.11 *The spiral model*

- the degree of system structure;
- familiarity with the technology; and
- project size.

Linear cycles are usually best suited to problems which are well understood and highly structured. In these cases it is possible to make accurate predictions about system behavior in the early design stages and to proceed toward a problem solution in a sequence of well-defined steps. Problems that are unstructured and harder to understand require more experimentation in the early stages. The evolutionary or prototype approaches become attractive for these problems.

Familiarity with technology also influences the choice of problem-solving cycle. Again, if one is familiar with the technology, better predictions can be made earlier and the linear cycle becomes more attractive. New and unfamiliar technology calls for more early experimentation.

Problem size also affects the choice. The most pressing need for some problems is to produce early results and maintain user commitment to the project. A staged approach is often attractive for large problems (provided that the whole system can be broken up into useful subsystems).

SUMMARY

Different systems can be developed in different ways. This chapter described various ways of developing systems. For well-defined problems, a linear cycle was suggested. The chapter described the linear cycle, which is composed of a number of phases used to build the system. It also includes a project review and maintenance that take place after the system is built. Project development proceeds in sequence through these phases. Each phase in the linear cycle has a defined objective and uses a number of activities to achieve this objective. Each phase produces an output that includes the phase product, together with a management report describing any difficulties encountered in the phase and including a plan for the subsequent phase. The chapter concluded by suggesting that the linear cycle may not be appropriate for all projects, particularly for systems that do not have clearly defined objectives. Alternative cycles may be needed to build such systems.

Where the problem is not well defined, an evolutionary or prototype approach may be more appropriate. Prototypes and evolutionary cycles call for design methodologies that allow easy system changes. They also require project management systems that support controlled change.

 DISCUSSION QUESTIONS

7.1 Why is a life cycle needed for the development of information systems?

7.2 What is the difference between highly structured teams and adaptive teams?

7.3 What kind of team structure would you expect to be best for evolutionary problem solving or prototyping?

7.4 Describe some roles that you could expect to find in a team.

7.5 Define the phases used in the linear cycle.

7.6 What kinds of problems would not be amenable to the linear problem-solving cycle?

7.7 What is the difference between the linear cycle and staged development? Where would you use staged development?

7.8 Why is the division between broad and detailed design necessary?

7.9 Describe what information you would keep for the post-implementation review.

7.10 What is the difference between system maintenance and the development of a new system?

7.11 What are the advantages of top-down problem solving?

7.12 Define what you understand by *system quality*.

7.13 Why is it difficult to build decision support systems using a linear cycle?

7.14 Explain the difference between the staged approach described in Chapter 3 and the evolutionary approach.

7.15 Explain how the linear cycle meets top-down problem-solving requirements.

7.16 Are you familiar with any systems where a prototype problem-solving approach would be useful?

7.17 What are the advantages of reusing existing modules?

EXERCISES

7.1 Suppose you are responsible for preparing a budget for advertising products that your organization sells. You have the figures for advertising costs in various media at different times and locations. You also have estimates of sales increases that may occur as a result of different volumes of advertising.

You are responsible for allocating the advertising budget to maximize the revenue increase. However, because of the number of products, media types and locations, you find it difficult to do so without assistance. A computer-based decision support system has been suggested. How would you break up your problem into the stages suggested by Alter, and what kind of output would you expect at each stage?

7.2 What kind of problem-solving cycle would you recommend for the project goal suggested for Text Case B?

BIBLIOGRAPHY

Alavi, M. (June 1984), 'An assessment of the prototyping approach to information systems development', *Communications of the ACM*, Vol. 27 No. 6, pp. 556–63.

Alter, S.L. (1984), *Decision Support Systems: Current Practice and Continuing Challenges*, Addison-Wesley, Reading, Massachusetts.

Anriole, S.J. (1992), *Storyboard Prototyping: A New Approach to User Requirements Analysis* (2nd edn), QED Information Sciences, Inc., Wellesley, Massachusetts.

Arnatt, R.J. (March 1979), 'From inception to beyond implementation—a system development case history', *Canadian Datasystems*, pp. 44–53.

Avison, D.E. Fitzgerald, G. (1988), *Information Systems Development*, Blackwell Scientific Publications, Oxford.

Baker, F.T. (1972), 'Chief programmer team management of production programming', *IBM Systems Journal*, Vol. 11, No. 1, pp. 56–73.

Bally, L., Brittan, J. and Wagner, K.H. (1977), 'A prototype approach to information systems design and development', *Information and Management*, pp. 21–26.

Bennaton, E.M. (1995), *Software Project Management: A Practitioners Approach*, McGraw-Hill, London.

Bersoff, E.H. and Davis, A.M. (April 1991), 'Impact of life cycle models on software configuration management', *Communications of the ACM*, Vol. 34, No. 8, pp. 105–118.

Boehm, B.W. (May 1988), 'A spiral model of software development and enhancement', *The Computer*, pp. 61–71.

Brittan, J.N.G. (February 1980), 'Design for a changing environment', *The Computer Journal*, Vol. 23 No. 1, pp. 13–19.

Constantine, L.L. (October 1993), 'Work organization: paradigms for project management and organization', *Communications of the ACM*, Vol. 36, No. 10, pp. 34–43.

Dearnley, P.A. and Mayhew, P.J. (1983), 'In favor of system prototypes and their integration into the systems development cycle', *The Computer Journal*, Vol. 26 No. 1, pp. 36–42.

Hirschheim, R. and Klein, H.K. (October 1989), 'Four paradigms of information systems development', *Communications of the ACM*, Vol. 32, No. 10, pp. 1199–216.

IEEE (1993), *Software Engineering, IEEE Standards Collection*, The Institute of Electrical and Electronic Engineers, New York.

Keen, P.G.W. (1978), *Decision Support Systems: An Organizational Perspective*, Addison-Wesley, Reading, Massachusetts.

King, D. (1984), *Current Practices in Software Development*, Yourdon Press, New York.

Kumar, K. (February 1990), 'Post implementation evaluation of computer-based information systems: Current Practices', *Communications of the ACM*, Vol. 33, No. 2, pp. 203–12.

Lucas, H.C. (Winter 1978), 'The evolution on an information system: from key-man to every person', *Sloan Management Review*, pp. 39–52.

Madsen, K.H. and Aiken, P.H. (June 1993), 'Experiences using cooperative interactive storyboard prototyping', *Communications of the ACM*, Vol. 36, No. 4, pp. 57–66.

Mason, R.E.A. and Carey, T.T. (May 1983), 'Prototyping interactive information systems', *Communications of the ACM*, Vol. 26, No. 5, pp. 347–54.

Mumford, E. (1981), 'Participative systems design: structure and method', *Systems, Objectives and Solutions*, Vol. 1, No. 1, pp. 5–19.

Rettic, M. (October 1993), 'A project planning and development process for small teams', *Communications of the ACM*, Vol. 36, No. 10, pp. 45–55.

Walz, D.B., Elam, J.J. and Curtis, B. (October 1993), 'Inside a software design team: knowledge acquisition, sharing and integration', *Communications of the ACM*, Vol. 36, No. 10, pp. 62–77.

Data flow diagrams

8

CONTENTS

KEY LEARNING OBJECTIVES

Why it is necessary to model data flows
Data flow diagrams
Context diagrams
The difference between physical and logical data flow diagrams
How to level data flow diagrams
Good practices in naming and conservation of data

INTRODUCTION

This and the next two chapters describe the modeling methods used in structured systems analysis to create analysis models, and very often the requirements model during the system specification phase. These methods center around modeling both the system and subject worlds, although they use mainly system world terms. Consequently, they require analysts to have particular skills in expressing subject world requirements in system world terms. Models in structured systems analysis are made up of three components: the process, the data and the system functions. Data flow diagrams model system processes and are one of the most important modeling tools used by systems analysts. The use of data flow diagrams as modeling tools was popularised by DeMarco (1978) and Gane and Sarson (1979) through their structured systems analysis methodologies. They suggested that a data flow diagram should be the first tool used by systems analysts to model system components. These components are the system processes, the data used by these processes, any external entities that interact with the system, and the information flows in the system.

This chapter will describe data flow diagrams and how to use them to model systems. Subsequent chapters will describe the other data and function components.

DATA FLOW DIAGRAM SYMBOLS

Data flow diagram (DFD)
A method to illustrate how data flows in a system.

Data flow diagrams (DFDs) use a number of symbols to represent systems. Most data flow modeling methods use four kinds of symbols to represent four kinds of system components: processes, data stores, data flows and external entities. Various writers use different symbols to represent these components. In this book we will use the symbols first introduced by DeMarco, but we will also indicate some alternative symbols that are often used. The symbols used by DeMarco are shown in Figure 8.1 and described in the text that follows.

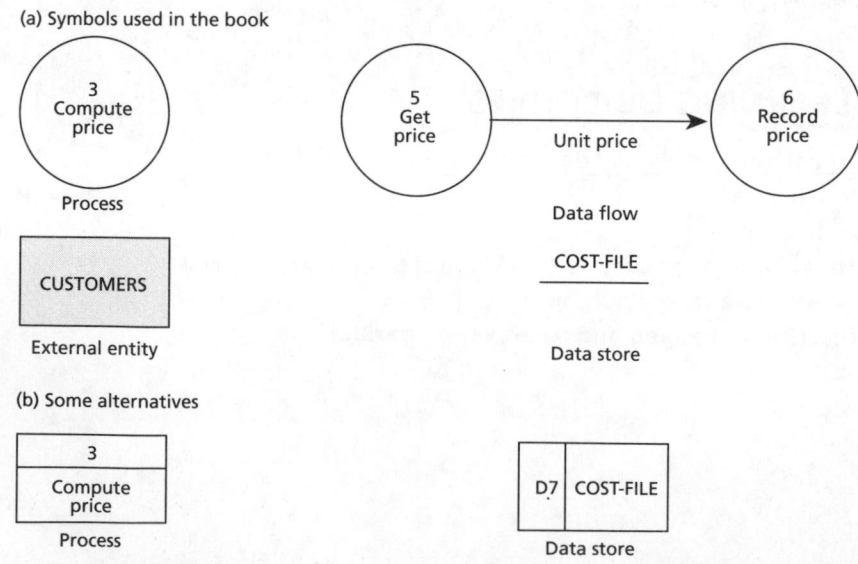

Figure 8.1 *Symbols used in DFDs*

PROCESSES

Processes show what systems do. Each process has one or more data inputs and produces one or more data outputs. Processes are represented by circles in a DFD. DeMarco sometimes uses the alternate term *bubble* to refer to a process in a DFD. Each process has a unique name and number which appear inside the circle that represents the process in a DFD.

FILES OR DATA STORES

A file or **data store** is a repository of data. It contains data that is retained in the system. Processes can enter data into a data store or retrieve data from the data store. Each data store is represented by a thin line in the DFD and each data store has a unique name.

Data store
A component of a DFD that describes the repositories of data in a system.

EXTERNAL ENTITIES

External entities are outside the system, but they either supply input data into the system or use the system output. They are entities over which the designer has no control. They may be an organization's customers or other bodies with which the system interacts. Alternatively, if we are modeling one section in an organization, other sections are modeled as external entities. External entities are represented by a square or rectangle.

External entities that supply data into a system are sometimes called *sources*. External entities that use system data are sometimes called *sinks*.

External entity
An object outside the scope of the system.

DATA FLOWS

Data flows model the passage of data in the system and are represented by lines joining system components. The direction of the flow is indicated by an arrow and the line is labeled by the name of the data flow. Flows of data in the system can take place:

Data flow
Data flowing between processes, data stores and external entities.

- between two processes;
- from a data store to a process;
- from a process to a data store;
- from a source to a process; and
- from a process to a sink.

We have no control of flows between external entities, so we do not model them. Similarly, stores are passive and cannot have data flows between themselves.

Figure 8.1 also shows some alternative symbols that sometimes appear in DFDs. A process is sometimes represented by a box, with the number appearing on top of the box. Data stores are also sometimes represented by a rectangular box, with a special number and a name inside the box.

DESCRIBING SYSTEMS BY DATA FLOW DIAGRAMS

We will now illustrate how systems are modeled using these symbols. A common way to begin is to model the whole system by one process. The DFD that does this is known as the **context diagram**. It shows all the external entities that interact with the system and the data flows between these external entities and the system.

Figure 8.2 is an example of a context diagram. It models the 'budget monitoring system'. This system interacts with three external entities: DEPARTMENTS, MANAGEMENT and SUPPLIERS. In Figure 8.2, the main data flows from DEPARTMENTS are 'spending request'. In response, DEPARTMENTS either receive 'rejected request' data flows or 'delivery advice' data flows. MANAGEMENT receives 'request for special approval' data flows to which it responds. MANAGEMENT also sends 'budget allocation' data flows to the system and gets 'spending summaries' data flows. Suppliers receive 'part order' data flows and return 'supplier delivery advice' data flows.

Of course, a model like that shown in Figure 8.2 does not describe the system in detail. For more detail it is necessary to identify the major system processes and draw a DFD made up of these processes and the data flows between them. The DFD that shows the major system processes is called the top-level DFD (shown in Figure 8.3). The top-level DFD shows the various processes that make up the system. Each process has a unique name and number. From Figure 8.3 we see that data flow 'spending request' from DEPARTMENTS goes to the 'check funding' process. This process looks up the allocated budget and determines whether special permission is needed from MANAGEMENT to proceed with the request. Approved requests go to the 'classify expenditure' process where they are entered into data stores, DEPARTMENTAL-ACCOUNTS and TYPE-ACCOUNTS. Finally, if required, a 'part order' for parts originally specified in a 'spending request' is placed with suppliers. There are also two other processes in Figure 8.3. One is to 'set up budget' and the other to 'provide spending summaries'.

We could continue to expand each process in Figure 8.3 into a more detailed DFD. As an example, Figure 8.4 is a detailed description of the 'classify expenditure' process labeled as Process 3 in Figure 8.3. Each process in this detailed DFD is labeled with a 3 and followed by a number to show that each is an expansion of Process 3. The input to this DFD is the data flow 'approved request'. Process 3.1 classifies the entries in each 'approved request' by expense type (such as material and capital overhead), and Process 3.2 uses this classification to update data store TYPE-ACCOUNTS. All

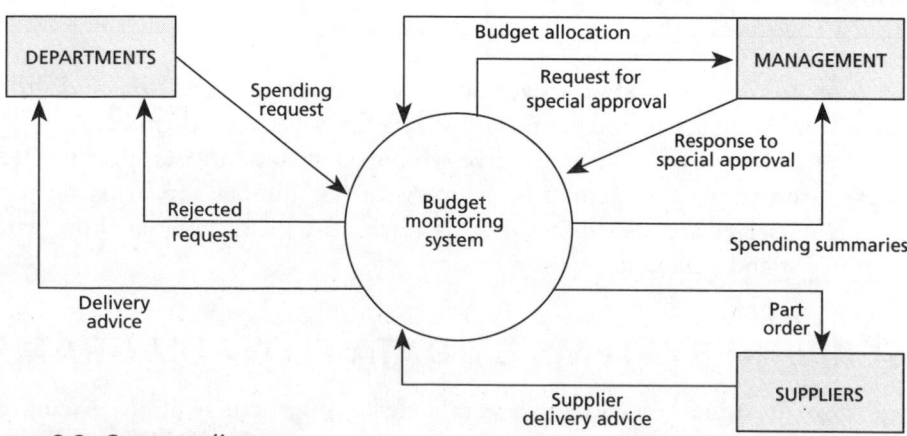

Figure 8.2 *Context diagram*

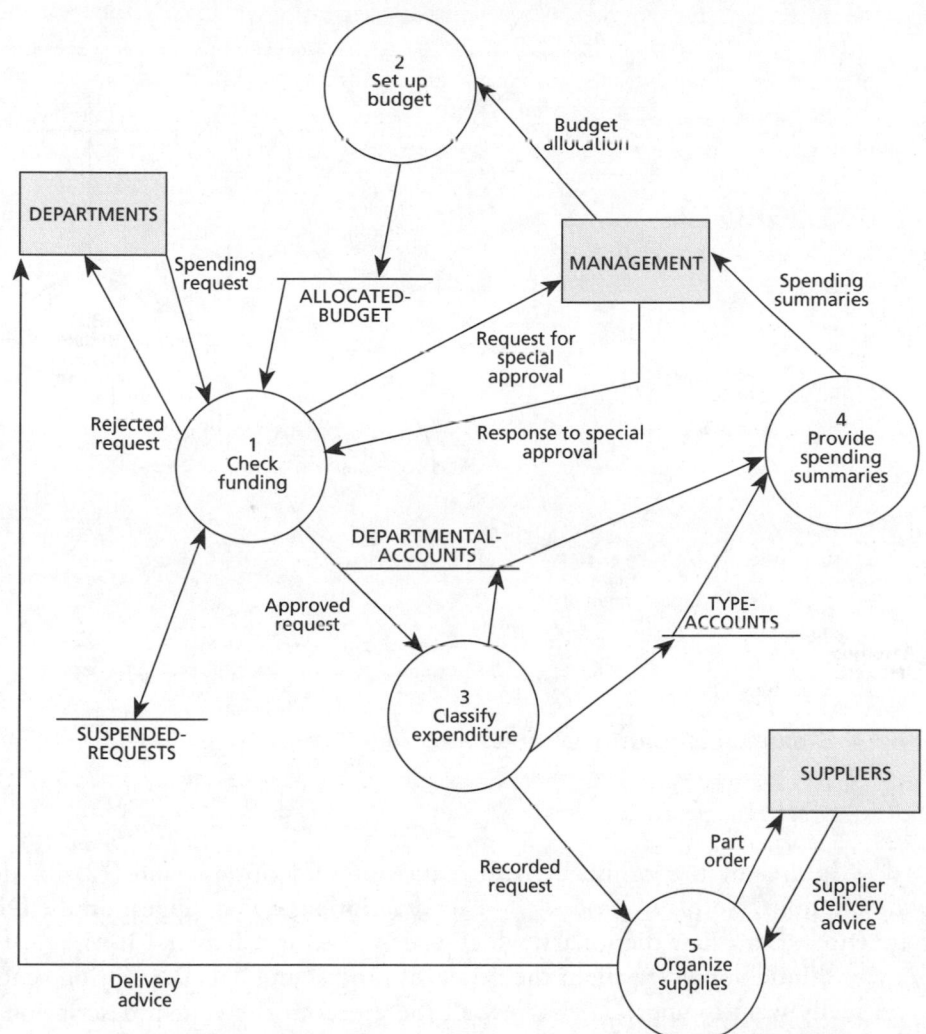

Figure 8.3 *A top-level DFD diagram*

the entries for the whole request are summed by Process 3.3, and Process 3.4 uses the total to update data store DEPARTMENTAL-ACCOUNTS.

We could expand each of the processes in Figure 8.4 by even more detailed DFDs. However, eventually we must stop this expansion. If we don't, then we will get DFDs containing processes describing simple computations such as the addition of two numbers. DFDs which reached that level would be awkward and unduly complex. However, it is necessary to get down to a level that describes detailed arithmetic computation. This is done by using process specifications, rather than DFDs.

Process specifications and detailed data definitions are described in detail in later chapters. A brief description of process and data specifications is given here to show you how all the constructs of a structured system description fit together.

Figure 8.5 illustrates a detailed description of processes, data stores and data flows. In Figure 8.5, detailed process descriptions are marked by the symbols (*) and detailed

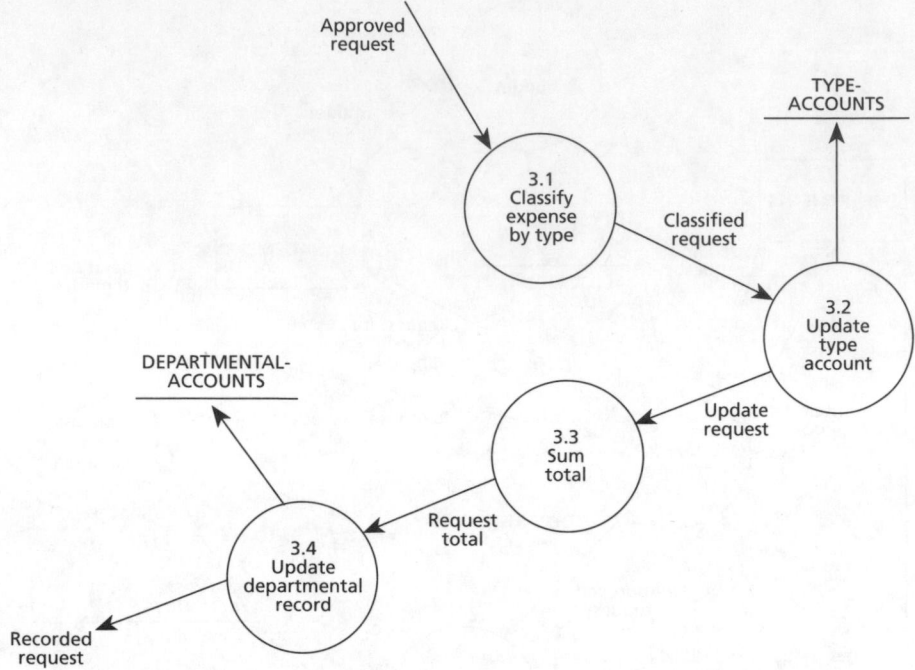

Figure 8.4 *Expansion of 'classify expenditure' process*

data descriptions by the symbols (*l) for data store descriptions and (*2) for data flow descriptions. Normally, process and data descriptions do not appear on the DFD but are entered in a data dictionary, which is described in Chapter 13. Also, at this stage, you should not worry about the details of process and data description syntax. All you really want to appreciate is how all the pieces of the system description fit together. You will find out about the details in later chapters.

Figure 8.5 shows that an 'approved request' is made up of the data items DEPT-NO, REQUEST-NO and a number (as indicated by the asterisks) of request lines, each made up of data items AMOUNT and DESCRIPTION. The data changes as it passes through the processes. After Process 3.1, DESCRIPTION in data flow 'approved request' is replaced by TYPE in data flow 'classified request' and then, after Process 3.3, all the values of AMOUNT are summed to REQUEST-SUM.

The data stores are also defined in Figure 8.5. Thus the data store DEPARTMENTAL-ACCOUNTS contains any number of entries made up of two items, DEPT-NO and TOTAL-EXP. The TOTAL-EXP means the total expenditure in requests so far made by the department identified by DEPT-NO.

In Figure 8.5, process specifications use formal methods and refer to data item names defined for data structures. For example, the description of Process 3.2 shows that TYPE in the classified request is used to locate an entry in the TYPE-ACCOUNTS data store. The TOTAL-AMOUNT in this entry is updated and the entry written back to the data store.

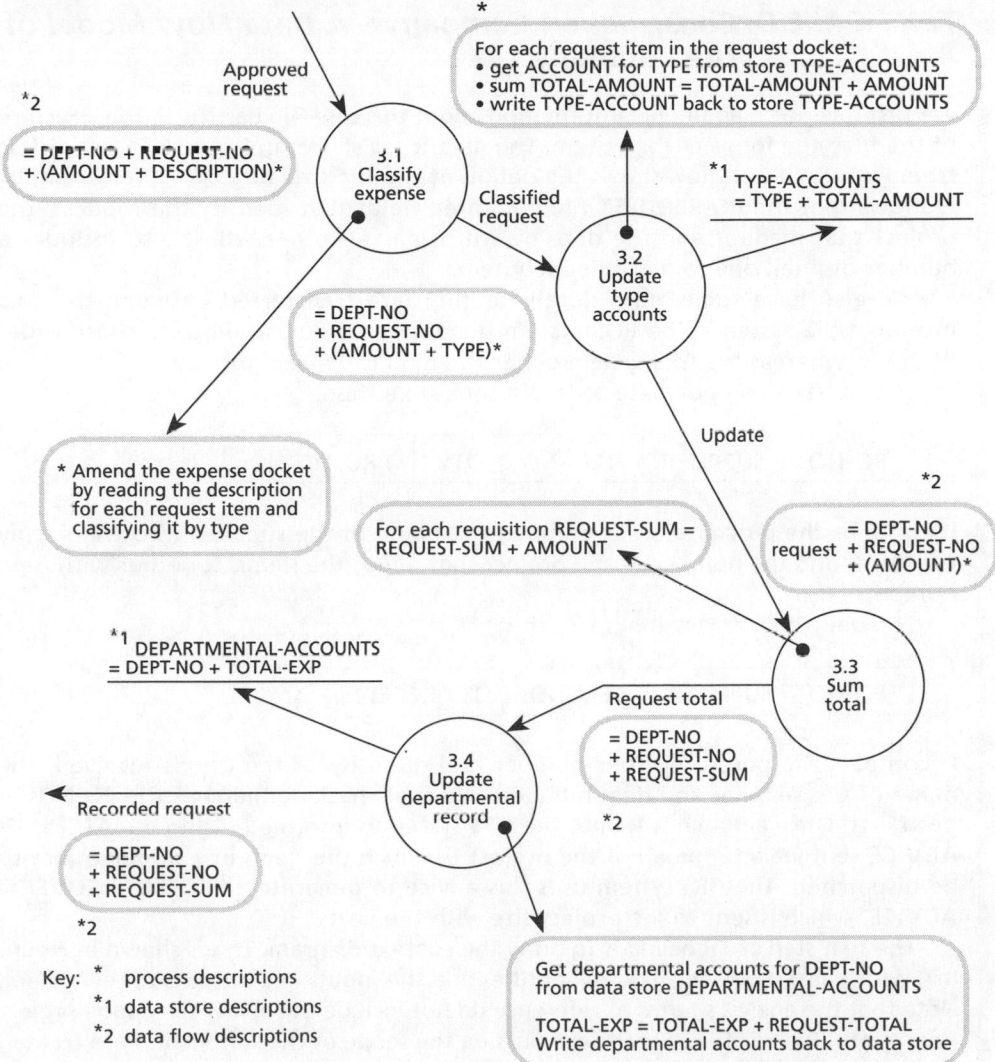

Figure 8.5 *Describing processes and data for 'classify expenditure' process*

So far we have tried to provide an idea of what structured analysis is all about. It may look quite simple on the surface, but there are a number of difficulties that can arise once you get into detailed work. First, you should note that there are many ways to draw a DFD for a system. Some of these may be better than others. Ideally, a DFD is self-explanatory, complete and unambiguous. Nevertheless, a number of conventions and rules have been developed to make your work easier. The rest of this chapter will describe some of these conventions, beginning with a description of the properties of a good DFD.

Let us now see how we can apply some of these techniques to the case we introduced in Chapter 4.

TEXT CASE D: Construction Company—A Data Flow Model of the Company

We first give some additional information about this case—in particular, the structure of the files and forms of the system. The details are shown in Figure 8.6. This differs from Figure 4.1 as it now shows the details of the file structure. Thus, for example, it shows that the PO-REQUEST file has three fields that identify the request, the project that made it and the date by which parts are needed. It also includes a number of lines, one for each needed item.

We also have some more details of the data transferred between the two incompatible systems. The POS system generates an outstanding purchase order list daily, whereas the GRS system generates a daily delivery list.

The outstanding purchase order list looks like this:

PO-NO	SUPPLIER	ITEM-NO	QTY	PROJECT-NO

It contains the purchase order number, the name of the supplier who will supply the items and the number of the project that needs the items, together with item numbers.

The daily delivery list looks like this:

PO-NO	SUPPLIER	ITEM-NO	QTY-RECEIVED

It contains the purchase order number and quantity of the goods received, the name of the supplier and item numbers. Manual checking matches the PO-NOs in both lists. Once a match is found, the GRS system is informed (using a MATCHING-ADVICE sent via a terminal) of the project to which the items in a shipment are to be dispatched. The GRS system uses this advice to generate a PROJECT-DELIVERY-ADVICE, which is sent to the project site with the parts.

The first step of modeling is to draw the context diagram. This is shown in Figure 8.7, which also shows the external entities and the inputs and outputs to the system. Note that the analyst's terms of reference do not include the ability to change project operations. PROJECTS are therefore outside the scope of the system and are treated as external entities.

Before drawing the top-level DFD, we describe one important aspect of data flow diagrams, namely—the difference between logical and physical DFDs.

LOGICAL VERSUS PHYSICAL FUNCTIONS

Many designers make a distinction between logical and physical functions. Another way to consider the difference is to see the physical-level functions as closer to the usage world, whereas the logical diagram more closely mirrors the subject world. Figure 8.8 illustrates the difference between these two kinds of functions. Figure 8.8(a) is a DFD that models what is going on. It says that orders are received, the location of ordered parts is determined and delivery notes are dispatched. It does not, however, tell us how these things are done or who does them. Are they done by computer or manually and, if manually, who does them?

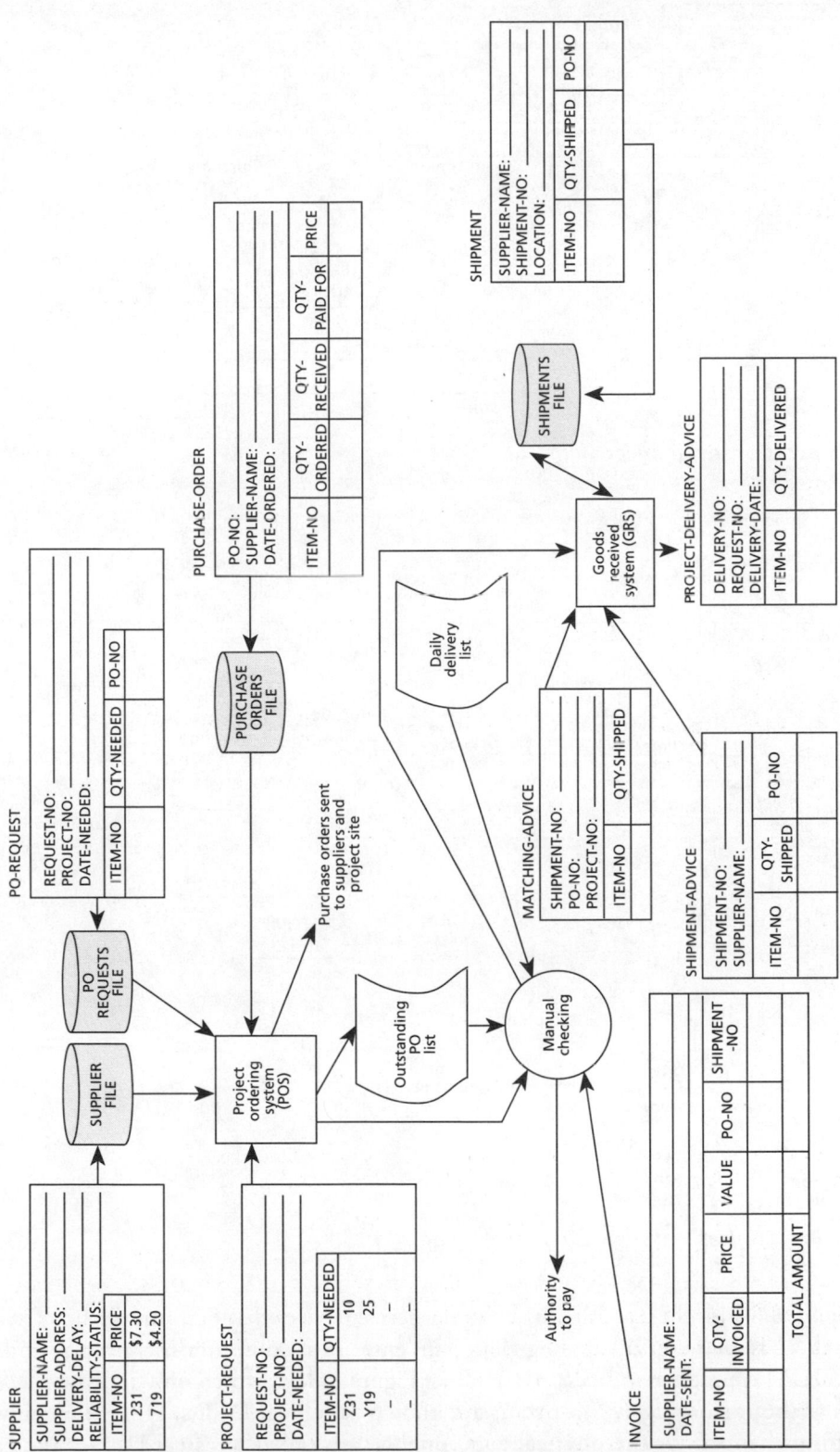

Figure 8.6 *Project ordering and goods received systems*

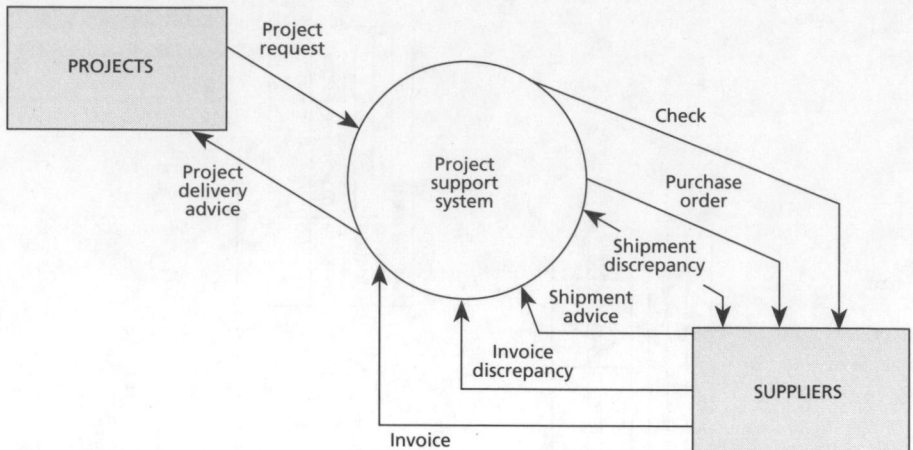

Figure 8.7 *Context diagram*

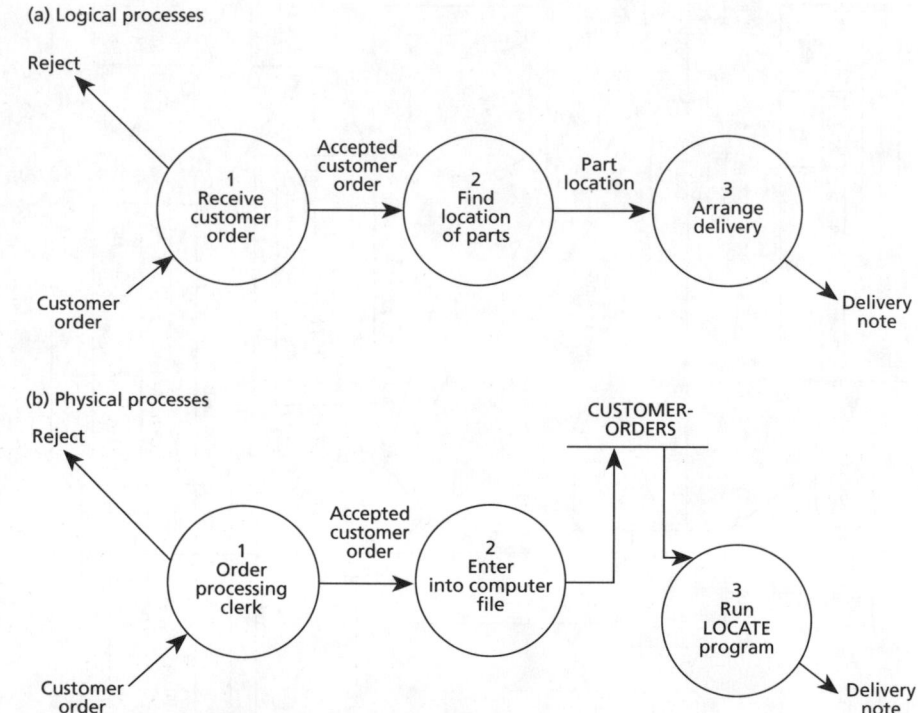

Figure 8.8 *Logical and physical data flow design*

Logical DFD
Describes the flow of logical data components between logical processes in a system.

Physical DFD
Describes the flow of physical data components between physical operations in a system.

Figure 8.8(b) is the opposite. It shows the actual devices that perform the functions. Thus, there is an 'order processing clerk', an 'enter into computer file' process and a 'run LOCATE program' process. DFDs, like Figure 8.8(a), which only illustrate *what* occurs without showing *how* it occurs are known as **logical DFDs**. DFDs that show *how* things happen, or the physical components, are called **physical DFDs**. Typical processes that appear in physical DFDs are methods of data entry, specific data transfer or processing methods, and processes that depend on the physical arrangement of data. Often DFDs include both physical and logical processes.

What are the advantages of these two kinds of DFDs? It is often argued that logical models assist designers to gain a clear perception of what the system is to achieve without getting confused by its current implementation details. After all, one of the objectives of systems analysis is to improve system operation. It is easier to do this if one initially concentrates on what is to be done without considering the limitations imposed by physical devices.

However, it is easier to start modeling the physical system because physical components can be readily identified during analysis. Analysts therefore often begin by building a physical model and then convert this physical model to a logical model.

CONVERTING PHYSICAL DFDS TO LOGICAL DFDS

There are a number of steps that can be followed when converting physical DFDs to logical DFDs. These steps are illustrated by using the DFD shown in Figure 8.9, which includes four processes:

1. *The reception clerk* receives an order and checks to determine if it is of the type made by the organization. If the answer is no, the order is not accepted; if yes, it goes to the production section.
2. The orders are *sorted* into areas.
3. *The production section* checks if the machines for making the order are available. If not, the order is not accepted; otherwise, resources for order production are committed.
4. *The production section* produces the ordered part.

All of these processes are **physical processes**. During conversion to logical DFDs, we first remove all the processes that refer to physical activities only and do not transform information. The two processes of this kind in Figure 8.9, for example, are 'sort into areas' and 'send to production section'.

The remaining processes are physical because they describe physical components. However, they cannot be removed from the DFD because they transform data. These two processes are then expanded into their logical functions. To do this, take each physical process, find out what it does, and replace it by a leveled DFD of logical functions that represent the physical object's logical activities, or what the object does. All physical processes can be expanded in this way and their expansion combined into a lower-level logical DFD. Thus, in Figure 8.9, the reception clerk is replaced by the two reception clerk functions, 'record order' and 'check type of order'. Similarly, 'production section' is replaced by its two functions, 'check available resources' and 'commit resources to production'.

This lower-level DFD is then examined. Any common or similar functions are combined, and these combined higher-level processes become the higher-level DFD. Examination of the expanded DFD in Figure 8.9(b) shows that 'check type of order' and 'check available resources' have a similar purpose—they determine whether the

Physical process
Usually a physical device used to transform data—for example, computer, person, and so on.

(a) Top-level physical DFD

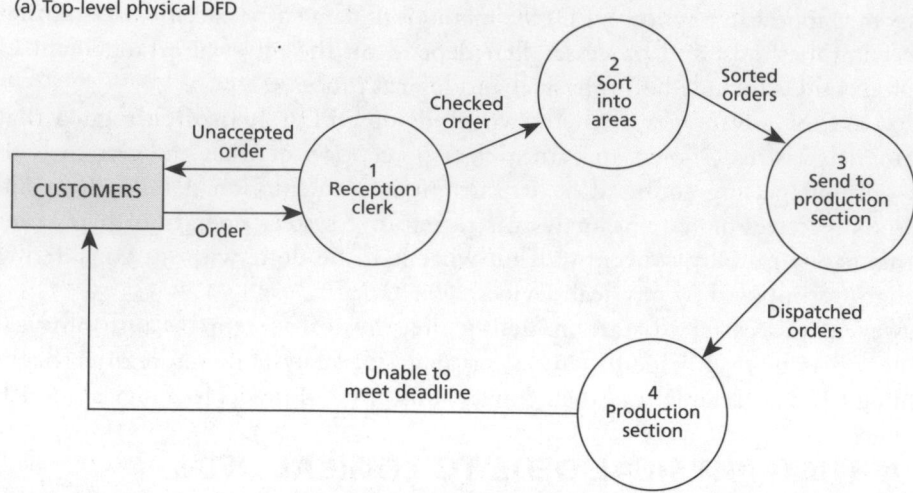

(b) Expanded processes

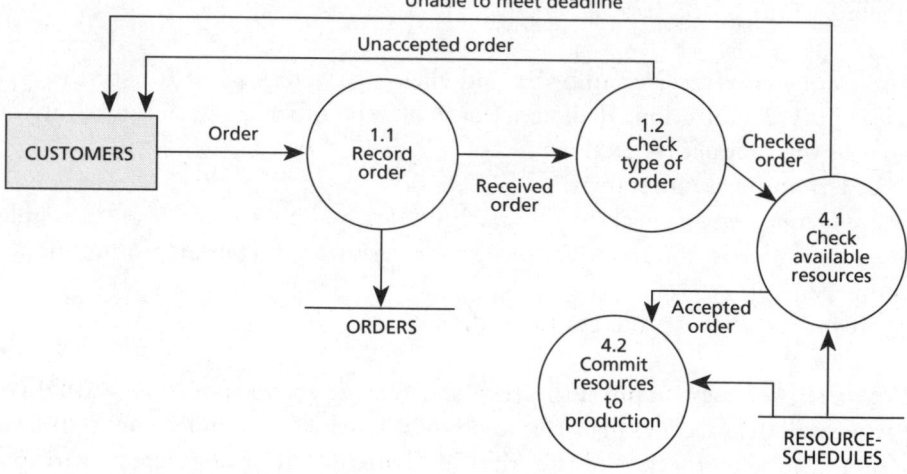

(c) Recombined logical processes

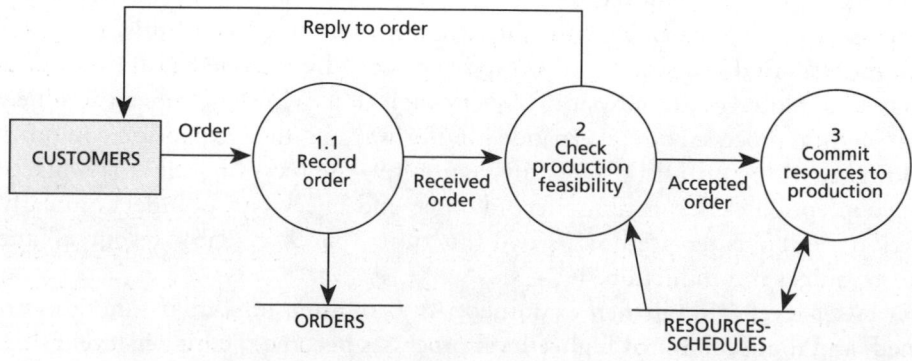

Figure 8.9 *Converting physical DFDs to logical DFDs*

job can be done. Hence they are combined into a higher-level logical function, 'check production feasibility', in Figure 8.9(c). This process becomes the only process to interface with the users. It replies to the users, either accepting or rejecting their orders, and carries out any other dialog with them. The processes 'record order' and 'commit resources to production' are then also added to the DFD in Figure 8.9(c). The result is that, in Figure 8.9(c), we have the logical DFD equivalent of the physical DFD shown in Figure 8.9(a).

More examples of typical physical DFDs and their conversion to logical DFDs are shown below. Figure 8.10(a) shows a DFD that contains all data in one physical database. This often happens when we are modeling systems with an existing centralized database. The centralized physical database can be replaced by its logical components— that is, the logical data structures stored in the database as shown in Figure 8.10(b).

Models that include generalized retrieval packages are further examples. In Figure 8.11(a), many processes are combined into the general process enquiry package. Again the DFD does not show explicit logical processing. Thus the general enquiry package can be replaced by logical functions, as shown in Figure 8.11(b).

In general, physical DFDs are often characterized by the kind of structures shown in Figure 8.12. Physical processes usually have many functions and consequently have many flows in and out of them. Whenever you see a structure like the one shown in Figure 8.12, you can be fairly sure that it is a physical process and you should, if necessary, convert it to a **logical process**.

Let us now return to Text Case D and expand its context diagram.

Logical process
Describes any changes of value made by the processes on logical data.

TEXT CASE D: *Construction Company—Expanding the Context Diagram*

Figure 8.13 illustrates a first attempt at a top-level DFD. The system is modeled by four obvious physical components: the GRS system, the POS system, the manual checking system and the payment section. This top-level DFD is physical in nature. Because it is difficult to go directly from this physical top-level DFD to a top-level logical DFD, we use the idea shown in Figure 8.9 and first level the physical system into its logical components.

The leveled processes are shown in Figure 8.14. This figure shows the leveled diagrams for Processes 1, 2 and 4 of Figure 8.13. Thus, for example, Process 2, which receives parts from suppliers, has been leveled into three parts. Process 2.1 simply records a shipment received from a supplier. Process 2.3 generates the shipment list for manual checking (Process 3). Process 2.2 generates delivery advices, as indicated by the matching advices obtained from Process 3.

You should note that leveled Processes 1.1, 1.2, 1.3 and 2.1 still represent physical computer system components. Processes 1.4 and 2.3 also represent physical processes because they describe a particular sort order of data. Process 3 describes a physical processing component (manual processing) and Process 1.2 a physical method of data entry. Process 4.1 also refers to a physical component—checks.

You should note that Figure 8.14 contains the leveled DFD for a number of top-level processes. Normally, each of these DFDs would appear on a separate page. In Figure 8.14 they appear on the same diagram for illustrative purposes only.

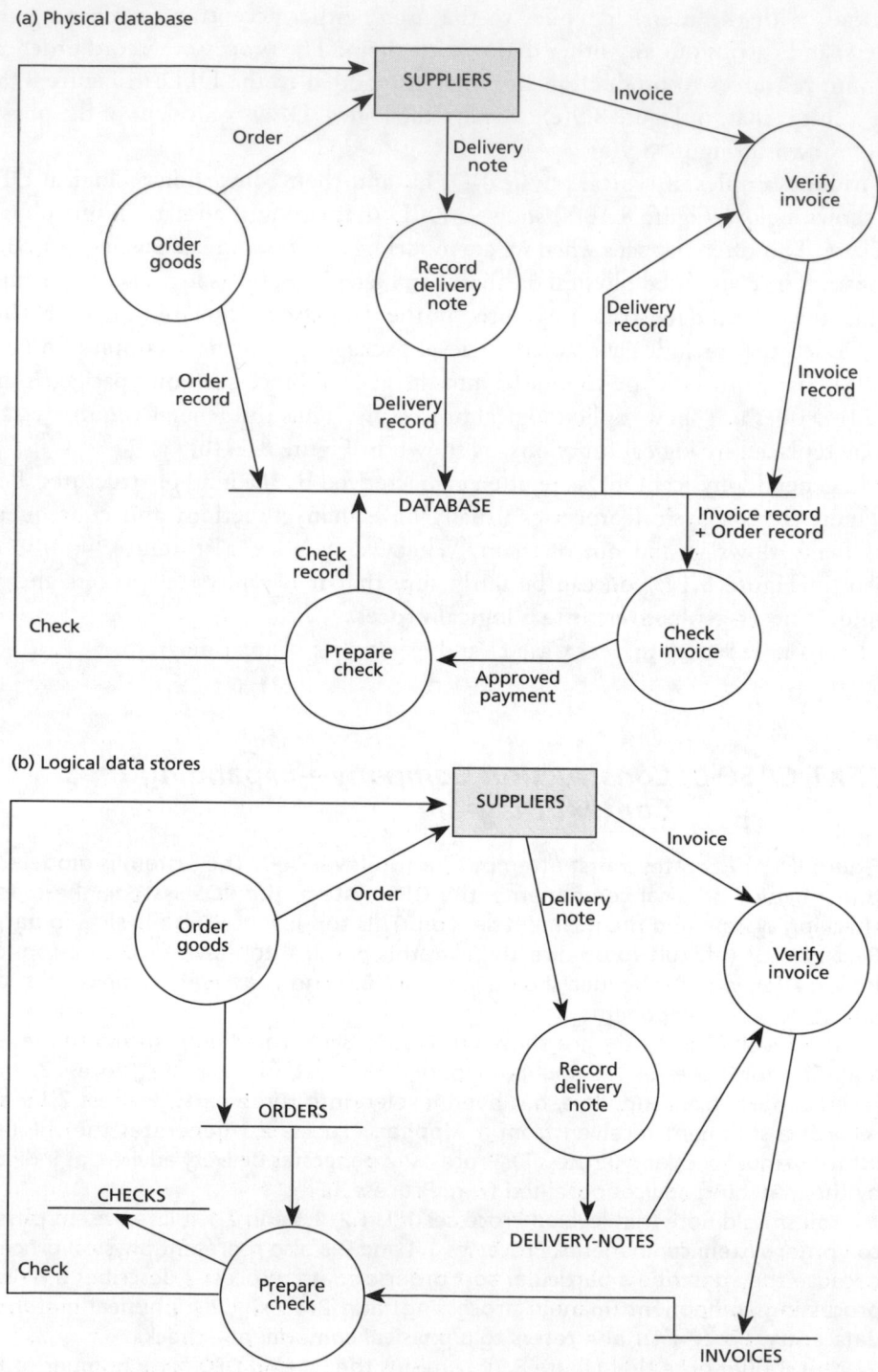

Figure 8.10 *Conversion of physical database*

(a) A physical enquiry package

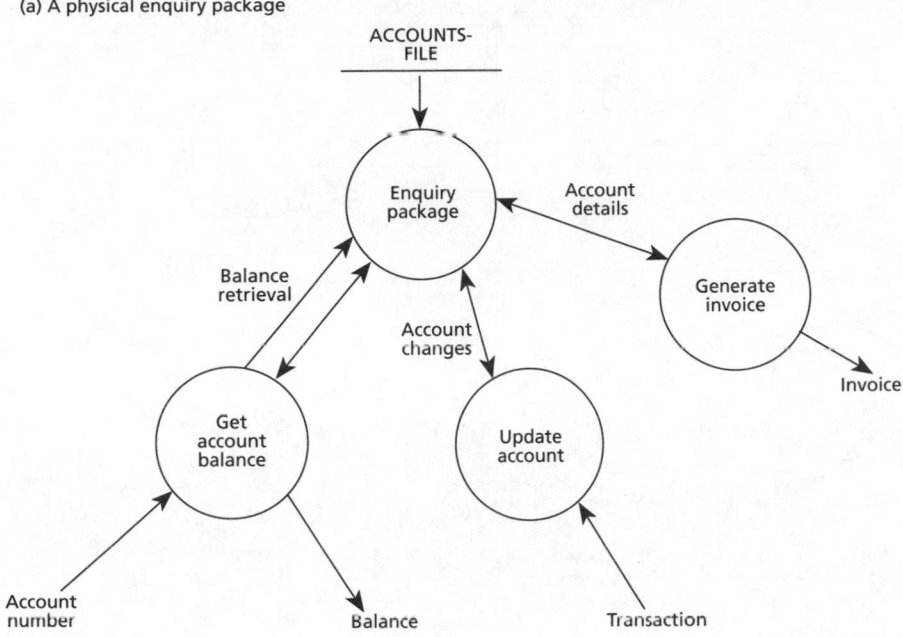

(b) Removing enquiry package

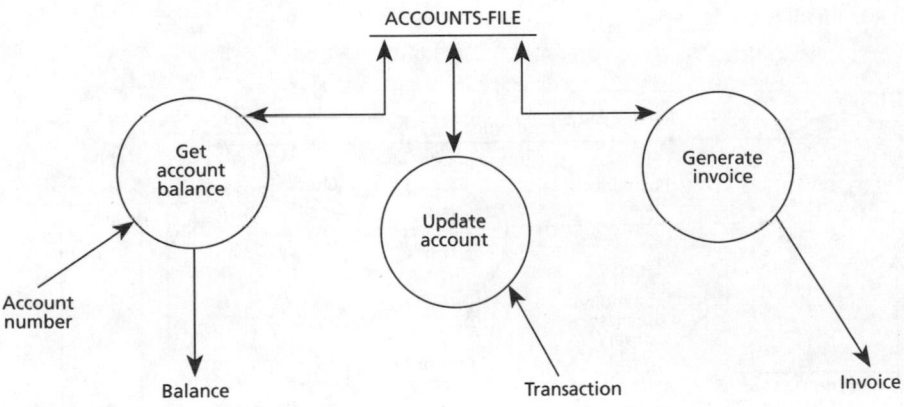

Figure 8.11 *Modeling file access*

To create the top-level logical DFD it is necessary to eliminate references to physical systems and devices and to remove any processes that describe purely physical transformations. It is also necessary to level Process 3 before any recombination into higher-level logical processes. Figure 8.15 shows DFD 3, which is the leveled DFD of Process 3. It describes what is currently done manually. The first step, Process 3.1, is to take the shipment list and match it with the outstanding purchase orders. Any matches are followed by identifying the project involved (Process 3.3) and an advice to store on where to send the items (Process 3.4). Any discrepancies found in Process 3.1 are brought to the attention of suppliers. All received parts are recorded on the PURCHASE-ORDER file, which is used to authorize payments (Process 3.5). Process 3.5 also checks for any discrepancies between the received part and the invoice and brings them to the attention of suppliers.

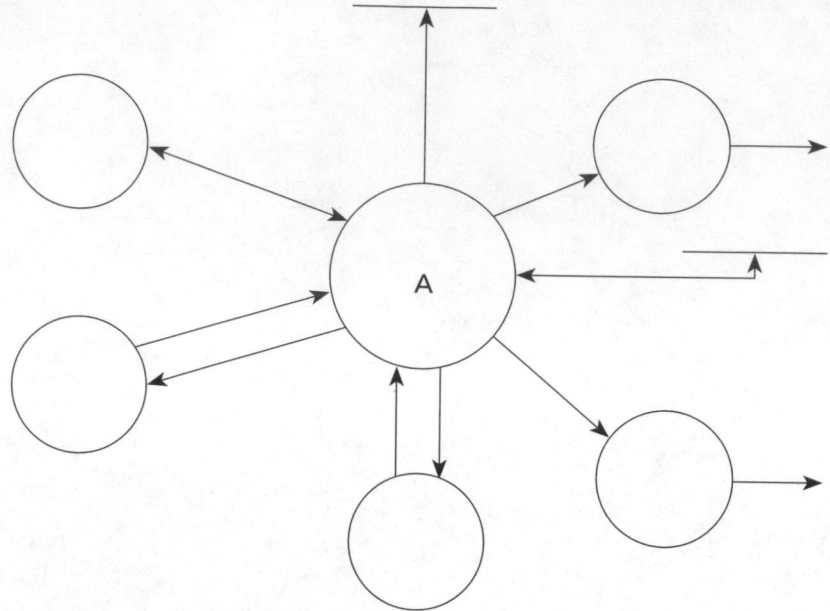

Figure 8.12 *Typical physical process interface*

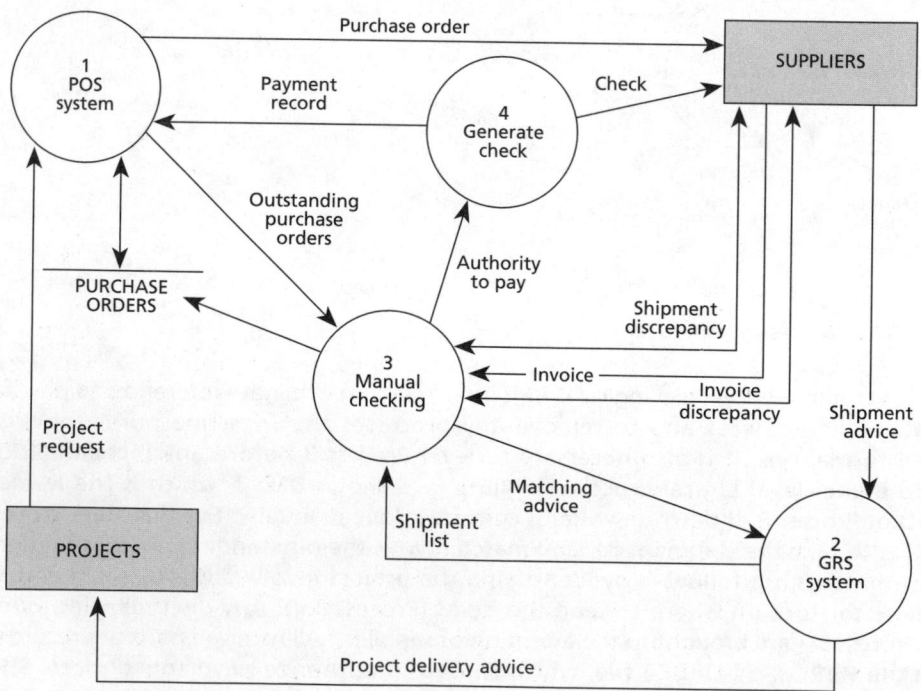

Figure 8.13 *Physical top-level DFD*

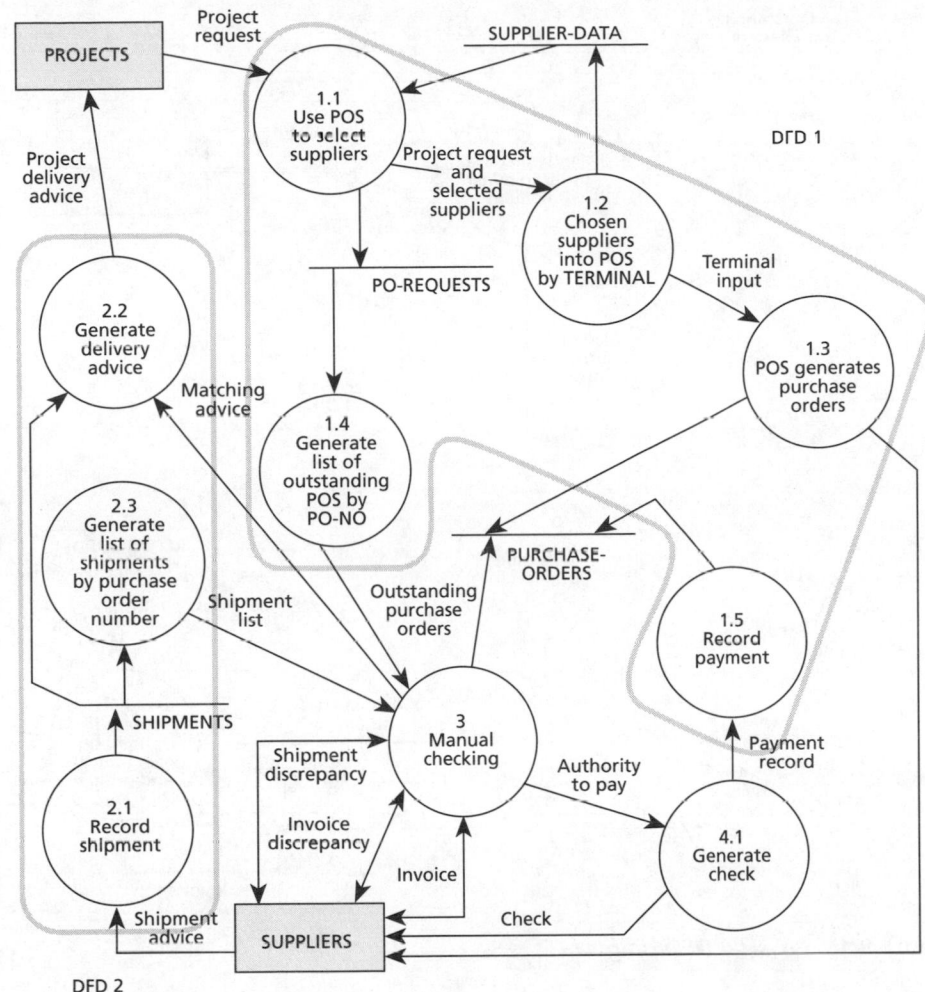

Figure 8.14 *Leveling of physical processes*

Let us examine how to construct a logical top-level DFD from the leveled diagrams. First, purely physical processes like Process 1.2 are removed, and references to physical devices are removed from process descriptions. Thus the words 'use POS to' are removed from Process 1.1 and this process becomes Process 1 in the top-level DFD, shown in Figure 8.16. Similarly, the reference to POS is removed from Process 1.3 and this becomes Process 2 in Figure 8.16.

Processes 1.4 and 2.3 are removed because they are purely physical. The leveled Processes 3.1, 3.2, 3.3 and 3.4 in Figure 8.15 are recombined into Process 4 in the logical top-level DFD in Figure 8.15. Note that data store PO-REQUESTS is used by logical Process 4 to find a destination for shipments. The 'shipment destination' is sent to Process 5, which generates the 'project delivery advice'. Process 3.5 in Figure 8.15 becomes Process 6 in the logical top-level DFD. Processes 2.1 and 2.2 become logical Processes 3 and 5 respectively in the logical top-level DFD. Finally, Process 4 is combined with Process 1.5 into logical Process 7.

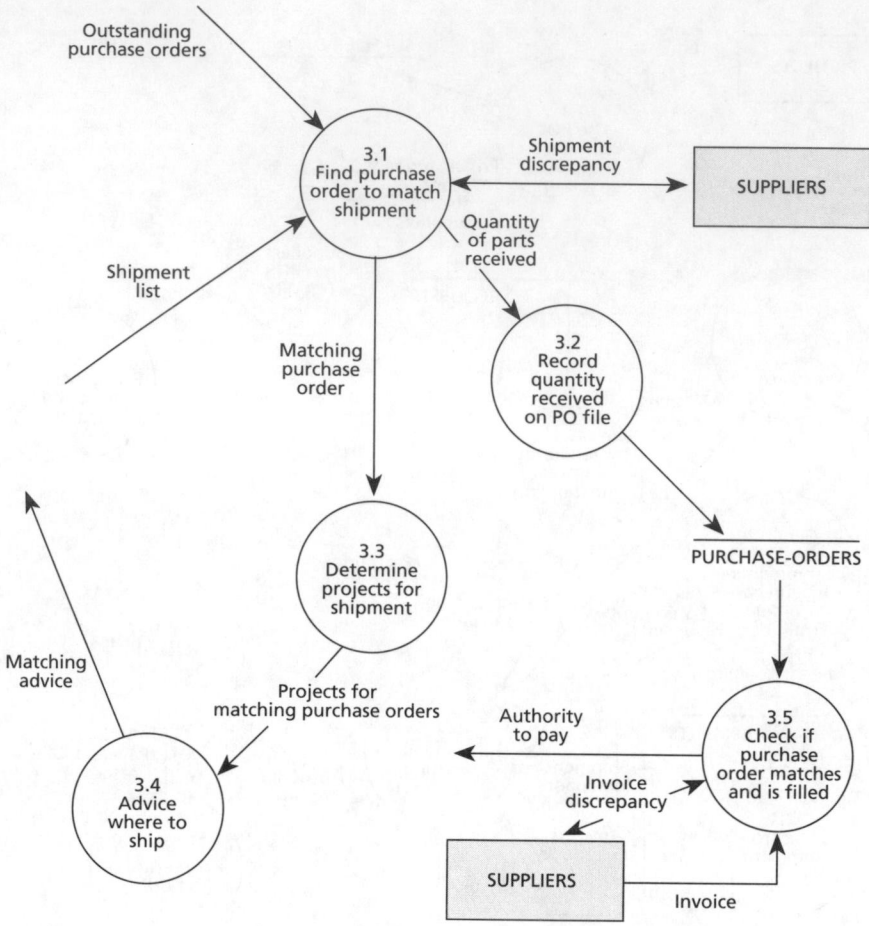

Figure 8.15 *Physical DFD diagram 3*

One question that designers often ask is: 'How can I tell if this is a good DFD?' Unfortunately, this is not an easy question to answer. One part of the answer is whether all the information about the system has been captured. This can only be checked by validating the DFD with the users. The other part of the answer is whether the structure or syntax of the DFD is correct. Again, there is no easy answer. However, it is possible to suggest some features of good DFDs, which we will do in the remainder of this chapter. Designers can then determine whether their DFDs violate any of these features. You may postpone reading this part until you have done some detailed diagramming.

 ## WHAT IS A GOOD DATA FLOW DIAGRAM?

DFDs have a number of features which can be used to ensure that they are self-explanatory, complete and unambiguous. The features are:

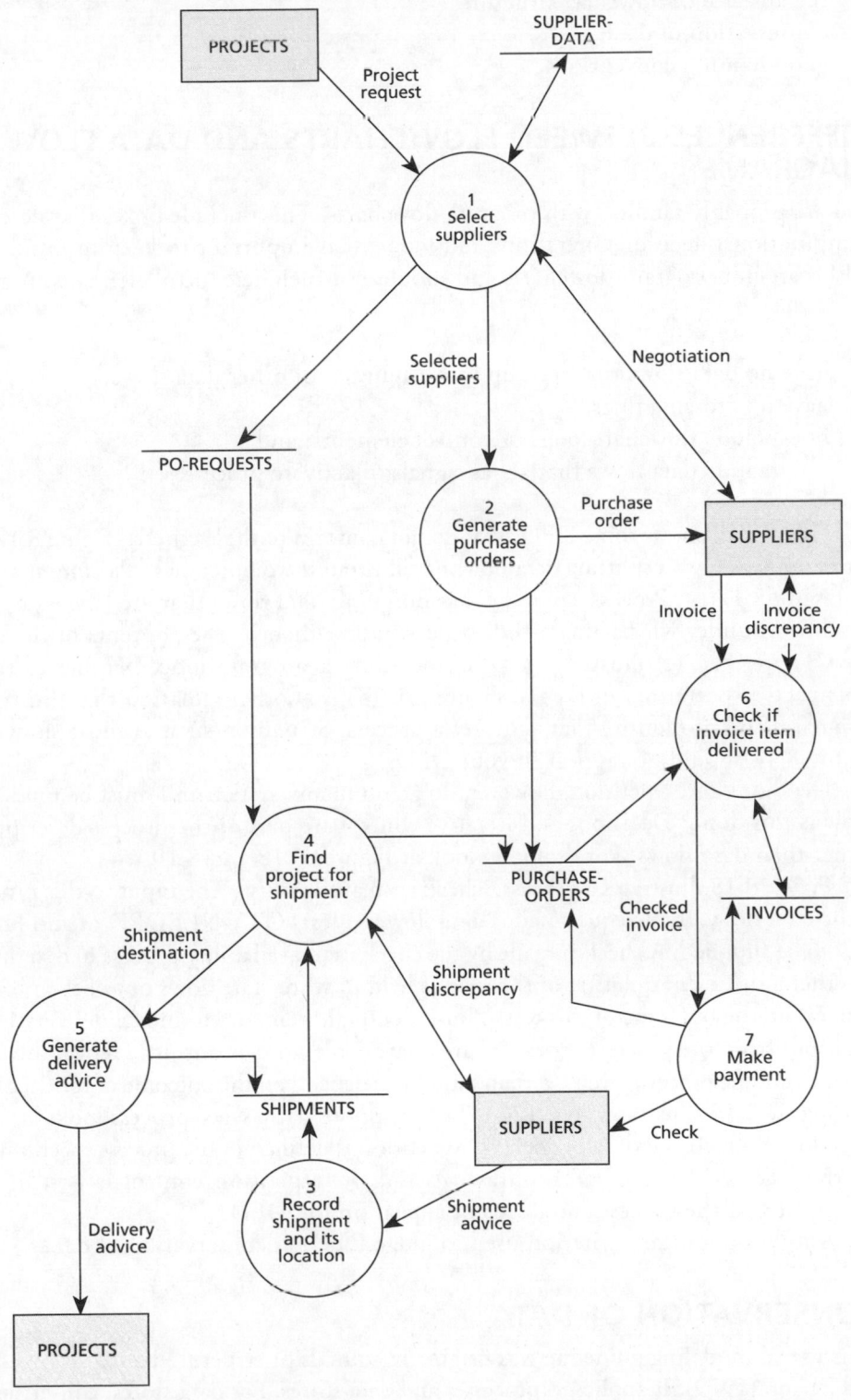

Figure 8.16 *Logical top-level DFD*

- the absence of flowchart structures;
- conservation of data; and
- good naming conventions.

DIFFERENCES BETWEEN FLOWCHARTS AND DATA FLOW DIAGRAMS

You are probably familiar with program flowcharts. They include boxes that describe computations, decisions, iterations and loops. It is important to keep in mind that DFDs are not program flowcharts and should not include control elements. A good DFD should:

- have no data flows that split up into a number of other data flows;
- have no crossing lines;
- not include flowchart loops of control elements; and
- not include data flows that act as signals to activate processes.

Figure 8.17 shows some DFDs that do not conform to these criteria. Figure 8.17(a), for example, shows a splitting data flow that illustrates two outcomes of a computation. In Figure 8.17(b), Process 'compare' has outgoing data flows that are labeled by the conditions under which a data flow occurs, rather than by the contents of the data flow. Figure 8.17(c) illustrates a DFD modeling a program loop. Neither of these constructs is permitted in DFDs. Figure 8.17(d) is another violation that illustrates a signal ('End of month') that activates a process. Structures such as those shown in Figure 8.17 should not appear in your DFDs.

Decisions and repetition, however, do go on in any system and must be modeled. How is this done? Decisions and iterative control are part of the process description rather than data flows. For example, look at Figures 8.18 and 8.19.

Figure 8.18 illustrates a process, 'check item availability'. The input to this process is the data flow, 'Item-request'. This data flow requests QTY-NEEDED of an ITEM-NO to be supplied. A check is made by the check item availability process to determine whether a sufficient quantity of the item is held in store. The flows out of the process depend on the outcome of this test. Thus, if enough items are found, a 'delivery note' is output from the process; otherwise an 'unavailable note' is output. Hence, the data flows out of the process, given a certain input, will depend on the outcome of the decision.

Figure 8.19 illustrates repetition. The 'compute daily sales' process looks at each sales docket in a batch of sales dockets. Repetition is defined in the process specification by the REPEAT . . . UNTIL phrase. Again, the repetition control is part of the description of the process and does not appear on the DFD.

Another important criterion used to judge DFDs is conservation of data.

CONSERVATION OF DATA

This useful modeling guideline was originally coined for structured analysis by Gane and Sarson (1979). It applies to processes and data stores. For data stores, conservation of data says that what comes out of the data store must first go in. It is not possible

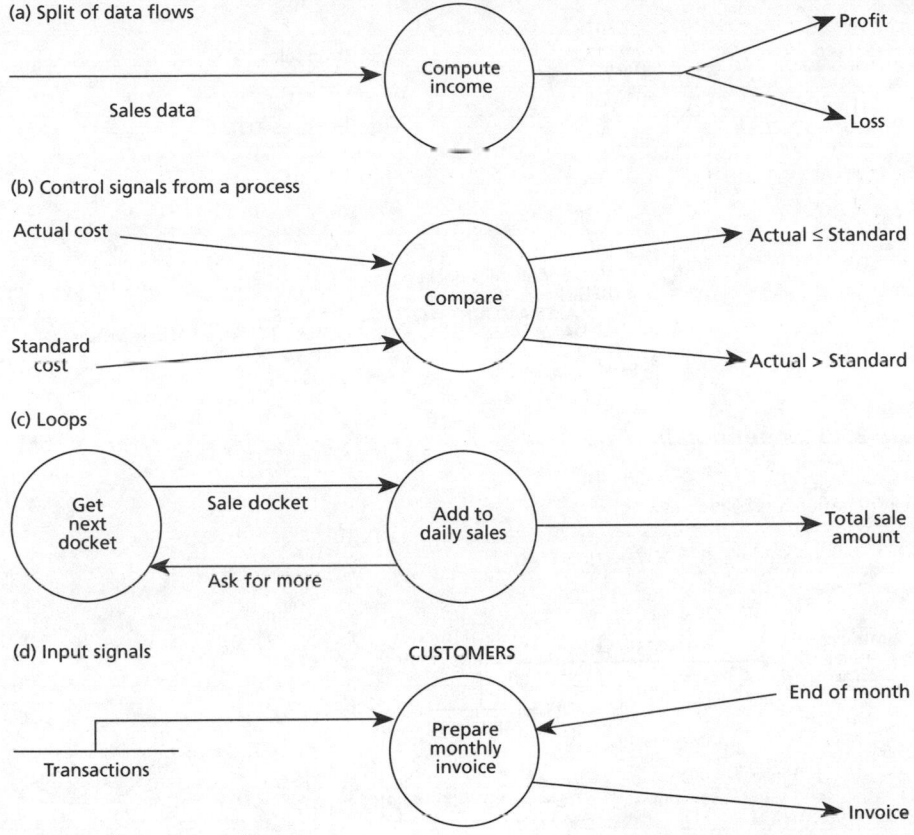

(a) Split of data flows

Sales data → Compute income → Profit / Loss

(b) Control signals from a process

Actual cost, Standard cost → Compare → Actual ≤ Standard / Actual > Standard

(c) Loops

Get next docket — Sale docket → Add to daily sales → Total sale amount
Ask for more

(d) Input signals

CUSTOMERS

Transactions → Prepare monthly invoice ← End of month → Invoice

Figure 8.17 *Illegal data flows*

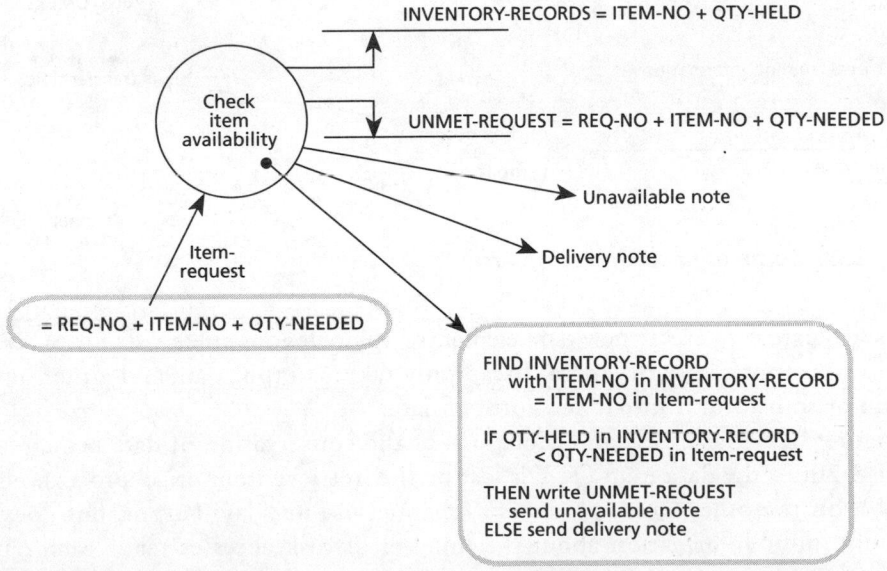

INVENTORY-RECORDS = ITEM-NO + QTY-HELD

UNMET-REQUEST = REQ-NO + ITEM-NO + QTY-NEEDED

Check item availability → Unavailable note / Delivery note

Item-request
= REQ-NO + ITEM-NO + QTY-NEEDED

FIND INVENTORY-RECORD
    with ITEM-NO in INVENTORY-RECORD
    = ITEM-NO in Item-request

IF QTY-HELD in INVENTORY-RECORD
    < QTY-NEEDED in Item-request

THEN write UNMET-REQUEST
    send unavailable note
ELSE send delivery note

Figure 8.18 *Decisions in DFDs*

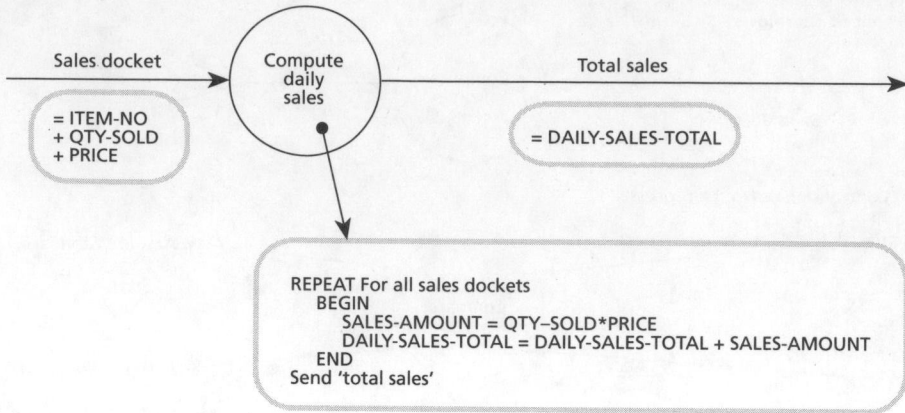

Figure 8.19 *Repetition in DFDs*

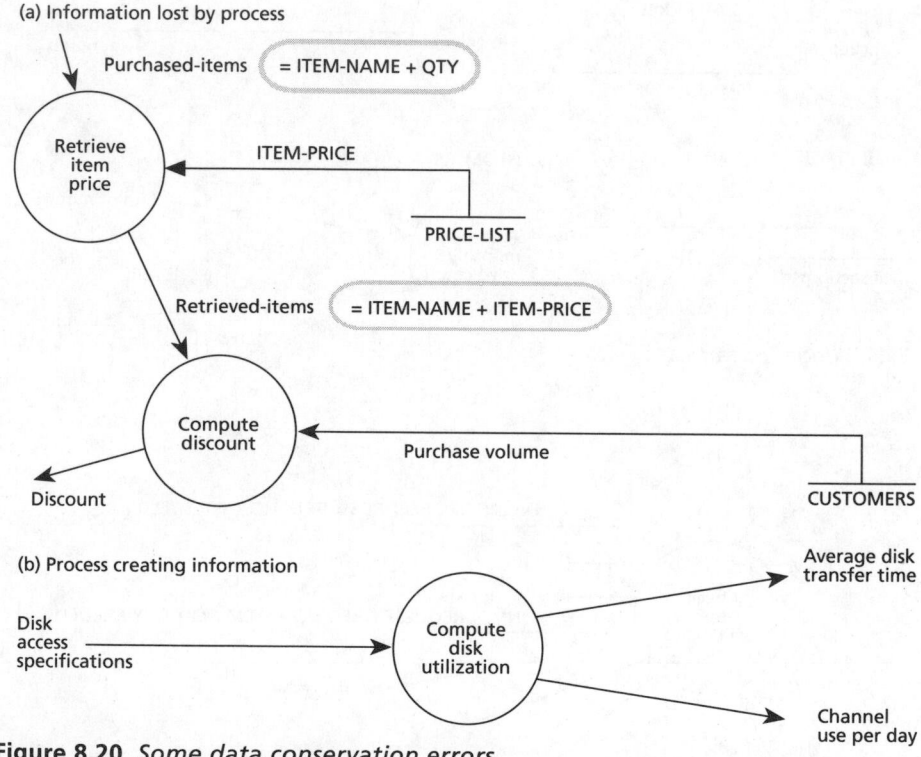

Figure 8.20 *Some data conservation errors*

for the data store to create new data elements. An analogous rule exists for processes. A process cannot create new data. It can only take its input data and either output it again or transform it into a new form of data.

Figure 8.20 illustrates some violations of the conservation of data principle. In Figure 8.20(a), the data item QTY is lost by the 'retrieve item price' process. Figure 8.20(b), on the other hand, produces a 'channel use per day' output, but does not have any input information about the number of disk accesses made each day. A process should also not lose any data.

NAMING

To make a DFD readable, analysts should avoid using meaningless names. Little information is conveyed by the labels shown on Figure 8.21. Names such as 'needed data', 'standard operations' and so on should be avoided. Specific names should be used at all parts of the DFD. The choice of these names depends on the type of component named.

Figure 8.21 *Meaningless names*

Naming processes

A process name should be one single phrase and it should be possible to describe a process in one sentence. The process name should define a specific action rather than a general process. For example, the following names are acceptable:

- 'edit a withdrawal transaction';
- 'compute weekly salary'; and
- 'compute discount on order'.

However, process names should not be general (e.g. 'examine transaction'). Such general terms are only necessary when a process is not a single function. Such a process may, for example, be: 'Read a transaction and process its detail lines if the heading is correct. Also check if the transaction is useful to the sales department.' This process describes more than one function and should be broken up into more than one process. A good guide for evaluating a DFD is to check whether all the process names are single phrases and whether each process can be described in one sentence.

Naming data stores

The same comment applies to naming data stores. Again, use specific names and avoid general terms such as: USER-DATA, CENTRAL-REPOSITORY or PRODUCTION-DEPT-FILE. Helpful specific terms like: CUSTOMER-ORDER, LAST-YEARS-RECEIPTS or MACHINE-SCHEDULE should be used.

Furthermore, each data store should contain only one specific set of structures and not combinations such as 'MACHINE-SCHEDULES and PARTS-USED by PRODUCTION-DEPT'. MACHINE-SCHEDULES and PARTS-USED are different kinds of structures and should be modeled by separate data stores.

Naming data flows between processes

Data flows should normally be named as one word (e.g. 'invoice', 'check', etc.). However, there are many instances in DFDs where using only a single word for a data flow can lead to ambiguity and loss of self-description. One frequently occurring instance is where a particular document goes through a number of processes and can be modified by each process. In Figure 8.22, for example, an invoice goes through a number of processes. The 'edit invoice' process checks if the invoice contains all the needed

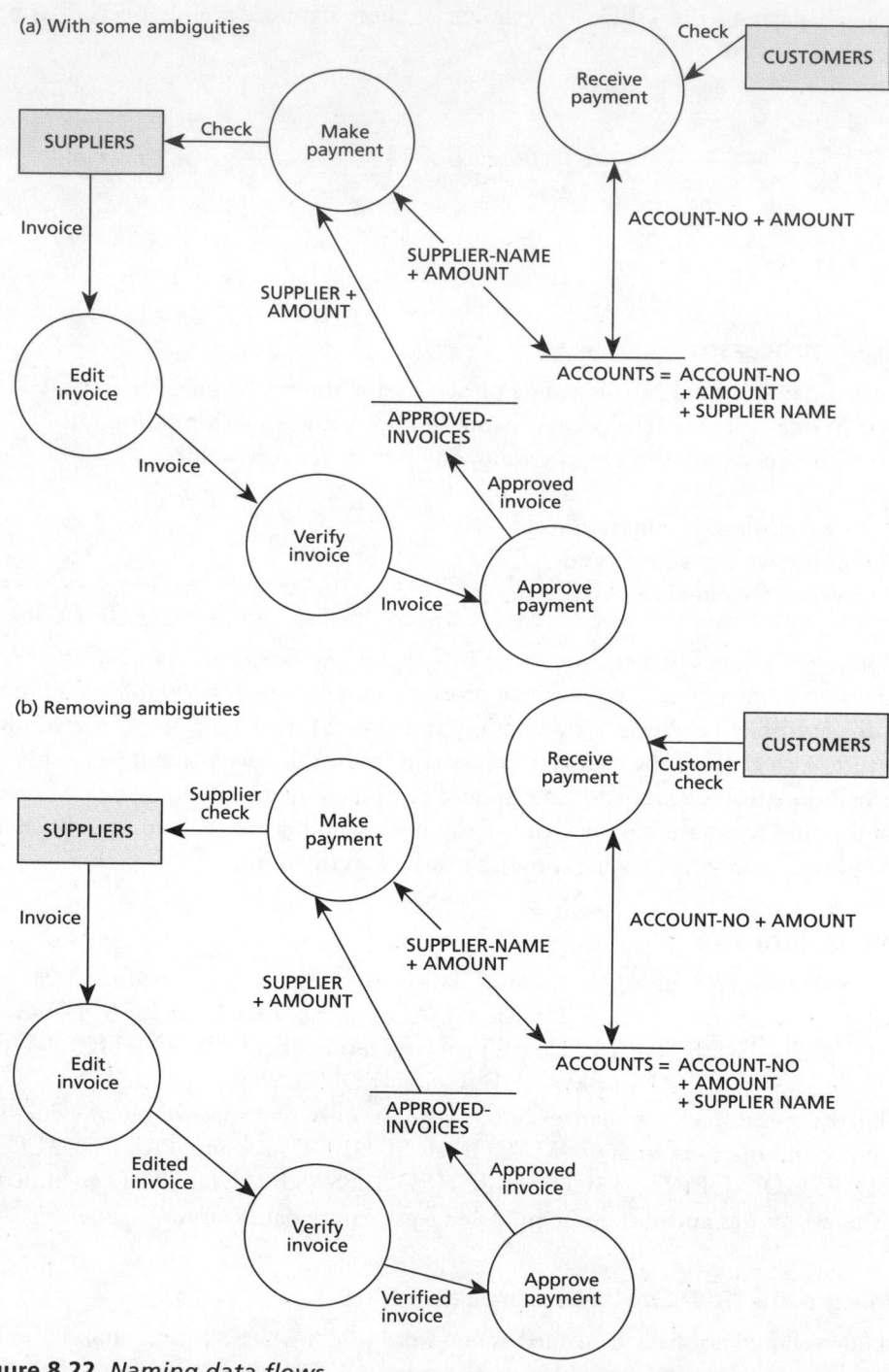

Figure 8.22 *Naming data flows*

data. The 'verify invoice' process checks if the invoiced items have been actually delivered. Finally, the invoice is checked against budgetary provisions and approved for payment.

Figure 8.22 has 'invoice' on all data flows even though it could have been amended or had additional data attached to it at each process. Figure 8.22(b) shows a better naming technique. Now the term 'invoice' is prefixed by a qualifier that specifies the process through which the invoice has just passed.

Figure 8.22(a) has another instance where names should be qualified. Note that in the top part, 'check' appears twice although obviously the type of check in each case is different. The labeling used in Figure 8.22(b) is preferred. Now each check is qualified as either a 'supplier check' or a 'customer check'.

Some final notes about naming flows between processes and data stores are needed. Often, data flows store or read the whole record in the data store. For example, in Figure 8.22, the 'approve payment' process stores the whole of the 'approved invoice' record into data store APPROVED-INVOICES. By convention, data flows that carry the whole data store record between processes and data stores are not labeled. However, if a process uses only part of a data store record, the data flow must be labeled to indicate the referenced part. Thus, in Figure 8.22(b), the 'make payment' process uses only the data items SUPPLIER and AMOUNT from data store APPROVED-INVOICES. Note that data flows between data store and processes that contain part of the data store can be labeled by the names in capital letters of the accessed data store items.

Another DFD convention concerns bidirectional flows between processes and data stores. For example, the 'make payment' process reads a SUPPLIER-NAME and AMOUNT from data store ACCOUNTS, updates the AMOUNT and stores the updated AMOUNT, back into data store ACCOUNTS. In this case the flow is labeled with two arrows to show that it is bidirectional.

SOME OTHER NOTATIONAL SUGGESTIONS

There are many other suggestions for notations on DFDs. You can, for example, allow an external entity to appear more than once in a DFD. Each new appearance has a line added to one of its corners. Another suggestion is to differentiate between accesses which update a data store and those which retrieve data from the data store. Updates are indicated by a double arrow.

Modeling material flows

DFDs are intended to model information and not material flows. Sometimes, however, it is desirable also to include material flows. Gane and Sarson illustrate one way of doing this. They include a bottom portion in each process and show the physical location associated with the process—for example, 'store' and 'machine room' in Figure 8.23. Material flow is modeled by a thick line between physical locations. The name of materials is placed inside the thick arrow (see 'parts' in Figure 8.23). Note that Figure 8.23 uses Gane and Sarson's convention to represent processes by rectangular boxes.

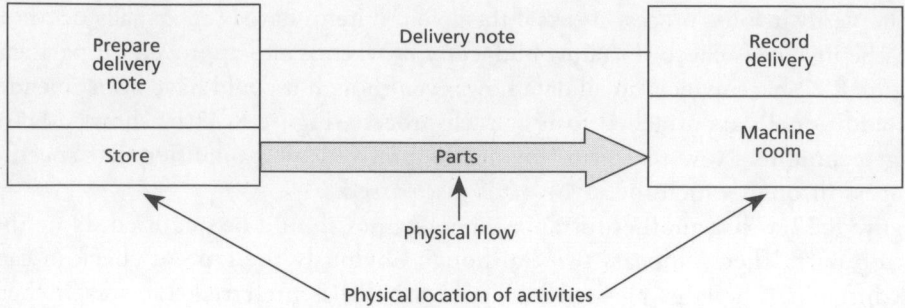

Figure 8.23 *Information and material flows*

SOME MORE ON LEVELING TECHNIQUES

So far this chapter has concentrated on the structure of the DFD and not on the procedures used to develop system models. Structured systems analysis also includes a number of modeling methods and conventions that can assist model development. One, called **leveling**, concerns the top-down elaboration of a DFD. Leveling is examined next and then differences between physical and logical DFDs are described.

Leveling
Expanding a process into more detailed processes.

LEVELING DATA FLOW DIAGRAMS

Leveling allows an analyst to start with a top-level function and to elaborate it in terms of its more detailed components. These detailed components are modeled as lower-level DFDs. In Figure 8.2 we started with a context diagram, which was then elaborated in terms of the top-level system functions in Figure 8.3. Each of these functions can then be elaborated further by lower-level DFDs, as shown in Figure 8.4. Finally, the functions are described by process logic.

Apart from supporting a natural top-down problem-solving process, leveling improves the readability of the DFD. One ought to be able to understand what the system is doing just by looking at a DFD. If one had a relatively large system and wished to include all the detailed system functions on the DFD, the DFD could become quite large. In fact, it could become so large that it would be difficult to understand and would no longer serve as a communications tool. However, each level of a DFD is small enough to be clearly understood. If someone wishes to know about a particular function or functions at one level, they can refer to it at the next level. This improves the clarity and communication value of the DFD.

SOME LEVELING CONVENTIONS

Although leveling is a very useful tool, a number of conventions must be observed to ensure that no information is lost as a DFD is leveled. These conventions use documentation practices that assist analysts to maintain consistency between DFDs at different levels.

One important convention is numbering. The context diagram is usually given the number 0. Processes in a top-level DFD are numbered consecutively, starting with 1 and continuing until all processes have been labeled. In Figure 8.24, the top-level DFD has five processes numbered 1, 2, 3, 4 and 5.

As each process is leveled, its DFD is given the same number as the process. Thus, in Figure 8.24, the leveled DFD of Process 1 is named Diagram 1. Each process in the leveled DFD receives a number made up of its diagram number, followed by a period (i.e. ' . '), followed by a number within the leveled DFD. Thus the processes in Diagram 1 have process numbers 1.1, 1.2 and 1.3.

Another important leveling convention is data flow balancing. Fundamentally, balancing requires that all the data flows entering a process are the same as those entering its leveled DFD. Similarly, all the data flows leaving the process are the same as those leaving its leveled DFD. If you look carefully at Figure 8.24 you will see that this requirement is satisfied for all leveled diagrams. For example, look at Diagram 2, which is the leveled DFD of Process 2. You will see that the only input data flow to Process 2 in the top-level DFD is Y and its outputs are V and W. You should note that the inputs and the outputs of Diagram 2 are the same as the inputs and outputs of Process 2 in the top-level DFD.

Leveling can also introduce data stores which are local to the leveled diagram. In Figure 8.24, data store DS2 contains data that is local to Process 3. Hence, this data store does not appear in the top-level DFD but only in its leveled diagrams. The consequence of this rule is that a data store is only used on a DFD if it is referenced by more than one process in the DFD.

External entities are never part of a process and analysts should avoid introducing new external entities at lower DFDs. All external entities should appear on the context diagram. They should also appear with a DFD if any process in the DFD has a flow to or from the external entity. Thus, in Figure 8.24, external entity EXT1 has flows to and from Process 1. This external entity appears on the leveled DFD for Process 1.

You should, however, note that, if we strictly adhere to data flow balancing, all the detailed flows that occur at the lower-level DFDs must eventually appear at the top-level DFD. If this were to happen, then the top-level DFD could become unmanageable, as it would contain every conceivable flow between the top-level processes. For this reason, a number of modeling techniques are used to apply leveling ideas to data flows. These techniques expand data flows as we level the DFD.

EXPANDING DATA FLOWS

Detailed flows, such as dialog between a process and an external entity, error conditions and detailed variations of a flow, do not appear at the higher-level DFDs but appear in the more detailed DFDs. Figure 8.25 shows how such detailed flows can be introduced into the lower-level DFDs while maintaining data balancing. In Figure 8.25(a) the top-level DFD models the establishment and maintenance of a loan. Process 1 is used to receive new applications and approve or reject them, Process 2 records payments against established loans, and Process 3 handles any queries from an applicant about a loan. Note that the top-level DFD has a data flow named 'clarification dialog' between Process 1 and the APPLICANT, but details of this flow are not included. The double-arrow on this flow shows that the flow occurs in two directions. Similarly, the data

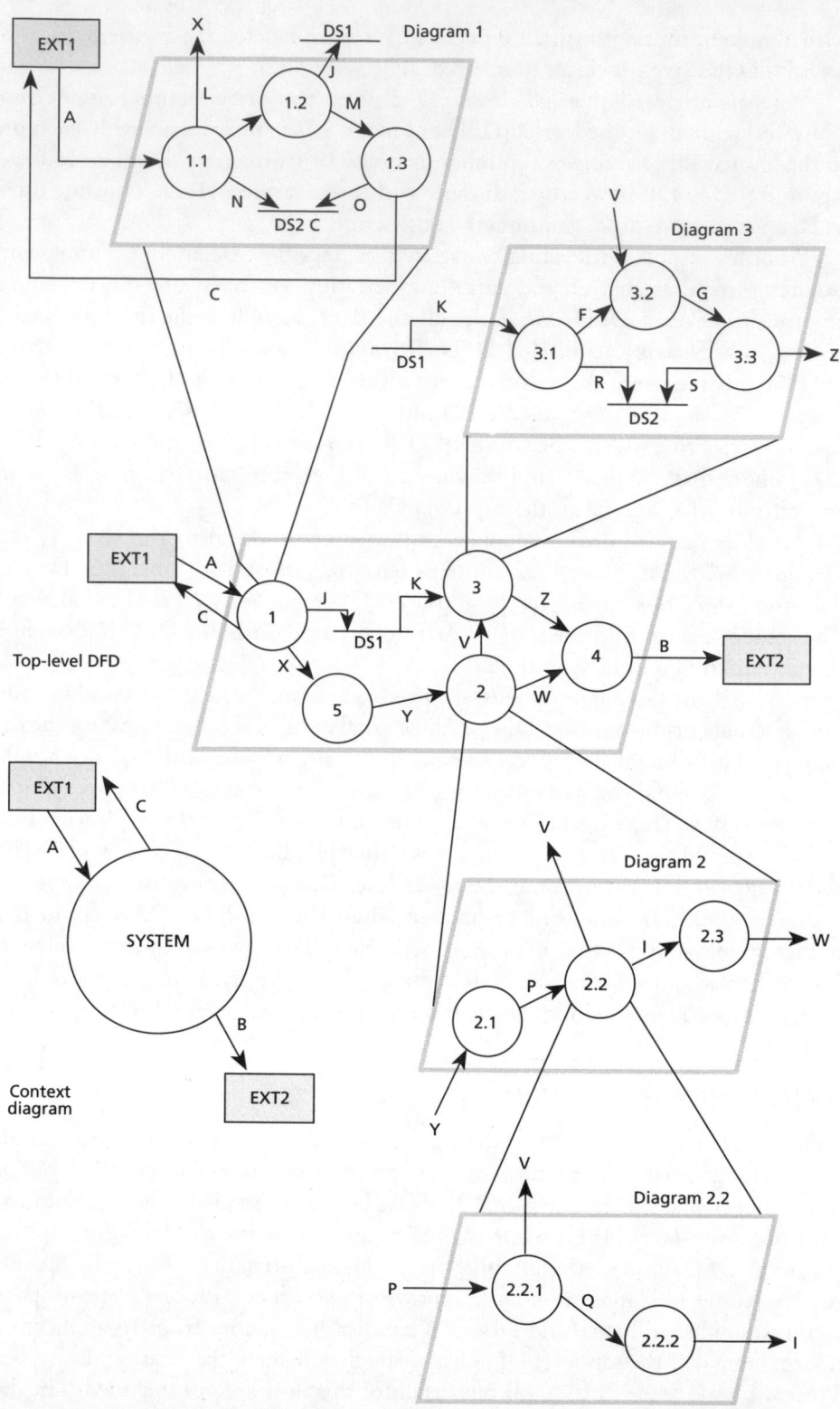

Figure 8.24 *Leveling*

flow between Process 3 and the APPLICANT is labeled 'query and reply' but details of possible queries are not given.

Figure 8.25(b) shows an expansion of Process 1, which includes some data flow expansions. Data flow 'loan application' remains the same but data flow 'reply to application' is expanded into two flows—namely, 'approved application' and 'rejected application'. You should note that the numbering on both the top-level and leveled diagrams is used to check for data conservation. Thus the data flow 'reply to application' is labeled R in the top-level DFD and its expansion in Diagram 1 is labeled Rl and R2.

The data flow 'clarification dialog', which is labeled C in the top-level DFD, is expanded in Figure 8.25(b) to show the kind of clarification sought. Thus, Figure

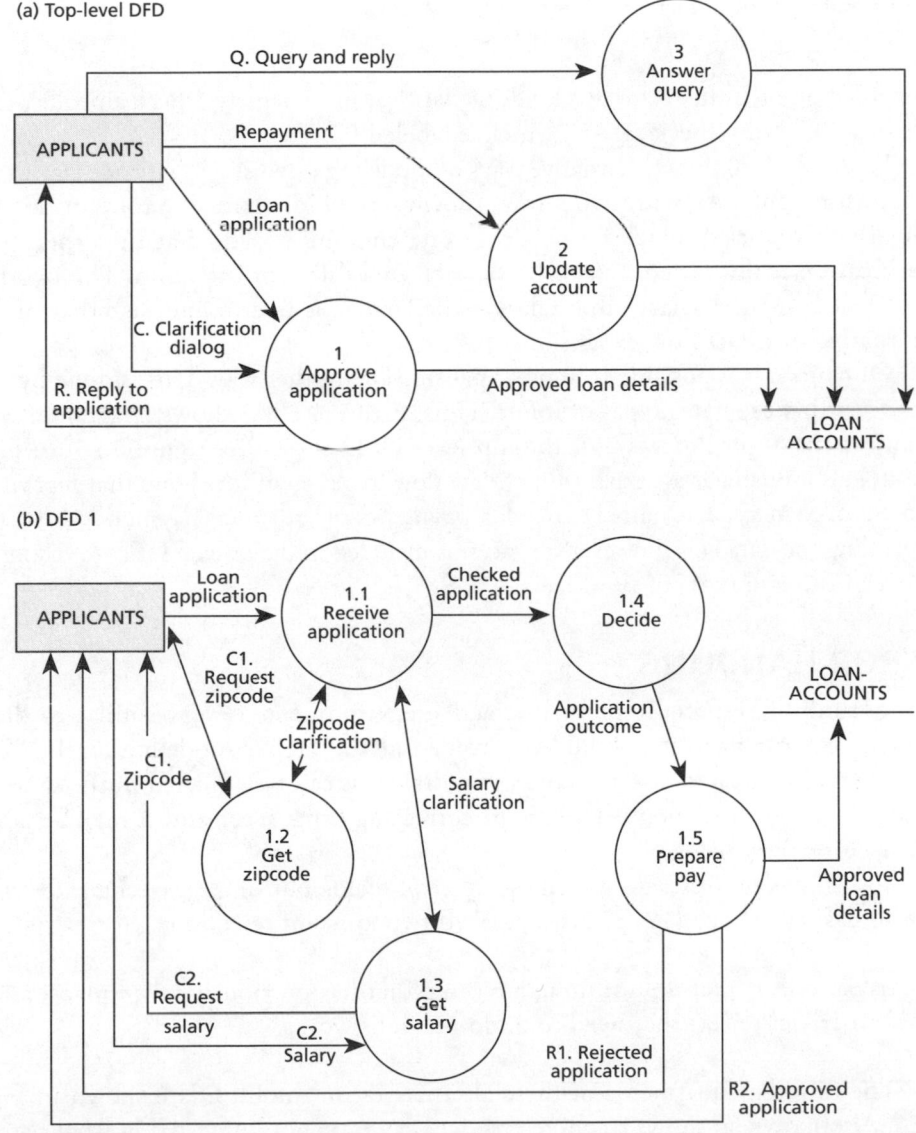

Figure 8.25 *Expanding data flows*

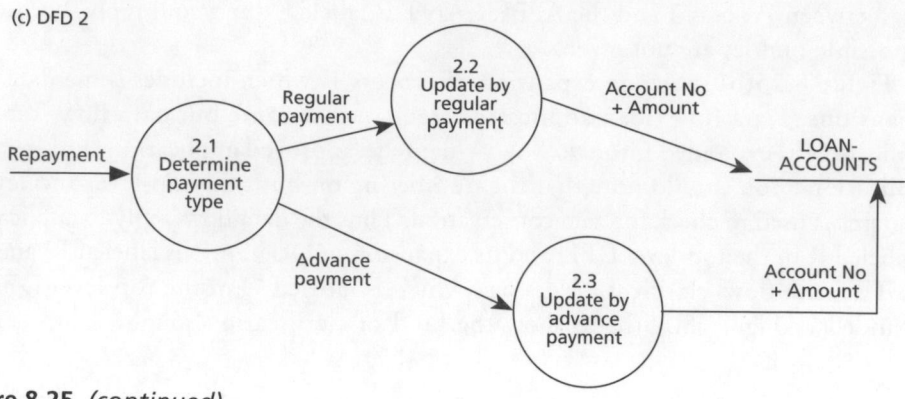

(c) DFD 2

Figure 8.25 *(continued)*

8.25(b) shows that there are two kinds of clarification—namely, 'check zipcode', which is labeled Cl, and 'check salary', which is labeled C2.

Figure 8.25(b) shows alternative ways of modeling expansions. Zipcode clarification is shown by one flow with two arrows showing the bidirectional nature of this flow. This flow is labeled 'request zipcode' at one end and 'zipcode' at the other. Salary clarification is illustrated by two flows, each in a different direction. The two flows are labeled 'request salary' and 'salary'. The analyst is free to choose either of these alternatives for data flow expansion.

Of course, it is possible to show expansion in another way. This is done by using a process that separates types of input. Thus, Figure 8.25(c) shows Diagram 2 which is an expansion of Process 2 of the top-level DFD shown in Figure 8.25(a). Figure 8.25(c) also illustrates an expansion of data flow 'repayment'. It shows that repayments can be of two types—namely 'regular payment' or 'advance payment'. Instead of expanding the data flow, however, a process is included in the leveled DFD to distinguish between the two types of flow.

ERROR HANDLING

Error handling, especially in an interactive environment, is very similar to dialog. Details of error handling should be avoided at the higher modeling levels. Where error handling creates an error-correction dialog, it can be modeled in the same way as dialog. Now the dialog is specific to correcting some error and it may be labeled 'error-correcting dialog'.

Sometimes processes do not engage in error dialog but simply reject a given input. In this case DeMarco (1978) distinguished two kinds of rejection:

- trivial rejects that do not undo anything that has previously taken place; and
- non-trivial rejects that need to undo previous works.

The different treatments of these alternatives on the DFD are shown in Figure 8.26. Alternative (a) shows trivial rejects, where we are not interested in what happens to the rejected data. Thus in Figure 8.26(a) the system does not take any further

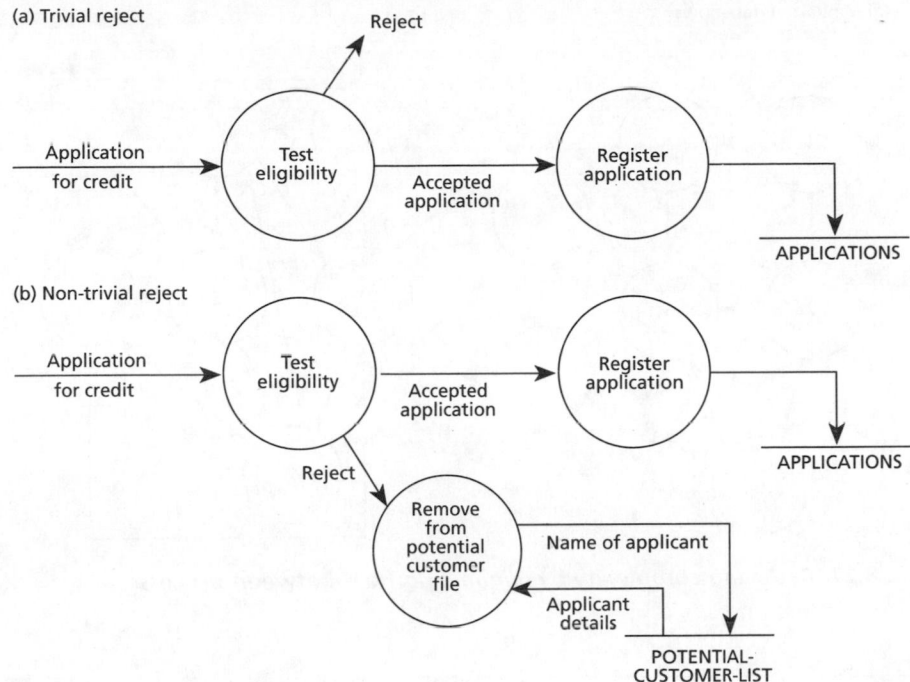

Figure 8.26 *Modeling error conditions*

interest in rejected applications. Alternative (b) shows a rejection that is followed by some action. The rejection is used to remove the rejected applicant from a POTENTIAL-CUSTOMER-LIST.

HOW MANY LEVELS?

It is sometimes difficult to know how far to level down, how many processes to include on a data flow diagram or even where to start. It is impossible to give precise answers, but some guidelines can be suggested.

Most practitioners say that about seven, plus or minus two, is the ideal number of processes on a DFD. This number can be clearly understood by a visual examination but is not too small to be trivial. A larger number is sometimes too hard to understand; a smaller number often includes too little information to be useful.

However, one should not take a trivial approach and suggest that leveling simply involves taking a higher-level process and partitioning it into seven lower-level processes. Consider, for example, Figure 8.27. It contains two DFDs, each with seven processes. One of these diagrams is clearly less complex and hence easier to understand than the other. Figure 8.27 thus illustrates another requirement of leveling—the interfaces between processes must be minimized. This can only be done by the correct choice of lower-level functions and this is where the true nature of analysis comes in. The analyst must carefully analyze the top-level process, determine what its self-contained functions are and represent them on the DFD. If the interconnections are too complex,

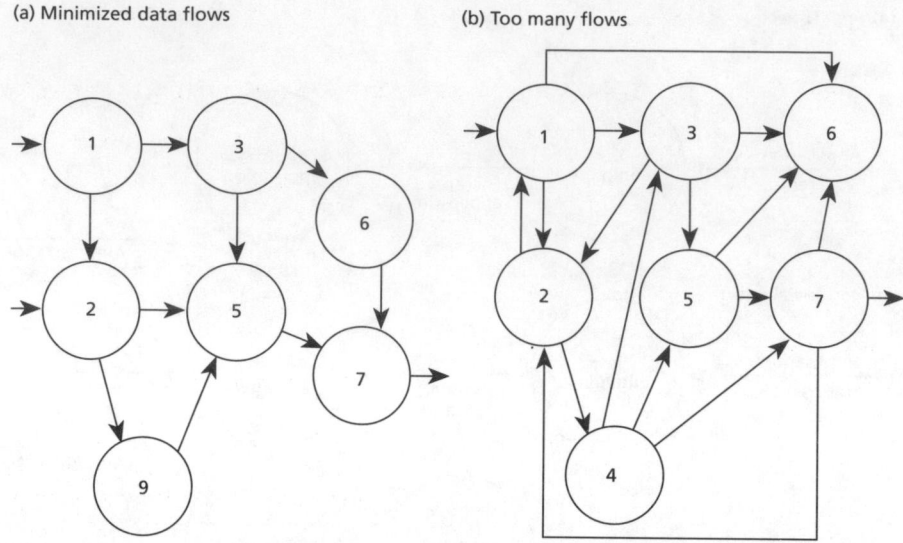

Figure 8.27 *Reducing complexity by minimizing flow between processes*

the leveling should be re-examined and, if necessary, restarted. This may continue over a number of iterations until a satisfactory solution is found.

Minimizing the complexity of interfacing is one leveling guideline. There are some other informal leveling guidelines, based on the idea of creating functions that are *linguistically modular*. This means that we must actually look at what the higher-level function does or means and describe it in one, or at least a very few, precise sentences. The phrases in these sentences will identify the lower-level functions. For example, the process 'order parts' may be described as:

'For the requisition from a project, select a supplier and then make an order to the supplier.'

This immediately suggests that process 'place an order' should be decomposed into three processes, namely, 'get requisition', 'select supplier' and 'make order'.

For how long does leveling continue? Generally, until you reach a set of processes that can be described by about one page of detailed process specifications.

 # SUMMARY

This chapter has described how systems are modeled using data flow diagrams. It described what a DFD looks like and how DFDs can be developed in a top-down manner using leveling. The chapter made an important distinction between modeling what a system does and how a system works. A logical DFD defines what a system does and a physical DFD defines how a system works. The chapter described how to develop logical DFDs using conversions between logical and physical DFDs. Some characteristics of good DFDs were also described.

DISCUSSION QUESTIONS

8.1   Where would structured system models be used in the system specification?

8.2   Do you think DFDs are more appropriate to the subject, usage or system world?

 ## EXERCISES

8.1   Detect any errors in the DFDs in Figure 8.28.

8.2   Consider the DFDs in Figure 8.29. Do they satisfy the conservation of data rules?

8.3   Figure 8.30 is a DFD that describes a system to satisfy user requests for parts. Whenever a parts request is received, a search is made to determine whether the part is available in store. If so, the part is dispatched together with a dispatch notice. Otherwise a non-availability notice is sent.

Suppose the system is now changed, as follows:

- Check with suppliers to see if any parts not in store can be obtained immediately. If so, a purchase order is made out to the supplier and a copy

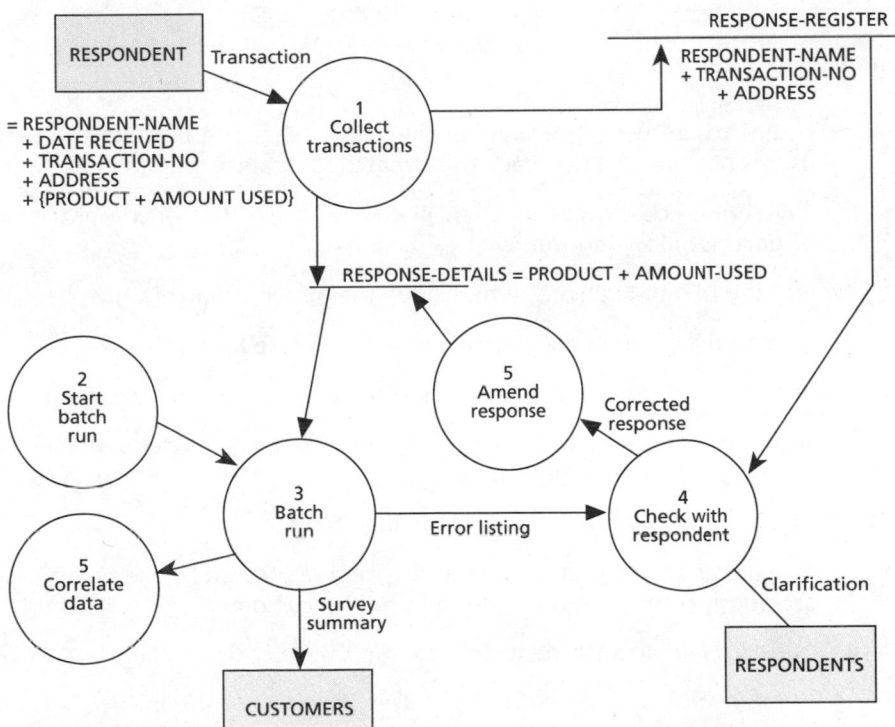

Figure 8.28 *Processing DFDs*

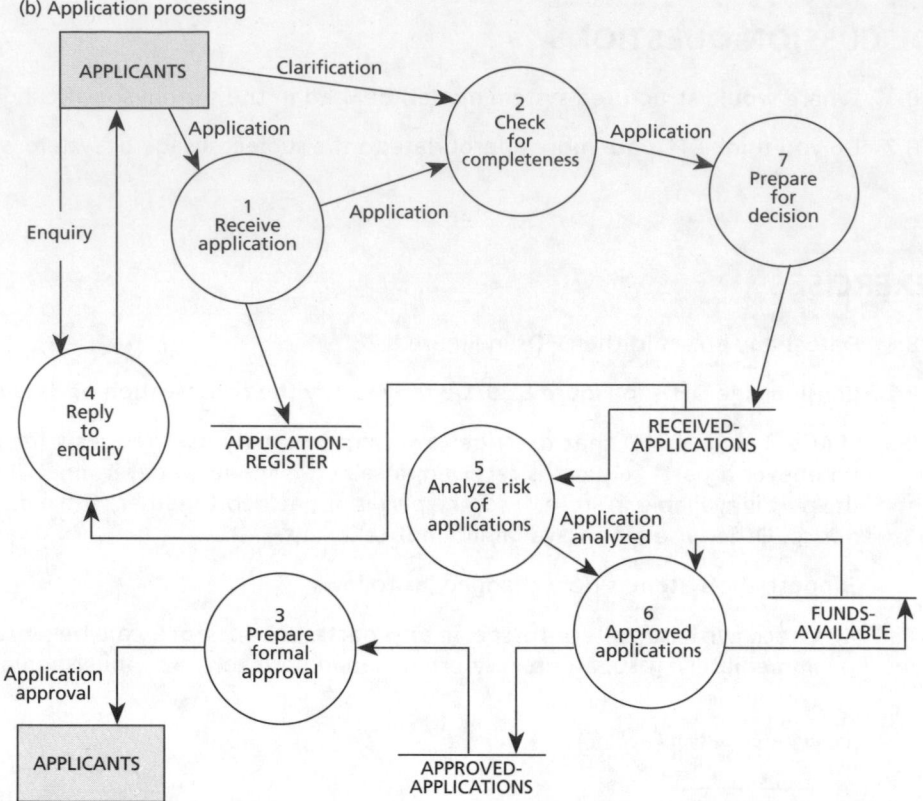

(b) Application processing

Figure 8.28 *(continued)*

is sent to the user. The supplier then dispatches the parts to the user. The user sends the dispatch back to be matched against the purchase order.

- Regularly check the inventory and place purchase orders whenever the number of parts is below reorder level.

Amend the DFD in Figure 8.30 to include the above changes.

8.4 Can you find any data balancing problems in Figure 8.31?

8.5 Draw a top-level logical DFD for the system made up of the following:

1. Selling customers request the organization to sell various items on their behalf. A record of these requests is kept.

2. Buying customers make requests to buy items.

3. A sale is arranged with a buyer if the item requested by the buyer has been previously put forward for sale by a selling customer.

4. During a sale arrangement:

   - An invoice is prepared for the buyer. A record of the invoice is kept.

   - A notification is sent to the seller whose item was sold. The seller will now hold the item.

(a) Daily sales of items are recorded and totals of each term sold computed:

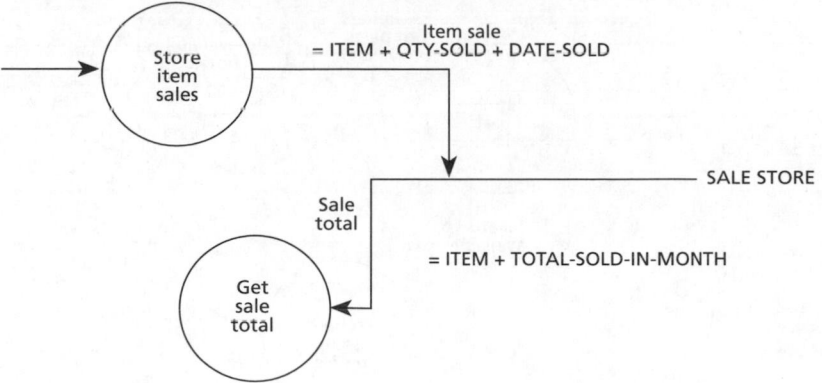

(b) The expenses on a trip are computed:

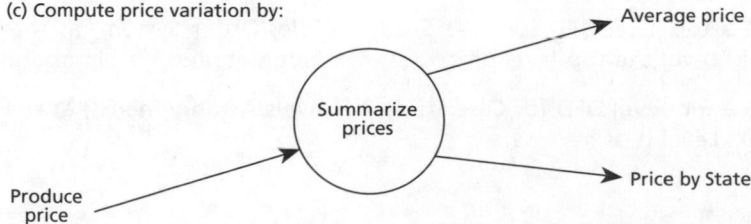

(c) Compute price variation by:

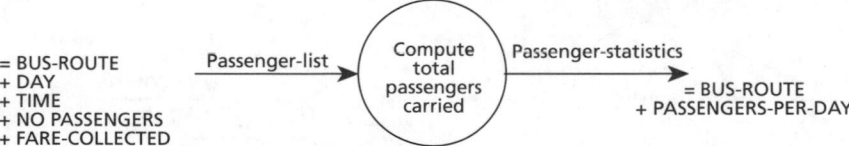

(d) Compute passengers carried per day on a bus-route:

= BUS-ROUTE
+ DAY
+ TIME
+ NO PASSENGERS
+ FARE-COLLECTED

Passenger-list → Compute total passengers carried → Passenger-statistics

= BUS-ROUTE
+ PASSENGERS-PER-DAY

Figure 8.29 *Conservation of data problems*

- A commission is computed and debited to the selling customer. This commission is subtracted from the amount sent to the selling customer and advice of the commission is given in the sale advice.

5. The sale is completed when payment is received from the buyer. A cheque is then sent to the seller together with a dispatch request for items to be sent to the buyer.

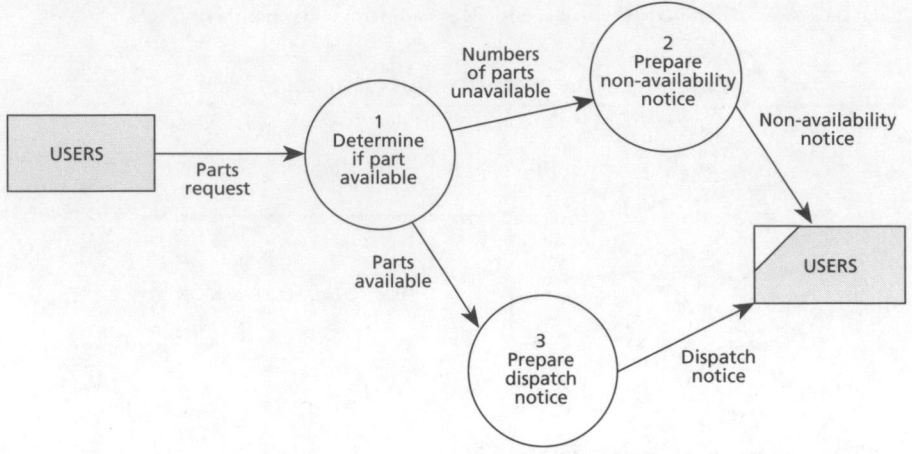

Figure 8.30 *Requests for parts*

8.6 Figure 8.32 is a DFD made up of three processes: 'invoice maintenance', 'invoice monitoring' and 'make payment'. These processes have been leveled down one level to illustrate the information flows between them. Rearrange the bottom-level processes into higher-level processes that have fewer data flows between them.

8.7 Figure 8.33 illustrates two top-level DFDs containing a mixture of physical and logical processes. Examine both these DFDs and state which processes are logical and which are physical.

8.8 Develop a top-level DFD for Case Study 1 (Sales/Order System) at the end of the book. Level the top-level processes to obtain detailed system operations.

8.9 Develop a top-level DFD for Case Study 2 (Travels/Arrangements) at the end of the book. Level it as necessary.

(a) Top-level DFD

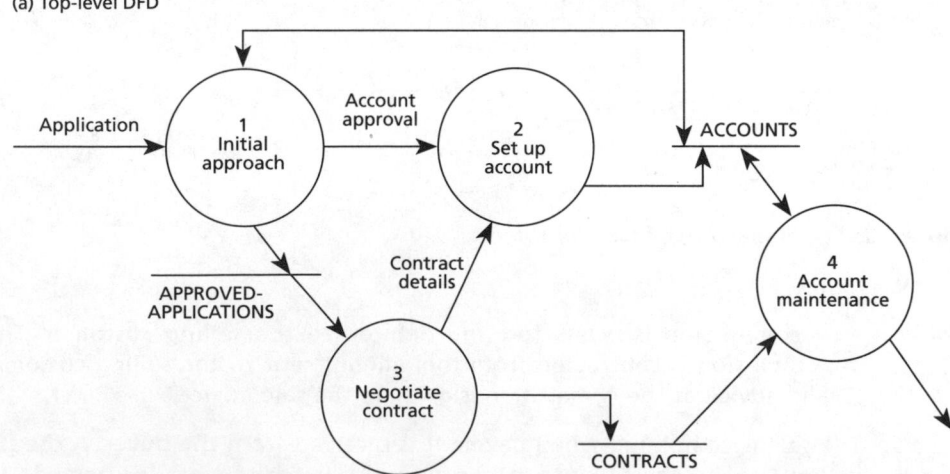

Figure 8.31 *Leveling a DFD*

(b) Leveled DFD

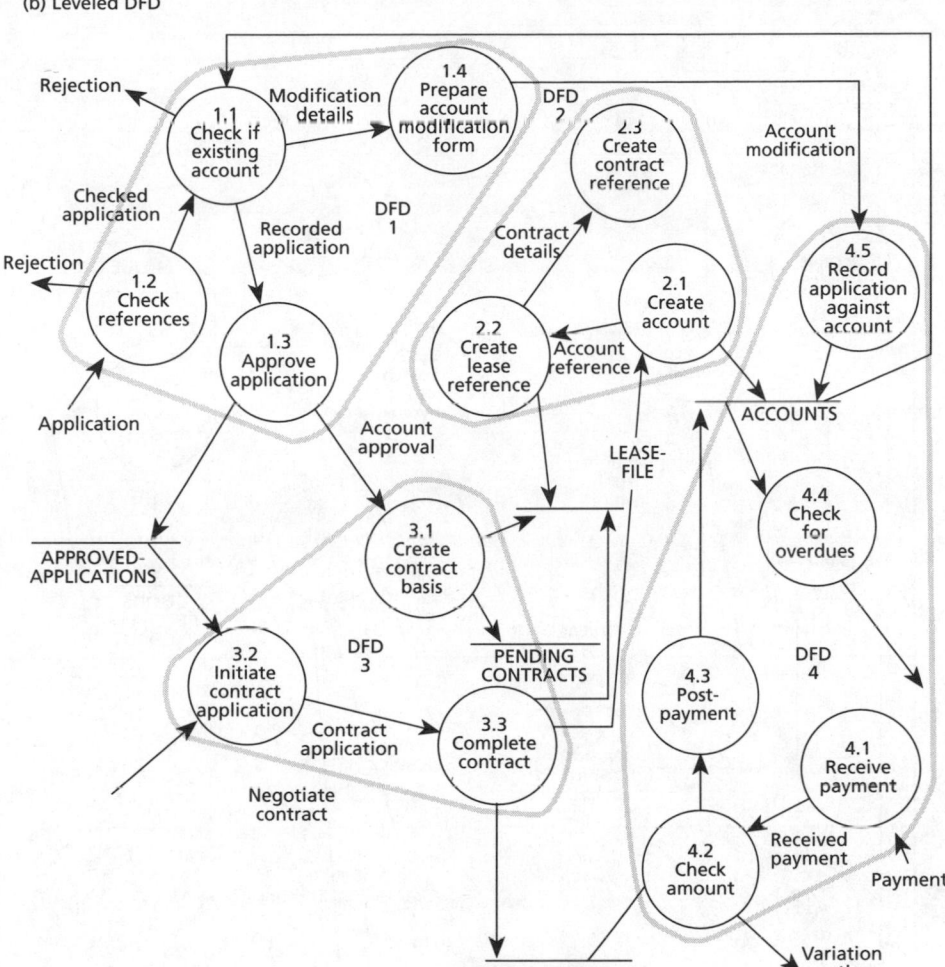

Figure 8.31 *(continued)*

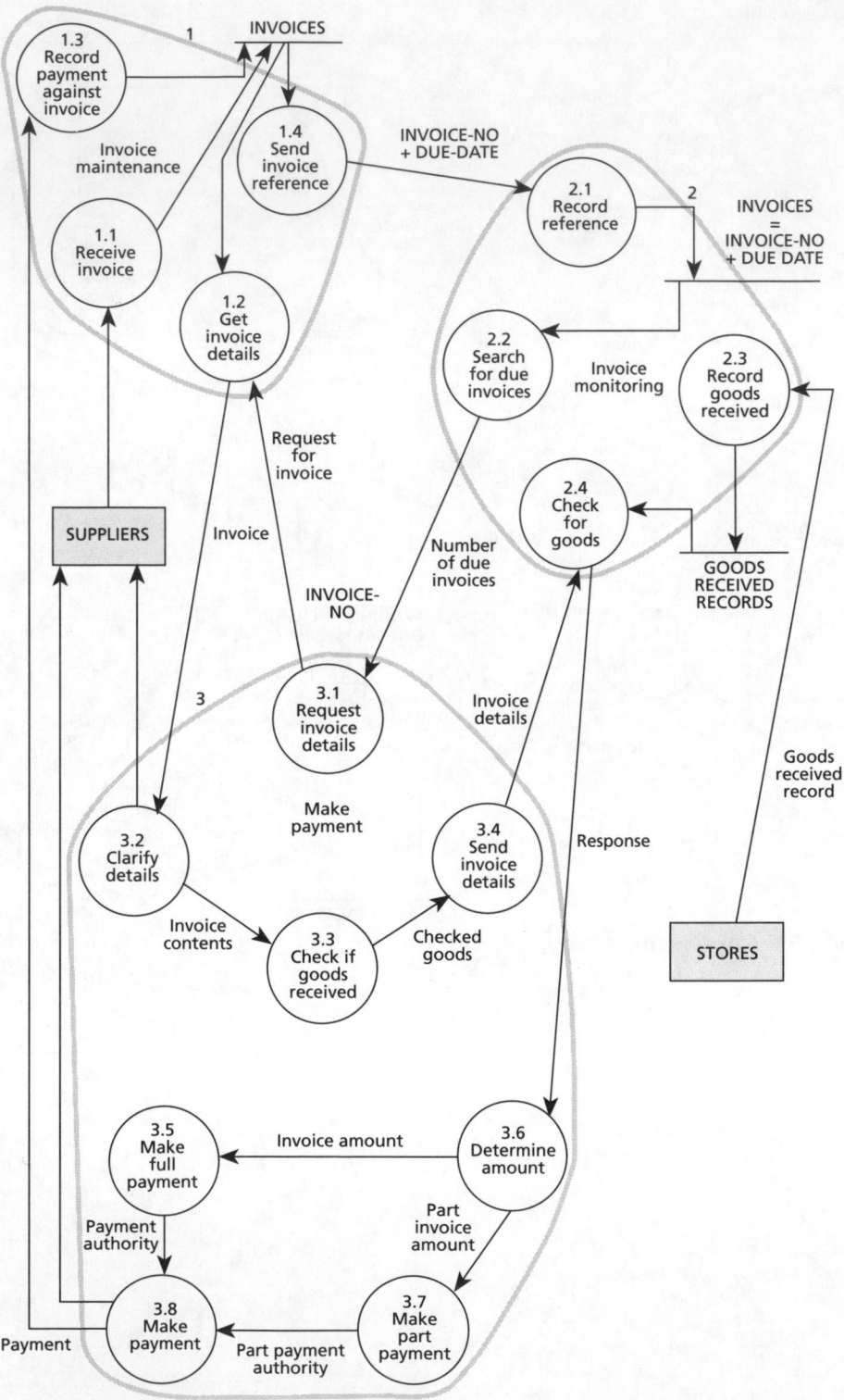

Figure 8.32 *Reducing flows between processes*

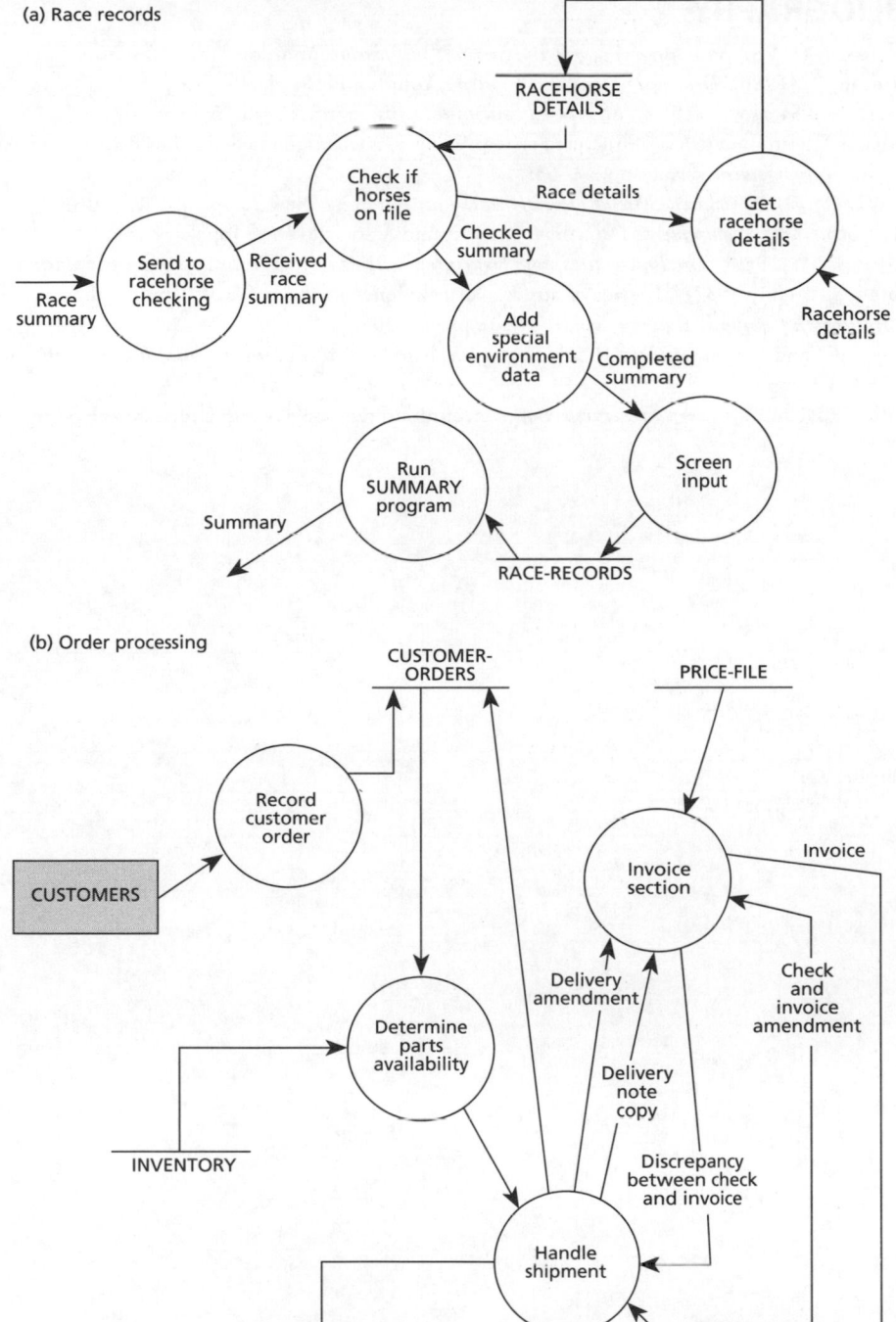

(a) Race records

RACEHORSE
DETAILS

Check if
horses
on file

Race details

Get
racehorse
details

Send to
racehorse
checking

Received
race
summary

Checked
summary

Race
summary

Racehorse
details

Add
special
environment
data

Completed
summary

Run
SUMMARY
program

Screen
input

Summary

RACE-RECORDS

(b) Order processing

CUSTOMER-
ORDERS

PRICE-FILE

Record
customer
order

Invoice
section

Invoice

CUSTOMERS

Determine
parts
availability

Delivery
amendment

Check
and
invoice
amendment

Delivery
note
copy

INVENTORY

Discrepancy
between check
and invoice

Handle
shipment

Discrepancies
resolution

DELIVERIES

Delivery note

CUSTOMERS

Figure 8.33 *Physical and logical processes*

BIBLIOGRAPHY

DeMarco, T. (1978), *Structured Analysis and System Specification*, Yourdon Press, New York.

Dickinson, B. (1980), *Developing Structured Systems*, Yourdon Press, New York.

Gane, C. and Sarson, T. (1979), *Structured Systems Analysis*, Prentice Hall, Sydney.

Mendes, K.S. (Summer 1980), 'Structured systems analysis: a technique to define business requirements', *Sloan Management Review*, pp. 51–63.

Orr, K.T. (1977), *Structured Systems Development*, Yourdon Press, New York.

(1981), *Structured Requirements Definition*, Ken Orr and Associates Inc., Topeka, Kansas.

Page-Jones, M. (1980), *The Practical Link to Structured Systems Design*, Yourdon Press, New York.

Simpson, J.A. (July 1982), 'Impact of structured techniques in the Bank of New South Wales', *The Australian Computer Bulletin*, Vol. 6, No. 6, pp. 18–20.

Teague, L.C. and Pidgeon, C.W. (1985), *Structured Analysis Methods for Computer Information Systems*, SRA, Chicago.

Yourdon, E. (1989), *Modern Structured Analysis*, Yourdon Press, Englewood Cliffs, New Jersey.

Describing data

CONTENTS

KEY LEARNING OBJECTIVES

Why data modeling is important
Semantic concepts of entity, relationship and attribute
How to represent data using semantic concepts
The relationship between data modeling and data flow modeling
Dependent entity sets and subsets

181

INTRODUCTION

An important aspect of systems modeling is the analysis of system data. As with a data flow diagram (DFD), an abstract or implementation independent model of the data is developed as part of the system specification, which is later converted to a physical implementation.

Data modeling is a more difficult subject than data flow modeling. You will find that a data abstraction is not as obvious as a DFD abstraction. A DFD looks almost like a system. It has boxes that you can actually envisage as physical operations, and its flows can be imagined just as easily. A data model, however, is often more abstract and difficult to relate to actual system components—for example, data associations, which are not visible as physical things in the system.

Data modeling is part of the development process. In the linear development cycle, it is used during the system requirements phase to construct the data component of the analysis model. This model represents the major data objects and the relationships between them. It should not be confused with data analysis, which takes place in the system design phase. System design organizes data into a good shape. Usually this means removing redundancies, a process often called normalization, which uses ideas from relational theory. This normalized model is then converted to a physical database.

Most designers develop only the high-level conceptual model in the system specification phase. The more detailed analysis using normalization is carried out during design. This chapter describes one commonly used set of techniques for developing the conceptual data model—namely, entity–relationship modeling. Normalization is described in later chapters when we turn to design.

As in a DFD, a model of data consists of a number of symbols joined up according to certain conventions. We will describe conceptual modeling using symbols from a modeling method known as entity–relationship *analysis. This method was first introduced by Chen in 1976 and is now widely used.*

 # ENTITY–RELATIONSHIP ANALYSIS

Entity–relationship (E–R) model
A model that represents system data by entity and relationship sets.

Entity–relationship (E–R) analysis uses three major abstractions to describe data. These are:

- *entities*, which are distinct things in the enterprise;
- *relationships*, which are meaningful interactions between the objects; and
- *attributes*, which are the properties of the entities and relationships.

Entity
A distinct object in a system.

Entity set
A component in an E–R diagram that represents a set of entities with the same properties.

The idea of E–R analysis is illustrated by Figure 9.1. Similar objects or things are grouped into entity sets. In Figure 9.1, all the persons have been put into a PERSONS entity set and all the projects into a PROJECTS entity set. You should note the difference between the terms *entity* and *entity set*. Each individual object is called an **entity**. A collection of such entities is an **entity set**. Thus, each person or each project is an entity. A collection of persons is the entity set, PERSONS, and a collection of projects is the PROJECTS entity set.

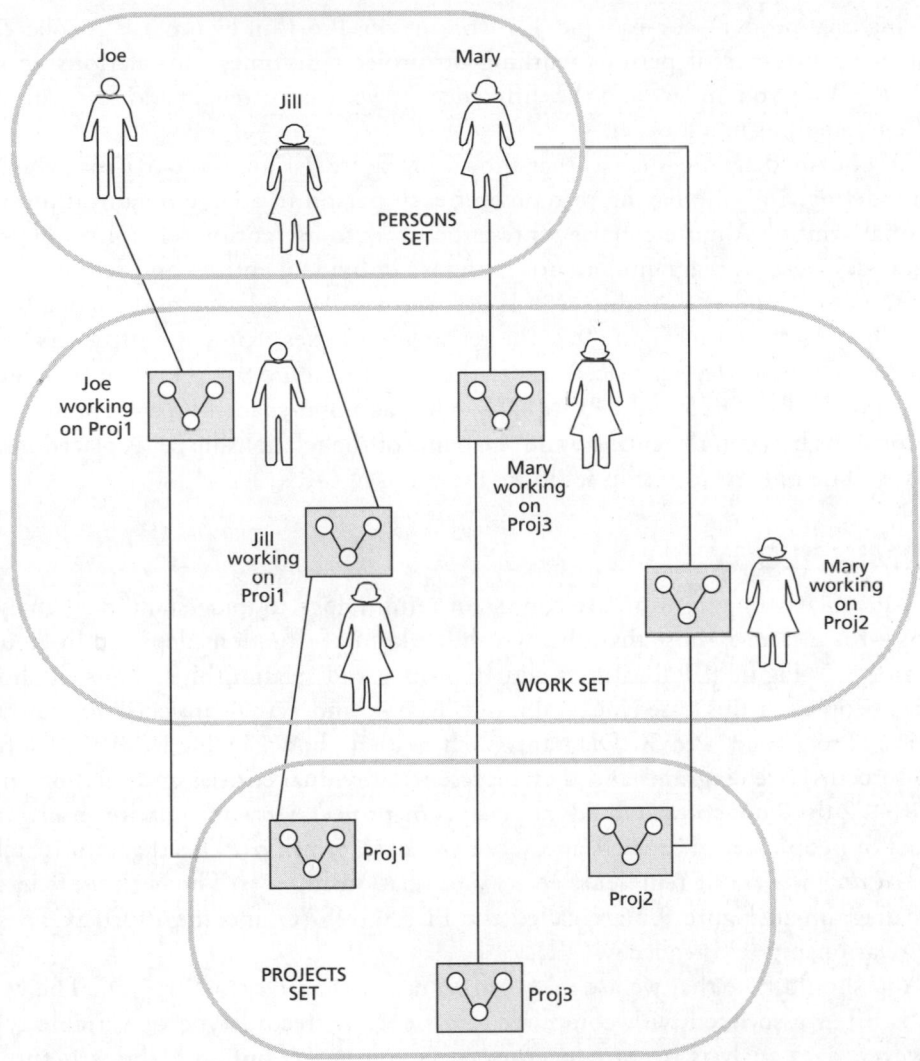

Figure 9.1 *E–R modeling*

We then model all interactions between the things in entity sets by relationships and relationship sets. Just as with entities, there is a difference between the terms *relationship* and *relationship set*. If a person works on a project, then there is a **relationship** between that person and the project. A **relationship set** is a collection of such relationships. In Figure 9.1, a collection of relationships of persons working on projects is modeled by the WORK relationship set. This set is a relationship set because it represents a collection of relationships between things in two different entity sets. Each relationship in the WORK relationship set is one person working on one project.

Relationship sets are harder to perceive than entity sets. We can actually see entities, but we cannot see relationships. This makes data analysis difficult because it is necessary to create models of things that do not physically exist as single objects. However, if you stretch your imagination you should perceive a relationship occurrence as a person

Relationship

One interaction between one or more entities.

Relationship set

A component in an E–R diagram that represents a set of relationships with the same properties.

working on a project—for example 'Jill' working on 'Proj1' in Figure 9.1. A collection of such occurrences of persons working on projects becomes the relationship set, WORK. Once you understand the difference between occurrences and sets, you will find data analysis much easier.

Of course, diagrams such as that shown in Figure 9.1 are not particularly useful for modeling. Imagine having to represent each person in a large organization by a personal symbol! A more concise representation is to use entity–relationship (E–R) diagrams. The E–R diagram does not represent individual entities and relationships, only the entity and relationship sets. It uses rectangular and diamond-shaped boxes to do this. As shown in Figure 9.2, the rectangular boxes represent entity sets, with the name of the entity set placed inside the box. In Figure 9.2 there are two entity sets, named PERSONS and PROJECTS. The diamond-shaped boxes represent the relationships between the entities, and the name of the relationship set is placed inside the box. The only relationship set in Figure 9.2 is WORK.

TERMINOLOGY

It is particularly important to use consistent terminology to understand data analysis terms—for instance, those that distinguish the kind of situations depicted in Figures 9.1 and 9.2. Figure 9.1 illustrates actual entities and relationships. Thus, it shows actual people, in this case 'Joe', 'Jill' and 'Mary', and actual projects, in this case 'Proj1', 'Proj2' and 'Proj3'. Diagrams such as that shown in Figure 9.1 are often called **occurrence diagrams** and they represent individual entities and relationships. Figure 9.2 does not show individual persons or projects or work relationships, only the set of people, set of projects and set of work relationships. This diagram is called an *E–R diagram* and it represents entity and relationship sets. The entity sets in the E–R diagram in Figure 9.2 are called the PERSONS set and the PROJECTS set. The relationship set is called WORK.

You should note that we use the word *set* rather than *type* for a reason. The word *type* is often associated with computer terms such as record type or variable type. However, data analysis is not concerned with computers but with the structure of system data and uses terms more natural to data properties rather than the definition of data in computer terms. Data analysis avoids computer terms as much as possible

Occurrence diagram
A diagram that represents entities and relationships.

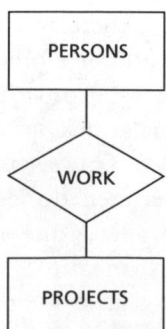

Figure 9.2 *An E–R diagram*

to prevent any preconceptions about computer structures slipping into the analysis. Of course, sets are converted to record types later during computer system design. This conversion is described in Chapters 16 and 17.

ENTITY–RELATIONSHIP STRUCTURES

Figure 9.2 illustrates the simplest E–R construct. It shows two entity sets with one relationship set between them. It is also possible to have more complex structures. There can be a large number of entity and relationship sets in an E–R diagram. Each entity set in the E–R diagram can be linked to more than one relationship set. Figure 9.3, for example, contains the entity set PERSONS, which is associated with two relationship sets. One relationship set is WORK-ON with projects. This relationship set shows that persons work on projects. The other relationship set, ARE-IN, shows that persons are in departments. There are also a number of other entity and relationship sets in Figure 9.3. Entity set PARTS, for example, is associated with three relationship sets: USE with PROJECTS to show that projects use parts, SUPPLY with SUPPLIERS to show that suppliers supply parts, and HOLD with WAREHOUSES to show that parts are held in warehouses.

Figure 9.3 shows each relationship set linked to two entity sets and at most one relationship set between any two entity sets. This, however, is not a general requirement of E–R diagrams. There are, in fact, very few restrictions placed on drawing E–R diagrams. For example, it is possible to have two or more relationship sets between the same two entity sets. One example of this is illustrated in Figure 9.4. Here there are two relationship sets, OWNS and LEASES, between COMPANIES and VEHICLES. It is necessary to have these two different relationship sets because there are two different ways in which companies can interact with vehicles. Each of these ways has different properties. Relationship OWNS occurs between a company and a vehicle if that company purchases the vehicle. This relationship may have properties such as DATE-PURCHASED or PRICE-PAID. Relationship LEASES exists when a company rents a vehicle. In that case, the properties may be LEASE-TERMINATION-DATE and MONTHLY-RENTAL.

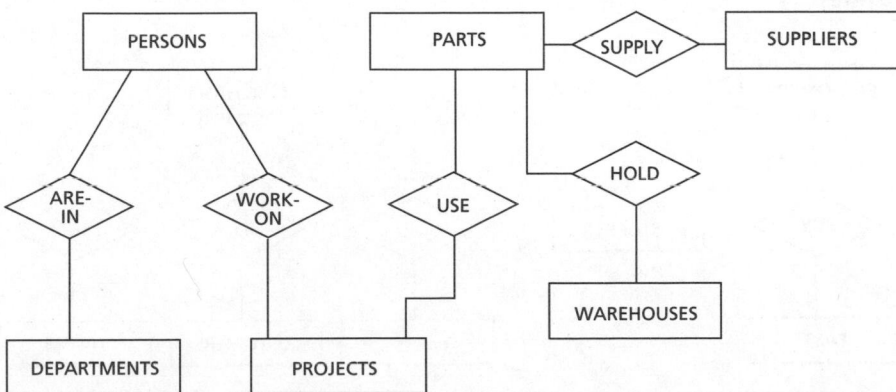

Figure 9.3 *An E–R diagram with many entity and relationship sets*

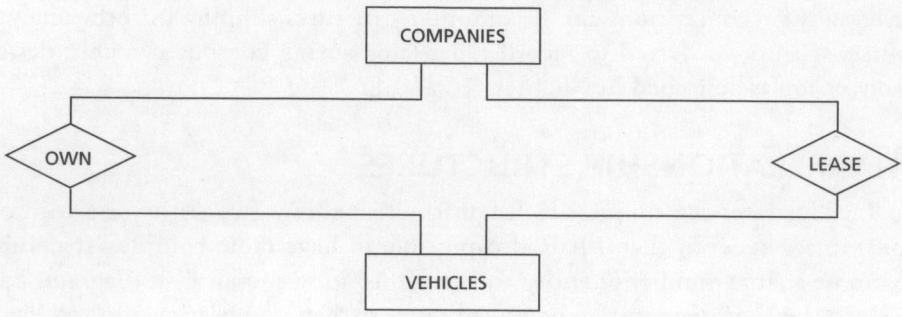

Figure 9.4 *Two relationship sets between the same two entity sets*

It is also possible for more than two entity sets to be associated with the same relationship set. Figure 9.5(a), for example, shows the relationship set BUY, which models an interaction between CUSTOMERS, STORES and PARTS. Each relationship in this set includes a person, a part bought by the person, and the store where the purchase was made. Relationship sets that include more than two entity sets are known as **N-ary**. Relationship sets that include only two entity sets are known as **binary**. However, N-ary relationship sets should be avoided in E–R diagrams because they include more than one concept. For example, the relationship in Figure 9.5(a) describes both the store where a customer bought the goods, as well as the details of the purchase. It is always possible to remove an N-ary relationship by replacing it with an entity set. Relationship sets are then created between this new entity set and those entity sets that participated with the N-ary relationship set. In this way, the E–R diagram in Figure 9.5(a) can be converted to the E–R diagram in Figure 9.5(b). The E–R diagram Figure 9.5(b) contains only binary relationship sets.

There are some things you should avoid. For instance, the system itself should not appear as an entity set in the E–R diagram. Thus, for example, we should not have the entity set BUSINESS in the E–R diagram in Figure 9.6(a) if we are modeling the business. The entity set BUSINESS would include only one entity. The correct E–R diagram here is shown in Figure 9.6(b). This E–R diagram does not include the entity set BUSINESS but only includes those entity sets that are of interest to the business.

N-ary relationship
A relationship that includes entities from more than two entity sets.

Binary relationship
A relationship that contains entities from at most two entity sets.

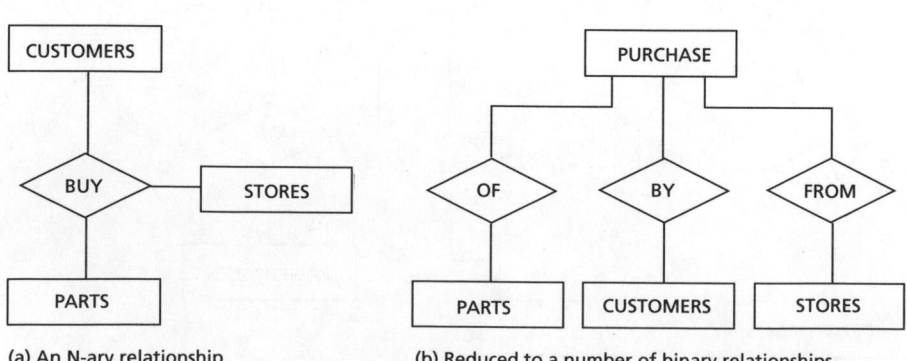

(a) An N-ary relationship   (b) Reduced to a number of binary relationships

Figure 9.5 *Reducing N-ary relationship sets*

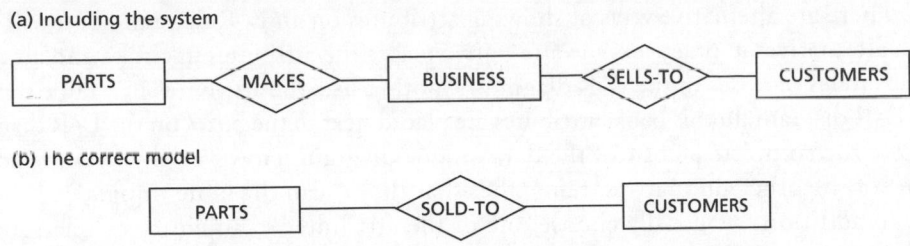

(a) Including the system

(b) The correct model

Figure 9.6 *Excluding the system from the E–R diagram*

You should also avoid derived relationship sets in an E–R diagram. Figure 9.7 includes one such derived relationship set. The E–R diagram in Figure 9.7 contains three relationship sets. Relationship set HAVE describes the sections in each department, and relationship set EMPLOY describes the persons employed in each section. Relationship set ARE-IN then models the persons in each department. However, we can find all the persons in a department through relationship sets HAVE and EMPLOY. Once we know all the sections in a department through relationship set HAVE and then find all the persons in each section through relationship set EMPLOY, we will know all the persons in the department. The relationship set ARE-IN is thus not needed because it contains information that can be derived from the other relationship sets. Relationship sets that include derived information should not appear in an E–R diagram.

MORE ABOUT ENTITY–RELATIONSHIP MODELING

After the entity and relationship sets are identified, the next step is to determine the **attributes** (or properties) of objects in the sets. For example, what is of interest to us about persons? This may be a person's NAME, their ADDRESS or their unique identifier, PERSON-ID, in the organization. These properties are written alongside the boxes of the E–R diagram.

Attribute in an E–R diagram
A property of a set in an E–R model.

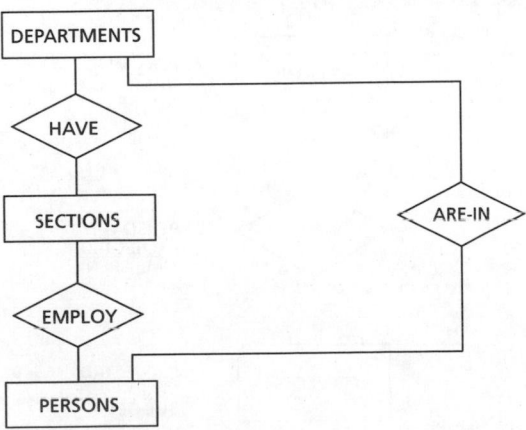

Figure 9.7 *The derived relationship set, ARE-IN*

There are alternative ways of showing attributes on an E–R diagram. You will find such alternatives in practice. One alternative places the attributes in circles and attaches these circles to boxes in the E–R diagram. Another lists the attributes in a table next to the E–R diagram. In this book, attributes are placed next to the boxes on the E–R diagram to give the complete picture of the data on one diagram. However, if you come across some of the other alternatives, remember that they mean the same thing.

In addition, we usually choose one of the attributes of an entity or relationship set to be the **identifier**. The identifier has one important property: its values identify unique entities in the entity set. The identifier attributes are underlined in the E–R diagram.

Thus, in Figure 9.8, PERSON-ID is the identifier of the PERSONS entity set. Each person in the PERSONS entity set has a unique value of PERSON-ID. Similarly, PROJECT-ID is the identifier of the PROJECTS entity set, as each project has a unique value of PROJECT-ID. Choosing identifiers for relationship sets is somewhat more complex.

The convention used in this book is to use the identifiers of the entities that participate in the relationship as the relationship identifiers. In most cases it is necessary to know the value of both of these identifiers in order to identify a unique relationship. Thus, in Figure 9.2, we need to know both the value of the person identifier, PERSON-ID, and the value of the project identifier, PROJECT-ID, to identify a particular relationship in relationship set WORK. A value of the person identifier on its own would not be enough, because that person can work on more than one project and hence appear in more than one relationship. Similarly, a value of the project identifier is not enough, because there may be more than one person working on a project. Thus, we must know both the person and the project identifiers to identify one relationship. In some cases, however, one identifier is sufficient to identify a relationship— for example, when entities in one entity set are restricted to one relationship. Thus, if a person could work on only one project at the most, the value of the person identifier would be enough to identify a unique WORK relationship.

The convention used in this book, however, is to use all the entity identifiers to make up the relationship identifier. Some people may point out that such identifiers

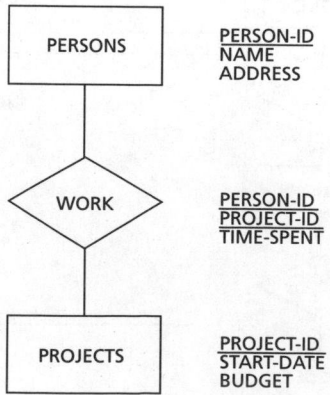

Figure 9.8 *Adding attributes*

do not correspond to file keys, but you should remember that data analysis does not imply any computer implementation and identifiers have nothing to do with file keys. It is true that if sets are converted to files, the identifiers can become the file keys. However, at this stage, relationship identifiers are not file keys but are the identifiers of entities that participate in the relationship.

On the E–R diagram, we show the number of relationships in which an entity can appear. This value is sometimes known as the relationship cardinality.

MODELING RELATIONSHIP CARDINALITY

One property often shown on E–R diagrams is relationship **cardinality**, which specifies the number of relationships in which an entity can appear. An entity can appear in:

- one (1) relationship;
- any variable number (N) of relationships; and
- a maximum number of relationships.

Cardinality
The number of relationships in which one entity can appear.

If you refer to Figure 9.1 you will see that a person can appear in more than one WORK relationship, and so can a project. This is shown by the letters N and M on the E–R diagram links (see Figure 9.9). These letters stand for variables and can take any value. If there was a limit to the number of times an entity can take part in the relationship, then N or M would be replaced by the actual maximum number. N and M are used (rather than N to N) to show that entities in the different sets may participate in a different number of relationships.

Figure 9.10 illustrates a 1:N relationship. Here a project has one (1) manager, whereas a manager can manage any number (N) of projects. Thus, the occurrence diagram shows that manager 'm1' manages two projects: 'p1' and 'p2'. Thus manager 'm1' appears in two MANAGE relationships. Every project, however, in Figure 9.10 appears in one MANAGE relationship only. You should note that in the E–R diagram, '1' appears opposite the PROJECTS set and the diagram indicates that a project is managed by one manager.

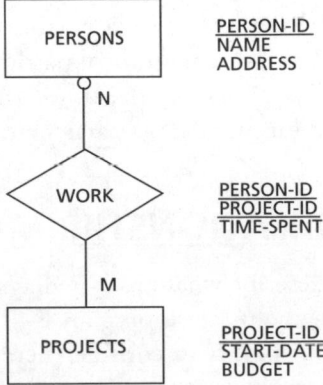

Figure 9.9 *Adding cardinality*

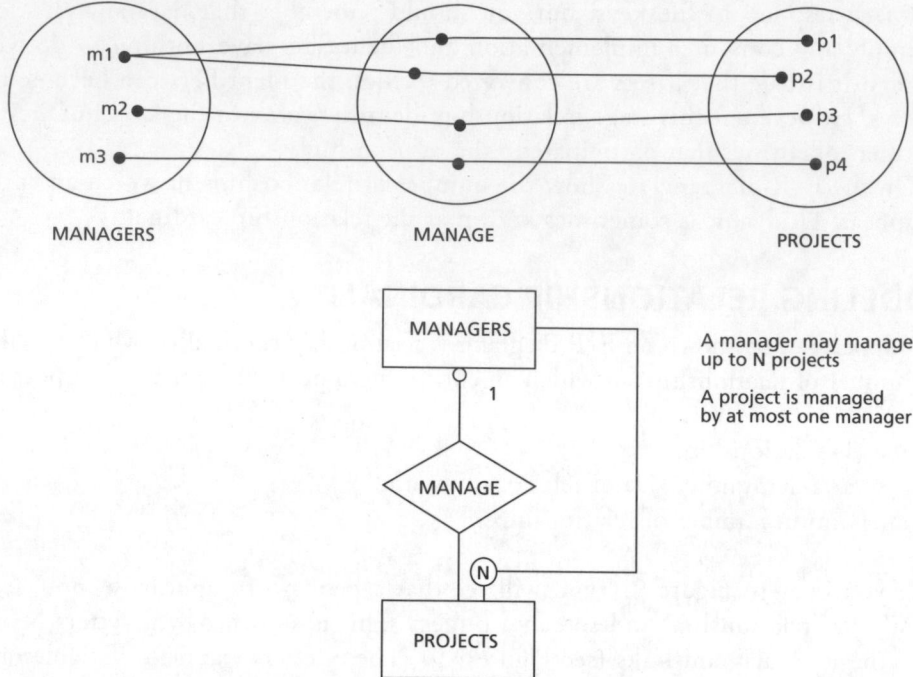

Figure 9.10 *A 1: N relationship*

MODELING RELATIONSHIP PARTICIPATION

E–R diagrams often specify the manner of participation of entities in a relationship set. The participation of entities in a relationship set can be mandatory, optional or conditional. If all entities in a given set must appear in at least one relationship in a relationship set, then their participation in the relationship set is mandatory. If each entity need not appear in the relationship set, then its participation in the relationship set is optional. Thus, suppose that a project must have at least one person working on it. The project must appear in at least one WORK relationship and the participation of each project in the WORK relationship set is mandatory. A person, however, need not work on a project. The participation of each person in a WORK relationship set is optional. The notation used to indicate optional participation is shown in Figure 9.9. An optional participation has a small circle, 0, on the link next to the entity set. There is no mark on the link for mandatory participation.

 ## BUILDING ENTITY–RELATIONSHIP MODELS

Although it is relatively easy to describe what an E–R diagram looks like, it is much harder to describe how one goes about developing an E–R diagram for a particular system. There are some important points to consider here: how to choose entities, relationships and attributes; how to choose names; and what steps should be followed in analysis.

EACH SET TO MODEL ONE CONCEPT

One of the most important things to remember is that in analysis we are trying to capture the precise semantics of a system. To do so it is necessary to identify the fundamental components of a system and relationships between them. For this reason, each set in the E–R diagram should model only one concept. Thus, each entity set models only the one concept—that is, entities with some common properties. Each relationship set models the one concept of two entities, each from the same set interacting in the same way. If you adhere to this idea you can only place things with the same properties into the same entity set. Thus, all persons would fall into one entity set named PERSONS, all parts into one entity set named PARTS, and so on. In any case, you would not place persons and parts into the one entity set.

What kinds of things are to be modeled as entity sets? The most common system entities are distinct physical things in the organization, things such as persons, parts, projects, invoices and so on. However, other things that are not so clearly visible are also modeled as entities. The most common of these are organizational entities such as projects, departments or budgets. Finally, things that happen, such as deliveries, faults or examinations, may also be modeled as entities.

CHOOSING ATTRIBUTES

Attributes, just like entity and relationship sets, should express simple concepts. For this reason, attributes should also be simple. Any attribute in an E–R model should therefore take a simple value. E–R diagrams should not contain multivalued or structured attributes, as shown in Figure 9.11(a).

In Figure 9.11(a), entity set PERSONS has four attributes. Attribute PERSON-ID is the person's identifier and attribute DATE-OF-BIRTH is the person's birthdate. Both of these attributes take one value for each person entity. Attribute

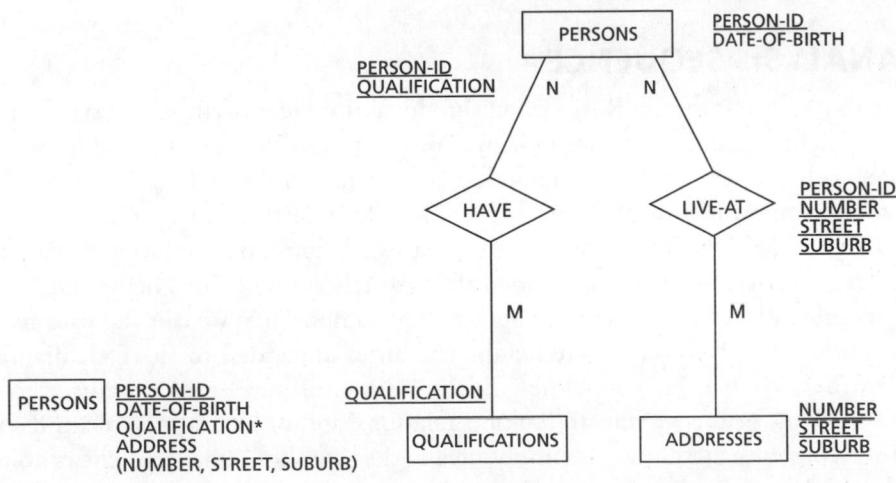

(a) Non-simple attributes   (b) Removing multivalued and structured attributes

Figure 9.11 *Reducing to simple attributes*

QUALIFICATION is another, and this may take many values for one person because a person can have many qualifications. The asterisk (*) indicates that QUALIFICATION is a multivalued attribute. Attribute ADDRESS, on the other hand, is itself made up of other attributes—namely, SUBURB, STREET and NUMBER. Attribute ADDRESS is known as a structured attribute.

Any multivalued or structured attributes should not appear in the final E–R diagram. They can be removed by converting them to relationship sets, as shown in Figure 9.11(b). Here there are two new entity sets: QUALIFICATIONS and ADDRESSES. The multivalued attribute, QUALIFICATION, now becomes an attribute of the new entity set, QUALIFICATIONS. The structured attribute ADDRESS has now become the entity set ADDRESSES, and its components have become the attributes of this new entity set. Entity set PERSONS is associated with these two new entity sets through relationship sets HAVE and LIVE-AT. These relationship sets are used to find a person's qualifications and address.

CHOOSING OBJECT SET NAMES

Proper choice of names often helps in E–R modeling. Remember that one goal of E–R modeling is to produce a model that is easily understood by users as well as computer personnel. To do this we must choose set names that make the diagram readable. In an E–R diagram, entity sets are usually labeled by nouns, whereas relationship sets are labeled by verbs. This is quite natural in E–R modeling, because entities are usually distinct objects that are best described by nouns. Relationships are actions and are better described by verbs. Often, however, relationship sets are named by prepositions. This is particularly so when modeling structural relationships, like that shown in Figure 9.5(b). This shows that each entity in entity set PURCHASES is made up of a part, a customer and a store. Such structural relationships often appear in E–R diagrams. For example, a building can consist of rooms, or parts can be made up of other parts.

AN ANALYSIS SEQUENCE

Most analysts suggest that E–R modeling should start by identifying the system entity sets. After defining entity sets, we look at how entities in the entity sets can interact with each other and model this interaction by relationship sets. Thus, once we find out that persons work on projects, we would add a relationship set between the PERSONS and PROJECTS entity sets and give this relationship an appropriate name—in this case, WORK. We then go on identifying further interactions between entities and model them by relationships with appropriate names. Then we can add cardinality to the system. As we go into more detail, attributes are added to the E–R diagram and identifiers chosen. However, the guideline does not mean that we must choose all the entity sets before we start to look for relationships, or have all the relationships before starting with attributes. It simply means that we should have an entity to use in a relationship and not propose a relationship set first or define attributes and have no sets to attach them to. Thus we can define some entity sets, then some relationship sets between them. We can then add more entity sets, then perhaps add some attributes to existing sets, then add some more entity sets, and so on. The model thus grows in an evolutionary manner.

This evolution calls for a continuous refinement of the model. We may initially draw a top-level diagram that may include N-ary relationships or even multivalued and structured attributes. We may then refine the model by replacing such components using the techniques shown in Figures 9.5 and 9.11. We may at the same time remove any derived relationships. Thus E–R modeling is a continuous and evolutionary process, and a model gradually evolves which correctly represents the semantics of a system.

We now develop an E–R diagram for our Text Case D.

TEXT CASE D: Construction Company—Drawing the E–R Diagram

The E–R diagram for Text Case D is developed in two steps, the first of which is to develop a top-level E–R model. This model is shown in Figure 9.12. It will then be refined further. To develop the top-level model, we first define the entity sets, then the relationship sets and then add attributes to these sets.

The first two entity sets defined are the SUPPLIERS and PROJECTS entity sets, after which each data store in Figure 9.12 becomes an entity set. This creates the entity sets PURCHASE-ORDERS, SHIPMENTS and INVOICES. A dependent entity set PROJECT-REQUESTS is defined to model project requests. It is defined as a dependent entity set because a project request cannot arise without there being a project. Its identifier is made up of the identifier of projects, PROJECT-NO and REQ-NO, which identifies a request within a project. The entity set PROJECT-DELIVERIES is also included to model deliveries made to projects.

Next, relationship sets are defined. A number of relationship sets are first defined between entity set SUPPLIERS and the documents that suppliers use. Thus there is a relationship set TO between entity sets SUPPLIERS and PURCHASE-ORDERS, because purchase orders are sent to suppliers. Similarly, there are relationship sets SEND and FROM between entity sets SUPPLIERS and SHIPMENTS and entity sets SUPPLIERS and INVOICES, because suppliers send these documents to the organization. A number of relationship sets between documents are then added. The relationship set OF between entity sets SHIPMENTS and PURCHASE-ORDERS models the fact that shipments are made to satisfy purchase orders. The relationship set INCLUDE between entity sets INVOICES and SHIPMENTS models the fact that invoices are sent for items delivered in shipments. The relationship set FOR shows that invoices are for payments against purchase orders. The relationship set MET-BY between entity set PROJECT-DELIVERIES and dependent entity set PROJECT-REQUESTS models the fact that the project deliveries are made in response to project requests.

Now, attributes are added to the entity and relationship sets. The attributes added to the sets can be found by examining Figure 9.12. For simplicity, some fields are modeled as multivalued fields in the top-level E–R diagram. Thus, for example, look at PURCHASE-ORDERS in Figure 9.12. This is modeled by the entity set PURCHASE-ORDERS. Document PURCHASE-ORDERS has three heading fields, PO-NO, SUPPLIER-NAME and DATE-ORDERED. PO-NO and DATE-ORDERED become attributes in entity set PURCHASE-ORDERS. SUPPLIER-NAME does not become an attribute in set PURCHASE-ORDERS but is associated to entity set PURCHASE-ORDERS through relationship set TO. Document PURCHASE-ORDERS has a number of lines, each made up of the five fields, ITEM-NO, QTY-ORDERED, QTY-RECEIVED, QTY-PAID-FOR and

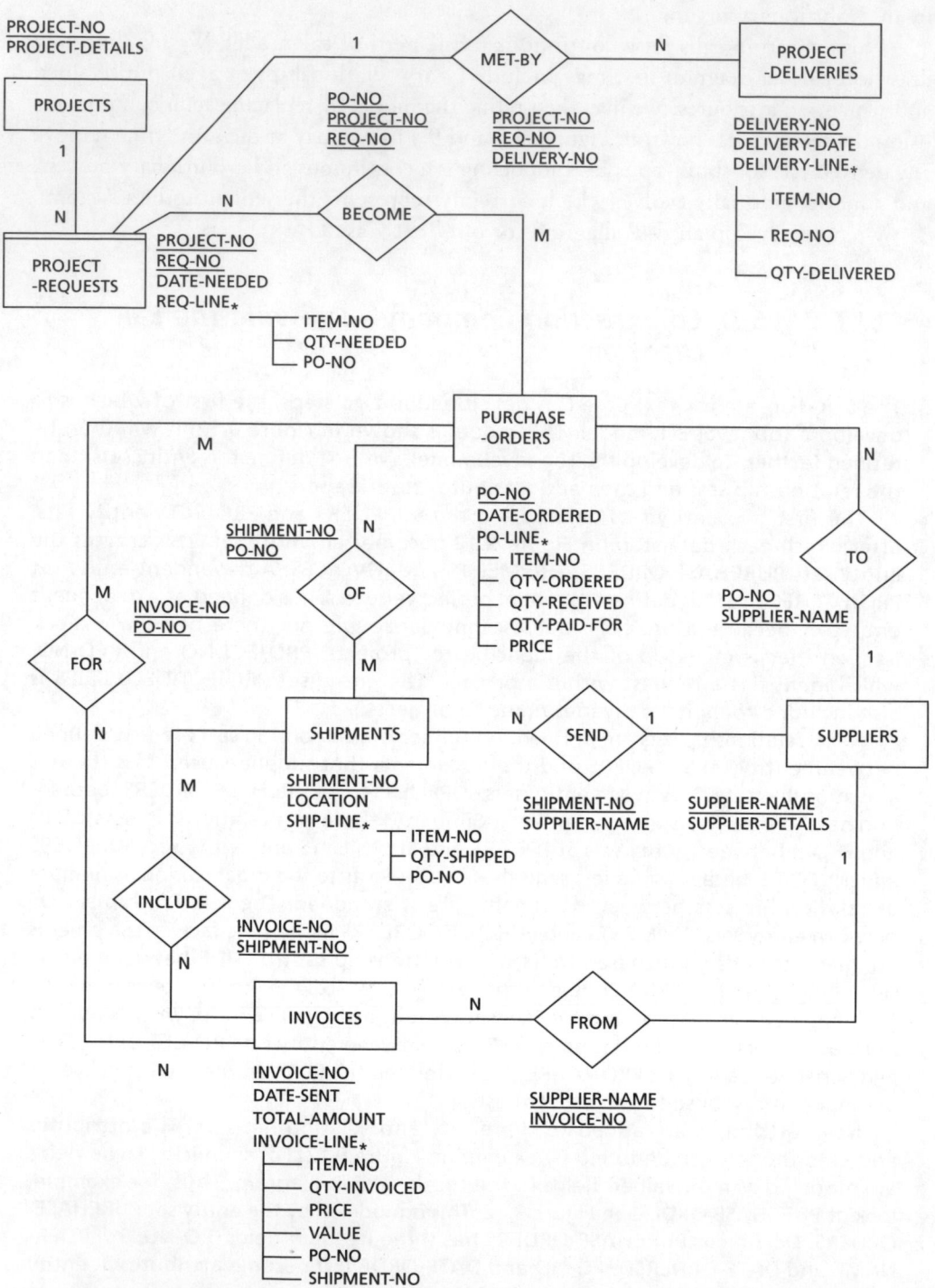

Figure 9.12 *A first attempt at an E–R diagram*

PRICE. These lines are modeled by the multivalued attribute PO-LINE, which is made up of these five fields. The asterisk next to PO-LINE indicates that there may be more than one PO-LINE for each PURCHASE-ORDER. You should note that a new attribute, INVOICE-NO, has been added to entity set INVOICES. This attribute is an internal identifier added to distinguish invoices received from different suppliers. You may wish to examine all the documents in Figure 9.12 and study how they have been converted to the E–R diagram.

SOME ADDITIONAL CONCEPTS

The most common extensions to the E–R model are dependent entity sets and subsets. This book will introduce these extensions here. For more elaborate descriptions, you should go to more advanced database texts (e.g. Hawryszkiewycz, 1991).

DEPENDENT ENTITIES

The first E–R model extension is the concept of **dependent entity set**. Dependent entity sets are also sometimes known as **weak entity sets**. You should recall what is meant by the word *set*. An entity or relationship set is made up of objects that have the same properties. All objects in the same dependent entity set not only have the same properties, but also another property in common: their existence depends on the existence of a parent entity in another set. If that parent is not of interest to the system, its dependent entities also cease to be of interest to the system.

The dependent entity set is shown in the E–R diagram by a rectangular box with a second line drawn across the top. Figure 9.13 shows two E–R models that include dependent entities. Figure 9.13(a) models INVOICES and INVOICE-LINES. An invoice line obviously cannot exist without there being a corresponding invoice and only appears in the system if a corresponding invoice exists. This dependence is modeled by an arrow directed from the parent entity set (in this case, INVOICES) to its dependent entity set (in this case, INVOICE-LINES). Figure 9.13(b) is another example of dependence. Here project tasks are set up for projects in the system. Thus, a project to build a computerized payroll system may include tasks such as analysis, design and implementation.

A task cannot be set up without there being a project. In an E–R model, tasks are modeled by dependent entity set TASKS, projects are modeled by entity set PROJECTS, and the dependence is shown by the arrow from PROJECTS to TASKS.

Dependent entity set
A set of entities whose existence depends on other entities.

Weak entity set
Another term for a dependent entity set.

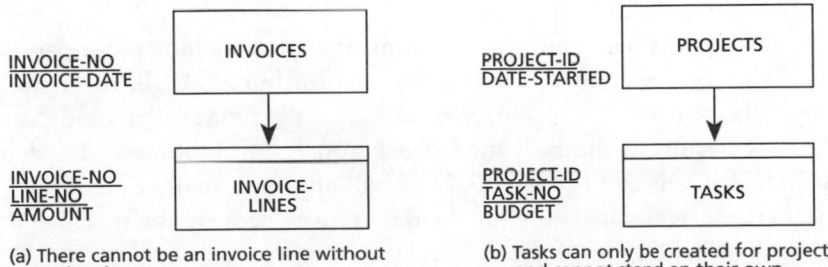

(a) There cannot be an invoice line without an invoice

(b) Tasks can only be created for projects and cannot stand on their own

Figure 9.13 *Dependent entities*

Dependent entity set

Note that dependent entities have composite identifiers. Their identifier consists of the identifier of their parent entity, together with another attribute that uniquely identifies the dependent entity within the parent. Thus an invoice line is made up of the attribute INVOICE-NO (which identifies the invoice in which the invoice line appears) and the attribute LINE-NO (which identifies the particular line in the invoice). Similarly, a task identifier is made up of the attribute PROJECT-ID (which identifies the task's project) and the attribute TASK-NO (which identifies a task within the project).

Using dependent entity sets

Dependent entities are very useful for modeling historic information. Historic information must be kept whenever two entities interact more than once. Each such interaction may be at a different time, and each interaction may have different property values. An example of historic information is the amount of machine time used by projects each day. The amount of time used by the same machine on the same project may be different each day. The obvious way to model machine use by projects without using dependent entity sets is shown in Figure 9.14(a). The machines are modeled by entity set MACHINES and projects by entity set PROJECTS. The use of machines by projects is modeled by the relationship set USE.

The occurrence diagram in Figure 9.14(a) shows that a machine in entity set MACHINES interacts more than once with the same PROJECTS entity in relationship set USE. Machine 'Mach1', for example, appears in two USE relationships, 'u1' and 'u2', with project 'Proj1'. There is one such relationship between the same machine and the same project for every day that the machine uses that project. Relationships between the same two objects in the same relationship set are sometimes known as **multiple relationships**.

Without historic data, the identifiers of relationships in relationship set USE would be the identifiers of MACHINES and PROJECTS—namely, MACHINE-NO and PROJECT-ID. To model historic information, relationship USE contains an additional identifier, DATE-USED, to distinguish the different relationships between the same machine and project. The attribute TIME-SPENT-ON-PROJECT in relationship set USE is the amount of machine time used by a project on one day. Relationship set USE also has the attribute MACHINE-CONDITION-FOR-DAY to store the machine condition for the day. The machine condition is the same for all projects on a given day.

Relationship sets with multiple relationships often include redundancy because they model more than one concept. Thus relationship set USE, in Figure 9.14(a), describes both the condition of a machine as well as the projects that used the machine. If you look carefully at the E–R model in Figure 9.14(a), you will see that a value of MACHINE-CONDITION-FOR-DAY will appear as many times as the number of projects that use the machine for the day. This is because the machine condition for the day is independent of the projects that use the machine.

A better way to model this system is to use a separate dependent entity set to model the machine condition of the day. In Figure 9.14(b), the dependent entity

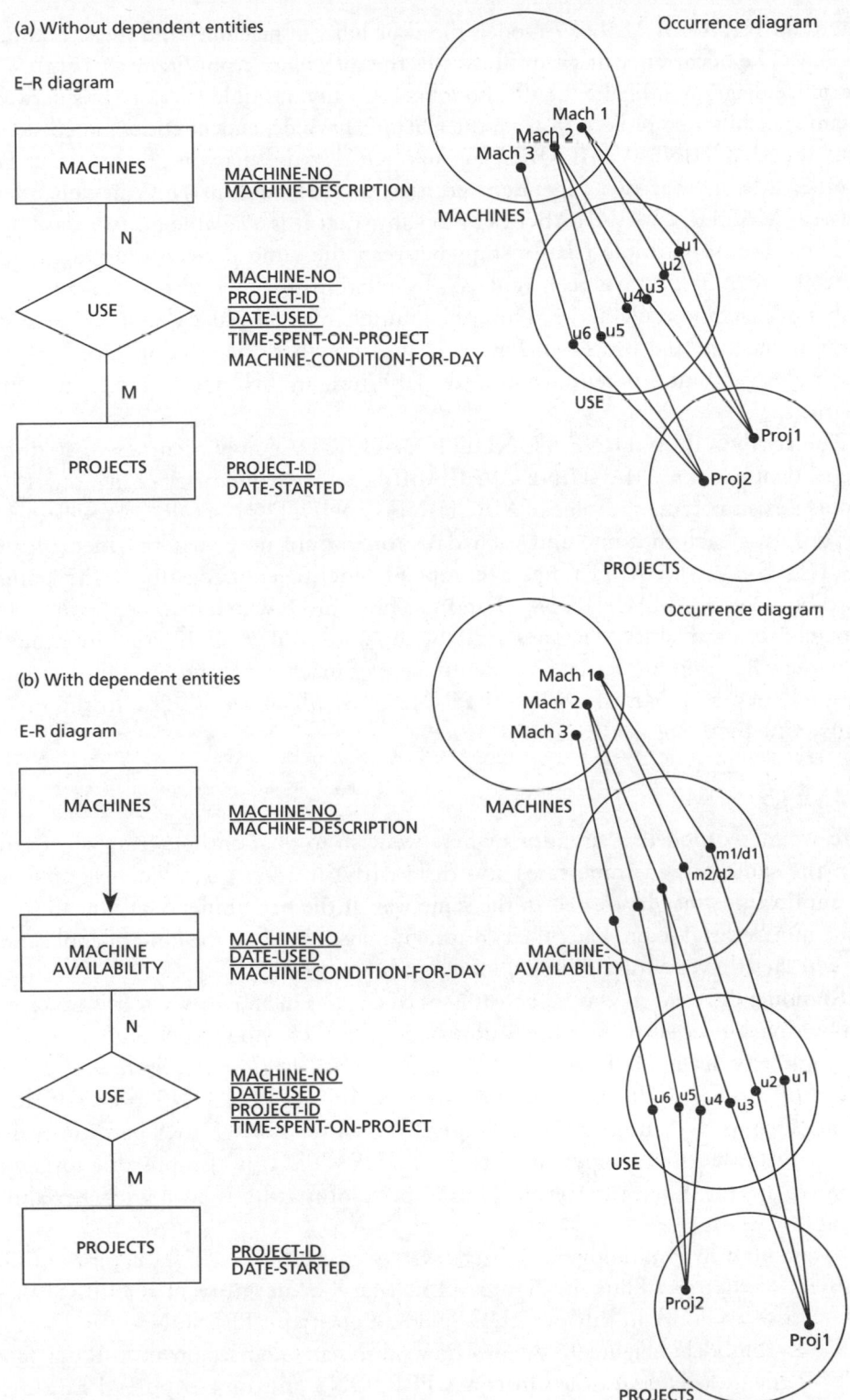

(a) Without dependent entities

E–R diagram

MACHINES — MACHINE-NO
MACHINE-DESCRIPTION

N

USE — MACHINE-NO
PROJECT-ID
DATE-USED
TIME-SPENT-ON-PROJECT
MACHINE-CONDITION-FOR-DAY

M

PROJECTS — PROJECT-ID
DATE-STARTED

Occurrence diagram

MACHINES

USE

PROJECTS

(b) With dependent entities

E-R diagram

MACHINES — MACHINE-NO
MACHINE-DESCRIPTION

MACHINE
AVAILABILITY — MACHINE-NO
DATE-USED
MACHINE-CONDITION-FOR-DAY

N

USE — MACHINE-NO
DATE-USED
PROJECT-ID
TIME-SPENT-ON-PROJECT

M

PROJECTS — PROJECT-ID
DATE-STARTED

Occurrence diagram

MACHINES

MACHINE-
AVAILABILITY

USE

PROJECTS

Figure 9.14 *Modeling historic data*

set MACHINE-AVAILABILITY models the availability of machines and their condition each day. The occurrence diagram illustrates the difference from Figure 9.14(a). The occurrence diagram in Figure 9.14(b) no longer has any multiple relationships between the same machine and project. Instead, the machine has a dependent entity in dependent entity set MACHINE-AVAILABILITY for each day the machine is available. For example, 'Mach1' has two dependent entities, 'm1/d1' and 'm1/d2', in dependent entity set MACHINE-AVAILABILITY, to show that it is available on two days.

There are no multiple relationships between the same project and machine in Figure 9.14(b). They have been replaced by relationships between a project and a number of machine availabilities. Thus, the multiple relationship 'u1' and 'u2' between the same machine and project in Figure 9.14(a) now become relationships between the same project but different machine availabilities, 'm1/d1' and 'm1/d2', in Figure 9.14(b).

The attribute MACHINE-CONDITION-FOR-DAY now becomes an attribute of dependent entity set MACHINE-AVAILABILITY. The redundancy of Figure 9.14(a) no longer exists because the value of MACHINE-CONDITION-FOR-DAY will appear once only for each machine and each day. You should note that the identifier of MACHINE-AVAILABILITY has a composite identifier made up of the parent identifier—namely, MACHINE-NO and DATE-USED, which is the date on which the machine is available. Machines available on a given day can be used by projects on that day. Relationship set USE models the use of machines by projects and contains attributes such as TIME-SPENT-ON-PROJECTS, which are specific to the use of the machine by the project.

SUBSETS

There are many modeling situations where we wish to treat entities from one entity set in the same way in some cases and differently in other cases. For example, all loan applications may be treated in the same way at the beginning. They are all filed, given a number, and so on. Later their treatment may depend on the kind of application (e.g. whether they are for a personal loan or a home loan).

Subset
Some of the objects from one entity set.

To model different methods of treatment of entities in an entity set, it is necessary to show division of entity sets into **subsets**. Figure 9.15 shows how such a division can be modeled using the E–R model. The occurrence diagram in Figure 9.15 shows the idea of subsetting. It shows five persons in entity set PERSONS. Some of these persons, such as 'Jill', are teachers and appear in subset TEACHERS and some, like 'Mary', are students and appear in subset STUDENTS. It is also possible for some persons to appear in both subsets—for example, 'John', who is both a teacher and a student.

To extend our terminology to subsets, we say that entities of a set can be entities in subsets of that set. Thus, in Figure 9.15, 'Mary' is an entity in set PERSONS. 'Mary' is also an entity in subset STUDENTS of entity set PERSONS.

The E–R model in Figure 9.15 shows how subsets are modeled on an E–R diagram. The E–R diagram includes the entity set PERSONS and its attributes PERSON-ID, NAME and ADDRESS. PERSON-ID is the identifier of persons in entity set PERSONS. The subsets are modeled by rectangular boxes with a second line on the

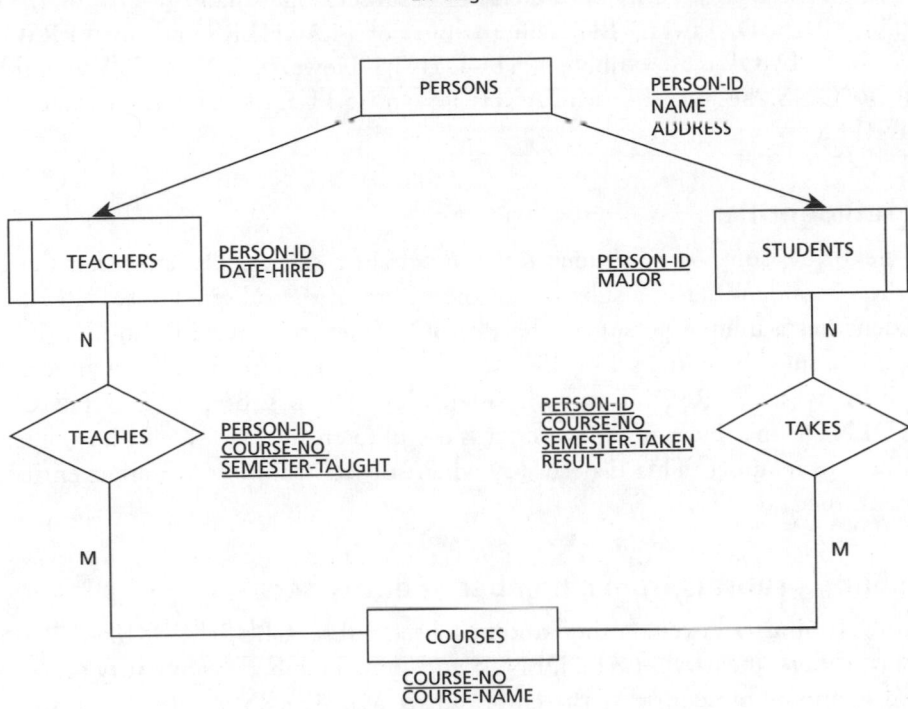

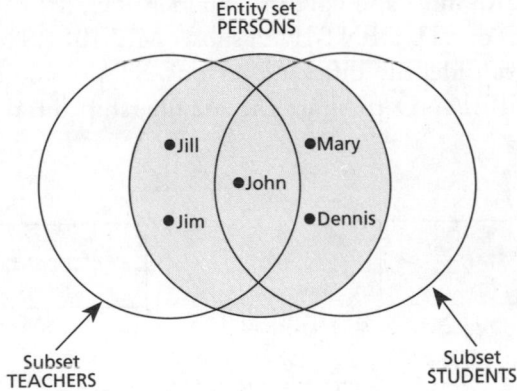

Figure 9.15 *Subsets*

left-hand side of the box. Two subsets of entity set PERSONS, namely TEACHERS or STUDENTS, are modeled by the E–R model in Figure 9.15. The directed arrows from PERSONS to TEACHERS and STUDENTS show that STUDENTS and TEACHERS are subsets of PERSONS.

It is also common for entities in different subsets to have some different attributes and some common attributes. The common attributes are shown as attributes of the parent entity set, whereas attributes particular to a subset are shown only as attributes of that subset. Thus, a person who is a teacher may have the attribute DATE-HIRED, and a person who is a student may have the attribute MAJOR. Attributes which depend on the type of entity are stored in the subset rather than the entity set. Thus, in Figure 9.15, DATE-HIRED is an attribute of TEACHERS and not PERSONS. Similarly, a MAJOR is an attribute of STUDENTS. However, ADDRESS is an attribute of PERSONS, because both TEACHERS and STUDENTS have the attribute ADDRESS.

Subset identifiers

The next question is how to identify members of a subset. The simplest way is to use the same identifier in a subset as in the parent of the subset. Thus, if PERSON-ID identifies a unique person in the PERSONS set, then it will also identify that person in a subset of entity set PERSONS. In Figure 9.15, PERSON-ID is an identifier of an entity set PERSONS and the identifier of two subsets, TEACHERS and STUDENTS. In some cases, however, it is useful to create a new identifier to identify members of a subset. This is necessary when subsets from two different entity sets are combined.

Combining subsets from a number of entity sets

Figure 9.16 illustrates yet another kind of subset. Subset CLUB-MEMBERS contains some members of entity set STUDENTS and some members from entity set STAFF. These members use courts at the club. Subset MEMBERS is called non-uniform, or merged because it contains entities from more than one entity set.

Subset MEMBERS must also have its own identifier, MEMBER-NO. We cannot use either STAFF-ID or STUDENT-ID in subset MEMBERS because the same value of these identifiers can identify different persons. STAFF and STUDENTS include the attribute MEMBER-NO to show the membership numbers allocated to staff and students.

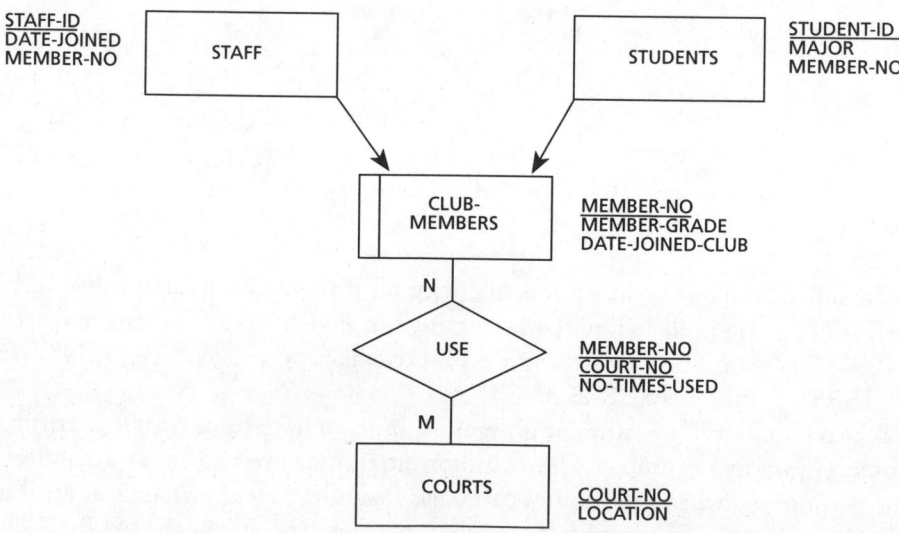

Figure 9.16 *A non-uniform subset*

TEXT CASE D: Construction Company—Refining the E–R Diagram

An initial E–R diagram for Text Case D was illustrated in Figure 9.12. The next E–R modeling step is to refine this initial E–R diagram. The refined E–R diagram is shown in Figure 9.17. Each multivalued attribute in the top-level E–R diagram is replaced by a dependent entity set in the refined E–R diagram. For example, PO-LINE of PURCHASE-ORDERS is replaced by the dependent entity set ORDER-LINES. All the fields of the multivalued attribute become attributes of the newly created dependent entity set. In addition, a new identifier is added to the dependent entity set to identify the dependent entities within their parent. The attribute PO-LINE-NO is, thus, used to identify lines within a PURCHASE-ORDER.

Another refinement is to add entity sets ITEMS to the E–R diagram. This entity set is added because a reference to items appears in most documents. Relationship sets are added between the entity set ITEMS and all the dependent entity sets for document lines that refer to items.

Relationship sets that previously existed between documents are now replaced by relationship sets between the document lines. This calls for a detailed analysis to precisely determine the relationships between document lines. The refined E–R diagram shows that:

- one purchase order line is related to many shipping lines, because items in one purchase order line may be delivered in more than one shipment;
- one shipment line is related to many invoice lines, because items in one shipment line may be spread across a number of invoices;
- one purchase order line is related to many invoice lines, because items in a purchase order line may be invoiced over a number of invoices;
- one order line is related to many request lines, because a purchase order line may combine requests from more than one project request; and
- one request line is related to many delivery lines, because items in one project request line can be delivered in a number of deliveries to the project site.

E–R DIAGRAMS AND DFDs

So far E–R analysis and data flow analysis have been discussed as two separate modeling methods. However, in practice, both of these techniques are used together in system modeling. Data flow analysis is used to model system flows, whereas E–R analysis is used to model system data. There are two implications in this. First, as both models describe the same system, they must be consistent in their use of system names. Second, each model can be used to help develop the other, and to check that the other model is complete so that if something is missed in one model it can be found in the other, and vice versa.

However, it should be pointed out that one cannot derive one model from the other. Hence it is possible to start modeling with either the DFD or the E–R diagram, or to use both together. Most methodologies start with the DFD diagram and then use the data stores or flows as indicators of the major system entities. However, it is possible to use the information gathered in developing one model to help develop the other. The DFD diagram can also suggest what to include in an E–R diagram. Typical guidelines here include:

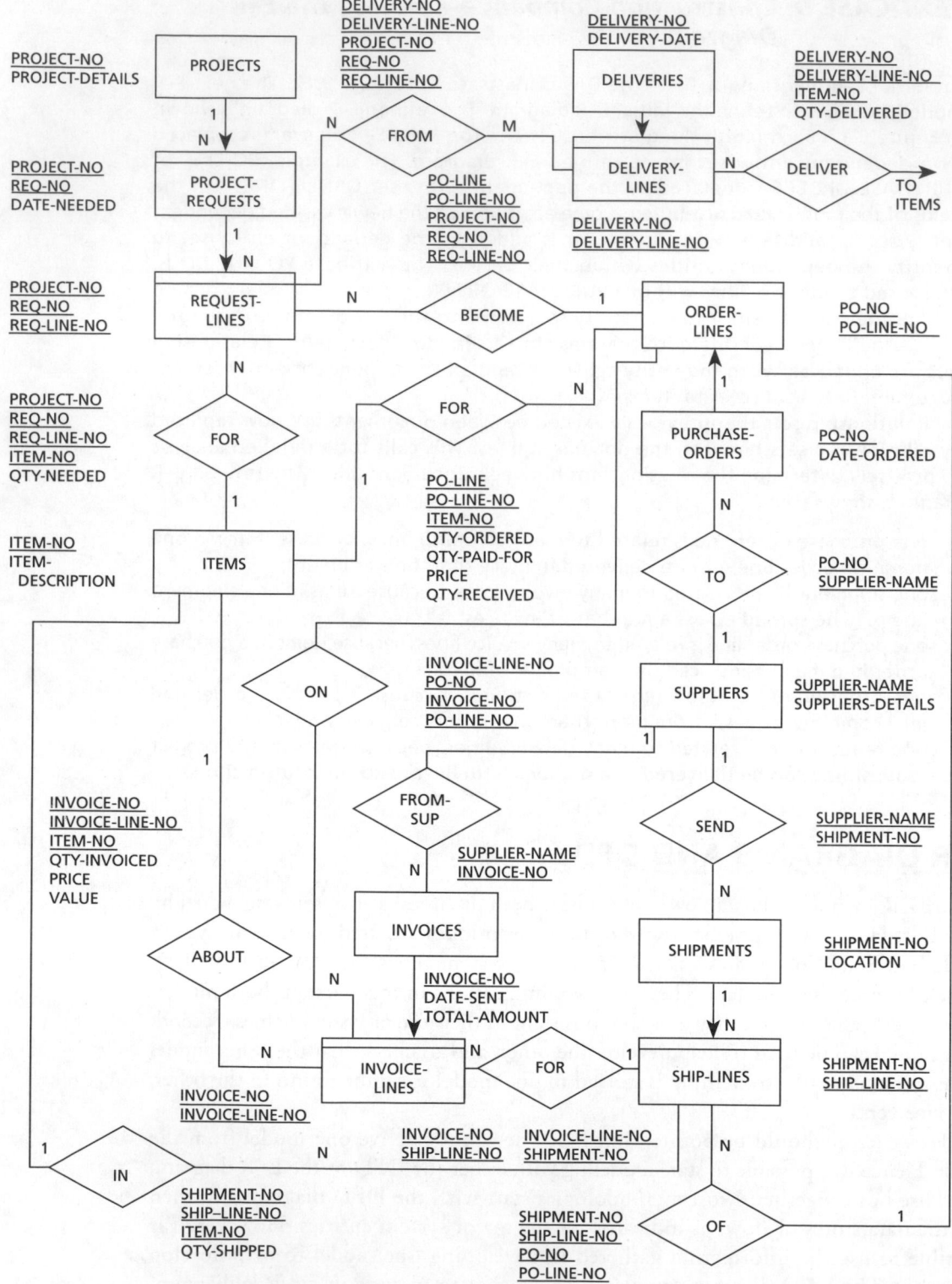

Figure 9.17 *A refined E–R diagram*

- Each external entity is usually modeled by an entity set. We often need information about such external entities—for example, their addresses—and this would be modeled as part of this entity set.
- Data stores often indicate possible entity sets. A detailed examination of a data store often suggests entity sets and their attributes.
- Processes often suggest relationships. A process that uses two components often suggests a relationship between these components. Thus a process that uses two stores often suggests that a relationship exists between the entities in those stores. A process that uses flows with an external entity and a store often suggests a relationship between the external entity and entity sets in the store.

In contrast, data flows often do not suggest entity sets. They often move information from one source to another. Such information may be collected from more than one entity set and need not be restricted to one set. However, some data flows may sometimes carry information related to one entity, such as an order or a delivery.

As an example, consider the DFD in Figure 8.3 and how it can be used to suggest an E–R diagram. The first step may be to create an entity set for each of the three external entity sets. These three entity sets are shown in Figure 9.18 as entity sets DEPARTMENTS, MANAGERS and SUPPLIERS. Then we note that there are data stores for budgets and accounts and set up the ACCOUNTS and BUDGETS entity sets. A relationship is then set between BUDGETS and DEPARTMENTS to show the departments to which a budget applies. REQUISITIONS is the next entity set that we might set up. You might ask why have REQUISITIONS as an entity set? There are no data stores for requisitions in Figure 8.3. However, the flow from the external entity, DEPARTMENTS, does suggest a requisition and there might be a data store that contains requisitions, probably in one of the processes such as 'Check funding'. We may also add entity set ORDERS, because this would be part of process 'Organize supplies' and is sent to suppliers. Again, there is no data store of orders, but the flow to SUPPLIERS suggests that ORDERS might be stored in process, 'Organize supplies'. We then assume that process 'Organize supplies' uses requisitions to create orders and thus set up a relationship between ORDERS and REQUISITIONS and

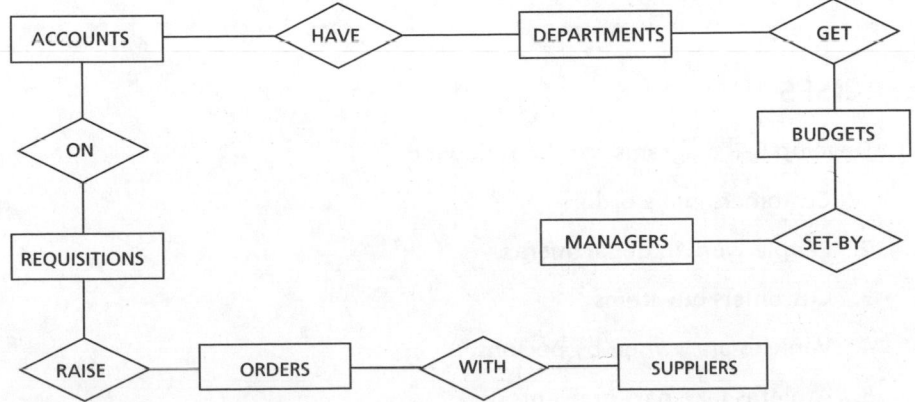

Figure 9.18 *An initial E–R diagram*

also between ORDERS and SUPPLIERS because orders are sent to suppliers. Finally, we might set up a relationship between REQUISITIONS and ACCOUNTS because of the checking in process 'Check funding'. The DFD in Figure 9.18 may then be a good starting point for E–R modeling.

The idea of using a DFD to suggest an initial E–R model does not in any way imply that E–R models should be derived from DFD diagrams. They are in fact developed in parallel, and one usually suggests improvements to and completeness of the other. Thus it is possible to check model consistency and to ensure that no information is missed during analysis. Names in the E–R model and DFD model are often checked to ensure that both contain all the information. Documentation is frequently designed to check for such consistency. Many CASE tools also provide consistency checks.

The question, of course, is how tight to make the link between the two models. One way is to keep a fairly loose link. Here we ensure that there is a consistency between the names used in each model and that each model can provide leads for detailed searches or corrections in the other. Alternatively, there may be a more comprehensive set of link requirements. For example, we may require each data store to correspond to an entity set, a relationship set, or a combination of the two.

SUMMARY

This chapter described ways to describe data as part of a system and methods used to develop data models during systems analysis. The goal at this early stage is to capture the important characteristics of data. This is done by using a high-level semantic model. This chapter described how entity–relationship (E–R) modeling techniques are used to develop such a model. Later in design, some further refinements are made to the E–R model. This model is then refined by converting it to a relational model. The relational model provides a number of criteria to construct normal form relations. The chapter also discussed the relationship between the E–R model and DFD diagrams and how this can be used to ensure that correct and complete models are developed during analysis.

EXERCISES

9.1 Develop E–R diagrams for the following:

1. Customers make orders.

2. People work in departments.

3. Customers buy items.

4. Vehicles are owned by persons.

5. Athletes take part in events.

6. Deliveries of parts are made to customers.

9.2   Draw E–R diagrams showing the cardinality for the following:

1.   An invoice is sent to one customer and there can be many invoices sent to the same customer.

2.   A part is used in many projects and many projects use the part.

3.   A person works in one department and there are many persons in a department.

4.   A vehicle is owned by one person and a person can own many vehicles.

5.   Students take subjects. Each subject can be taken by many students and each student can take many subjects.

6.   Persons apply for loans. Each loan must be made to one person but each person can make many applications.

7.   An operator can work on many machines and each machine has many operators. Each machine belongs to one department but a department can have many machines.

9.3   Draw E–R diagrams with attributes, cardinality and identifiers for the following:

1.   Customers identified by a CUSTOMER-NAME and with an ADDRESS buy items. Items are identified by an ITEM-NO and have a COLOR. The QTY-BOUGHT of an item by each customer is recorded. An item can be bought by many customers.

2.   Departments are identified by a DEPT-NO and have a budget. A department can manage many projects but each project is managed by one department. Projects are identified by a PROJECT-NO and have a START-DATE.

3.   An order with a unique ORDER-NO and ORDER-DATE can be made for any number of parts (identified by ITEM-NO and with a COLOR). QTY-ORDERED is the amount of each part ordered. Each order is made to one supplier (who has a unique SUPPLIER-NAME and one ADDRESS).

4.   A fault occurs on one item of equipment. A log book contains FAULT-NO, FAULT-DATE and FAULT-DESCRIPTION. Each item of equipment has a unique EQUIP-NO and an EQUIP-DESCRIPTION and TYPE. Each such item is located in one building, which has a unique BUILDING-NAME and one ADDRESS.

5.   A student (with STUDENT-ID, ADDRESS and SURNAME) takes any number of subjects, which have a unique SUBJECT-NAME and a SUBJECT-DESCRIPTION. The student is enrolled in a major that has a unique MAJOR-NAME and LENGTH. The date on which a student started a major is recorded. A subject is taken by one teacher, who is identified by a TEACHER-ID and has a TEACHER-ADDRESS.

9.4   Convert the N-ary relationship set shown in Figure 9.19 to a set of binary relationship sets.

9.5   You have gathered the following data: you are required to draw an E–R diagram from the data.

- Persons (identified by PERSON-ID) work on machines (identified by MACHINE-NO) to produce garments.

- Various GARMENT-KINDS can be produced. Each GARMENT-KIND has a description (GARMENT-DESCRIPTION) and is made up of a variety of materials

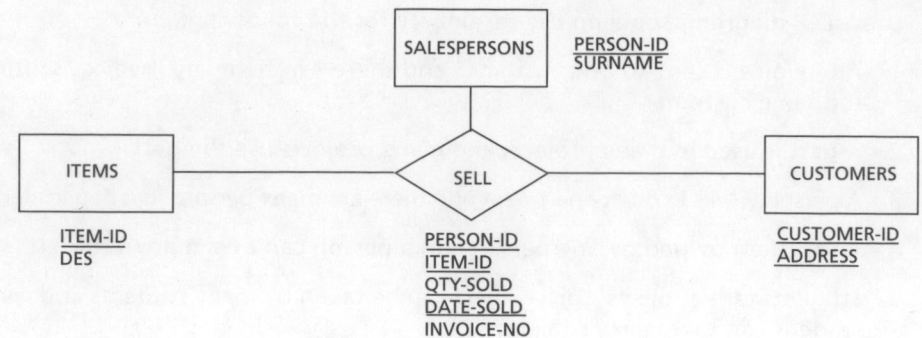

Figure 9.19 *A N-ary relationship set*

(identified by MAT-KIND). A record of the QTY-NEEDED of each MAT-KIND for each GARMENT-KIND is stored.

- The production of each garment is recorded as a job identified by JOB-NO. Each JOB-NO has a START-TIME and an END-TIME and is performed by one person on one machine. A number of garments of the same kind can be produced on one job.

- Other information of interest is:

  (a) the NAME and DATE-OF-BIRTH of each person;

  (b) the DATE-PURCHASED of each machine;

  (c) the DESCRIPTION of each MAT-KIND;

  (d) the TIME-SPENT by a person on a job; and

  (e) the NUMBER-OF-GARMENTS produced on one job.

9.6 Below are some statements about order processing in an organization. You are required to construct an E–R diagram from these statements.

- Persons in the organization are identified by a PERSON-ID and have a SURNAME, FIRST-NAME and DATE-OF-BIRTH.

- The persons are responsible for orders, which are identified by an ORDER-NO and have an ORDER-DATE, DESCRIPTION and QUOTED-PRICE. Each order is from one customer. Only one person is responsible for a given order but a person may be responsible for many orders.

- The organization manufactures the order in a series of jobs. A person responsible for an order makes formal requests to sections to carry out these jobs. The requests are identified by a REQUEST-NO. They nominate a START-DATE and an END-DATE for each request.

- A number of jobs can be created by a section in response to a request. Each job is identified by a JOB-NO and has a COST. All jobs for one request go to the same section, which is identified by SECTION-ID and has one MANAGER.

- Each job uses a QTY-USED of one or more materials. Materials are identified by MAT-ID and have a MAT-DESCRIPTION.

9.7   Draw E–R diagrams for the following using dependent entities if necessary. Where required, make sensible assumptions and carefully specify those assumptions.

1.   A department has a number of sections. Each department has a unique DEPT-NO and BUDGET and each section has a unique SECTION-NO within the department.

2.   An office (identified by OFFICE-NO) in a building (with a unique BUILDING-NAME) is occupied by a person (identified by PERSON-ID and with a SURNAME). The building has a unique ADDRESS and the office has an OFFICE-SIZE.

3.   A vehicle is identified by a REGISTRATION-NO and is of a given MAKE. Vehicles are used every day to make deliveries. A driver is assigned to a vehicle for the whole day and that driver can make any number of deliveries during the day. Each delivery is identified by a DEL-NO and is to a given ADDRESS.

4.   A student identified by a STUDENT-ID and with a given ADDRESS can enrol for any number of semesters. The enrolment in a semester can be of a given TYPE ('part-time' or 'full-time'). The student can take any number of subjects in the semester and get a GRADE for each subject taken. The subject is identified by SUBJECT-NAME and has a DESCRIPTION.

9.8   EMPLOYEES in an organization can be 'part-time' or 'full-time' employees. The organization keeps the PERSON-ID and SURNAME for each employee. In addition, for each part-time employee, the organization keeps that employee's START-TIME and END-DATE.

The DATE-JOINED is kept for each full-time employee. In addition, each full-time employee occupies one POSITION. Each position is identified by a POSITION-NO and is in one DEPARTMENT. The date the full-time employee was appointed to the position is also stored.

9.9   Draw an E–R diagram for the following:
An exhibiting organization keeps information about paintings and sculptures. Each painting has a PAINTING-NAME, PAINTER-NAME and PAINTING-DESCRIPTION. Each sculpture has a SCULPTOR-NAME, SCULPTURE-NAME and SCULPTURE-DES.
    Paintings and sculptures may appear in the same gallery. For the purpose of keeping track of the location of items, each painting and sculpture is given a unique identifier, ART-NO.
    Each gallery has an identifier, GALLERY-NO, and a size. Each gallery can store any number of art objects. Each art object appears in one gallery only. The DATE-PLACED-IN-GALLERY is kept for both paintings and sculptures.
    Note that PAINTING-NAME is unique within PAINTER-NAME, and SCULPTURE-NAME is unique within SCULPTOR-NAME.

9.10 Draw an E–R diagram that describes the following message transmission system:
Messages are sent in an organization. Messages have a DATE-SENT and LOCATION-MAILED. Messages may be of bulletin or letter type. A bulletin is identified by a unique BULLETIN-NO, whereas a letter is identified by a SENDER-NAME and TIME-SENT.
    Persons (identified by a unique PERSON-ID and with NAME and DATE-OF-BIRTH) in the organization belong to groups (identified by GROUP-NO and with a given GROUP-LOCATION and FUNCTION). Each person is assigned to a group on a given DATE-ASSIGNED and a person can belong to more than one group. Similarly, a group is made up of more than one person.

Letters may be addressed to either groups or individual persons. Only individual persons can send bulletins or letters. Bulletins are addressed to groups only.

BIBLIOGRAPHY

Chen, P.P. (March 1976), 'The entity–relationship model—toward a unified view of data', *ACM Transactions on Database Systems*, Vol. 1, No. 1, pp. 9–36.

Davenport, R.A. (1979), 'Data analysis for database design', *Australian Computer Journal*, Vol. 10, No. 4, pp. 122–37.

Flavin, M. (1981), *Fundamental Concepts of Information Modeling*, Yourdon Press, New York.

Hawryszkiewycz, I.T. (1991): *Database Analysis and Design* (2nd edn), Macmillan, New York.

Herman, M. (Fall 1983), 'A database design methodology for an integrated database environment', *DATA BASE*, pp. 20–7.

Howe, D.R. (1983), *Data Analysis for Data Base Design*, Edward Arnold, London.

Nijssen, G.M. and Halpin, T.A. (1987), *Conceptual Schema and Relational Database Design: A Fact Oriented Approach*, Prentice Hall, Sydney.

Robinson, H. (1981), *Database Analysis and Design*, Chartwell-Bratt, Bromley, Kent.

Process descriptions

CONTENTS

KEY LEARNING OBJECTIVES

How to specify processes in detail
How to describe processes in data flow diagrams
Decision trees and tables

INTRODUCTION

The modeling methods described in the previous two chapters all used a graphical representation. This has been done for a reason. Graphs are easier to understand, and they often give a total picture of the system. However, graphical models become unwieldy when used to specify processes in detail. Instead, such detailed process descriptions tend to use languages or scripts rather than diagrams. This chapter describes a number of ways of describing processes in detail. These range from natural language descriptions through scripts that must satisfy structure rules. The chapter then concentrates on the way in which detailed processes are defined in structured systems analysis.

Process descriptions have to satisfy a number of desirable properties. These depend on the level of the specification. At the usage level, they must be sufficiently rich to capture detailed user operations. At the system level, they must be more precise as they become the system specification. Processes in the system specification should be specified in such a way that they can be converted to a computer program. Such specifications are often called executable specifications. *An alternative to executable system specifications are specifications that can be converted to a computer program using a specific set of rules. A third desirable property of process descriptions is that they should be easy to read and understand.*

 NATURAL LANGUAGE SPECIFICATIONS

Most early design methods used natural language to specify system requirements. Such natural language specifications were generally found unsuitable because they often led to ambiguities. For example, consider the description: 'Add the expense to the travel budget if the trip exceeded two days or was longer than 250 miles and a company vehicle was used.' What do we do if the trip was 300 miles long, took three days and used a private vehicle? It depends on whether we group 'was longer than 250 miles' with 'exceeded two days' (in which case, the answer is 'do not add') or we group it with 'company vehicle was used' (in which case, the answer is 'add'). The process description is therefore ambiguous.

For this reason, natural language is not generally used for detailed process specification but is sometimes used at higher specification levels to define broad process goals.

 SCRIPTING

Script
A description of a process.

Basically, **scripting** means a structured written description of something. This book has described a number of ways of scripting. One method uses scenarios together with rich pictures to describe processes in the usage world. Ethnographic scripts were used for a similar reason. Both of these were relatively informal methods, describing a set of steps followed by people in their work. They both described specific instances of work practice in organizations. Use cases tend to introduce more formality, as they are generalizations of a number of scenarios. Examples of use case specifications will be given in Chapter 11.

Computer specifications, however, often require even more structured scripts. Such scripting can be anything from a program to a structured specification. The important thing is that such scripts have a structure that encourages precision. They must leave no doubts in the mind of the reader as to what they mean. Often this means that the scripts follow a logical structure. They may also use key words to shorten the amount of script. The scripts may also have to follow rules, be limited to predefined constructs, use specific instructions, or closely approximate computer programs themselves. There are some advantages in using scripts that follow precise rules, as they can be directly converted to a program code.

One example of scripts that follow a predefined structure comes from the work of Schank and Abelson (1977), who defined scripting as a method of defining knowledge. Here, scripts are defined as scenes that describe the interaction between roles in an environment. Such scripting methods can be adapted in defining processes in systems analysis.

TEXT CASE A: Interactive Marketing—A Script for Arranging a Sale

We assume that the following are involved in marketing:

> C—Consumer;
> V—Vendor;
> T—Trader.

We now define a script made up of four scenes—namely, initiating a purchase, agreeing on a price, arranging a purchase or aborting it.

Scene: initiating purchase:

> C—ASK (for PRODUCT) from T;
> T— PRESENTS (list of product);
> C— ASK (for price) from T;
> do bargaining;

Scene: bargaining:

> C—ASK (for price) from V;
> V—PRESENTS (price) to T;
> T—PRESENTS (price) to C;
> C—REPLIES (accept)—do arrange purchase;
> C— REPLIES (reject)—do abort purchase;
> C— REPLIES (ask again)—repeat bargain.

Additional scripts would be written for arranging a purchase, which would create a sales record, and abandoning a purchase, which would delete any record of negotiation.

In the above example, scripting described the interaction between three roles. One important requirement of scripting is that it must use a precise syntax to be unambiguous. In the example above, each line of the script has a VERB, such as ASK, as well as some arguments and the source and target of each interaction. The important thing to remember about scripts is that they must be precise and describe unambiguously the steps followed in a system. Precise methods for scripting have also been developed for DFDs and are described below.

SCRIPTING PROCESSES IN DATA FLOW DIAGRAMS

All processes in a DFD must have a process description. Different methods can be used to describe processes in a DFD diagram. The scripts used to describe top-level processes, for example, differ from those used to describe detailed processes. Top-level processes are usually brief and can use natural language. The process is usually described by one sentence that states what the process does. For example, Process 1 in Figure 8.3 may be described as 'Check whether there are sufficient funds in the department's budget to meet the spending request'.

What is needed at detailed levels are specifications that are unambiguous and can be easily understood by both users and programmers. The main techniques proposed for this purpose are:

- structured English;
- tight English;
- decision tables; and
- decision trees.

Structured English and tight English put verbal descriptions into a logical structure which removes logical ambiguities. This provides the best of two areas: the logic structure removes logical ambiguities, but English narrative can still be used to describe activities. The logical structures used to remove ambiguity are the logic constructs of structured programming. Thus process descriptions look very similar to program structures which appear in block structured languages.

The next two methods—*decision tables* and *decision trees*—are preferred where one of a large number of actions is to be selected. The action selected depends on a large number of conditions. Structured or tight English is not usually used for this purpose because the logic structure would become repetitive.

The differences between the four methods are illustrated in Figure 10.1, where there is a description of a process that determines whether a customer is to be given credit. The process is described using each of the four methods. The process chooses one of the three possible actions ('allow credit', 'refuse credit' or 'refer to manager'). The chosen action depends on whether customers have exceeded their current credit limit, the size of the purchase and the customer's payment history. Note that credit is allowed if the credit level has not been exceeded. If the credit limit has been exceeded, then a customer's credit history and amount of credit are examined. Customers with a bad credit history are refused credit. Customers with a good credit history can be allowed a further credit of up to $200 at the discretion of a manager.

You will note that in structured English these conditions are expressed by logic on the IF . . . THEN . . . ELSE construct. The first statement checks the condition 'credit limit exceeded'. Statements that follow THEN specify what is to be done if the condition is true. Statements which follow the ELSE (which falls directly under the THEN) specify what is to be done if the condition is false. Further conditions are tested if the condition 'credit limit exceeded' is true. These tests are indented to the right to be within the first THEN clause. The first test is condition 'customer has bad payment history'. The THEN and ELSE clauses indented under this test

(a) Using structured English
   IF credit limit exceeded
      THEN
         IF customer has bad payment history
            THEN refuse credit
            ELSE
               IF purchase is above $200
                  THEN refuse credit
                  ELSE refer to manager
      ELSE allow credit

(b) Using tight English
    5.1 IF credit level exceeded
    5.1.1 THEN (credit limit exceeded)
        IF customer has bad payment history
            5.1.1.1 THEN refuse credit
            5.1.1.2 ELSE (customer has good payment history)
                IF purchase is above $200
                5.1.1.2.1 THEN refuse credit
                5.1.2.2.2 ELSE (purchase is below $200)
                   refer to manager
    5.1.2. ELSE (credit level not exceeded) allow credit.

(c) Using a decision table

Conditions	Credit limit exceeded	Y	Y	Y	Y	N	N	N	N
	Customer with good payment history	Y	Y	N	N	Y	Y	N	N
	Purchase above $200	Y	N	Y	N	Y	N	Y	N
Action	Allow credit					X	X	X	X
	Refuse credit	X		X	X				
	Refer to manager		X						

Key:
Y = Yes, condition true
N = No, condition not true

(d) Using a decision tree

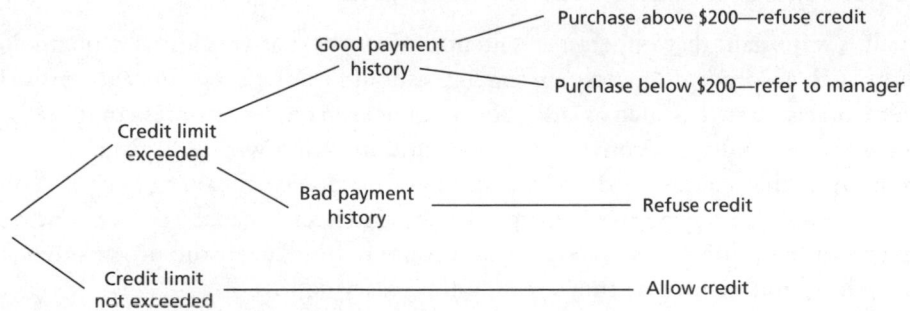

Figure 10. 1 *Specifying processes*

specify what is to be done for the 'true' and 'false' outcomes of this test. A 'false' outcome leads to a test of condition 'purchase above $200' and the outcomes of this test appear as further indentations. Too many indentations often lead to confusion in a structured English specification and should be avoided. The term *nesting* refers to indentation levels.

Tight English uses a numbering scheme to simplify indentation. Statement 5.1 checks whether the credit limit has been exceeded. Statement 5.1.1 specifies what has to be done if the credit limit has been exceeded. Statement 5.1.2 specifies what is to be done if the credit level has not been exceeded. Tests within other tests use a further level of numbering. Thus 5.1.1.1 and 5.1.1.2 specify the outcomes of condition 'customer has bad payment history' within level 5.1.1.

A decision table shows each possible set of conditions in one column and the corresponding actions in the same column. The decision tree defines the conditions as a sequence of left to right tests, commencing with credit limit, then, depending on the outcome, looking at the payment history and, finally, on the size of the purchase.

You should also note that tight English is similar to structured English and decision trees use the same ideas as decision tables. Structured English and decision tables are described in detail in the remainder of this chapter.

 # STRUCTURED ENGLISH

Structured English syntax is very similar to block structured languages. It provides the keywords to structure process specification logic as a block structured language while leaving some freedom when describing the activities and data used in the process. As with block structured languages, process specification logic consists of a combination of sequences of one or more imperative sentences with decision and repetition constructs.

IMPERATIVE SENTENCES

An imperative sentence usually consists of an imperative verb followed by the contents of one or more data stores on which the verb operates. For example:

> add PERSONS-SALARY to TOTAL-SALARY

It is important that imperative sentences use verbs that are clear and unambiguous. Verbs such as 'process', 'handle' or 'operate' should not be used. Instead verbs should define precise activities such as 'add' or 'compute average'. Sometimes computer general words such as 'edit' or 'convert' have specific meaning within a given context and are used in that context. Adjectives that have no precise meaning such as 'some' or 'few' should also not be used in imperative sentences because they cannot be used later to develop programs. These adjectives are redundant in the process description and should not be used as they create unnecessary confusion.

Additional standards are often used in imperative statements. For example, data flow names often appear in lower case between quotes, while specific data items in the data flows are capitalized. Data store names, as well as specific data store items, appear in capitals in imperative statements. If necessary, specific item names can be qualified by their data flow names or data store names to avoid ambiguity.

Boolean and arithmetic operations can be used in imperative statements. The exact operators used will depend on the standards adopted by a particular organization and usually include the following:

arithmetic multiply (*)
divide (/)
add (+)
subtract (−)
exponentiate (**)

Boolean   add
or
not
greater than (>)
less than (<)
less than or equal to (<=)
greater than or equal to (>=)
equals (=)
not equal to (π)

STRUCTURED ENGLISH LOGIC

Structured English uses certain keywords to group imperative sentences and define decision branches and iterations. These keywords are:

BEGIN	REPEAT	IF
END	UNTIL	THEN
CASE	WHILE	ELSE
OF	DO	FOR

GROUPING IMPERATIVE SENTENCES

A sequence of imperative statements can be grouped by enclosing them with the BEGIN and END keywords. For example, Process 2.3 in Figure 10.2(a) can be defined as:

```
BEGIN
    Receive 'sale report'.
    Get SALES record for PART-NO in 'sale report'.
    TOTAL-QTY = TOTAL-QTY + QTY-SOLD.
    SALE-VALUE = QTY-SOLD * UNIT PRICE.
    TOTAL-VALUE = TOTAL-VALUE + SALE-VALUE.
    Write SALES record.
    Send 'summary advice'.
END
```

This sequence defines what happens when a 'sale report' is received. Each 'sale report' reports a sale of one part-kind to a customer. The part-kind is identified by PART-NO; QTY-SOLD is the number of parts sold, whereas UNIT-PRICE is the sale price of one such part. The item CUSTOMER in 'sale report' identifies the customer.

Process 'record sale' maintains data store SALES which keeps an accumulated total of the number of parts sold and total moneys received for each part-kind. To do this, the process uses PART-NO from 'sale report' to select a record about the

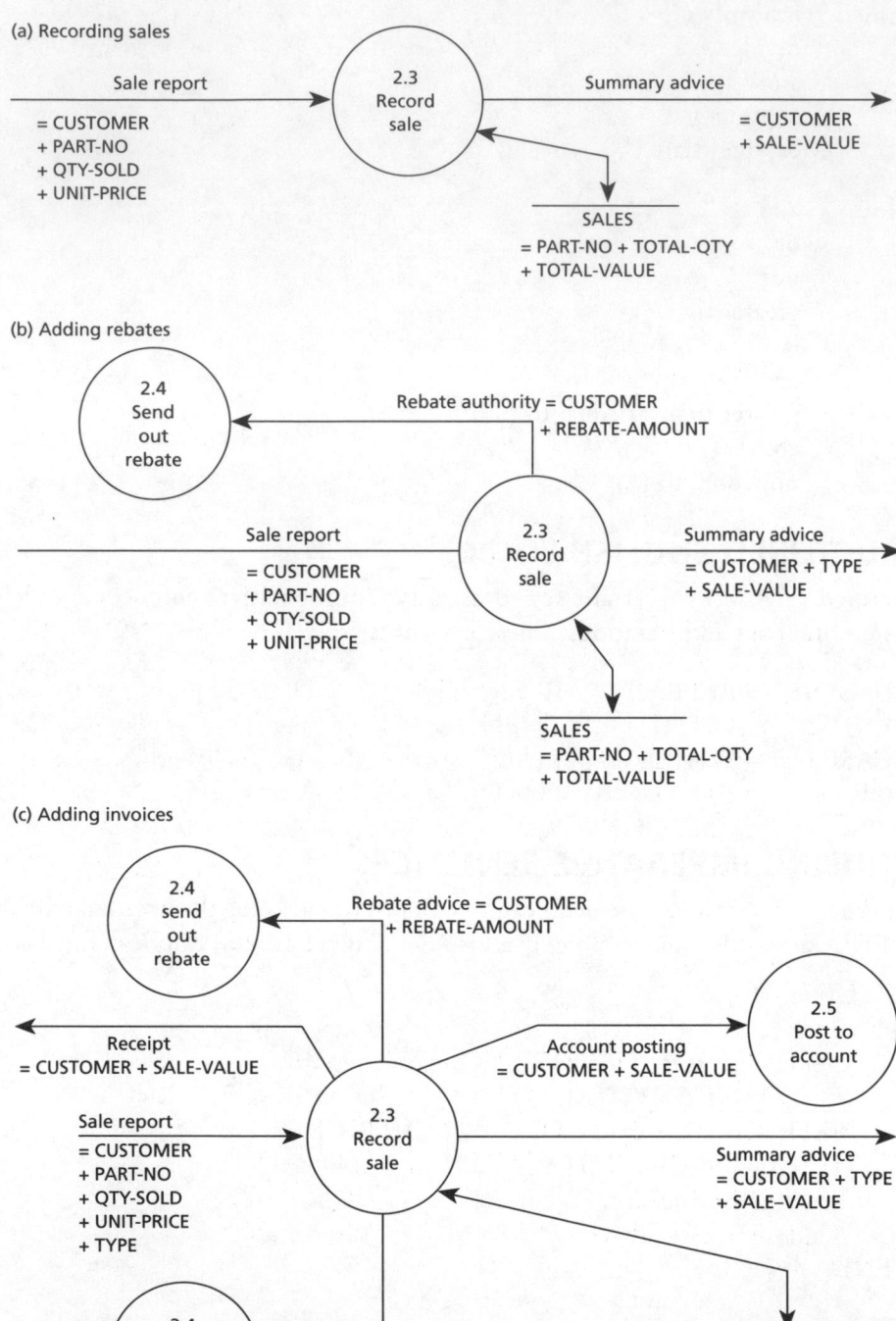

(a) Recording sales

Sale report
= CUSTOMER
+ PART-NO
+ QTY-SOLD
+ UNIT-PRICE

2.3
Record
sale

Summary advice
= CUSTOMER
+ SALE-VALUE

SALES
= PART-NO + TOTAL-QTY
+ TOTAL-VALUE

(b) Adding rebates

2.4
Send
out
rebate

Rebate authority = CUSTOMER
+ REBATE-AMOUNT

Sale report
= CUSTOMER
+ PART-NO
+ QTY-SOLD
+ UNIT-PRICE

2.3
Record
sale

Summary advice
= CUSTOMER + TYPE
+ SALE-VALUE

SALES
= PART-NO + TOTAL-QTY
+ TOTAL-VALUE

(c) Adding invoices

2.4
send
out
rebate

Rebate advice = CUSTOMER
+ REBATE-AMOUNT

Receipt
= CUSTOMER + SALE-VALUE

Account posting
= CUSTOMER + SALE-VALUE

2.5
Post to
account

Sale report
= CUSTOMER
+ PART-NO
+ QTY-SOLD
+ UNIT-PRICE
+ TYPE

2.3
Record
sale

Summary advice
= CUSTOMER + TYPE
+ SALE–VALUE

2.4
Send
out
invoice

Invoice data
= CUSTOMER
+ PART-NO + INVOICE-AMOUNT

SALES
= PART-NO + TOTAL-QTY
+ TOTAL-VALUE

Figure 10.2 *Editing records*

part-kind from data store SALES. It updates the value of TOTAL-QTY by QTY-SOLD and the value of TOTAL-VALUE by the SALE-VALUE of the sale and writes the record back to data store SALES. The process also sends out a 'summary advice' for each sale. The 'summary advice' contains the total value of a sale, SALE-VALUE, and the customer identifier, CUSTOMER.

Remember that structured English is not a programming language and that imperative statements are as brief as possible. There are no unnecessary move statements such as:

MOVE CUSTOMER in 'sale report' to CUSTOMER in 'summary advice'

which would normally be found in a programming language. It is assumed that the value of CUSTOMER remains the same as it passes through the process. Data items are not qualified unless there is ambiguity. Thus TOTAL-QTY is not qualified as TOTAL-QTY in SALES because the qualification does not add any useful information but makes the specification longer.

DECISIONS

Two types of decisions structure usually appear in structured English. These are as shown in Figure 10.3. Figure 10.3(a) shows a structure which allows a choice between two groups of imperative sentences. The keywords IF, THEN and ELSE are used in this structure. If a condition is 'true', then GROUP A sentences are executed. If it is false, then Group B sentences are executed.

The structure shown in Figure 10.3(b) allows a choice between any number of groups of imperative sentences. The keywords CASE and OF are used in this structure. The value of a variable is first computed. The group of sentences executed depend on that value. In Figure 10.3(b), the value of TEST is first computed. If that value is 'A', Group A sentences are executed. If it is 'B', Group B sentences are executed, and so on.

Suppose Process 2.3 in Figure 10.2(a) is amended to compute rebates for sales above a certain amount. The amended process is shown in Figure 10.2(b) and its process description now becomes:

```
BEGIN
    Receive 'sale report'.
    Get SALES record for PART-NO in 'sale report'.
    TOTAL-QTY = TOTAL-QTY + QTY-SOLD.
    SALE-VALUE= QTY-SOLD * UNIT-PRICE.
    TOTAL-VALUE = TOTAL-VALUE + SALE-VALUE.
    Write SALES record.
    Send 'summary advice'.
    IF SALE-VALUE > 500.00
        THEN
            BEGIN
                REBATE-AMOUNT = SALE-VALUE * .02.
                Send 'rebate authority'.
                END
END
```

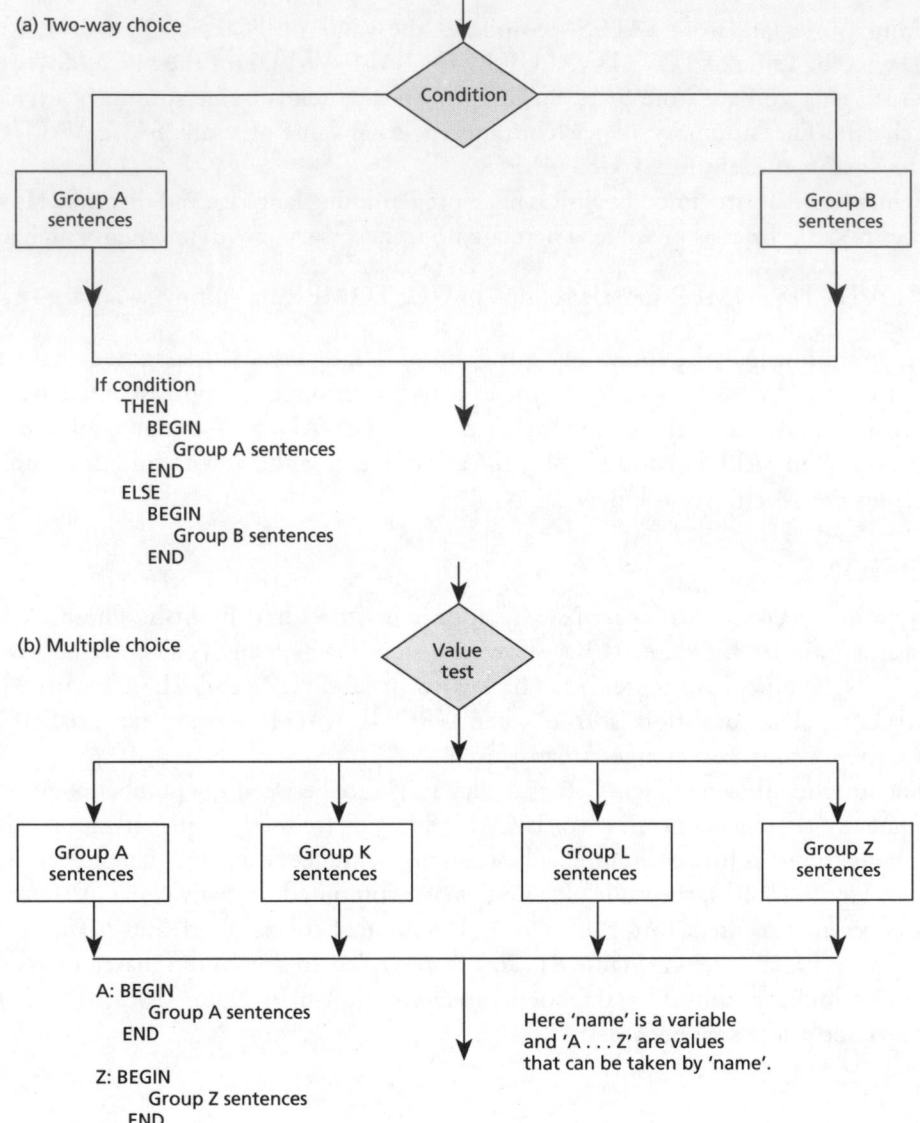

(a) Two-way choice

Condition

Group A sentences

Group B sentences

```
If condition
    THEN
        BEGIN
            Group A sentences
        END
    ELSE
        BEGIN
            Group B sentences
        END
```

(b) Multiple choice

Value test

Group A sentences

Group K sentences

Group L sentences

Group Z sentences

```
A: BEGIN
        Group A sentences
    END

Z: BEGIN
        Group Z sentences
    END
```

Here 'name' is a variable and 'A . . . Z' are values that can be taken by 'name'.

Figure 10.3 *Decision structure*

An IF clause has now been added. It checks whether the total amount of the sale exceeds $500 and sends out an authority for a 2 percent rebate to the customer.

A further change is made to process 'record sale' to illustrate the CASE structure. Figure 10.2(c) shows the changed process. Now each 'sale report' contains the field TYPE. The value of type shows the way that payment is to be made. A payment can be 'cash', 'cheque', 'credit' or 'account'. Process 'record sale' is now changed to cater for these types of payment.

An invoice must be sent for each 'credit' sale. An 'account' sale must be posted to an account and only 'account' sales attract a rebate. A receipt is returned for all 'cash' and 'cheque' sales. A 'summary advice' is still sent for all sales.

The changed process is shown in Figure 10.3(c) and its process description is as follows:

```
BEGIN
    Receive 'sale report'.
    Get SALES record for PART-NO in 'sale report'.
    TOTAL-QTY = TOTAL-QTY + QTY-SOLD.
SALE-VALUE = QTY-SOLD – UNIT-PRICE.
TOTAL-VALUE = TOTAL-VALUE + SALE-VALUE.
Write SALES record.
Send 'summary advice'.
CASE TYPE OF
    'account':
        BEGIN
            Send 'account posting'.
            IF SALE-VALUE > 500.00.
                THEN
                    BEGIN
                        REBATE-AMOUNT = SALE-VALUE* .02.
                        send 'rebate authority'.
                    END
        END

    'cash', 'cheque':
        BEGIN
            Send 'receipt' .
        END
    'credit':
        BEGIN
            INVOICE-AMOUNT = SALE-VALUE + SALE-VALUE * .01.
            send 'invoice data'.
        END
    END
END
```

Note that each sentence sequence for a CASE outcome is enclosed by a BEGIN and END statement.

REPETITION

Figure 10.4 shows two ways of specifying iterations in structured English. One way is to use the WHILE . . . DO structure. Here a condition is tested before a set of sentences is processed. The other way uses the REPEAT . . . UNTIL structure. Here the group of sentences is executed first and then the condition is tested.

As an example, consider process 'finalize order' in Figure 10.5. This process computes the value of an order for parts. The 'preliminary order' is identified by ORDER-NO

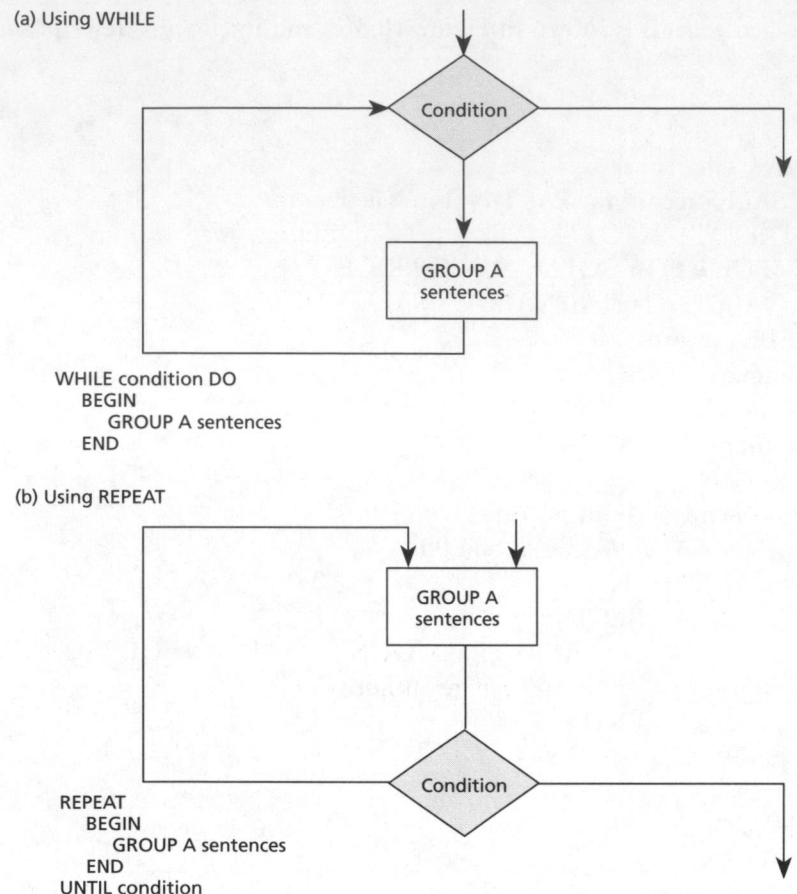

(a) Using WHILE

```
WHILE condition DO
    BEGIN
        GROUP A sentences
    END
```

(b) Using REPEAT

```
REPEAT
    BEGIN
        GROUP A sentences
    END
UNTIL condition
```

Figure 10.4 *Repetition structures*

and is made up of a number of lines. Each line contains PART-NO to specify a needed part and QTY-NEEDED to specify the quantity of that part ordered. The process looks up the price of each part in file PRICES and computes the total value of the order. The process is specified as:

```
Get 'preliminary order'.
ORDER-VALUE = 0.
WHILE there are more order lines DO
    BEGIN
        Get next 'order line'.
        Get PRICES record for PART-NO in 'order line'.
        PART-VALUE = QTY-NEEDED * PRICE.
        ORDER-VALUE = ORDER-VALUE + PART-VALUE.
        Create order line in 'finalized order'.
    END
Send 'finalized order'.
```

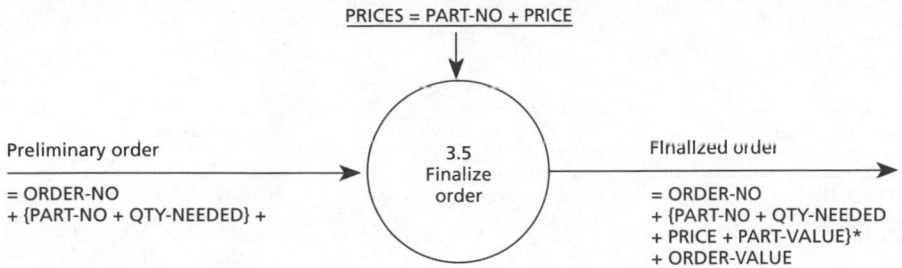

PRICES = PART-NO + PRICE

Preliminary order

= ORDER-NO
+ {PART-NO + QTY-NEEDED} +

3.5
Finalize
order

Finalized order

= ORDER-NO
+ {PART-NO + QTY-NEEDED
+ PRICE + PART-VALUE}*
+ ORDER-VALUE

Figure 10.5 *Finalizing orders*

An alternative to the WHILE . . . DO structure is to use the FOR structure.
The same process is now specified as:

Get 'preliminary order'.
ORDER-VALUE = 0.
FOR each order line in an order DO
    BEGIN
        Get next 'order line'.
        Get PRICES record for PART-NO in 'order line'.
        PART-VALUE = QTY-NEEDED * PRICE.
        ORDER-VALUE = ORDER-VALUE + PART-VALUE.
        Create order line in 'finalized order'.
    END
Send 'finalized order'.

A small change is made to process 'finalize order' illustrating the REPEAT . . .
UNTIL construct. The amended process is shown in Figure 10.6. Each order now
has an ORDER-LIMIT. Order values must fall below the limit. Process 'finalize order'
is now specified as:

Get 'preliminary order'.
ORDER-VALUE = 0
REPEAT
    BEGIN
        Get next 'order line'.
        Get PRICES record for PART-NO in 'order line'.
        PART-VALUE = QTY-NEEDED * PRICE.
        ORDER-VALUE = ORDER-VALUE + PART-VALUE.
        IF ORDER-VALUE < ORDER-LIMIT
            THEN create order line in 'finalized order'.
    END
UNTIL (ORDER-VALUE > ORDER-LIMIT) or
        (there are no more order lines).
Send 'finalized order'.

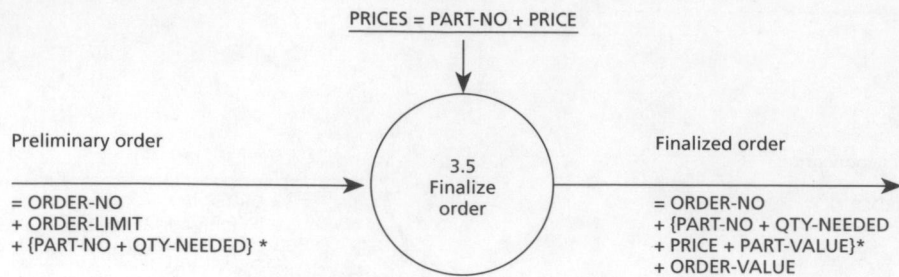

Figure 10.6 *Finalizing values with order limit*

Order lines are now priced only until the accumulated total for the value of the order is below the value of ORDER-LIMIT. Once this limit is exceeded, no more lines are added to 'finalized order'.

SOME COMMENTS ON USING STRUCTURED ENGLISH

Those familiar with programming (especially with using block structured languages) may ask whether we can use structured English to nest decisions within iterations and iterations within decisions, and have a number of levels nesting. This can be done but should be avoided as much as possible. Remember that what we are trying to achieve are process specifications that can be readily understood by those reading them. Complex levels of nesting should not be necessary, as we try (through leveling) to reduce processes to their most fundamental function. The guideline is that the structured description of a procedure should not exceed one page. If it does, you should try to level the process down further.

 ## DECISION TABLES

Although structured English can describe most processes, such process descriptions can become clumsy if we try to specify a process that selects one of a possible set of actions using a set of complex rules. This particularly applies if it is necessary to repeat a decision or to do the same process more than once to retain the logic structure. For example, consider Figure 10.7. The structured English specification in Figure 10.7 specifies two tests (one for type of account and one for type of transaction) and different combinations of the same actions (additions to or subtraction from accounts and counters), depending on the tests. You will find that either the tests or the actions must be repeated in the specification.

A better way of describing such logic is to use decision tables. A decision table for this process is illustrated in Table 10.1.

A decision table is first divided into two parts: the conditions and the actions. The conditions part states all the conditions that are applied to the data. The actions are the various actions that can be taken depending on the conditions. The table is constructed by using columns so that each column corresponds to one combination of conditions.

```
IF a trade account
THEN
      BEGIN
          IF withdrawal
              THEN
                  BEGIN
                       make an account deduction
                       add 1 to trade withdrawal
                  END
              ELSE (a deposit)
                  BEGIN
                       make an account addition
                       add 1 to trade deposits
                  END
          END
      ELSE (a personal account)
          BEGIN
              IF withdrawal
                  THEN
                      BEGIN
                           make an account deduction
                           add 1 to personal withdrawal
                      END
                  ELSE (a deposit)
                      BEGIN
                           make an account addition
                           add 1 to personal deposits
                      END
              END
          END
```

Figure 10.7 *Multiple conditions described by structured English*

The entry in the column indicates the existing condition. In Table 10.1, condition 'account type' can take two values: P for 'private' and T for 'trade'. Condition 'activity type' can also take two values: W for withdrawal and D for deposit. In many decision

Table 10. 1 *Multiple conditions with decision tables*

			P	P	T	T
Conditions	Account type		P	P	T	T
	Activity type		W	D	W	D
Actions	Add to account			X		X
	Subtract from account		X		X	
	Add 1 to trade withdrawal				X	
	Add 1 to personal withdrawal		X			
	Add 1 to trade deposits					X
	Add 1 to personal deposits			X		

Key:
P = Personal
T = Trade
W = Withdrawal
D = Deposit

tables there are only two values for a condition (i.e. T for true or F for false). It is possible for conditions to take more than two values. Condition 'activity type' could, for example, take the additional value B to get the balance of an account. Decision tables where conditions take more than two values are sometimes called *extended decision tables*.

The actions taken for the combination of conditions in the column are given by the crosses in the column. If the action line is crossed then that action is taken, given the set of column conditions. For example, if 'account type' is P and 'activity type' is W, then two actions follow: 'subtract from account' and 'add 1 to personal withdrawal'.

SOME ISSUES IN PROCESS DESCRIPTION

The two most important issues in process description in structured systems analysis are, first, when to abandon graphical modeling and begin scripting, and, second what scripting method should be used. Only guidelines can be provided here. One is to use graphical techniques as long as possible, as these tend to give a total picture of a system, but not to use them to extreme to describe detailed computations. Thus, as a guideline, any graphical object should be represented by a fairly substantial script, otherwise it is a graphical script.

SUMMARY

This chapter described methods used for process descriptions. It began by describing why precise process specifications are needed and continued by presenting some of the main description methods used in structured systems analysis.

The first method was structured English. This is a mixture of natural language prose and keywords used to define logic. Structured English thus endeavors to get the best of two worlds, program logic to define precision and natural language to get the convenience of the spoken word.

The chapter described another method that is often used to describe processes: decision tables. Decision tables are used where a large number of conditions must be tested to select one of many possible actions.

DISCUSSION QUESTIONS

10.1 Why is natural language not useful as a system-level specification?

10.2 What is the difference between scripts at the usage and system levels?

10.3 Would structured English be useful in describing informal interactions between people?

EXERCISES

10.1 Use structured English to describe the following system. The system receives a batch of transactions, each of which has a key value. The system examines each transaction in the batch and, depending on the type, does the following:

- For Type X transactions, the system stores the transaction as a Type X record but only if there is a Type Y record with the same key value. Otherwise the system writes out an error line. If there is a Type W record with the same key value as the Type X transaction, the Type W record is converted to a Type Z record.

- For Type Y transactions, the system stores the transaction as a record of Type Y in the main file.

- For Type Z transactions, the system stores the transaction Type Z record but only if there is a pair of Type X and Type Y records with the same key value as the Type Z transaction. If there is no such pair, then the Type Z transaction is stored as a Type W record but only if its date is before 1982. If none of these conditions hold, then an error line is output.

The system ensures that no two records of the same type have the same key value.

10.2 Develop a decision tree and a decision table for the following:

The gatekeeper at an amusement park is given the following instructions for admitting persons to the park:

- If the person is under three years of age, there is no admission fee.

- If a person is under 16, half the full admission is charged and this admission is reduced to a quarter of full admission if the person is accompanied by an adult (the reduction applies only if the person is under 12).

- Between 16 and 18, half the full admission fee is charged if the person is a student; otherwise the full admission is charged.

- Over 18, the full admission fee is charged.

- A discount of 10 percent is allowed for a person over 16 if they are in a group of 10 or more.

- There are no student concessions during weekends. On weekdays under-12s get one free ride.

10.3 Convert the DFD in Figure 10.8 into structured English. You should note that, dependent on transaction type, one or more of the four processes are applied to the transaction. Thus, for one transaction we need only determine the material, for another the personnel and computing cost, and for another still some other combination of processes. Do you feel that structured English is a better way of describing this process than the DFD in Figure 10.8? Alternatively, do you think there is a better way to represent the system in Figure 10.8?

10.4 An invoice clerk receives invoices from suppliers. Each invoice contains information on:

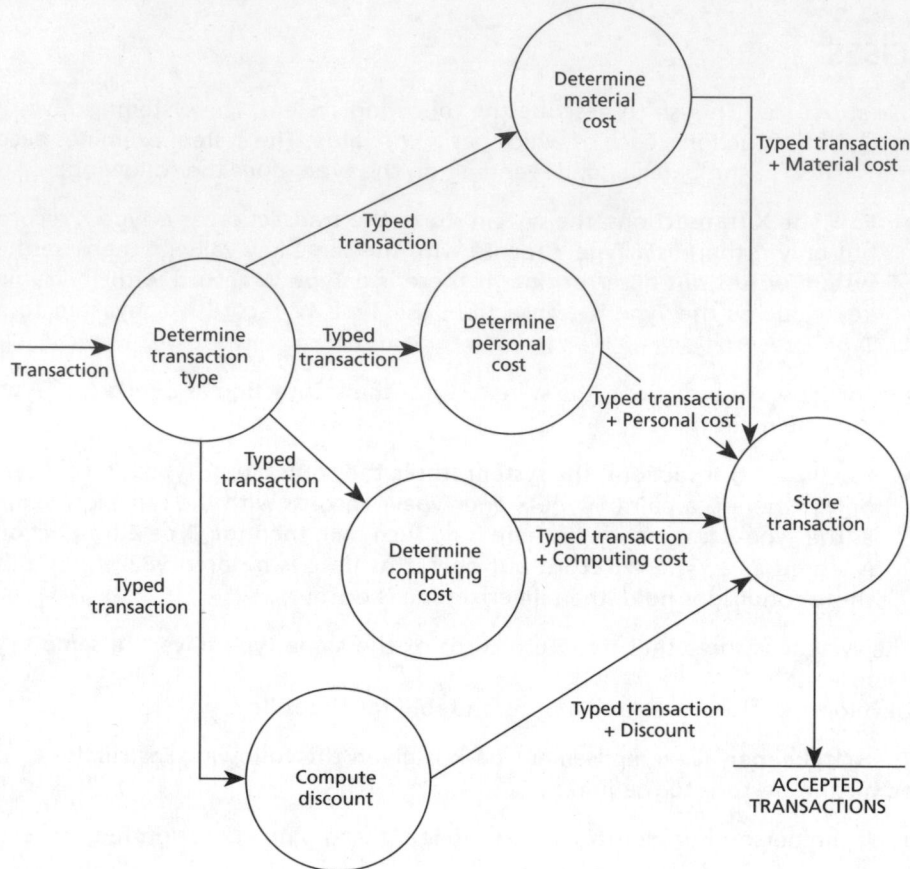

Figure 10.8 *Processing transactions*

- an order and supplier number;
- items delivered;
- quantity of each item delivered;
- price of each item; and
- total invoice amount.

The invoice clerk examines the invoice and compares it with both the order and a stock report. The stock report contains data on the goods received in the organization's store from various suppliers. This data includes the order number and the supplier who delivered the items.

If the items on the order, the invoice and the stock report match, then the invoice clerk checks the total invoice amount. If the amount is correct, the invoice clerk sends an authority to the accounts department to issue a check for the invoice. If the amount is incorrect, the invoice clerk adjusts the invoice and authorizes the accounts department to issue a check for the adjusted amount. At the same time, the invoice clerk prepares and dispatches a vendor memo advising of the adjustment.

If the items on the invoice do not match the stock report, but do match the order, the invoice clerk first checks the correctness of the report. If it is correct, the invoice clerk first makes an adjustment to the invoice amount, authorizes accounting to prepare a check for the adjusted amount, and prepares a vendor memo advising of the adjustment. At the same time, a stock memo is sent advising of further items to be received against the order and issuing a supplementary order number to both the store and the supplier.

1. Prepare a decision table to illustrate the activities of the invoice clerk as described above.

2. Is any further information required to completely describe all possible situations that the invoice clerk may meet? If not, what other information would you need to completely describe the activities of the invoice clerk?

BIBLIOGRAPHY

McDaniel, H. (1978), *An Introduction to Decision Logic Tables*, Perocelli Books, Princeton, New Jersey.

Pollack, S.L., Hick, H.T. Jr. and Harrison, W.F. (1971), *Decision Tables: Theory and Practice*, Wiley-Interscience, New York.

Schank, R.C. and Abelson, R.P. (1977), *Scripts, Plans, Goals and Understanding*, Lawrence Erlbaum Associates, Hillsdale, New Jersey.

Object modeling

CONTENTS

KEY LEARNING OBJECTIVES

The object-oriented paradigm
The important object characteristics
How to design objects
Object representations
Use cases
Methods used to model behavior

INTRODUCTION

This chapter and the following one describe the object-oriented (OO) approach to system development. The object-oriented approach differs from structured systems analysis and design because it provides a way of modeling that integrates data and processes. Thus, rather than modeling systems by data flows, E–R diagrams or process descriptions, all three components are integrated together into objects.

This chapter introduces the object-oriented approach and describes how systems can be represented at the system level. It outlines some of the characteristics of object structures—in particular, encapsulation of data and methods—and explains how these characteristics can be used to advantage in system development. The chapter then describes how object dynamics can be modeled. This is the objective of dynamic modeling. Modeling behavior is not just an activity in its own right, but must also be an integrated part of the development process and must lead to identification of methods.

 THE OBJECT ENVIRONMENT

Object modeling was recently introduced into system development. It emphasizes:

- combining processes, data and flows into the one modeling paradigm, thus allowing objects to be modeled as independent entities that can be flexibly combined into cooperating systems;
- easy conversion from analysis to design models, through the use of similar terms; and
- supporting multimedia information and not only record structures.

In object analysis it is not necessary to think in terms of building one large system. Instead, we identify objects as independent entities with their own local goals. Such objects can then exchange messages between themselves to achieve a global goal of the large system. This idea is illustrated by the simple client-server example shown in Figure 11.1. Here we have two objects—a client and a server. The data and processes are all **encapsulated** in each object. Processes are often called **methods**, which are implemented as programs within the object. Objects communicate with each other through messages. The client object can send a message that requests a service from the server object. A message activates a process, or method, in the receiving object.

Encapsulation
Inclusion of many features in the one object.

Methods
A feature that describes programs within an object.

Figure 11.1 *Objects*

Often the message has the same name as the method. The message causes the execution of the method program, which carries out any processing required by the message, and returns the response. A server object can provide a service like computing a statistical average or looking up a file. It is also possible to model other kinds of communication between objects, such as one object issuing a command (e.g. update a database) to another object. Some other characteristics of the OO approach are discussed below.

OBJECT ORIENTATION AND AUTONOMY

The encapsulation of data and processes means that objects can be designed independently of each other with, usually, only their interfaces specified. Interface specifications are made in terms of messages that can be accepted by each object. Using the same paradigm to represent these two features eliminates some of the disadvantages of storing data, process and flows separately. Thus the analyst need no longer maintain separate models for data and process but can include everything in one system model. It is not necessary, therefore, to develop and validate links between models based on these different techniques. It is also easier to change systems, as only one model has to be changed. Simplifying change is important, with the evolution toward systems that emphasize greater autonomy and coordination using the client-server concept.

Greater autonomy between objects increases the flexibility in building and changing systems. Thus we can model the system as a collection of independent components and allow these components to communicate with each other. Such autonomy results in models that are closer to the evolving structures that tend to favor the idea of independent and asynchronous objects cooperating with each other, often in a client-server relationship. For example, one object can represent a business process that calls on functional units for service. We can thus replace a server by another server without changing the client, or add another client that uses the same server.

OBJECT-ORIENTED IMPLEMENTATIONS

There is now a growing number of software products that support objects at the implementation level. Such systems are either languages or object-oriented database management systems. They provide another advantage for using the OO approach by making it possible to directly, or seamlessly, convert a system model to an implementation model. Implementation-level systems allow the system to be programmed as a set of objects, which must satisfy the structural rules supported by the implementation.

OBJECT ORIENTATION IN SYSTEM DEVELOPMENT

The existence of software systems that directly support objects offers a number of advantages for system development. First, it leads to an easy conversion of models to an implementation, as the same terms are used in the system and implementation models. This leads to the possibility of directly converting a model developed during analysis to an implementation.

It also supports another idea of system design. This is the idea of *reuse*. As objects are autonomous, they should be easily plugged together into systems. All we need to do is design objects in a way that makes them widely applicable to many problems in a problem domain. Reuse has a further property: it supports quick changes to functions or interactions between people.

In summary, we point out the difference between what is sometimes known as the *object-oriented model* and object-oriented programming systems. The OO paradigm implies a way of thinking. We see systems as collections of objects, each with some functional purpose but connected in some way to reach a common goal. We must then identify such objects and find ways of connecting them in order to reach that common purpose. This is not what we do with conventional analysis. In conventional analysis, we see the system itself as a set of functions, data and processes.

OBJECT STRUCTURE

Objects encapsulate all modeling components, including the data structure and the processes that operate on the data structure. Thus a simple kind of object would be like the one shown in Figure 11.2. This object includes only two kinds of features: properties and methods. It also shows that properties themselves can be of different kinds. One kind takes simple values, as for example PROJECT-NO, START-DATE and BUDGET, while another kind can be a reference to another object. Thus MANAGER in Figure 11.2 does not include a person name but is a reference to the object that represents the project manager. Another example of a reference is PEOPLE-ASSIGNED, where the N indicates that this property can contain a number of references rather than one reference. TASKS is another kind of property that defines objects included in projects. These objects, like dependent entities, cannot exist on their own. The term *composite* is sometimes used to indicate that one object, in this case PROJECTS, contains other objects. So far this is similar to an entity set. Thus PROJECT-NO, START-DATE and BUDGET can be seen as entity attributes.

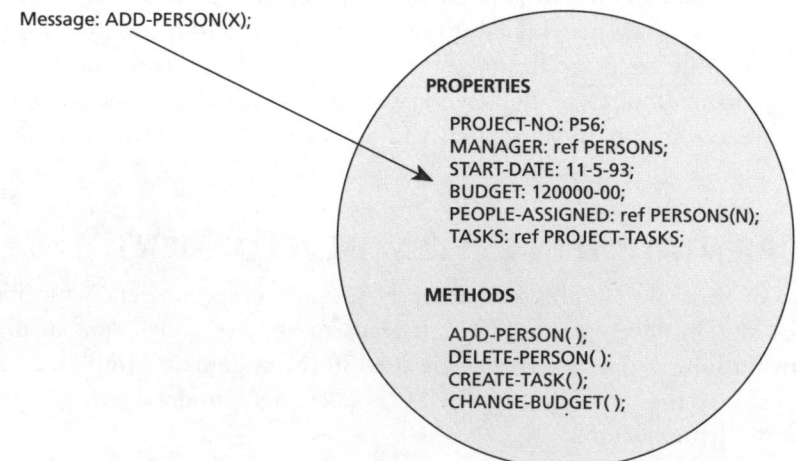

Figure 11.2 *An object with encapsulated data and methods*

MANAGER and PEOPLE-ASSIGNED can be seen as relationships, and TASKS as dependent entities. There is, however, one important difference from E–R modeling: the object also contains methods. The methods shown in Figure 11.2 are ADD-PERSON, DELETE-PERSON, CREATE-TASK and CHANGE-BUDGET. These methods are activated by messages outside the object and can change object properties. Thus an ADD-PERSON message would add another reference

Methods are programs that can change property values. The object interfaces to its environment through messages, where each message activates a method within the object. Thus, in Figure 11.2 the message 'add-person' would activate method ADD-PERSON, which would add a new person, X, to the project. Thus both the properties and programs are encapsulated in the one object.

OBJECT FEATURES

We often talk about objects as having **features**. Objects in an object **class** can have other features in addition to properties and methods. OO modeling does not have a standard set of features, and objects can have as many different features as we like. Thus we can have features such as:

- object states that can initiate methods;
- constraints maintained between object properties;
- checks on pre- and post-conditions to be satisfied on messages and replies; and
- triggers that activate messages for given data conditions.

The question is to select those features that allow autonomous objects to be modeled in the most natural yet simple way. There is no agreement on what these features should be, although there is recognition that properties and methods must be included in any model. Each programming language or implementation, however, will support only some of the features.

CLASSES AND OBJECTS

Another interesting characteristic of object modeling is that it is also possible to represent an *object class* as an object, as well as individual objects or *object instances* of that class. Thus we can have an object class, PROJECTS, and each project is an instance of that class. It is possible in an implementation to store the class, PROJECTS, as a separate object. Individual projects become **instances** of the class, much the same as entities were instances in entity sets. Each project instance is stored as a separate object. Object methods are often stored once in the class object rather than being duplicated in each instance of that class. Thus all object instances inherit their methods from their class object.

REPRESENTATION

Another important issue is the method used to represent object models. There is no standard representation and a number of representations have been proposed. All of these representations use notations that include both the object structure and its methods. The usual approach is a graphical one that illustrates the major features of objects, as well as connections between objects. However, object feature details may be specified in a more algorithmic way. An example of a graphical notation is shown in Figure 11.3, where we represent an object as a square box with subdivisions for each of the object features. Two subdivisions in Figure 11.3 describe the properties and methods. Figure 11.3 also illustrates another feature—namely, constraints. This places a limit on the number of people in a project.

Note that this notation is used here for the purpose of illustration and is not in any way a standard notation. There is at this stage no standard notation for the OO model, although all methods proposed use a notation similar to that in Figure 11.3. Many have additional notations to describe object components.

Note, also, that a system can be made up of a large number of objects. Thus, although objects can be developed independently of other objects, they also have a relationship to other objects. One such relationship is to use a link directly from one object to another. Thus MANAGER in PROJECT in Figure 11.3 represents such a link. Another important relationship is where we compose objects from other objects. Thus in Figure 11.3 the PROJECT object contains a number of TASKS objects. We now show how such relationships can be illustrated using our notation.

ASSOCIATIONS AND CONTAINMENT

An object model is usually made up of many objects related to each other. Such relationships are shown by references between the objects. A reference to an object is usually made through an object **property**. Some such properties were shown in Figure 11.3, and Figure 11.4 shows associations from projects to managers and persons assigned to the project. Thus, for example, there is a link from MANAGER to that object instance that represents the project's manager. There are also links to the persons who work on the project and the tasks that make up the project. It also shows that a PROJECT contains a number of tasks.

Properties
A feature that describes values stored within an object.

```
┌─────────────────────────────────┐
│            PROJECT              │
├─────────────────────────────────┤
│ PROJECT-NO: P56;                │
│ MANAGER: ref PERSONS;           │
│ START-DATE: 11-5-93;            │
│ BUDGET: 120000-00;              │
│ PEOPLE-ASSIGNED: ref PERSONS(N);│
│ TASKS: PROJECT-TASKS(N);        │
├─────────────────────────────────┤
│ Add-person( );                  │
│ Delete-person( );               │
│ Change-budget( );               │
│ Create-task( );                 │
├─────────────────────────────────┤
│ ensure                          │
│    number (PEOPLE-ASSIGNED) < 50│
└─────────────────────────────────┘
```

Figure 11.3 *A notation for object modeling*

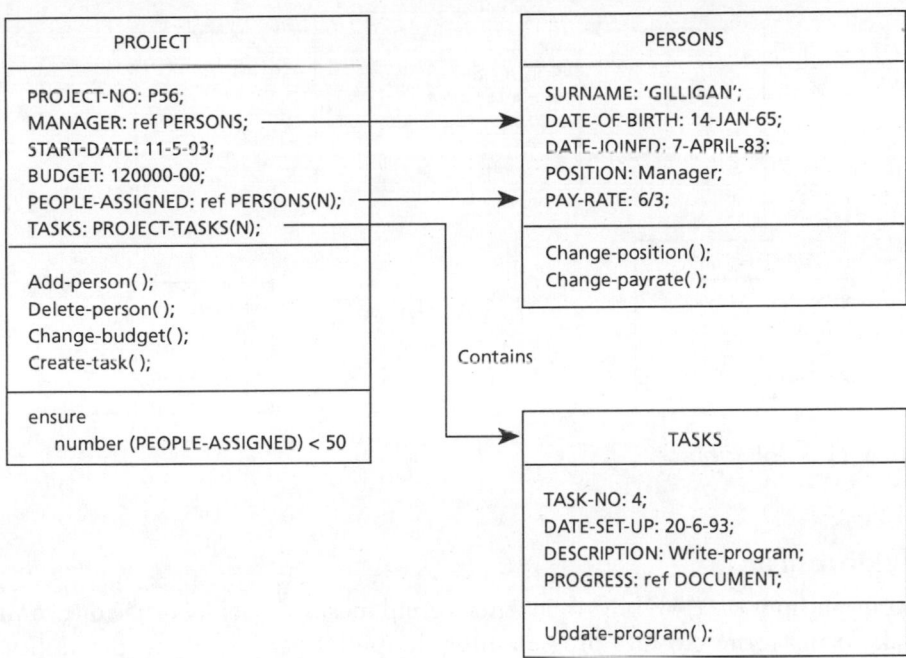

Figure 11.4 *Object relationships*

INHERITANCE

Inheritance is very similar to the idea of subsets in E–R models. An object can inherit features from another object. It can also have some additional features or, if needed, replace some of the object features. Figure 11.5 illustrates a very simple inheritance structure. It shows that there can be two different kinds of OFFERS, one based on individual items and the other on item quantities. Both these kinds of offers inherit the features of OFFERS and also have additional properties and methods. For example, both ITEM-OFFERS and VOLUME-OFFERS will have the properties PRODUCER and TIME-AVAILABLE. ITEM-OFFERS also has the additional properties QUANTITY and PRICE/ITEM, whereas VOLUME-OFFERS has the properties WEIGHT and PRICE/KG. Similarly, they each have the additional method, 'compute-value', although the computation used by 'compute-value' will be different in both cases. It will multiply QUANTITY by PRICE/ITEM in one case and WEIGHT by PRICE/KG in the other.

The term **specialization** often comes up when discussing inheritance. We can say that ITEM-OFFERS and VOLUME are a specialization of OFFERS. They inherit all the features of OFFERS but are also specialized with additional features.

Inheritance is important because it gives designers the ability to specialize objects while at the same time not requiring a change to calling messages. We may, for example, decide to provide yet another kind of offer, say, a FIXED-PRICE. This could be added as yet another specialized object of OFFERS.

Inheritance
Using the same features as another object.

Specialization
Taking on features in addition to those inherited from another object.

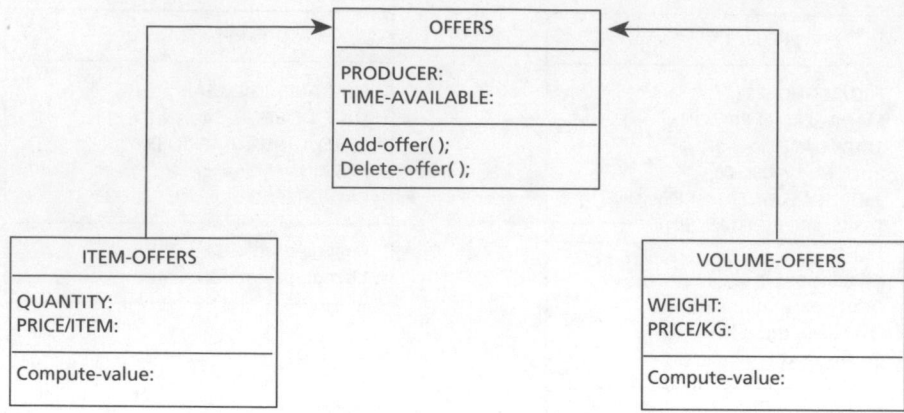

Figure 11.5 *Inheritance*

Polymorphism

Polymorphism
Selecting the method
appropriate for the
class of object called.

Polymorphism is closely related to inheritance and means the ability of the one construct to take many forms. In OO programming, it applies particularly to the ability of a message to change its effect depending on the instance of object called. Thus a message 'compute-value' addressed to OFFERS will select the appropriate method depending on the type of offer being considered. Furthermore, adding a new specialized object with a new specification of 'compute-value' will mean that the message 'compute-value' will select that method if addressed to an instance of the new class.

MULTIPLE INHERITANCE

The subject of inheritance is crucial to object orientation. What we have shown so far is objects inheriting their properties from only one other object. It is also possible to have structures where an object inherits properties from more than one other object. This is generally known as *multiple inheritance*.

Figure 11.6 is an example of multiple inheritance. Here we make SALES, some of which are over-the-counter sales whereas others require delivery to the buyer. These two kinds of sales are modeled as specialization of SALES. They have all the features of SALES, as well as additional features. Thus LOCAL-SALES has a receipt, as receipts are issued at the time of sale. DISTANT-SALES inherit the properties of SALES as well as properties of another object, called DELIVERIES, because every distant sale results in a delivery. A DISTANT-SALE is a union of all the properties of SALES and DELIVERIES. It inherits properties concerned with selling from SALES and properties of delivering from DELIVERIES. Thus processes such as making a transportation arrangement come from DELIVERIES, whereas arranging a sale comes from SALES.

DISTANT-SALES thus illustrates the idea of multiple inheritance—that is, inheritance of features from more than one object. It would, of course, be possible to include the properties and methods concerned with transportation in DISTANT-SALES. However, DELIVERIES is modeled as a separate object because there is more

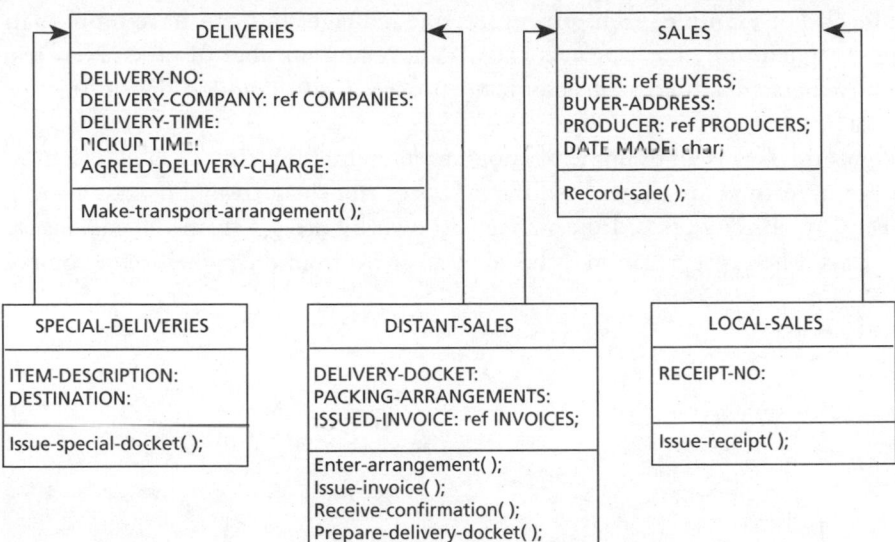

Figure 11.6 *Multiple inheritance*

than one kind of delivery in the system. It is also possible to arrange deliveries of special items that are not part of the sales system but which use the same process as deliveries made through the sales system. Hence, all features common to delivery of both of these kinds of deliveries are abstracted into the object class, DELIVERIES.

Multiple inheritance introduces a problem when both of the parents have a feature with the same name. The question is which of these two features to inherit.

OBJECT REPRESENTATION METHODS

There are a number of methodologies now used in practice that apply their own representation methods. These methods differ in a number of ways. For example, the actual graphical notation can differ in the way it represents object features, links and inheritance, as well as participation and cardinality. Also, different notations are used at different development phases. The representation method we have used so far is that used in the analysis to represent the system. It closely approximates that used by Coad and Yourdon (1990) to represent object features, but not the links between objects. At the analysis level, most of the other representations have a similar set of components but may have a different notation. Grady Booch (1994), for example, describes a notation like that shown in Figure 11.7(a). Here object classes are represented by cloud-shaped objects, with attributes and methods listed in the object. The method is distinguished by the fact that it has a set of parentheses to represent methods.

Associations between objects are shown by lines. There are four kinds of associations. For example, a 'managed-by' association may exist between projects and persons. There is also a 'has' association—as, for example, a project has many tasks. This is shown by a line with a solid dot. An inheritance association is shown by an arrow, and a using association is shown by a line with an empty dot. Cardinality is also shown on the lines, using a notation similar to that described for E–R diagrams in

Chapter 9. For example, each project has one manager but can have more than one person assigned to it. Each project can also have any number of tasks. New features and constructs are added as development proceeds into detailed design (for details, see Booch, 1994).

Figure 11.7(b) is an example of another representation, that of Henderson-Sellers. Here again, features are shown in different boxes and the arrows show the associations between the object classes. Inheritance is shown by arrows from the subclass to the owner class, whereas aggregation is shown by an arrow from the owner to the component.

(a) Grady Booch

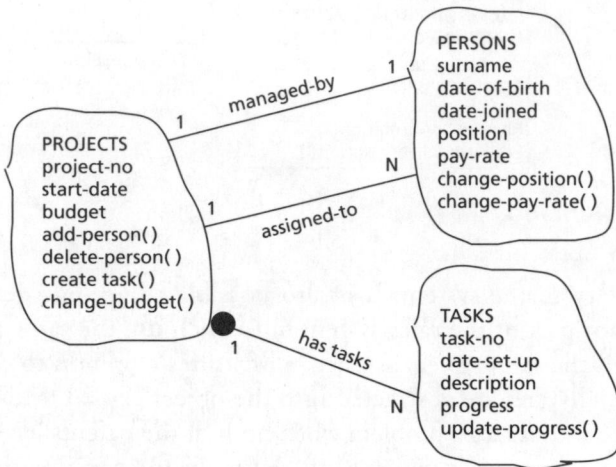

(b) Henderson-Sellers

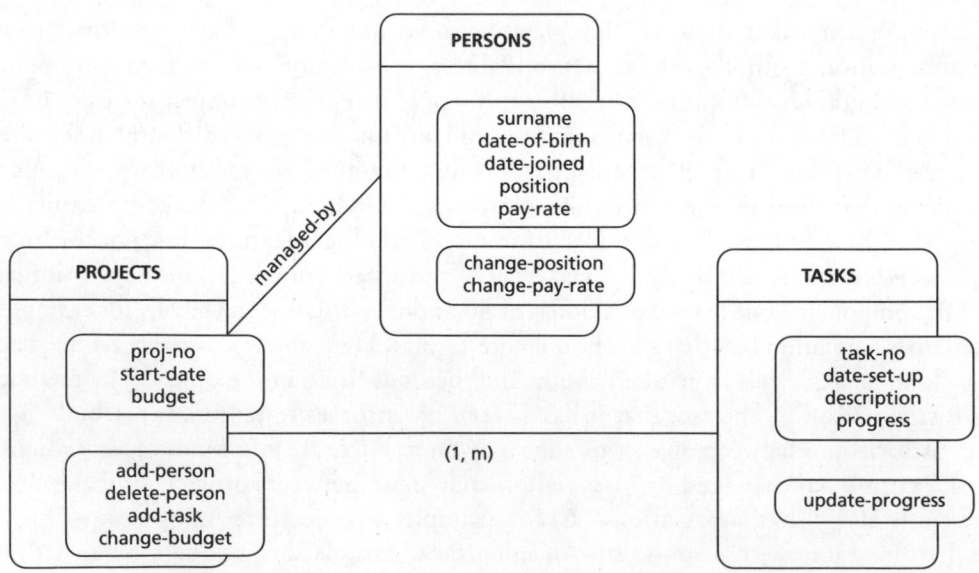

Figure 11.7 *Representation methods*

(c) Jacobson

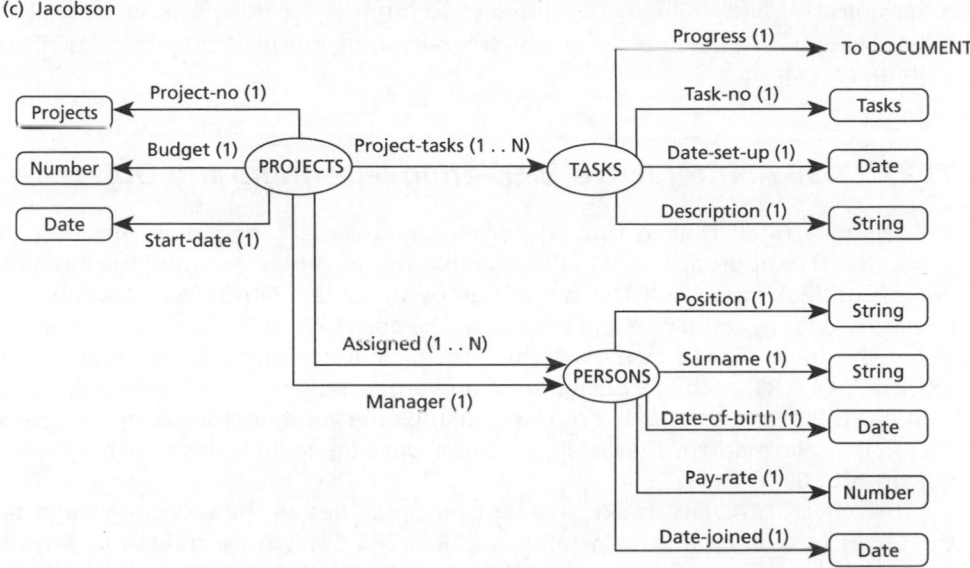

Figure 11.7 *(Continued)*

Yet another representation is that by Jacobson shown in Figure 11.7(c). This representation method concentrates on the objects without their methods. It shows the links between the classes and the class attribute types. Thus in Figure 11.7(c), the attribute 'Budget' is of type Number and there is only one value of budget for each project. Links to objects also show cardinality. For example, there is one manager for each project but any number of persons assigned to the project. Methods for the objects are derived from use cases, which are described later.

DEFINING OBJECTS

During analysis, one of the most important activities is to identify object classes and the components of each object. There are different ways of doing this. One of the first ways was to start with an existing method, such as an E–R model, and add additional features to it. New modeling methods are being developed for designing objects.

EXTENDING THE E–R MODEL

One of the simplest ways use to the OO approach is to start with an E–R model. This approach was widely used when object orientation was first introduced. It begins by representing each entity as an object. Entity and relationship attributes become object properties. However, we can go one step further and add methods, or what some people call services, to each entity and relationship object. These methods can update particular object properties or define the local behavior of objects. They can also be computations that the object can do for other objects.

The next step is to define global behavior, or how objects interact with each other. This is much the same as defining a business process object that uses the services of other objects. Methodologies use different techniques for this purpose.

We now provide an example of an object model using our marketing case described initially in Chapter 1.

TEXT CASE A: Interactive Marketing—Defining the Objects

Readers may recall that in this case producers are marketing their products to consumers. The approach used in this example was to center it around the business process of 'Making a Sale'. This is modeled by the object TRADERS to provide the services needed by consumers and producers. The object PRODUCTS keeps information about the items traded in the system. Each product can include any number of PRODUCT-OFFERS, each offer being from one producer, giving QTY-AVAILABLE and an ASKING-PRICE. It also keeps a record of all the offers of items for sale by producers and all the sales made by the system. An initial object model for this system is shown in Figure 11.8.

The object 'TRADERS' is like an agent that provides all the services needed by the buyer to arrange a sale. Instances of TRADERS objects are created by buyers whenever they wish to initiate a purchase. The BUYER states the required product and quantity through the method 'initiate-trade'. The TRADERS object will request

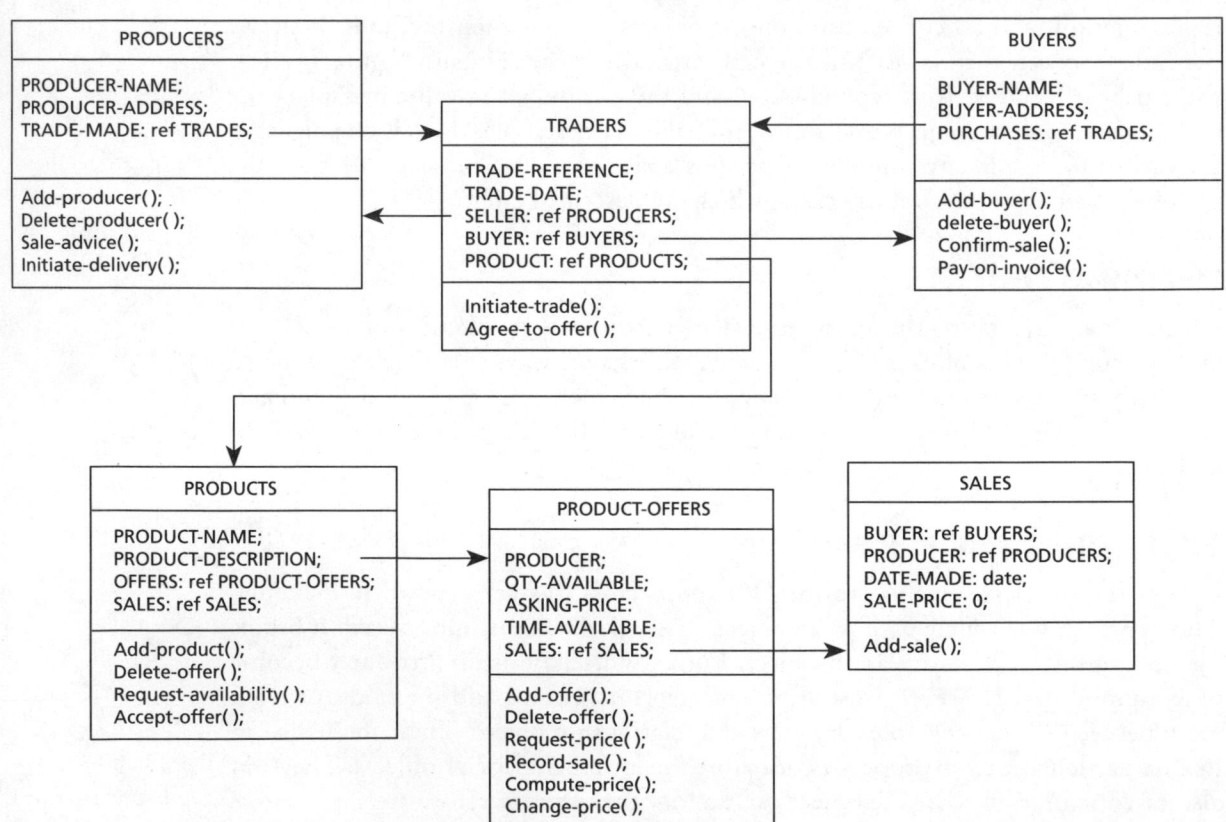

Figure 11.8 *Object diagram for interactive marketing*

all PRODUCT-OFFERS for that product and present them to the buyer. The BUYER then examines these offers to find one that is acceptable and, if so, instructs the TRADES object to complete the sale through method 'agree-to-offer'. The TRADERS object provides the necessary services for arranging a trade.

The object TRADERS can easily be extended to manage additional services for producers and consumers. For example, we can eventually add an object TRANSPORT that has a record of possible means for arranging the delivery of sold parts.

The methods in the objects support the interactive trading. These include:

Method 'initiate-trade' receives a request from a buyer. It sends a message 'request-availability' to PRODUCTS, which returns the relevant offers and their prices to TRADERS, who then passes them on as an answer to the buyer.

Method 'request-price' searches PRODUCT-OFFERS asking them to 'compute-price' for the requested item. It returns the volumes and prices to TRADERS.

Method 'accept-offer' from TRADERS to PRODUCTS requests PRODUCTS to complete the purchase following acceptance of a quote. This method initiates 'record-sale' in PRODUCT-OFFERS to record the sale by creating a SALES object.

Other solutions would also be possible here. For example, instead of TRADES managing all sales, we could design a system where BUYERS objects send messages to PRODUCERS objects. In this case, each PRODUCER object manages its own OFFERS and SALES. TRADES can also be extended later to arrange transportation of purchased items.

In our example, we used the idea of TRADES as representing a business process that primarily serves the BUYER. Using the idea of an object that represents a business process is only one approach to modeling systems. Of course, there are other ways of modeling. We could model the systems as BUYERS directly communicating with PRODUCERS, who could then use PRODUCTS as a server object to make offers to the buyer. Thus, having an independent set of objects provides many options for combining them into systems and does not guarantee that any option is better than another. There are as yet few guidelines on how one can combine objects into systems and guarantee correct operation; this is still an area of research.

MODELING BEHAVIOR IN OBJECT MODELING

Another way to build object models is to start with behaviour. Representations of behaviour must cover all the levels used in design, going from the usage world to the subject and system worlds. The most common way used to describe behavior in the usage world is through use cases.

USE CASES

Use cases were introduced into object analysis by Jacobson (1992) as a means of communication with users. They are scripts that describe typical ways that a system is or will be used. A use case is general in the sense that it does not describe instances of how a system is used, but generalizes a number of instances into a general script.

Use case
A description of work in usage world terms.

In developing a use case, we identify the main actors or roles in the system and then describe the way they use or interact with the system, or their behavior in the system. Use case identification usually begins by looking at particular examples, sometimes called scenarios, of how these actors carry out their activities. We then use these scenarios to identify the usual way in which these actors carry out their activities. Some common alternatives are also outlined. For example, a scenario in the interactive marketing case could be: 'the seller, Mary, usually counts the number of items available for sale, computes their prices and then begins to advertise them through the interactive system.' Of course, if one tried to specify the system in this way, one would finish with a huge number of such scenarios. What use cases do is try to generalize such scenarios into use case classes, where each use case class covers what might be called a large number of typical scenarios. An example of a use case class is given in Figure 11.9. The figure shows the usual procedure followed to make a sale and arrange. It also describes an alternative to this usual way.

A system is usually described by a number of use cases, which together become the use case model.

OBJECT STATES

Object states are commonly used at both the subject and system levels. They were earlier used in E–R modeling but are now also commonly used in object modeling. They describe how objects and entities change as a system evolves. For example, an order for a part may be placed and approved, the part ordered and, finally, the payment made and the application completed. It is common to refer to the way the order progresses by its state. For example, the statement that 'the order has been initiated' implies that it is in the 'initiated' state. The statement that 'the order has been approved'

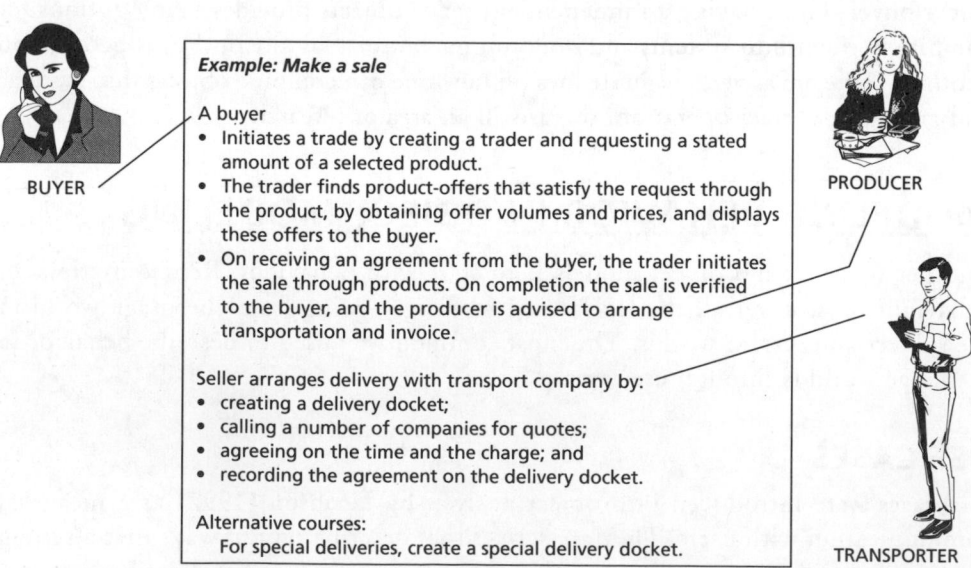

Figure 11.9 *A use case*

implies that it is in the 'approved' state, and so on. The earliest forms of **state diagrams** were entity life histories.

State diagram
A diagram showing
how objects evolve.

STATE DIAGRAMS

State diagrams tell us what happens to objects in the system. Each object in the system goes through a number of states. An application object may be received, in which case it becomes a 'received' application. It may then be checked, following which it becomes a 'checked' application. Next, the application may be approved, in which case it becomes an 'approved' application.

The application thus passes through a number of *states*—that is, the 'received application' state, the 'checked application' state, the 'approved application' state and, finally, the 'accepted application' state. An application moves from state to state during its life in the system. The movement of an application from state to state is called a *state transition*. The object states, and the transitions between them, are represented by a state transition diagram. Each state is represented by a circle, and the transitions between the states are represented by lines between the states. The state name is placed inside the circle and the transition name is placed on the transition between circles.

Figure 11.10 is an example of a state transition diagram. It shows several states of an application passing through the system. You will find that some circles in the state transition diagram have a double circumference. The three shown in Figure 11.10 are 'rejected application', 'refused application', and 'paid off loan'. Objects that enter these states are no longer of interest in the system.

Transition names are usually names of processes that cause the transition. They can also be the outcome of a process, or a combination of the process and the outcome of the process. Thus the 'check application' process causes a transition from the 'received application' state to the 'checked application' state. The checked application usually goes to the process normally called 'approve application'. The transitions from the 'checked application' state are labeled by the outcome of the process—namely, 'accept application' or 'reject application'. Rejected applications go into the 'rejected application' state and are of no further interest to the system. Approved applications can be taken up by applicants and become 'accepted applications'. If applicants change their mind and no longer wish to proceed, then the application enters the 'refused application' state and is of no further interest to the system.

The state transition diagram in Figure 11.10 illustrates some other characteristics of object state modeling. There are activities which operate on an object but do not cause a change of state. Two such transitions are illustrated in the figure, and both apply to the 'accepted application' state. One is a transition that looks up something about an object. This is labeled by the enquiry name—in this case, 'look up balance'. There are also transitions that change object attribute values. Thus the 'make payment' transition may alter the amount owing on a loan, but the object state remains the same.

State transition diagrams are useful later in design because they indicate system transactions. Each transition in the diagram becomes a transaction which operates on the entity. State transition diagrams are also used to verify DFDs. We may find a transition that does not appear as a process in the DFD. We would then return to the DFD and add the process to it.

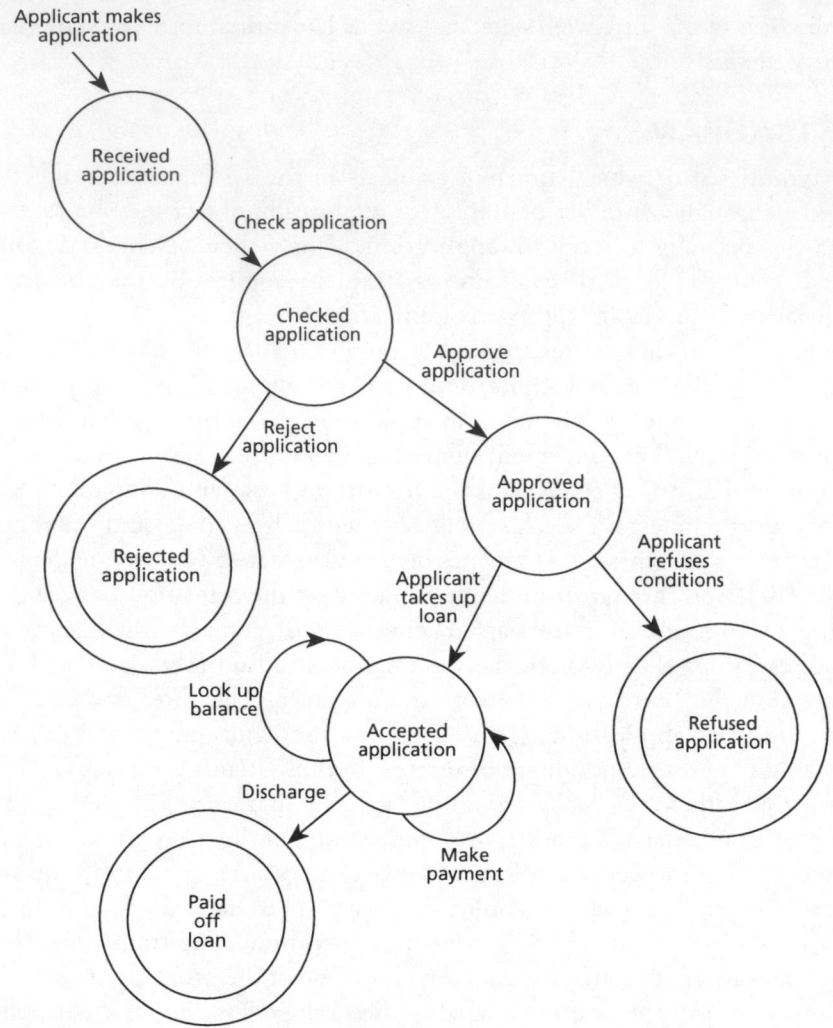

Figure 11.10 *A state transition diagram*

EVENT TRACE DIAGRAMS

Event trace diagram
A diagram showing dynamic relationships between objects.

Event trace diagrams, also known as scenario diagrams, or interaction diagrams, form a powerful tool when combined with Jacobson's use cases. A use case usually follows a set of steps that define actions by objects. Each step involves one object passing information to another object. As an example, consider the following scenario when making a purchase in the interactive marketing system.

The potential buyer initiates a request for one or more products, stating the required volumes and delivery times. This creates a trader to manage the request. The trader will enquire whether the requested products are available in the required quantities and at the preferred prices. It will assemble this information and return a range of options to the buyer. The buyer may then accept one of the options. The trader will then initiate the purchase of goods specified by the option, and verify the completion of the purchase to the buyer. Information about available goods is maintained as a product list, which contains all the offers made by producers. A request for availability must examine the offers available under a product listing.

The event trace diagram for this scenario is shown in Figure 11.11. Here the main objects in the scenario are shown by the vertical lines labeled 'Buyer', 'Trader', 'Products' and 'Product-offers'. The horizontal lines between the vertical lines define *events* in the use case. These events usually result in the exchange of information between these objects. These lines closely follow the sequence portrayed by the use case. Thus the first line from the buyer to the trader shows the initiation of trade. This is followed by a line labeled 'Request availability' from the trader to products. Products then looks at offers to obtain volume and price. These are returned to the buyer through the trader through 'Display offers'. The next line emanating from the buyer is 'Agree to offer'. This initiates an 'Accept offer' from the trader to products. Once the trade is completed, a confirmation is sent to the buyer and a 'sale-advice' to the producer to arrange transport. Of course, a complete event trace diagram would also contain all the error conditions, as well as the possibility of rejecting offers or buyers making counter proposals to the offers.

THE EVENT FLOW DIAGRAM

There will be as many event trace diagrams as there are use cases. The same object can also appear in a number of different use cases. The **event flow diagram** groups all the flows in and out of objects in different event trace diagrams into the one diagram. This diagram can then be used to identify the methods to be included in the object. Figure 11.12 shows the event flow diagram derived from the event trace diagram shown in Figure 11.11. It shows objects as rectangular boxes, with all the events from all the event trace diagrams grouped by input and output.

Event flow diagram
A diagram that shows the sequence of information flows between objects.

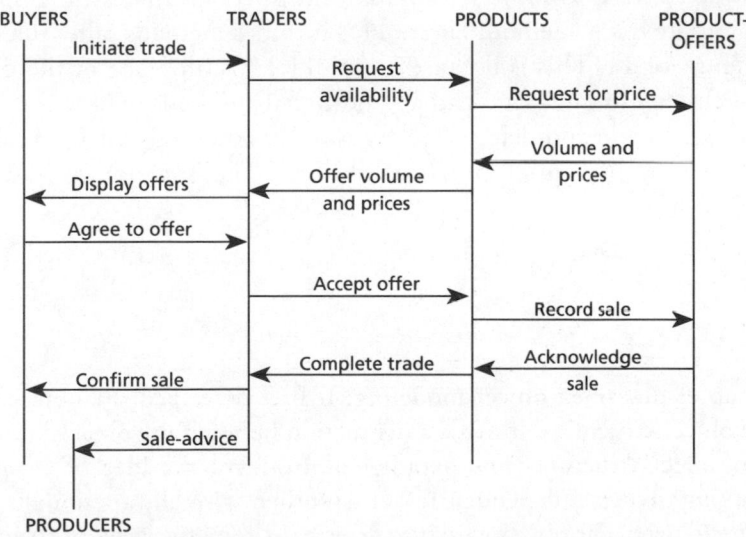

Figure 11.11 *Event trace diagram*

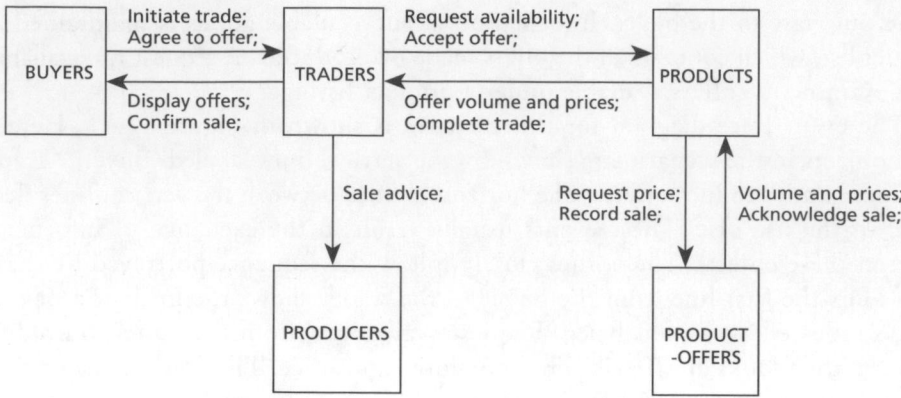

Figure 11.12 *Event flow diagram*

Figure 11.12 includes only those events shown in Figure 11.11. However, other events from other use cases could be added to this diagram, which could then be used to identify the object classes and their methods resulting in the model shown in Figure 11.8. Each object becomes an object class and each incoming event must have a matching method. The event can thus be seen as an incoming message that needs a method to process it. Thus Figure 11.8 includes a method to process each of the incoming events. For example, TRADERS has methods 'Initiate trade' and 'agree-to-offer' to process messages from BUYERS. The object PRODUCERS has a method 'sale advice' that is activated by a message from TRADERS whenever a sale is made. Some of the events on the event flow diagram are responses to messages and need not have their own method. For example, an 'initiate trade' method in TRADERS can send a 'request availability' message to PRODUCTS. PRODUCTS responds with 'offer volume and prices' to TRADERS. There is no corresponding method in TRADERS for 'offer volume and prices' as this is the response expected by the 'initiate trade' method. Figure 11.8 includes methods other than those derived from Figure 11.11. This is because Figure 11.11 is only one of the use cases in the system. Other use cases can lead to additional methods. Thus, for example, there are methods to add and delete objects, as well as methods for internal computation such as compute-price in PRODUCT-OFFERS. These are not shown in Figure 11.12 for clarity.

◥ SUMMARY

This chapter described object modeling. It first described the object paradigm and defined object structures. It made a distinction between the object-oriented paradigm and the object structure. The paradigm introduces the idea of encapsulation and constructing objects independently of each other, with all functionality encapsulated within the object. The object structure describes alternative ways of structuring objects. Each programming language can support a different kind of structure.

The chapter then covered some ways of developing analysis objects, starting with use cases and reducing them to object classes through event flow and event trace diagrams.

DISCUSSION QUESTIONS

11.1 What do you understand by the term *object-oriented paradigm* as compared to *object-oriented languages*?

11.2 What are the advantages of combining all modeling components into one object?

11.3 What are some common object features?

11.4 Describe what you understand by inheritance.

11.5 What is multiple inheritance?

11.6 What is the difference between a use case and a scenario?

11.7 What are the important components of a use case?

EXERCISE

11.1 One way to develop an object is to start with data and identify the main data objects as was the case with E–R modeling. Repeat Exercises 9.5, 9.6, 9.8 and 9.9 in Chapter 9 to construct object class diagrams showing any relationships between object classes.

11.2 Another way is to start with use cases and reduce them to class diagrams using event flow and event trace diagrams. Use this method to develop a class diagram for Case 4.

11.3 Extend the model in Figure 11.8 by including objects that model transport arrangements. It is assumed that there are a number of transportation companies that are regularly hired to pick up products from producers and deliver them to buyers. Each delivery has a stated delivery and pick-up time and a fixed price.

BIBLIOGRAPHY

Bancillon, F. et al. (1988), 'The design and implementation of O2, an object oriented database system', in Dittrich (ed.), *Proceedings of the Second International Workshop on Object Oriented Database Systems*, Springer-Verlag, Berlin.

Banerjee, J., Chou, H.-T., Garza, J.F., Kim, W., Woelk, D., Ballou, N. and Kim, H. J. (January 1987), 'Data model issues for object oriented applications', *Transactions of Office Information Systems*, Vol. 5, No. 1, pp. 3–26.

Booch, G. (1994), *Object Oriented Analysis and Design with Applications* (2nd ed), Addison-Wesley, Menlo Park, California.

Coad, P. and Yourdon, E. (1990), *Object-Oriented Analysis* (3rd edn), Yourdon Press, Englewood Cliffs, New Jersey.

Coplien, J.O. and Schmidt, D.C. (eds) (1995), *Pattern Languages of Program Design*, Addison-Wesley, Reading, Massachusetts.

Fishman, D.H., Beech, D., Cate, H.P., Chow, E.C., Connors, T., Davis, J.W., Derrett, N., Hoch, C.G., Kent, W., Lyngbaek, P., Mahbod, B., Neimat, M.A., Ryan, T.A. and Shan, M.C. (January 1987), 'Iris: an object-oriented database management system', *Transactions of Office Information Systems*, Vol. 5, No. 1, pp. 48–69.

Gibbs, S., Tsichritzis, D., Casais, E., Nierstrasz, O. and Pintado, X. (September 1990), 'Class management for software communities', *Communications of the ACM*, Vol. 33, No. 9, pp. 90–103.

Glassey, C.R. and Adiga, S. (November/December 1990), 'Conceptual design of a software object library for simulation of semiconductor manufacturing systems', *Journal of Object Oriented Programming*, pp. 39–43.

Henderson-Sellers, B. and Edwards, J. (September 1990), 'The object oriented systems life cycle', *Communications of the ACM*, Vol. 33, No. 9, pp. 142–59.

Jacobson, I. (1992), 'Basic use-case modeling', *ROAD*, Vol. 1, No. 2, pp. 15–19 and Vol. 1, No. 3, pp. 7–9.

Jacobson, I., Christerson, P.J. and Overgaard, G. (1992), *Object-Oriented Software Engineering*, Addison-Wesley, Reading Massachusetts.

Kim, W. and Lochovsky, F. (eds) (1989), *Object Oriented Concepts, Databases, and Applications*, ACM Press, Addison-Wesley, New York.

McGregor, J.D. and Korson, T. (eds) (September 1990), *Communications of the ACM, Special Issue on Object-Oriented Design*, Vol. 33, No. 9.

Meyer, B. (1988), *Object-Oriented Software Construction*, Prentice-Hall, New York.

Prieto-Diaz, R. (May 1991), 'Implementation faceted classification for software reuse' *Communications of the ACM*, Vol. 34, No. 5, pp. 88–97.

Psankake, C.M. (October 1995), 'The promise and the cost of object technology: A Five-Year Forecast', *Communications of the ACM*, pp. 32–49.

Rumbaugh, J., Blaha, M., Premerlani, W., Eddy, F. and Lorensen, W. (1991), *Object-Oriented Modeling and Design*, Prentice-Hall, Englewood-Cliffs, New Jersey.

Schmidt, D.C. (October 1995), 'Using design patterns to develop reusable object-oriented communications software', *Communications of the ACM*, Vol. 38, No. 11, pp. 65–74.

Tomlinson, C., Scheevel, M. and Kim, W. (November/December 1989), 'Sharing and organizational protocols in object-oriented systems', *Journal of Object Oriented Programming*, pp. 25–36.

Weiberg, R., Guimares, T. and Heath, R. (Fall 1990), 'Object oriented systems development', *Journal of Information Systems Management*, Vol. 7, No. 4, pp. 18–26.

Object
development
methods

12

CONTENTS

KEY LEARNING OBJECTIVES

Object modeling methodologies
Unified methods
Object libraries and reuse
Subject world analysis
Synthesis

◇ INTRODUCTION

The previous chapter introduced the object-oriented approach and described object models of data and behavior. This chapter describes how these models can be used in design methodologies based on the OO approach. Discussion on methodologies must distinguish between the modeling representations used, the techniques used to convert from a model at one development phrase to a model at the next stage, and the design processes. To elaborate on this distinction it is necessary to return to Chapter 7, which described the development process. It identified the development phases and the models produced at the completion of each phase. These models use a representation to describe the system. The techniques are then used to convert from models at one phase to those at another. The design process describes the steps followed in the conversion. These same distinctions apply to object modeling, which must also follow a development process. The chapter describes some representations and techniques used at different life-cycle phases.

◇ OBJECT MODELING IN THE DEVELOPMENT PROCESS

Just like structured systems analysis, OO approaches must follow a development cycle. Many of the early object modeling methods concentrated on the data representations and usually applied to only a subset of the development process. Thus, for example, Coad and Yourdon (1990) concentrated on using objects to develop analysis models, whereas Booch (1993) primarily concentrated on the design model. A methodology requires models at each development phase with techniques to convert models developed at one phase to those at the next phase.

OBJECT MODELING AND THE LINEAR CYCLE

Figure 12.1 illustrates the most common approach now used to integrate OO design with the development process. It shows the four major phases from Figure 7.4. It is assumed that the concept formation phase is similar to any other methodology and that object methods begin to be used at the system requirements definition phase. During this phase, object methods are used to create a requirements model that is often a collection of a number of use cases, together with an analysis model which describes the system in terms of object classes and is very similar to that shown in Figure 11.8. A design model is then developed during the system design phase. It is made up of object classes, which can be implemented using OO languages.

There are, of course, other techniques that can be used at each of the development phases. For example, rather than using an OO implementation model, conventional systems, including relational databases, can be used in the implementation. Conversions to such implementation models are described in Chapter 16.

Object oriented methodologies can be compared by the models and notations that they use, where these models are applied in the development process, and by techniques they use to convert models at one phase to those at another. The next few sections of this chapter describe a number of methodologies using this framework.

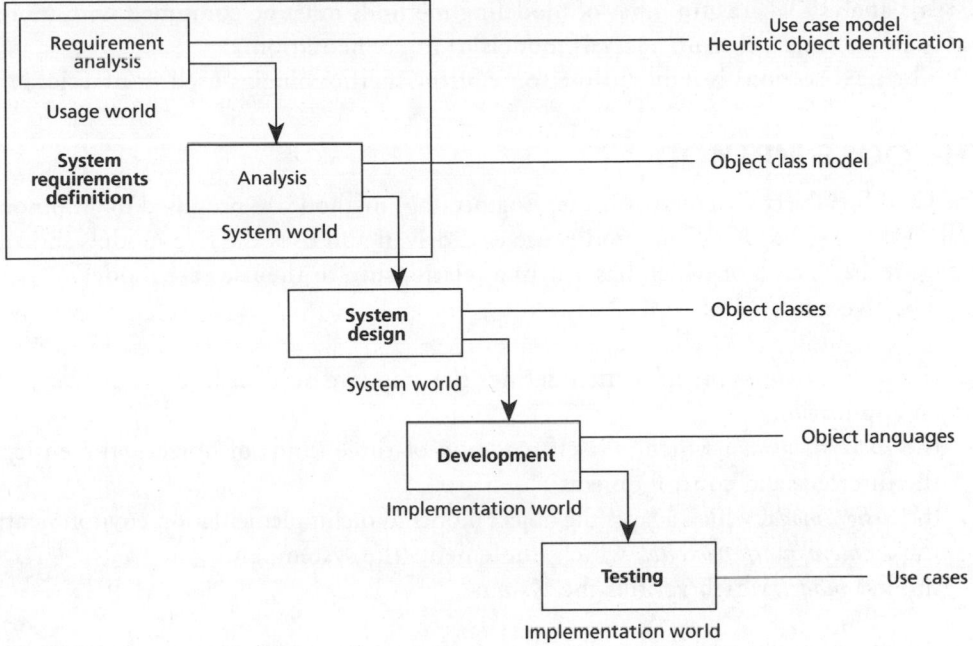

Figure 12.1 *Object orientation in the development cycle*

The descriptions given here describe only the general philosophy of each methodology. Readers should consult relevant manuals or texts for detailed descriptions of the methodologies and compare the techniques used at different life-cycle phases.

METHODOLOGIES

Object orientation is gradually becoming the major design method in the development process. However, it is perhaps fair to say that OO methods began to be used at the implementation phases of the development process through languages such as SMALLTALK. Other OO languages have included C++ and Eifel. Object orientation then became a popular method for developing analysis models during the system requirements definition phase. Thus, methodologies like that of Coad and Yourdon concentrated on representation for an analysis model, primarily at the system level. Subsequent models, such as that proposed by Booch, on the other hand, were seen to be applicable more to the system design phase. Jacobson stressed use cases and their importance in developing a requirements model using usage terms.

However, recently the trend has been to go beyond using object orientation in one or two development process phases and to integrate the approach into the entire development process. Such integration offers the possibility of using the OO approach throughout the entire development process. The advantage here is that analysis and design models can be converted directly into implementations. What it offers is the ability to commence at user level, then go directly to a systems specification and implementation using only one modeling method. This is in contrast to structured systems analysis where a number of modeling methods must be combined with more elaborate conversions from analysis models to implementation.

The next sections briefly outline some of the methodologies used in practice.

THE OOSE METHOD

The OOSE (Object Oriented Software Engineering) method was proposed by Jacobson et al. (1992). The OOSE method is use case driven and uses the five models shown in Figure 12.2, each of which has a strong relationship to the use case model.

The five models are:

- the *domain object model*, which defines the standard subject level terms used in an application;
- the *analysis model*, which is itself made up of three kinds of objects: the entity, the interface and control objects;
- the *design model*, which adapts the object model to the implementation environment;
- the *implementation model*, which implements the system; and
- the *test model*, which verifies the system.

Each of these models is used at different development process phases, and there are formal conversion rules as one passes from one phase to the next. Figure 12.3 shows where each of the models is used in the OOSE development cycle.

The analysis model that is produced during requirements definition is refined into a design model in system world terms. The interaction (or event trace) diagram is developed in this phase and used to drive object modules for the design model in ways described in Chapter 11. Methods are provided to convert the analysis model to system models for either of these alternatives.

Using use cases

Use cases are general descriptions of similar individual activities. Such individual instances of activities are often known as scenarios. For example, there may be a number of scenarios in the way different individuals may place orders. Analysts must then look at each of these scenarios and produce a use case that is sufficiently general

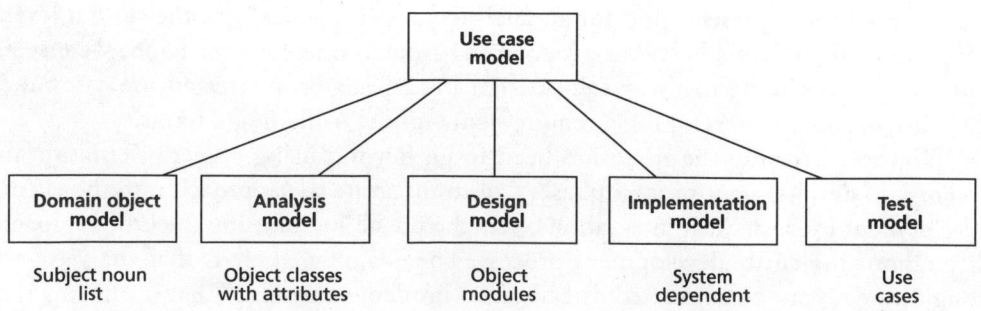

Figure 12.2 *Major models used in OOSE*

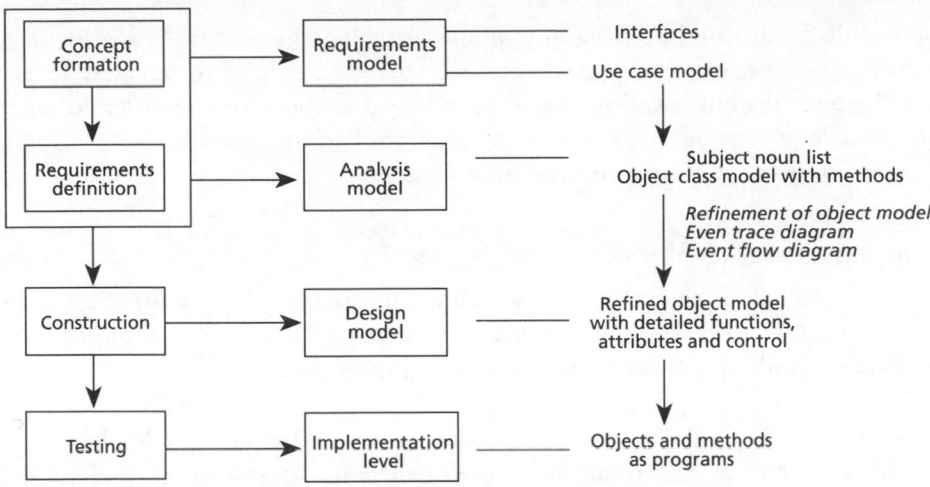

Figure 12.3 *The OOSE development process*

to include all of them. Another way to look at this is to look back on the discussion of languages in Chapter 5, and in particular Figure 5.3. In this framework, scenarios describe specific activities in the usage world, whereas a use case is a general descripton in the subject world using general subject world terms to describe subject domain processes in well-defined terms. Use cases are usually accompanied by a clear definition of subject domain terms, which is part of the domain model. Use cases were described in Chapter 11 and an example of one was given in Figure 11.9. There is some similarity between use cases and rich pictures, which were described in Chapter 5. Use cases in this sense are a somewhat restrained set of rich pictures, in that they restrict models to roles and use cases (or processes in the more general sense). For example, in Figure 5.4 in Chapter 5, we allowed rich pictures to include artifacts.

The use case model in Figure 12.4 identifies the three major roles in the interactive marketing system—namely, the seller, the buyer and the facilitator, who will be

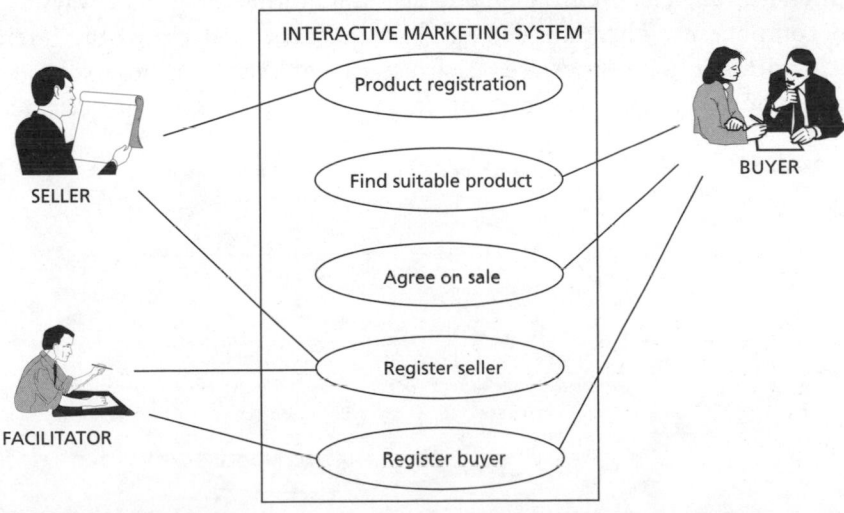

Figure 12.4 *Use case model*

responsible for maintaining the system and ensuring that it runs smoothly. It also includes a number of use cases and who is involved in each of these cases. Thus, for example, both the buyer and the seller are involved in the agreement on sale, whereas only the seller is responsible for product registration. Each of these use cases is elaborated in more detail in the manner described in Chapter 11.

From use cases to objects

Use cases are not in themselves objects, but serve as the driving force for finding good objects for a given system. One approach that may be used to develop the analysis model is to combine use cases with the entity approach, as follows:

1. Identify the most obvious objects (or entities)—for example, the roles themselves—then the artifacts that result or are used by the use cases—for example, product list or sale.
2. From the use cases, analyze how the system will be used and the interface objects that are needed by the users.
3. Identify any additional lower-level objects that may be reused in a number of use cases—for example, update account.

The last of these can also be initiated directly from the use cases, as suggested by Jacobson et al. The way to do this is to decompose some of the use cases using interaction diagrams to create the requirements model.

The requirements model

The requirements model is in OOSE centres around the use case model, and the analysis model. There is a close relationship between them, as the analysis model is derived from the use case model. The combined requirements model can then be considered as made up of the components shown in Figure 12.5: behavior, presentation and information. The OOSE method also has a number of specific ways to represent these components. These are derived from use cases and model the interaction of objects within the one use case. Each use case is seen as a process, and a special control object is created to represent the process. The control object is represented

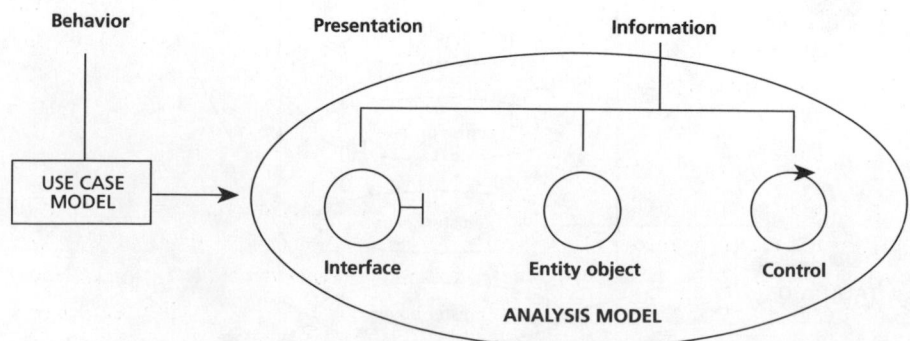

Figure 12.5 *The requirements model*

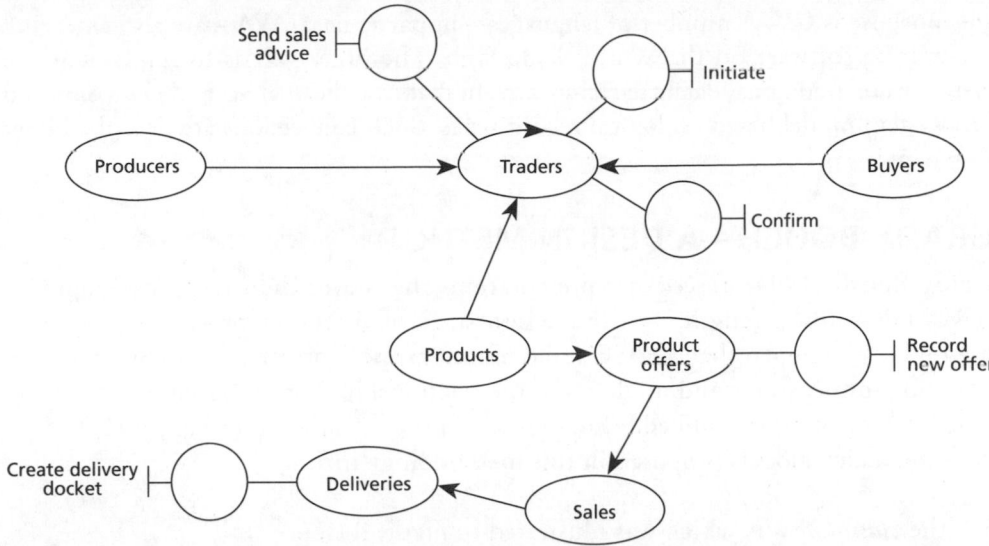

Figure 12.6 *An analysis model for interactive marketing*

by an ellipse with an arrow, as for example, Traders in Figure 12.6. This object initiates all the process steps by calling other objects as needed. There are also interface objects created for each user in a use case which show how the roles will use the system.

An example of an analysis model is shown in Figure 12.6. This figure illustrates the analysis model for interactive marketing. It shows the major objects that are identified from the use cases. They include the objects that were illustrated in Figure 11.9, together with links between the objects. Figure 12.6 also shows a number of interface objects and a control object. Thus there is an interface object to initiate a trade, another to confirm the trade and still another to send a sales advice. Each of these will eventually be implemented as a user interface by program modules or perhaps as World Wide Web pages. The best way to describe control objects is as objects that monitor processes. A rough rule is that there should be one control object for each case. Figure 12.6 illustrates one such object—namely, 'Traders'. A 'Traders' object will initiate the purchase of products for a buyer, commencing with finding a suitable offer, getting the buyer to agree, and then confirming the sale with the producer and the buyer. A system may be made up of a number of control objects—for example, there may be another control object to arrange deliveries. The actions taken by that control object will be defined by its use case.

From objects to implementation

Maximum advantage can be obtained from object analysis if the object model can be directly implemented on an OO system. There are two approaches here. One is based on object technology. Object implementations can use OO database management systems, where object classes are directly defined. Alternatively they can use an OO language to write programs. Object classes are declared in the language, and methods are written using language syntax. The most common language used for this purpose is C⁺⁺. A number of languages—in particular, JAVA—are also emerging for writing software on the World Wide Web. The other way is to implement the system using traditional database technology. In that case the analysis model is converted to a system model based on logical record types. Such conversions are described later in Chapter 16.

GRADY BOOCH—A DESIGN METHOD

Grady Booch (1993) describes representations that cover the various development stages but whose strength is in the design stage of the development process. This method is more open than OOSE and does not propose prescriptive steps. It defines a number of notations and models and the relationships between them, but is more open in how these are applied. One suggested process is shown in Figure 12.7.

The major models proposed in this methodology include:

- the *class diagram*, which was illustrated in Figure 11.7(a);
- the *object diagram*, which is shown in Figure 12.8;
- *interaction diagrams*, which are very similar to the event trace diagram in Chapter 11;
- *state transition diagrams*; and
- the *module diagram*, which becomes part of the system design model and is described in more detail in Chapter 16.

Booch suggests a very broadly defined development process that starts with conceptualization and is followed by the development of an analysis model. No formal specification is given for these steps, although the class diagrams, with their relatively informal notation, are useful here. The next step is to create an architecture for the new system, defined in terms of the class and object structures. An intermediate step is to use interaction diagrams when constructing object models. These interaction

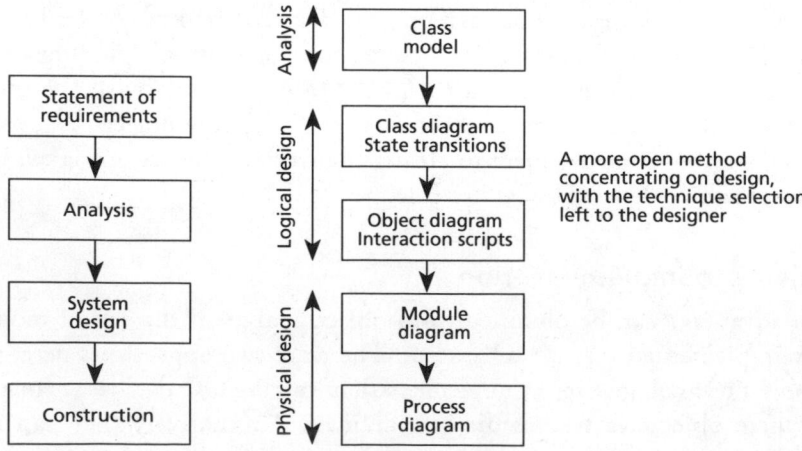

Figure 12.7 *Grady Booch—a suggested process*

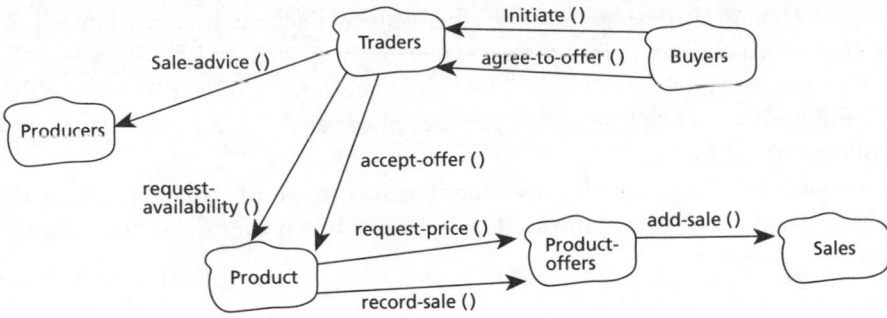

Figure 12.8 *An object diagram*

diagrams can contain a script, very similar to a use case, on the side to show how the transitions arise.

THE OMT METHOD

The OMT (Object Modeling Technique) method was originally proposed by Rumbaugh and others (1991) but has gone through substantive revision (Rumbaugh, 1996) since then. The original version is shown in Figure 12.9.

The method assumes that a statement of requirements is available and concentrates on developing an analysis model. It includes the following representations:

- The *object diagram*, which represents object properties in the way described in Chapter 11.
- The *dynamic model*, which represents the states of an object. The dynamic model is similar to the state transition diagrams. It shows the states that an object can assume over its lifetime and the transition between those states. For example, in Figure 11.10 an application goes through states like 'received', 'checked', 'approved', 'rejected', 'accepted' and so on. Each transition is activated by an

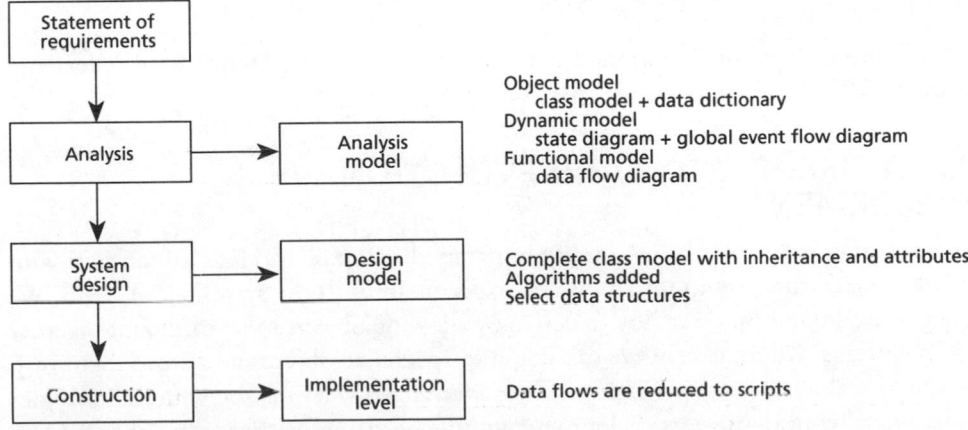

Figure 12.9 *The OMT modeling technique*

internal *event* or a message from another object. Each such transition requires a method to change to object properties in the way dictated by the event. Thus each arrow in Figure 11.10 would become a method in object APPLICATION. The methods would thus include 'receive application', 'check application', 'approve application', and so on.

- The *functional model*, which shows the transformation of each step on the object properties. Each such transformation is caused by an event and is modeled as a data flow diagram.

Later developments with OMT have placed more emphasis on the use case approach which has become part of the development of unified methods that use techniques from each of the above methodologies.

UNIFIED METHODS

The trend at the time of writing is to develop methods that unify many of the existing techniques into development processes that support the entire development cycle. One such method is the unified model, UML, which combines techniques from the methodologies defined by Rumbaugh, Jacobson and Booch (Rumbaugh, 1991; Jacobson, 1992; Booch, 1993). It combines the strengths of these methodologies to form a standard methodology that supports all the development process phases. A good reference to this method can be found on the World Wide Web site of Rational (http://www.rational.com), the company that is marketing the method. UML include the following main components:

- class diagrams, which follow the notation used in OMT but also incorporate technique from Booch and other modeling methods to describe the object structures;
- use case diagrams based on OOSE that are used in the requirements model and specification;
- interaction diagrams for OOSE but now called scenario diagrams;
- state diagrams which describe the changes in object states; and
- implementation diagrams.

Another approach to unified models is the OPEN method of Henderson-Sellers and Firesmith (1997).

OBJECT ORIENTATION AND EVOLUTIONARY DEVELOPMENT

Object orientation can also be used in evolutionary development. Here we can start with some objects, connect them into a system, experiment with the system, and so on. We can begin to add new functionality to design by allowing objects to be easily put together to form systems. Alternatively, we can begin to specialize objects and store them into a library, and then reuse them or reuse their specialized versions. New methodologies are slowly evolving to support cycles that combine both evolution and synthesis. One, called the *fountain cycle*, has been described by Henderson-Sellers (1990).

OBJECT LIBRARIES

Object orientation as a new paradigm has been slowly finding its way into system development since the early 1990s. Its adoption must often be justified if it is to replace established methodologies in organizations. Organizations that use existing methodologies have invested considerable effort in training their staff in methodology techniques and have developed or purchased the necessary documentation and support tools. All this will have to be replaced if object orientation is to be adopted. Management must therefore be shown that the OO approach will give advantages over existing methods. Two ways can be used to justify the introduction of OO methods, namely:

- better productivity is achieved using the OO approach when compared to existing systems; and
- it is possible to build systems or include functionalities that cannot be supported with existing methods.

To do this, it is necessary to develop convincing measures to illustrate such advantages. Alternatively, one can try to fit object orientation into existing methodologies gradually, usually by using it on new and challenging applications rather than by replacing existing applications.

REUSE

One important goal of object analysis and design is reuse. One approach is to build **libraries** of reusable objects and to provide methods for combining these objects into systems. The problem is how to design such object libraries. When we design, programs we usually have an objective in mind and design the program or module to satisfy that objective. We have deadlines to meet and so are not interested in thinking about how to add the additional structures or features needed to meet other and more general needs.

    An environment where the emphasis is on individual objects leads to the first option for constructing object libraries: to build objects for individual applications and to store every such object. Each of these objects is usually classified using a classification scheme to enable it to be retrieved by other potential users. Such users may use the object in its original form or perhaps modify it slightly to meet their particular needs. The approach of storing every object is heavily dependent on having a very good classification scheme. It is usually found that if a programmer cannot find an object to reuse within about 20 minutes or so, they will simply give up the search and write their own module. Consequently, there has been considerable research on developing such classification schemes. One approach is to support the idea of browsing, where a programmer finds an object and then browses around nearby objects to find one that is suitable.

    Another approach which encourages reusability is to develop a library specifically for reuse. This calls for what is commonly known as *problem domain analysis*. The library would contain generalized **skeleton objects** that can be **customized** to particular applications.

Library
A collection of objects that can be reused in many applications.

Skeleton object
An object that can be customized for more than one application.

Customization
Adapting an object for use in an application.

SUBJECT WORLD ANALYSIS

Problem domain analysis, or the analysis of the subject world, is a new and growing area in object analysis. Many approaches are suggested, one of which is based on semantics. Here we identify the *meaningful objects* that are frequently used in a general sense in the domain of discourse in the problem domain. For financial systems they may be things such as investment, accounts, transactions and so on. Once we identify the general objects, we may begin both to identify their general properties and to specialize them.

The analysis, rather than covering a particular application, now looks at a whole area and sees what are common, generic things that go on in this area. We base our objects on semantics meaningful to the problem domain but which are general across many applications in that domain. For example, in the area of finance, we may have a generic activity such as investment. There may, of course, be many kinds of investment, such as in real estate or in shares. Each of these kinds of investment has features in common, as well as features that are different. Common features include evaluation of the returns on investment.

We can go further and define object **patterns**. Object patterns are collections of objects and their connections that form skeletons for possible applications.

Patterns
A collection of objects that can be adapted to an application.

SYNTHESIS

So far we have assumed that a system is always built from scratch and that there is no existing software that we can use. A set of requirements is defined, and we begin to build the system that satisfies these requirements. This is not always the most effective way to be working. It is also possible to build parts of a system in a way that can be *reused* in other systems. In this case we would gradually build up a library of modules that can be used again and again to build new applications. This introduces a new dimension to the development process. While we need to develop the application, we must also ensure that consideration is given to making modules reusable. The idea of a system **synthesis** is illustrated in Figure 12.10.

Synthesis
Building a system from existing modules.

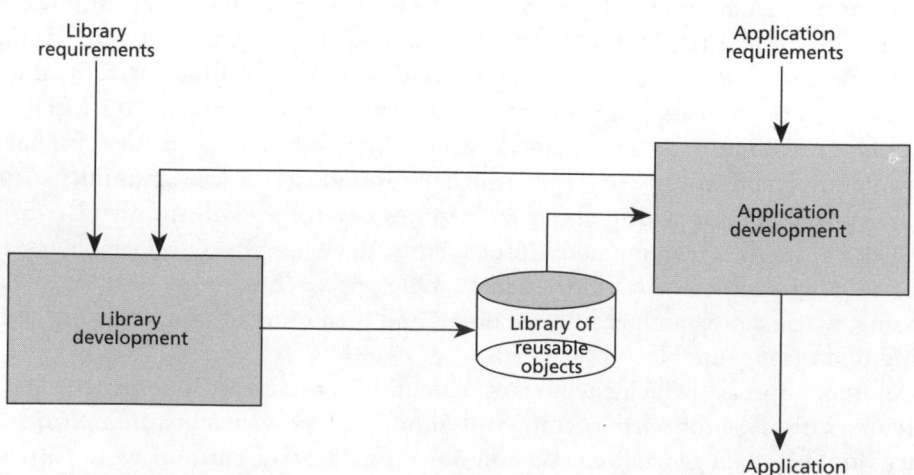

Figure 12.10 *System synthesis*

Figure 12.10 includes a library of reusable modules in the development process. In fact, there are now two processes—one for application development and one for library development for a particular problem domain. The two processes are usually closely integrated. Part of the application development process is to examine the library to see if it has modules that can be used in the development. The other is to identify possible new modules to be included in the library. Often the new modules are modifications to existing modules.

There is now an additional dimension to system quality here. What we need to do first is provide modules to cover the widest breadth of an application area. This should be done using the minimum number of library objects. Reducing the number of objects reduces the amount of storage while making it easier to select the best module for a given application.

CONTINUAL REFINEMENT

One important aspect of library development is the idea of continually refining or specializing existing objects to meet new needs. The object paradigm supports this idea. The concept of inheritance leads to the possibility of continual refinement of objects. It allows new objects that meet new needs to be created from existing objects by changing or replacing some features of the existing objects.

SUMMARY

This chapter described how object modeling techniques can be integrated into a life cycle and discussed various ways of using object orientation in system development methodologies. It described the methods used to design individual objects and then how object design is integrated into methodologies. The chapter concluded by discussing the importance of reuse and how to build libraries of reusable objects.

DISCUSSION QUESTIONS

12.1   Describe what you see as the difference between using objects for analysis and using them for implementation.

12.2   In what ways is object orientation used in system development methodologies?

12.3   In what ways are object libraries developed?

EXERCISE

12.1   Draw an event trace diagram for the agency management case described in Chapter 2.

BIBLIOGRAPHY

Booch, G. (1993), *Object Oriented Analysis and Design with Applications* (2nd edn), Benjamin-Cummings, Redwood City, California.

—(1996), *The Best of Booch*, SIGS Books and Multimedia, New York.

Coad, P. and Yourdon, E. (1990), *Object-Oriented Analysis* (3rd edn), Yourdon Press, Englewood Cliffs, New Jersey.

Henderson-Sellers, B. and Edwards, J. (September 1990), 'The object oriented systems life cycle', *Communications of the ACM*, Vol. 33, No. 9, pp. 142–59.

Henderson-Sellers, B. (1992), *A Book of Object-Oriented Knowledge*, Prentice-Hall, Englewood Cliffs, New Jersey.

Henderson-Sellers, B. and Firesmith, D., (1997), 'Choosing between OPEN and UML' *American Programmer*, Vol. 10, No. 3, March 1997, pp. 15–23.

Jacobson, I., Christerson, P.J. and Overgaard, G. (1992), *Object-Oriented Software Engineering*, Addison-Wesley, Reading-Masachusetts.

Pancake, C.M. (October 1995), 'The promise and cost of object technology: a five-year forecast' *Communications of the ACM*, *Special Issue on Object-oriented Experiences and Future Trends*.

Rumbaugh, J., Blaha, M., Premerlani, W., Eddy, F. and Lorensen, W. (1991), *Object-Oriented Modeling and Design*, Prentice-Hall, Englewood Cliffs, New Jersey.

Rumbaugh, J. (1996), *OMT Insights*, SIGS Books and Multimedia, New York.

Schmidt, D., Fayad, M. and Johnson, R. (eds), (October 1996); 'Software patterns', *Communications of the ACM*, *Special Issue on Software Patterns*.

Shlaer, S. and Mellor, S.J. (1988), '*Object Systems Analysis: Modeling the World in Data*, Yourdon Press, Englewood Cliffs, New Jersey.

13

Documentation

CONTENTS

KEY LEARNING OBJECTIVES

The importance of documentation
What is a project dictionary?
The configuration and components of a project dictionary
Cross-checking

INTRODUCTION

Previous chapters described an important requirement of good system development practice: the techniques used to develop precise system models at different phases of the development process. Also important is the documentation support needed to keep track of these models and other project documents. We do not want to develop models on loose pieces of paper and misplace them, or fail to maintain records about our work. There are a number of reasons why an organized approach is needed to keep track of documents. First, it allows us to manage complexity by cross-referencing model components. Second, it supports maintenance, because any work can be passed from one person to another. In addition, it can be used to manage change by using cross-references between documents to find documents that are effected by changes to earlier documents.

Documentation is thus both a communication tool and a management tool. It is a communication tool because it contains a repository of all work done to date and makes it available to all persons working on related parts of a large project. Such a repository can prevent unnecessary repetition when someone leaves the project team. Proper documentation ensures that all the information developed about the system is always available to new people joining the project.

Documentation is also a management tool. It supports management in two ways. First, it gives access to the latest work to all project personnel and thus reduces the chance of work having to be repeated. Second, it is the only project deliverable, especially in the early project phases, and thus serves to determine project status and progress. We know what documentation must be provided at the end of each project phase and can measure phase progress by estimating the proportion of phase documentation that has been completed. Finally, documentation becomes part of the phase output. This output includes the system model, as well as plans for subsequent project phases.

To be useful, documentation must be mandatory; most organizations that adopt formal design methods make documentation mandatory. Mandatory documentation requires formal techniques to be used in systems analysis and design, so avoiding an ad hoc *approach. It also ensures that the organization obtains the communication and management advantages of good documentation practices.*

DOCUMENTATION

System directory
Another term for project dictionary.

Project dictionary
A record of all documents produced during system design.

Document configuration
The structure of documents within a project dictionary.

Documentation primarily keeps records of all project information. This information includes any models of the system components, detailed description of these components, as well as information such as the organizational structure and user responsibilities within this structure. In some systems it can include the programs themselves. The documentation is organized in a way that makes it easy for any user to find out needed information about the system. For this reason, it contains many indexes and cross-references between documents. It is also usually maintained in one place.

Different organizations use different terms to refer to the collection of all documents about the system. Terms such as **system directory** or **project dictionary** are common. The terms *document configuration* and *configuration management* are also commonly used to describe documents associated with a project. The **document configuration** is the set of documents, whereas configuration management is the system used to keep track of these documents. Configuration management has a wide scope in that it can contain both models and specifications as well as program modules themselves. Each entry in a **configuration** can be a document or model produced during development.

Configuration
A set of documents used in a system development project.

The role of CASE tools is also important in documentation. CASE tools are specially designed software for maintaining models. They provide graphical interfaces to enable developers to enter their model constructs. CASE tools are described in more detail in Chapter 19.

 # THE DOCUMENT CONFIGURATION

A configuration management system:

- stores all documents created during the development process;
- provides access to the latest versions of documents or allows earlier versions to be examined;
- organizes documents in ways that allow work to be tracked throughout the development process, usually by linking documents to the development phases; and
- supports change by maintaining document **versions** as well as their status. Documents can go through status states like 'initial', 'accepted' and 'approved'. They may go through a number of versions as the system undergoes change.

Version
A variation of the same document.

The documents stored in a configuration management system depend on the development process and the modeling methods used. Figure 13.1, for example, illustrates a typical set of documents created in a development process that uses structured systems analysis. The configuration contains the major documents for each phase, including the statement of requirements produced during the concept formation phase, and the systems specification, analysis and requirements models produced during the system specification phase. The configuration also contains the design model and system modules. Each of these major documents can contain any number of parts. Figure 13.1 shows only the parts contained in the analysis model. These are DFD diagrams, E–R diagrams and process descriptions, as well as detailed descriptions of these components. These latter could have been produced using a CASE tool. Thus there may be descriptions of individual data flows, data stores, or the items that appear in the system. There may even be detailed descriptions of each kind of item. It is also possible to create entries for system users and how they use the system, or descriptions of forms within the system.

DFD DIAGRAMS

The project dictionary contains an entry for each DFD developed during analysis. Thus there is a context diagram, a top-level DFD, and detailed diagrams for all top-level functions and their components. Each DFD has a unique number and can be referenced by that number.

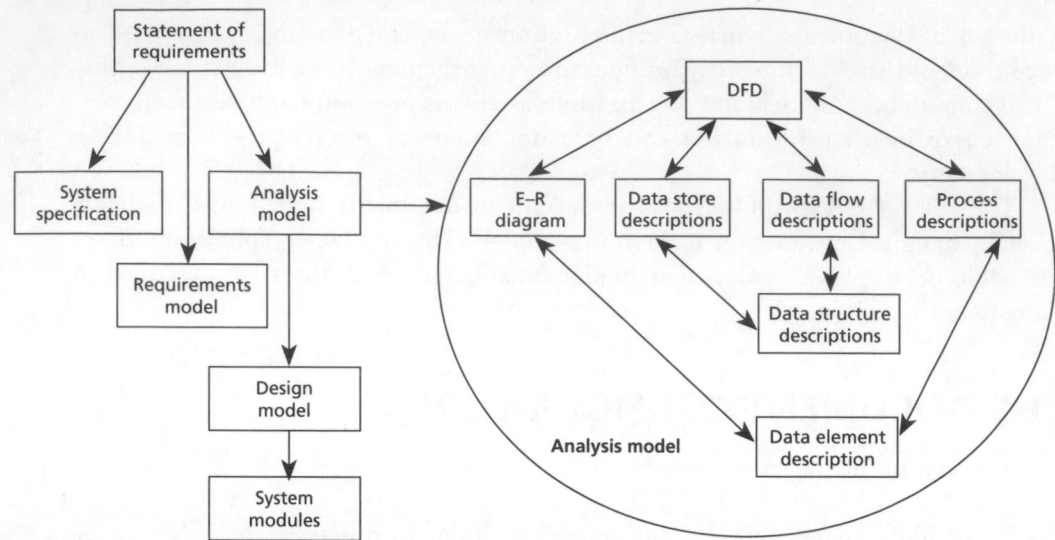

Figure 13.1 *Configuration components*

DATA STRUCTURE

Many project dictionaries also include detailed descriptions of the data components of the DFD. These include descriptions of both the data flows and the data stores, as well as the detailed data elements and structures that make up these flows or stores. These descriptions can then be referenced by the DFD or the E–R diagram. Figure 13.2 illustrates typical project dictionary entries and the cross-references between them. These entries are described below.

Describing data elements

Data dictionary
A document that contains the DFD and a description of all its components.

There is one entry in the **data dictionary** for each data element. One such data element entry is illustrated in Figure 13.2. This entry describes the data element PRODUCT-CODE. The entry describes any aliases or alternate names for the data element. For example, PRODUCT-NO can be used to mean the same thing as PRODUCT-CODE. The entry also includes the data element description, which includes the kind of values the element can take and the range of these values.

Describing structures

Data structures are combinations of data elements that appear in various parts of the DFD. Most data dictionaries describe structures by hierarchies. For example, the data structure described in Figure 13.2 is the INVOICE. The structure INVOICE is made up of a number of lower-level structures—namely, INVOICE-HEADING, INVOICE-LINE and SUPPLIER-DATA. INVOICE-HEADING is made up of two data elements: SUPPLIER and ORDER-NO.

Similarly, INVOICE-LINE is made up of three data elements—namely, PRODUCT-CODE, QTY and PRICE. The asterisk next to INVOICE-LINE indicates that this structure may be repeated any number of times in INVOICE.

```
Data element:  PRODUCT-CODE
Alias:  PRODUCT-NO
Description: A five-character code. The first two characters are alphabetic to
             indicate class. The last two characters are a number within the class.

Where used:  INVOICE
```

```
Data structure:  INVOICE
INVOICE-HEADING
    SUPPLIER
    ORDER-NO
INVOICE-LINE*
    PRODUCT-CODE
    QTY
    PRICE
SUPPLIER-DATA

Description:  Standard format constructed from supplier invoice

Where used:
Data stores:
Data flows:
    SUPPLIER-INVOICES
```

```
Data flow:  SUPPLIER-INVOICE

Source:
    External entity suppliers or process:
Destination:
    External entity or process:  1.3.1

Data structure:  Depends on supplier

Volume:  10/day

Physical description: Paper invoices, format depends on supplier
```

```
Data store:  INVOICES

Contents:  INVOICE + DATE-RECEIVED
                   + DATE-PAID
Processes used by:
3.7      STORE INVOICE
7.2.1    RECORD PAYMENT

Physical description:  Computer file

Size:  average of 20,000 records
```

Figure 13.2 *Data entries for structured system analysis*

The illustration in Figure 13.2 uses a hierarchical description of structures. A hierarchy is described by listing the data elements that make up a structure as a hierarchy, for example:

```
ORDER
    SUPPLIER-NO
    DATE-ORDERED
    DATE-REQUIRED
    ORDER-NO
```

Here ORDER is the structure name. The order is made up of four data elements: SUPPLIER-NO, DATE-ORDERED, DATE-REQUIRED and ORDER-NO. The indentation of the item names under ORDER implies that they are components of ORDER. Of course, most data structures are more complex than the ORDER structure shown above. Item values may be repeated, and there may be optional or alternative values and structures within structures.

An example showing structures within structures and repetition follows:

```
ORDER
    SUPPLIER-NO
    DATE-ORDERED
    DATE-REQUIRED
    ORDER-NO
    ITEMS-ORDERED*
        ITEM-NO
        QTY-ORDERED
```

Now ORDER contains the structure ITEMS-ORDERED. This structure is made up of two data elements. ITEM-NO specifies the item ordered, and QTY-ORDERED specifies the quantity of the ordered item. Because an order can contain many items, the structure ITEMS-ORDERED can be repeated many times. The asterisk after the structure name indicates that a structure or a data element can be repeated.

The notation also allows specification of alternative or optional items in a structure. This is done as follows:

```
ORDER
  { SUPPLIER-NO   }
  { SUPPLIER-NAME }
    DATE-ORDERED
    DATE-REQUIRED
    ORDER-NO
    [ORDER-STATUS]
    ITEMS-ORDERED*
        ITEM-NO
        QTY-ORDERED
```

Here the curly brackets { } indicate alternative structures. Thus an order may contain SUPPLIER-NO or SUPPLIER-NAME, but not both. The square brackets indicate an optional component. Thus an ORDER may or may not contain the data element ORDER-STATUS.

There are, of course, alternative ways of describing structures. One such alternative has been described by DeMarco (1978). In this notation, structure components are described by using the plus sign (+) instead of indentations. Thus ORDER is now described as:

```
ORDER = SUPPLIER-NO + DATE-ORDERED + DATE-REQUIRED
        + ORDER-NO
```

Repetition is described by placing the repeating structure within curly brackets; alternative structures are defined by square brackets and optional structures by round brackets. Thus the previous example, using DeMarco's notation, becomes:

$$ORDER = \begin{bmatrix} SUPPLIER\text{-}NO \\ SUPPLIER\text{-}NAME \end{bmatrix} + DATE\text{-}ORDERED$$
$$+ DATE\text{-}REQUIRED + ORDER\text{-}NO$$
$$+ (ORDER\text{-}STATUS) + \{ITEM\text{-}NO$$
$$+ QTY\text{-}ORDERED\}$$

Note that structures within structures do not have to be explicitly named using this notation. The structure {ITEM-NO + QTY-ORDERED} was given the name ITEMS-ORDERED using the hierarchical notation, but no such name is needed using DeMarco's notation.

DATA STORES AND DATA FLOWS

Data stores and data flows are made up of data structures and elements. Consequently, data store and flow entries contain data structures and data elements. The data in these entries is described using any of the above notations. Entries about data stores and flows also include other references. For example, in Figure 13.2, the data flow description contains the origin and destination of the data flow. It also contains the physical description of the data flow, in this case stating that it takes the form of paper invoices.

Data store descriptions also contain physical information, such as the medium used to store the data and where it is located.

ENTITY–RELATIONSHIP DIAGRAMS

The project dictionary contains the complete E–R diagram for the system. This diagram usually only shows the entity and relationship sets but not their attributes. The attributes and identifiers are recorded in entries for each entity set, each relationship set and each subset. The E–R diagram contains cross-references from these entries to the other entries in the project dictionary, such as data elements, data structures, flows and stores. Whenever an attribute is identified as part of the E–R diagram, it is added to the project dictionary. Similarly, any data stores or flows that include a set in the E–R diagram will include cross-references to that set. The set in turn will include a cross-reference back to the data stores or flows that contain the set.

PROCESS DESCRIPTIONS

Process description includes an entry for each process in a DFD. Each process entry includes the DFD number for the process together with the process description. The process description itself will depend on the process level.

High-level processes are usually described in an informal manner. They may be simple sentences that describe the overall process goal. Thus a top-level process like Process 3 in Figure 8.3 is described in the system dictionary by an entry like that shown in Figure

```
┌────────────────────────────────────────────────┐
│ DFD number:  3                                   │
│ Process name:  Classify expenditure              │
├────────────────────────────────────────────────┤
│ Input data flows:  Approved request              │
├────────────────────────────────────────────────┤
│ Output data flows:  Recorded request             │
├────────────────────────────────────────────────┤
│ Data stores used:  DEPT-ACCOUNTS, TYPE-ACCOUNTS  │
├────────────────────────────────────────────────┤
│ Description:  Approved reports are classified into│
│               one of a number of types           │
├────────────────────────────────────────────────┤
│ Method:  Users examine paper requests and their  │
│           type is entered into the computer       │
└────────────────────────────────────────────────┘
```

Figure 13.3 *Describing a high-level process*

13.3. The entry includes the process number and name. It also includes the names of the data flows coming in and out of the process and a narrative process description.

Low-level DFD descriptions are the same as those for the high-level process. Like Figure 13.3, they also include the process number and name, together with the incoming and outgoing data flows. The process description in this case, however, is more formal. Instead of narrative, the process description will now use structured English definitions or any of the other process description methods described in Chapter 10.

All the process entries are organized into their numeric sequence, according to which they are entered into the system dictionary.

ENTRIES IN OBJECT MODELING

Where object modeling rather than structured systems analysis is used, then a different set of documents is included in the document configuration. The kind of entries, however, will depend on the method used and will illustrate a wider variety than that used in structured system analysis, which is relatively standard. Typically, an object-oriented approach would include object classes and their descriptions. Attributes of object classes would be stored just as are data store or element descriptions; methods would replace process descriptions. Other components depend on the method—for example, use scenarios would be part of the configuration where these are used to model requirements.

OTHER KINDS OF ENTRIES

System users can be individuals or organizational entities. The system dictionary will include details of these users and their responsibilities. It will also describe the data that the users can access and the processes they use. Some project dictionaries can also contain descriptions of and displays and forms used in the system. The project dictionary can also contain many entries produced during design. These will be described in later chapters but include structure charts, program modules and file structures.

CROSS-REFERENCING

Apart from maintaining the entries, the project dictionary also maintains cross-references between the entries. These cross-references, which are illustrated by arrows in

Figure 13.1, show any relationships between the project dictionary components. Such cross-references make it easy to start at one point of the documentation and find other information related to that point. For example, there is a cross-reference between DFDs and process descriptions. These links can be followed by anyone who needs to find process descriptions for the processes in the DFD. Cross-referencing between different parts of a model makes it easier to trace components related to any part of a model. It includes methods to check consistency and thus makes it easier to develop correct models.

Ensuring completeness

One of the more difficult things in modeling is to make sure that all information about a system is captured and nothing is missed. Cross-checking between alternative models can help to point out any information missed during modeling. Thus a missing cross-reference from an E–R diagram to an existing data store in a DFD probably means that the data in that store is not represented in the E–R diagram.

Supporting system maintenance

Cross-referencing improves system maintenance. Whenever a change is proposed to one part of the system, the repercussions of that change can be quickly evaluated using the cross-references in the project dictionary. If, for example, we wish to add an element to a data structure, we can use the project dictionary entries to find the flows and stores where that structure appears, and from them, find the processes which use that data structure. Thus the repercussions of any change can be quickly evaluated. Furthermore, all parts of the system related to the change will be amended during the change, ensuring that no unforeseen errors arise when the change is implemented.

Common kinds of cross-references

The number of cross-references that can be made in project dictionaries is virtually unlimited. They range from the very simple to in-depth checks that may follow a cross-reference path. Considerable work is needed to maintain such cross-references and keep them up to date. Thus a particular project dictionary may only implement a subset of them.

Simple cross-references. Simple cross-references are used to check the correspondence of names in project dictionary entries. Data elements play an important role in these checks, because any data name used anywhere in the project dictionary must appear as a data element entry. There is cross-referencing between data element entries and data structure entries, with data element entries referring to the structures that contain the data element. The cross-reference from the structure to the data element uses the data element name. Typical checks for DFDs include:

- Any DFD can only include processes, data flows and stores that appear in the project dictionary.

- Process specifications must only refer to attribute names that appear in the data element listing.
- Data stores and all data flows must contain data elements that appear in the data element listing.
- Processes should reference the data stores and flows they use. References to data stores are necessary, because it is possible to have unlabeled flows between processes and stores. If we cross-reference flows only, these unlabeled flows would not appear in the process entry.

Cross-references to processes often use the number of the lowest order process. However, a cross-reference to a low-order process like Process 1.3.1 also implies a cross-reference to its top-level processes like Processes 1.3 and 1. Data flow entries include a cross-reference to their source and destination. They also cross-reference the data elements and data structures that appear in the data flow.

There are also a number of simple cross-references in E–R diagrams. All the attributes in the E–R diagram must be data element entries. Conversely, all data elements must appear in the E–R diagram.

In-depth cross-references. More complex checks apply to processes in a DFD and can be used to check for data conservation errors. Such checks can include:

- All elements that appear in a process description must also appear in the data flows into a process or in stores referenced by the process. This ensures that the process does not create any data.
- All elements produced by a process must appear in the output flows or in stores used by the process. This ensures that all data produced by a process is used.
- Checks that entities in E–R diagrams correspond to data stores and include as their attributes all the elements in related data stores.
- Data stores can only include data elements that appear in processes that enter data into the data store. This ensures that data stores do not create data.

DOCUMENTATION AS A STANDARD

Keeping records in easily accessible locations is just one purpose of documentation. It has one additional important purpose: documentation becomes the standard for analysis and design work, as all work produced must satisfy documentation standards. As a standard, documentation provides the guidelines for what is to be done next. It may include checklists to make sure that no important task is omitted. It may also suggest sequences for doing things and specify things to be done before each task. However, you should not see documentation as a set of things to be done with no particular benefit. It is there to help you.

 ## USING THE DOCUMENT CONFIGURATION

Document configurations are used for two purposes. One is to support the actual analysis and design process, as well as any changes to the system. The other is to produce reports needed by management.

PROJECT REPORTS

Project reports include information required by project management. They are the deliverables expected at the end of each phase. Project reports include general as well as phase-specific information. General information includes a summary and recommendation for the next phase. It also includes a plan for the next phase, together with proposed resources for that phase.

Phase-specific information depends on the project phase. A project report at the end of a feasibility study will include different components to that provided at the end of the systems analysis phase. The feasibility report will include expected project costs and a recommendation to proceed or abandon a project. The report at the end of systems analysis will describe the existing system and objectives for the new system.

Project reports also include parts of the system description or references to parts of that description. In some cases, project reports may include high-level DFDs and a high-level E–R model. Alternatively, they may include a list of references to these diagrams.

MAINTAINING A CONFIGURATION

The documents in the configuration management system include all the entries shown in Figure 13.1. It can be manual or automated.

MANUAL SYSTEMS

Manual project dictionaries usually have one page for each project dictionary entry. There is a separate entry for each data element, data structure, process description, user, data flow and store. Each entry described in Figure 13.1 is entered on one sheet of paper. These forms are then maintained in a central loose-leaf system folder, as shown in Figure 13.4. These entries are usually grouped by their type, and each entry has a unique number and can be cross-referenced by that number. New entries can be added to the manual, but change to an entry requires the page for that entry to be replaced.

Here a loose-leaf folder is made up of a number of sections, and each section contains entries of one particular kind. Thus there is a section for DFDs, another for data stores and flows, and still another for data structures. The project dictionary also contains the E–R diagram. Pages can be easily removed from or added to the project dictionary.

AUTOMATED SYSTEMS

Manual configurations are sometimes awkward to maintain. Every change requires a form to be replaced, and if there is more than one copy of the system dictionary this form must be replaced in each copy. Any cross-references must also be updated. Sometimes copies may not be updated and inconsistencies can arise.

Many organizations are now beginning to use computer tools to maintain document configurations. Two aspects are important in developing such support, namely:

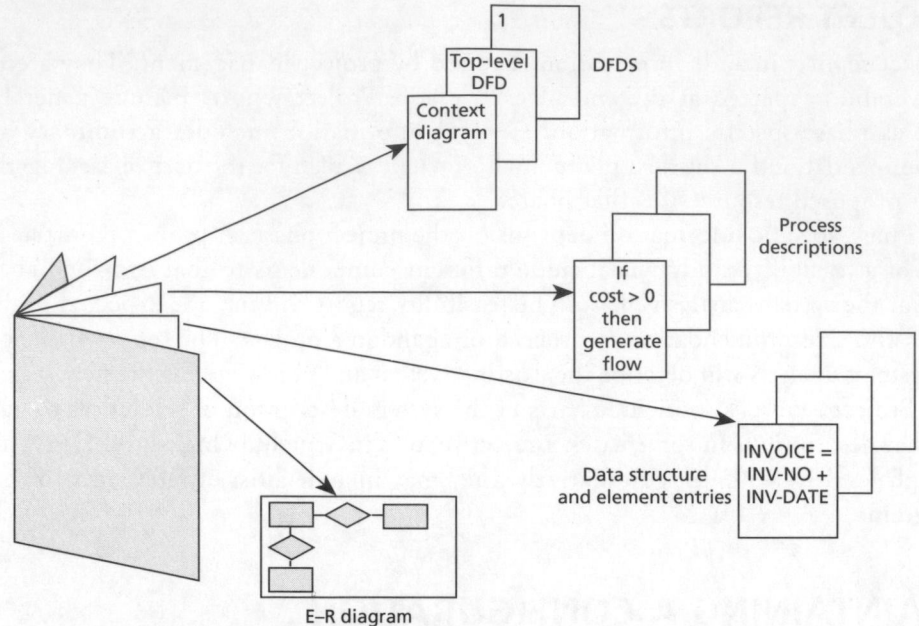

Figure 13.4 *Manual project dictionary*

- keeping track of the documents themselves; and
- using standard document structures.

Configuration management systems are now available to keep track of documents. They can be seen as extensions of the file management systems available on most computer systems but with additional facilities to automatically keep track of versions.

Document structures

Document structures are of two kinds. Some documents, such as statements of requirements, are primarily text. Others describe system models and must support precise structure. Sometimes a template can be provided for text-based documents to meet an organizational standard. Whenever the entry is to be created, the template is used to create a new word processor page for that entry. Each entry can be one word processor page. Updates are made to that page, and the entries can be made accessible to many users. Because there is only one central source of all entries, inconsistencies between different users will not arise.

Word processor systems, however, do not provide the assistance needed to maintain system models. For example, they cannot check for proper cross-referencing between dictionary entries, nor do they automatically generate modeling constructs. To do this, it is necessary to have software specially designed for this purpose. Such software is now known by the generic name, *CASE tools*. Here 'CASE' stands for Computer Assisted Software Engineering.

The kind of CASE tool depends on the modeling method that is used. However, irrespective of the modeling method, CASE tools will provide:

- *A repository of information.* Computer systems keep a record of all model components and any cross-references between them. A different screen is usually provided for each component. Cross-references are often updated automatically.
- *A tool for finding information.* Extensive indexing and numbering schemes are used to help users find information about the system. The user can then start a search using one of the indexes and find related information using the cross-references.
- *Carrying out cross checking.* One obvious assistance is to check model consistency. A number of checks have been suggested for DFDs. One of these is data flow balancing between levels of the DFD—that is, checking that a lower-order DFD has the same flows across its boundaries as its parent. Another check is to ensure that all data flow names appear in the data dictionary. A computer tool should be able to check this and report any violations to the analyst. The analyst can then do any necessary additional work to correct such discrepancies.

    Computer support can also provide valuable assistance in data analysis. For example, the computer can check the consistency of E–R models or determine whether relations are in normal form. It can also check naming consistency between the E–R diagram and the DFD.
- *Providing design support.* A computer tool can work in two ways: it can be passive or active. A passive tool relies on the analyst to input all the data about the model and then checks the model for consistency. An active tool actively guides analysts in their work. This kind of tool can suggest work to be done next, identify missing pieces of the model, and guide the designer by asking questions that fill in any model details. Later in design, such tools can be used to convert models to an implementation.

Computer support in structured systems analysis

CASE tools used in structured systems analysis provide a graphical interface for DFDs and E–R diagrams. The system will create a new DFD or E–R diagram. The designer can issue a number of commands that add, amend and delete components of the DFD or E–R diagram. The designer can also manipulate the position of the components. Thus a process can be moved from one point to another on the DFD. All the flows in and out of the process will also be moved as the process is moved. However, if a process is leveled, the designer must ensure that all the flows in and out of the leveled process are connected to processes in the new DFD. This ensures that data balancing is preserved during leveling.

Some CASE tools can assist users to develop correct models. They can, for example, ask simple questions to establish ranges and guide users to establish proper identifier structures for different kinds of sets. Finally, they can evaluate the model for inconsistencies and suggest possible changes to it.

A typical tool of this kind will be made up of the following components:

- Various *input modes.* One input guides the user through simple questions. Another allows the designer to work on a graph. Still another allows volume data to be input quickly.

- An *evaluation mode*, to check models for consistency and suggest changes to them.
- A *reporting mode*, to produce listings that describe the model object sets and attributes or to draw the E–R diagram.
- A *generation mode*, which creates database definitions from the model.

This kind of modeling tool is used in the way shown in Figure 13.5. The user first inputs the E–R model, starting by entering all known attributes as a volume input. Then the E–R diagram itself is drawn by entering the entity and relationship sets and adding attributes to them. Often, modeling tools have an alternative mode that guides the user toward developing a model. It asks the user, through a set of menus, what the user wants to do and then suggests possible actions the user can take.

Once a model is input, it is evaluated. During evaluation, the model is checked for consistency using the cross-references supported by the CASE tool. Whenever an inconsistency is found, it is reported to the designer and changes to the model are suggested. The designer can then follow up one of the suggestions or make some other change to the model. Reports about the model can be generated at any time. More details about such tools can be found in Chapter 19.

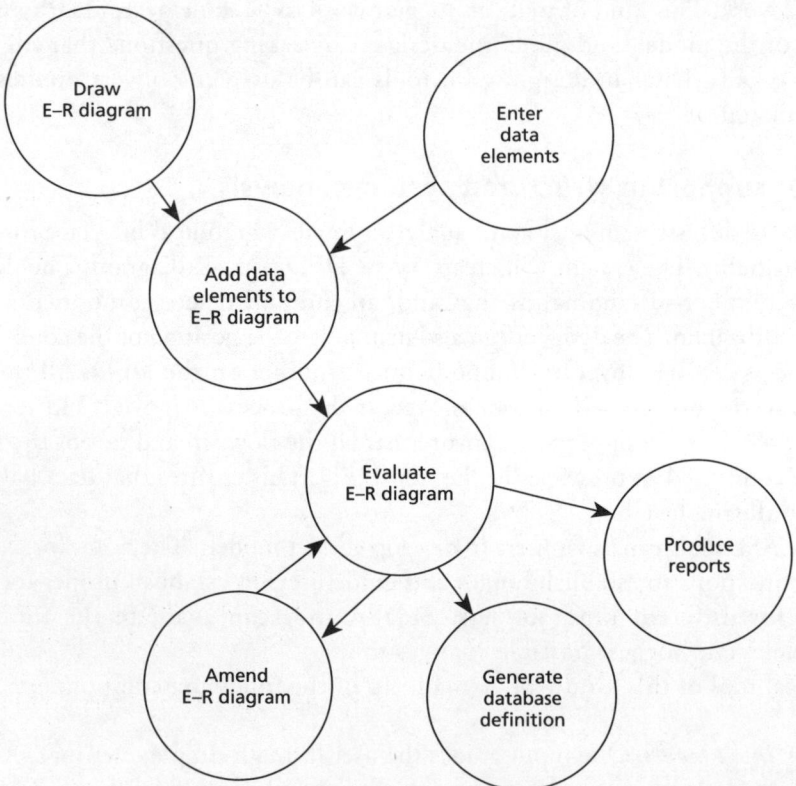

Figure 13.5 *Modeling using an E–R modeling tool*

SUMMARY

This chapter described documentation methods. Documentation is needed to support the development process. It keeps track of work done to date and makes this work available to all project personnel.

Documentation also assists analysts to maintain system consistency by storing cross-references between system components. It is up to the analyst to detect any inconsistencies in the model.

Computer tools can assist analysts even further by guiding the modeling process and detecting any modeling inconsistencies. Thus the inconsistencies are automatically brought to the analyst's attention, whereas in the manual case it is up to the analyst to detect them.

DISCUSSION QUESTIONS

13.1 What must be included in a configuration management system?

13.2 Describe how you would expect documentation to help analysts and designers.

13.3 What kind of cross-referencing checks should be supported for structured systems analysis?

13.4 What is needed to support an effective documentation system?

13.5 What are the components of a documentation system?

13.6 What is the difference between tools that keep track of documents and those that actively assist analysts to develop system models?

13.7 What kind of facilities would you expect from a computer structured system analysis and design tool?

13.8 What would you require from a computer system that supports E–R modeling?

13.9 What are the reasons for cross-referencing?

13.10 What kind of cross-reference checks can be used to ensure completeness of a model?

BIBLIOGRAPHY

Berlack, H.R. (1991), *Software Configuration Management*, Wiley, New York.

DeMarco, T. (1978), *Structured Analysis and System Specification*, Yourdon Press, New York.

Horton, W.K. (1990), *Designing and Writing On-line Documentation*, Wiley, New York.

Wertz, C.J. (1989), *The DATA Dictionary Concepts and Uses* (2nd edn), QED Information Sciences, Inc., Wellesley, Massachusetts.

Whitgift, D. (1991), *Methods and Tools for Software Configuration Management*, Wiley, Chichester.

Designing the new system

CONTENTS

KEY LEARNING OBJECTIVES

Design activities

Identifying design objectives

Developing logical and physical models of the new system

Specifying new business processes

Designing jobs for the new system

INTRODUCTION

Design is a much more creative process than analysis. It involves working with the unknown new system rather than analyzing the known system. Thus, in analysis, it is possible to produce the correct model of an existing system. There is, however, no such thing as a correct design. It is even harder to define the best design for a given system. A good design is very dependent on a particular system, and what is a good design for one system may be bad for another. It is not possible, therefore, to propose a set of standard solutions from which to select a good design for any system. Instead, design requires considerable creativity to propose the necessary system-specific changes and additions that are both acceptable to users and easy to implement. The designer, together with users, has to search for a solution using any special knowledge about the system until there is agreement that a satisfactory solution has been found. All a book can do is suggest how to search for a solution and propose some general methods that will assist you in the search. After that, it is up to the designer.

One question that is often asked is: when is the design complete? Is it an ongoing process, or is there some defined time of system development? The answer, to some extent, is that design is never complete. In fact, design is an ongoing process but its nature changes as the development process proceeds. Thus design is needed to define the concept, as we have to come up with a new idea. Then, during specification, the new system and its requirements are designed. In system design, we design the best computer structures, the programs, and so on. During this time, we are always clarifying issues and problems and thinking of possible things we could do, although we do not necessarily put them down on paper—at least not in a formal document.

This approach to design is consistent with the top-down approach of the waterfall cycle. Design models are developed throughout the cycle, being gradually reduced from high-level user world terms into detailed implementation models. Models in the early stages are usually expressed in user terms, and design centers on solving problems for users. In later stages, design centers on the computer system and uses system and later implementation models. This chapter will concentrate on design of the new system during the system specification stage, which begins with a statement of requirements from the concept phase.

STARTING WITH SYSTEM OBJECTIVES

Design of the new system begins by elaborating the statement of requirements in terms of more detailed objectives. Such objectives can be specified in terms of improvements to the organization's processes and functions and what is to be done to realize these improvements. It is therefore important to state the objectives in a way that is useful to design. What is needed is precision rather than generality, to give designers precise goals. For example, we would prefer:

'ensure that errors during input are less than 1 percent' instead of
'improve the data capture process'
or:

'ensure that all reports on stock movements are produced by the end of the month'
rather than
'improve the timeliness of the stock reporting process'.

KINDS OF OBJECTIVES

There are many kinds of objectives. Common types are:

1. *Functional objectives*, which state new or amended functional system requirements. For example:
   - new or changed output reports or displays;
   - new services to be provided by the system functions; and
   - revised security and access controls.
2. *Process improvements*, which include:
   - changes to the way data is accessed;
   - changes of sequence in which things are done;
   - changes to the process steps; and
   - changes to input and output methods—for example, regular instead of *ad hoc* reporting.
3. *Operational objectives*, which specify performance standards to be attained by the new system. These define system accuracy and various timing requirements.
4. *Personal and job satisfaction needs.* Important objectives include designing systems that are easy to use and which allow users to be creative rather than simply responding to computer outputs.

Different design ideas are needed to satisfy each of these objectives. Functional objectives may require changes to the kinds of computations in the system—for example, new accounting reports may be needed. It may also be necessary for new data to be stored in the system. Process objectives may require rearranging the way a service is provided or some internal objective is carried out.

The operational objectives, on the other hand, require different solutions. They may, for example, require a different physical implementation of some of the system processes to improve performance or flexibility, such as changing from a batch to a transaction-oriented environment. Another typical operational change may be to propose an *ad hoc* method of data access instead of regular reporting. Operational objectives may also call for a rearrangement of procedures used for some tasks, such as including more checks to improve accuracy, rearrangement of functions to reduce the number of steps in a procedure, or greater use of computers to increase throughput. Operational objectives will also identify the training needed to enable users to use the new system.

Personal and job satisfaction objectives may call for changes to the user interface to the computer, new report layouts or changes to the data flows. Presenting delivery advices sorted by area may improve the satisfaction of schedulers, as they will no longer have to perform this routine task. Instead, they can concentrate on the important problem of selecting routes for each vehicle.

Design must address all these issues. It must specify the layout of any input screens or forms. The outputs are also designed showing the layout of reports or screens. In addition, the files, structures and programs are specified, showing the different record types and program modules needed to make the system work. It must also specify what people in the system will have to do to make it work.

REDUCING OBJECTIVES

Objectives can be high-level, low-level, general or specific. Usually we start with high-level objectives and then reduce them as we proceed to detailed system analysis. Often, objectives are defined by starting with key performance factors. These are general statements about how the goal will be met by the new system.

These key factors are then analyzed. To do this, analysts talk to the users to define precisely what each key goal entails. Usually it is necessary to ascertain things like:

• the information requirements to satisfy the key goals;
• performance targets (such as time, volume, sample size);
• comparison to existing systems; and
• personnel issues such as skill levels.

New and specific values can then be set against each key goal. These target values become the system objectives. Often the process can be repeated through a number of levels. The objectives are defined, then they are broken down into more detailed objectives. Specific target values are assigned to these detailed objectives, and so on. Once we have the objectives, design can commence. The design process described here uses the problem-solving steps proposed for structured systems analysis.

> ### TEXT CASE D: Construction Company—Redefining the Objectives
>
> We review some of the objectives set earlier in Chapter 6 for the Construction Company. Primarily, the broad objective was to improve the process of parts distribution to projects. This is to be done by re-engineering two independent systems, the GRS and POS systems, so that the project ordering function, POS, is now more closely integrated with the purchasing function, GRS. This will eliminate the need to manually check delivery lists against purchase requests, thereby streamlining the distribution process.
>
> The detailed objective is to implement this on the existing system and to change the GRS system so that it can accept inputs from projects, while at the same time changing GRS for input from POS rather than projects.

DESIGN USING STRUCTURED SYSTEM MODELS

Proponents of structured systems analysis have suggested a set of problem-solving steps to develop the system specification model. Their approach is illustrated in Figure 14.1 in relation to the development process described in Chapter 7. It corresponds closely to the system requirements definition in Figure 7.4. Figure 14.1 also illustrates the next phase, system design, and the two models developed in that phase. System requirements definition follows the following four steps:

1. Develop an analysis model to describe how the system works now.
2. Develop an analysis model to describe what the system does now.
3. Develop a requirements model to describe what the new system will do.
4. Develop a requirements model to describe how the new system will work.

Of course, the first two steps are unnecessary if you are building a completely new system. All the steps, however, apply if you wish to change an existing system. Each of the models uses DFDs, E–R diagrams and process descriptions, as described in Chapters 8 and 9. The model of the new system can become part of the system specification and be converted to an implementation model during system design. Thus the DFD part of the model is converted to structure charts, as described in Chapter 18, and the E–R diagram is converted to a logical data model, as described in Chapter 16.

THE FIRST STEPS—SYSTEMS ANALYSIS

The first two steps in Figure 14.1 are to develop the analysis model. As described in Chapter 8, the process begins by analyzing the current operation and developing the current physical model, and identifying system problems. The physical model often uses user terms and is thus easier to develop as a first step. This is followed by

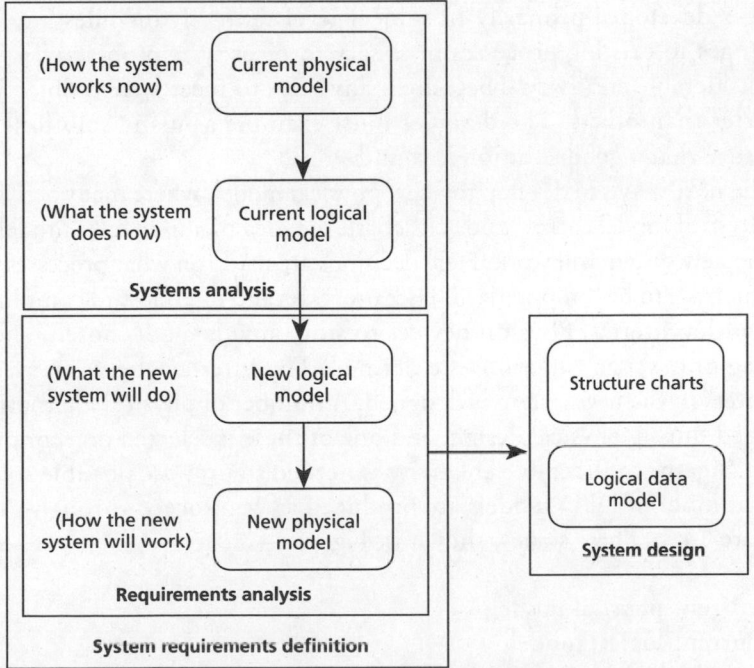

Figure 14.1 *Problem-solving steps in structured systems analysis*

developing the logical model—that is, a model that describes what the system does. This closely approximates the subject world model, described in Chapter 5.

Although we are after the logical, or subject world, model in systems analysis, in practice it is easier to build this model in two steps. The first step is to construct a physical model using user terms and then to convert the physical model to a logical model using the methods suggested in Chapter 8.

A physical model is built first because it is closer to the user world and it is easier to start by analyzing physical components. The analyst gathers the information needed about the system from interviews with system users and by examining documents, procedure manuals or existing computer programs. During this search, the emphasis is on the physical system components, and the tendency is to develop an initial DFD that includes these physical components. Once a physical model exists, it is elaborated in terms of its logical components in the way described in Chapter 8. In doing this, analysts often start by defining system-level terms and use them to name the logical model processes. These lower-level logical processes can then be recombined into a higher-level logical model in the manner described in Chapter 8.

THE NEXT TWO STEPS—SPECIFYING THE NEW SYSTEM

The design steps shown in Figure 14.1 commence once the logical model of the existing system is available. The goal of design is to develop a model of the new system. Development of the new system model is driven by the objectives for the new system, and it proposes a system that satisfies these objectives. It serves both to define the requirements and to create a system specification that is used in the system design stage.

Just like analysis, this development proceeds in two steps. First, the new logical model is developed primarily in subject-level terms. It includes any new processes or changes to existing processes necessary to meet system objectives. This step calls for considerable creativity. There are many ways to meet system objectives, and some are better than others. The designer must examine as many solutions as possible to make sure that a good solution is found.

The next step is to develop the new physical model, where many activities take place. The physical model corresponds closely to the idea of a user-level model and describes how the new system will work. Here decisions are made on what processes will be manual and which are to be computerized. User processes and interfaces to computers are defined in broad-level terms. Physical devices to store any data are chosen, and methods for carrying out system functions are defined. The interface between system users and computers in the new system is designed. A number of physical alternatives are usually produced during physical design, and one of these is selected on economic and social criteria. Again, considerable creativity is needed to propose possible solutions.

A number of DFD models are produced as we proceed through the cycle shown in Figure 14.1. These stages, shown in Figure 14.2, are:

- a current physical model;
- a current logical model;
- a new logical model; and
- a new physical model.

This does not mean that four separate models have to be maintained at all times. Rather, the goal is to gradually evolve to a model of the new system. Thus we may begin with a physical model and then convert it to a logical model using the techniques described in Chapter 8. Then we change the logical model of the existing system into a new logical model that satisfies the objectives of the new system. A physical model is then created to show how the new system is to work. It is, of course, possible, particularly if one is using computer support tools, to retain snapshots of the models as one proceeds through this cycle.

DESIGNING THE NEW LOGICAL MODEL

DeMarco (1978) has proposed a method for creating a new logical model from the logical model of the existing system. This method is shown in Figure 14.3. The first step is to see which processes are affected by the objectives for the new system. These processes are included in what is called the **domain of change**, which looks something

Domain of change
That part of the logical DFD of an existing system that will be changed in the new system.

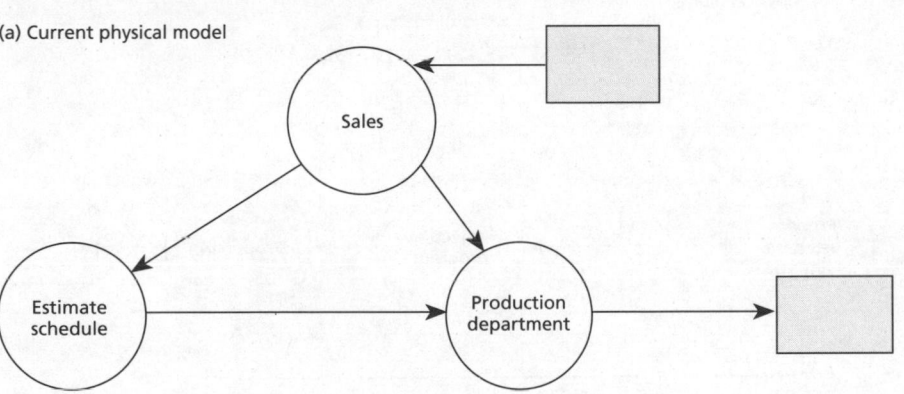

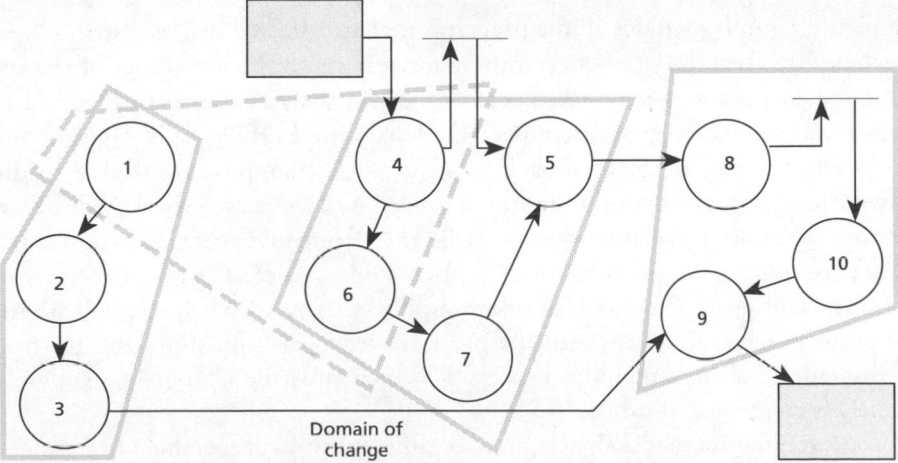

Figure 14.2 *The structured systems analysis problem-solving cycle*

(c) New logical model

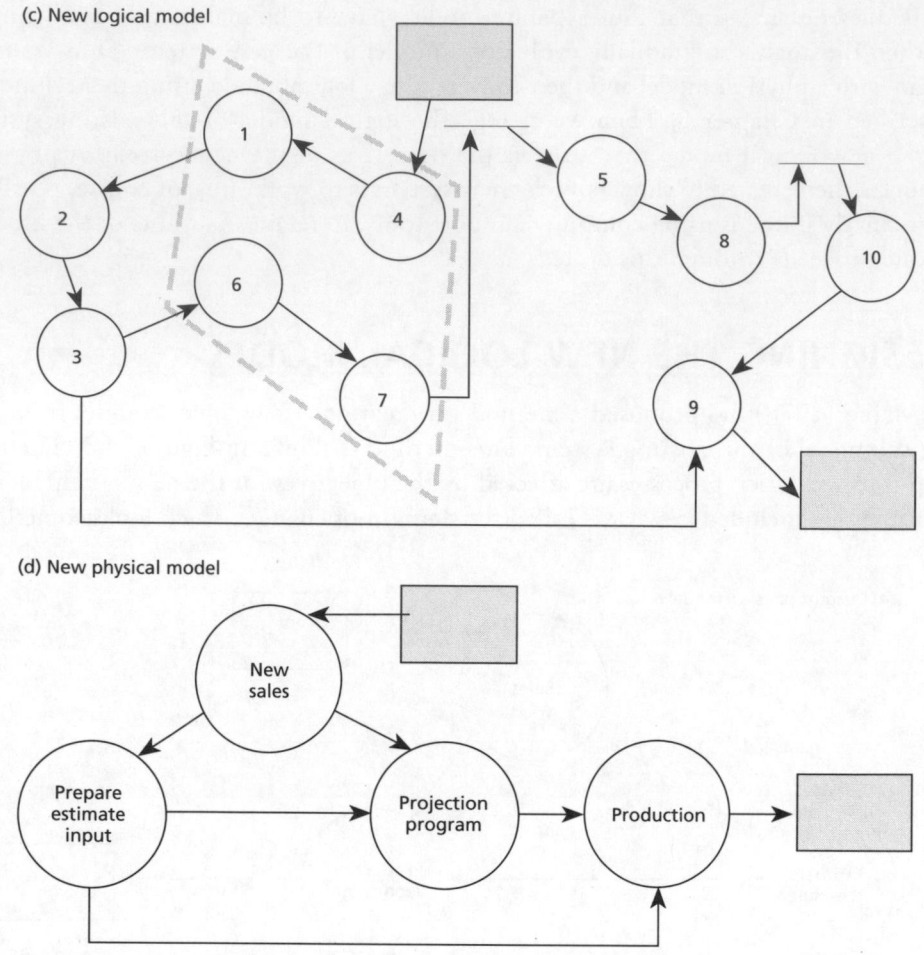

(d) New physical model

Figure 14.2 *(Continued)*

like Figure 14.4. It includes all the processes that are affected by the system objectives, together with the interface between these processes and the remainder of the system. The affected processes may be adjacent to each other, as shown in Figure 14.4(a), or they may be made up of disconnected or disjointed DFDs, as in Figure 14.4(b).

As an example, let us turn back to Figure 8.16. Suppose we decide to include an inventory system to contain frequently used parts. A new process will be needed to check whether a project request can be met from inventory or whether it must be met by purchasing parts from a supplier. Only project requests for parts not in inventory will go to Process 1 to select suppliers. Any such request will be held in data store PO-REQUESTS until the parts are received from suppliers. In this case, the domain of change includes Process 1, which must be changed to get its input from the newly created process.

You should note that designers may see different ways of meeting system objectives and thus define alternative domains of change. One of these alternatives must be selected during design.

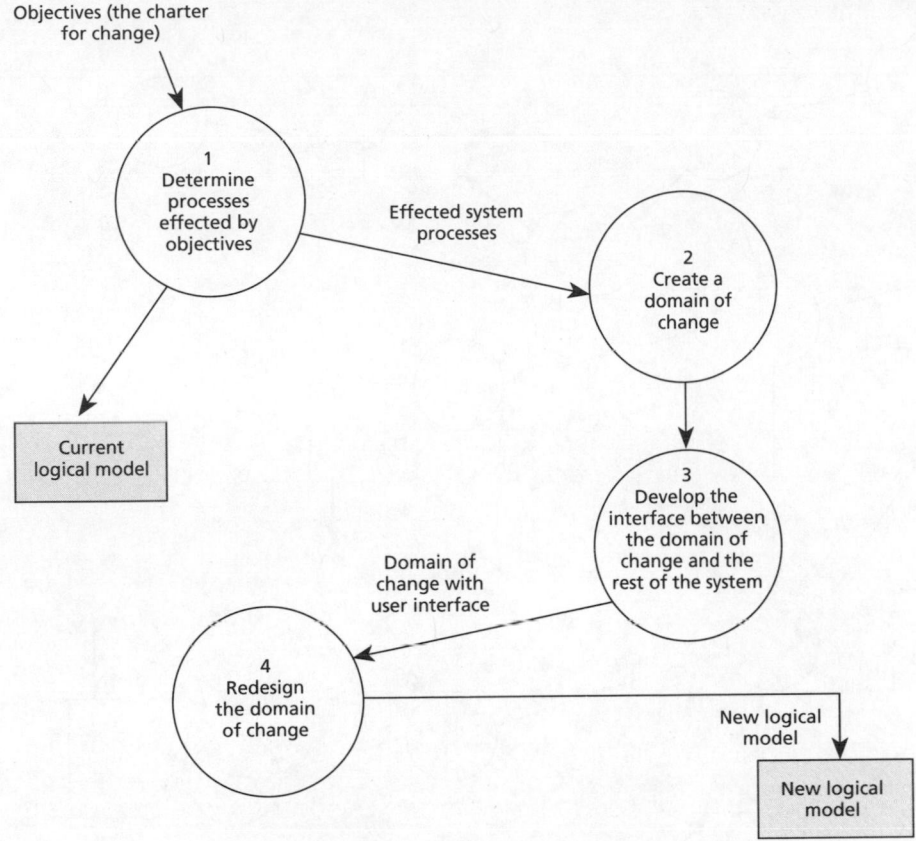

Figure 14.3 *Steps for developing the new logical problem*

The domain's processes, data flows and data stores are designed once a domain of change is selected. Design cannot be described as a prescriptive process. It is possible to suggest guidelines, but it is up to designers to use their knowledge of the system to suggest ways to satisfy system objectives. Two approaches can be identified. One is to completely redesign the domain of change, and the other is to amend it. A mix is also possible, where a part of the system is amended and another part is redesigned.

REDESIGNING THE DOMAIN OF CHANGE

A technique often used to redesign systems is illustrated in Figure 14.5. It starts with the domain of change, and data flows in and out of this domain. The design then proceeds in the following steps:

1. *Add data stores.* Identify the data needed inside the domain of change and construct data stores for this data.
2. *Define processes, data flows and data stores.* Take each input into the domain of change and define processes that the input data flows through before it is stored or used to produce an output.

(a) A single domain of change

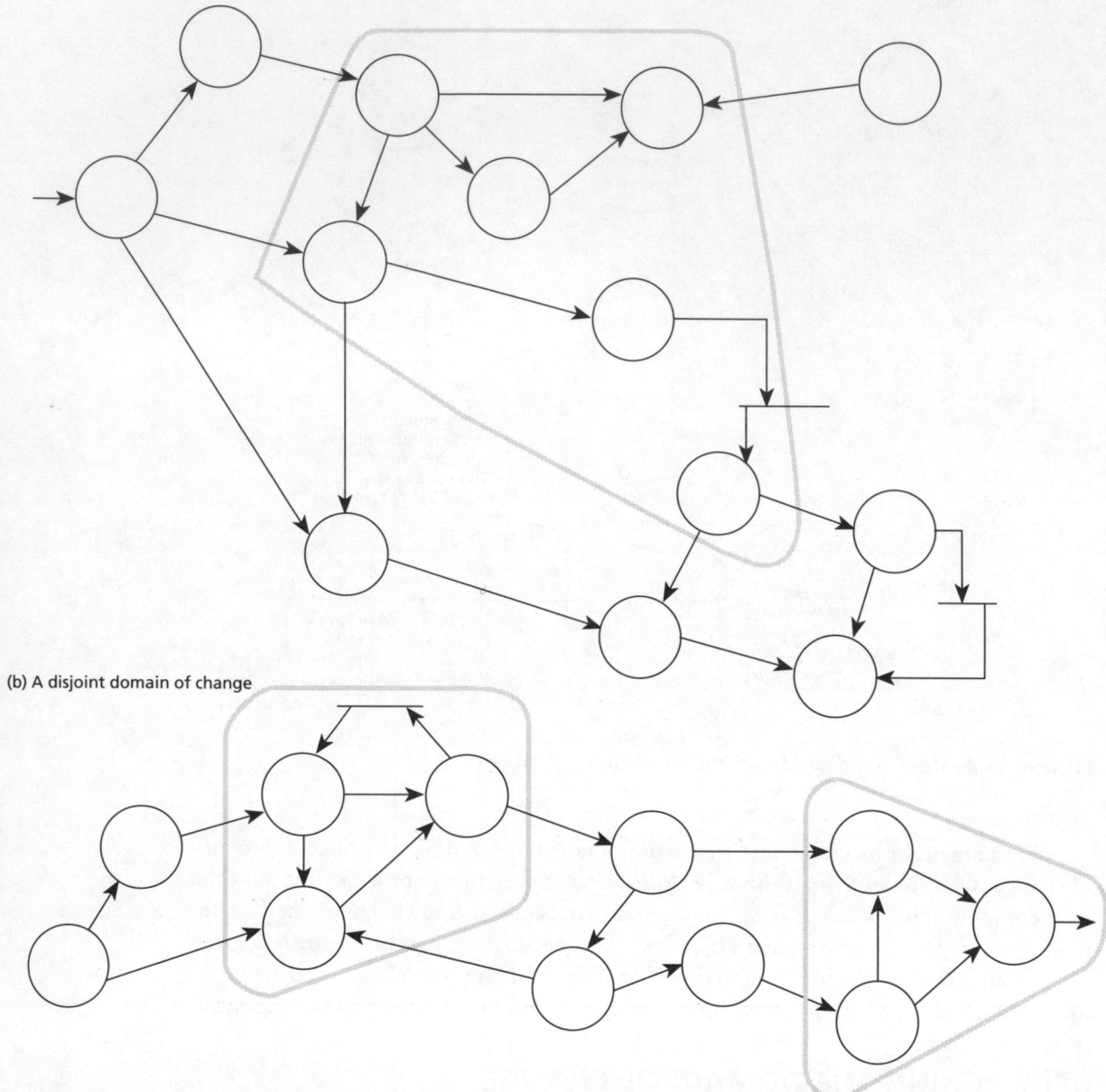

(b) A disjoint domain of change

Figure 14.4 *Domains of change*

3. *Add processes that transform data.* Define processes that use data in the data store and define how the processes use the data.

4. *Add processes to create outputs.* Look at each output produced and identify the data stores used to produce the output. Define the processes that the data goes through before being output.

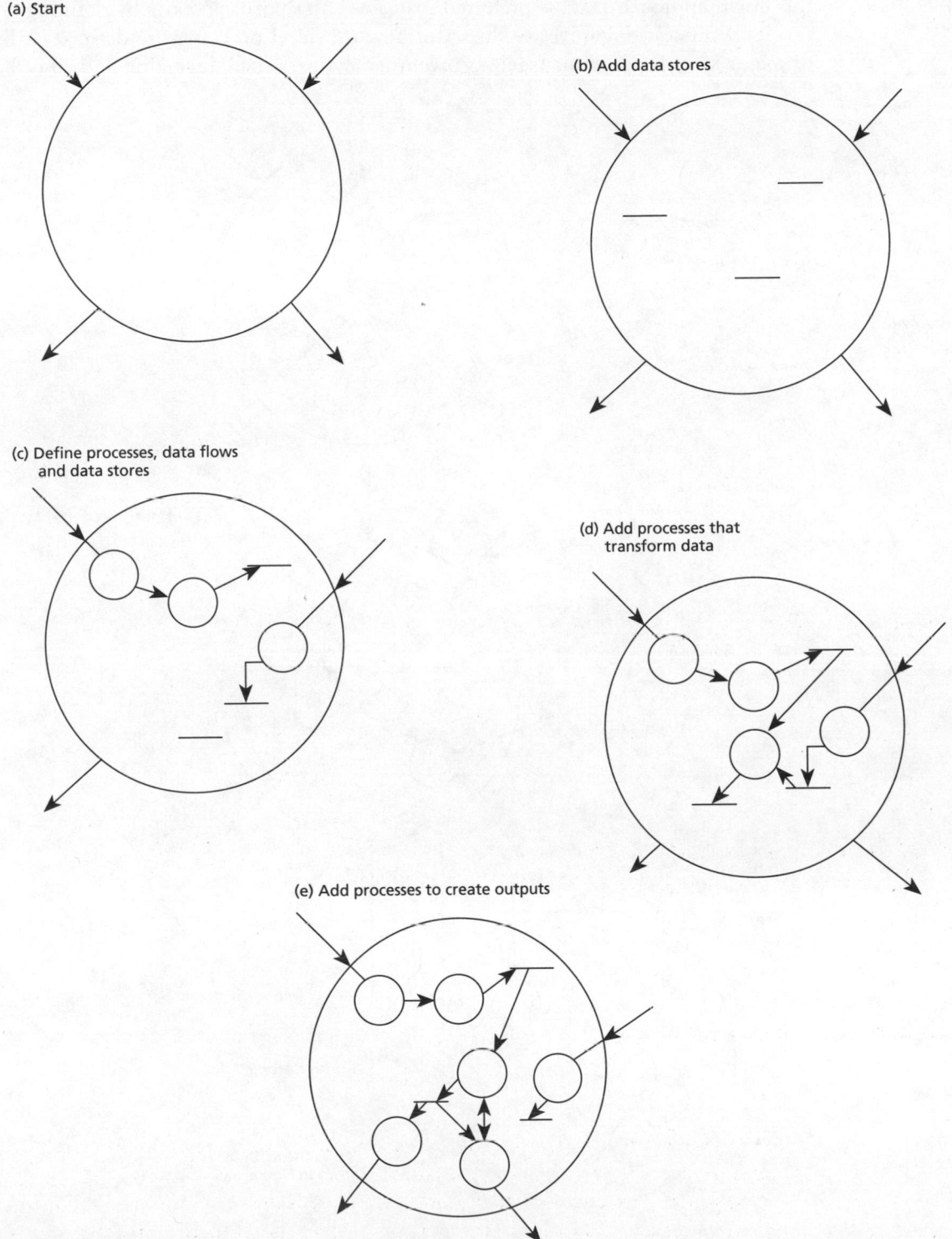

(a) Start

(b) Add data stores

(c) Define processes, data flows and data stores

(d) Add processes that transform data

(e) Add processes to create outputs

Figure 14.5 *A set of steps used to design the new system*

Of course, it may not be possible to proceed in this way for a large system. A top-down approach may be preferred instead. This approach starts by defining the top-level process. Figure 14.6 illustrates how top-level processes are defined. A list of major system functions (such as inventory maintenance, invoicing and so on) is

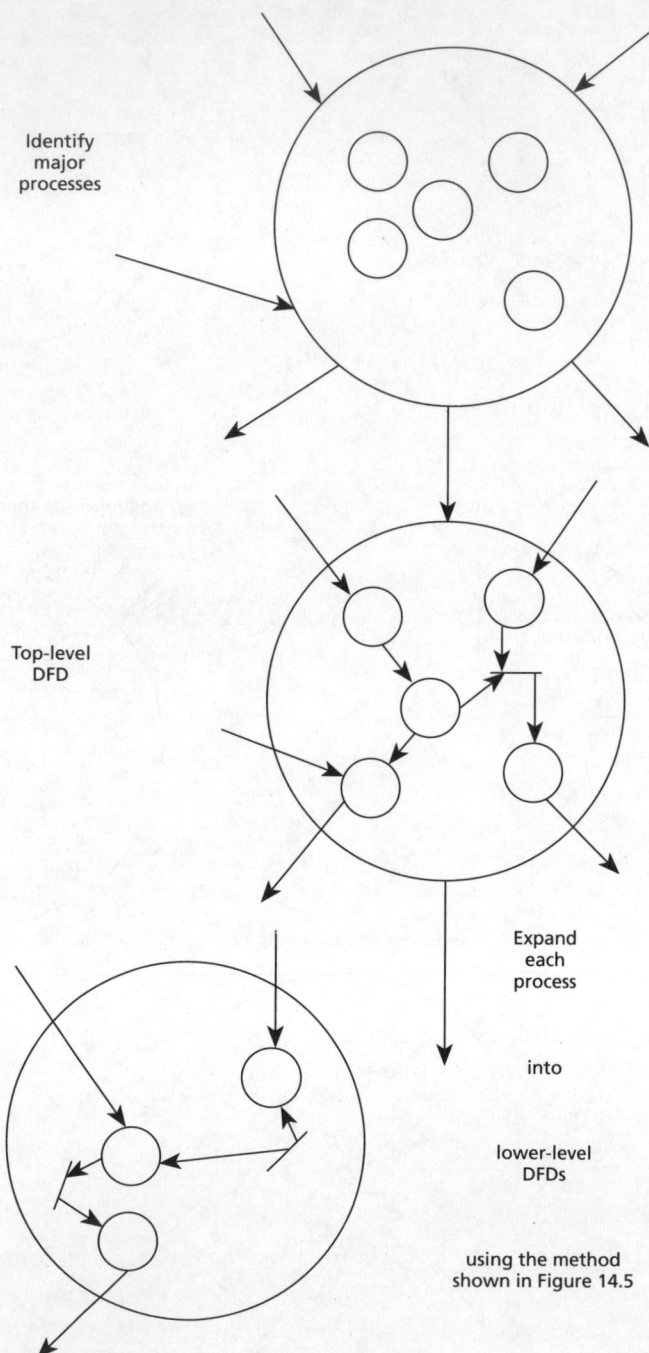

Figure 14.6 *Top-down design*

first made and their inputs and outputs are defined. These functions are then linked by data flows to construct a top-level DFD for the domain of change. The method shown in Figure 14.5 is now applied to each top-level function.

TEXT CASE D: Construction Company—The New Logical Diagram

We now develop the new logical model for the Construction Company. The logical model for the existing system in this case was illustrated in Figure 8.16. The system goal is to reduce the time between the project request and goods delivery. Feasibility analysis (see Solution 5 in Figure 4.3) indicated that this is to be realized by adding an inventory function and eliminating manual checking of deliveries and invoices against purchase orders.

These two objectives can be realized by making two changes to the existing logical model, shown in Figure 14.7, with the logical model for the existing system shown in Figure 8.16.

The first change is to add the new data store INVENTORY to represent the inventory. Process 8 is the new logical process that is added to check project requests against inventory. Project requests now go to Process 8 in the new system, rather than to Process 1 as in the existing system. A project request will only be forwarded to Process 1 if it cannot be met from current inventory. If a project request can be met from inventory, then it is sent directly to Process 5 as a 'store request' requesting the items to be withdrawn from store and sent to the project site. Project requests that require purchase orders to be sent to suppliers are stored in data store PO-REQUESTS and sent to Process 1. A project request directed to Process 1 has a purchase order number assigned to it by Process 8. This purchase order number is sent to Process 1, together with the project request. Data store PO-REQUESTS contains the requests sent to Process 1, together with purchase order numbers allocated to them. Process 1 will select a supplier to supply the requested items and Process 2 sends the purchase order to that supplier. A record of all purchase orders sent out by Process 2 is held in data store PURCHASE-ORDERS.

Process 5 is also changed to receive data flows 'store request'. These data flows are used to withdraw parts from inventory and to generate data flow 'delivery advice'.

Note that there is a new data store, PROJECT-REQUESTS, in Figure 14.7. This data store contains all requests made by the project. In Figure 8.16 all project requests appeared in data store PO-REQUESTS. In the new system, PO-REQUESTS contains only those requests whose items requirements cannot be met from INVENTORY. Thus, PROJECT-REQUESTS is added to the system to store all project requests. Note also that Process 4 would be simplified in the new system because of the more simplified matching.

DATA ANALYSIS IN DESIGN

As data stores are defined, the system data model is amended to include any new data requirements. The existing E–R diagram is amended to include any new entity sets, relationship sets and attributes, and an (E–R) diagram for the new system is produced. The newly designed E–R model should then be discussed with system users to gain their approval.

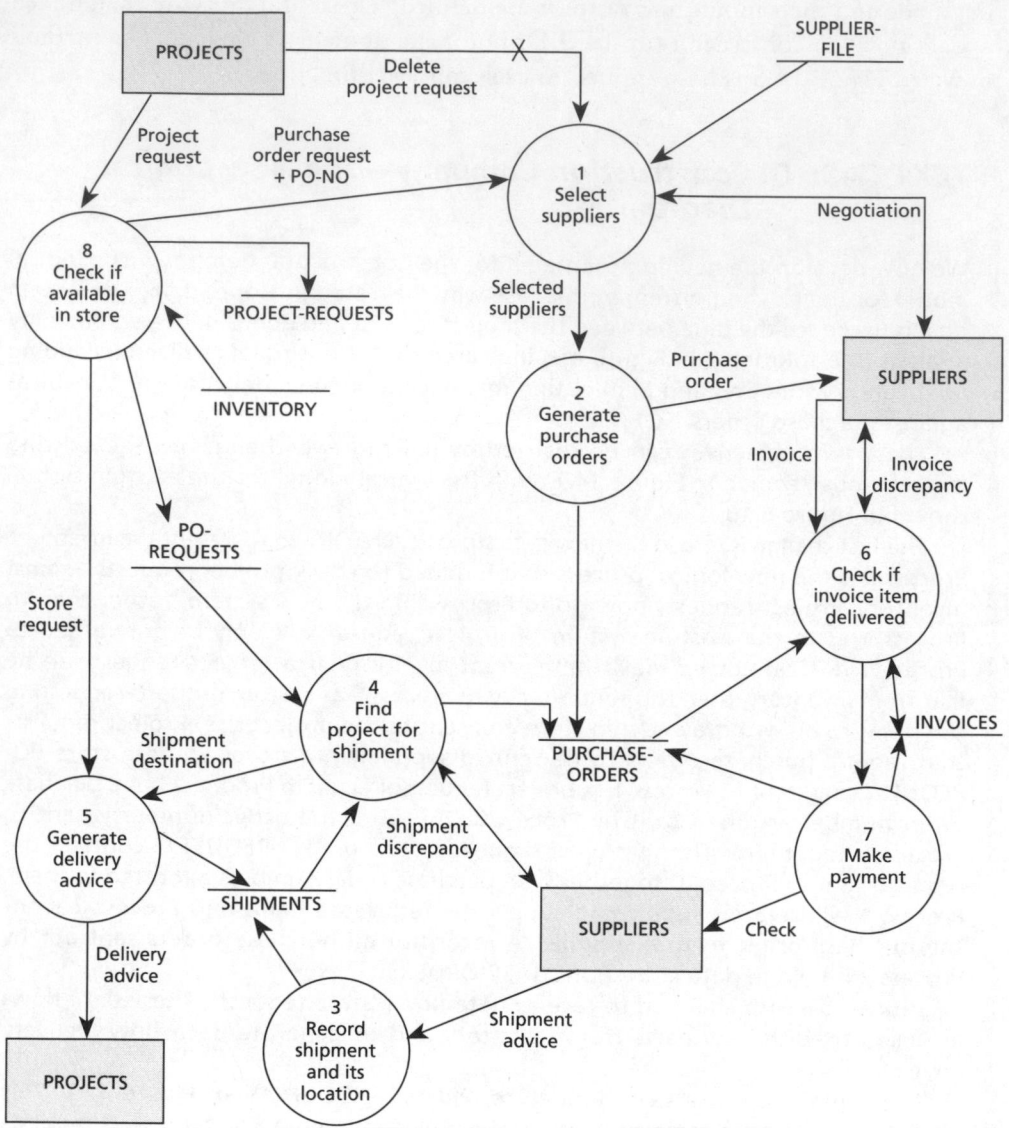

Figure 14.7 *Logical model*

During detailed design, the new E–R model is converted to a set of relations, normalized to eliminate data redundancies and then converted into a database. Techniques used to do this are described in Chapters 15 and 16.

AMENDING AN EXISTING SYSTEM

The alternative to a complete redesign of the domain of change is to make changes to individual components of the domain of change—that is, to redesign by parts.

Many different kinds of amendments can be made to an existing system, including:

- adding a new system process;
- creating a new data flow;
- changing the sequence of operations on information;
- eliminating redundant or unnecessary processes;
- combining two or more processes; and
- adding new data and changing processes to use this data.

Figures 14.8 to 14.11 illustrate some typical amendments. Figure 14.8 illustrates a simple addition: add a check on field 7 of the input data. This is achieved by adding one new process (Process 1.1.7 in Figure 14.8).

Figure 14.9 illustrates a slightly more complex addition. Here Processes 1, 2, 3 and 4 are used to make cost estimates for a project. The existing system takes too long to get project cost estimates and hence many enquiries cannot be satisfied. It is not possible to improve the speed of the existing Processes 1 to 4 because, first, it takes too long to get some external cost estimates and, second, breaking the project up into jobs is highly dependent on individual projects and must remain manual. Instead, the system is to be redesigned to make preliminary estimates based on internal historic data. A new logical Process 6 will be added to make the preliminary estimates. Figure 14.9 shows the new process. At this stage, the addition is logical only. It specifies what information is necessary to produce preliminary estimates but does not yet specify

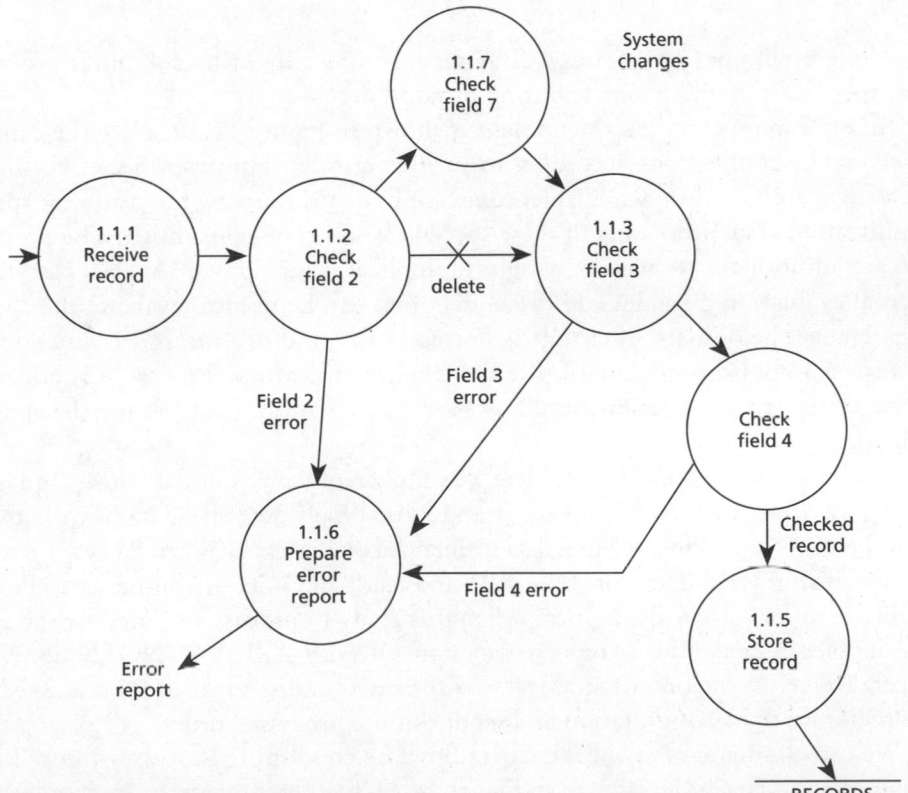

Figure 14.8 *Adding a simple process*

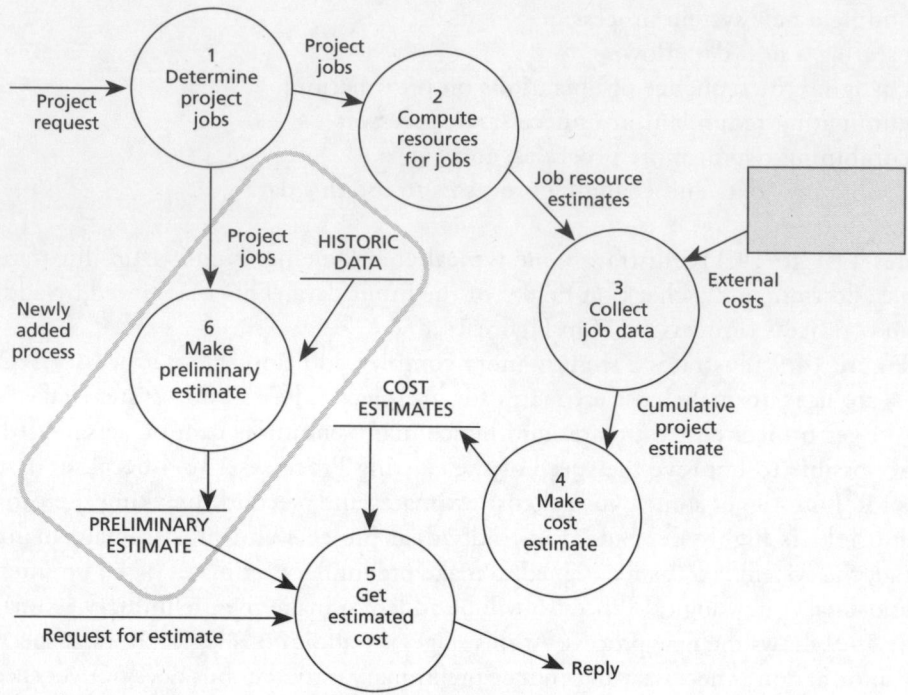

Figure 14.9 *Adding a more extensive new process*

how these preliminary estimates will be made—manually or by computer program. That specification will be made during physical design.

An even more complex amendment is shown in Figure 14.10. Here the existing system ranks applications according to various criteria. However, because some of the criteria are not always available, some applications must be put aside for special consideration. The processing of these special cases is time-consuming. The proposal is to get additional external evaluations of applications to process special cases. The external evaluation provides additional data that can be used to evaluate the special cases. Hence the domain of change is Processes 1, 2 and 3. Process 1 is amended to send special applications out to external evaluations, a new Process 4 is added to receive the external evaluations, and Processes 2 and 3 are amended to use the external evaluations.

Finally, we have Figure 14.11. Here we simply reorganize our data flows. In Figure 14.11(a) we start with two processes, 1 and 2, that have excessive data flows between them. This is because Process 2 uses data maintained by Process 1. When Process 1 receives an order, it stores it in data store ORDERS and sends an Order-arrival-notice to Process 2, which replies with 'order request' when it is ready to process an order. At the same time, it notes its request for an order in data store ORDER-ARRIVAL-NOTICES. When Process 1 receives the order request, it gets the order and sends it to Process 2, which uses the order in its computation and sends out the processed order.

We can eliminate many of these data flows by combining Processes 1 and 2 into the process 'process order' shown in Figure 14.11(b). The process 'process order' can be leveled into the two processes 'store' and 'compute' shown in Figure 14.11(c).

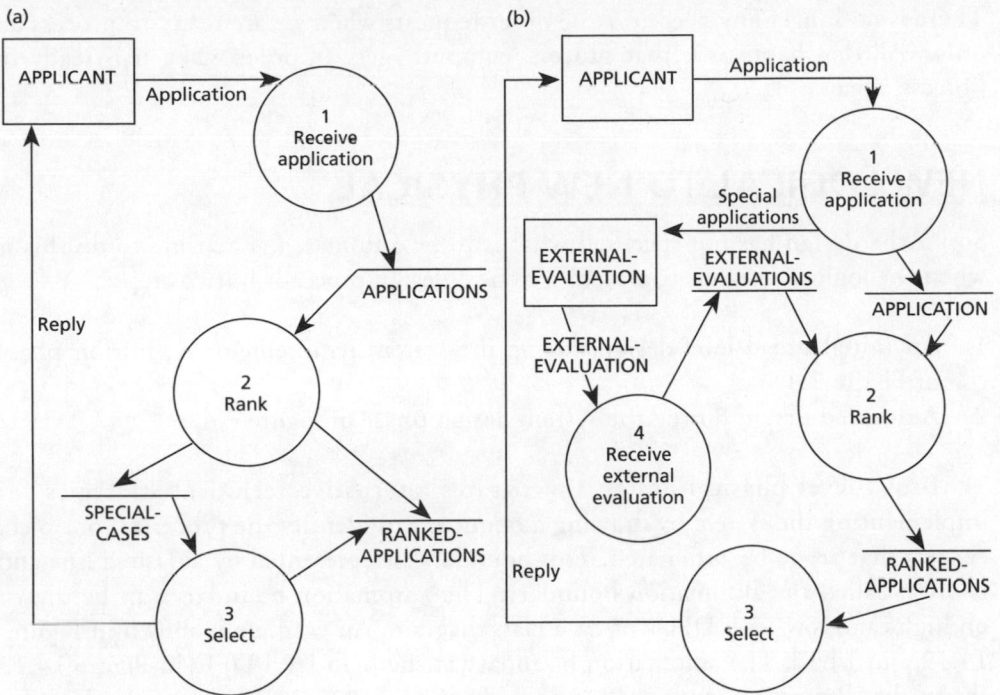

Figure 14.10 *Using new data*

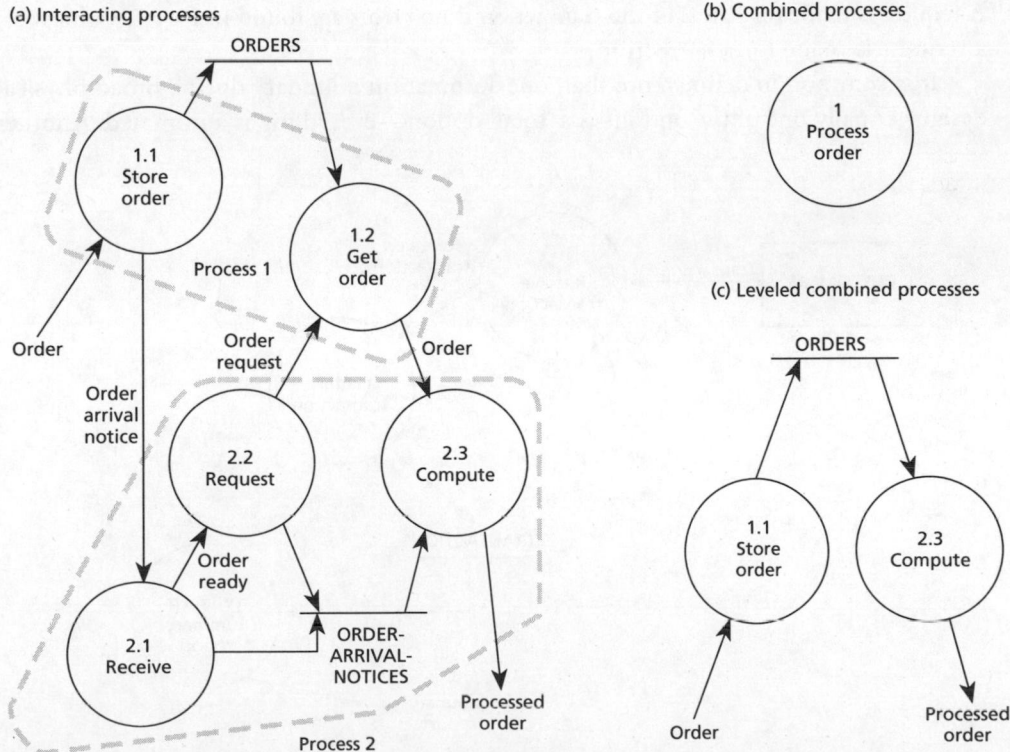

Figure 14.11 *Redesigning to simplify data flows*

There is no longer any need to issue order requests when we are ready to process an order. All that happens is that process 'compute' gets an order when it is ready to process one.

NEW LOGICAL TO NEW PHYSICAL

So far the design has not specified what is to be automated. The time to do this is when the logical design is complete. Physical design proceeds in two steps:

1. An initial broad-level design during the system requirements definition phase of Figure 7.4.
2. A detailed design during the system design phase of Figure 7.4.

Broad-level physical design investigates alternative technical strategies for implementing the system by drawing a boundary to identify the processes, or object classes, that are to be automated. This boundary is represented by a dashed line and is often called the automation boundary. The automation boundary can be drawn on high- and low-level DFDs or on a class diagram. An example is shown in Figures 14.12 and 14.13. The automation boundary at the high-level DFD in Figure 14.12 shows that Processes 2 and 3 are to be automated. Figure 14.13 illustrates the same boundary for leveled Process 2 of Figure 14.12. The leveled diagram shows that the transaction is entered in two parts. Part 1 is entered first and examined for errors. A request is made for Part 2 of the transaction if no errors are found in Part 1. Otherwise, a request is made for a correction.

It is common to define more than one automation boundary during broad physical design. Usually one of the options is a 'total' option—everything is automated. Another

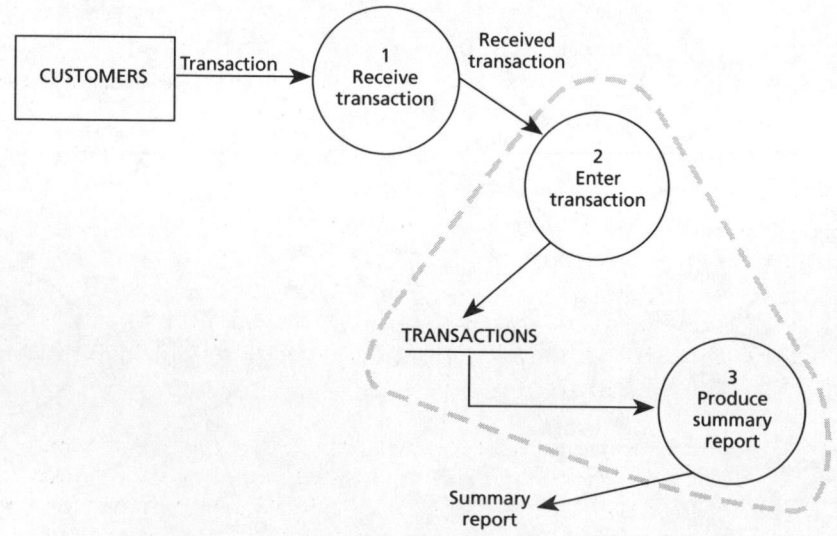

Figure 14.12 *High-level automation boundary*

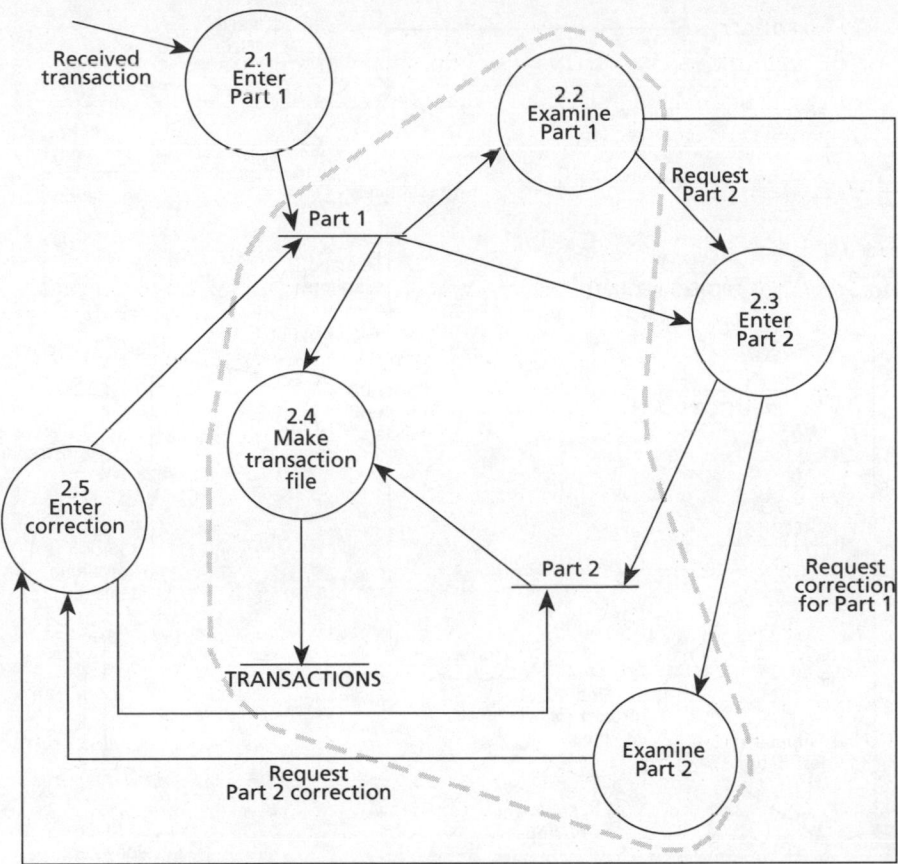

Figure 14.13 *Low-level automation boundary*

option is a minimum automation option, which only automates the processes necessary to realize the most important objectives while leaving a considerable portion of the system non-automated. Finally, an option that includes no additional automation but uses the revised logical flows should be considered.

The operational, technical and economic feasibility of the proposed designs is then evaluated, and a preferred alternative may be somewhere in between the three you started with. The evaluation uses the methods described in Chapter 5 but is now carried out in greater detail.

TEXT CASE D: Construction Company—Defining Automation Boundaries

The broad-level automation boundary for the new parts distribution system in the Construction Company is shown in Figure 14.14. Two boundaries are drawn on this figure. One Is for the new project ordering system (POS) and the other for the new goods received system (GRS). You should note that the boundaries between the two systems are now defined in more detail than shown in Figure 4.3 which was

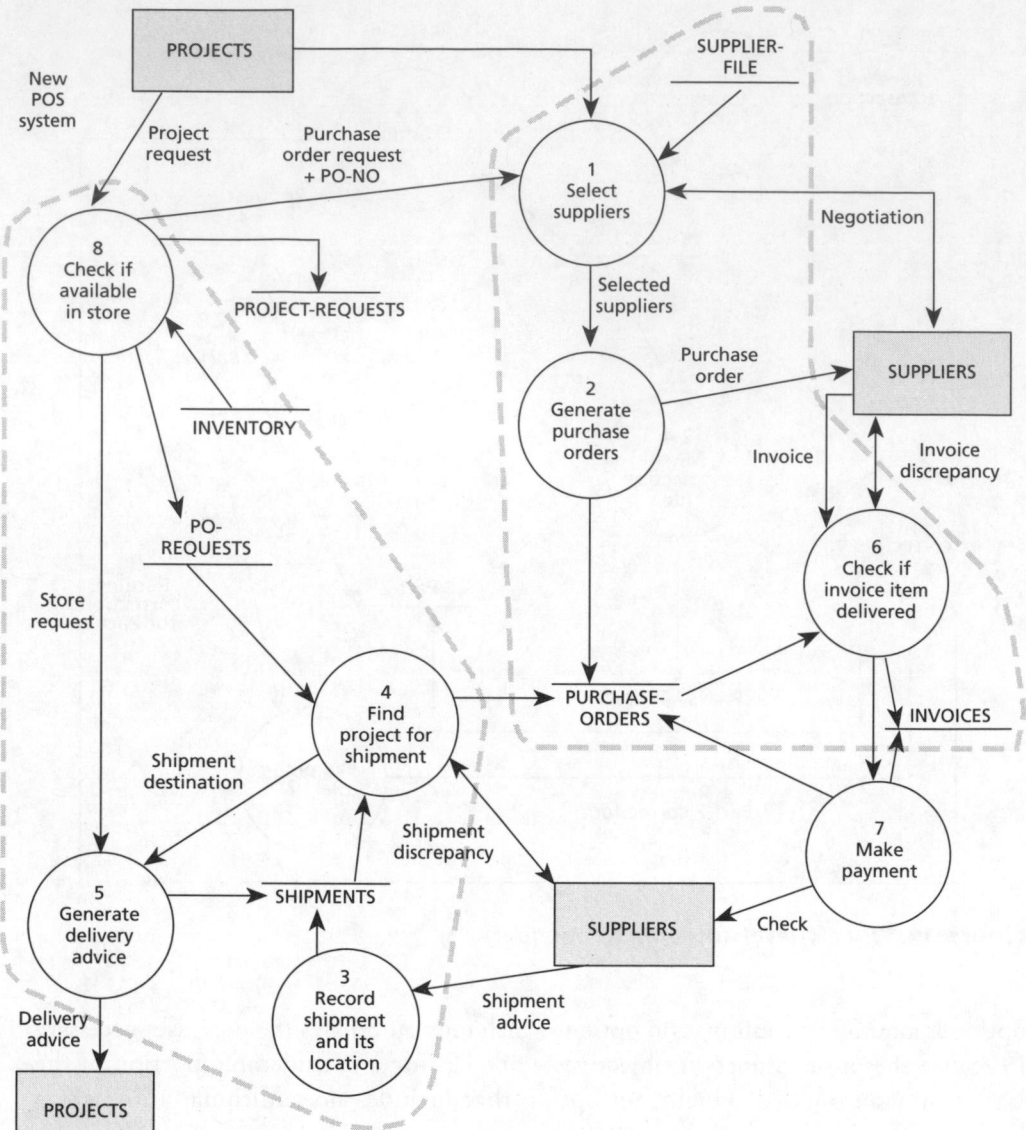

Figure 14.14 *Logical model*

only a very rough proposal. Now you can see that one flow from the new POS system to the new GRS system is the purchase order request. This request is generated when the requested items are not found in store. The purchase order request contains the purchase order number. A copy of the purchase order number and its matching project request are kept in data store REQUESTS in the new POS system.

The new POS system now checks incoming shipments against the data in data store PO-REQUESTS to find project requests that match the shipment and send 'delivery advices' to PROJECTS. Thus manual matching is no longer necessary. Advices about 'received shipments' are sent by the new POS system to the new GRS system where they are used to update the PURCHASE-ORDERS data store by the received goods. Process 6 in the new GRS system then checks any invoices against PURCHASE-ORDERS to see whether the invoiced goods have been received.

DESIGN USING OBJECT MODELING

Object-oriented methodologies are also beginning to provide more guidelines for designing new systems. Most OO methods described in Chapter 12 use models based on object classes at the system specification level, together with use cases or scripts. This, as is the case with structured systems analysis, again corresponds to a usage-level model and a subject-level model.

With a waterfall cycle the same steps as described for structured systems analysis are followed, but of course any changes must be expressed in terms of object classes rather than data flow constructs. For example:

- Design of a system requires a new model based on new object classes to be developed, or methods added to the object classes.
- To describe an existing system, an analysis class model, together with use cases, is developed. This can then be amended by changing existing classes or adding new object classes. Thus, for example:
  — adding a new process results in the addition of a new object class;
  — creating a new flow leads to a change in a use case, followed by a new method in one class that is called from another class.

  For example, the change in Figure 14.9 would result in the creation of a new method to make preliminary estimates with new object classes for preliminary estimates and historical data.

Another distinction when using object modeling is that it is easier to adapt to evolutionary design or prototyping cycles. In this case, objects are gradually added to the system. Thus it is possible to start development with a few object classes, prototype them and then add new classes as the design proceeds.

DESIGNING PROCESSES

Part of the implementation model must describe what people will do in the new system. It is not sufficient to do this simply by defining methods or programs. Processes that define what people must do to make the system work must also be included. A number of things are important in process design. One is to correctly define all the tasks in the processes and to ensure they fit together. These tasks must transform and move the data in the way specified by logical design. Another important part of detailed design is job design. Job design specifies what people must do to carry out the tasks. Jobs must then be combined into the process. Processes, jobs and tasks are thus related, and tasks must be designed so that they can be carried out by people and put together into an effective process. We will first describe job design and then discuss how to design define processes and include jobs in these processes.

JOB DESIGN

It is now generally accepted that systems will work much better if they are properly designed for users. Job design must encourage user involvement with the system.

People will be more likely to accept the system if they are satisfied with it, and their skills will improve while using the system.

Good job design involves a number of things. One is to ensure that people are not in the service of computers. This can be done in a number of ways. First, the interface to the computer should be made as easy and pleasant as possible. The interface should use dialog that approaches natural language rather than using computer jargon. Dependence on computers is also reduced by creating jobs that contain a variety of work, some dealing with computers and some independent of computing. Designing jobs with such variety is often called *job enrichment.*

Another important consideration in job design is the skills and skill levels required for jobs. A skill profile can be developed for each job and the skill level needed specified. Skills include dealing with people, various technical skills, and decision or supervision abilities.

Finally, once the skills needed for the job are defined, it is important to precisely define the duties required of the job and to ensure that these duties can be carried out within the allocated times. Precise specifications are needed to avoid uncertainties with the consequent indecision and loss of respect for the system. Procedures must specify clearly what is needed at each step and what is to be done at each step. They must specify any checks to be made on incoming data and what to do in case of errors. Such precise descriptions make the system easy to use and consequently increase user satisfaction with the system. Users who know precisely what to do under all conditions will avoid making mistakes and thus accomplish their work as quickly as possible.

Job descriptions are usually documented in a user manual which is produced in conjunction with users during system design. It includes an entry for each task and the jobs necessary to accomplish that task.

JOB ENRICHMENT

Job enrichment, now a common term in practice, is used to make jobs more interesting and rewarding to system users. It gives individuals greater initiative and responsibility, enabling people in the organization to improve themselves through involvement in a variety of activities. They also get more satisfaction from their work because they are contributing to the development of the organization rather than doing some minor and repetitive task.

An important part of job enrichment is to eliminate routine and repetitive tasks. For example, suppose we have a procedure where orders are received and checked for accuracy, then entered into the computer for processing. If the procedure calls for one person to receive the orders, another to check the orders and a third one to enter the orders into the machine, there is little scope for people to improve themselves as they are restricted to one small task and have no opportunity to do other work. They do not see the final outcome of their work, the completed order, because they are only a small cog in the ordering process. Consequently, there can be considerable dissatisfaction and lack of commitment to the work.

A better way would be for each person to follow the order through the whole ordering process; that is, one person takes an order, checks it, enters it into the machine and follows it through from there. Satisfaction is generally increased because people feel responsible for a larger task. In this method there are a number of people doing the same kind of work, and hence there are greater possibilities of team work and people can learn from each other.

Jobs can also be enriched by providing a good interface with the computer, ensuring that people do not feel they are in the service of computers rather than the reverse.

PROCESS DESIGN

Process design starts from the DFD of the new system. This specifies how data is obtained, the medium used to carry the data, and the format of the data on the medium. It also specifies the methods used to move the data and how to perform any calculations on the data. A design method must satisfy a number of requirements, one of which is to make sure that all the processes in the DFD are included in the user procedures. The simplest way to satisfy this requirement is to make each process in the DFD into a task. However, this method may result in many trivial tasks and other design methods are preferred in practice. These methods combine closely related processes into tasks.

Figure 14.15 illustrates such combinations. The system described by the DFD in Figure 14.15 maintains customer accounts. It receives payments for accounts and carries out such accounts maintenance functions as generating accounts statements, reading balances, changing conditions and sending out reminders. One way to divide the DFD into user tasks is shown in Figure 14.15. One task is made up of Processes 7.1, 7.2 and 7.3, which receive, edit and record payments. This task is assigned to one person or a group of people who are responsible for receiving payments from customers. The other task is made up of Processes 7.4, 7.5, 7.6 and 7.7, which carry out accounts maintenance. People assigned to that task are responsible for maintaining accounts.

The combinations used in Figure 14.15 illustrate some general rules used to combine DFDs into tasks. One rule is to combine all processes that operate on a transaction as it passes through the system. To apply the rule, we follow transactions through the system until they are eventually input into the computer system. A user procedure is then defined, describing what is to be done to each transaction as it passes through the system. Entity life-cycle diagrams are useful here. They define the movement of an entity, which can be a transaction, through the system. It is often possible to go directly from an entity life-cycle diagram to a set of procedure tasks.

Another rule is to combine all processes that operate on the same data store into a single task. People assigned to that task become responsible for the data.

One output from design must be a process description, which is usually physical in nature. Process descriptions must, for example, include the physical devices used by procedure users, as well as the physical forms used to carry data. Procedure descriptions also include the tasks in each procedure, the information used by the tasks, and how the information flows in the system.

Flowcharts

Flowcharting is one of the earliest representation tools for physical systems and it is still frequently used to describe physical procedures. A variety of flowcharting techniques are used in practice. A flowcharting technique uses a finite set of symbols to represent

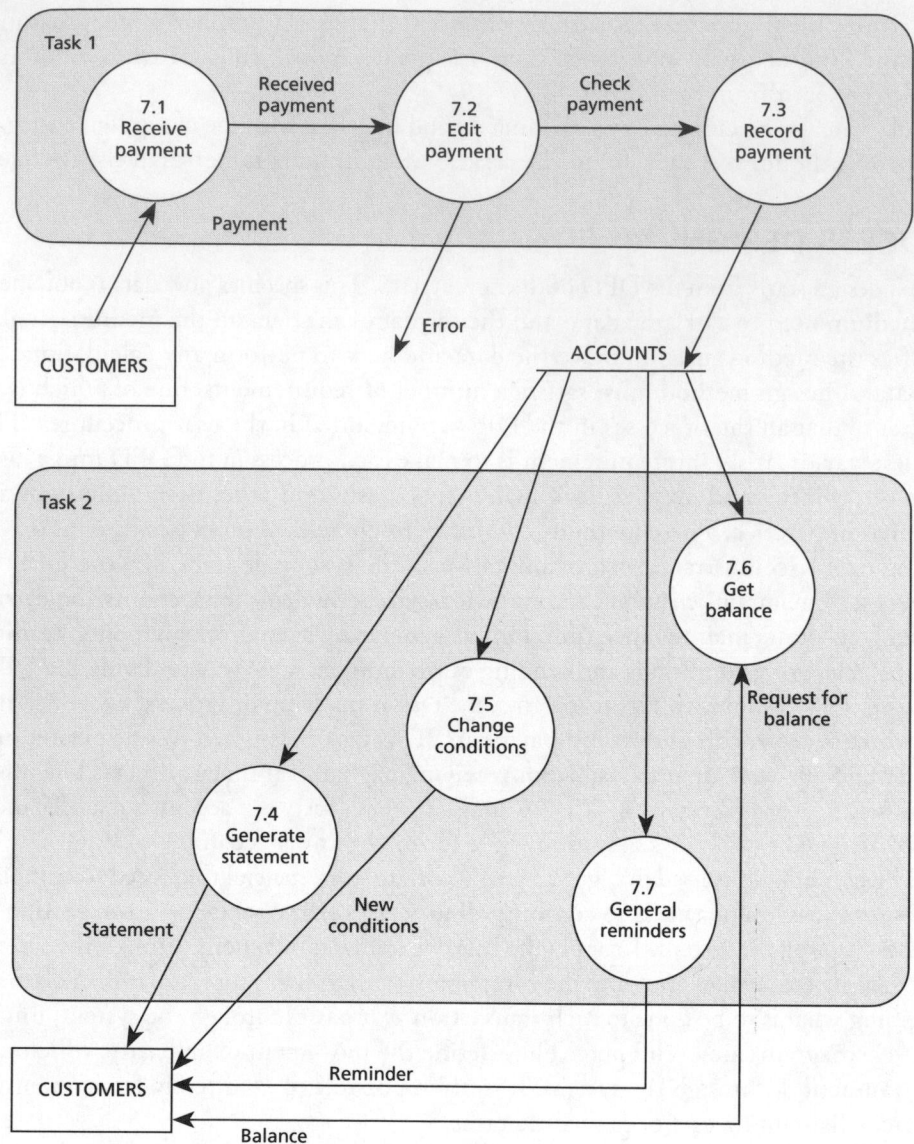

Figure 14.15 *Grouping processes*

system components, which may be physical hardware devices, information stores or flows, as well as processes. Figure 14.16, for example, shows symbols used to represent computer components such as punched cards, terminals, magnetic tape, and so on. Figure 14.17, on the other hand, illustrates symbols used to represent data storage devices and user activities in the procedure.

When drawing flowcharts, we represent each physical system component by one of the flowcharting symbols. Then we look at information flows between these components and join the corresponding representations on the flowchart.

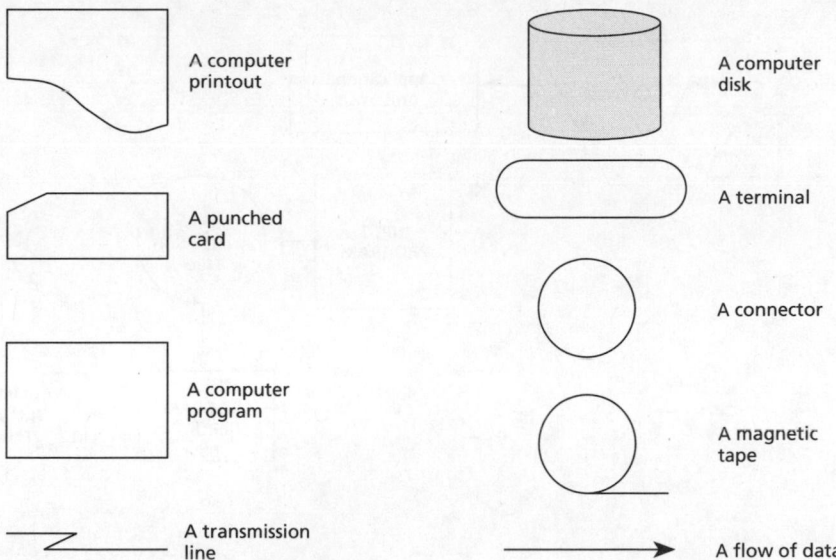

Figure 14.16 *Flowcharting symbols for computer components*

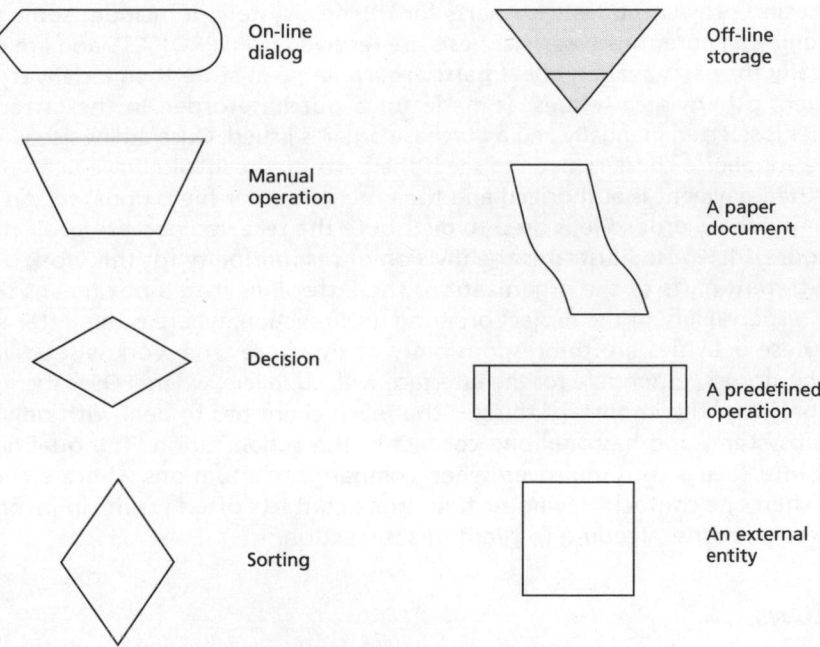

Figure 14.17 *Flowcharting symbols for non-computing components*

Figure 14.18 illustrates a typical flowchart. It illustrates how applications are collected and input into a computer. The applications submitted by the applicants are punched on to cards, which are read by INPUT PROGRAM and stored on tape as the RECEIVED-TRANSACTION-FILE. REPORT PROGRAM is then used to generate the 'application-summary-report' from the tape.

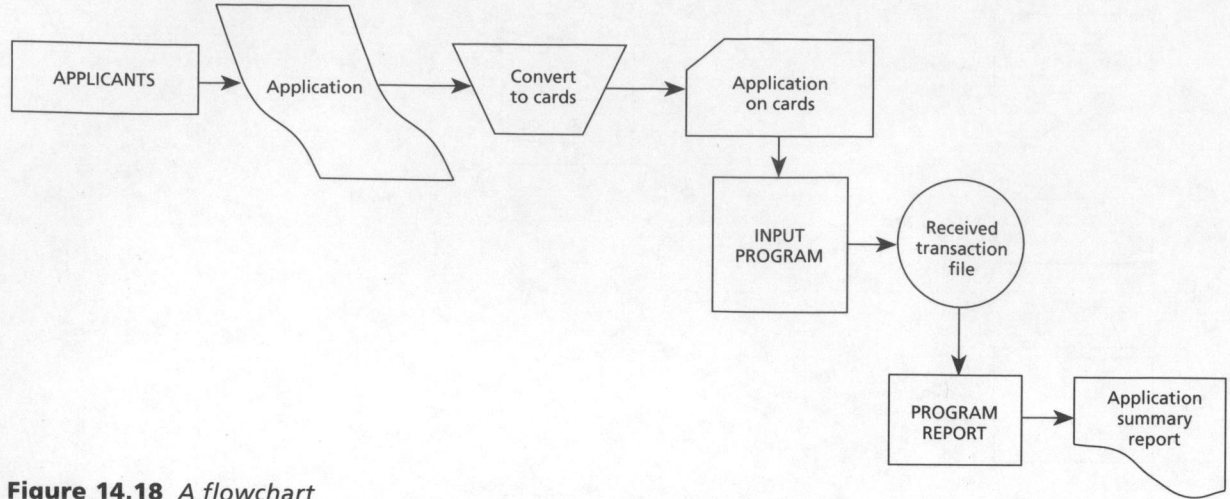

Figure 14.18 *A flowchart*

TEXT CASE D: Construction Company—A Flowchart

Figure 14.19 is a slightly more complicated flowchart which illustrates the process of meeting project requests for parts for the new system. It includes some manual and some computer processes. Requests are received from PROJECTS and are checked manually for parts availability. If parts are available in store then a delivery advice is issued; otherwise a request is made for a purchase order. In the latter case a supplier is selected manually and a purchase order is issued. Once an invoice is received from a supplier, a check is made to see if the parts on the invoice have been received. If so, then payment is authorized and the purchase order file is updated. An update to the purchase order file is used to distribute the received parts to projects.

Figure 14.19 also illustrates the division of responsibility for this work between the different parts of the organization. The letter P next to a box means that this is the responsibility of the project ordering (POS) section, whereas the letter S means that these activities are the responsibility of the store. The work is subdivided so that the store is responsible for the interface with suppliers, where POS is the interface with projects. The important thing is that each client has to deal with only one of the subsystems and has only one contact in the organization. The quality of the client interface is thus improved when compared to situations where a client has more than one contact. Having such multiple contacts often results in inconsistent answers to queries, leading to client dissatisfaction.

Workflows

A new way of talking about processes has emerged in the last few years. This is to use the term **workflow**. A workflow is a graphical representation of the business process, like that shown in Figure 14.20. This diagrammatic representation, which is similar to DOMINO (Kreifelts, 1991), an early office definition language designed at the National Computer Research Laboratory (GMD) in Germany, shows:

Workflow
An instance of a workflow process.

Workflow process
A process made up of a predefined set of steps.

- all the forms used in the procedure;
- the flow control of the forms, shown by the circles;

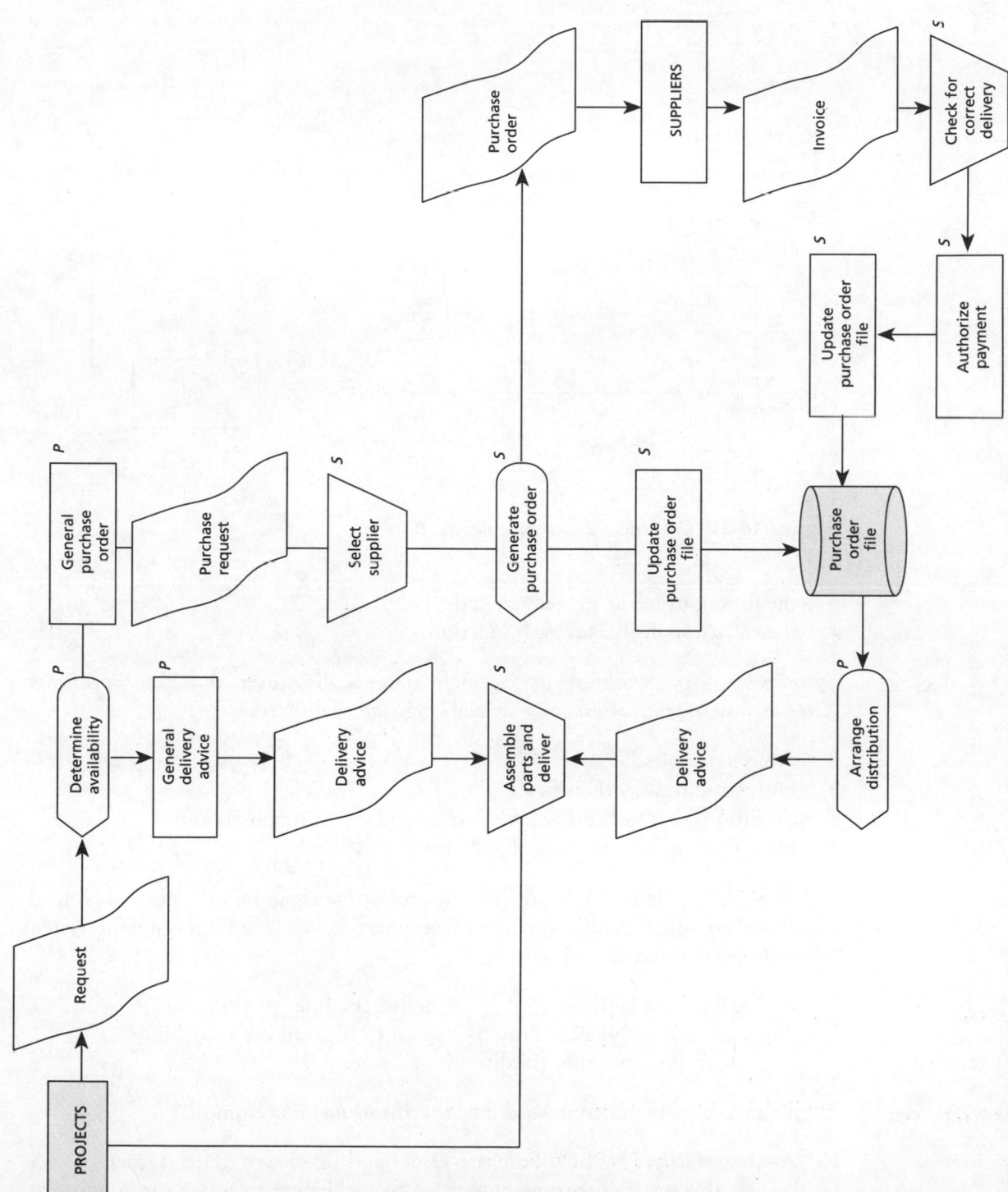

Figure 14.19 *A flowchart for the Construction Company*

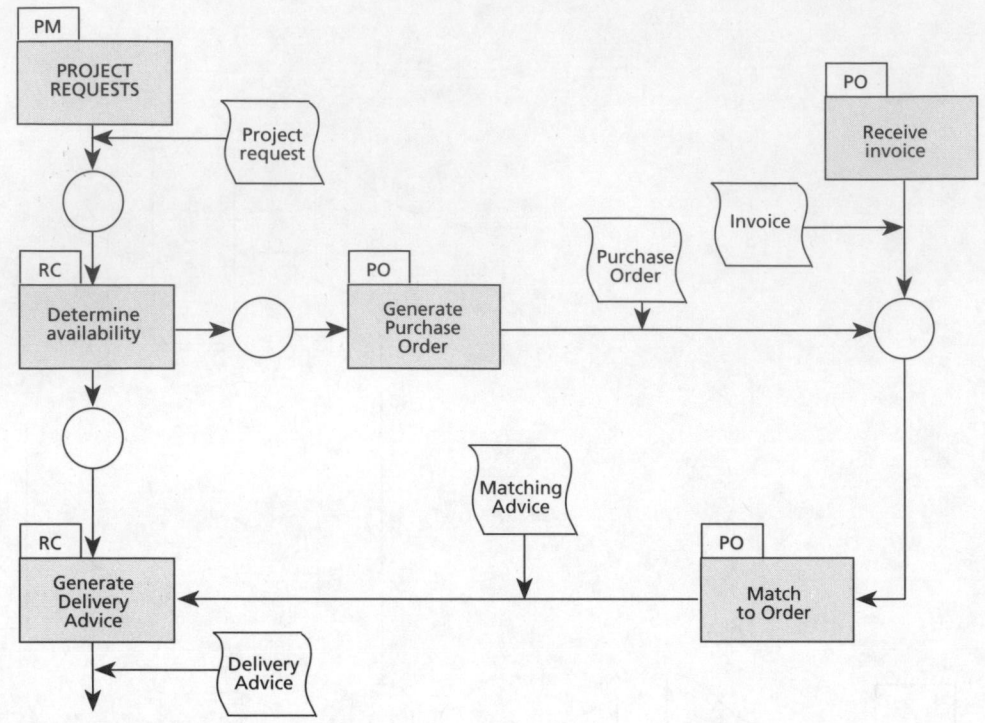

Figure 14.20 *Graphical procedure description*

- the functions in the procedure; and
- the roles responsible for each function.

Systems known as workflow management systems allow users to define workflows. They are often described using a special language that defines:

- the system roles;
- form structures by their fields;
- conditions that indicate when a form is to be sent to a user; and
- the actions to be carried out by the user.

The roles in Figure 14.20 are PM, the project manager, PO, the purchase officer, and RC, the request coordinator. The exact syntax can change from system to system but includes definitions such as:

ROLE Purchase-Officer: 'Jim' . . . to define the role,
Purchase-Officer NEEDS Project-Request to 'Determine availability'
    . . . to specify action conditions for a role.

Logic can also be included in workflow specifications. For example,

Purchase-Officer NEEDS Purchase-Order and Invoice to Match Order
    . . . this specifies that two inputs are needed before an action can commence.

The use of workflow management systems is increasing in practice. Most such systems cater for a specific class of systems—in particular, office clerical processing sequence, where electronic forms pass between users and each user is required to carry out some action on the form and send it, or a new form, to a subsequent user. Many of them allow workflows to be defined using a graphical interface.

Obviously, such a system can be very effective. We would do away with all the different kinds of modeling, the conversions and other design activities. All we need do is specify the business process and the system does the rest.

THE IMPORTANCE OF PROCESS DESIGN

In conclusion, it is perhaps worthwhile to reflect on the role of the process in system design. One may at this stage argue that perhaps the process should be the first thing that appears in the specification of the new system, particularly as it is increasingly realized that good business processes are essential in organizations. They define the way the organization works and must therefore be properly designed if we are to have a high-quality organization. Analysts will increasingly be required first to define the process, including the jobs in the process, and then to choose the technology to implement the process. This way will doubtless become more popular as the emphasis on business processes in analysis increases.

SUMMARY

This chapter described design as a creative problem-solving process. Some design methodologies use objectives to focus the design, whereas others allow objectives to evolve as the design proceeds. The waterfall development cycle focuses design by defining objectives and the chapter described ways of specifying the objectives. Broad design in the linear cycle is made up of two steps: producing a new logical model and following this with a new physical model. It defined some techniques used to define these new models. It then outlined how the physical model is used to derive processes within the new system. A similar approach can be followed in object modeling, although the object approach tends to favor prototyping or evolutionary development processes. The chapter showed how these processes are defined and emphasized the importance of defining jobs to be carried out by people within the process.

DISCUSSION QUESTIONS

14.1   What is the role of objectives in design?

14.2   Describe the four problem-solving steps suggested by DeMarco. Do you think they are natural to the way analysts proceed in analysis?

14.3   What are the advantages of developing an E–R diagram separately from a DFD? Consider the advantages in cases where you are developing a database intended primarily for on-line enquiry or where you are designing a system from scratch.

14.4   What is the domain of change and how would you create it?

14.5   What is the advantage of starting with a broad physical design? Discuss the role of the user interface in broad design. Does it illustrate what will be required of users in the new system?

14.6   What are the advantages of using object modeling in a prototyping development process?

14.7   Suggest some typical flowcharting symbols you would like to use.

14.8   Do you think physical flowcharts are useful, and could they be integrated into structured systems analysis?

 EXERCISES

14.1   Consider the logical model in Figure 14.7 and see if you can develop a different physical implementation than that shown in Figure 14.13. In this alternative physical implementation, inventory maintenance and supplier selection are to be on the same machine. This machine will also process invoices. The idea here is to integrate purchases for the store inventory with purchases for special project requests into one system. Would any changes to logical processing be required to implement such a system? Suggest any changes.

14.2   Look at the DFD and an E–R model for Case Study 2 (travel arrangements) at the back of this book. You should have developed this model as one of the problems in Chapters 6 and 7. Now it is time to propose some possible implementations for this system. Propose alternative automation boundaries for this system and comment on them. You may, for example, consider that some automation may be impractical here. For example, keeping all hotels or airline schedules on computer file may simply call for too much data collection and therefore be impractical. Be careful to suggest only alternatives that can be practically implemented for automation.

14.3   Suppose someone has proposed an additional extension to the project support system whose logical model is given in Figure 14.7. It has been suggested that projects be allowed to initiate their own orders for urgent parts requirements without going through the system. However, before doing so, they should check the inventory holdings. How would you amend the logical model to accommodate this suggestion, and what physical implementations would you suggest?

14.4   Draw a physical flowchart for the following process:

An organization services a variety of equipment. Following a fault report, which may be by letter or phone, a fault report form is filled in and sent to the dispatch center. A repairperson is selected at the dispatch center and a partially filled-in repair report is prepared. This report includes the person's name, the fault description, and the promised date or time of the repair. Following completion of the repair work, details of the work are entered on to the repair report. These details include the time spent and parts used. After the repair form is received, it is costed and an invoice is sent to the customer. Use the symbols shown in Figure 14.17 to describe this system.

BIBLIOGRAPHY

DeMarco, T. (1978), *Structured Analysis and System Specification*, Yourdon Press, New York.

Gane, C. and Sarson, T. (1979), *Structured Systems Analysis*, Prentice Hall, Sydney.

Jacobson, I., Christerson, P.J. and Overgaard, G. (1992), *Object-Oriented Software Engineering*, Addison-Wesley, Reading, Massachusetts.

Kreifelts, T.T., Hinrichs, E., Klein, K, H., Seuffert, P. and Woetzel, G. (1991), 'Experiences with the DOMINO office procedure system', in L. Bannon, M. Robinson and K. Schmidt (eds), *Proceedings of the European Conference on Computer Supported Cooperative Work*, ECSCW, 91, Kluwer, Doedrecht.

User
interface
design

15

CONTENTS

KEY LEARNING OBJECTIVES

How to judge a good interface
What is a user workspace?
Usability and how to measure it
Interface presentation and dialog
The different dialog methods
Characteristics of an interface used for problem solving
Characteristics of an interface for group support
When should off-line processing be used?

311

INTRODUCTION

This and the next three chapters cover system design and describe activities that are carried out during the system design phase. Usually system design is made up of three activities: database design, user procedure design, which includes the user interface, and program development. This chapter covers interface design.

The goal of interface design is to provide the best way for people to interact with computers, or what is commonly known as human computer interaction (HCI). Provision of good interfaces is becoming more important because of its impact on most organizations. This impact is increasing, because most people in organizations are spending more time interacting with computers as part of their normal work—they enter transactions, retrieve data, design artifacts, and do the other myriad things that need to be done in organizations. Their work and satisfaction are improved with better interfaces, leading to an improvement in their quality of work and the effectiveness of the organization.

Many people believe that improving interaction between people and computers is one of the most important activities in system design. One reason for paying more attention to HCI is that, nowadays, computers are used by nearly everyone, not only people closely associated with computers. People are no longer interested in the technology behind the computer; they simply want a tool that is easy to use and can help them with their problems. They don't want to spend a lot of time learning about computer software, they just want computers to make their own work easier. A good interface certainly helps to satisfy this goal.

The interface is usually defined in broad terms during system specification and designed in detail during system design. System specifications usually define how interfaces fit into the new processes and the kinds of input and output that they should provide. The second part describes the actual screen layouts that make up these inputs and outputs. It is often part of detailed design, but very frequently now is also part of prototyping during requirements analysis.

WHAT MAKES A GOOD INTERFACE?

How, then, do we design good interfaces? There are two aspects to interface design. One is to choose the transactions in the business process to be supported by interfaces. This will define the broad interface requirements in terms of what information is input and output through the interface during the transaction. The second is the design of the actual screen presentation, including its layout, and in fact the sequence of screens that may be needed to process the transaction.

CHOOSING THE TRANSACTION MODULES

Defining the transactions that must be supported through interfaces is part of the system specification. For example, the requirements model produced in Jacobson's method includes the interface objects and what information they should present. Each interface object defines one interface module which will interact with the user in some way. Each such interaction results in one transaction with the system. For example, if we return to the requirements model in Figure 12.6, we see that it defines five transactions—send sales advice, initiate, confirm, record new offer and create delivery docket. Each of these can be implemented as one or more screens, or perhaps as Web pages.

DEFINING THE PRESENTATION

Each interaction includes both the presentation and dialog. **Presentation** describes the layout of information, whereas **dialog** describes the sequence of interactions between the user and the computer. Designers must provide interfaces and dialog that will help users to solve their problems, and the presentation must include objects that the user can readily understand in terms of their everyday work. The dialog must also closely correspond to users' normal work and to their **mental model** of the system. The presentation and dialog often depend on what users are doing. There are many reasons for people to interact with computers. The most common are to:

- capture information for storage and later use by system users;
- retrieve information—often called the system output;
- support of everyday operations, such as keeping diaries or writing reports;
- solve a problem or make decisions, such as designing a computer;
- control remote facilities, such as a machine tool;
- develop an artifact, such as writing a report or proposing a budget; and
- support workgroup interactions, often when jointly developing an artifact.

This wide variety of interfaces and users means that interface design is not a straightforward process. The kinds of tasks that particular users do on a computer must first be identified and then the ideal interactions for these tasks sought and programs written to support these interactions. Such programs are often difficult to write because of the need to program displays and predict all possible actions, correct and incorrect, that a user can take on each display. Consequently, interface design tools have been developed that simplify the design and support easy change. As most users have different preferences for displays, even for the same problem, it has been suggested that presentations should be made adaptable to the user. This is an area of continuing research.

This chapter describes what makes a good interface and then describes some typical interfaces and the techniques used to develop them.

EVALUATING THE PRESENTATION

There are many ways of evaluating interfaces. One is to determine how **user-friendly** the interface is. User-friendliness means that the interface should be helpful, tolerant and adaptable, and the user should be happy and confident to use it. Thus, outputs or messages such as:

SYNTAX ERROR, or

IMPROPER DATA—TRY AGAIN

Presentation
The layout of information on a computer screen.

Dialog
An interaction sequence between a user and computer.

Mental model
The way a user sees a problem.

User-friendly
A helpful interface.

do not satisfy the criterion of friendliness. They simply say 'you made a mistake' and it's up to you to find out what it is, and fix it. Instead, the interface should be explanatory and helpful. For example, it might say:

AT THIS POINT YOU SHOULD PUT IN THE DATE IN THE FORMAT DAY/MONTH/YEAR.

YOU SEEM TO HAVE A MONTH WHOSE VALUE IS HIGHER THAN 12 BUT I EXPECT A VALUE IN THE RANGE 1 TO 12.

It is these simple things that must be kept in mind when designing interfaces. Paying attention to friendly interactions results in better interfaces, which not only make users more productive but also make their work easier and more pleasant. The terms 'effectiveness' and 'efficiency' are also often used to describe interfaces. An interface is effective when it results in a user finding the best solution to a problem, and it is efficient when it results in this solution being found in the shortest time with least error. Often, effectiveness is improved by providing an interface that closely parallels the user's *mental model* of their problem—that is, the way the user perceives the problem. What we need to do is design interfaces that support the user's mental model so that the user can easily recognize the issues and work on the problem in a natural way. Mental models, especially for dialog, are different for different kinds of problems. Thus a model for information input and retrieval is different from one used in decision making, because users can quickly consider many options and come up with a better solution. Users must therefore be provided with a suitable *computer workspace* that enables them to do their work easily.

WORKSPACES

The idea that the computer interface is part of a user workspace is an important one. A **workspace** defines all the information that we need for our work, as well as the layout of this information. When we work, we usually lay out information before us in a way that will simplify our tasks. A good workspace will support the mental model of our task and provide facilities for carrying out the actions associated with it. The computer **screen**, then, is seen as part of a user's workspace and must become part of their information and be integrated with other media that forms the workspace, including documents, books, tables and so on.

According to some, the ultimate goal is for computers eventually to make up most, if not all, of a user's workspace. We now have multimedia systems that include images, video and voice. Thus we can support communication in all these media. Why, then, do we need phones, faxes and other devices when all of these can be integrated in the computer screen? All we need to do is link the computer to the phone system and dial through the computer, or have the computer dial numbers for us. Representing the entire workspace on a computer may be the way of the future, but at the moment most computer interfaces are restricted to only a part of the user's workspace. Designers must identify the part of a user's workspace to be represented on the screen, while at the same time presenting information in a way that is natural

Workspace
The space and facilities provided for a user on a screen.

Screen
All the information presented to a user by a computer.

to use and complements the remainder of the user's workspace. This information can include reports, tables and documents, and should be provided in a way that can easily be manipulated in natural chunks rather than through computer-specific commands.

ROBUSTNESS

Another important feature of the interface is its **robustness**. This means that the interface should not fail because of some action taken by the user, or indeed that a user error leads to a system breakdown. This in turn requires checks that prevent users from making incorrect entries.

A good interface can deal with incorrect inputs and prevent errors from entering the system. It also helps the user to correct any errors. There are usually **controls** associated with the input to ensure that no erroneous data enters the system. Similarly, output design must ensure that all data needed by users is provided by the output and that this output is laid out in an easy-to-read way. Furthermore, it must capture this data without introducing any errors.

Robustness
Ability to prevent interface errors from corrupting the system.

Controls
Checks to ensure that system inputs are correct and will not destroy system integrity.

USABILITY

It is important for a designer to know how to evaluate interfaces. While it may be easy to devise an interaction, it is often harder to tell how good it will be in practice. Effectiveness and efficiency are ways to evaluate interfaces. For example, a simple criterion for data capture is to minimize the number of key strokes required of the user. Inputs must be well laid out and easy to understand and use. They must use precise names and allow abbreviations where necessary to speed up input. Repetitive inputs should be avoided.

The term **usability** is often used when evaluating interfaces. The computer interface defines how users interact with a computer and it has an important bearing on users' acceptance of a system. There is considerable work in progress on how to define and measure the usability of an interface or, to use more contemporary terminology, to define the **usability metrics**. Metrics are the things about usability that can be measured. What we need to do next is to choose their method of measurement. Metrics cover objective factors as well as subjective factors. These are:

Usability
A term that defines how easy it is to use an interface.

Usability metrics
The things that can be measured to describe usability.

- *Analytical metrics*, which can be directly described—for example, whether all the information needed by a user appears on the screen.
- *Performance metrics*, which include things like the time used to perform a task, system robustness, or how easy it is to make the system fail.
- *Cognitive workload metrics*, or the mental effort required of the user to use the system. It covers aspects such as how closely the interface approximates the user's mental model or reactions to the screen.
- *User satisfaction metrics*, which include such things as how helpful the system is or how easy it is to learn.

The next question is how to measure these factors.

Measuring usability

Usability is becoming more important, and consequently many software providers emphasize this issue and often require interfaces to be evaluated for their usability. Since no standard usability measures exist at present, this is an issue facing the computer community. Usability measurement depends on the kind of metric being measured. It is usually measured by questionnaire or observation. Thus, analytical metrics, such as 'is all the needed information on the screen?', can often be observed. Performance metrics, or how long it takes to carry out some task, can often be measured by observing how long users take to carry out a task. Other metrics may be harder to measure because they must consider the mental effort that is required of a user. Metrics on cognitive overload often center on the stress level of the user, which can be measured by a user's heart rate or blood pressure, and it is important that these measurements are made under actual working conditions. User satisfaction metrics can usually be evaluated through questionnaires or by interviewing users to find out their general attitude to the system.

It is agreed that usability itself depends on many factors, sometimes called the context, which include:

- the kind of user, ranging from the expert to novice user;
- the kind of task carried out by the user;
- the organizational environment;
- the workplace conditions; and
- the technical system.

The whole area of selecting usability metrics and their measurement is outside the scope of this text. Nevertheless, readers should note that considerable work is in progress to define standards for usability. The approach is usually to provide guidelines for selecting factors from the context and then proposing tools to measure the factors. A user could then analyze their context, obtain the recommended factors and then proceed to measure them.

Designing for usability

Having introduced the notion of usability, the next question is how to design for usability. Do we simply build a system and then test and adjust interfaces, or do we progressively check for usability as the system design proceeds? The second approach is obviously preferable, as it minimizes the amount of rework. To make it work, however, we have to integrate usability considerations into the system development cycle. Design for usability must be user-centered and must ensure user participation. It is also experimental and iterative. This means that we must get the users involved early in system design and thus integrate usability design into the development cycle.

 ## INTERACTIVE INTERFACES

The ideal interactive interface would be one where the user can interact with the computer using natural language. The user types in a sentence on the input device (or perhaps speaks into a speech recognition device) and the computer analyzes this sentence and responds to it. The user could then follow up with another sentence to which the computer would respond, and so on. However, technology has not yet advanced to the stage where it can support such natural interfaces, and most dialogs between users and machines take a much more restricted form. It is, however, important to ensure that interaction supports problem-solving methods that are natural to the user.

Consequently, the form of dialog and presentation depends on the kind of system supported. There are different kinds of interaction—for example:

- dialogs in transaction processing that allow the input of one transaction that describes an event or action, such as a new appointment, or a deposit in an account;
- designing an artifact such as a document or a report, or the screen layout itself;
- making a decision about a course of action, such as what route to take to make a set of deliveries; and
- communication and coordination with other group members.

Each of these kinds of interaction is different. Thus, interfaces for transaction-based systems will be different than those for decision support. There will also be additional differences if groups rather than individuals are supported. Each of these requires a different workspace. Workspaces for simple transactions are usually bounded and predictable, whereas those for design can dynamically change as new ideas come to mind.

Transaction design is perhaps the simplest of all the interactive designs. It deals with one user, usually entering one or at most a very few related facts. Transactions are usually made through a terminal, with messages interchanged in a relatively short space of time. One important property here is that an output is obtained from the computer very soon after the input, allowing the user to make additional inputs if necessary. Transaction outputs need to produce the minimal information for a particular purpose. If the information is insufficient, then the user can ask for more information. Thus the computer can be selective in the information it outputs. Interactive interface design calls for user–machine dialogs that permit rapid interchange of information between computers and their human users.

USER DIALOG FOR TRANSACTIONS

Interactive transaction dialog is usually an interchange of messages between the user and the computer in a relatively short space of time. The dialog concerns one fact and centers around the attributes related to that fact. Different presentation methods are used in on-line user dialog for entering transaction data. The most common methods are menus, commands or templates. The difference between these methods is described below and illustrated in Figure 15.1, where alternative ways of entering a person's name, address and telephone number using different dialog methods are shown.

Menus

A **menu** system presents the user with a set of actions and requires the user to select one of those actions. Once an action is selected, another menu is presented. This next menu depends on the selected action. In Figure 15.1(a), the computer asks the

Menu
A set of alternative selections presented to a user in a window.

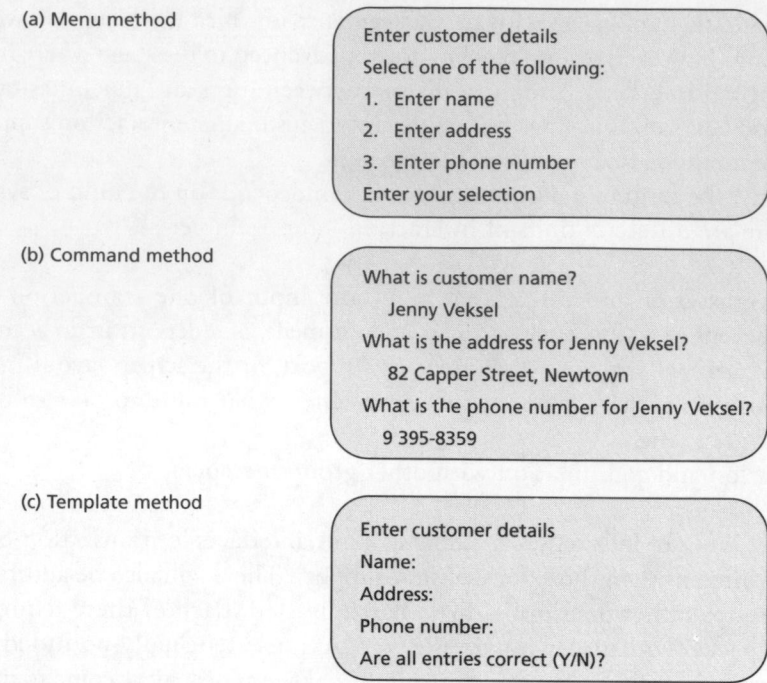

Figure 15.1 *Methods used in dialog design*

user to select one of a number of possible actions, in this case whether to enter a name, an address or a telephone number. After one of these is selected, the computer may ask the user to select another set of actions, and so on.

Note that actions are selected by typing in a number rather than entering the actual name. This saves keystrokes and makes the system easier to use.

Commands and prompts

In this case the computer asks the user for specific inputs. On getting the input, the computer may respond with some information or ask the user for more information. This process continues until all the data has been entered into the computer or retrieved by the user. In Figure 15.1(b) the system prompts the user for successive pieces of data. It first asks the user for the person's name. When the user enters the name, the computer asks the user for the address. Then it asks the user to enter the phone number.

Templates

Templates are equivalent to forms on a computer. A form is presented on the screen and the user is requested to fill in the form. Usually several labeled fields are provided and the user enters data into the blank spaces. Fields in the template can be highlighted or blink to attract the user's attention. The advantage templates have over menus or commands is that the data is entered with fewer screens.

COMPARING DIALOG METHODS FOR TRANSACTION PROCESSING

Different methods may be appropriate for different purposes. The template is probably the best way to enter information about an entity, like a person, because all the data is on the screen at the time of input. The user can view it, check it and decide to input it in one screen. However, a template may not be the best way to change certain details about a person, such as their address or telephone number. A menu system may be more useful in this case, because it displays the changes that can be made and asks the user to select that change.

Most dialogs, however, use combinations of all these methods. A dialog usually goes through a number of screens, with the response to one screen usually resulting in a new screen being displayed. A response to that screen leads to yet another screen, and so on. Often dialogs are described by screen hierarchies.

One such screen hierarchy is shown in Figure 15.2. It starts with a menu that asks the user to select one of three actions—enter a new customer, delete a customer or change customer details. A new screen is displayed, depending on the choice. If a new customer is to be entered, then a template asking for customer details may be displayed. If deletion is specified, there may be a command asking for the name of the customer to be deleted. If details are to be changed, then another menu may be displayed asking the user to define the kind of change.

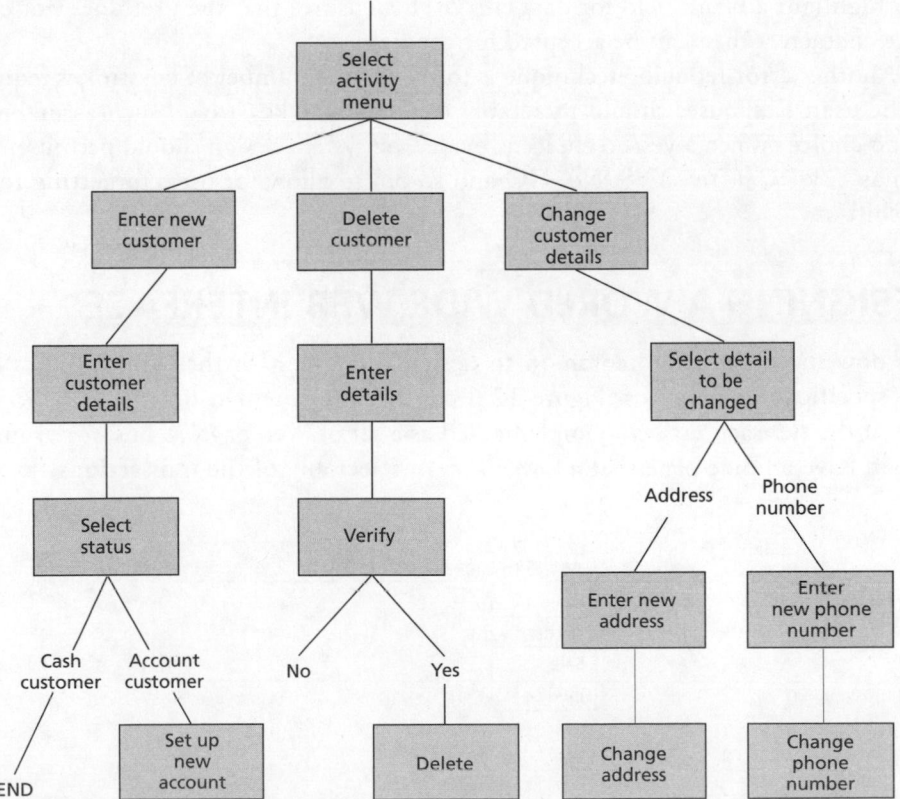

Figure 15.2 *Dialog hierarchy*

The dialog hierarchy may go down any number of levels. In Figure 15.2, the hierarchy goes down a number of levels to enter a new customer. First it gets the customer details, then it asks for customer status. If the customer is to be an account customer, the hierarchy goes down one more level to set up an account for the customer.

A very common menu presentation that illustrates such hierarchical structures are *pop-up menus*, illustrated in Figure 15.3. Here one level of the menu is the top of the screen. The user can click on one entry at this level, say 'Update'. This causes the next level to pop up. In Figure 15.3 this level gives additional options—that is, whether to update 'Project', 'Account', 'Sale' or 'Invoice'. One of these is selected and its menu replaces the top menu. The process can then repeat through any number of levels.

An alternative is to replace menu lists by sets of icons. There may be an icon for projects, another for accounts, and so on. The user selects the option by clicking on the icon.

CONTROLS FOR INTERACTIVE TRANSACTION INPUT

Most transaction input systems include controls to prevent erroneous data from entering the system. Such controls are made by edit programs which check every field of data entry at the time of input and inform the user as soon as there is an error. The user is usually informed by a loud beep, together with a message that describes the error.

Some techniques are also commonly used to help users avoid errors. One method is to highlight a blank field for data entry. This ensures that the user does not enter more characters than can be accepted for the field.

Another error-reducing technique is to reduce the number of keystrokes required by the user. Responses should preferably use only one keystroke, such as making a yes/no choice. When a yes/no choice is made, the system design should permit entries such as Y, y, N, n, Yes, YES, No, NO and so on, to allow for users forgetting to use the shift key.

DESIGNING A WORLD WIDE WEB INTERFACE

It is now more and more common to design interfaces for the World Wide Web. The specification shown in Figure 12.6 can be implemented on the WWW, with each of the transactions being implemented as a set of Web pages. Thus, for example, we can have a home page that allows users to select any of the transactions through

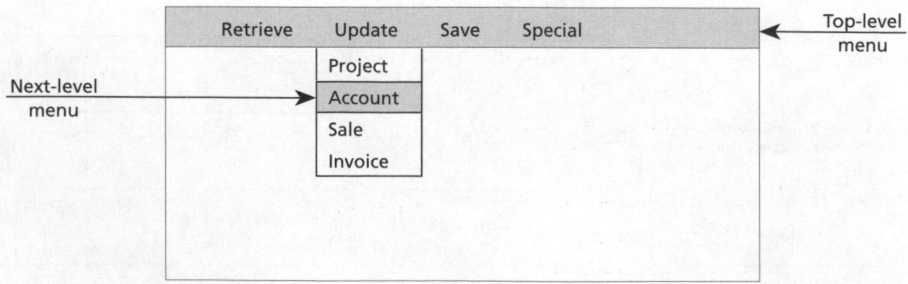

Figure 15.3 *Pop-up menus*

a menu. Selecting a transaction will open up new pages that allow users to provide the inputs needed by the transaction.

Figure 15.4 illustrates a skeleton set of pages used to initiate a trade. It is assumed there is a home page for the interactive trading system. The HOME PAGE may include a description of the system, together with a menu (often a set of graphic images on the WWW) that allows the user to select any transaction available to that user. The menu selections open pages that are indicated by the lines emanating from the page. On selecting the initiate trade transaction, new options are provided to the user on a TRADE PAGE. One of these is to search through the products. A particular product may be selected through an entry in a form field, and this in turn will allow the user to view details about the product in a PRODUCT PAGE. Alternatively, the user may select a particular producer. If on searching a PRODUCT PAGE, the user becomes interested in purchasing that product, then the user may open up a page to set up a trader for the product, or alternatively look at the product's sales history, prior to initiating a trade.

The World Wide Web also supports a new kind of interface, commonly known as the site map. This is a page that has a pictorial representation of all the major pages on the site. These pages can then be selected by clicking on an icon that represents the page on the map.

INTERACTIONS FOR PROBLEM-SOLVING

The type of interface described in Figures 15.1 and 15.2 supports a relatively simple mental model. The mental model usually concerns a bounded fact and its entry into the computer, or a simple response to a transaction screen—for example, entering a simple fact like a person's attendance record. The model can be extended by allowing users to relate the entry to other information and thus extend the scope of their work. For example, prior to making the entry the user may need to refer to other information to make decisions. Thus, before approving a purchase a manager may

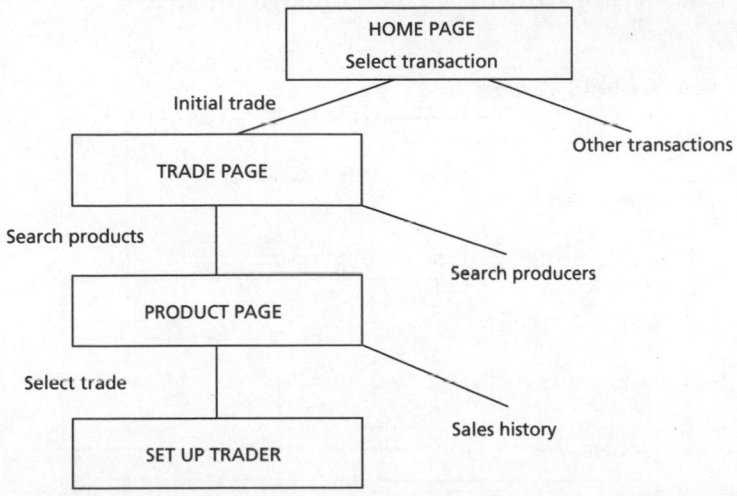

Figure 15.4 *Web pages to initiate a trade*

wish to examine the budget, the previous record of purchases and supplier history. This may be done either by preprogramming all these actions or by allowing the user to select what they want to see. Such selections can be made using pop-up menus and the auxiliary information displayed as separate **windows** on a multi-window display.

Window
An enclosed area on a screen.

MULTI-WINDOW DISPLAYS

By allowing a multi-window display, users have all the information in front of them. This supports a mental model that allows all the factors to be jointly considered when making a decision. A multi-window presentation is illustrated in Figure 15.5.

The presentation in Figure 15.5 includes four windows. One window is the order, another is a window of project budgets, a third window shows prices quoted by the suppliers, and a fourth shows supplier records. Users are presented with all the information needed to make a decision about placing the order. They can look up the prices for the parts, select the supplier and make an entry in the order. Windows can be selected, usually by clicking on them with a mouse, one at a time, when the menu for the selected window appears on the screen. A further extension is to include a work window used for simple computations, such as computing the total value of an order following supplier selection. In that case, the screen would be the total workspace for the user. Finally, it should be possible to move information from one window to another, thus supporting simple integration of information from different functions—for example, moving a supplier price to an order.

MULTIMEDIA DISPLAYS

Screen presentations are now becoming richer because it is possible to use more than one medium in a display. A screen may now contain some text, an image, a video and even speech. Each of these may use their own window. This provides more options to the screen designer. For example, a user may be controlling tools in a machine shop. There may be a video that monitors such tools and displays them on a multimedia display. The user can then activate such tools through the screen.

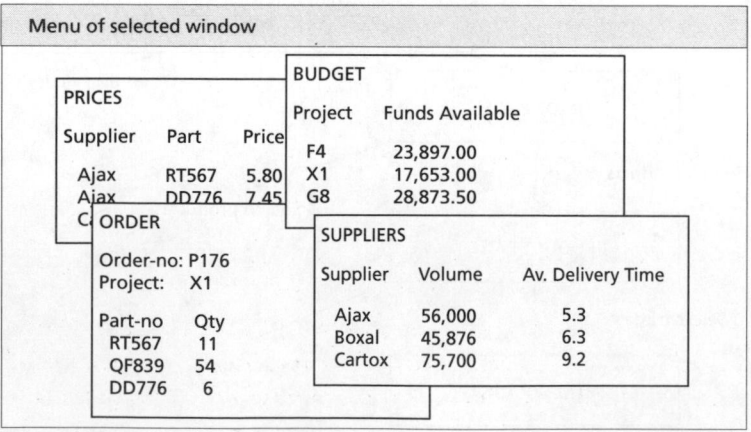

Figure 15.5 *A multi-window presentation*

INTERFACES FOR PERSONAL SUPPORT

Transaction interfaces often specify a user action as part of a business process. Apart from being involved directly in a business process, many users must do some personal work to develop information that they can use in the business process. The most common example is working on an artifact such as a report, a budget or a diagram. Parts of these artifacts may then be used in a business process. The computer can be used to develop the artifact and to transfer parts of it into the business process.

The kinds of support provided in personal work includes document processing software, such as word processors, spreadsheets and so on. Such personal support systems pay special attention to the presentation and layout of artifact information so that the user can select and view parts of the artifact and apply various transformations to them. There is also more emphasis on using a variety of media in preparing artifacts and in combining information from more than artifact. This includes such processes as:

- combining a document from many parts, such as moving a drawing into a text; and
- using reference material.

The artifact itself may be presented using different media such as text, graphs, images, sound or video. The usual approach is to use windows to allow users to lay out their work in front of them, and menus in order to select transformation commands to apply to the artifact.

Again, an important consideration in problem solving is to accurately represent the user's mental model on the computer screen. Close correspondence to the mental model allows the user to quickly recognize the problem and thus simplify the decision to reach a solution. This requires special attention to the layout of the screen.

Important features of such interfaces are:

- defining the mental domain concepts and their representation by *icons*;
- identifying the actions to be taken by users; and
- subdividing the problem space and representing each part by a separate window.

Similar features are needed to move information from personal artifacts on to screens provided by a business process. What we need is a multi-window display, where one window is part of a business process, and the other is a personal document. We should be able to select part of a personal document and move it into the business process window.

 ## INTERFACES FOR WORKGROUPS

Workspaces for workgroups have some additional features when compared to those used for personal support—for example, showing interaction between users. Furthermore, the idea of awareness must be included in the interface. Awareness is a feature that enables each user to be aware of what other users in the group are doing. Responsibility for artifact manipulation may be distributed, and the user may be working on one part of a document but at the same time must be aware of what other users are doing to other document parts.

WISIWYS
'What I see is what you see' interface.

The kind of interface depends on the group characteristics. For example, suppose a group of people are working at the same time but at different places and all group members need to share the information. What is needed is an interface known as a **WISIWYS** (What I see is what you see) interface, where any change made by one user appears on the screens of all the other users, as shown in Figure 15.6. Each user has a window or windows for a personal workspace and another window for a group workspace. The group workspace also has a set of identifiers, which may be faces, of all the group members. One is shaded to show who currently has control of the workspace. The entry made by that member appears in the workgroup window of all the other users. Control from one user to another may be through a shared mouse. A controlling member must 'park' a mouse at some spot and it can then be grabbed by another member. Alternatively, control can rotate from one member to another, perhaps with a predetermined time limit.

The kinds of additional windows needed to support coordination vary with the kind of group. Figure 15.6 assumed a simple interchange of messages, or perhaps changes made on an artifact in a sequence. These windows may show other group members, or they may contain information on who is working on particular parts of a jointly owned artifact. WYSIWYS is only one possible kind of group support. It caters for synchronous interaction between participants. There are also other kinds of support, such as WISIWYD (What I see is what you did) or WISIWIG (What I see I what I get.

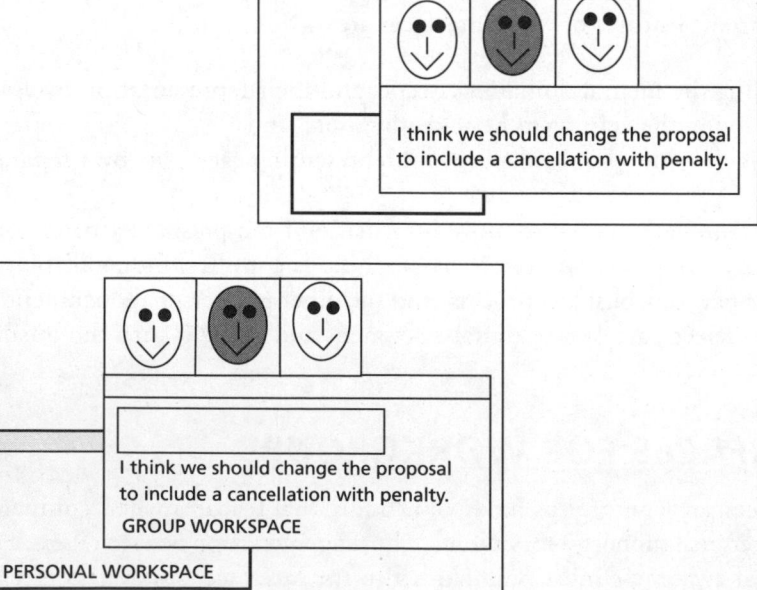

Figure 15.6 *Additional windows for group support*

INTERFACE DESIGN TOOLS

Interface design must center on usability, and users must participate in the design process. It is not possible to design usable interfaces without some experimentation. Few people can anticipate how users will react to an interface and consequently one cannot expect to design an acceptable interface, directly from user requirements. Instead, the design becomes iterative, with experimentation and testing, until a suitable interface is produced. Such experimentation must also be integrated with the development cycle.

Interface design can thus be quite a complex and laborious process unless we have tools that enable us easily to construct trial interfaces and quickly change them. Such experimentation is not possible if each new trial requires us to write programs for the presentation, as well as to program the often complex dialogs between the user and the computer. Often compromises are made in designing screens to reduce programming cost, but these may result in reduced interface effectiveness. Effective interfaces can only be designed by using higher-level tools for defining interfaces without such laborious programming. Such tools are now becoming available.

However, it has not yet been possible to define a general language or system for defining interfaces, because a common set of characteristics have not yet been found for such diverse interactions as entering a simple transaction or helping with a complex decision. Consequently, tools for interface design can be classed into different layers, and dialogs are built up using these layers. Some of the better-known layers are:

- the *basic layer*, which includes window support or menu support;
- *presentation layers*, which allow users to define presentations particular to their problem; and
- the *dialog layer*, which allows users to define dialogs for their particular problem.

The idea is that by defining the tools in layers, one can build a tool at one layer using functions provided by tools at a lower level. We can use a window support system to define presentation using the window constructs—for example, the various screen painters provided by application generators or database systems. We can then define dialogs by rules that use the attributes of the defined screens. Eventually, further layers will be developed to provide more powerful tools which can include the object level to define generic interface concepts, and the application level to define customized screens for particular application classes.

Various tools are becoming available for developing interfaces and publishing on the World Wide Web. The primary tool here is HTML (HyperText Markup Language). A number of editors are now available to generate HTML to set up Web pages.

User interface tools are an important area of research in computing. They are particularly important for prototyping, because they make it easy to set up interfaces to illustrate proposed systems to users. The goal of such research is to provide tools where trial prototype interfaces can be gradually improved and become part of the new system. As a result, software that is developed as part of a prototype is not thrown away but becomes part of the system, so that ultimately what starts off as a storyboard can become a system. To achieve this goal, interface design tools must be integrated with the other software systems used in application development, such as transaction processing systems and database management systems. Again, this goal is now being actively addressed in research and development.

OFF-LINE TRANSACTIONS

This chapter would not be complete without referring to off-line interfaces and interactive interfaces. In off-line interfaces there is no direct response to transactions. Instead, a number of transactions may be collected and input as a batch. This batch is processed later, sometimes overnight, and outputs are distributed later to users. Thus, considerable time can elapse from the time transactions are input into the computer to the time the response is obtained. A typical batch run is shown in Figure 15.7. It begins by collecting a set of transactions which are entered on to a form. The form is then passed to data entry operators who enter the data into machine-readable form. One early method was to enter the data on to punched cards which were then read into the computer. A more common way now is to enter the data through a computer terminal.

The transactions are stored on an input file and the input file goes through an edit run, which outputs any errors found in the transactions. The error transactions can be corrected and input again on a subsequent batch run. The correct transactions are passed to a FILE UPDATE program which updates existing files using transaction data. The file is then processed by a report program to produce a set of reports.

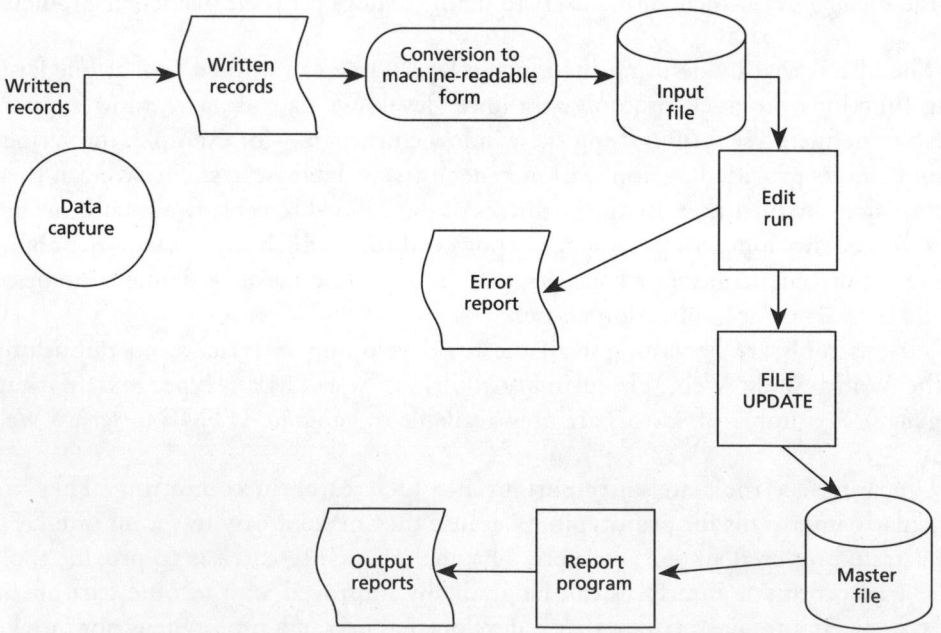

Figure 15.7 *A batch run*

OFF-LINE INPUT INTERFACE

The term **data entry** is often used to describe transaction input. Here, transactions are collected on to forms at the point of capture. A batch of these forms may then be given to a data entry operator, who will input them into the computer. The form that is used to capture the transactions can be an important component of batch processing. Form design is quite important. Forms must be easy to fill in and should not lead to unnecessary delays while users decide how to enter an unusual transaction. Form layout must be clear and must capture the complete data necessary for the transaction. Sometimes forms allow codes to be used to minimize the time needed to fill them out.

Data entry
Transaction input for later batch processing.

Figure 15.8 illustrates a typical form, called 'on-site sales'. This form is used to collect information about sales made by salespersons in an organization. One form is filled out following each sale, at the time and place of the sale. The items sold are also recorded. The form is then sent to a central computer site for data entry.

The 'on-site sales' form is divided into a number of parts. One part records information about the customer, another contains information about the salesperson, a third part contains the items sold to the customer, and finally the method of payment is recorded.

Some efforts have been made to make it easier to fill in the form. The salespersons have a code and must enter that code. This reduces the number of keystrokes later, because a short code rather than a long name must be entered into the computer. Similarly, only a circle is needed to select an area for a user, and one key stroke will be needed to enter the area code into the computer. Only a tick is needed to enter the method of payment.

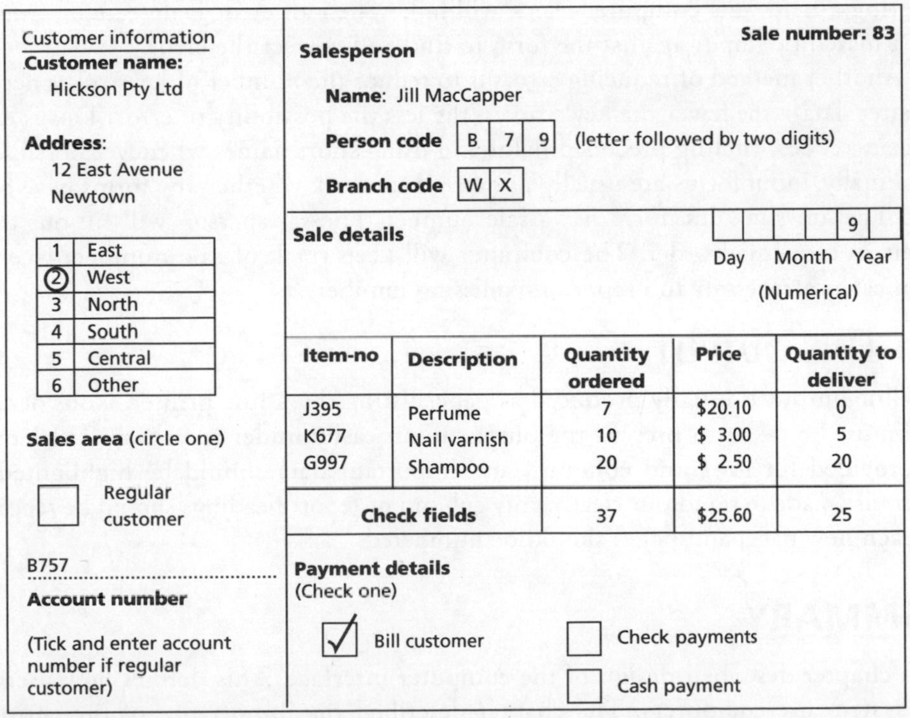

Customer information
Customer name:
Hickson Pty Ltd

Address:
12 East Avenue
Newtown

1	East
(2)	West
3	North
4	South
5	Central
6	Other

Sales area (circle one)

☐ Regular customer

B757
Account number

(Tick and enter account number if regular customer)

Sale number: 83

Salesperson

Name: Jill MacCapper
Person code B 7 9 (letter followed by two digits)
Branch code W X

Sale details 9
Day Month Year
(Numerical)

Item-no	Description	Quantity ordered	Price	Quantity to deliver
J395	Perfume	7	$20.10	0
K677	Nail varnish	10	$ 3.00	5
G997	Shampoo	20	$ 2.50	20
	Check fields	37	$25.60	25

Payment details
(Check one)

☑ Bill customer
☐ Check payments
☐ Cash payment

Figure 15.8 *ON-SITE SALES form*

CONTROLS WITH OFF-LINE INPUT

One important off-line input requirement is to ensure that all data is correct and no errors are entered into the computer. If erroneous data is entered, then incorrect data will be stored in the computer. This in turn will lead to errors in the system when the data is used.

Two types of errors commonly appear in inputs. One occurs when the transaction data itself is incorrect—for example, incorrect dates, errors in data formatting and so on. The other type occurs when there is an error in entering the transaction on to the form or transcribing the data from the form into the computer. This is called a transcription error. Finally, there is the possibility of someone forgetting to input a transaction into the computer.

Different methods are used to protect the system against these kinds of errors. First, guidelines are included on the input form to guard against erroneous entries being made by the user. Thus, the 'on-site sales' form includes simple instructions such as those telling the user how to enter a date. The day comes first, then the month and then the year. Computer edit programs are used to check data input to the computer. The computer system contains information about expected data formats and ranges, and it checks the incoming data to see if it satisfies these requirements.

Transcription errors are detected by including check fields with the transaction data. The 'on-site sales' form includes a number of check fields. For example, there is a check field for QTY-ORDERED. Thus all entries in the QTY-ORDERED column are summed and the sum is entered into the check field. The computer checks whether the input check field equals the sum of the fields. If the operator makes an error entering a field, this computer check will fail. When an error is detected, someone must match the input against the form to find and correct the error.

Another method of reducing errors is to reduce the number of keystrokes needed to enter data—the fewer the key strokes, the less the possibility of error. This is done by using codes, circling precoded fields and using short names whenever possible.

Finally, input forms are usually numbered to check whether any forms have been lost. The 'on-site sales' form has a sale number. The salesperson will fill out these forms in sequential order. The computer will keep track of sale numbers received from each salesperson and report any missing numbers.

OFF-LINE OUTPUT

Off-line output is usually produced as paper listings by a line printer. Considerable care must be taken to present the output in an easily understood way. Titles must be provided for rows and columns, and important data should be highlighted or otherwise made to stand out clearly. Any column or report headings should be repeated on each new page, and pages should be numbered.

◖ SUMMARY

This chapter described design of the computer interface. This defines how users in the system use computers. The chapter described the importance of presenting a meaningful user interface and discussed some criteria that interfaces should meet and the need to measure these criteria. It introduced the idea of the computer workspace and how this should be designed to simplify the work of users. The interface must be designed to capture all the information without error and to provide, in an easily readable form, any information needed by the users. The chapter concluded by describing tools that can be used to design interfaces and off-line input of data.

DISCUSSION QUESTIONS

15.1 What do you understand by the term *meaningful interface*?

15.2 What do you understand by the term *transaction*?

15.3 How would you design a transaction?

15.4 What is a user-friendly interface?

15.5 Why is usability measurement important?

15.6 What factors are important when measuring the usability of an interface?

15.7 What kinds of interactions are commonly found in organizations?

15.8 What do you understand by the term *workspace*?

15.9 Do you think the computer should encompass all of a user's workspace?

15.10 Compare different types of on-line user dialog for transaction processing and describe the advantages of each.

15.11 What features distinguish group support workspaces from workspaces that support one user?

15.12 Why are user interface tools built up in layers?

15.13 What are the better-known layers?

15.14 Why is it important to link user interface design tools with other software systems used in application design?

15.15 How would an interaction for computer entry differ from that used in decision making?

15.16 List some criteria for good form design.

EXERCISES

15.1 Design a transaction dialog for entering a project request for the Construction Company.

15.2 Suggest useful windows for a multi-window display for the schedulers in Universal Electronics.

BIBLIOGRAPHY

Barfield, L. (1993), *The User Interface: Concepts and Design*, Addison-Wesley, Wockingham.

Bass, L. and Dewan, P. (eds) (1993), *User Interface Software*, Wiley, Chichester.

Bullinger, H. J. and Fahnrich, K. P. (1991), 'User interface management—the strategic view', in H. J., Bullinger (ed.), *Human Aspects in Computing: Design and Use of Interactive Systems and Work with Terminals*, Elsevier Science Publishers B.V.

Dix, A., Findlay, J., Abowd, G. and Beale, R. (1993), *Human-Computer Interaction*, Prentice-Hall, New York.

Harrison, M.D. and Monk, A.F. (eds) (1986), *People and Computers: Designing for Usability*, Cambridge University Press, Cambridge.

Hurley, W.D. (1992), 'Integrating user interface development and modern software development', *International Journal on Software Engineering and Knowledge Engineering*, Vol. 2, No. 2, pp. 227–50.

Mayhew, D.J. (1992), *Principles and Guidelines in Software User Interface Design*, Prentice-Hall, Englewood Cliffs, New Jersey.

Molich, R. and Nielsen, J. (March 1990), 'Improving a human-computer dialog', *Communications of the ACM*, Vol. 33, No. 3, pp. 338–48.

Nielsen, J. (1993), *Usability Engineering*, Academic Press, San Diego, California.

Shafran, A. (1996), *Creating and Enhancing Netscape Web Pages*, QUE, Indianapolis.

Shneiderman, B. (1992), *Designing the User Interface* (2nd edn), Addison-Wesley, Reading, Massachusetts.

Database design

16

CONTENTS

Introduction   332

KEY LEARNING OBJECTIVES

Defining logical data structures

How to draw access paths

How to satisfy access requirements

◇ INTRODUCTION

One component of the system specification is data requirements, which are converted to a database specification during system design. The database specification is then used to construct a database during implementation. The kind of conversion used during system design depends on the kind of implementation model.

Figure 16.1 illustrates the main conversion alternatives. One is the common path followed in structured systems analysis. Here the requirements specifications use the E–R model. During system design the E–R model is first converted to a set of record types with each record made up of a number of fields. The set of record types is here called the logical record structure. The logical record structure is then converted to a definition for a database management system. The database definition, which is the implementation model, depends on the database management system (DBMS). Consequently, techniques that depend on the DBMS are used in this step because different DBMSs support different kinds of links between their records. Design at the implementation level also defines how data is to be accessed. Access requirements, which define access needs, are used later to choose DBMS structures.

Such conversion is not needed with object models that are converted to object-oriented implementations. In that case, the system model is based on object classes, as is the implementation. There is also the alternative where the user requirements are specified as object classes but the implementation uses a record-based DBMS. In that case, the object model must be converted to a logical record structure, which is then converted to a database implementation in the same way as occurred with structured systems analysis.

This chapter first describes logical record structures and how to derive them. It then describes DBMS software and physical design. Because database design is a complex process, it cannot all be described in detail in one chapter. This chapter therefore gives a brief outline only. It will give you an idea of how to go about database design, but you will have to read one of a number of books devoted totally to database design to get the details.

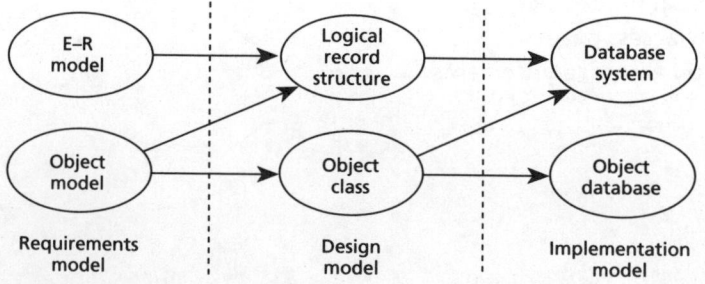

The requirements model is converted to a system model.
The system model is then converted to an implementation model.

Figure 16.1 *Database design steps*

WHAT DO LOGICAL RECORD STRUCTURES LOOK LIKE?

There is no standard for logical record structures at the system level. A typical **logical record structure** is shown in Figure 16.2. The logical record structure is made up of a number of record types. Each record type is represented by a rectangular box and has a unique name. The three record types in Figure 16.2 are named PROJECTS, USE and PARTS. Each record type is made up of a number of fields. In Figure 16.2, record type PROJECTS is made up of three fields: PROJECT-NO, START-DATE and BUDGET. To distinguish the logical structure from the E–R diagram, the record type name appears outside the box inside which the record type fields are placed.

The logical record structure also contains links between record types. Each logical record link is labeled by the fields that appear in both linked record types and is directed from one record to another. Thus, the link between PROJECTS and USE is labeled PROJECT-NO, because PROJECT-NO is a field in both the PROJECTS and USE record types.

The following convention is used to determine link direction. The link originates on the record type that contains only one record with a given value of the link label. Thus, in Figure 16.2, the link labeled PROJECT-NO originates from the PROJECTS record type, as there will be only one PROJECTS record with a given value of PROJECT-NO. The link terminates on a record type that may have one or many USE records with that value of label. Thus, in Figure 16.2, there may be many records with a given value of PROJECT-NO because a project may use many parts. Another interpretation of the link semantic is that it originates on a record that must exist before a record type with the same value of the link label can be created. Thus a record with a given value of PROJECT-NO in PROJECTS must exist before a USE record with the same value of PROJECT-NO can be created. Otherwise, no existent projects would be using parts.

There is semantic reason for such links. Links define owner records of other records. In Figure 16.2, PROJECTS records own USE records. The common field, PROJECT-NO, identifies the particular records owned. Thus a PROJECTS record with a given PROJECT-NO value will own all USE records with that PROJECT-NO value. There is reason for this link. Suppose we want to find all the parts used on a project. We would first find the PROJECTS record with the required PROJECT-NO. The links are then used to find all the USE records owned by that PROJECTS record. These USE records contain the PART-NO of parts used by a given project.

It is, of course, possible to use other conventions for linking records, and different conventions can be found in different methodologies.

Logical record structure
A way of describing records at the system level.

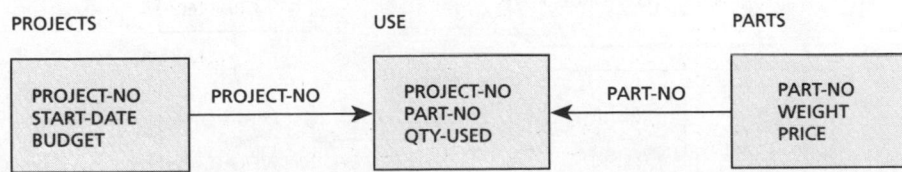

Figure 16.2 *Logical record structure*

◇ CONVERSION TO A LOGICAL RECORD STRUCTURE SYSTEM MODEL

Now we have described what a logical record structure looks like, we can begin to describe how to derive it from the E–R model. Both E–R diagrams and object models can be converted to system designs that use logical record structures.

STRUCTURED SYSTEMS ANALYSIS—CONVERTING E–R MODELS TO LOGICAL RECORD STRUCTURE

The first database design step in structured systems analysis converts the E–R analysis model to logical record types and specifies how these records are to be accessed. These access requirements are later used to choose keys that facilitate data access. Quantitative data such as item sizes, numbers of records and access frequency are often also added at this step. Quantitative data is needed to compute the storage requirements and transaction volumes to be supported by the computer system.

The combination of logical record structure, access specifications and quantitative data is sometimes known as the system level database specification. This specification is used at the implementation level to choose a record structure supported by a DBMS.

The simplest conversion is to make each set of the E–R diagram into a record type. However, there is one small variation to this, where we combine object sets. One such conversion is illustrated in Figure 16.3. Here sets PROJECTS, FOR and

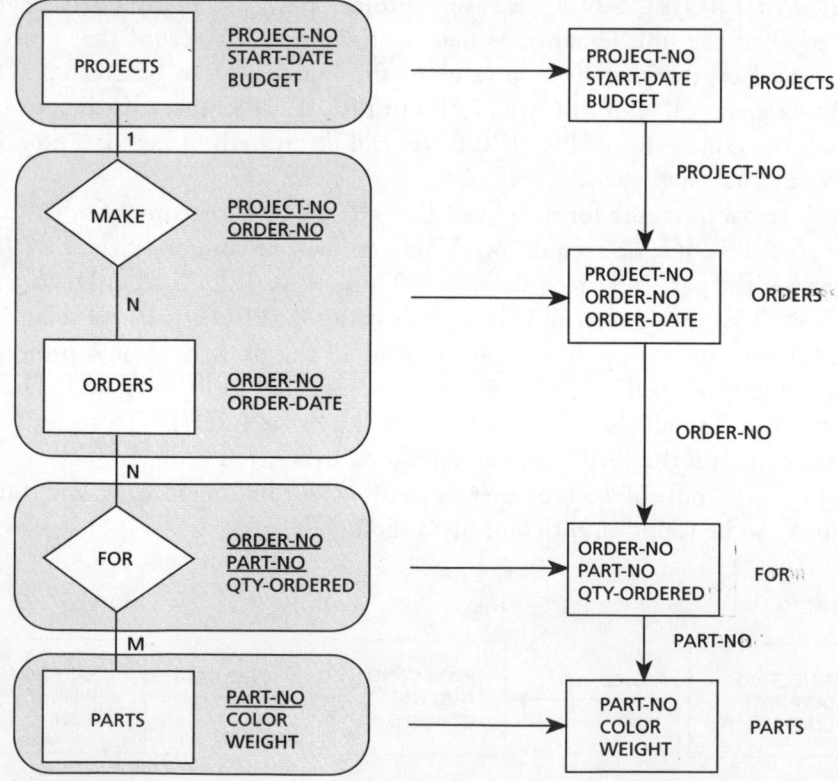

Figure 16.3 Converting an E–R diagram to a logical structure

PARTS are each converted to a logical record type. The entity set ORDERS and the relationship set MAKE are combined into the one logical record type. You will find that such combinations are always possible in l:N relationships. In a l:N relationship, entities in one of the entity sets appear in one relationship only. In Figure 16.3, each order in the ORDERS set appears in one MAKE relationship only and hence they are combined.

Links are then added. Links start on logical record types that represent entities and terminate on logical records that represent relationships. There is a link from PARTS, which represents an entity set, to FOR, which represents a relationship set. The same rule applies where sets have been combined. There is a link from PROJECTS, which represents an entity set, to ORDERS, which contains the relationship MAKE.

Each dependent entity set is also converted to one logical record type. A link is then added from the entity set to its dependent entity sets. The label on the link will be the entity set identifier.

Subsets and dependent entity sets can also be converted to logical record structures. One example of this conversion is given in Figure 16.4. This shows the E–R diagram previously illustrated in Figure 9.15 but changed to model course offerings as a dependent entity set. Here COURSE-OFFERINGS are dependent on COURSES. Thus, a course must exist on the university's statutes before it can be offered. It can then be offered in many semesters, with a different room used for each semester. Each of the sets is now converted to a record type in a logical record structure, with links labeled by the common attribute names. The links point from the owner record to the subset, as the owner must exist before it can become part of a subset—teachers must be

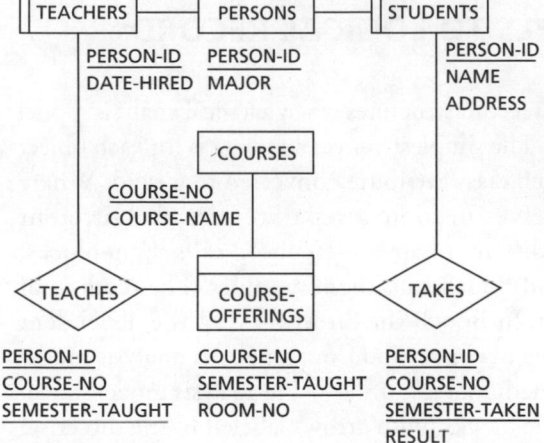

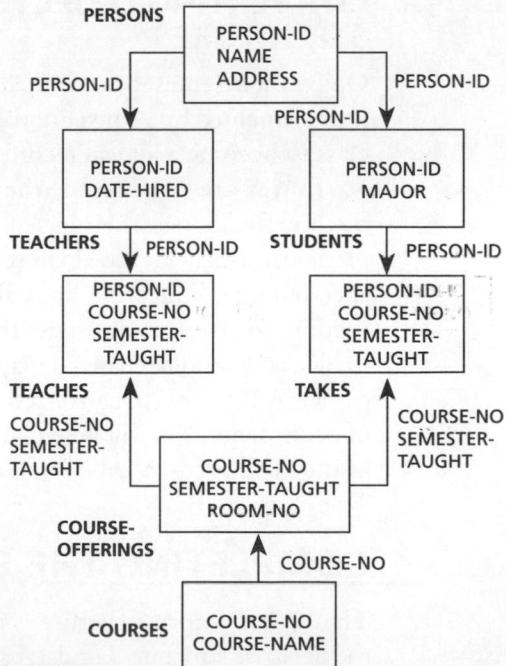

Figure 16.4 *Converting subsets and dependent entity sets*

hired before they can teach. Similarly there is an arrow from the set to the dependent entity set— a course must exist before it can be taught.

> ### TEXT CASE D: Construction Company—Developing the Logical Record Structure
>
> We now illustrate the application of these techniques to the data of the Construction Company. The logical structure for it is shown in Figure 16.5. You may wish to go back to Chapter 9 and see if you can derive the logical structure in Figure 16.5 from the E–R diagram in Figure 9.17.
>
> The method illustrated in Figures 16.3 and 16.4 is used to convert the E–R model in Figure 9.17 to the logical record structure in Figure 16.5. Each entity set or dependent entity set is combined with any 1:N relationships, in the manner shown in Figure 16.3, to form one logical record type. For example, dependent entity set INVOICE-LINES can be combined with relationship sets ABOUT, ON and FOR to construct the logical record INVOICE-LINES. Such combinations are made for all other entity sets and dependent entity sets.
>
> The next step is to add links to the logical record structure. Again, the method used in Figures 16.3 and 16.4 is used. The links always terminate on logical records that represent relationship sets or contain relationship sets. Logical record type INVOICE-LINES contains relationship sets ABOUT, ON and FOR. There are three links terminating on INVOICE-LINES for these relationship sets. There is also a fourth link from logical record type INVOICES to show the dependence of INVOICE-LINES on INVOICES. You may like to go through Figure 9.17 and see how the rest of the LRS in Figure 16.5 is constructed.

CONVERTING OBJECT MODELS TO LOGICAL RECORD STRUCTURES

Object models must be converted to logical record structures when a logical analysis model is implemented by a conventional DBMS. The simplest conversion here is for each object class to become a logical record, with each class attribute converted to a field. Where attributes are structured, they themselves become a separate record. Different methodologies give their logical records different names—Jacobson calls them blocks, Henderson-Sellers calls them schema, and Booch calls them modules. The method of specifying and directing links also varies. In Booch the direction is to the dependent module. Figure 16.6 illustrates the first step of conversion from an object analysis model to blocks or modules based on Jacobson's methodology. It shows the analysis model shown earlier in Figure 12.6 converted to module blocks, with arrows labeled in the direction of dependency. You will note that the interface objects have also been converted to blocks, as they will eventually be implemented as program modules.

 ## COMPLETING THE SYSTEM MODEL

The logical record structure is just one part of the system model. It serves to define the database structure. For database design, we need additional information, in particular:

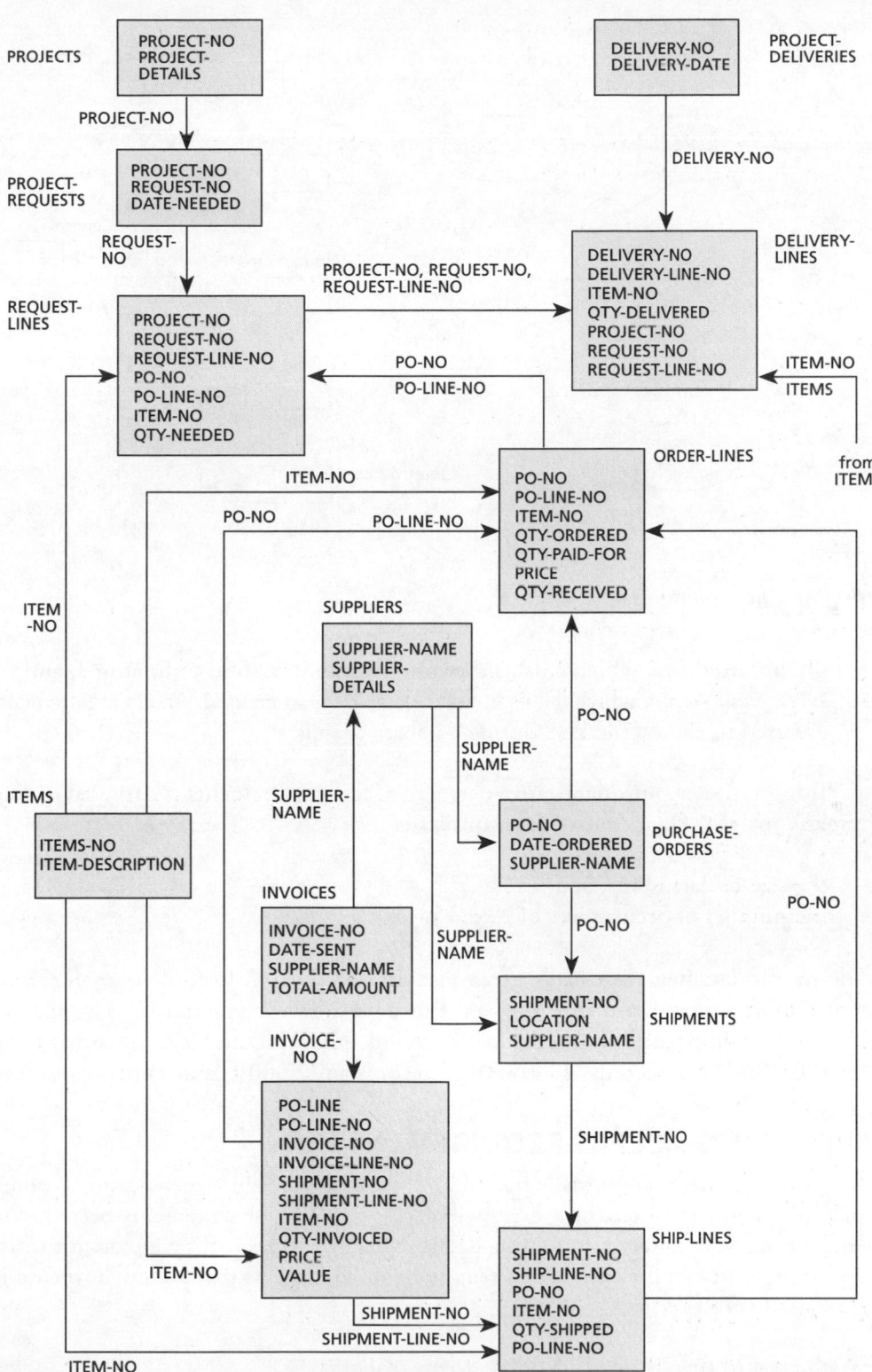

Figure 16.5 *A logical record structure for Text Case B*

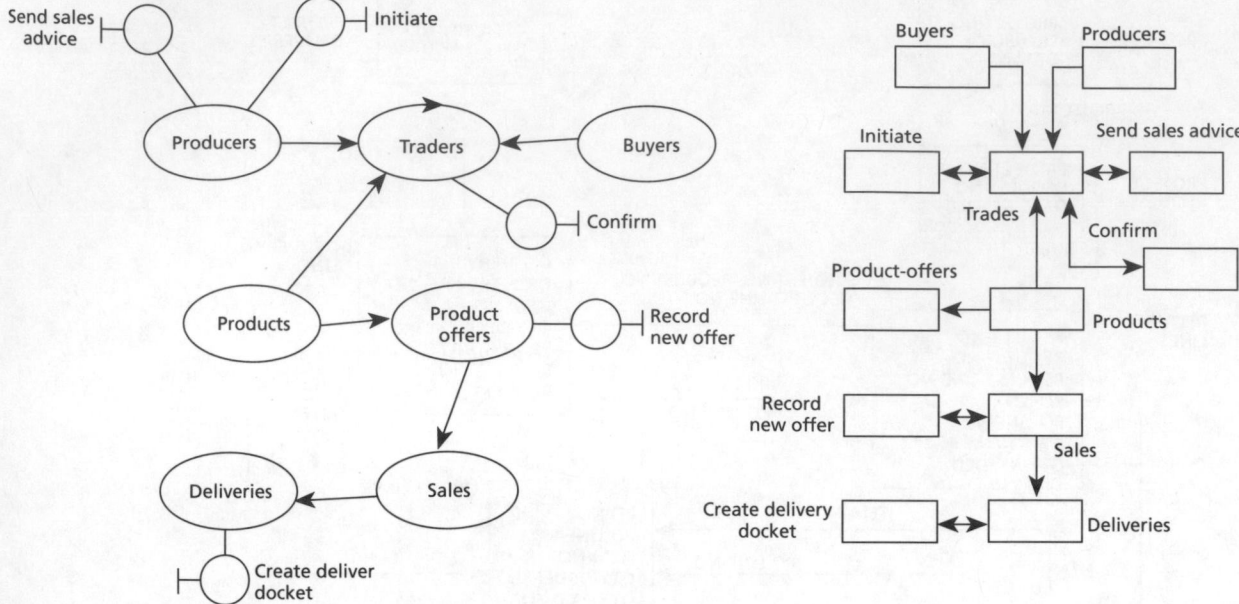

Figure 16.6 *Conversion of object modules*

- *quantitative data*, which tells us the volume of information to be stored; and
- *access requirements*, which tell us how the database is to be used. Access requirements are used to choose file keys during database design.

Information about quantitative data and access requirements is gathered during systems analysis. Quantitative data consists of:

- the size of data items; and
- the number of occurrences of record types.

The size of data items is usually given in a data dictionary. Record volumes can be added to the logical record structure by the method shown in Figure 16.7. The number of records is simply added into the logical record. Thus, Figure 16.7 shows that there are 100 PROJECT records, 2000 PARTS records and 5000 USE records.

SPECIFYING ACCESS REQUIREMENTS

Access requirements
Defining how databases are accessed.

Access requirements are initially picked up from user procedure specifications, which include statements about how users will access data. These statements become the database access requirements. During database design, access paths are plotted against logical record types for each access requirement. The access paths show how data is to be used and describe:

- the record types accessed by each access request;
- the sequence in which the record types are accessed;

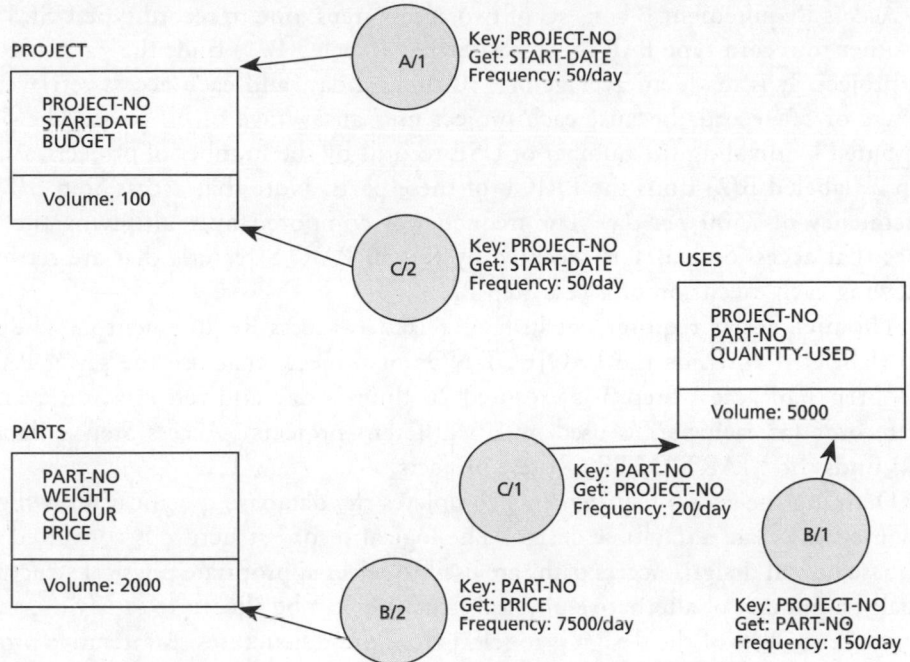

Figure 16.7 *Access paths to the logical structure level*

- the access keys used to select record types;
- the items retrieved from each record; and
- the number of records accessed.

There are many ways to draw access paths. One method is illustrated in Figure 16.7. This figure shows three access requirements plotted against three logical record types. The three access requirements are:

A—find the START-DATE for a given project.
B—find the PRICE of parts used on a project with a given PROJECT-NO.
C—find the START-DATE of projects that use a given PART-NO.

There is one access path for each access requirement, and each access path can be made up of one or more access steps. Each access step has a label that is made up of the mnemonic that describes the requirement and a sequential number. The access step is labeled with an access key. The access keys are the names of fields whose values are known at the time of the access step. The access step also includes a description of the activity at the step.

Access Requirement A is specified by one access step, which is labeled A/1 in Figure 16.7. This access step is used to access PROJECTS records. The access uses the value of PROJECT-NO as the access key and retrieves the value of START-DATE. It is made an average of 50 times a day and retrieves one record.

Access Requirement B consists of two access steps, one to record type USES and the other to record type PARTS. Access Step 1 (labeled B/1) finds the parts used by the project. It is made an average of 150 times a day, and each access retrieves an average of 50 records because each project uses an average of 50 parts. The 50 is computed by dividing the number of USE records by the number of projects. Access Step 2 (labeled B/2) finds the PRICE of these parts. Note that access Step B/2 has a frequency of 7500 per day. The frequency is computed by multiplying the 150 times that access Step B/1 is executed by the 50 PARTS records that are retrieved following each execution of access Step B/1.

The final access requirement in Figure 16.7 is access Requirement C. The first step (labeled C/l) finds the PROJECT-NOs of projects that use the given PART-NO. Step 1 of access Step 3 is executed 20 times a day and retrieves, on average, 2.5 records (as each part is used by 2.5 different projects). Access Step 2 (labeled C/2) finds the START-DATE of these projects.

Defining the access requirements completes the database specification, which is now used to create a database design. The logical record structure is converted to a database logical design. Access paths are used to select appropriate physical structures. Usually, a number of alternative physical structures can be chosen to satisfy the access requirements. Part of the design is to select from these structures. An iterative process is used to make such choices and performance estimates are made at each iteration to compare the alternatives.

The kinds of design techniques used will depend on the software to be used to implement the database. The simplest conversion is to a set of files. Alternatively, the database may be implemented on a DBMS. We will first describe conversion to a set of files, then DBMS. We will also give you a brief outline of design techniques used to convert the logical record structure to a database structure.

 ## IMPLEMENTATION MODELS

Before describing conversion to implementation models, we briefly describe database management systems, one of the most common forms of implementation model. These store information as sets of records with links between them. Each record type is made up of a number of fields. As an example, Figure 16.8 is a record type called PERSONS. Each record of this type has three fields: NAME, DATE-OF-BIRTH and WHERE-BORN.

Records can be retrieved from database management systems in a variety of ways. One way to do this is to use serial access and read records serially, starting with the first record and continuing until all the records have been read. Often, however, it is necessary to retrieve only one record from the database. For example, we may want to find Bill's record to see where Bill was born. To do this, we could start at the beginning and read records until we get to Bill's record. This, however, can be time-consuming because, in a large database, many records may have to be read until the required record is found. What is needed is the ability to access one record directly rather than read the whole database until the required record is found.

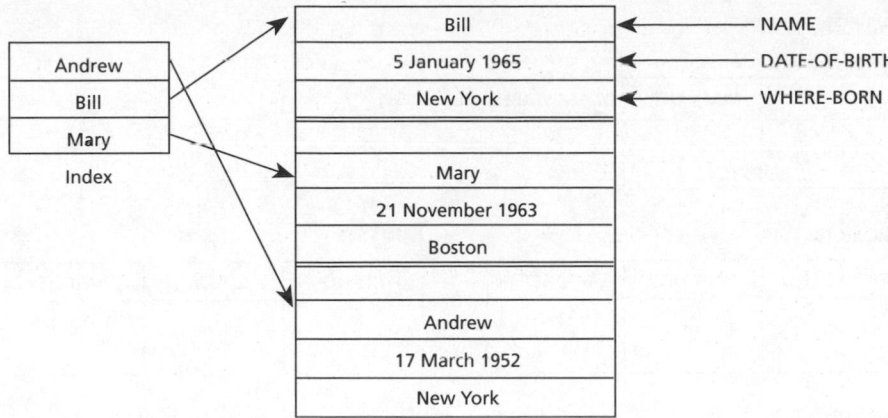

Figure 16.8 *File PERSONS*

Direct access is provided by using indexes. An index uses one of the record fields as a key, and there is an entry in the index for each record in the database. This entry contains the value of the records key and a link from the index to the record. Thus, record type PERSONS in Figure 16.8 has an index whose key is NAME. It is made up of three entries with values 'Bill', 'Mary' and 'Andrew'. Each entry has a link to a record with that key value, and programs can access records through the index. A program specifies the value of the key, and file software will use the index to directly access the record with that key value.

Every DBMS supports a different kind of link structure between record types. Thus virtually every DBMS supports a unique structure. However, there are some common features found in some DBMS. These common features arise because of efforts made to standardize DBMSs. There are now a number of DBMSs that support the relational model. These DBMS are known as relational DBMSs. There are also a number of DBMSs that support network structures. The network structure was once proposed as a standard and a number of DBMS suppliers have followed this standard. DBMSs that support network structures are known as network DBMSs. Finally, there are a number of DBMSs that support the hierarchical structures. These are known as hierarchical DBMSs.

We will illustrate the structures supported by each of these three kinds of DBMSs. This is shown in Figure 16.9, which presents the DBMS record structures for the system where:

- projects are assigned to departments;
- projects are made of any number of jobs; and
- each project uses different part kinds.

RELATIONAL DATABASE MANAGEMENT SYSTEMS

The relational model stores data as a set of tables or relations, as shown in Figure 16.9(a) where each record is a row in the table. In a relational DBMS, each such relation would be defined using the system's definition language. Commands provided by the DBMS would then be used to store and retrieve data. The next chapter will cover the relational model in greater detail.

Direct access
Retrieval of records based on keywords.

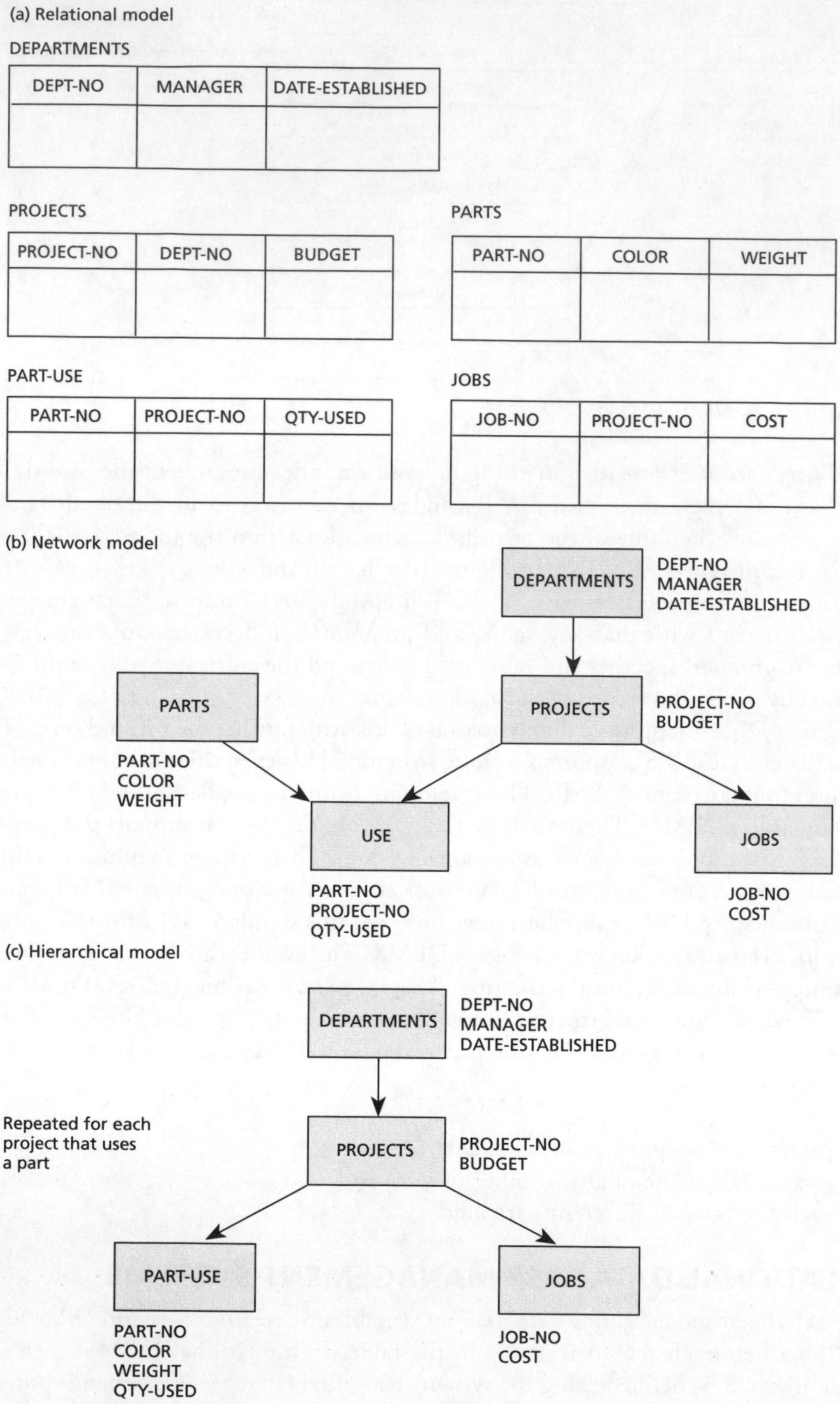
(a) Relational model
DEPARTMENTS
DEPT-NO
MANAGER
DATE-ESTABLISHED
PROJECTS
PROJECT-NO
DEPT-NO
BUDGET
PARTS
PART-NO
COLOR
WEIGHT
PART-USE
PART-NO
PROJECT-NO
QTY-USED
JOBS
JOB-NO
PROJECT-NO
COST
(b) Network model
DEPARTMENTS
DEPT-NO
MANAGER
DATE-ESTABLISHED
PARTS
PART-NO
COLOR
WEIGHT
PROJECTS
PROJECT-NO
BUDGET
USE
PART-NO
PROJECT-NO
QTY-USED
JOBS
JOB-NO
COST
(c) Hierarchical model
DEPARTMENTS
DEPT-NO
MANAGER
DATE-ESTABLISHED
Repeated for each project that uses a part
PROJECTS
PROJECT-NO
BUDGET
PART-USE
PART-NO
COLOR
WEIGHT
QTY-USED
JOBS
JOB-NO
COST

Figure 16.9 *Data models*

NETWORK DATABASE MANAGEMENT SYSTEMS

DBMSs that support network structures store data as record types. Furthermore, parent–child relationships can be established between these record types. Such relationships are illustrated in Figure 16.9(b). Here each DEPARTMENTS record will own any number of PROJECTS records. A DEPARTMENTS record will own PROJECTS records of projects that are assigned to that department. Each PROJECTS record owns the JOBS records of jobs that make up that project. Each PROJECTS record also owns those USE records that represent a project's usage of items. The parent–child links are called set types in network terminology.

In a network model, each record type can be a parent of any other record types. It can also have any number of parents. This, however, is not the case for hierarchical database management systems.

HIERARCHICAL DATABASE MANAGEMENT SYSTEMS

The hierarchical data model differs from the network model because each record type can have only one parent. We can no longer have a record type such as USE which had two parents in the network data model. The designer has to decide whether USE is to be modeled as a child of record type PARTS or a child of record type PROJECTS. Figure 16.9(c) represents the case where record type USE has become a child of record type PROJECTS. In that case, PARTS record fields are now combined with the USE record to make the PART-USE record which is a child of PROJECTS record. PART-USE records now store the details of each part used by each project. The disadvantage of this approach is that the COLOR and WEIGHT for a part are stored more than once. In fact, they are duplicated for each project that uses a part.

Alternative hierarchical representations of the same user data are possible. For example, we could make USE records a child of PARTS records and PROJECT records a child of PARTS records. In that case, PROJECT data would be duplicated for each part used by the project. Alternatively, we could store each USE record twice, once as a child of record PROJECTS and once as a child of record USE. Designers must choose between these alternatives.

CONVERSION TO A DATABASE MANAGEMENT SYSTEM (DBMS) STRUCTURE

During implementation the logical record structure is converted to a **database definition** supported by a DBMS. This proceeds in two steps:

Database definition
A definition of a database used as an input to a DBMS.

1. *Logical design*, to convert the logical record structure to a data model supported by the DBMS. The database is defied by a database definition, which is inputed directly into the DBMS and sets up the database record structures.
2. *Physical design*, to choose the physical structure for the database.

The conversion method depends on the type of data model supported by the DBMS.

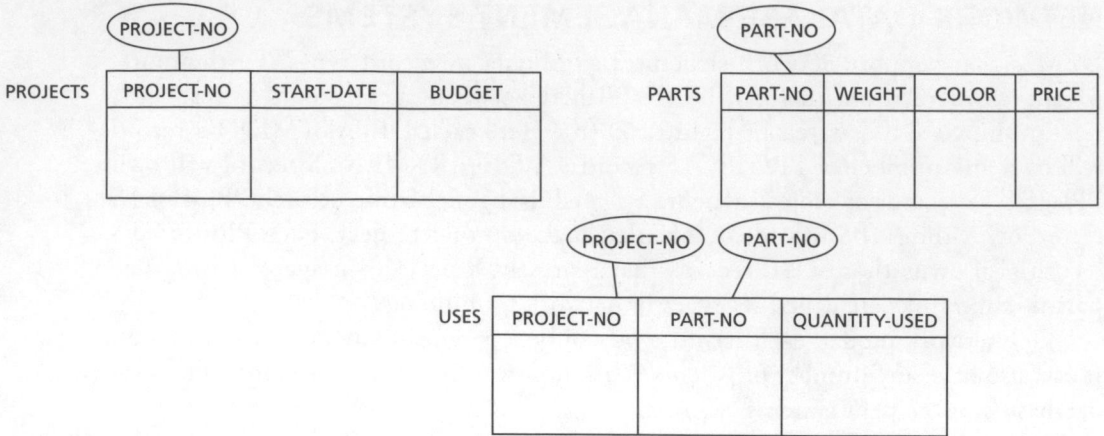

Figure 16.10 *A relational database for the logical structure of Figure 16.5*

CONVERSION TO RELATIONS

The simplest conversion is where the DBMS supports the relational model. Here each logical record type becomes a relation in the relational DBMS. Thus the logical record structure in Figure 16.2 would be converted to three relations: PROJECTS, PARTS and USE, shown in Figure 16.10. The logical record fields would become the relation columns. Thus, relation PROJECTS would contain three columns: PROJECT-NO, START-DATE and BUDGET. The fields of records in each relation are shown next to the relation in Figure 16.10. Thus, records in relation PARTS have four fields: PART-NO, WEIGHT, COLOR and PRICE.

The keys in the access steps shown in Figure 16.7 are used to choose keys for the relations. Relation PROJECTS has two access steps: A/l and C/2. The key in each step is PROJECT-NO. PROJECT-NO is now made the key of an index to the relation PROJECTS. All accesses to the relation can now be direct using a value of PROJECT-NO.

Similarly, PART-NO is chosen as the key of an index to relation PARTS. File USES also has two access steps terminating on it. However, each is labeled with a different key. Access Step C/l has key PART-NO, and access Step B/l has key PROJECT-NO. If all accesses are to be direct, then relation USE must have two indexes. One index uses the key PART-NO, and the other uses the key PROJECT-NO.

CONVERSION TO A NETWORK DATABASE MANAGEMENT SYSTEM

The logical record structure can be converted to a network model in a relatively simple way. Each logical record is converted to a record type, and each logical record link becomes a set type. An example of such a conversion is shown in Figure 16.11. The logical record structure to be converted is shown in Figure 16.11(a). This logical record structure is converted to the network structure shown in Figure 16.11(b).

Each logical record becomes a record type in the network structure, and all the links in the logical record structure become links in the network representation.

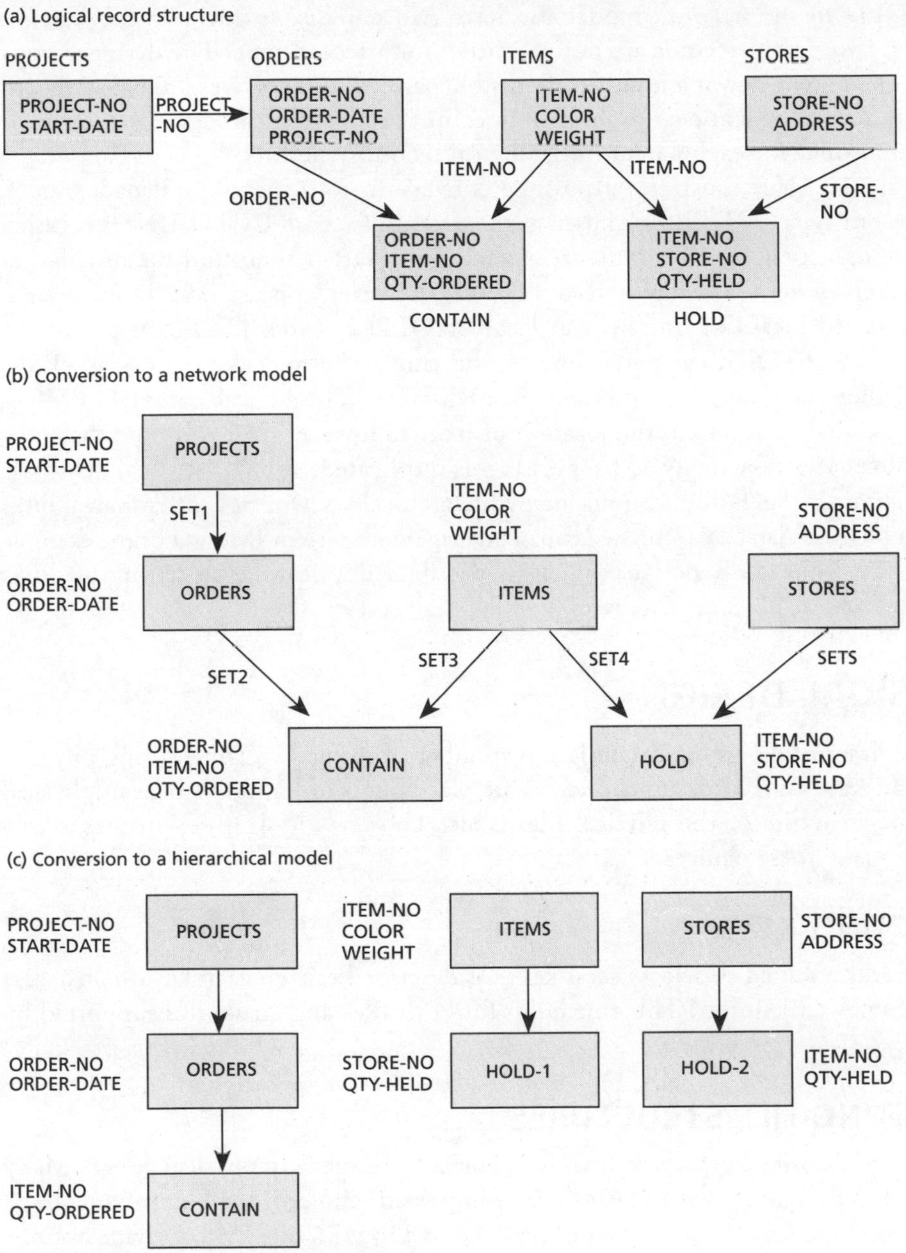

(a) Logical record structure

(b) Conversion to a network model

(c) Conversion to a hierarchical model

Figure 16.11 *Conversion to a data model*

CONVERSION TO A HIERARCHICAL DATABASE MANAGEMENT SYSTEM

Conversions to a hierarchical model impose an additional constraint. Each record type in a hierarchical model can have only one parent. This was not the case in network model design. For example, records CONTAIN and HOLD in Figure 16.11(b) have two parents in the logical record structure. After conversion, record types CONTAIN and HOLD in the network model also have two parents. In hierarchical systems, however, two parent records are not permitted for a record type. The designer must choose one parent out of a number of possible parents. Alternatively, a logical record structure record may appear more than once in the hierarchical logical structure. It will appear once for each parent in the logical record structure.

Figure 16.11(c) illustrates a possible conversion to a hierarchical data model. Here, record type ORDERS is chosen as the parent of record CONTAIN. It is easier, in this design, to access the contents of each order rather than find the orders that contain a given item. The logical record HOLD, however, appears twice in the design, once as record HOLD-1 and once as record HOLD-2. It has ITEMS as parent the first time and STORES as parent the second time. The logical parent STORES is used to allow easy access to holdings in each store. The logical parent ITEMS is used to allow easy access to the location of items. However, you will note that now some information—namely, QTY-HELD—is duplicated.

To eliminate such duplications, many hierarchical systems now offer logical links between physical databases. IBM's database management system IMS is a prime example here. These links allow designs which reduce data duplication by setting up links between separate physical databases.

 # PHYSICAL DESIGN

Physical design follows logical design. A number of things are done during physical design. Indexes to records are chosen, as are placements of logical records in physical files. The structure of the physical files is also chosen. Physical design uses access paths to make these choices.

SELECTING KEYS

Access paths are used to select access keys. As described earlier, each key on an access step becomes a file index. This rule holds for both files and structures supported by a DBMS.

SELECTING FILE STRUCTURES

Apart from choosing keys, there are other choices to be made in physical design. Many of these depend on the type of DBMS. One important choice is the file structure to be used to store records of a given record type. Some DBMSs, like IMS, provide options for record storage; in IMS, which is a DBMS supported by IBM, sequential, indexed-sequential or direct files (specialized to IMS hierarchical data structures) can be used to store record types. The access paths can be used to guide this choice, as on-line accesses generally suggest direct files. The way this is done depends on the particular DBMS.

IMPROVING ACCESS PERFORMANCE

Access paths can also be used to select physical links between records. This is done by examining successive access steps and physically linking records, which are accessed in successive steps.

The number of access steps can be reduced by combining fields, retrieved in successive access steps, into one record. For example, in Figure 16.7, the value of PRICE could be added to record USES. Access Step C/2 now becomes unnecessary and performance of access Requirement C is improved. The performance improvement, however, is made at the price of losing normal form because record type USES is no longer in normal form. Thus redundancy is introduced in a controlled manner to improve performance. It is up to the designer to make the tradeoff between improved performance and good data representation.

DESIGN TRADEOFFS

Designers usually choose design options in an iterative manner, as shown in Figure 16.12. A design problem is identified and a solution proposed. Usually the solution requires the designer to make some tradeoff. The major tradeoffs are:

- *Performance against storage use.* The introduction of new physical links usually improves performance but requires additional storage to store the physical links.
- *Performance against structure.* The controlled introduction of redundancy improves performance but requires additional storage and introduces restructuring problems.

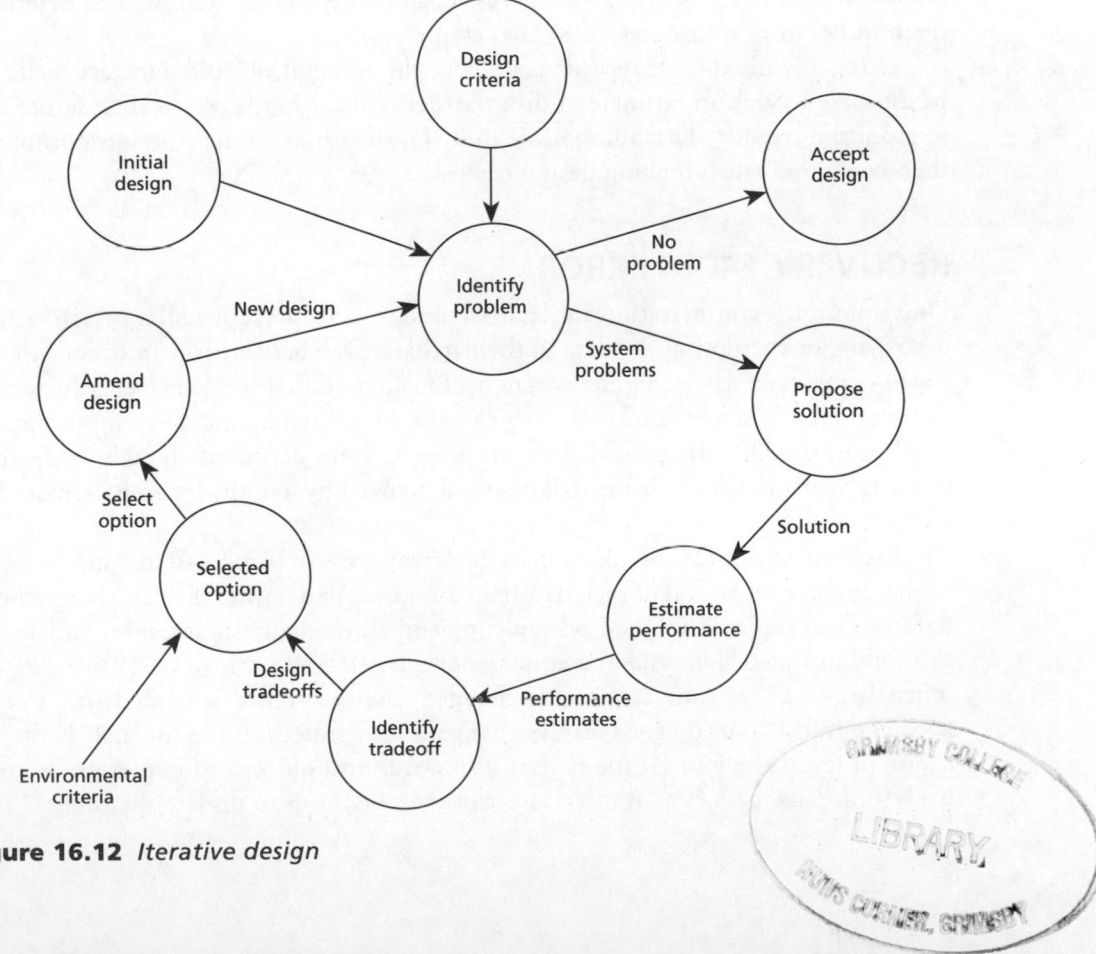

Figure 16.12 *Iterative design*

To make these tradeoffs, designers first estimate any improvements of performance and the cost required to achieve this improvement. Usually a number of options are evaluated and the tradeoffs for each option are identified. Environmental criteria are then used to select the appropriate option. Typical criteria include:

- the availability of storage;
- the importance of improved performance for a given requirement; or
- the probability of restructuring a particular database part.

A particular option is then selected, given the criteria and the user environment. The user environment is usually important in such choices. In microprocessor systems, for example, where storage is at a premium, it is unlikely that designers would be prepared to sacrifice storage for marginal performance improvements. However, such a tradeoff will be quite reasonable in large systems which are tightly integrated with user functions.

LOGICAL RECORD ANALYSIS

Designers are required to make performance estimates during the iterative process shown in Figure 16.12. The usual method for doing this is called logical record analysis. Logical record analysis uses access paths. Each access step is examined to determine the number of records accessed by that step.

Once this number of records is known, the number of disk transfers made can be estimated. Such an estimate of disk transfers considers the physical structure used to store the records. The numbers of disk transfers for different design options are then compared when making design tradeoffs.

RECOVERY FROM ERROR

One important consideration in database design is to prevent faults or errors from destroying or corrupting the data in the database. Database errors can occur in many ways—errors caused by computer system malfunctions, disk drives which crash, operating system faults or power failures. Errors can also be caused by incorrect input data.

Recovery is usually provided by keeping back-up copies of the whole database or parts of the database. If the database is destroyed by a fault, it can be replaced by its back-up copy.

Back-up copies can be made in various ways. Early batch systems made a copy of the database at the end of each day. If an error occurred during the day, the corrupted database was replaced by the back-up copy and all the daily transactions run again.

On-line transaction systems use more sophisticated recovery methods. They maintain journal files. Every time a record is changed, the old record is copied to a journal file. The transaction that makes the change is also stored on the journal. If there is a system fault, the journal file is read backwards and old record copies are restored back to the database. The transactions can then be rerun to update the file.

SUMMARY

This chapter described database design. It described a design process that proceeds by converting analysis models to system models and then to implementation models. Such conversions are needed where the analysis model uses E–R techniques or object modeling techniques. The system model in most cases is based on logical record structures, which are sometimes known as block or module structures.

The conversion from a logical record structure to a DBMS structure usually proceeds in two steps—logical design followed by physical design. The conversion to a DBMS also depends on the type of structures supported by the DBMS. DBMSs also are often classified into three kinds: relational, network or hierarchical. This chapter showed how logical record structures can be converted to logical relational, network and hierarchical structures. It then described the tradeoffs made during physical design to get satisfactory database performance.

EXERCISES

16.1 Convert the following set of relations to a logical record structure:

APPLICATIONS (<u>APPLICATION-NO</u>, APPLICANT-NAME, APPLICATION-DATE, DATE-APPROVED)

APPLICANTS (<u>APPLICANT-NAME</u>, ADDRESS, DATE-OF-BIRTH)

REPAYMENTS (<u>APPLICATION-NO</u>, <u>REPAYMENT-DATE</u>, AMOUNT)

16.2 Convert the following set of relations to a logical record structure:

FAULTS (<u>FAULT-ID</u>, DATE-OCCURRED, DATE-FIXED, EQUIPMENT-ID)

EQUIPMENTS (<u>EQUIPMENT-ID</u>, DESCRIPTION, LOCATION)

REPAIR-STAFF (<u>PERSON-ID</u>, DATE-OF-BIRTH)

REPAIR (<u>PERSON-ID</u>, <u>FAULT-ID</u>, TIME-SPENT-ON-FAULT)

16.3 You are given the logical record structure shown in Figure 16.13. The logical record structure describes a delivery system. Each trip is by one driver using one vehicle. A number of deliveries can be made on each trip. Any number of part kinds can be delivered in each delivery. Draw access paths on the logical record structure for the following access requirements:

1. List the NAME of drivers who made deliveries to a customer with a given CUSTOMER-NAME.

2. List the NAME of drivers who used a vehicle with a given REGISTRATION-NO.

3. List the REGISTRATION-NO and MAKE of vehicles used on a given TRIP-DATE. Assume that a trip never takes more than one day.

4. List QTY-DELIVERED of a given PART-NO on a given TRIP-DATE.

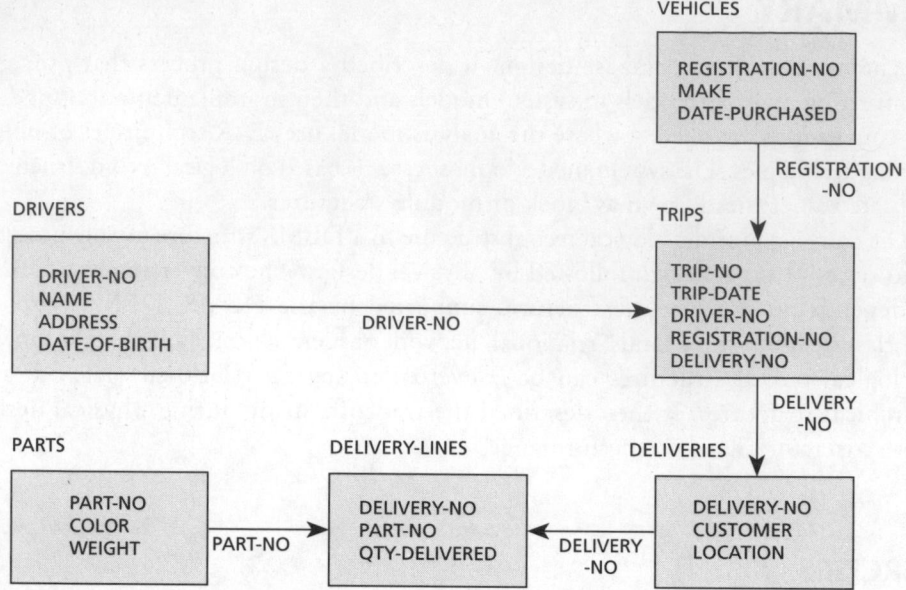

Figure 16.13 *A logical record structure*

16.4 Convert the logical record structure in Figure 16.13 to a network and a hierarchical DBMS.

BIBLIOGRAPHY

Davenport, R.A. (1979), 'Logical database design—from entity model to DBMS structure', *Australian Computer Journal*, Vol. 11, No. 3, pp. 82–97.

Korth, H.F. and Silberschatz, A. (1991), *Database System Concepts*, (2nd edn) McGraw-Hill, New York, 1995.

Relational analysis

17

CONTENTS

KEY LEARNING OBJECTIVES

Defining a relation
Why we should avoid redundancy
Normal relational forms
Functional dependencies

INTRODUCTION

One design goal is to create a design that is in some way a good design. The criteria for good design are provided by relational theory, which has been used for this purpose for a number of years. The way this is done is to first specify the design as a set of relations. The relations are then examined for redundancy and, if necessary, changed into a non-redundant form. The output of this step is a non-redundant relational model of the user system. If the development uses a relational database management system, then these relations are directly defined to be the database. The next step is to convert the relational model to a database definition. This chapter describes relational analysis.

RELATIONS

Relational model
A set of tables that describes the data in a system.

Relation
A table or list of values.

Attribute in a relational model
A column of the table or list of values.

There are two ways of describing the **relational model**. One method uses formal terms such as relation, attribute and tuple. The other describes the model using more familiar terms, such as table, column and row. The relational model describes data as a set of **relations** or tables. Each relation or table has a table name. Each such relation has a set of **attributes**, and each attribute has a unique name in the relation. The relation attribute is the same as a table column. Each relation has a set of tuples, or rows in a table.

There is a close correspondence between the relational model and E–R diagrams. Figure 17.1 shows how the E–R diagram of Figure 9.9 has been converted to a set of tables or relations. Here each entity set is converted to a table and each entity set attribute is converted to a column. Individual entities in an entity set become rows in the relation that represents the entity set. Similarly, relationship sets are converted to relations.

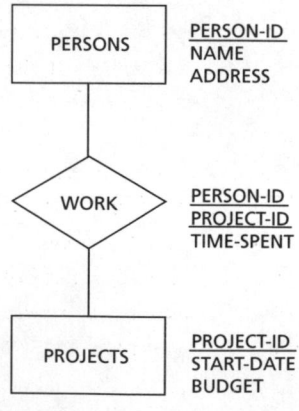

PERSONS

PERSON-ID	NAME	ADDRESS
PX1	Jackson	London
PX2	Maine	Liverpool
PZ5	Oldham	London

WORK

PERSON-ID	PROJECT-ID	TIME-SPENT
PX2	Proj3	30
PX1	Proj2	15
PZ5	Proj2	40
PX2	Proj5	30
PZ5	Proj3	75

PROJECTS

PROJECT-ID	START-DATE	BUDGET
Proj3	1 Mar 98	50
Proj2	15 Feb 98	30
Proj5	1 Nov 98	60

Figure 17.1 *E–R diagram and relations*

A tabular representation of data can be useful in explaining the data structure to users. However, representing a system by tables can become clumsy, especially if the system is large. Besides taking a lot of space and drawing effort, we are always faced with providing columns for data and either leaving these columns blank or filling them with example values. To avoid such drawing effort, it is convenient to use a relational notation, which shows only the relation name and its attributes. The relational notation for the tables shown in Figure 17.1 is:

PERSONS (PERSON-ID, NAME, ADDRESS);
WORK (PERSON-ID, PROJECT-ID, TIME-SPENT);
PROJECTS (PROJECT-ID, START-DATE, BUDGET).

In this notation, each relation is represented by one line. Each line starts with the relation name and is followed by the names of the relation attributes in brackets. The underlined attributes are the relation key. Values of the relation key identify unique rows in the relation. You will recall that when 1:N relationship sets are converted to relations, the relationship set relation has the same relation key as one of the entity set relations. The relations with the same relation key are then combined into one relation. Thus if a person worked on one project, the key of relation WORK would be PERSON-ID. Relations WORK and PERSONS would then be combined into the one relation:

PERSONS (PERSON-ID, PROJECT-ID, NAME, ADDRESS, TIME-SPENT)

There are two reasons for converting the E–R model to a set of relations. First, such a conversion is a convenient step for going from an E–R model to a set of files. Each table eventually becomes a database file. Each attribute becomes a field in the file, and each row becomes a record occurrence. The other reason is more important. There is a theory based on sound mathematics that specifies how we should construct tables to avoid data redundancies. What we are after is a set of 'normal' relations. If we organize the data into a set of such relations, we are guaranteed a good data design.

A number of normal forms have been defined for relations. They are commonly known as first normal form (1NF), second normal form (2NF), third normal form (3NF) and Boyce-Codd normal form (BCNF). Two other normal forms are known as the fourth normal form (4NF) and fifth normal form (5NF). Relations in 1NF, 2NF, 3NF and BCNF must satisfy a different set of constraints than those in 4NF and 5NF. Database designers must ensure that their relations are in the highest normal form.

It should also be pointed out that, although much of the work on relations has been of a mathematical nature, the beauty of the relational model is that the mathematical results can be explained in terms of constraints relevant to practical database design. There are two main constraints to be met by normal relations. First, relations must be flat—that is, all the column values must have simple values and cannot be groups of values. Flat file structures are easier to access and to change in order to meet new user requirements. Normal relations must also not contain redundancy—normal relations store each fact once only. In order to explain how to obtain a set of normal relations we must first define some terminology.

TERMINOLOGY AND PROPERTIES

Tuple
A row in the relation.

Relations can be thought of as tables made up of columns and rows. In relational work, columns are often called attributes and rows are called **tuples**. Each relation has a unique name within the system, and each column or attribute has a unique name in the relation. In Figure 17.1, the relations were given the names PERSONS, WORK and PROJECTS. Individual rows describe objects modeled by the relation. Thus, in relation PERSONS, each row (or tuple) describes one person, whereas each column is one property of the person. The column NAME contains the person's name, the column PERSON-ID contains the person's identifier, and the column ADDRESS contains the person's address.

Another property of relations is that the order of columns and rows is insignificant. Furthermore, a relation cannot contain two identical rows.

NORMAL FORM AND NON-NORMAL FORM RELATIONS

The difference between relations in normal form and those that are in non-normal form is illustrated in Figure 17.2. The relation ORDERS, in Figure 17.2(a), is not in any normal form. Each row in relation ORDERS represents one order. This order is identified by the value of ORDER-NO and has one value of ORDER-DATE.

(a) Non-normal form relations

ORDERS

ORDER-NO	ORDER-DATE	ORDER-LINES	
Ord1	6 June 1998	**PART-NO** / P1 P6	**QTY-ORDERED** / 10 30
Ord2	3 May 1998	**PART-NO** / P5 P6 P2	**QTY-ORDERED** / 10 50 30

(b) First normal form relation

ORDERS

ORDER-NO	ORDER-DATE	PART-NO	QTY-ORDERED
Ord1	6 June 1998	P1	10
Ord1	6 June 1998	P6	30
Ord2	3 May 1998	P5	10
Ord2	3 May 1998	P6	50
Ord2	3 May 1998	P2	30

Figure 17.2 *First normal form and non-normal form relations*

Each order is for any QTY-ORDERED of parts with a given PART-NO. The parts ordered in the order are themselves modeled by a relation in column ORDER-LINES in relation ORDERS. Thus, an order identified by a value of 'ord1' of ORDER-NO is for 10 parts identified by 'P1' and 30 parts identified by 'P6'. The important thing to notice for relation ORDERS is that one of the attributes (ORDER-LINES) does not have simple values. Attributes ORDER-NO and ORDER-DATE have only one single value for one row and, thus, are said to have simple values. Attribute ORDER-LINES has a value made up of a number of rows in another relation and this value is not simple. Normal form relations can have only simple values and, thus, relation ORDERS in Figure 17.2(a) is not in normal form.

Figure 17.2(b) illustrates a normalized relation that contains the same data as the relation in Figure 17.2(a). Each value in each column of this relation is a simple value. Relations that are not in normal form can always be normalized. To do this, take each row in the unnormalized relation and look at the relation in the non-simple column of the unnormalized relation. Now combine each row of the relation in the non-simple column with the values of other columns in the unnormalized relation to make a row in the normalized relation. For example, take the first row in the unnormalized relation ORDERS. Now take the first row in the relation in column ORDER-LINES. In this row, PART-NO= 'Pl' and QTY-ORDERED = 10. Now combine these values with the values in the other columns in ORDERS—that is, ORDER-NO = 'ordl' and ORDER-DATE = '6 June 1993'. All of these values now become the first row in the normalized relation ORDERS in Figure 17.2(b). This combination is now repeated for every row of the relations in column ORDER-LINES of the unnormalized relation ORDERS.

Relations with only simple attribute values, such as that shown in Figure 17.2(b), are in the first normal form (lNF) or are normalized. The important advantage of normalized relations is that each attribute has the same importance. This is useful when we convert the relation to computer software. It then becomes possible to add an index on any attribute field and retrieve data using any attribute as key.

The relation ORDERS in Figure 17.2(b) is in lNF. Relations in 1NF can still contain redundancy. For example, in relation ORDERS, the ORDER-DATE for a given order can be stored more than once for the same order. To have no redundancy, relations must satisfy additional constraints. Relations that satisfy such constraints and contain no redundancy are in higher normal forms. Constraints satisfied by relations in higher normal forms are defined in terms of functional dependencies and relation keys.

FUNCTIONAL DEPENDENCIES

Functional dependencies describe some of the rules that hold between attributes in a system. In particular, they state whether a particular value of one attribute (X) in a relation determines a particular value of another attribute (Y) for that relation. That is a way of saying that if we know the value of X, then we can determine a unique value of Y. For example, if we know the value of PERSON-ID for a person, then we can determine the value of NAME for that person. A functional dependency is often expressed as:

$$\text{PERSON-ID} \quad \rightarrow \quad \text{NAME}$$

Functional dependency
Where one value of an attribute determines a single value of another attribute.

We can now say that attribute NAME is **functionally dependent** on attribute PERSON-ID. Alternatively, we sometimes use the terminology that PERSON-ID *determines* a unique value of NAME or that NAME is determined by PERSON-ID. The important thing to remember is that for each value of PERSON-ID there is *one* value of NAME.

Functional dependencies often involve more than one attribute on the left-hand side. Thus to know how much time a person spent on a given project, we must know both the value of the project identifier, PROJECT-ID, and the value of the person identifier, PERSON-ID. The functional dependency then becomes:

$$\text{PERSON-ID, PROJECT-ID} \quad \rightarrow \quad \text{TIME SPENT}$$

Again, there will be only one value of TIME-SPENT for a given combination of PERSON-ID and PROJECT-ID.

DERIVED FUNCTIONAL DEPENDENCIES

Sometimes, one functional dependency can be derived from other functional dependencies. For example, a project identifier PROJECT-ID may determine one value for attribute BUDGET. Now suppose each manager manages one project. Given a manager, we at once know the project managed by that manager and from the project we can derive the budget managed by that manager. Mathematically, we would say that if:

$$\text{MANAGER} \quad \rightarrow \quad \text{PROJECT-ID and PROJECT-ID} \quad \rightarrow \quad \text{BUDGET}$$
then
$$\text{MANAGER} \quad \rightarrow \quad \text{BUDGET}$$

This simply says that if you know the one project managed by the manager, and the one budget of this project, then you know the one budget for which the manager is responsible.

It is up to the designer and analyst to ensure that there are no derived functional dependencies in their model.

HOW TO FIND FUNCTIONAL DEPENDENCIES

Functional dependencies are not just mathematical relationships. They arise from the nature of the information system and must be found by careful and detailed analysis. They usually arise from rules that hold in a system. For example, a rule that a person can only work on one project will lead to the functional dependency:

$$\text{PERSON-ID} \quad \rightarrow \quad \text{PROJECT}$$

However, if a person could work on more than one project, then this dependency would no longer be true. The functional dependencies require careful and detailed examination of the system rules. This detailed analysis is carried out during design. Analysts must question the relationships between attributes and the detailed rules that determine these relationships to find the functional dependencies. Collections of the dependencies are usually documented as a functional dependency diagram.

FUNCTIONAL DEPENDENCY DIAGRAMS

Functional dependency diagrams show all the functional dependencies between a set of attributes in a pictorial way. One example of such a functional dependency diagram is shown in Figure 17.3, where there are eight attributes and each attribute is enclosed by a rectangle. Other enclosures could, of course, be used—for example, an oval-shaped ellipse. Directed arrows are drawn from attributes that determine other attributes. Thus, if you find that each project has a single budget, then there is a directed arrow from PROJ-NO to BUDGET. Similarly, if you discover during analysis that each supplier has one address, then this is represented by a directed arrow from SUPPLIER-NAME to ADDRESS on the functional dependency diagram. Also, there is a directed arrow from PART-NO to WEIGHT, because each part has one weight. Whenever two attributes determine a single value of a third attribute, these two attributes are enclosed and a directed arrow drawn from the new enclosure to that third attribute. Because there is a single value of QUANTITY-USED for each combination of PART-NO and PROJ-NO, then a directed arrow originates from an enclosure that contains PART-NO to PROJ-NO and terminates on QUANTITY-USED. There is also a directed arrow from the enclosure of SUPPLIER-NAME and PART-NO to QUANTITY-SUPPLIED. This states that there is one value of QUANTITY-SUPPLIED for a given combination of SUPPLIER-NAME and PART-NO.

There are two things that you should note about functional dependency diagrams. First, each attribute appears once only on the functional dependency diagram. Second, all the attributes of interest to the system appear on the one diagram.

Let us return to the discussion about relations in higher normal forms. Such relations must satisfy additional constraints to having only simple attribute values. To describe such constraints it is necessary to define a relation key.

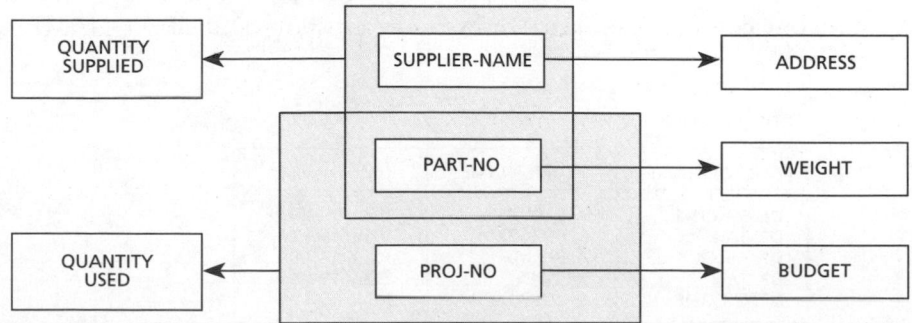

Figure 17.3 *A functional dependency diagram*

RELATION KEYS

Relation key
A set of attributes whose values identify a unique row in a relation.

A **relation key** is a set of columns whose values select unique relation rows. Thus PERSON-ID is the relation key of relation PERSONS in Figure 17.1. Once we are given a value of PERSON-ID we can immediately select one unique row.

Relation keys can be made up of more than one column. For example, the relation ORDERS in Figure 17.2(b) stores all the facts about orders (i.e. ORDER-DATE) and the facts about the parts (i.e. QTY-ORDERED) in those orders. The relation key of ORDERS is the two columns, ORDER-NO and PART-NO. ORDER-NO is not sufficient on its own, as there can also be more than one row with one value of PART-NO. There is, however, only one row for each order-part combination. We use the notation {ORDER-NO, PART-NO} to describe relation keys made up of more than one column.

Relations can have more than one relation key, as illustrated in Figure 17.4. This relation stores records of patient consultations with doctors. It is assumed that there is only one patient in each consultation and that only one doctor participates in each consultation. This relation has two relation keys. One is {DOCTOR-NO, TIME-OF-VISIT}, because a doctor can be in only one place at a time. The other is {PATIENT-NAME, TIME-OF-VISIT}, because each patient can be in only one place at a time.

One important thing to remember about relation keys is that they must apply for all possible contents of the relation. For example, if you look at relation PROJECTS in Figure 17.1 you may think that BUDGET is also a relation key because each row has a different value of budget. However, the uniqueness property of BUDGET does not hold for all possible relation contents. As soon as there are two projects with the same budget value (which is quite possible), a value of BUDGET no longer identifies one row only. PROJECT-ID, however, is a relation key because for any possible contents of the relation PROJECTS, there can never be two rows in the relation with the same value of PROJECT-ID.

There are two other definitions related to relation keys. These definitions are needed to define normal relations. An attribute is a *key attribute* if it is at least part of one relation key. It is a *non-key attribute* if it is not part of any relation key. Thus, in relation CONSULTATIONS, each attribute is a key attribute because each attribute is part of the relation key. In relation ORDERS in Figure 17.5, only ORDER-NO is a key attribute whereas the other attributes are non-key. You should bear in mind the distinction between a relation key and a key attribute. An attribute may be a key attribute but not a relation key. For example, attribute DOCTOR-NAME is a

CONSULTATIONS

DOCTOR-NAME	PATIENT-NAME	TIME-OF-VISIT
DR. SMYTHE	A. BLAND	10am 15/1/94
DR. TAN	B. JACKO	10am 15/1/94
DR. MACK	A. BLAND	10am 17/1/94
DR. TAN	J. COPES	11am 15/1/94
DR. SMYTHE	K. BLISS	11am 15/1/94

Figure 17.4 *A relation with two relation keys*

ORDERS

ORDER-NO	ORDER-DATE
Ord1	6 June 1998
Ord2	3 May 1998

ORDER-CONTENTS

ORDER-NO	PART-NO	QTY-ORDERED
Ord1	P1	10
Ord1	P6	30
Ord2	P5	10
Ord2	P6	50
Ord2	P2	30

Figure 17.5 *Relations in second normal form*

key attribute in relation CONSULTATIONS because it is part of the relation key {DOCTOR-NO, TIME-OF-VISIT}. It is not a relation key in its own right because, on its own, a value of DOCTOR-NAME does not identify a unique row.

NORMAL FORM RELATIONS

The concept of **normal form relations** is based on functional dependencies and relation keys. Informally, we would like relation keys to determine unique values of the non-key attributes. For example, look at the PERSONS relation in Figure 17.1. The relation key here is PERSON-ID. The other columns—namely, the person's NAME and the person's ADDRESS—are functionally dependent on the value of PERSON-ID. Note that there is no redundancy in relation PERSONS, because a person's NAME and ADDRESS are stored once for each person.

Normal form relations
A set of relations that describes the data in a system, but where each data component is a simple value.

DATA REDUNDANCIES

Now let us consider a relation that stores some facts more than once. The relation ORDERS, in Figure 17.2(b), is such a relation. As explained before, the relation key of relation ORDERS is made up of two columns, ORDER-NO and PART-NO. You should note that in relation ORDERS, the value of ORDER-DATE is determined by part of the relation key only. It is determined by ORDER-NO only and not by the combination of ORDER-NO and PART-NO. You will also note that the ORDER-DATE for the same order can appear more than once in relation ORDERS. It is stored as many times as there are parts in the order. When facts are stored more than once, a relation is no longer in the highest normal form.

The design goal is to eliminate such redundancies. Relations that do not have such redundancies satisfy a number of constraints. The constraints are defined in terms of functional dependencies and relation keys.

SECOND NORMAL FORM

Relations in second normal form (2NF) must satisfy the additional constraint that all non-key attributes must be functionally dependent on the whole of each relation key. Relations in 2NF cannot have non-key attributes that depend on only part of a relation key. To show how this constraint applies, let us turn to relation ORDERS in Figure 17.2(b). Here the relation key is {ORDER-NO, PART-NO}. The key attributes are ORDER-NO and PART-NO. The non-key attributes are ORDER-DATE and

QTY-ORDERED. The value of ORDER-DATE, however, depends only on ORDER-NO because all you have to know to determine ORDER-DATE is ORDER-NO. The relation is therefore not in 2NF.

Relations that are not in second normal form can always be decomposed into second normal form relations. To do this we can use a very simple rule:

Remove the offending functional dependency.

This means that we take the functional dependency that violated the 2NF constraint and make a new relation out of all the attributes in this functional dependency. We then remove the attributes on the right-hand side of this functional dependency from the original relation to make another new second relation.

For example, the relation ORDERS in Figure 17.2(b) is not in 2NF. The offending functional dependency is:

ORDER-NO $\rightarrow$ ORDER-DATE

As shown in Figure 17.5, we make a new relation ORDERS from this functional dependency and remove ORDER-DATE from the original relation. Relation ORDERS now stores facts about orders only. The original relation is now replaced by relation ORDERS-CONTENTS, which stores facts about order lines (or the parts ordered in orders). The relation key of relation ORDERS is ORDER-NO and the relation key of ORDER-CONTENTS is {ORDER-NO, PART-NO}. You will note that in these relations, non-key fields are determined by the whole (and not part) of the relation key and hence these relations are in second normal form.

THIRD NORMAL FORM

Relations in 2NF can still contain redundancies, and additional constraints must be satisfied to eliminate such redundancies. Relations in third normal form (3NF) must satisfy yet another constraint. In such relations, there must be no dependencies between non-key attributes.

An example of a relation that is in 2NF but not 3NF is relation VEHICLES in Figure 17.6. Relation VEHICLES stores information about cars. Each car is uniquely identified by its REGISTRATION-NO and has one owner. Values in all the other columns—that is, its OWNER, MODEL, MANUFACTURER and NO-CYLINDERS—are determined by the value of REGISTRATION-NO. The column REGISTRATION-NO is the relation key; the values of the non-key attributes are determined by the whole relation key and therefore the relation is in second normal form.

However, you may note that there are functional dependencies between the non-key attributes of relation VEHICLES. For example, NO-CYLINDERS is functionally dependent on a combination of MODEL and MANUFACTURER. If there are more than two cars of the same MODEL and MANUFACTURER in relation VEHICLES, then the NO-CYLINDERS of this model and manufacturer will be stored twice—again an undesirable characteristic. Here facts are stored more than once, because

(a) Relations not in third normal form

RELATION KEY

VEHICLES

REGISTRATION-NO	OWNER	MODEL	MANUFACTURER	NO-CYLINDERS
YX-01	George	Laser	Ford	4
YJ-77	Mary	Falcon	Ford	6
YW-30	George	Corolla	Toyota	4
YJ-37	Mary	Laser	Ford	4
YJ-83	Andrew	Corolla	Toyota	4

(b) Relations in third normal key

RELATION KEY

REGISTRATION

REGISTRATION-NO	OWNER	MODEL	MANUFACTURER
YX-01	George	Laser	Ford
YJ-77	Mary	Falcon	Ford
YW-30	George	Corolla	Toyota
YJ-37	Mary	Laser	Ford
YJ-83	Andrew	Corolla	Toyota

RELATION KEY

VEHICLE 1

MODEL	MANUFACTURER	NO-CYLINDERS
Laser	Ford	4
Falcon	Ford	6
Corolla	Toyota	4

Figure 17.6 *Decomposing relation to third normal form*

NO-CYLINDERS (which is a non-key column) is functionally dependent on other non-key attributes, MODEL and MANUFACTURER.

Relation VEHICLES is in second but not third normal form. To be in third normal form, a relation must first be in second normal form. In addition, it should not have any functional dependencies between non-key attributes.

Relations in second but not third normal form can always be decomposed into third normal form relations. Again, we can use our simple rule, 'remove the offending functional dependency'. In this case, the offending functional dependency is:

MODEL, MANUFACTURER $\rightarrow$ NO-CYLINDERS

Thus relation VEHICLES can be decomposed into the two relations shown in Figure 17.6(b). The relation key of relation REGISTRATION is REGISTRATION-NO, and the relation key of relation VEHICLE1 is {MODEL, MANUFACTURER}. You will note that in Figure 17.6(b), each relation:

- contains facts about the relation key only; and
- has no facts between non-key columns.

Each relation in Figure 17.6(b) is therefore in third normal form.

OPTIMAL NORMAL FORM

All the relations discussed so far had one relation key. Normal forms must also cover relations that have more than one relation key. The particular problem with relations that have more than one key is that part of one key may be functionally dependent on part of another key. For example, look at relation WORK in Figure 17.7(a). This relation describes the TIME-SPENT by persons working on projects. It also includes the MANAGER of each project, and in this system each project has one manager and a manager can at most manage one project. Relation WORK in Figure 17.7(a) has two overlapping keys. One relation key is (PROJECT-ID, PERSON-ID) and the other is (MANAGER, PERSON-ID). These keys overlap because they have a common attribute—namely, PERSON-ID. The only non-key attribute in relation WORK is TIME-SPENT.

In relation WORK, part of relation Key2—namely, MANAGER—is functionally dependent on part of Key1—namely, PROJECT-ID (i.e. the manager of the project). Similarly, PROJECT-ID is functionally dependent on MANAGER, as it gives the project managed by the manager. Note also that the MANAGER for a project identified by a given PROJECT-ID can be stored more than once. However, using the strict third normal definition, relation WORK in Figure 17.7(a) is in third normal form. The only non-key attribute in relation WORK is TIME-SPENT. This attribute depends

(a) A non-normal form relation with overlapping keys

		RELATION KEY 2	
	RELATION KEY 1		
PROJECT-ID	PERSON-ID	MANAGER	TIME-SPENT
Proj1	J1	Vicki	30
Proj2	J1	Joe	12
Proj1	J2	Vicki	11
Proj2	J2	Joe	79
Proj3	J2	Belinda	17
Proj2	J3	Joe	3

WORK

(b) Decomposing to normal form relations

RELATION KEY

PROJECTS

PROJECT	MANAGER
Proj1	Vicki
Proj2	Joe
Proj3	Belinda

RELATION KEY

WORK

PROJECT-ID	PERSON-ID	TIME-SPENT
Proj1	J1	30
Proj2	J1	12
Proj1	J2	11
Proj2	J2	79
Proj3	J2	17
Proj2	J3	3

Figure 17.7 *Non-normal form relations with overlapping keys*

on the whole of each relation key. There are no dependencies between non-key attributes (as there is only one of them).

What is needed is a higher normal form—one that takes overlapping keys into account. Such a higher normal form is the Boyce-Codd normal form (BCNF). A relation R is in BCNF if for every functional dependency $(X \rightarrow Y)$ between any relation attributes, the attributes on the left-hand side (that is, X) are a relation key.

Relations where this property holds are in BCNF, which is sometimes called **optimal normal form**. The relation WORK in Figure 17.7(a) is not optimal. Here there is a functional dependency:

PROJECT $\rightarrow$ MANAGER

but PROJECT is not a relation key of WORK.

Again, a non-BCNF relation can be decomposed into a set of optimal relations by removing the offending functional dependency. The result of decomposing Figure 17.7(a) is shown in Figure 17.7(b).

Optimal normal form
Set of relations that have no single-valued redundancy.

TEXT CASE D: Construction Company—Constructing Relations

Let us now see how we convert the E–R diagram for our Construction Company into relations. Figure 17.8 shows the relational model of the system shown in Figure 8.6 and modeled by the E–R diagram in Figure 9.17. The conversion proceeds in two steps. First, each set in Figure 9.17 is converted to a relation. Then, relations with the same relation key are combined. This means that on the E–R diagram, a relation for a 1:N relationship set is combined with a relation for one of the entity sets that participate in that relationship set. For example, the relation for entity set PURCHASE-ORDERS is combined with the relation for relationship set TO into one relation, PURCHASE-ORDERS. The combination is made to reduce the number of relations. It is possible because each purchase order is sent to one supplier and the relation key of relation TO is PO-NO. Hence, both PURCHASE-ORDERS and TO have the same relation key and combining them does not destroy normal form.

PROJECTS (<u>PROJECT-NO</u>, PROJECT-DETAILS)

PROJECT-REQUESTS (<u>PROJECT-NO, REQ-NO</u>, DATE-NEEDED)

REQUEST-LINES (<u>PROJECT-NO, REQ-NO, REQ-LINE-NO</u>, ITEM-NO, QTY-NEEDED, PO-NO, PO-LINE-NO)

PURCHASE-ORDERS (<u>PO-NO</u>, DATE-ORDERED, SUPPLIER-NAME)

ORDER-LINES (<u>PO-NO, PO-LINE-NO</u>, ITEM-NO, QTY-ORDERED, QTY-PAID-FOR, PRICE, QTY-RECEIVED)

ITEMS (<u>ITEM-NO</u>, ITEM-DESCRIPTION)

SUPPLIERS (<u>SUPPLIER-NAME</u>, SUPPLIER-DETAILS)

SHIPMENTS (<u>SHIPMENT-NO</u>, LOCATION, SUPPLIER-NAME)

SHIPLINES (<u>SHIPMENT-NO, SHIP-LINE-NO</u>, PO-NO, PO-LINE-NO, ITEM-NO, QTY-SHIPPED)

INVOICES (<u>INVOICE-NO</u>, DATE-SENT, SUPPLIER-NAME)

INVOICE-LINES (<u>INVOICE-NO, INVOICE-LINE-NO</u>, SHIPMENT-NO, SHIP-LINE-NO, ITEM-NO, QTY-INVOICED, PRICE, VALUE, PO-NO, PO-LINE-NO)

DELIVERIES (<u>DELIVERY-NO</u>, DELIVERY-DATE)

DELIVERY-LINES (<u>DELIVERY-NO, DELIVERY-LINE-NO</u>, ITEM-NO, QTY-DELIVERED, PROJECT-NO, REQ-NO, REQ-LINE-NO)

Figure 17.8 *Relations for Text Case D*

FINDING THE HIGHEST NORMAL FORM OF A RELATION

It is perhaps worthwhile here to outline a procedure for finding the highest normal form of a relation. This procedure is illustrated in Figure 17.9. It follows the arguments described in the previous paragraphs. We begin by finding the relation keys and then listing the key and non-key attributes. We then check whether each non-key attribute depends on the whole key. Relations that satisfy this constraint are in at least second normal form. Then we check whether there are any dependencies between non-key attributes. Relations that have no such dependencies are in at least third normal form. We then check if the relation has more than one relation key. If not, then a 3NF relation is also in BCNF. If the relation has more than one relation key, then one more check is needed. It is necessary to check if the left-hand side of each functional dependency is a relation key; if so, the relation is in BCNF.

Of course, in practice it is not always necessary to follow such a procedure. What we are really interested in is whether a relation is in optimal form. To find this out, we must first find all the functional dependencies and all the relation keys. All we need to do then is see whether the left-hand side of each functional dependency is

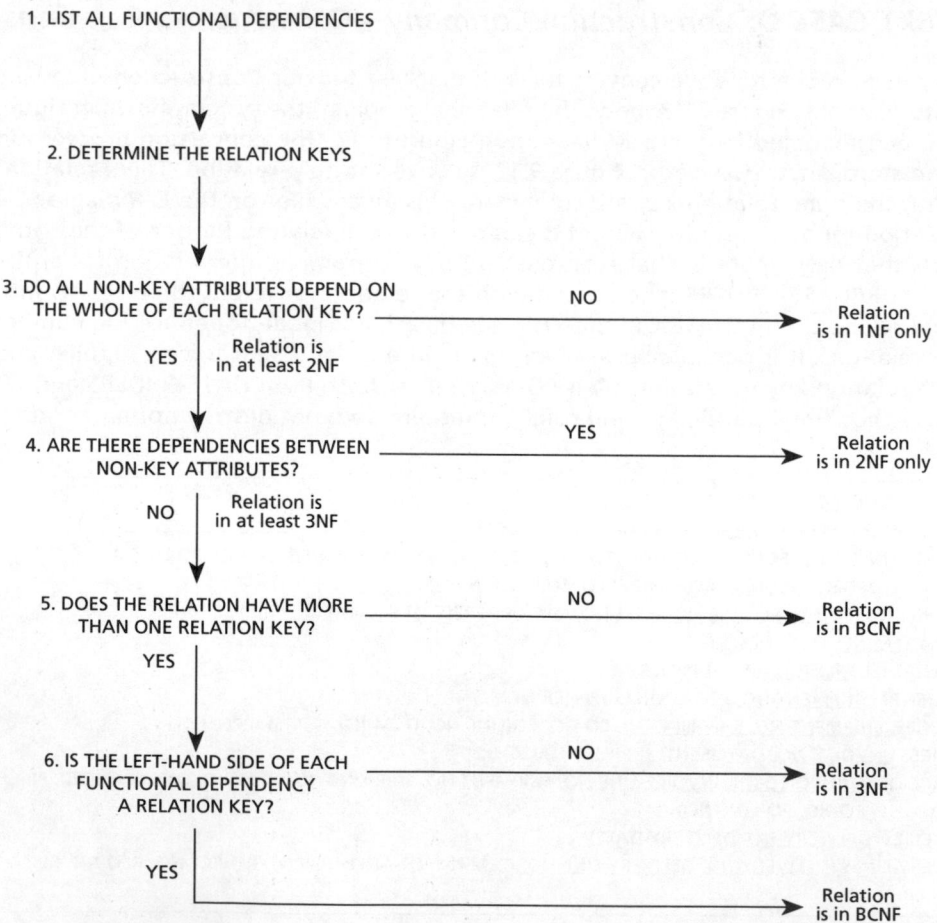

Figure 17.9 *Finding the highest normal form of a relation*

a relation key. If so, the relation is in optimal normal form. If not, we may try to determine the highest normal form in order to work out how to decompose the relation into optimal normal form.

NORMAL FORM RELATIONS AND MULTIVALUED DEPENDENCIES

Normal forms up to and including the optimal form have to satisfy constraints defined in terms of functional dependencies. There are also a number of problems that can arise with multivalued dependencies, and higher normal forms have been developed to deal with them. A **multivalued dependency** exists in a relation when a value of one column or set of columns, X, determines a set of values in another column, Y. Multivalued dependencies are often expressed by the notation:

Multivalued dependency
Where one value of an attribute determines a set of values of another attribute.

PERSON-ID $\twoheadrightarrow$ SKILL

This means that a value of PERSON-ID always determines a set of values of SKILL.

Some problems that are caused by multivalued dependencies are illustrated in Figure 17.10. Here a person identified by PERSON-ID has a number of SKILLS and works on a number of projects, identified by PROJECT-ID. Thus, both SKILL

(a) Storing different multi-fact values in different rows

PERSONS

PERSON-ID	SKILL	PROJECT-ID
Jill	Computing	—
Jill	French	—
Jill	—	Proj1
Jill	—	Proj3
Arnold	French	—
Arnold	Economics	—
Arnold	—	Proj1
George	Computing	—
George	—	Proj2
George	—	Proj1

(b) Minimizing number of rows

PERSONS

PERSON-ID	SKILL	PROJECT-ID
Jill	Computing	Proj1
Jill	French	Proj3
Arnold	French	Proj1
Arnold	Economics	—
George	Computing	Proj1
George	—	Proj2

(c) Cross product

PERSONS

PERSON-ID	SKILL	PROJECT-ID
Jill	Computing	Proj1
Jill	French	Proj1
Jill	Computing	Proj3
Jill	French	Proj3
Arnold	French	Proj1
Arnold	Economics	Proj1
George	Computing	Proj1
George	Computing	Proj2

Figure 17.10 *Storing multiple facts*

and PROJECT-ID are multivalued dependencies about PERSON-ID (because a person can have many skills and work on many projects). Now, how do we store SKILLS and PROJECT-ID for persons in the one relation? Some possibilities are shown in Figure 17.10. In Figure 17.10(a), each row contains a value from either one SKILL or one PROJECT-ID and the other column is blank. The problem with this method is that there are excessive null fields (resulting in wasted storage) and that system programs would have to handle these null fields.

Figure 17.10(b) minimizes the number of rows by storing values from both SKILL and PROJECT-ID in the same row. If the number of SKILL and PROJECT-ID values for a given person is the same, then there are no blank values (as for 'Jill'). If the number of values is different, however (as is more likely), then there will be blank values. System programs in this case can become difficult, due to the following:

- *Insertions of a new value may have different effects.* For example, adding a new project for 'Jill' adds a new row (with a NULL skill value). Adding a new project for 'Arnold' changes a NULL value to a project identifier.
- *Deletions also have different effects.* Deleting 'Economics' for 'Arnold' would delete a row. Deleting 'French' for 'Arnold' would mean that 'Proj1' would have to be moved to another row and then a row deleted. Deleting 'French' for 'Jill' would replace a value by a blank value.

All these effects would make the processing program complex and difficult to write and test.

Figure 17.10(c) is an alternative representation which does not make use of NULL values. We simply have one row for each possible SKILL-PROJECT-ID combination for each person. Thus, all skills possessed by 'Jill' appear in combination with all projects that 'Jill' works on. In this case, to insert or delete a new value we must insert or delete more than one row. Thus if 'George' gained a new skill 'Accounting', we would have to add two rows to relation PERSONS in Figure 17.10(c). One row would contain < 'George', 'Accounting', 'Proj1'> and the other <'George', 'Accounting', 'Proj2'>. You will now note, however, that there is redundancy in Figure 17.10(c). For example, we store all of 'Jill's' SKILLS once for each project on which 'Jill' works. Relations must satisfy additional constraints to avoid such redundancies. These constraints are expressed in terms of multivalued dependencies.

FOURTH NORMAL FORM

All the relations in Figure 17.10 are in 3NF or optimal form because there are no functional dependencies between their attributes. However, they are not in fourth normal form (4NF). Relations in 4NF must satisfy a constraint in terms of multivalued dependencies. A relation in 4NF must not contain more than one independent multivalued dependency or one independent multivalued dependency together with a functional dependency.

In Figure 17.10, SKILL and PROJECT-ID are independent multivalued dependencies of PERSON-ID. A person's skills are independent of the projects they work on, and the projects a person works on are independent of their skill. Therefore, a person's skills and their projects should be stored in separate relations, as shown in Figure 17.11. A relation is in 4NF if it does not contain independent multivalued dependencies.

It can be shown that any relation in 4NF is automatically in BCNF. This arises because each functional dependency is also a multivalued dependency.

FIFTH NORMAL FORM

Fifth normal form (5NF) can be viewed as an extension of 4NF in the sense that now the multivalued dependencies are no longer independent. For example, let us return to Figure 17.10(c). Suppose that instead of containing information about a person's SKILLs and PROJECT-ID, the relation also stores information about what skills the person uses in a given project. It is assumed that if a person possesses a skill, then that person will apply that skill to a project if the project needs it. Thus, suppose 'Proj1' only needs 'Computing' and 'Economics' skill but not 'French'. The relation would now be as shown in Figure 17.12(a).

Fifth normal form
A set of relations that have no multivalued redundancy.

The relation in Figure 17.12(a) differs from the relation in Figure 17.10(c) in that it does not contain rows that include both 'French' and 'Proj1'. This relation is in 4NF but still has undesirable properties in that:

- some facts are stored twice (e.g. 'Jill' and 'George' possess the skill 'computing'); and
- there are blank fields (e.g. 'Arnold' has skill 'French' which he is not currently applying to any project).

These undesirable properties arise because APPLYING-SKILLS contains dependent multivalued dependencies—that is, the value of SKILL that is associated with PROJECT-ID depends on the SKILLs needed by the project. A property of a relation that is in 4NF but not in 5NF is that it cannot be decomposed into two relations but must be decomposed into three relations. Thus, to remove the undesirable properties in relation APPLYING-SKILLS in Figure 17.12(a), we must decompose it into the three relations shown in Figure 17.12(b).

The relations in Figure 17.12(b) differ from the decomposed relations in Figure 17.11 because they contain the additional relations NEEDS-SKILL. The NEEDS-SKILL relation eliminates some of the rows in relation PERSON in Figure 17.10(c).

There is yet a third possibility where a person may not apply all their skills to a project even if they are needed. Thus, for example, 'Jill' may not use her 'computing'

KNOWLEDGE

PERSON-ID	SKILL
Jill	Computing
Jill	French
Arnold	French
Arnold	Economics
George	Computing

ASSIGNMENTS

PERSON-ID	PROJECT-ID
Jill	Proj1
Jill	Proj3
Arnold	Proj1
George	Proj1
George	Proj2

Figure 17.11 *Relations in 4NF*

(a) Relation with dependent multivalued facts

APPLYING-SKILLS

PERSON-ID	SKILL	PROJECT-ID
Jill	Computing	Proj1
Jill	Computing	Proj3
Jill	French	Proj3
Arnold	French	—
Arnold	Economics	Proj1
George	Computing	Proj1
George	Computing	Proj2

(b) Decomposing into 5NF relations

KNOWLEDGE

PERSON-ID	SKILL
Jill	Computing
Jill	French
Arnold	French
Arnold	Economics
George	Computing

ASSIGNMENTS

PERSON-ID	PROJECT-ID
Jill	Proj1
Jill	Proj3
Arnold	Proj1
George	Proj1
George	Proj2

NEEDS-SKILL

PROJECT-ID	SKILL
Proj1	Computing
Proj1	Economics
Proj2	Computing
Proj3	Computing
Proj3	French

Figure 17.12 *Fifth normal form*

skill in project 'Proj3' even if 'Proj3' requires a 'computing' skill. For that reason relation APPLYING-SKILLS would not contain the row <'Jill', 'Computing', 'Proj3'>. In that case, relation APPLYING-SKILLS could not be decomposed and would be in 5NF. However, the other three relations in Figure 17.12 must be in the database to avoid null fields in relation APPLYING-SKILLS. Thus, an informal definition of a 5NF relation is a relation that cannot be decomposed without losing information.

CONSTRUCTING RELATIONS FROM FUNCTIONAL DEPENDENCY DIAGRAMS

So far we have assumed that relations are first constructed. They are then checked to see if they are in the highest normal form and, if not, they are decomposed to higher normal forms. Sometimes, however, an alternative approach works. Why not start with functional dependencies and construct normal form relations from them?

A simple way to convert functional dependencies to relations is illustrated in Figure 17.13. It is to convert each set of dependencies with the same determinant to a relation. In this case, the left-hand side of the dependency will become the relation key. All the other non-prime attributes will be dependent on that key and thus the relation will be in at least 2NF. To ensure that such relations are also in optimal

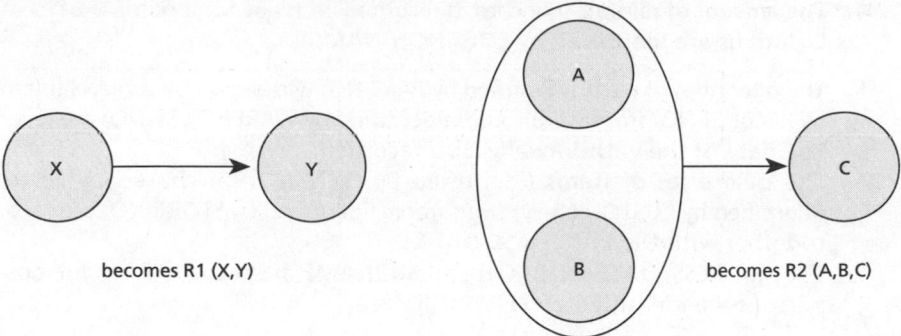

Figure 17.13 *Converting functional dependencies to relations*

form, it is necessary to remove any redundant functional dependencies before conversion takes place. The functional dependencies in Figure 17.3 would be converted to the following relations:

SUPPLIERS (<u>SUPPLIER-NAME</u>, ADDRESS)
PARTS (<u>PART-NO</u>, WEIGHT)
PROJECTS (<u>PROJ-NO</u>, BUDGET)
SUPPLY (<u>SUPPLIER-NAME</u>, PART-NO, QUANTITY-SUPPLIED)
USE (<u>PROJ-NO, PART-NO</u>, QUANTITY-USED)

 # SUMMARY

This chapter described the first database design step: to convert the E–R model to a relational model, which is then checked to see if it contains any redundancies. A number of criteria for such tests were described. These criteria were defined in terms of functional dependencies and relation keys. Relations that satisfy the criteria are known as normal relations. A number of normal forms were defined in this chapter. Designers should ensure that their data model contains only relations in the highest normal form.

 # EXERCISES

17.1 Construct relations for the following. Give each relation a name and specify all its attributes.

1. Deliveries (identified by DELIVERY-NO) of parts (identified by PART-NO) are made. The QTY-DELIVERED of each part is stored.
2. The number of miles cars (identified by REGISTRATION-NO) are driven on trips (identified by TRIP-NO) are stored, together with the driver (identified by DRIVER-NO) and TRIP-DATE.
3. A person's weight is recorded each day. The person is identified by PERSON-ID.

4. The amount of rainfall, in inches, is recorded each day for a number of locations. Locations are identified by LOCATION-NAME.

5. The quantities of parts (identified by PART-NO) withdrawn by projects (identified by PROJECT-NO) from warehouses (identified by WAREHOUSE-NO) are recorded. The date of the withdrawal is also recorded.

6. The quantities of items (identified by ITEM-NO) purchased by customers (identified by CUSTOMER-ID) from stores (identified by STORE-NO) are recorded, together with the PURCHASE-DATE.

7. The ADDRESS, DATE-OF-BIRTH and SURNAME are recorded for persons. The persons are identified by PERSON-ID.

17.2 Draw a functional dependency diagram showing functional dependencies between the capitalized attributes in the following problem:

Policies identified by a POLICY-NO can be established in an organization. Each policy has one DATE-SET-UP and is set up for one customer. Each customer has a CUSTOMER-ID. The customer also has an ADDRESS but addresses can change. The START-DATE is kept for each address. There is one RISK-LOCATION for each policy.

A policy can include any number of special items. Each special item has a unique SPECIAL-ITEM-NAME within the policy. The VALUE of each special item is recorded.

Claims can be made against policies. Each claim has a unique CLAIM-NO and is made on a given CLAIM-DATE and a CLAIM-AMOUNT. Any special items included in the claim are recorded, together with the ADDITIONAL-AMOUNT-CLAIMED for each special item.

17.3 Convert the E–R diagrams shown in Figure 17.14 to relations.

17.4 Examine the four relations in Figure 17.15. The rules for these relations are given below. Find the relation key for each relation and state the highest normal form for each relation.

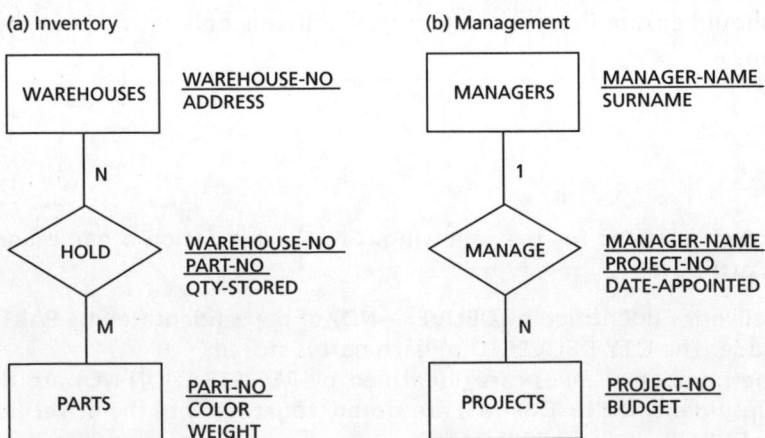

Figure 17.14 *E–R diagrams for Exercise 17.3*

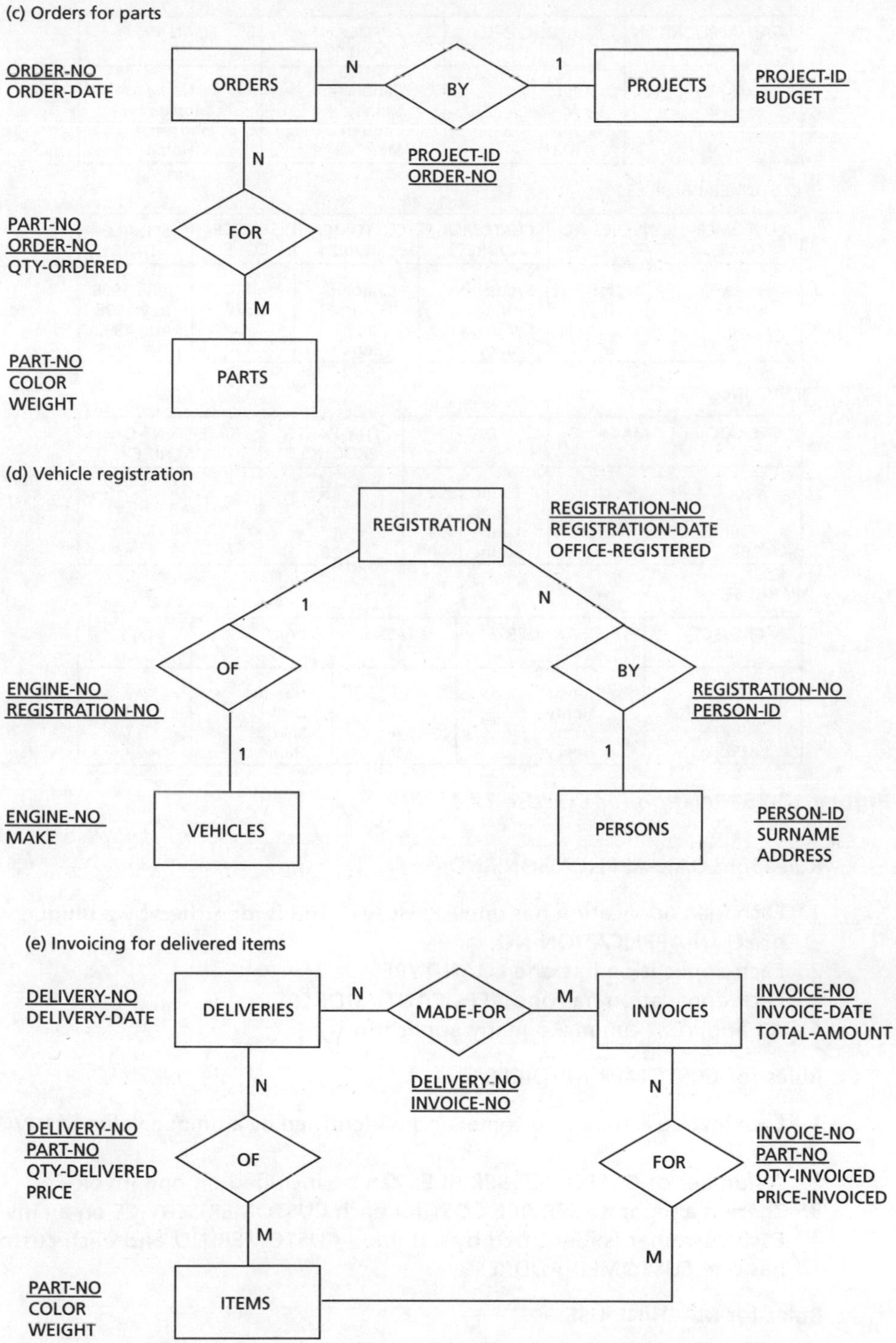

(c) Orders for parts
ORDER-NO
ORDER-DATE
ORDERS
N
BY
1
PROJECTS
PROJECT-ID
BUDGET
PROJECT-ID
ORDER-NO
N
PART-NO
ORDER-NO
QTY-ORDERED
FOR
M
PART-NO
COLOR
WEIGHT
PARTS
(d) Vehicle registration
REGISTRATION
REGISTRATION-NO
REGISTRATION-DATE
OFFICE-REGISTERED
1
N
OF
BY
ENGINE-NO
REGISTRATION-NO
REGISTRATION-NO
PERSON-ID
1
1
ENGINE-NO
MAKE
VEHICLES
PERSONS
PERSON-ID
SURNAME
ADDRESS
(e) Invoicing for delivered items
DELIVERY-NO
DELIVERY-DATE
DELIVERIES
N
MADE-FOR
M
INVOICES
INVOICE-NO
INVOICE-DATE
TOTAL-AMOUNT
DELIVERY-NO
INVOICE-NO
N
N
DELIVERY-NO
PART-NO
QTY-DELIVERED
PRICE
OF
FOR
INVOICE-NO
PART-NO
QTY-INVOICED
PRICE-INVOICED
M
M
PART-NO
COLOR
WEIGHT
ITEMS

Figure 17.14 *(Continued)*

LOAN APPLICATIONS

LOAN-APPLICATION-NO	APPLICANT	APPLICANT-ADDRESS	LOAN-TYPE
1	Jill	Canberra	Home
2	Joe	Sydney	Mortgage
3	Jill	Canberra	Personal
4	Max	Melbourne	Home

CUSTOMER-INVOICES

CUSTOMER-NAME	INVOICE-NO	CUSTOMER-ADDRESS	CUSTOMER-SERVICES	SERVICE-COST	SERVICE-DATE
Joe	6	Sydney	Repair	120	June 1998
Joe	6	Sydney	Course	320	July 1998
Jill	3	Canberra	Repair	80	Aug 1998
Joe	6	Sydney	Repair	150	Oct 1998

MACHINE-USE

OPERATOR	MACHINE	DATE	QTY-PARTS-PRODUCED	TIME-SPENT-ON-MACHINE
Joe	Mach1	1 June 1998	15	10
Joe	Mach2	1 June 1998	20	12
Bill	Mach3	1 June 1998	12	6
Bill	Mach2	2 June 1998	20	14

PART-USE

PROJECT-ID	MANAGER	TASK	PART	QTY
Proj1	Jenny	3	Hammer	7
Proj2	Henry	9	Drill	9
Proj1	Jenny	4	Saw	11
Proj2	Henry	9	Hammer	6

Figure 17.15 *Relation for Exercise 17.4*

Rules for LOAN-APPLICATIONS-NO:

1. Each loan application has one APPLICANT and is identified by a unique value of LOAN-APPLICATION-NO.
2. Each application has one LOAN-TYPE.
3. Each application has one APPLICANT-ADDRESS.
4. An applicant can make many applications.

Rules for CUSTOMER-INVOICES:

1. Each invoice is to one customer and is identified by a unique value of INVOICE-NO.
2. A number of CUSTOMER-SERVICES can be included on one invoice.
3. There is a separate SERVICE-COST for each CUSTOMER-SERVICE on an invoice.
4. Each customer is identified by a unique CUSTOMER-NO and each customer has one CUSTOMER-ADDRESS.

Rules for MACHINE-USE:

1. A machine can be used by only one operator on a given date.
2. An operator can use any number of machines on the one day.
3. TIME-SPENT-ON-MACHINE is the time spent by an operator on the machine on a given DATE. QTY-PARTS-PRODUCED is the quantity of parts produced on that machine by the operator on the given date.

Rules for PART-USE:

1. Each PROJECT-ID has one MANAGER.
2. Each MANAGER manages one PROJECT.
3. Each TASK belongs to one PROJECT.
4. Each task uses a given QTY of a PART and may use any number of parts.

17.5   Construct a set of normal relations described by the following statements.

1. Persons (identified by PERSON-ID and a SURNAME) are given AUTHORITY-NOs by PROJECTS (identified by PROJECT-NO and a given BUDGET). Each such AUTHORITY-NO authorizes the person to place orders for a project. A person can have many authority numbers and many persons can have an authority for a given project.
2. The AUTHORITY-NO is assigned on a given AUTHORITY-DATE and is for a given MAX-AMOUNT and for one project only.
3. The order is made to one supplier on a given ORDER-DATE. It can be for any number of different PART-KINDS. The order includes a QTY-ORDERED for each PART-KIND. Each order is placed under one authority number.
4. Each PART-KIND has a PRICE. The PRICE depends on the supplier.
5. The supplier is identified by SUPPLIER-ID and can have any number of ADDRESSes. An order is placed at one ADDRESS.

17.6   What is the highest normal form of the following relations?

1. | JOB-NO | PLACE | PERSON-ID | DATE STARTED |

   A job is in one place and a number of people are working on a job. Each person starts once only on each job.

2. | ROOM | COMMITTEE | CHAIRPERSON | TIME | DATE |

A committee can meet any number of times in different rooms. The committee has the same chairperson at each meeting, and can meet more than once on the same day, possibly in different rooms.

3. | LOT-NO | DESCRIPTION | PURCHASER | DATE | PURCHASER | ADD |

Lots are sold to any purchaser at auction. A lot can be sold only once on any given day. A lot has one description and the purchaser has one address. There can at most be one purchase with a given LOT-NO on any day, but the same LOT-NO can be used on different days.

4. | ACCOUNT-NO | NAME | DATE | BALANCE | ADDRESS |

Account balances change over time. Address is for account. Each account has one address only.

5. | PROGRAM | DAY | TIME | CHANNEL |

   A television program guide.

BIBLIOGRAPHY

Aho, A.V. et al. (1979), 'Theory of joins in relational databases', *ACM Transactions on Database Systems*, Vol. 4, No. 3, pp. 297–314.

Armstrong, W.W. (1980), 'Decompositions and functional dependencies in relations', *ACM Transactions on Database Systems*, Vol. 5, No. 4, pp. 404–30.

Beeri, C. (August 1977), 'A complete axiomatization for functional and multivalued dependencies', *SIGMOD International Conference on Management of Data*, Toronto.

Codd, E.F. (1971), 'A relational model of data for large shared data banks', *Communications of the ACM*, Vol. 13 No. 6, pp. 377–87.

Date, C.J. (1990), *An Introduction to Database Systems* (4th edn), Addison-Wesley, Reading, Massachusetts.

Hawryszkiewycz, I.T. (1991), *Relational Database Design: An Introduction*, Prentice Hall, Sydney.

Kent, W. (1983), 'A simple guide to five normal forms in relational database theory', *Communications of the ACM*, Vol. 26 No. 2, pp. 120–25.

Korth, H.F. and Silberschatz, A. (1986), *Database System Concepts*, McGraw-Hill, New York.

Program design

KEY LEARNING OBJECTIVES

Steps to be followed in program design
Structure charts
Coupling and cohesion
Good characteristics of structure charts
How to convert data flow diagrams to structure charts

 **INTRODUCTION**

Implementation is usually made up of three activities: database design, user procedure design and program development. Database design uses the data requirements model to produce a database design in the way described in Chapters 16 and 17. User procedure design uses those parts of the data flow diagram outside the automation boundary to design user procedures in the way described in Chapter 14 and to define user interfaces in the way described in Chapter 15. We now come to the last component of the development process—developing programs. Programs are needed for a number of reasons in systems. They are needed to make enquiries of databases, update the database with new transactions, support interaction with users, or to produce reports. This again goes through two steps: developing the system model during system design, and converting this model to an implementation.

One objective of system design is to specify modules that satisfy a variety of good design criteria. Such designs result in programs that are easy to develop and, later, to change. These design objectives are achieved by modular program design. Modular program design localizes each well-defined user system function to one program module or object class. Note that modularity and structured programming are consistent with the criteria for good DFDs. In a well-designed DFD, each process represents one well-defined function. Furthermore, each process is described using structured English, which uses constructs similar to structured programming. These DFDs must be converted into programs in a way that passes on the good DFD structure to the program specification.

Once system design is completed, a variety of tools are available to develop programs during implementation. For example, enquiry packages or languages are available to make database enquiries. Reports are often produced using report generators, and screens for interaction with users can be developed using screen painting software.

In many cases, specific programs need to be written using the wide variety of available programming languages. Developers use structured programming to make programs readable.

 FROM SPECIFICATION TO SYSTEM MODELS

Figure 18.1 shows the steps usually followed in progressing from system specifications to program development, and the activities carried out in each of these phases. In structured systems analysis, the design follows Processes 5, 6, 7, 8, 9 and 10 in Figure 18.1. It begins with Process 5 by selecting processes to be automated and dividing them into subsystems. These are then converted to charts, which then become program modules. Database design proceeds seperately as Process 4. Where there is an object-oriented implementation, then Steps 4, 6, and 7 can be combined to convert the class objects to object classes in the implementation. In that case, Process 8 becomes the detailed design of an object class.

DIVIDING INTO COMPUTER SUBSYSTEMS

System design starts with DFDs or objects inside the automation boundary and uses outputs from database design and user procedure design to produce working programs. In structured systems analysis, the first system design step is to divide the DFD into

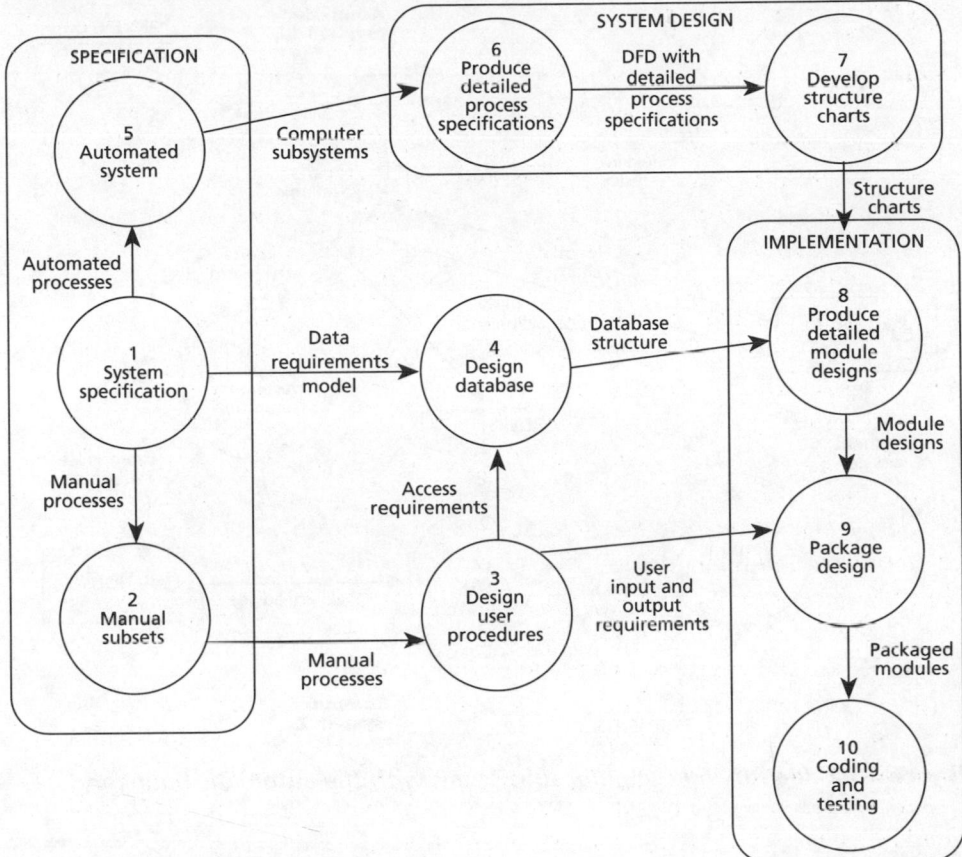

Figure 18.1 *Program design*

computer subsystems. The way this is done is to group logically connected processes into computer subsystems. These subsystems usually involve one transaction or some connected transactions and become transaction programs or batch suites of programs.

The most common method of grouping DFD processes is to follow through one kind of input, which usually identifies a part of a business process. Figure 18.2 shows how DFD processes can be broken up into computer subsystems. The DFD in Figure 18.2 describes a business process that takes a customer order and delivers the parts requested in the order. In Figure 18.2 this business process is subdivided into two parts. Processes 3.1, 3.2 and 3.3 form the part of the process that takes the order and converts it to a warehouse requisition. They check if the ordered parts are in the warehouse and create a warehouse requisition for the parts. Processes 3.4 and 3.5 form the part of the process that delivers the parts requested in the warehouse requisition. They remove the requisitioned parts from the warehouse, package them, and check if they meet the order prior to delivery to the customer.

The DFD processes in Figure 18.2 are grouped into two computer subsystems. The first subsystem contains Processes 3.1, 3.2 and 3.3. These processes follow through customer orders until a warehouse requisition is generated. The requisition requests

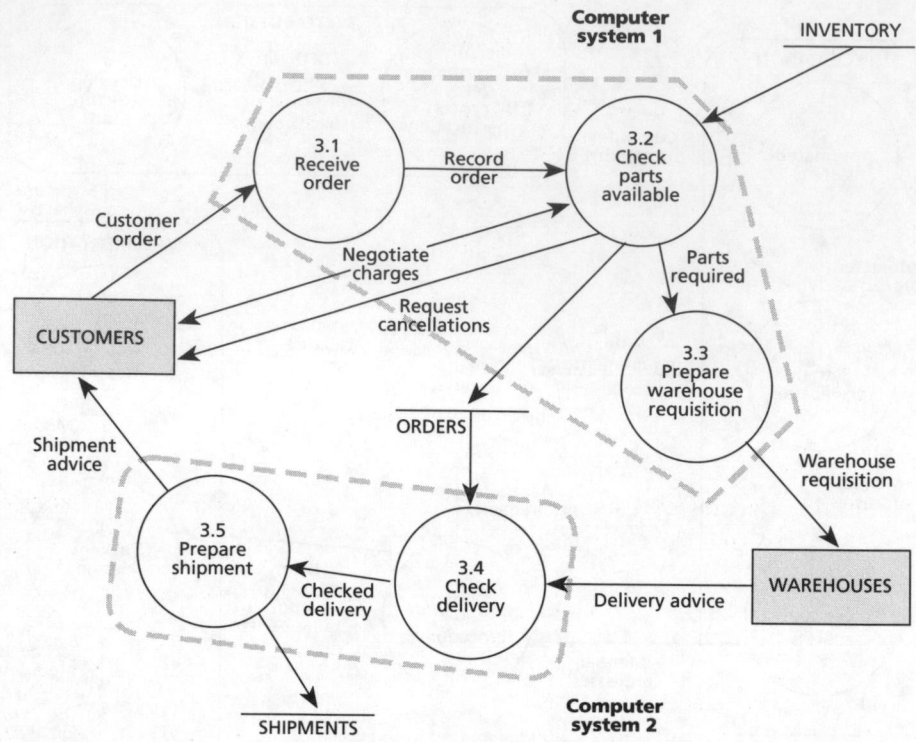

Figure 18.2 *Identifying computer subsystems with the automatic boundary*

the warehouse to prepare the ordered parts for delivery. The second subsystem is made up of Processes 3.4 and 3.5. These processes follow delivery advices until a shipment advice is sent to the customer.

After computer subsystems are chosen, detailed process specifications are developed for each DFD process in each subsystem. The DFD processes are then converted to program modules, which are shown on a **structure chart**. The program modules are grouped into load modules during implementation.

Structure chart
Program modules and their interconnection.

STRUCTURE CHARTS

Structure charts are one of the most commonly used methods for system design. In a structure chart, each program module is represented by a rectangular box. Modules at the top level of the structure chart call the modules at the lower levels. The connections between modules are represented by lines between the rectangular boxes. The connections describe data flows between the called and calling modules. Figure 18.3 illustrates a simple structure chart made up of four modules. The top module is called COMPUTE-SALE-TOTAL. This module calls three lower-level program modules to accomplish its task. It calls module READ-SALES-TRANSACTION to read individual sales transactions. It then calls module ADD-TO-TOTAL to sum the amount in each transaction. Finally, it calls module OUTPUT-TOTAL to output the sum.

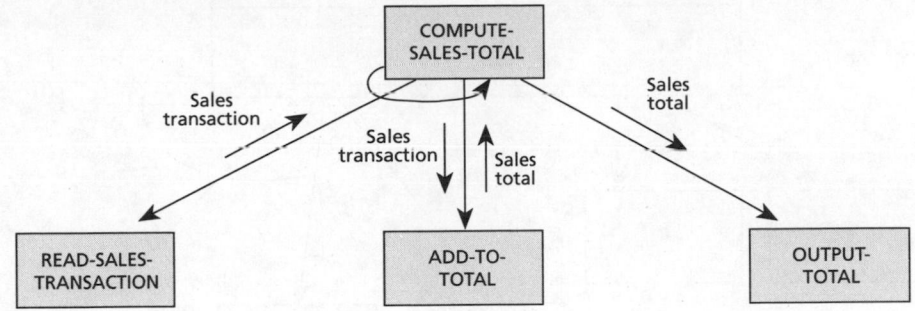

Figure 18.3 *A structure chart*

Structure chart conventions

Structure charts use a number of conventions to describe system operation. The most important conventions specify the execution sequence and parameter passing between modules.

Parameter passing

The calling module passes a set of values to the called module and receives a set of values in return. These values are passed as parameter values. The parameters are shown in the structure chart next to the connection. Thus, in Figure 18.3, a value of 'sales transaction' is passed from module READ-SALES-TRANSACTION to module COMPUTE-SALES-TOTAL. Module COMPUTE-SALES-TOTAL then passes the value of 'sales transaction' to module ADD-TO-TOTAL and gets a value of 'sales total' in return. The value of 'sales total' is then passed from module COMPUTE-SALES-TOTAL to module OUTPUT-TOTAL.

Execution sequence

By convention, modules are executed from left to right. Thus, in Figure 18.3, module READ-SALES-TRANSACTION is called before module ADD-TO-TOTAL. Module OUTPUT-TOTAL is the last module to be called.

Certain conventions are also used to represent decisions and repetition. Decisions occur whenever a calling module has to decide to call only one of a number of modules. Repetition, on the other hand, occurs when some modules are called repetitively by the calling module.

Repetition is modeled by a looping arrow. As an example, in Figure 18.3, module COMPUTE-SALES-TOTAL calls modules READ-SALES-TRANSACTION and ADD-TO-TOTAL any number of times.

Decisions are modeled by a diamond symbol. An example of decisions is given in Figure 18.4. Here, module A:

- calls either module B or module C; and then
- executes a loop which calls module D, E and sometimes F.

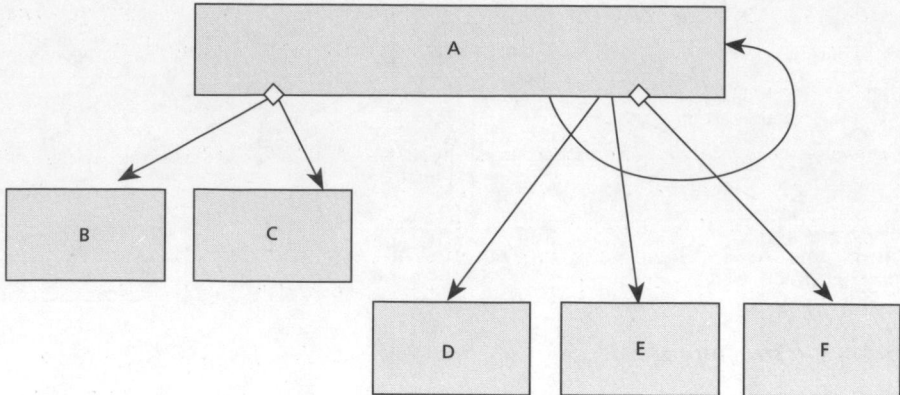

Figure 18.4 *Procedural annotations*

STRUCTURE CHARTS AND STRUCTURED DESIGN

Structure charts are developed by a process called *structured design*. The objective of structured design is to produce structure charts with properties commensurate with good programming practice. A number of properties are used to judge how well structure charts satisfy these objectives. These properties are usually known as *module coupling* and *cohesion*. Module cohesion is also sometimes called *module strength*.

Coupling describes the nature, direction and quantity of parameters passed between modules, while cohesion describes how system functions are coded into modules. A goal of structured design is to minimize the complexity of coupling between modules. Structure charts with simple coupling are said to have low coupling. Another goal of structured design is to represent a well-defined system function by one module. When this happens, we have high strength. Structure charts with low coupling and high strength result in greater independence between modules and easier maintenance, as one module can be changed independently of other modules.

The proponents of structured design have devised measures of coupling and module strength. A number of terms are used to describe coupling and cohesion. These terms are ordered into a range starting with the least desirable to the most desirable.

Module coupling

Module coupling measures the quality of the connections between modules in the structure chart. The objective is to design structure charts that only pass data and not control information between program modules. However, a first-cut design may not meet this objective and the structure chart may exhibit other kinds of coupling. There are a number of ways to describe coupling. The best coupling is data coupling, followed by control coupling, common-environment coupling and content coupling.

Content coupling. Two modules are content coupled if one module makes a direct reference to the contents of another module. This kind of coupling allows the calling module to modify a program statement in the called module or to refer to an internally defined data element of the called module. It also allows one module to branch into another module. Content coupling should be avoided at all costs, and structure charts should ensure that the only way to pass information between modules is by parameter values passed during sub-routine calls.

Common-environment coupling. Two modules are common-environment coupled if they refer to the same data structure or data element in a common environment.

Examples of common-environment coupling include common areas in user programs or shared files. The effect of common-environment coupling is that modules that appear unrelated in a structure chart are coupled through their use of common data.

Control coupling. Two modules are control coupled if one module passes a control element to the other module. This control element affects the processing in the receiving module. Typical examples of control coupling are flags, function codes and switches.

Control coupling violates the principle of information hiding. Passing a control element from a calling module to a called module implies that the calling module must know the method of operation of the called module. Any changes made to the called module can then require changes in the calling module.

Data coupling. Two modules are data coupled if they are not content coupled, common-environment coupled or control coupled. Only data elements are passed as parameters between two data coupled modules.

Data coupling is seen as the most desirable form of coupling. The calling module passes data values by parameters to the called module and expects some computations to be made on these values. The results of the computation are then returned as parameter values to the calling module. The calling module need not be aware of how the program does the computation.

Common examples of data coupling are calls to input or output modules. A calling module may require some input; it calls another module, INPUT, to provide this input. The calling module does not care how the called INPUT module obtains the input—it is only concerned with the data it receives.

Calls to output modules are of a similar nature. The calling module passes the data that is to be output, to module OUTPUT; it is not concerned with how the called module OUTPUT outputs the data.

Module strength

Module strength measures reasons why code appears in the same module. Many writers use the following six levels of module strength (listed from the least to the most desirable):

- coincidental;
- logical;
- temporal;
- procedural;
- communicational; and
- functional.

A brief outline of these six levels follows, with more detailed descriptions to be found in Yourdon and Constantine's *Structural Design* (1979).

Coincidental strength. Coincidental strength exists if there is no meaningful relationship between the parts in a module. It often occurs when existing code is modularized. Modularization often proceeds by searching existing code for multiple occurrences of sequences of commands and replacing these sequences by modules. Often such modules are not related to well-defined system functions, but result from techniques that have been used to write the program.

Logical strength. Logical strength occurs when all elements in a module perform similar tasks—for example, modules that include all editing, or modules that include all accesses to a file.

Considerable duplication can exist in the logical strength level. For example, similar edit checks may be made on more than one data item—for instance, more than one data item in an input transaction may be a date. Separate code would be written to check that each such date is a valid date. A better way is to construct a DATE-CHECK module and call this module whenever a date check is necessary.

Temporal strength. Temporal strength is very similar to logical strength. All functions related to time are grouped into one module. Typical examples are INITIATION and TERMINATION modules.

Temporal strength is generally regarded as stronger than logical strength, but it still has some undesirable features as far as change is concerned. For example, adding a new file to a system will result in changes to both the INITIATION and TERMINATION modules, as well as to those modules directly concerned with operations on the new file.

Procedural strength. Procedural strength often results when a flowchart is divided into a number of sections and each section is represented by one module. This division may not be ideal, as the flowchart can represent one well-defined system function; division distributes this self-contained function among a number of modules.

Communicational strength. Communicational strength occurs when processes that communicate with each other are included in the same module. Thus all actions concerned with a file may be included in the same module. This module will read the file, process it and write the output back to the file.

The most often-quoted problem with communicational strength is the interdependence of processes in the module. For example, we may include code that uses the input from a file in the same module as the code that reads the file. However, the file 'read' and the use of the information from the file may occur in different time frames and may share common buffers. A change that allows concurrent 'reads' and 'writes' to the file may result in unexpected problems.

Functional strength. A module that has functional strength carries out one well-defined function. This module does not have those properties that characterize coincidental, logical, temporal, procedural or communicational strength.

In addition, some writers define sequential strength and informational strength. Sequential strength occurs where outputs from elements in a module serve as inputs to other elements in a module. In terms of a flowchart or data flow graph, sequential strength combines a chain of successive transformations on the data. Information strength exists where modules perform multiple functions, with each function represented by a different entry point to the module. Each such entry point has the characteristics of a module of functional strength. Sequential and informational strengths fall between communicational and functional strengths in the scale of module strength.

Morphology

Coupling and cohesion are criteria applied locally to a few modules. Apart from such local criteria, structure charts can also be evaluated by considering their total structure. Some criteria used in this evaluation are span of control, fan-in, and the scope of control and scope of effect rules.

Span of control. Span of control comprises the number of immediate subordinates of a module. In Figure 18.5, modules B, C, D, E and F are the immediate subordinates of module A. Hence, the span of control of module A is five. Ideally, the span of control should not exceed seven.

Fan-in. The fan-in is the number of modules that call a particular module; in Figure 18.5, module A has a fan-in of one, while module C has a fan-in of two. Ideally, structure charts should have a high fan-in. This means that self-contained functions that can be used at a number of places have been identified.

Scope of control. The span of control comprises all the subordinates of a module. It includes the immediate subordinates of a module, *their* immediate subordinates, and

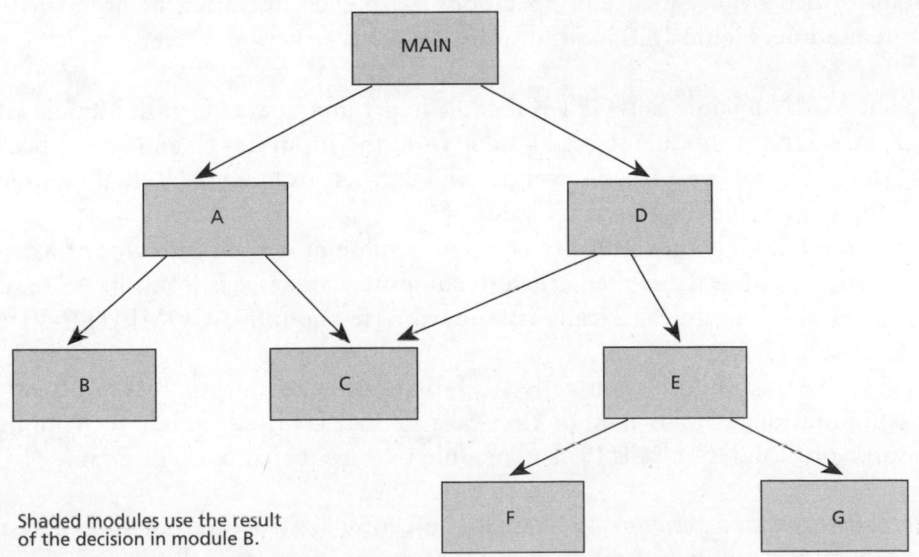

Shaded modules use the result
of the decision in module B.

Figure 18.5 *Scope of effect*

so on. Thus, the scope of control of the MAIN module in Figure 18.5 is all the modules A, B, C, D, E, F and G. The scope of control of module A is modules B and C.

Scope of effect. The scope of effect of a decision consists of all modules whose processing is conditional on the outcome of the decision. In Figure 18.5, for example, suppose that a decision (d1) is made in module B. If this decision affects processing in modules A, E and F, then modules A, E and F are said to be in the scope of effect of module B.

Good design calls for the effects of a decision to be confined to as few modules as possible. If this is done, then the tests based on one decision will not be unnecessarily repeated or the results of a decision will not be passed through an excessive number of modules. In Figure 18.5, for example, the result of decision d1 (in module B) would need to be passed through modules A, MAIN and D to be useful in modules E and F. To eliminate such passing of control parameters, the scope of effect of a decision should be within the scope of control of the module where the decision is made. The decision need not then be returned to calling modules. Indeed, it is desirable that the decision be made as close as possible to the modules that use the decision. One way to achieve this is to have only immediate subordinates within the scope of effect of a decision.

Some common structures

Structure charts are often characterized by some constructs that tend to reappear in many applications. Two such important constructs are transform-centered and transaction-centered structures.

Transform-centered structures. Transform-centered structures receive an input which is transformed by a sequence of operations, with each operation being carried out by one module. Figure 18.6 is a transform-centered structure where:

- The MAIN module calls GET-X module to get input parameter, X. Module GET-X calls GET-Y module to read a value from the input device and pass it back to GET-X as a value of parameter Y. GET-X then calls CHANGE-Y module to compute a value of X from the value of Y.
- A module (Tl) is then called to compute a value of A from the value of X.
- Another module T2 is then called to compute a value of B from the value of A. To do this, module T2 calls its subordinate modules, COMPUTE-VI and COMPUTE-B.
- The MAIN module then calls PUT-B module to output the result of the computation. PUT-B module first calls COMPUTE-C module to compute a value of C and then calls PUT-C module to output that particular value of C.

Transaction-centered structures. A transaction-centered structure describes a system that processes a number of different types of transactions. It is illustrated in Figure 18.7. Here the MAIN module controls systems operations. Its function is to:

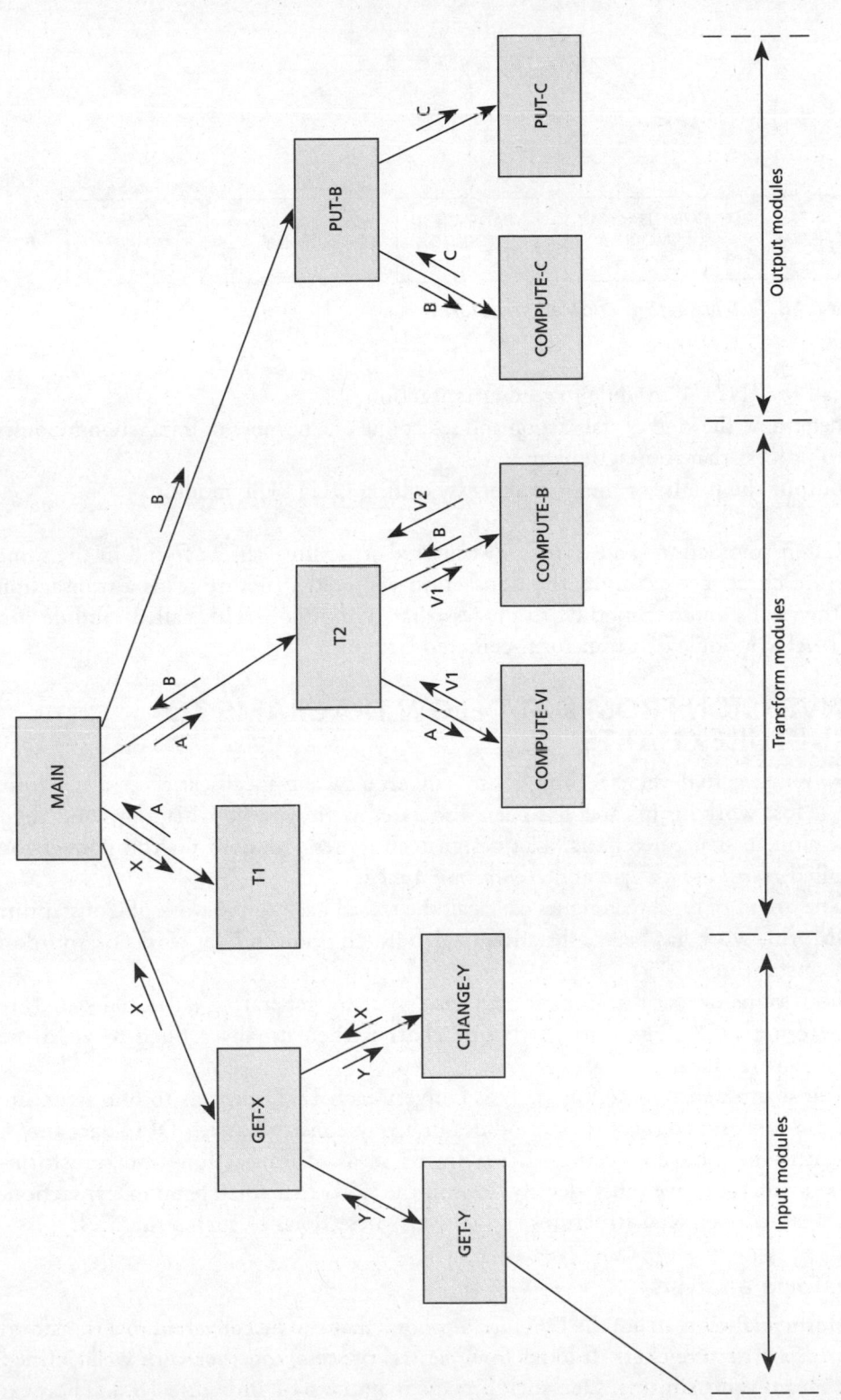

Figure 18.6 *Transform structure*

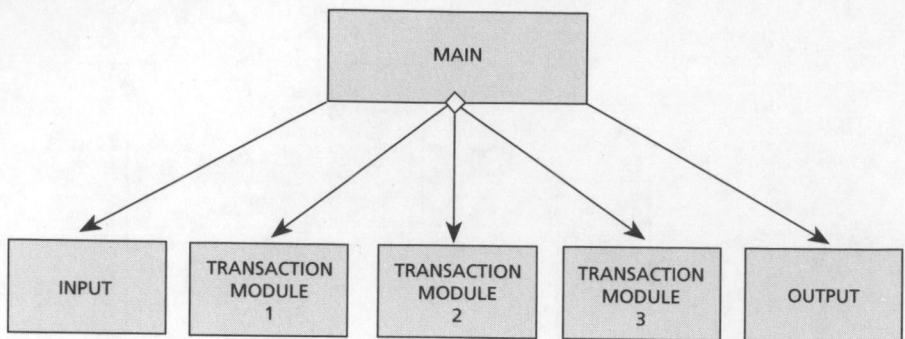

Figure 18.7 *Transaction-centred structure*

- call the INPUT module to read a transaction;
- determine the kind of transaction and select one of a number of transaction modules to process that transaction; and
- output the results of the processing by calling OUTPUT module.

Often transaction- and transform-centered structures can be found in the same structure chart. For example, the transaction-centered structure reads a transaction and then calls another module to process that transaction. This called module can be a MAIN module of a transform-centered structure.

CONVERSION FROM DATA FLOW DIAGRAMS TO STRUCTURE CHARTS

It now remains to develop techniques to convert a system specification to a structure chart. Most work in this area has been associated with data flow diagrams and their conversion to structure charts. The design techniques proposed for this conversion are called *transform analysis* and *transaction analysis*.

The origin of these techniques can again be traced back to the work of Constantine at IBM; this work has been substantially elaborated upon in later works of Yourdon and Constantine (1979).

Both transform and transaction analysis start by generating an initial structure chart from a DFD. The initial structure chart is then usually refined to yield the final structure chart.

Transform and transaction analysis convert each DFD process to one structure chart module and connect these modules in a way consistent with DFD data flows. The nature of these connections lies with the ideas of transaction- and transform-centered structures. We must identify flows in the DFD that correspond to transaction- and transform-centered structures and convert these flows to such structures.

Transform analysis

Transform analysis searches the DFD for a process that can be converted to a transform center in a structure chart. It looks for a central process, together with well-defined input and output streams. One such process is Process F2 in Figure 18.8. The next

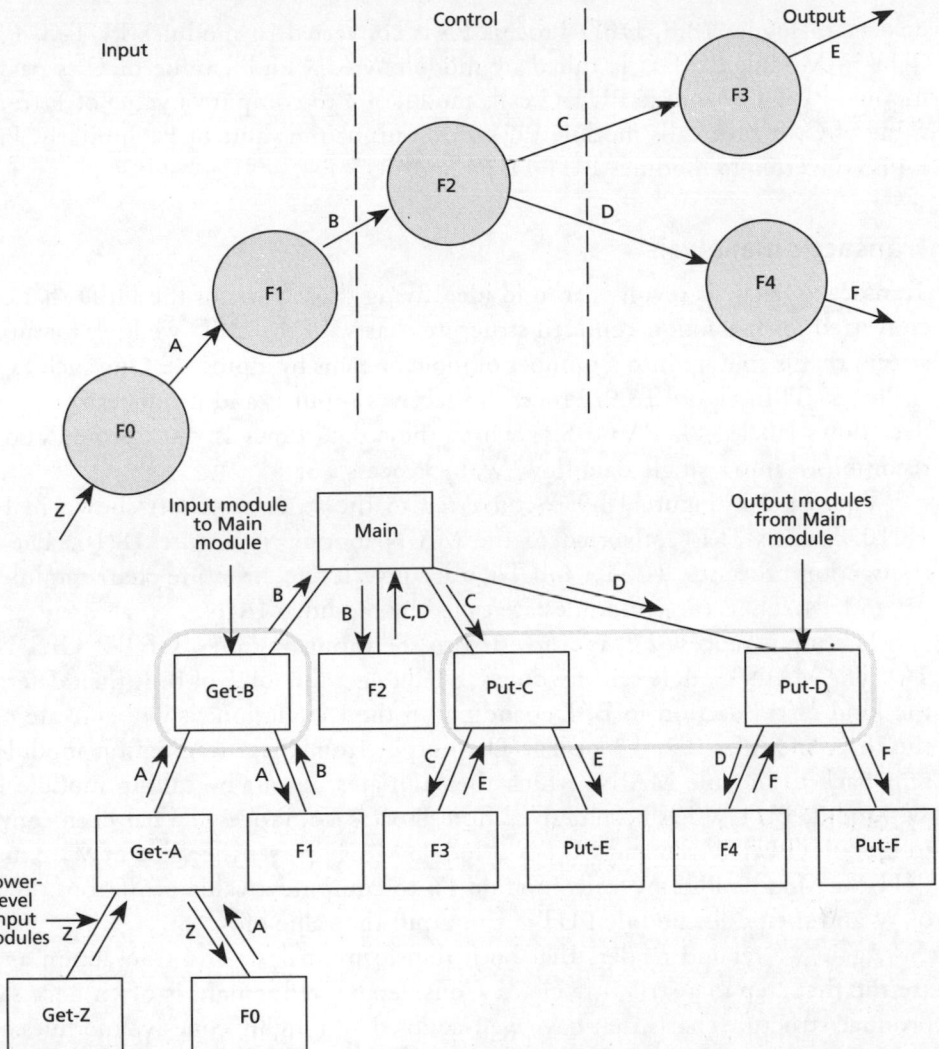

Figure 18.8 *Transform analysis*

step is to create a MAIN module and another module for the central process, then have the MAIN module call the central processing module (in this case, F2).

The next step is to convert the processes that provide input to Process F2 to structure chart modules. These modules will provide the input to module MAIN, which in turn passes it to module F2. Thus, in Figure 18.8, input modules are created for DFD processes F0 and F1. Process F0 is converted to three modules. Module GET-A calls module GET-Z to read a value and pass it in parameter Z. It then calls module F0 to compute a value of A from the value of Z and passes the value of A to module GET-B. Module GET-B and module Fl are derived from Process Fl. Module GET-B first calls module GET-A to get a value of A and then calls module Fl to compute a value of B from the value of A. B is then passed to module MAIN.

Finally, the DFD processes that take the outputs from F2 are converted to output modules that obtain outputs from the MAIN module and deliver them to an output device. In Figure 18.8, DFD Process F3 is converted to modules PUT-C, F3 and PUT-E. Module PUT-C is called by module MAIN and a value of C is passed to module PUT-C. Module PUT-C calls module F3 to compute a value of E from the value of C. It then calls module PUT-E to output the value of E. Similarly, Process F4 is converted to modules PUT-D, F4 and PUT-F.

Transaction analysis

Transaction analysis revolves around identifying those parts of the DFD that can be converted to transaction-centered structure charts. In the DFD we look for an input stream that is split up into a number of input streams by a process. One such example is Process Tl in Figure 18.9. Process Tl receives input P and produces three output data flows labeled Q, R and S. Each of these data flows is transformed and then recombined into a single data flow, W, by Process TS.

The DFD in Figure 18.9 is converted to the structure chart shown in Figure 18.10. Process Tl is converted to the MAIN module in Figure 18.10. The three transaction processes, T2, T3 and T4, are converted to structure chart modules T2, T3 and T4. These three modules are called by module MAIN.

The input process TO is converted to the input modules, GET-P, GET-N and TO. The MAIN module calls module GET-P to get the value of B. It then determines the kind of transaction in B. Depending on the transaction, it will activate one of the three modules, T2, T3 or T4. The output from these transaction modules are sent back to module MAIN, which then initiates output by calling module PUT-W. Module PUT-W has been derived from Process T6. Process T6 has been converted to modules PUT-W, T6 and PUT-X. Module MAIN passes the value of W to module PUT-W. Module PUT-W calls module T6 to compute a value of X from the value of W and then calls module PUT-X to output the value of X.

Again we remind readers that both transform analysis and transaction analysis are the first step to a structure chart. Considerable refinement is often necessary to produce structure charts that have well-coupled and highly cohesive modules.

SYSTEM MODELS FOR OBJECT DESIGNS

Most object-oriented design methodologies include a system model that is centered on object classes. Chapter 17 described how an object model can be converted to blocks or modules. These blocks then become classes in the implementation if the implementation uses an object-oriented system. If the implementation uses procedural programming, then the blocks become structure charts. The system model often includes interfaces that are derived from interaction or event-flow diagrams, as is the case with Object Oriented Software Engineering (OOSE).

 ## IMPLEMENTATION

The goal of implementation is to convert the system model, specified as a structure chart, into a set of program modules. Figure 18.10 describes the implementation steps in more detail. They start by producing a detailed module specification, which

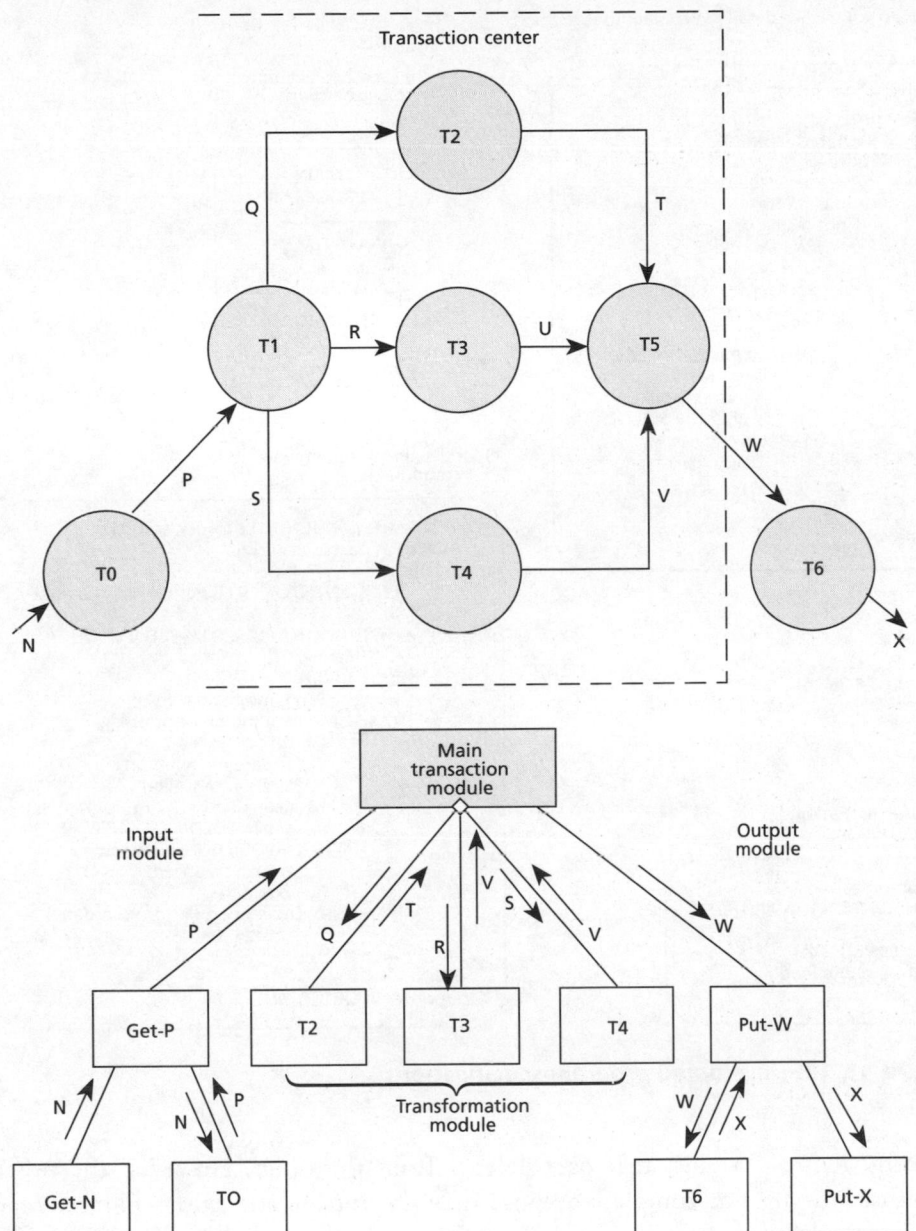

Figure 18.9 *Transaction analysis*

is then converted into program code. Figure 18.10 illustrates these steps by using Process 3.2 in Figure 18.2 as the example. The first step develops detailed process specifications for the process. As shown in Figure 18.10, detailed process specifications are written in structured English and begin to approximate program code. They include all the conditions that can arise in the process and how they are treated. Thus, for example, Step 1 in Figure 18.10 defines that three things can happen if sufficient parts are not found in store to meet an order: the order can be cancelled, the order

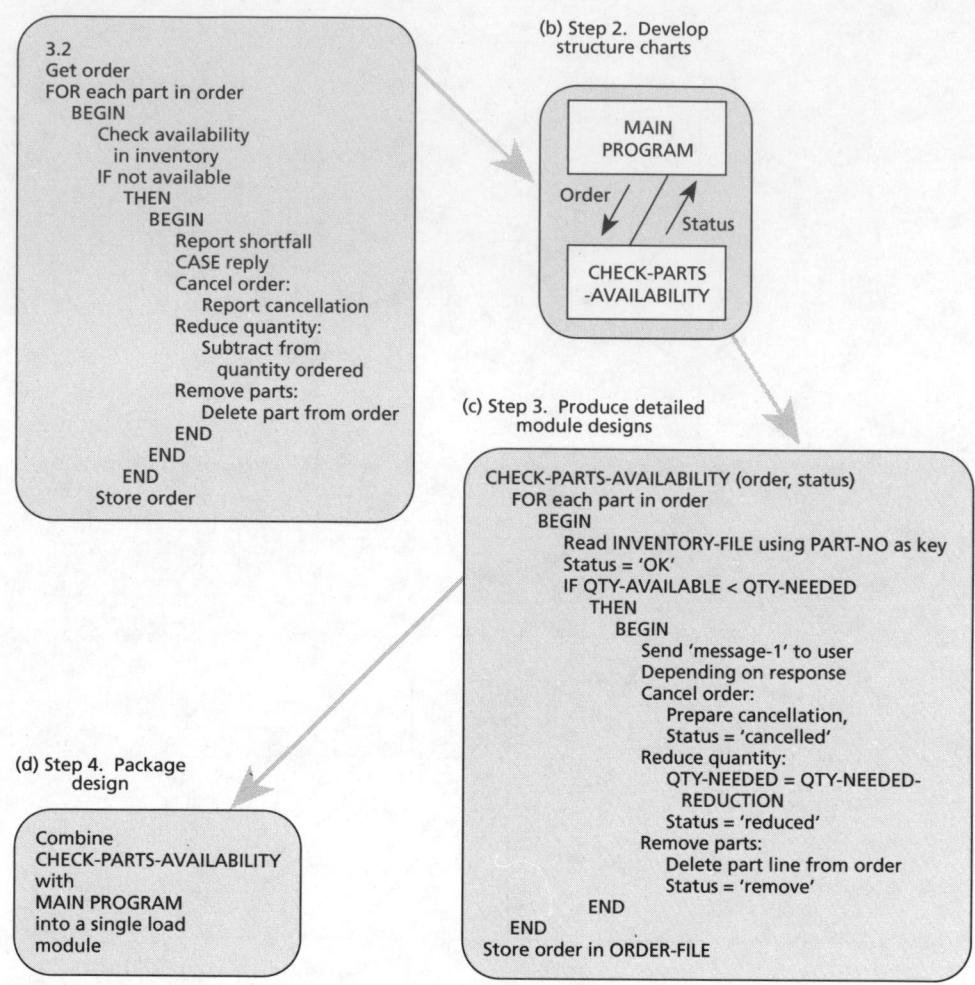

(a) Step 1. Produce detailed program specifications

```
3.2
Get order
FOR each part in order
    BEGIN
        Check availability
          in inventory
        IF not available
          THEN
            BEGIN
                Report shortfall
                CASE reply
                Cancel order:
                    Report cancellation
                Reduce quantity:
                    Subtract from
                      quantity ordered
                Remove parts:
                    Delete part from order
            END
    END
END
Store order
```

(b) Step 2. Develop structure charts

```
MAIN
PROGRAM
```
Order   Status
```
CHECK-PARTS
-AVAILABILITY
```

(c) Step 3. Produce detailed module designs

```
CHECK-PARTS-AVAILABILITY (order, status)
    FOR each part in order
        BEGIN
            Read INVENTORY-FILE using PART-NO as key
            Status = 'OK'
            IF QTY-AVAILABLE < QTY-NEEDED
              THEN
                BEGIN
                    Send 'message-1' to user
                    Depending on response
                    Cancel order:
                        Prepare cancellation,
                        Status = 'cancelled'
                    Reduce quantity:
                        QTY-NEEDED = QTY-NEEDED-
                          REDUCTION
                        Status = 'reduced'
                    Remove parts:
                        Delete part line from order
                        Status = 'remove'
                END
    END
Store order in ORDER-FILE
```

(d) Step 4. Package design

```
Combine
CHECK-PARTS-AVAILABILITY
with
MAIN PROGRAM
into a single load
module
```

Figure 18.10 *Developing program specifications*

quantity reduced or just that part deleted from the order. However, the process specifications are not complete because they do not include things like references to records, detailed error checks, 1/0 operations and user dialogs. These are added to the specification later.

PACKAGING INTO LOAD MODULES

Computer systems work by bringing a module into the memory when that module is called and then executing that module. Some system time is used up every time a module is loaded into the memory.

Ideally, all the program modules should be brought into the memory when the program starts. Thus all the modules would be in store at all times and would not need to be brought into the memory when they are called. However, this ideal cannot be realized for large programs because of memory size limitations. The whole program simply will not fit into the memory.

The next alternative is to make each structure chart module into a 'load' module. This approach may have to be used if all the modules are relatively large and the amount of memory is small. However, in most practical systems it is possible to fit more than one module into the memory at the same time. System performance can be improved by bringing all closely related modules into the memory at the same time. When these modules call each other, no additional computer time is used because all the modules are already in the memory. The question then becomes how to group modules so that the time spent moving 'load' modules in and out of storage is minimized.

There is no magic formula or rule that can be used to group structure chart modules into 'load' modules. Such grouping is usually made in a trial-and-error fashion and depends on factors such as memory size, module size and module-calling frequency. Obviously we want to put as many modules as we can into one 'load' module, while ensuring that such modules are related and call each other.

Some guidelines for constructing 'load' modules are given in Figure 18.11. The method shown in Figure 18.11(a) groups all modules on an input stream into a 'load' module. Once module B is called, modules C and D are also brought into memory. Subsequent calls to C and D do not require more 'load' modules to be brought into memory.

Another frequently used method is shown in Figure 18.11(b). Here all the lower-order modules are placed into one 'load' module. This method, however, is only useful if that low-level 'load' module contains a number of shared modules and can be continually resident in storage. It is frequently used where common data access modules are used at a number of points on a structure chart.

When more elaborate analysis is called for, we need to look at iteration and the decisions required to make 'load' module choices. Take Figure 18.11(c) as an example. Here we have found that the most common decision outcome is to select B rather than D. Furthermore, B calls C a number of times but calls E only once. It therefore makes sense to group A, B and C into one 'load' module. If this is done, the outcome of the decision will, in most cases, not require a new 'load' module to be brought in, nor require continual loading of a module during each loop. Of course, E and D should also be included in the loaded module if there is sufficient space. However, in the example, we have assumed that such space is not available.

PROGRAM DEVELOPMENT

Each kind of program is different and needs to be specified differently. Usually all that is needed to specify enquiries or reports is the statement of the enquiry or the report layout. Specially written programs usually require more detailed specifications, which define the steps followed by the program as well as any changes made to the database.

Specially written programs, in addition to satisfying user requirements, must be easy to read and understand, as well as to maintain. A good structure usually means that well-defined functions appear in the same section of program code, and changes

(a) Grouping by logical flow

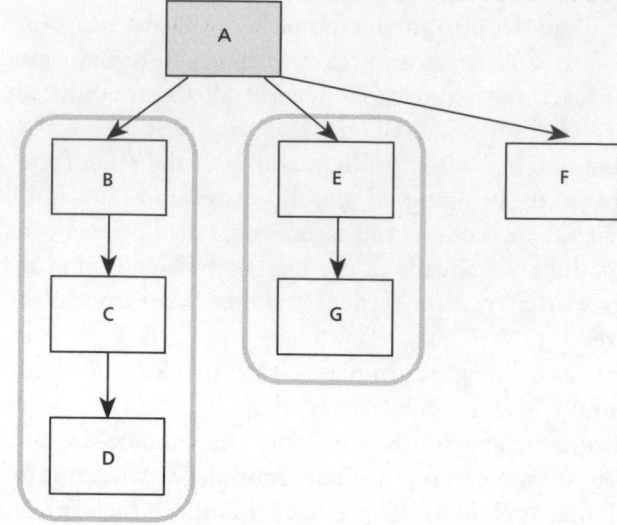

(b) Grouping by level

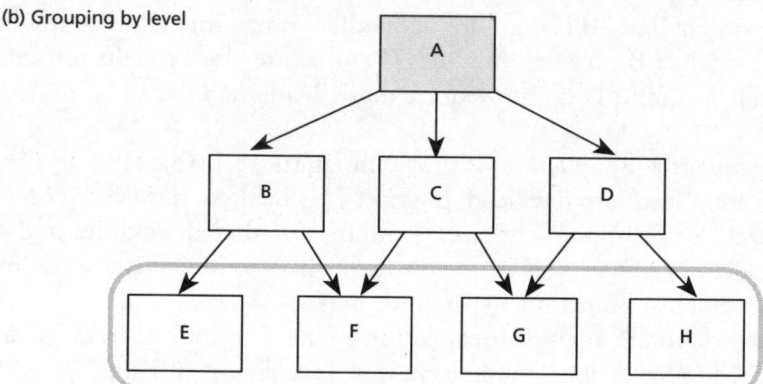

(c) Using decision and iteration structures

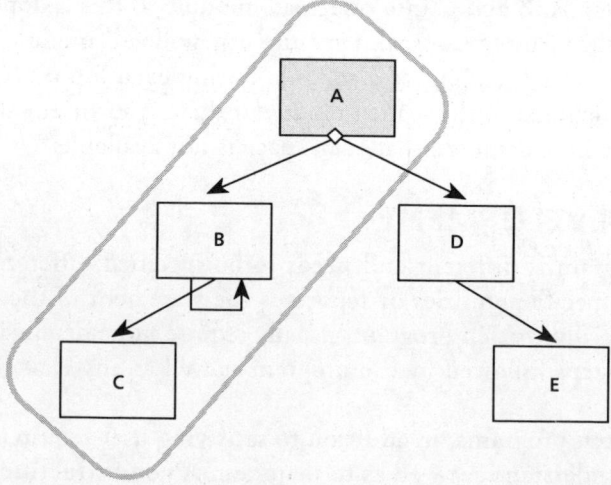

Figure 18.11 *Creating level modules*

to these functions only affect that section of code and not the entire program structure. Good structure makes it easier for people other than those who originally produced the code to later amend the program to accommodate the changes in user requirements that always occur after a system is built. Programs should also be written to use computer resources in the most effective manner.

Structured programming

Once 'load' modules are designed, programming and coding begins. We need to correctly transfer the process definitions into computer code while maintaining the criteria required of good code. It is now generally recognized that production of good code is realized by what is known as structured programming. Structured programming uses standard control structures to improve program clarity and maintenance. The control structures encourage top-down program development by orderly expansion of program blocks. Designers specify each top-level function by one program block and the block is then expanded into more detailed components.

To facilitate this top-down development, program blocks are made up of three main constructs—namely, SEQUENCE, IF-THEN-ELSE and REPEAT. Each block in the code should implement some well-defined function.

Good programming practice also calls for in-line comments to improve readability. Each block in the control structure should be defined and its purpose described. Links to outside descriptions of code should also be included in the documentation.

It is relatively easy to use process specifications to create well-structured code. Process specifications use key words very similar to the constructs used in structured programming. Thus, conversion from process specification to structured code can be very straightforward. The key words of the process specification are replaced by the key words used in the programming language. The arithmetic or transformation statements used in the process specifications are replaced by the grammar used in the programming language.

Object programming

Object implementation directly programs the class modules. The programming method will depend on the programming language and the ways it provides for defining object classes. Typical languages here include C^{++} and Eiffel (Meyer, 1988).

REPORTS AND ENQUIRIES

So far this chapter has described how to design programs that will be written using high-level languages. There are also other ways to develop programs. Enquiries, for example, can now be made using special enquiry languages, and output reports generated using report generators.

Enquiry languages

The idea behind enquiry languages is that a user should not have to write a special program to get data from a database but simply state what conditions the retrieved data must satisfy. Structured Query Language (SQL) is an example of a widely used enquiry language and is available with most relational systems. It specifies the rows to be retrieved from relations and what conditions these rows must satisfy. As an example, consider the following two relations.

PROJECTS (PROJ-NO, DEPT-NO, BUDGET)
JOBS (JOB-NO, PROJ-NO, START-DATE)

Here relation PROJECTS describes the projects in the organization and departments to which they are allocated. Relation JOBS describes the jobs and projects to which they are allocated. To find out the projects in a department, all that one needs to do is enter the statement:

SELECT PROJ-NO
FROM PROJECTS
WHERE DEPT-NO = 'Dep1';

A list of projects in 'Dep1' is then displayed on the screen. The SELECT-FROM-WHERE is the standard SQL clause used for data retrieval. It defines the data needed and conditions to be satisfied using the following syntax:

SELECT <data to be displayed>
FROM <relations that contain the data>
WHERE <conditions satisfied by the retrieved data>.

The user is free to select the data, relations and conditions at the time the query is input, and no special preprogramming is necessary. SQL supports a large variety of queries. Data displayed can include arithmetic statements, and conditions can include a large number of clauses separated by AND and OR and evaluated using Boolean logic. One SQL statement can be used to retrieve data from more than one relation. For example, to find all the jobs in a department we must first find all the department's projects from relation PROJECTS, and then find all the jobs for each project from relation JOBS. The jobs can be retrieved by the following SQL statement:

SELECT JOB-NO
FROM PROJECTS, JOBS
WHERE DEPT-NO = 'Dep1'
AND PROJECTS.PROJ-NO = JOBS.PROJ-NO;

Here the first part in the WHERE clause selects those rows in relation PROJECTS with the given value of DEPT-NO, 'Dep1'. The second part of the WHERE clause then matches the selected row in PROJECTS with rows in relation JOBS with the same value of PROJ-NO. The value of JOB-NO in the matched row is then output. Functions can also appear in SQL statements. For example, the statement:

```
SELECT SUM(BUDGET)
FROM PROJECTS
WHERE DEPT-NO = 'Dep1';
```

will output the sum of the value of BUDGET for all rows with a given value of 'Dep1'. That is, the output is the total project budget of a department. There are many additional facilities available with SQL, and its flexibility has now made it the standard language for relational systems.

Report generators

The idea behind reports is somewhat similar to that for enquiries. It is to get away from writing programs to generate reports but simply define the report contents and their layout using a report definition language. Usually the contents of a report are defined using a statement from a query language. The report layout is defined using special commands which may include specifications of report heading and footing, column names, any totalling or subtotalling, and the size of each column.

World Wide Web interfaces

Increasingly there will be many interfaces developed between an organization's information systems and external clients through the World Wide Web. Such Web sites will include interface components, which were discussed in Chapter 15, as well as programs that reside on servers, sometimes known as CGI (Common Gate Interface) programs. These CGI programs can be modules in a structure diagram, but the trend there is to use object-oriented languages such as Java.

SUMMARY

This chapter described one important component of detailed design: program design. The chapter defined three ways for writing programs—namely, enquiries, report generation, and specially written programs. It then concentrated on specially written programs, defining a good program structure and showing how the structure could be obtained by direct conversion from a data flow diagram. The conversion goes through a number of steps. The DFD is divided into subsets and each subset eventually becomes a structure chart. The chapter described how to go about developing structure charts and described the difference between good and bad structure charts. Good structure charts exhibit good coupling and cohesion.

The modules of the structure chart are then grouped into 'load' modules. Finally, the modules in the structure chart are coded. Good program design requires programmers to follow the ideas of structured programming. The chapter concluded by suggesting that conversions from process specifications to well-structured code can be very straightforward.

◇ EXERCISES

18.1 What is the cohesion of modules shown in Figure 18.12? In Figure 18.12 there is a brief process description of each module next to the module. Note that in Figure 18.12(a) it is necessary to sort by area before computing delivery amount for each area. Furthermore, truck requirements can only be estimated after amounts are computed for each area. In Figure 18.12(b), the sort operations are independent of each other. In Figure 18.12(c), the same algorithm is used to achieve functional cohesion.

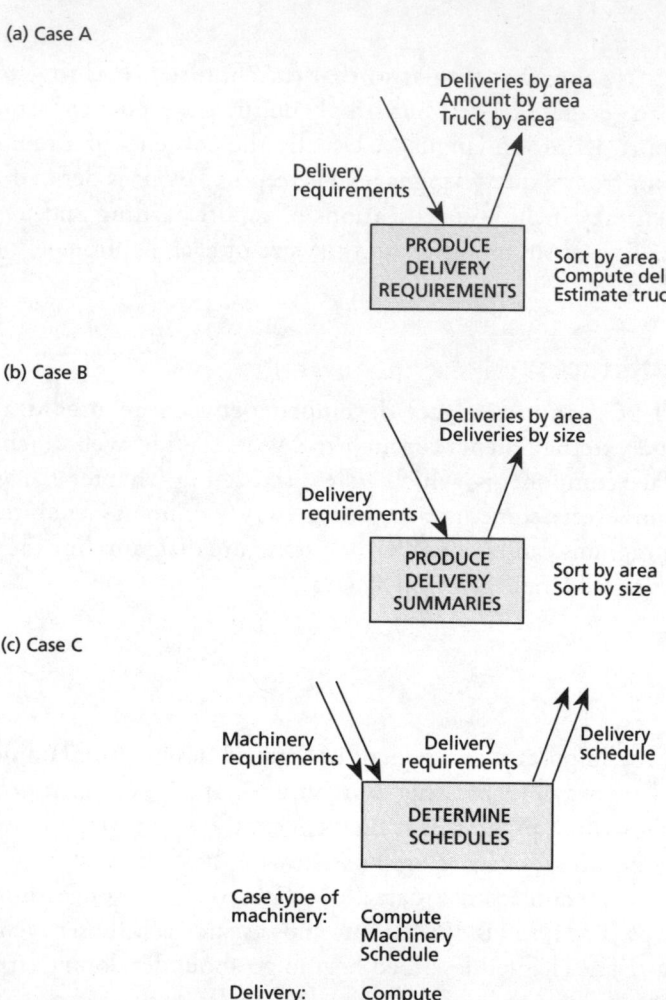

(a) Case A

Deliveries by area
Amount by area
Truck by area

Delivery requirements

PRODUCE DELIVERY REQUIREMENTS

Sort by area
Compute delivery amount by area
Estimate truck requirements for area

(b) Case B

Deliveries by area
Deliveries by size

Delivery requirements

PRODUCE DELIVERY SUMMARIES

Sort by area
Sort by size

(c) Case C

Machinery requirements   Delivery requirements   Delivery schedule

DETERMINE SCHEDULES

Case type of machinery: Compute Machinery Schedule

Delivery: Compute Delivery Schedule

END;

Figure 18.12 *Module cohesion*

18.2 Identify any coupling problems in the structure chart shown in Figure 18.13. If you identify any problems, then suggest a new structure chart where all coupling between modules is data coupling.

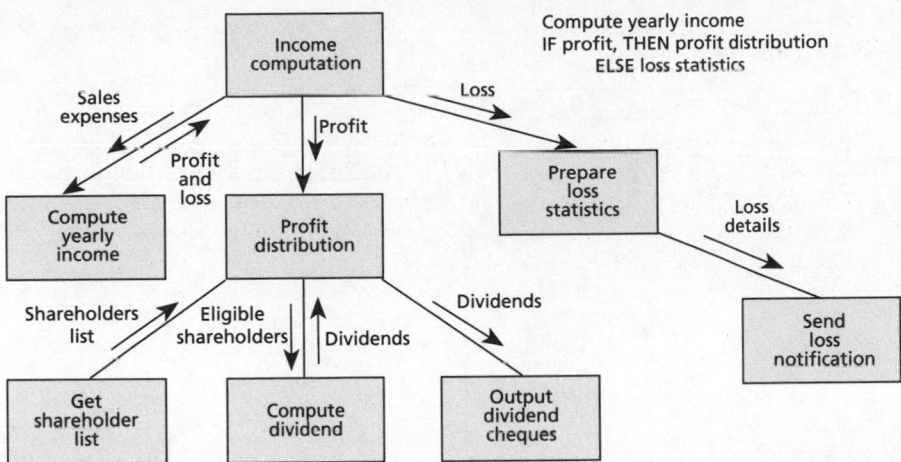

Figure 18.13 *Coupling*

18.3   Use transform analysis to convert the data flow diagram in Figure 18.14 to a structure chart.

18.4   Use a combination of transform and transaction analysis to convert the data flow diagram in Figure 18.15 to a structure chart.

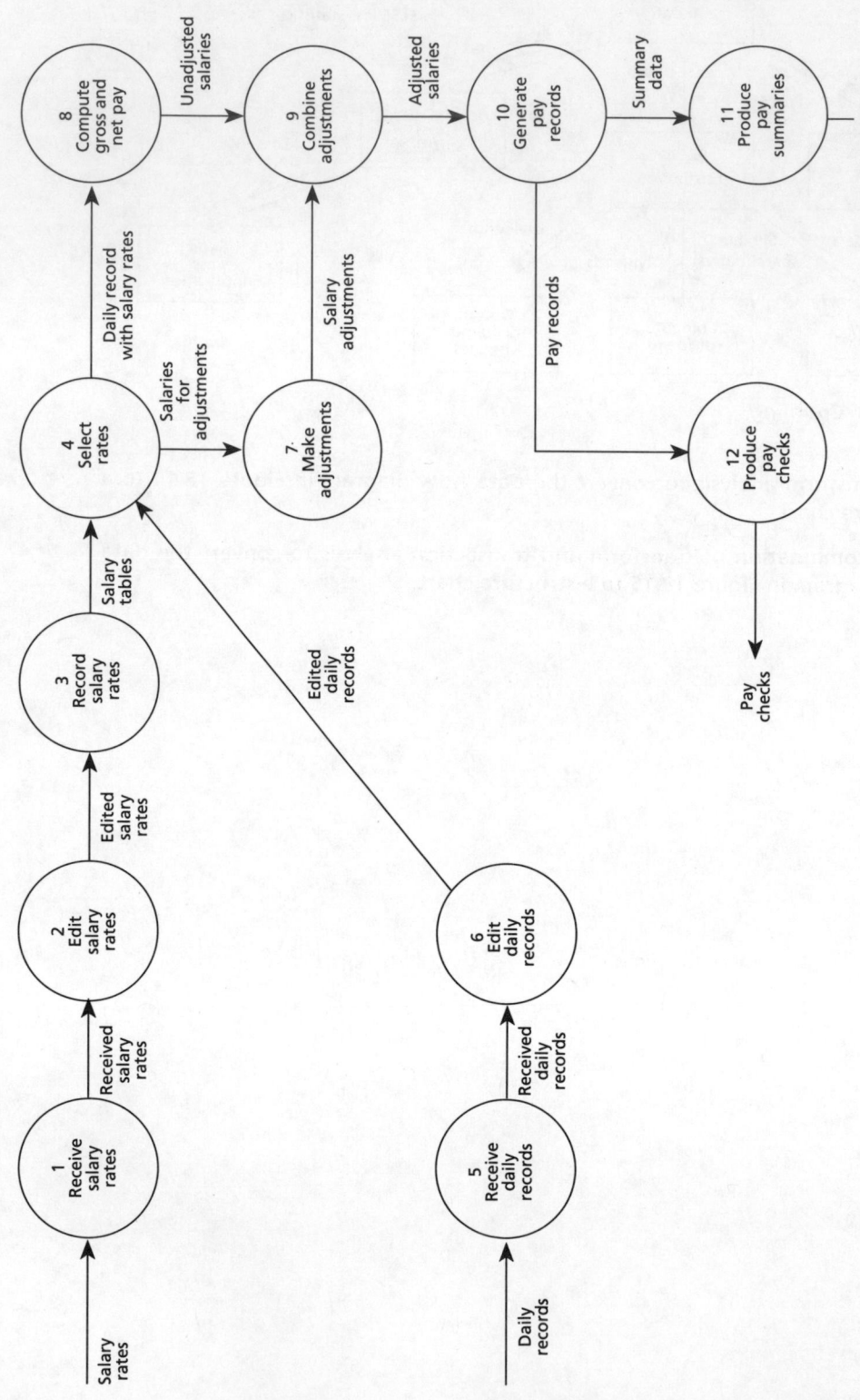

Figure 18.14 *Data flow diagram 1*

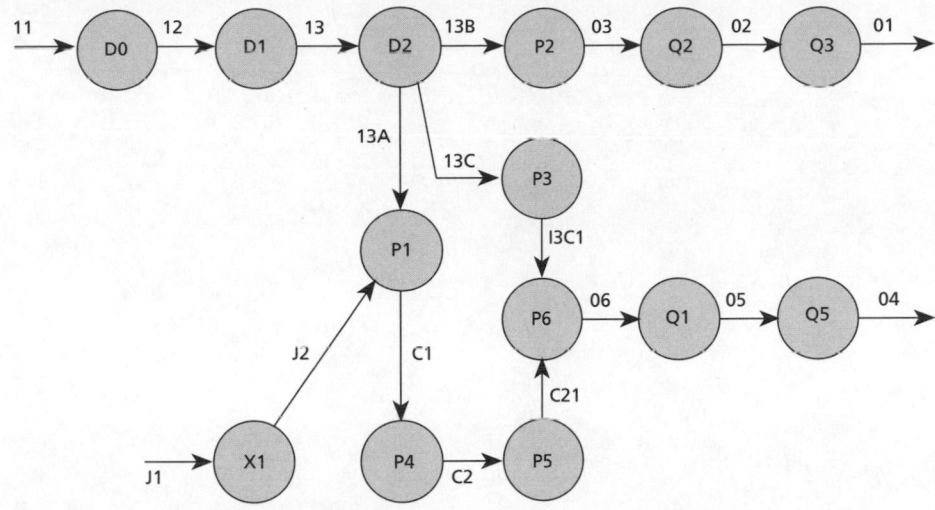

Figure 18.15 *Data flow diagram 2*

BIBLIOGRAPHY

Date, C.J. (1987), *A Guide to the SQL Standards*, Addison-Wesley, Reading, Massachusetts.

Dwight, J. and Erwin, M. (1996), *Using CGI*, QUE, Indianapolis.

Jackson, M.A. (1975), *Principles of Program Design*, Academic Press, New York.

Juliff, P. (1990), *Program Design* (2nd edn), Prentice Hall, Sydney.

Lans, van der, R.F. (1988), *Introduction to SQL*, Addison-Wesley, Reading.

Meyer, B. (1988), *Object-oriented Software Construction*, Prentice-Hall, New York.

Nassi, I. and Schneiderman, B. (August 1973), 'Flowchart techniques for structured programming', *SIGPLAN Notices*, pp. 12–26.

Page-Jones, M. (1988), *The Practical Guide to Structured Systems Design* (2nd edn), Prentice-Hall, International, Englewood Cliffs, New Jersey.

Warnier, J.D. (1974), *Logical Construction of Programs*, Van Nostrand, Reinhold Company, New York.

Wasserman, A.1. (ed.) (1981), Tutorial: 'Software development environments', *IEEE Computer Society*, Los Alamitos, California.

—(March 1982), 'The future of programming', *Communications of the ACM*, Vol. 25, No. 3, pp. 196–206.

Yourdon, E. and Constantine, L.L. (1979), *Structured Design*, Prentice-Hall, Englewood Cliffs, New Jersey.

Productivity tools

CONTENTS

KEY LEARNING OBJECTIVES

Why productivity tools are needed in system development
The different kinds of productivity tools
How CASE tools are used in system development
Vertical and horizontal integration of CASE tools
The necessary characteristics of a good CASE tool
Packages

◇ INTRODUCTION

This chapter describes how computer tools can be used to assist in the development of computer-based information systems. A variety of tools, commonly known as CASE (Computer Assisted Software Engineering) tools, are available for this purpose and make up the support systems for the development process. Earlier, Chapter 13 described the support provided by configuration management systems to keep track of documents. Other tools are used to assist team members to build models, and to convert models developed in one phase to those needed in another phase. This chapter concentrates on the tools used to assist system development. It should, however, be noted that there is a large number of support tools and they are continually evolving. This chapter concentrates on the evolution of such tools, rather than describing them in detail. Such detailed descriptions can be found in the relevant manuals.

Support tools must support the techniques used in the development process. Earlier chapters described a number of system development processes and the different models and methods used in these processes. For instance, entity–relationship methods may be used to describe data, and data flow analysis used to describe data flows in analysis models. Alternatively, object-oriented methods may be used to build models. Another set of methods may then be used to build system design models. By now you will have noticed that there is considerable work associated in building and keeping track of models with any development process. First, for any system other than the trivial, there are many diagrams and models. Furthermore, the iterative nature of design means that these diagrams and models are continually changing. As a result, designers must continually redraw their models, validate them against each other and eventually convert them to an implementation. A large volume of information must be documented during this process, and designers must keep track of this documentation.

CASE tools have been developed to help people build and keep track of models. There are a large number of CASE tools and each is applicable to some part of the development process. For example, 47 different case tools for database design are reported in the Time 15 issue of DBMS. This includes tools for E–R analysis, for data flow diagramming, a tool for object-oriented models, and so on. Designers must select the right tools for their work and use them during system development. Furthermore, designers are often required to use a different tool in different development phases and to use outputs produced by one tool as inputs to another.

Ideally, as more routine work is passed to tools, more time can be spent on the creative aspects of design. However, this only holds true if CASE tools are easy to use. If they are not, then using them may become a problem in itself and detract effort from the real design problem. CASE tools are only one of a set of possible productivity tools. There are also trends to develop other and more powerful tools. The trend is toward tools where we can specify a system in user terms and use this specification to generate a working system. This means that we do not have to go through any conversions leading to reduced development times.

 # CASE TOOLS

CASE tools first became prominent in the mid-1980s by supporting modeling techniques used in structured systems analysis and design and relieving designers of much of the manual work. There are now CASE tools that support E–R diagrams, others are used for data flow diagrams, and still others support techniques such as structure charts or logical database design. A new range of CASE tools is being developed to support object-oriented modeling. Using a range of CASE tools can become unsatisfactory if designers must manually convert outputs from one tool in order to use them as inputs to another, or manually validate the models by cross-checking them against each other. The trend thus is to develop a suite of CASE tools that are integrated and can support the entire development process. One way to distinguish CASE tools is by the degree of integration and assistance they offer.

INTEGRATION

Tools can be **integrated** both horizontally and vertically. **Horizontal integration** is where we connect tools at the same stage of the development process—for example, a connection between an E–R modeling tool and a DFD modeling tool during analysis. This allows the designer to cross-check the data in the two tools to validate both models. It also allows the designer to use information in one model as an input to the other. **Vertical integration** applies to different stages of the development process, and the output from one tool can become the input to the next tool. Thus, for example, we may use a tool to convert an E–R diagram to a relational model. A sequence of such tools can automate the whole design process.

Most support systems provide integrated sets of tools that cover either major parts or the entire development process. An example of integrated tools that cover a part of the development process is shown as the shaded part in Figure 19.1. Here there are three tools that cover the analysis part of the cycle, as well as conversion of the E–R diagram to a database design. These tools cover only some of the development tasks—the shaded tasks in Figure 19.1. They do not, for example, cover project planning or the implementation phases. Some of these may be integrated and others may be stand-alone tools. The goal is to provide a set of integrated tools that cover the entire development process.

INTELLIGENT DESIGN SUPPORT

Another CASE tool characteristic is the level of intelligent design support they provide. Most CASE tools simply act as repositories of models and design decisions. They do not assist in the creative part of model development nor in the decisions that lead to the model. They simply record the modeling decisions made by analysts or designers. Designers should not make the mistake of thinking that once a model is accepted by a CASE tool then the model is correct. It simply means that the model satisfies the syntactic rules of the CASE tool but may not be the correct representation of the system. A number of CASE tools attempt to provide some assistance, ranging from simple prompts, through syntax checking, to explanations of possible errors and suggestions for their correctness.

CASE tools
Computer Assisted Software Engineering tools used to keep track of system models.

CASE tool integration
The ability of one CASE tool to accept the input from another.

CASE tool horizontal integration
CASE tools from adjacent life-cycle stages integrated.

CASE tool vertical integration
CASE tools integrated at the same life-cycle stage.

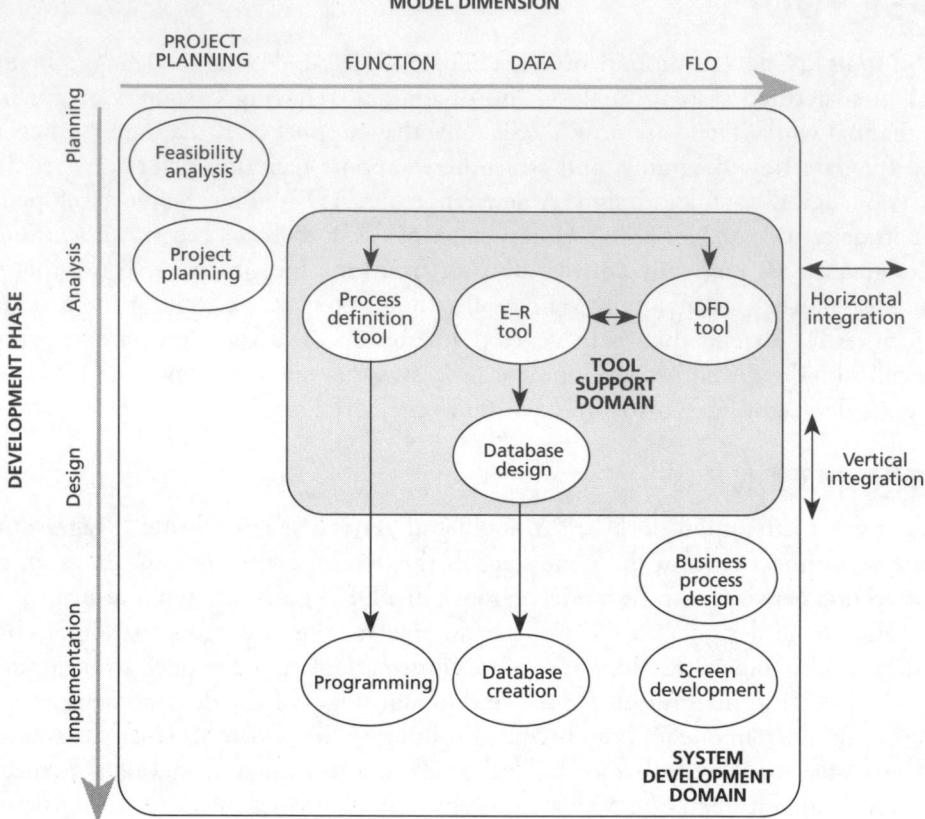

Figure 19.1 *Support domain*

Figure 19.2 illustrates the general structure of displays. Usually in an integrated system there will be one window for each model dimension. Figure 19.2 has one window for E–R diagrams and another for processes. There could also be another one for data flows. The display of all windows simultaneously has the advantage of allowing the designer to correlate and verify the models. Most CASE tools also allow designers to select one component of the diagram and explode or zoom in on it. In this way, for example, a process in a DFD can be selected and expanded to show its leveled components. Or an entity set may be exploded to show its attributes. There is usually also a HELP window to assist designers to use the CASE tool.

USER-FRIENDLINESS

An important characteristic of CASE tools is the interface they present to the designer. The trend now is to window support, where different model dimensions are represented by different windows on a screen. Designers can select items in more than one window to either validate the models or link the items in modeling. However, screen limitations often place constraints on what can be displayed in each window, and tool designers must use ingenuity to ensure that displays can assist designers.

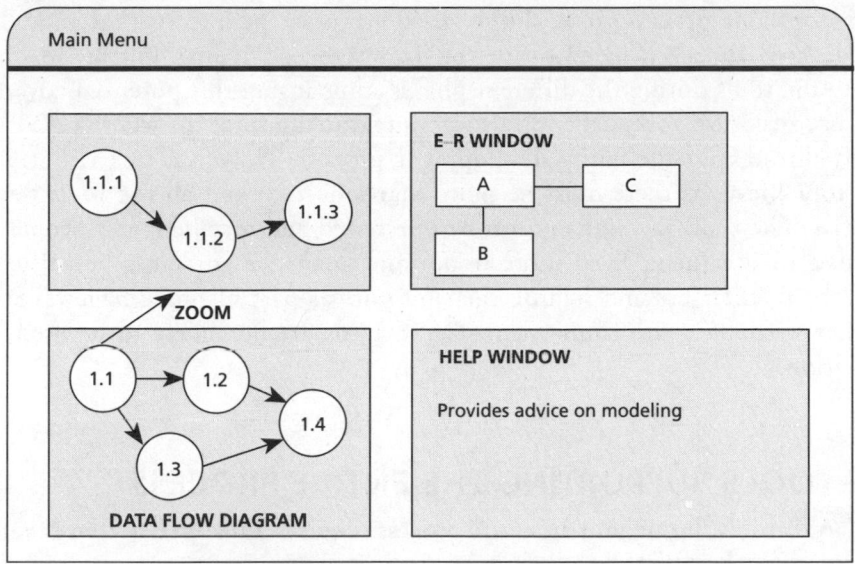

Figure 19.2 *Multi-window displays*

TOOL INTEGRATION

Ideally, a designer should be able to select a tool needed for each design activity and then vertically integrate the tools. This is easier said than done, because each tool is usually developed by a different organization and the outputs from one tool are not usually easily acceptable by others. It requires a set of standards to be widely adopted by tool developers. It may be some time, if indeed it ever happens, before such standards are developed and widely accepted. The usual practice is to use tools that are all developed by the same developer, as individual developers usually take care to ensure that their tools can be vertically integrated.

USING TOOLS IN SYSTEM DEVELOPMENT

CASE tools have been used from the early 1980s in a variety of ways. Historically they were introduced to support the modeling techniques used in structured systems analysis, with some object-oriented tools now appearing. Perhaps the two most common ways of using them are:

* as independent tools used as in some phases of the development process; or
* as a collection of integrated tools supporting the complete development process usually following a prescribed set of steps.

Structured design methodologies are likely to be found with highly structured cycles, whereas adaptive teams or prototyping are more likely to use tools as they suit their purpose. Using a tool in one development phase is usually the personal preference of the person responsible for the task and is often not integrated into the development process. It is simply used to assist people in that task. In an uncoordinated approach based on personal preferences, it may not be possible to integrate the tools during the different phases, thus losing this potential advantage. Proper use of CASE tools calls for a more integrated approach, where CASE tools are used throughput the entire development process. However, this is not always simple to achieve, as there must be more than one tool and all the tools must be integrated. The tools themselves must be purchased and installed, and people must be trained to use them. Even more important, management must be sufficiently committed to their use and require their outputs as part of phase reviews. Studies show that without such commitment, CASE tools are not likely to be used in an organization.

CASE TOOLS SUPPORTING THE ENTIRE PROCESS

Using CASE tools throughout an entire process requires a match between the design methodology and the CASE tools. It requires an organization to use standard design methods throughout its projects. A combination of such methods is often called a **design methodology**. Using standard methods offers a number of advantages. First, designers do not have to spend time selecting design techniques and developing new documentation methods for every project. Second, a standard supporting documentation method is available, thus encouraging the use of the methodology. Finally, system designers and users need only be trained in one method. Thus training costs are reduced and, over time, most users can become familiar with the modeling techniques used by designers. Users are then able to contribute more toward project development.

Design methodology
A collection of modeling methods and conversion techniques that start with a model of the user system and produce a computer system.

An organization can develop a standard methodology in two ways: it can construct its own methodology, or it can purchase an off-the-shelf design methodology. Of course, it is also possible to purchase and modify an off-the-shelf methodology.

First, let us look at what must be done to develop a methodology. The major steps are:

1. Identify the tasks to be carried out at each development process phase.
2. Define the models to be used at each phase.
3. Find CASE tools that can support these models.
4. Define the configuration management system to store the models.

Such a choice must ensure that:

- the chosen models are consistent in the sense that the output of a model at one phase becomes the input to the model at the following phase; and
- the models contain the three main system components: data, processes and flows.

Usually models follow either structured systems analysis method or object orientation. Earlier chapters described the kinds of techniques available for methodologies and how they can be integrated into system development cycles.

DEVELOPING OR ADOPTING A METHODOLOGY

As you see, a lot of effort is needed to create a design methodology. We have to spend time choosing techniques, developing a documentation method and perhaps providing computer support for it. For this reason, most organizations prefer to purchase a design methodology. There are now a large number of practical methodologies available which can save an organization the time and effort needed to develop its own methodology. Often, organizations choose an available methodology and modify it to suit their own special requirements.

A large variety of methodologies is available and a number of texts, manuals and articles have been written to compare them. We will not describe all such methodologies or compare them in detail, but will outline some ideas behind the more common methodologies to give you an idea of what a methodology looks like. You should, however, remember that the descriptions given here are very broad. They are included to give you an insight into what practical methodologies look like, but are in no way a substitute for the detailed instructions necessary to use the systems.

SOME EXAMPLES OF CASE TOOLS

CASE tools are continuously evolving in the marketplace. This book only gives a brief overview of the trend in CASE tools emphasizing the trend to open systems. Readers are advised to read manuals of particular tools for the most up-to-date information. Historically, CASE tools began by supporting structured systems analysis. Tools were used either to:

- support a prescribed set of steps with specific tools prescribed for each phase; or
- allow more flexibility in the selection of tools in each development phase. Systems that provide such flexibility are known as open systems.

The first approach is useful in the development of large projects, whereas the second is more commonly used in prototyping or a system where an adaptive team experiments and builds a system.

In the last few years there has been a trend towards more open systems that allow designers to choose from alternate tools and integrate them into a development process. The flexible or open approach is attractive, but it assumes that both vertical and horizontal tool integration is easy to achieve. Such integration, however, is often not easy to achieve, due to lack of standards, and it is often difficult to take a model produced by one tool and use it as an input to another. However, there are now vendors who will produce a set of tools that can be integrated in an open way, and support the entire development process. Integration is usually achieved by using a repository to hold modeling data while interfacing an ever increasing number of tools to the repository.

The ultimate goal of such development is to produce tools that can be used to develop a model in the repository and actually generate applications from the model for a variety of platforms. Apart from providing such tools, the vendor can often suggest a structured

methodology for using them, although users are free to choose their own development process. The rest of this chapter gives a brief outline of some of the tools and their general architecture. Details of these can be found in relevant manuals and there is now much more additional information about them on the World Wide Web.

SSADM—STRUCTURED SYSTEMS ANALYSIS AND DESIGN METHOD

SSADM (Structured Systems Analysis and Design Method) has become a standard methodology in the British Civil Service, and its detailed description can be found in a reference manual published by the Stationery Office (St. Crispins, Duke Street, Norwich NR3 1PD, UK). The methodology has evolved over a number of years, and is into its fourth version (Hares, 1994) at the time of writing. It began as a relatively prescriptive methodology that combined the structured systems analysis techniques described in the previous chapters of this book and integrated them into a system development life cycle. The fourth version has opened up the methodology, by concentrating on the development process and support, while allowing users to choose from a variety of analysis and design methods including object-oriented methods.

SSADM proposes a development process made up of five modules that include tasks, which can be combined into step-by-step procedures. Figure 19.3 illustrates the five modules that make up SSADM. The SSADM development process follows the basic flow of the linear cycle described in Chapter 7. Thus SSADM goes through

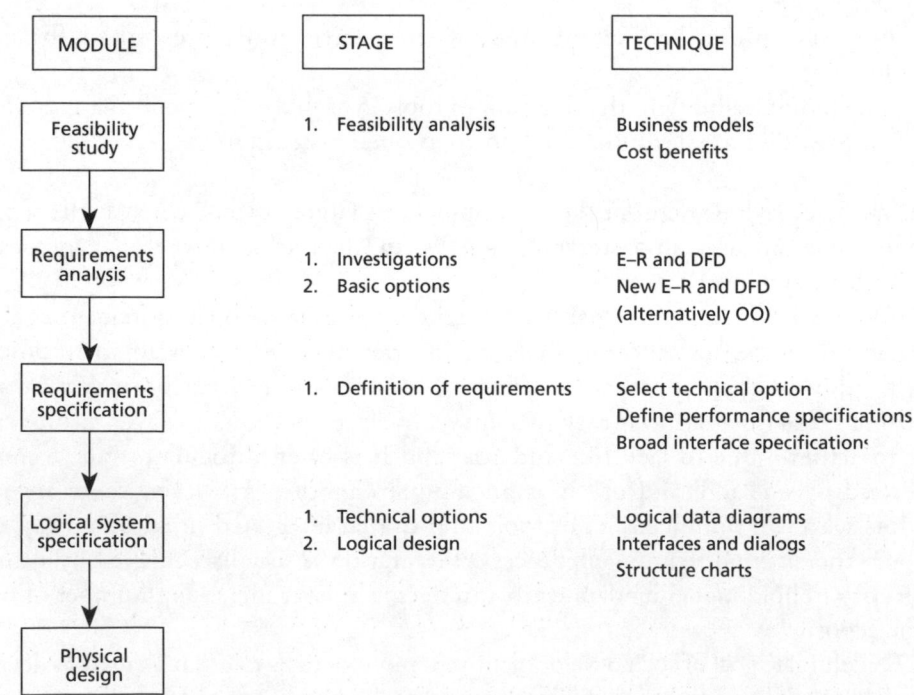

Figure 19.3 *SSADM development process*

concept formation and feasibility analysis, then develops an analysis model followed by a system specification, then a logical design and finally physical implementation. These activities are divided into modules that roughly correspond to the development phases described in Chapter 7.

Figure 19.3 also illustrates the techniques that can be used at each module. Keep in mind, however, that the methodology has now become more open (compared to earlier versions) and users are free to select alternate techniques at different modules. Thus for example, in module requirements analysis it is possible to use either structured systems analysis or object orientation

Concept formation takes place in module 1, that provides a problem definition statement emphasizing business rather than computing needs. The next two modules correspond to the system requirements phase in Chapter 7, although they include aspects of feasibility analysis and place more emphasis on defining the options. Thus, the requirements analysis module of SSADM is made up of two stages, First there is a detailed investigation that corresponds to data gathering, that can include development of an analysis model, followed by outlining a number of solution options. The analysis model can use the methods described in Chapters 8 to 12, whereas the options can be developed using the ideas described in Chapter 14 and described by high level models. These options are then used in the next module, requirements specification, to select one of the options and develop it into the system specification.

The module logical system specification corresponds to system design in Chapter 7. It results in detailed models of data, process and flow and can include any of the methods described in Chapters 15 to 18.

SSADM also specifies the documentation support for the development process. Case tool support was earlier provided by a tool specially developed for SSADM and based on an earlier method known as LSDM. However, the more open approach of Version 4 allows users to choose their own tools at each phase. This choice must obviously match tools at one phase to those at the next phase.

ORACLE PRODUCTS

ORACLE, a well-known vendor of database products supports them with a suite of tools. The major tools are Designer/2000 and Developer/2000. The architecture of their system centers around a repository that stores models and is broadly shown in Figure 19.4. Many more details can be found from the ORACLE Web site (http://www.oracle.com).

The tools provided by ORACLE are broadly divided into two major suites, one known as Designer/2000 that contains modeling tools, and another known as Developer/2000 that contains a set of development tools. For more detail, you should refer to the ORACLE Web site. In summary, Designer/2000 begins with tools for business process reengineering for redesigning business processes. For analysis, it supports entity relationship modeling, dataflows, functional hierarchy and matrix modeling techniques. Developer/2000 supports the generation of design models from the analysis model, that includes data structure diagrams and relational tables. It also supports the generation of module structures.

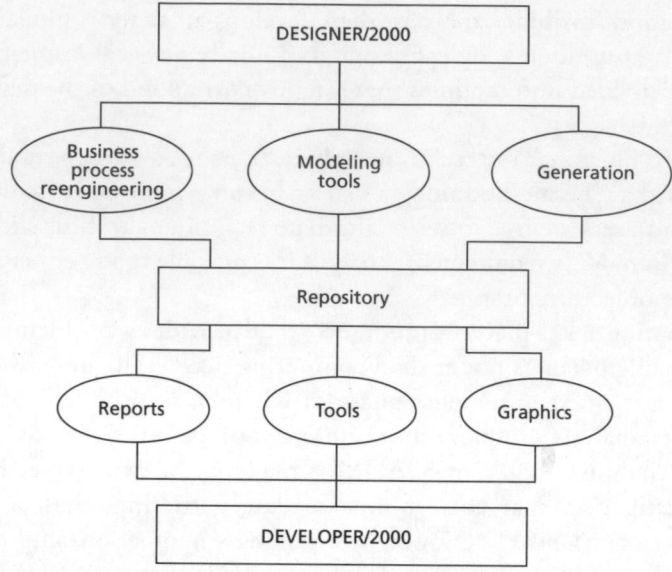

Figure 19.4 *ORACLE CASE tools*

 # RATIONAL ROSE SUITE OF TOOLS

Rational, the organization that is supporting the development of the Unified Modeling Language (UML) also has a family of tools that support analysis and design based on the object-oriented methodology. Details of these tools can be found in manuals that can be located on the Rational World Wide Wed site (http://www.rational.com). Broadly, the architecture of this family of tools is illustrated in Figure 19.5 and again centers on a repository that maintains the data models.

A set of tools are provided for model construction and another set for application generation. The analysis and design tools support the OO notation including both the Booch and OMT methods described in Chapter 12. Modeling support is also provided for the techniques used in UML and include (among others):

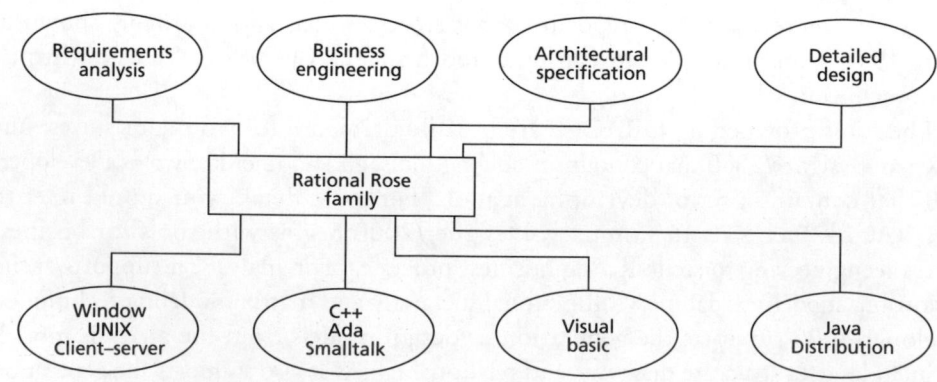

Figure 19.5 *The Rational Rose family of tools*

- using case modeling to create use case models;
- scenario modeling; and
- state modeling.

There are also a set of tools to generate applications on a variety of platforms, including C++, Ada, Smalltalk, Visual basic as well as Java for Web-based applications.

EXCELERATOR

Excelerator is another set of tools that supports the open approach. It was initially developed by Index Technologies and is now provided by Intersolv as Excelerator II. The initial version, illustrated in broad conceptual form in Figure 19.6, was made up of a number of products that can be used to develop system models. Its various tools are integrated through a data dictionary to allow validation between the models. Typical functions provided by the toolset include:

- *Graphics*: this allows analysts to draw six different types of models: DFDs, structure charts, E–R diagrams, logical data models, structure diagrams and presentation graphs. It is possible to choose the kinds of symbols used in the diagrams. Thus, for example, users can configure the tool to use either DeMarco or Gane and Sarson data flow symbols.
- *XL dictionary*: this is a data dictionary stored in Excelerator to keep track of the various graph objects produced by designers.
- *Analysis:* analyzes different models to see if they are properly connected. This supports validation of data models against each other.
- *Screens and reports*: assists designers to prepare reports of the current status of a design. It can also be used to support prototyping by designing screens and reports that will be made available in the application.
- *Documentation*: prints out any reports prepared by the screens and report function. It can print a document graph that shows in a tree form the contents of the data dictionary, generate specification documents to a variety of formats and track the progress of design work.

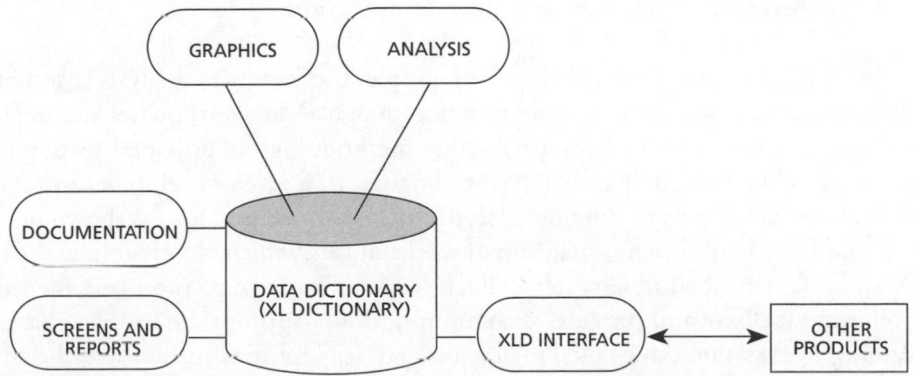

Figure 19.6 *The Excelerator CASE tool*

- *XLD interface:* supports transfer of models from some CASE tools. It contains a transfer function between other tools or can convert data into ACSII-format.
- *Housekeeping:* allows sharing of the information by a number of groups. It carries out functions such as back-up and maintains user profiles and passwords.

A user can select any of these functions from the main menu and use the facilities provided by them. There are no specified steps for using the different tools and members of the development team can make their own decision on the way they will be used. Thus designers can start with developing an E–R diagram, then develop an E–R diagram using the graphics tool. It can then check the diagrams, for example, data balancing for DFDs. The analysis tool can then be used to validate the diagrams against each other. Excelerator II now also provides support for object modeling with access to traditional tools provided by SSADM or other methods. What is also interesting is enhanced integration with supporting tools such as configuration management, using Intersolv products.

A FLEXIBLE WORKBENCH

The last example described here is the flexible workbench, which originated with James Martin and was one of the first to use the idea of a central repository, called the Encyclopedia in this case. Although there are a number of variants, the methodology follows four major phases:

1. *Information systems planning,* which examines the organization's business plans and produces an enterprise-wide model of the whole organization. It then subdivides the model into individual business areas.
2. *Business area analysis,* which develops a logical model for individual business areas. This uses DFDs, E–R diagrams and other tools. It allows the designer to define the business problem and divide the business into parts. It can then be used to develop and examine a number of alternative designs. It produces the business area information model and the technical requirements of new systems, and develops an initial project plan.
3. *System design,* which establishes the requirements and produces a detailed specification, including user interfaces and a test plan.
4. *Construction,* which generates and tests the programs, creates an operational database, trains users and brings new systems into operation.

In some cases, phases are split—for example, business area analysis is sometimes split into business system design and technical design. Additional phases are sometimes included in construction. Support for this methodology is provided through a set of workbenches, not all of which need to be used in a given development process.

It allows developers to combine tools in a flexible manner. Thus, as shown in Figure 19.7, the IEW workbench is made up of workstations, which closely follow the linear design cycle described in Chapter 7. Each workstation groups tools suitable for one development phase and provides diagramming tools appropriate to that phase. The planning workstation can be used to develop a strategy for the organization, the analysis workstation supports the development of the system specification and the designer's workstation supports system design. Each workstation provides a number of tools, and

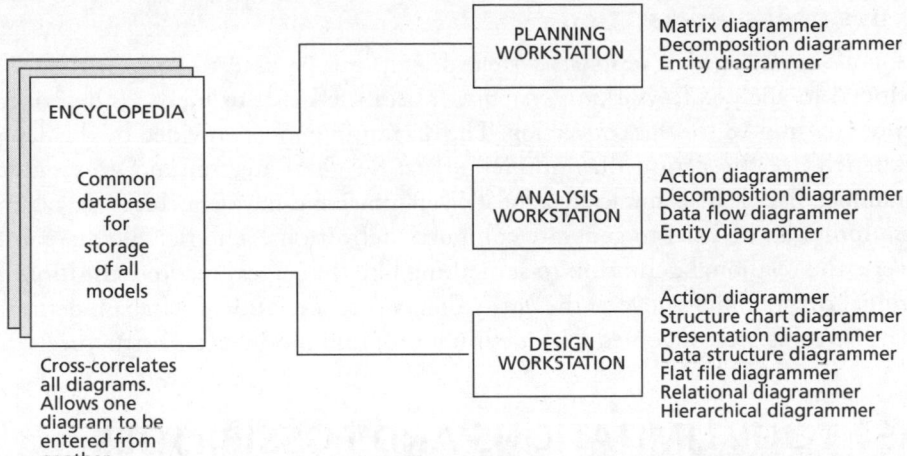

Figure 19.7 *The IEW workbench*

each tool supports one kind of system diagram. Information about all diagrams is kept in an integrated database, called an encyclopedia. Using a common encyclopedia makes it possible to cross-correlate information stored using the various diagrams. In fact, it is possible to work on one diagram and from this diagram to open other diagrams.

The IEW idea is to provide strong diagramming support to assist documentation, and cross-checking to assist quality maintenance. The development process phases and management reporting requirements may be chosen by the designer. The three workstations, however, suggest three major phases: planning, specification and design. We will give an outline of these three workstations and describe one in detail.

Planning workstation

This workstation supports initial information systems planning and the collection of high-level user requirements. It provides three diagramming tools: the matrix diagrammer, the decomposition diagrammer and the entity diagrammer. The entity diagrammer supports the entity diagram, which is very similar to the E–R diagram. The decomposition diagrammer models the system processes. The idea of the matrix diagrammer is similar to that in Figure 16.7(b). It maintains cross-references between functions and data. The output from this workstation would state the requirements of the system, together with a high-level model that shows the system functions and data.

Analysis workstation

The analysis workstation supports business system analysis. It is oriented around the DFD and entity modeling and provides two tools known as the data flow diagrammer and the entity diagrammer. These two diagramming tools support the development of DFDs and entity diagrams. This workstation also includes two additional tools: the action diagrammer and the decomposition diagrammer, which support process specifications.

The designer's workstation

This workstation, which supports system design, can be used to convert the models developed in analysis to working systems. It uses the kinds of methods described in Chapters 17 and 18 for this conversion. The diagraming tools provided by the designer workbench are the action diagrammer, structure chart diagrammer, presentation diagrammer, flat file diagrammer, relational diagrammer and the hierarchical diagrammers. These tools can be used to generate computer definitions. The flat file diagrammer converts the relational definition to something like the logical record definition. The relational diagrammer converts the entity diagram to a relational database definition. The other tools are concerned with defining program modules and structures.

CASE TOOL LIMITATIONS AND POSSIBILITIES

In summary, CASE tools do not guarantee a correct or good design; they simply assist the designers to build their models. There is very little experimental data to claim that CASE tools in fact require fewer resources to build a system. However, it is acknowledged that they improve the correctness of systems and are easier to maintain.

Research in the area of CASE is concentrating on how to provide better assistance both in modeling and supporting a process. It addresses the issue of developing a knowledge base about system design and using it to assist designers.

CASE tools assist designers to build new systems and to generate systems from existing software. The first kind of approach taken here was to use packages.

USING PACKAGES

Packages are software written to support the more common business functions. The idea is that a user should be able to buy a package and immediately use it in their work. Popular packages, for example, are accounting or inventory packages. Packages, however, are written in a very general way and must often be adapted or modified for use in particular organizations. Care has to be exercised when choosing a package for an application in order to reduce the amount of modification needed. If the modifications take as long as writing a new system (which sometimes happens) then there is no advantage in using the package. Consequently, packages tend to be used only in very special circumstances.

Another approach is to provide systems that satisfy only a small generic set of applications. The classification of systems described in Chapter 2 serves as a guideline to such classification. Thus we could have systems to support decisions, design cooperation or workflows. One common set of applications are those that correspond to workflows.

SUMMARY

This chapter described productivity tools used in system development. Such tools, known as CASE tools, support modeling used in analysis and design. They can be used as part of a structured methodology or on a needs basis. The chapter also discussed integration of such tools so that outputs of one can be used as inputs to another. A number of representative available methodologies and tools were then described. The chapter described a trend to open systems and outlined three systems that follow this trend—SSADM, and the family of tools provided by ORACLE and RATIONAL ROSE. An outline of the facilities provided by Excelerator AND THE IEW WORKBENCH was also given. The chapter concluded by describing some limitations of CASE and how packages can be used.

DISCUSSION QUESTIONS

19.1   Describe the idea behind CASE tools.

19.2   What are the current trends in the design of CASE tools?

19.3   Describe how structured systems analysis is integrated with the linear problem-solving cycle.

19.4   What are the different ways of using CASE tools?

19.5   How should a CASE tool assist a design methodology?

19.6   What is the difference between prescribed and flexible support tools?

19.7   Why is it preferable to buy an off-the-shelf methodology rather than developing one yourself?

19.8   Describe the SSADM stages and how they relate to the linear life cycle described in Chapter 6.

19.9   Describe the major phases used in information engineering.

19.10 Describe some common features of all design methodologies.

19.11 What kind of support is provided by IEW?

19.12 What are the limitations in using packages?

BIBLIOGRAPHY

Baker, J.M. (1992), 'Project management utilizing an advanced CASE environment', *International Journal on Software Engineering and Knowledge Engineering*, Vol. 2, No.1, pp. 251–61.

Deiters, W. and Gruhn, V. (December 1990), 'Managing software processes in the environment MELMAC', *Proceedings of the 4th Symposium on Practical Software Development Environments,* Irvine, California.

Dixon, R.C. (1992), *Winning with CASE*, McGraw-Hill, New York.

Downs, E., Clare, P. and Coe, I. (1988), *Structured Systems Analysis and Design Method*, Prentice-Hall, Englewood Cliffs, New Jersey.

Finkelstein, C. (1989), *An Introduction to Information Engineering*, Prentice-Hall, Englewood Cliffs, New Jersey.

Gane, C. (1990), *Computer-Aided Software Engineering: The Methodologies, the Products, and the Future*, Prentice Hall, Englewood Cliffs, New Jersey.

Hares, J.S. (1992), *Information Engineering for the AdvancedPractitioner*, John Wiley and Sons, Chichester.

— *(1994) SSADM: Version 4*, Wiley, City.

Hunnekens, H., Junkermann, G., Peuschel, B., Schafer, W. and Vagts, J. (1990), 'A step towards knowledge based software process modeling', in N. Madhavji, W. Schafer and H. Weber. (eds), *Proceedings of the First Conference on System Development Environments and Factories*, Pitman Publishing, London.

Iivari, J. (October 1996), 'Why are CASE tools not used?', *Communications of the ACM*, Vol. 39, No. 10, pp. 94–103.

King, S.F. (July 1996), 'CASE tools and organizational action', *Information Systems Journal*, pp. 173–94.

Martin, J. (1990), *Information Engineering: Book II Planning and Analysis*, Prentice Hall, Englewood Cliffs, New Jersey.

Napier, R. (1991), *Information Engineering and Application Development using KnowledgeWare CASE Tool Set*, Prentice-Hall, Englewood Cliffs, New Jersey.

Norman, R.J. and Forte, G. (eds) (April 1992), *Communications of the ACM, Special Issue on CASE Tools*, Vol. 35, No. 4.

Peuschel, B., Schafer, W. and Wolf, S. (1992), 'A knowledge-based software development environment supporting cooperative work', *International Journal of Software Engineering and Knowledge Engineering*, Vol. 2, No. 1, pp. 79–106.

Rothstein, M., Rosner, B., Senatore, M. and Mulligan, D. (1993), *Structured Analysis and Design for the CASE User*, McGraw-Hill, New York.

Vessey, I. and Sravanapudi, A.P. (January 1995), 'CASE tools as collaborative support technologies', *Communications of the ACM*, Vol. 38, No. 1, pp. 83–95.

Project management

20

CONTENTS

KEY LEARNING OBJECTIVES

The project management process
How to organize resources for a project
How to monitor project progress
The difference between project and process monitoring
Project management tools

◇ INTRODUCTION

The project management process goes alongside the system development process. In essence, the goal of the management process is to provide the necessary support for development to proceed smoothly and to reduce any development problems.

The project management process is made up of three main components: creating a project plan, monitoring whether the project is proceeding according to the plan, and putting in place the procedures for quality assurance. Quality assurance is managed by putting in place the quality assurance steps for reviews of project deliverables.

The project management process must be integrated with the development process. A common practice in project management is to break development down into a number of well-defined management entities, which are called phases, tasks, activities or some similar term. Such tasks have a single objective and produce a well-defined deliverable. Thus it would be extremely unlikely to have detailed analysis and hardware installation in the same management task. However, all tasks associated with hardware installation may be one project management entity. Each task also has a clear beginning and end.

The management and development processes are integrated by making each task into one component of the project plan and then defining the monitoring and review steps in terms of these tasks. Thus Figure 20.1 illustrates the idea of project management for a project made up of a number of tasks with time relationships between them. The time relationships show that Task 4 starts after Tasks 2 and 3 are completed, and that Tasks 2 and 3 can start after Task 1 is completed. Project management requires that resources, particularly personnel, be moved from a task that has been completed to tasks that are about to start.

As well as coordinating tasks, other important project management activities are to organize resources to do the work, provide the necessary documentation and team support, and monitor work progress while making sure that the work meets quality standards.

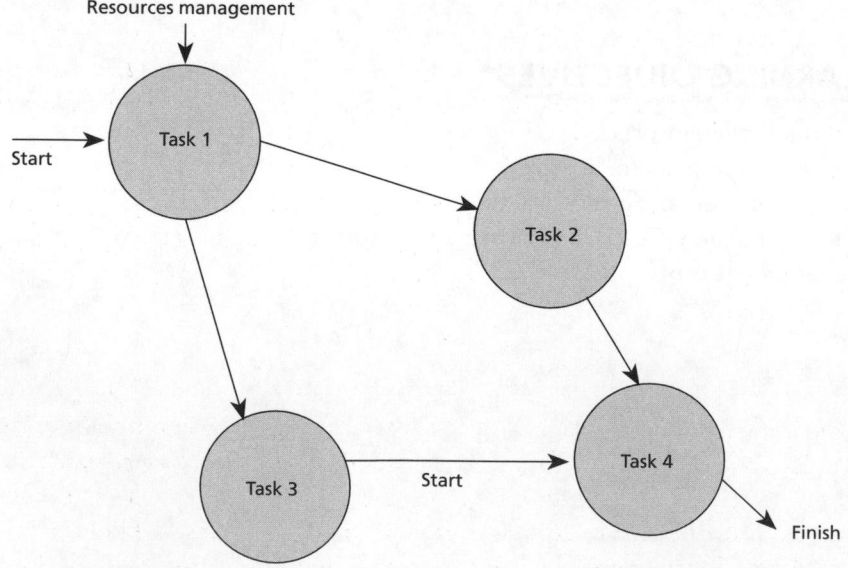

Figure 20.1 *Coordinating tasks*

Project management has been closely associated with the linear cycle, and this chapter will concentrate on describing how the management process is integrated with the linear cycle. It will then describe the variations found with other cycles.

MEASURING THE PROCESS

Before we describe the main components of project management, we will look at process management itself. Thus, as well as managing individual projects, a good project management practice is to measure the performance of the development process itself and, if necessary, change and improve the development process from one project to the next. Measurement of the process is different. Its goals, as outlined by Humphrey (1989) of the Software Engineering Institute (SEI), are first to measure the development process, and then to identify ways of improving it. The process is measured in terms of maturity levels, which are:

- *Level 1: Initial*—where the process is *ad hoc.*
- *Level 2: Repeatable*—where there is a basic development process together with a project management process to track costs, schedules and functionality.
- *Level 3: Defined*—where the project management process is documented and integrated with the development process, with quality reviews in place.
- *Level 4: Managed*—where detailed measures of the development process are made and correlated with product quality.
- *Level 5: Optimized*—where measures are used as feedback to improve the process.

Formal assessment procedures are provided by the SEI to measure the maturity level of development processes in an organization. The goal here is to reach the optimized level where any problems encountered in development are identified and used to improve the development process to ensure that such problems do not occur in future projects. In an optimized process, those parts of the process that caused the problem are changed to prevent the problem from recurring. Thus, for example, suppose it is found that a particular user requirement was not met. A check is made to find where the deviation from the user requirements took place and a validation check is added to that part of the process.

Most processes in practice have not reached an optimized level, although an increasing number are reaching Level 3. At Level 3 maturity, a development process is closely adhered to and monitored by a management process.

PLANNING

Planning must determine how each task fits into the process. This includes stating how long a task will take, and defining its start and completion times. In addition, a plan defines the sequence in which tasks are carried out. To make a plan requires estimates of the effort needed to complete each of the required tasks. These estimates are then used to allocate resources to a task and in turn determine how long it will take.

ESTIMATING

Estimating involves evaluating the amount and complexity of work to be done in each task. This information is used to determine the resources needed to complete the work. Estimates will depend on the type of work carried out in the task. Most software estimates take into account the organization's experience related to the type of task. This can be where:

- Existing software is used—this involves minimal risk, although often some compromise is needed to ensure a good fit to other system components.
- Previous experience exists—estimates use historical information about resources used in similar tasks to estimate the resource needs for a task in the new project. These estimates are usually quite accurate. However, a check should be made that this experience has been retained—in particular, people with this experience can participate in the new project.
- similar experience exists—the risk here is higher, although there is always some part which is familiar and can be used to make an estimate.
- totally new development—this is a high-risk task which will call for closer monitoring during development and suggests the need for prototyping.

A detailed discussion of the ways in which estimates are produced is beyond the scope of this book and would include alternatives for developing cost models for projects. There are methods—for example, function point analysis—whose goal is to measure software complexity. They do this by identifying functions such as external input/output, file operations, data and control operations. The complexity of each function is then estimated, and this is then used to compute a function point measure.

IDENTIFYING AND EVALUATING RISK

The idea of risk management has also become important. The idea here is to determine the most likely factors that could cause projects to fail or estimates to be incorrect and then take precautions either to avoid them or to deal with them. One way to minimize risk is to use evolutionary or prototype cycles where we are dealing with systems that are unique in some way and have no historical precedents to suggest needed resources.

Proper risk management will require additional planning to evaluate the difficulties of achieving project goals. An important consideration in many plans is to evaluate the risks of not achieving project goals within the available resources. Where there is the potential of risk, it may be necessary to spend more time in planning to assess the risk and reduce it. The way this is done depends on the type of risk. For example:

- *Risk of incorrect requirements leading to frequent change*—provide for change management, use evolutionary or prototype development cycles or prototyping, better customer involvement.
- *Risk posed by new technologies*—hire or train technology experts in the technology.

ORGANIZING RESOURCES

An important part of the project management process is to organize the resources needed to carry out a project. Project organization includes a variety of resources, perhaps the most important of which is choosing the right people for the project and organizing them into teams that support the chosen methodology. There are also other resources to be organized, such as the necessary computers and terminals, building space or productivity tools. Arrangements must be made for user departments to contribute to the project.

Users and computer professionals are often included in each team, thus ensuring the user involvement that is essential to good system design. Users know what the system does, and are familiar with its problems and objectives, so they should contribute to its development. Modeling methods and productivity tools make it easier for users to become involved in system design. These models and tools provide the necessary vehicles for communication with users and also enable greater experimentation and prototyping to improve user input.

DEFINING A PROJECT SCHEDULE

Once the project tasks are determined and their time requirements known, then it becomes necessary to determine their sequence. One choice which needs to be made is which problem-solving cycle to use. Do we use a linear cycle, a staged cycle or some other cycle? In our particular problem, we have opted for a staged cycle. The project plan will define the timing of tasks, including start and end times, and the resources, including the people needed for each task.

TOOLS USED IN PROJECT SCHEDULING

You will find that considerable information is necessary to keep track of project estimates and to monitor project progress. It is usually necessary to maintain a database on project status and resources. As shown in Figure 20.2, such a database must allow inputs that indicate any changes to project status and resources, and produce reports that can be used in project reviews.

The database assists management with quantitative controls. Planning and usage data is input to the database, and reports about current resource status can be produced. The project management database also contains project scheduling data. Activity start and end dates can form part of the inputs. These start and end dates can be monitored and deviations from the planned schedules output as exception reports.

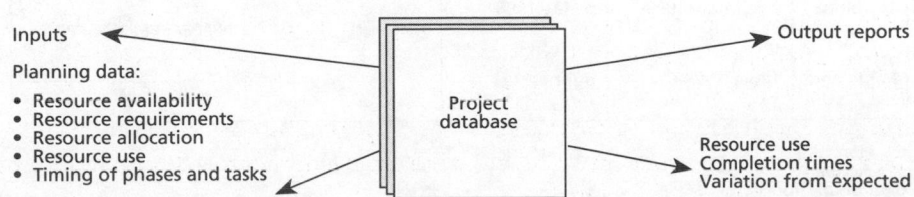

Figure 20.2 *A project database*

Management may request status reports on project progress from the project database. A project database, maintained on a computer, can provide a large variety of such reports. Typical reports produced by existing systems include:

- personnel availability by skill and by time;
- personnel schedules for a project or for a number of related projects;
- resource summary reports by project, and by tasks within projects;
- summaries by project size and type;
- summaries of resource usage within regular time periods;
- possible manpower shortages over a given period; and
- budget reports.

Schedule data is often presented in the form of bar charts or by project networks, sometimes better known as project evaluation and review techniques (PERT) charts. These charts or networks can be prominently displayed to make sure that everyone is aware of project progress.

Bar charts

A bar chart is illustrated in Figure 20.3. Four project phases are included in the bar chart: analysis, design, development and implementation. Two bars are plotted for each phase. One bar is plotted using the letter P, and the other bar is plotted using the letter A. The bar plotted with the letter P shows the planned time for each phase, and the bar plotted with the letter A shows the actual time for each phase. An A bar terminated with a C shows that a phase has been completed. Thus Figure 20.3 shows that analysis has been completed and we are now in the design phase.

19 January 1998

Activity	Start-date	End-date	September	October	November	December	January	February	March	April	May	June
Analysis	5 September 1997	11 October 1997	PPPPP AAAAAAAAC									
Design	1 December 1997	3 March 1998				PPPPPPPPPPPPPPP AAA						
Develop	2 February 1998	5 May 1998							PPPPPPPPPPPPPPPPPP			
Implement	1 May 1998	6 June 1998									PPPPP	

P = Plan
A = Actual
C = Completion

Figure 20.3 *A bar chart*

Network charts

A network chart, as well as showing the scheduled times for each task, also shows the dependence of one task on other tasks. There is one line for each task on the PERT chart. The line for each task is a continuation from lines of a previous task. A task cannot start until all its incoming tasks have been completed. Figure 20.4 illustrates a network chart for eight project tasks. A bar chart for the same tasks is also shown in this figure for comparison. This figure shows that Tasks 1 and 2 can both start as soon as a project is initiated. It also shows that Task 6 cannot start until Tasks 4 and 5 are completed. Outputs from PERT networks:

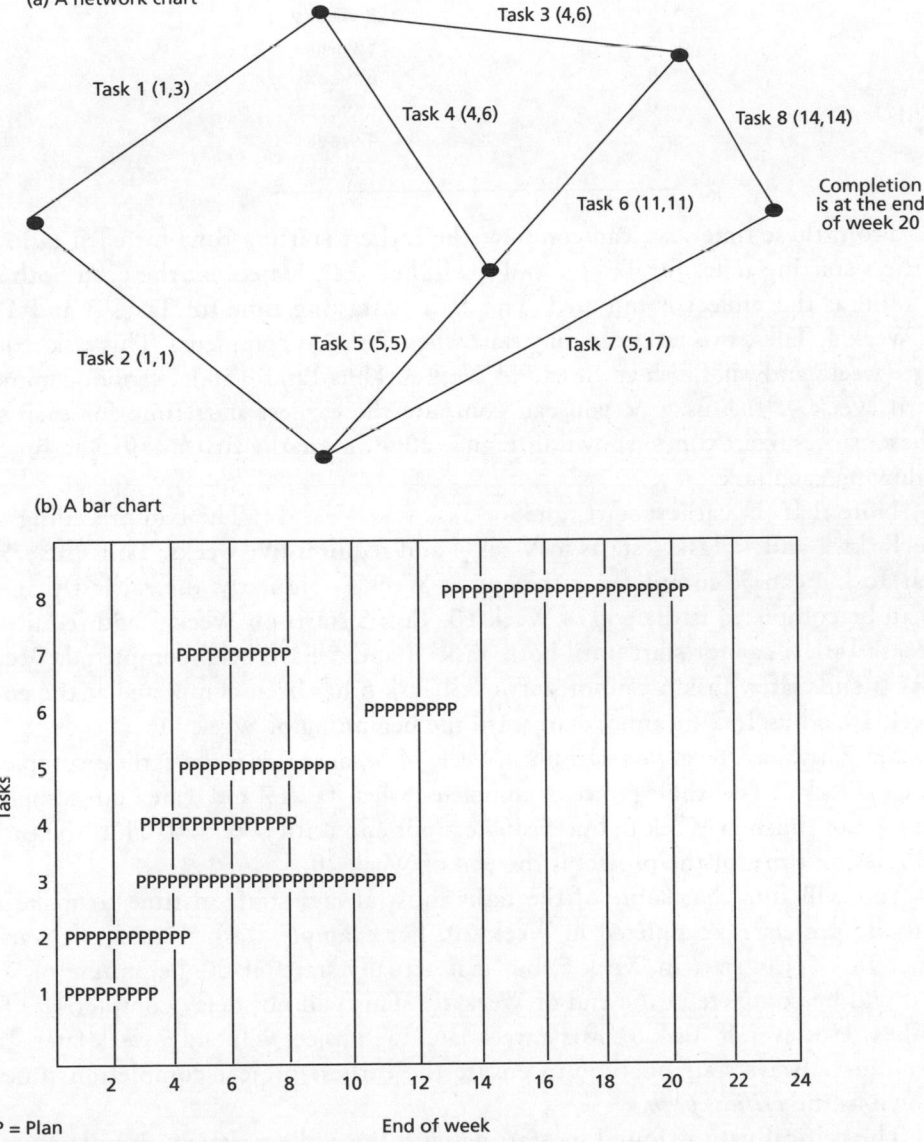

Figure 20.4 *A network chart and a bar chart*

- determine a critical path—These are the activities that must commence on time;
- determine the earliest and latest start time for each activity.

To illustrate these outputs, we need the expected time to complete each task. We assume these times to be as shown in Table 20.1.

Table 20.1 *Time to complete tasks*

Task	Time needed
1	3 weeks
2	4 weeks
3	8 weeks
4	5 weeks
5	6 weeks
6	3 weeks
7	4 weeks
8	7 weeks

From these times, we can compute the earliest starting time for each task. The earliest starting times for Tasks 1 and 2 will be Week 1, because they can both start as soon as the project is initiated. The earliest starting time for Tasks 3 and 4 will be Week 4. These two tasks can only start when Task 1 is completed. This task requires three weeks and will finish at the end of Week 3. Thus Tasks 3 and 4 cannot commence until Week 4. In this way, you can compute the earliest start time for each task. These earliest start times, shown in Figure 20.4(a), are the first number in brackets following each task.

Note that the earliest start time for Task 6 is Week 11. The two preceding tasks are Tasks 2 and 4. Task 4 starts in Week 4 and requires five weeks. Thus the earliest that Task 4 can be completed is the end of Week 8. Similarly, the earliest that Task 5 can be completed is the end of Week 10. Task 5 starts on Week 5 and requires six weeks. Task 6 cannot start until both Tasks 4 and 5 have been completed. Because Task 5 ends later, Task 6 cannot start until Task 5 has been completed at the end of Week 10. Thus Task 6 cannot start until the beginning of Week 11.

Similarly, Task 8 cannot start until Week 14 because this is the earliest completion time for Task 6. The whole project is completed when Tasks 7 and 8 are both completed. Task 7 can finish in Week 8, but Task 8 cannot end until Week 20. Thus the earliest completion time for the project is the end of Week 20.

You will find that some of the tasks must always start on time to make sure that the project is completed in Week 20. For example, Task 7 need not start on time. Task 7 can start in Week 5, but if it actually starts at the beginning of Week 9, it will be complete at the end of Week 12. This will not delay completion of the project. However, if Task 8 starts a week late, the project will end a week later. Tasks that must always start on time to ensure the earliest project completion time are known as the *critical path*.

The critical path is found by starting with the earliest project completion time and working backwards to compute the latest start time for each task. For Task 7, the latest start time is the beginning of Week 16. If Task 7 starts in Week 17, it will be complete at the end of Week 20 and project completion will not be delayed. The latest start time for Task 8 is Week 14. The latest start times for each task in Figure 20.4(a) are shown as the second number in brackets following each task.

Tasks whose earliest starting times and latest starting times are the same have no slack and must start on time if project completion is not to be delayed. In Figure 20.4(a), these tasks are 2, 5, 6 and 8. They are on the critical path. Other tasks have some slack and their starting time can be delayed. Task 7 can start anywhere between the beginning of Week 5 and the beginning of Week 17. It may in fact make sense to delay Task 7. If you look at the bar chart in Figure 20.4(b), you will see that there are four tasks in progress during Weeks 5 to 8. If we delay the start of Task 7 until after Week 8, there will never be a week that has more than three tasks in progress. This can mean that we reduce peak demands for resources and the project cost.

TEXT CASE D: Construction Company—A Project Plan

The problem for this case seems to be well defined and not too large, so an evolutionary or prototype approach would not be appropriate. There seem to be two well-defined tasks—namely, improving and rearranging current operations and then adding the inventory system. It is proposed that these tasks be done in two stages. First, we will change existing operations and then add inventory. This means some of the benefits (in particular, the replacement of manual checking) can be obtained more quickly with fewer staff employed.

Once a decision to use a staged approach is made, we specify the times and resources needed for each phase of each stage. Table 20.2 shows one way of representing such an allocation. It includes the start and finish times for each phase and the user and data processing personnel needed. Thus, for example, an average of one person from the information systems (IS) department would work in Stage 1 of the analysis for two months. There would also be an average of one person from the user area working on the analysis for two months, giving a total of four man-months for Stage 1 of the analysis.

Table 20.2 *A project plan*

(a) Stage 1 — Convert project request processing

	Personnel		Person-month effort	Start	End
	IS	User			
Analysis	1	1	4	1 May 1998	30 June 1998
System design	1	1	4	1 July 1998	30 August 1998
Detailed design	1	1/2	3	1 September 1998	30 October 1998
Implementation	2	1	12	1 November 1998	28 February 1998

(b) Stage 2 — Inventory function

	Personnel		Person-month effort	Start	End
	IS	User			
Analysis	1/2	1/2	2	1 November 1998	31 December 1998
System design	1/2	1/2	1.5	15 January 1999	28 February 1999
Detailed design	1	1/2	2.25	1 March 1999	15 April 1999
Implementation	1	1/2	3.75	16 April 1999	30 June 1999
Total amount of person-month effort			32.5		

Another common way to illustrate project plans is to make a chart that shows project phases graphically over time, and particularly how different projects overlap. Such charts are often known as Gantt charts. A Gantt chart for our project is shown in Figure 20.5. Here the horizontal dimension shows time, and each project or project stage is plotted on the time scale. The overlap of the projects is clearly shown here. For example, the implementation phase of Stage 1 and analysis of Stage 2 quite clearly overlap. A chart like the one shown in Figure 20.5 gives a total picture of what will be going on at each time, when phases finish, and when they start.

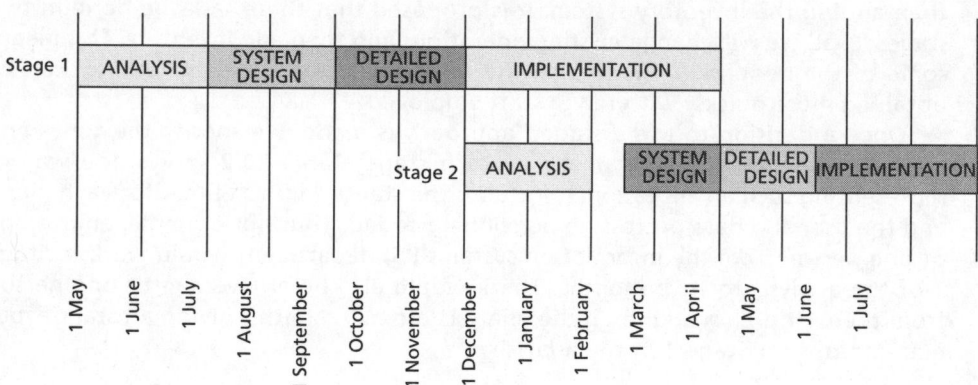

Figure 20.5 *A Gantt chart*

 # MONITORING

Monitoring keeps track of project progress. Project schedules contain statements of how long each task should take and how it utilizes resources. Monitoring collects information to determine whether these goals are being met. Any problems or defects found are usually traced back through the process to find the cause of the problem and the process is amended to prevent its future occurrence. For example, if it were found that a requirement has not been met, the part of the process where the deviation from requirement first appeared is found and a further validation requirement introduced at that point. Successful monitoring requires regular collection about the status of each task.

REVIEWING PROJECT PROGRESS

Project reviews have now been accepted as an essential activity in good project management practice. The project reviews may be quite complex and there may be more than one kind of review. There may be technical reviews to see if the best technical approach has been adopted. There may be user reviews that check system models, see if user requirements are met and seek agreement on future actions. Finally, there are management reviews to check resource levels and decide whether project objectives have been met. They are also necessary to decide what is to be done in further project phases.

It is usual, if not mandatory, to review a project at the completion of each phase and to produce a project phase report that describes the outcome of each task, including:

- the actual starting and completion dates of activities;
- the actual use of resources compared to the estimates;
- the level of expenditure in each activity;
- the quality of output; and
- any problems found with the supporting process.

Any variations from plans are analyzed and appropriate corrective action is taken. Management can take action in a number of ways. First, it can vary the project scope. Alternatively, project resources can be increased or changes made to activity schedules. Finally, the process itself can be improved by changing it in light of experiences with this project.

VARIATIONS WITH LIFE CYCLES

There are variations in the way project management is used with other development processes.   Project management is harder to apply to these alternative cycles because their objectives are not as well defined as in the linear cycle and because of greater iteration in these cycles. The difference is that we can define a precise deliverable for each linear cycle phase. Such a precise deliverable, however, cannot be specified for cycles where outcomes cannot be so clearly defined. It is thus harder to estimate the resources needed for the phase. It is also harder to define the beginning and end of particular tasks.

In this case, there is greater emphasis on risk management. The goal is to take steps to reduce uncertainty. As more is learned, better estimates are made for the next step, and so on. This is one of the principles of the spiral cycle described in Chapter 7, where every prototyping step is preceded by risk analysis.

With no certain outcomes guaranteed, it is often difficult to commit management to allocate resources for the whole project before the project starts. Resources are therefore often allocated in piecemeal fashion. This contrasts to the linear cycle, where all resources can be committed at the beginning of the cycle. Similarly, the management entities can also evolve during project progress. With other cycles, resources are allocated for a fixed period of time and the results are closely monitored. If nothing emerges after this time, then the project may be terminated. If a structure gradually evolves, more resources may be added to the project and its time gradually expanded. If uncertainties are removed, then we may continue project development using linear controls.

Objectives must therefore be defined in some other way for project management in these alternative cycles. Project entities are then defined to correspond to these objectives, which are experimental in nature, and consequently project entities can be defined in terms of elements of uncertainty removed or simply as blocks of time. The former is usually appropriate to decision support systems, whereas the latter is used in imprecise systems or for prototyping.

DECISION SUPPORT SYSTEMS

In a decision support system, it is never clear how much of the decision-making abilities can be passed on to the system. Rather than trying to build the whole system, it is advisable to break the project up into parts, so that each part resolves some well-defined problem. The framework suggested by Alter (1984) and briefly described in Chapter 7 can be usefully applied for this purpose. Each of Alter's phases becomes a management entity. Resources are allocated to one management entity at a time.

The suggested phases are:

- a data-analysis phase to collect data useful to decision making;
- an information-analysis phase to automatically extract data needed for decision making;
- a phase to develop a representation model to define the expected system behavior; and
- a phase to develop optimization models.

Each phase can be allocated a certain resource level, and a completion time can be specified for the task. The phase is then managed using the linear life cycle approach, often using ideas from the spiral model. If we find at one phase that there is a high risk of getting no further useful outcomes by proceeding further, then the project stops.

IMPRECISE SYSTEMS AND PROTOTYPING

In this case we cannot precisely define system requirements, but we know more or less what the system is to do. We are certain that a satisfactory solution can be reached, but we don't know what that solution will look like. One example here is dialog design for a given system. Hence a management entity may be to develop the user dialog, and a certain amount of time will be devoted to it. The dialog at the completion of that time will be the dialog used in the system.

Prototyping is also often used in imprecise systems. Its goal is to develop a better understanding of the system, where typical objectives concern:

- seeking knowledge about the capability of a technical system or procedure; and
- testing the feasibility of an algorithm.

It is more difficult to break objectives up into smaller components than was the case with evolutionary design. A more likely approach would be to develop a rough and limited system for part of the data inputs only. Thus, for our racehorse problems (introduced in Chapter 5), we may build an experimental system for only a limited number of tracks and horses. Experiments would then be run with this limited system to see if it should be extended. The results of the experiment are used to decide whether to continue the project.

The management objective in prototyping is usually to find out whether it is worthwhile to continue with a project. The only project control is a time restriction. The experiments are run for a given period of time; if no satisfactory result is found in that time, the project is terminated.

SUMMARY

Project management is based on defining a set of management entities. These entities are set up to support project phases that have an objective as well as a start and an end. Project management organizes resources to ensure that this project phase objective is achieved in the most effective way. This calls for:

- allocation of adequate resources;
- use of proper tools and documentation methods; and
- organization of the resources.

This chapter described how management entities can be defined for the different problem-solving cycles. It also described how resources can be organized to accomplish the project, and described the detailed activities that make up project management and the tools used to keep track of them.

Finally, it is important to realize that project ideas are not always fully accepted. Some practitioners consider project management activities and good problem solving to be in conflict. For example, many problem solvers consider that reviews standards and documentation inhibit creative problem solving by forcing designers into prescribed ways of thinking. Many also see documentation and reviews as unnecessarily consuming resources that otherwise could be used for productive development work. Such views are particularly strong if the documentation and reviews become too excessive. Managers, however, desire to accomplish project goals with limited resource use. They see documentation and reviews as necessary to preserve continuity should personnel change, to disseminate any decisions reached, and to distribute procedures developed during the phase to appropriate personnel in the organization.

Clearly, a balance must be reached. There must be sufficient freedom allowed for creative problem solving, but at the same time resources must be expended in an effective manner. A major objective of any project management system must be to ensure that such creativity is maintained. To do this, it is essential to remember that any additional work called for by project management helps rather than hinders problem solving.

DISCUSSION QUESTIONS

20.1 Why must the management and development processes be integrated?

20.2 Do you think that the same team should work through the whole project, or that project teams should be changed as the project proceeds?

20.3 Explain what you understand by the term *risk*.

20.4 Why is it difficult to make project estimates?

20.5 Why is additional effort often needed in projects with unclear goals?

20.6 Explain why project reviews are important.

20.7 Explain why documentation is essential for an effective review process.

20.8 What would you expect the documentation to include in a feasibility study that uses prototyping?

20.9 Why does time become one of the major controls for imprecise or decision support systems?

20.10 Discuss the importance of making correct estimates in project management.

20.11 What is the difference between project and process measurement?

 EXERCISES

20.1 Take the evolutionary cycle described in Chapter 7. How would you devise a documentation system that fits in with this cycle? In particular, consider the reusable aspects of documentation, as you would expect documents produced at one phase to be amended in subsequent phases.

20.2 One goal of successful project management is to break the project up into well-defined tasks and establish methods for coordinating these tasks. PERT and GANTT charts can be used for coordination.

Suppose you have the following set of tasks and task relationships:

Task	Duration	Waits for
T1	6	—
T2	9	T1
T3	7	T2
T4	11	T1
T5	3	—
T6	6	T5
T7	3	T4, T6
T8	6	T5
T9	3	T4, T6
T10	11	T8, T9
T11	4	T3, T7, T10

1. Draw GANTT and PERT charts for these tasks.
2. What are the earliest and latest start times for each task?
3. What is the earliest completion time for the project?
4. What tasks make up the critical path?

BIBLIOGRAPHY

Bennaton, E.M. (1995), *Software Project Management: A Practitioner's Approach* (2nd edn), McGraw-Hill, London.

Brooks, F.P. Jr (1974), *The Mythical Man-month: Essays on Software Engineering*, Addison-Wesley, Reading, Massachusetts.

Burrill, C.W. and Ellsworth, L.W. (1990), *Modern Project Management*, Burrill-Ellsworth Associates, Inc., Tanalfy, New Jersey.

Constantine, L.L. (October 1993), 'Work organization: paradigms for project management and organization', *Communications of the ACM*, Vol. 36, No. 10, pp.34–43.

Cotterell, M. and Hughes, R. (1995), *Software Project Management*, International Thomson Computer Press, London.

Curtis, B., Kellner, M.I. and Goldberg, A. (September 1992), 'Process modeling', *Communications of the ACM*, Vol. 35, No. 9, pp. 75–90.

Humphrey, W. (1989), *Managing the Software Process*, Addison-Wesley, Reading, Massachusetts.

Johnson, J.R. (1991), *The Software Factory: Managing Software Development and Maintenance* (2nd edn), QED Information Science, Wellesley, Masachusetts.

Jones, C. (July 1996), 'How software estimation tools work', *The American Programmer*, Vol. 9, No. 7, pp. 18–27.

Perry, D. (March 1991), 'Models of software development environments', *IEEE Transactions on Software Engineering*, Vol. 17, No. 3, pp. 283–95.

Putnam, L.H., Putnam, D.T. and Myers, W. (June 1996), 'Adapting project estimation to advancing technologies', *The American Programmer*, Vol. 9, No. 6, pp. 23–29.

Rettic, M. (October 1990), 'Software teams', *Communications of the ACM*, Vol. 33, No. 10, pp. 23–7.

Thomsett, R. (1980), *People and Project Management*, Yourdon Press, New York.

Yourdon, E. (1982), *Managing the System Life Cycle*, Yourdon Press, New York.

Strategic planning

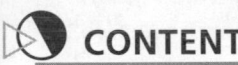

CONTENTS

KEY LEARNING OBJECTIVES

Why it is necessary to plan the development of the information system
Why information systems plans must be fitted into the organization's business plan
The planning cycle
The planning process
What happens during planning?
The plan components
What is included in an information systems plan?
Re-engineering the system

INTRODUCTION

Many things have to be done to design and build computer-based information systems. In any organization it is necessary to improve or re-engineer existing systems, while at the same time new systems must be developed to satisfy new needs. Re-engineering is a term that is now coming into frequent use; it means redesigning the system to work in a different way to fit in with the organization's changing business plan. Early examples of re-engineering included changing a system from batch to on-line, or integrating two systems to support a business process that needs data from more than one business unit. The general aim of re-engineering in the current climate is to move toward more flexible client-oriented systems which provide better client service, while reducing development costs.

There are always many ideas on how to change existing systems, but resource limitations prevent us building new systems and re-engineering all the existing systems at the same time. Many earlier designers, who often underestimated the complexity of large systems, made unrealistic promises to deliver working systems, only to find later that they could not deliver because unforeseen complexities had arisen. Meanwhile, considerable funds and effort had been invested and the promised results did not appear. It is wiser to plan any changes carefully and to make them in an orderly manner.

Planning is an ongoing process that sets the goals for the whole organization. It also defines how computer-based information systems will help to achieve these goals. Planning must also set priorities. Often there are many things that people in an organization wish to do, but only limited resources are available to do them. A plan must determine what is most important to the organization and set development priorities. Prioritizing includes determining what share of an organization's resources, including funds and people, will be used to develop new and re-engineer existing information systems.

Usually organizations develop both long-term and short-term plans for information systems. Long-term plans are often defined as being over five years or more; they are less precise and define the organization's **strategy***. The strategy is realized gradually over time as new systems are developed to replace existing systems. Long-term plans are often amended in the light of experience. Short-term plans are of one or two years' duration and define what needs to be done in the following year. They are usually quite precise and often identify actual projects, together with specific project goals and the resources needed to achieve them.*

Strategy
The broad objective for an organization.

 THE PLAN STRUCTURE

A plan is often a complex document that specifies the relationships between an organization's business units, as well as its relationship to its stakeholders and environment. The plan must:

- set objectives or a mission for the organization;
- be futuristic and project a vision of the organization in the future;
- look outside the organization;
- consider the organization as a whole and not just its component parts;
- consider all parts of the organization and their relationship to each other; and

- identify opportunities for the organization, match them to what it does now and see how it can make the most of these opportunities.

It is now common to develop plans by first defining the organization's **mission**. The mission basically defines the organization's role in its environment. This may be to provide specified kinds of insurance to the home market, or to provide investment services to a defined set of clients. The next step is to develop a **strategic business plan** to realize this mission. The organization's busines plan is made up of a number of components. There will be a marketing plan and strategy, a production plan and strategy, a financial plan and strategy, and an information systems plan and strategy.

Often, at an organizational level, the strategy determines the percentage of the total resources of an enterprise to be allocated to new information systems developments and the maintenance of new and existing information systems. We then use an estimate of such funds and the broad statement of organizational needs to determine how to use these funds to develop information systems that are consistent with these needs. The information systems plan also has its components.

Mission
A reason for the existence of an organization.

Strategic planning
Determining the broad objectives for an organization.

COMMITMENT TO THE PLAN

Effective planning requires commitment from the whole organization to achieve its plan. To ensure that all the people in the organization are committed to the plan, they must be made aware of what the business plan is and how they should contribute to it. People in each unit know what they are doing, but they also know their planned relationship to other groups. Commitment is often gained by including action points in the plan. These action points specify what individual units, or even individuals, must do to realize the plan objective.

It is also necessary to maintain coordination between people and units to achieve the plan. Such coordination must ensure that everything is ready at the right time to start any planned activities. For example, it ensures that equipment is obtained on time to begin system development. If the equipment is brought in too early, then it is idle and resources are not utilized. If it is too late, people are idle waiting for it to arrive. Planning must contain the information needed for proper coordination of all activities. Such coordination often requires regular reviews to monitor progress in relation to the plan and take any corrective action if needed. Such corrective action may sometimes call for changes in the plan itself.

PLANNING FOR UNCERTAINTY

It is perhaps fair to mention here that any strategic plan that assumes a steady external state is no longer valid as the external environment is always changing. Customer preferences change, new laws are enacted, and production methods can quickly change. Many organizations cater for this by including contingencies in their planning. These are actions to take if the strategic plan cannot be met. However, if the contingency plan tends to dominate strategic plans, then strategic planning can be seen to be unproductive. Another suggestion is that strategic planning should change its emphasis and cover new planning concepts related to change. These include building up human resource capabilities, improving links to the external world and facilitating the learning process.

INFORMATION SYSTEMS PLANNING

This chapter concentrates on information systems plans. However, it is important to remember that an information systems plan cannot be considered in isolation to its other activities. It is necessary to show how the information systems plan fits into the organization's plan. This can be done in a variety of ways. The importance of linking it to a financial plan is obvious, for example, as information systems can only be developed if funds are available to do so.

Links to other business units can often be specified in terms of services that will be provided by the information system and how these services help the business units to achieve their goals. Thus, for example, provision of a mobile network may mean that a sales force becomes more effective because it always has access to the latest information in the field. Setting up a system to track client requests will help to keep clients who might otherwise seek services elsewhere.

DEFINING THE TECHNICAL STRATEGY

Technical strategy is an important component of the information systems plan. Computer technology is continuously evolving, and new developments can be used to provide an ever-growing number of new services. It is therefore necessary to choose the technical strategy that best matches the business plan and provides services consistent with that plan. The major strategic choices to be made here include:

- the database strategy—is a warehousing approach needed, or should responsibility lie with the operating departments;
- the networking strategy—centralized, distributed or client server;
- the external networking strategy of how to link internal networks to clients or public networks;
- the degree of commitment to electronic commerce;
- the development strategy—integrated or distributed responsibility,
- the development framework—what development, support and management processes should be used; and
- the development tools—whether to use structured system analysis or object orientation, and the role of CASE tool support.

Just like the business plan, the components of the technical plan must be linked and coordinated. They should cater for uncertainty by being modular whenever possible to allow new technical components to be quickly introduced.

DEVELOPING THE STRATEGIC PLAN

Planning is a complex process that can be characterized in a number of ways. It is important to remember that the planning process must be creative, proceed in an organized way and involve a wide cross-section of people to get wide commitment.

THE PLANNING CYCLE

A question that may arise is: how often do we make a plan, and who will be involved? One often finds the term *planning cycle* used in this context. This is the time horizon of the plan and can be long- or short-term. The most common long-term time horizons are three- and five-year plans. This does not mean that we make a plan once every three or five years. On the contrary, since planning is an ongoing process a five-year plan will be amended every year, modifying some of the later years in the light of this year's experience. Most organizations also have a one-year plan. The one-year plan is more concrete and often defines specific things that will be done. Long-term plans, on the other hand, tend to be futuristic and state where we want to be in three or five years' time. Thus, as the planning horizon contracts, so does its precision and certainty.

Organizations choose the planning cycle that suits their style. An organization's plan may in reality be a set of plans, each for a different time period, which will be coordinated and can be adjusted. Most organizations have a planning process that is followed every year to develop their plan for the next year and to amend their longer term plans.

THE PLANNING PROCESS

Having outlined the planning cycle, we must now consider how to go about planning. Perhaps one can characterize the planning process by a lot of discussion and idea generation, followed by idea evaluation. Newly generated ideas should take into account the current status. They should also look at the external environment and try to match it to the organization's internal capabilities, including the funds available for new initiatives.

Such discussion and idea generation is usually carried out by teams that represent a wide cross-section of the organization. It often has a top-down component, where senior executives may define wider plans, and a bottom-up component where specific internal problems are considered. A good process will combine both of these components into an integrated plan. Thus in the context of information system planning the top level would consider the broad objective of the system, whereas the bottom-up component would be more concerned with ways to achieve this through re-engineering or infrastructure development.

THE PLANNING GOAL

Planning must reach a balance between the pressures of the external environment and the use of total resources to meet these pressures. As shown in Figure 21.1, the external environment produces opportunities for the organization to make some gains. The plan must decide how the organization must deploy its resources to make these gains. Thus there are limits to the number of computers we can buy for the system and to the number of people we can hire to build the systems. Planning must make the tradeoffs between the various organizational constraints. Given limited resources, a system planner is faced with the problem of deciding what to begin now and what to leave until later. Thus priorities must be set during planning that will ensure the

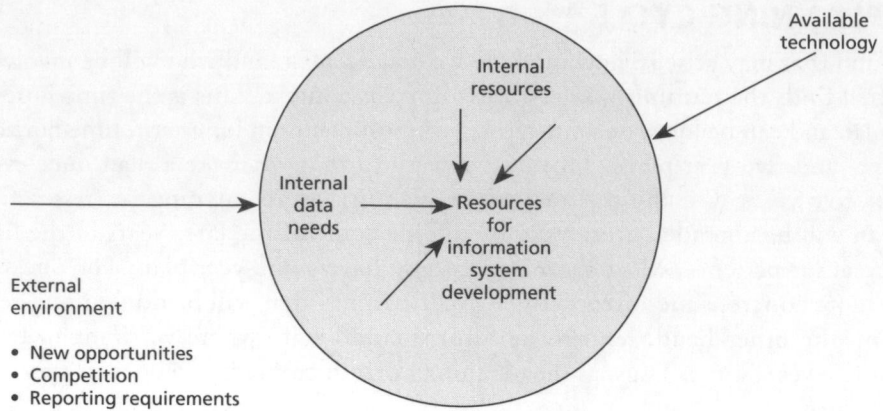

Figure 21.1 *The environment for strategic planning*

maximum return for funds invested in information system development. How is this choice made and how are priorities set? The questions that must be answered are: what new demands can the business easily satisfy, and what new equipment will improve the organization's operations? Answers to these questions are usually speculative and based on assumptions.

At an organizational level, many such questions are about the role of information systems. Re-engineering existing information systems is only one of the possibilities for improving an organization's standing. This must be evaluated against other possibilities, such as to increase research into new products, spend more on advertising, or replace production machines. All these possibilities must compete for the organization's funds.

 ## SOME GUIDELINES FOR PLANNING

Planning must generate alternatives, examine them, and consider the consequences given the various scenarios. We must evaluate each scenario to see what will be the most likely consequences of the proposed action.

It is also important to keep in mind that planning must consider information systems in the context of the whole organization. It considers how the information system can best help the organization to achieve its goals and ensure that the information systems plan fits into the organization's plan. The fit between information system and organization has a number of perspectives—namely, how the information system can:

- support the organization's ongoing operations and make them as effective as possible;
- change the organization's business strategy by making it possible for the organization to develop new products and services because of the availability of the information system, or to make a significant commitment to electronic commerce; and
- improve the quality of service provided to the organization's clients.

Most information systems have been used for the first of these reasons. They have enabled organizations to ensure that information is provided at the right time and place to support the organization's operations. The second capability of information systems has also been increasingly exploited. This has begun with financial industries where computer-based information systems provide additional scope to introduce new services, such as financial investment advisory services or new types of investment accounts. The third capability is now increasingly realized by making it easier to customize products, assist in providing help support services and enable customers to better track their service requests.

The planning process must be designed to take all these factors into account. It must ensure that there is interaction between information system planners and the rest of the organization. It must also require documentation that describes and evaluates the plan.

Discussion on planning is often based on guidelines or techniques. We outline some of these guidelines in this section.

STAGES OF GROWTH

A systems plan is often based on stages of growth within an organization. Nolan and Gibson (1974) in what has now become a famous paper, identified the stages of growth that all systems seem to go through. His four stages are:

1. Initial use and experimentation, where people in the organization use computers to support their local needs and see the benefits of using computers.
2. After some initial use, many people see the benefits of using a computer and this initial success encourages considerable proliferation and experimentation in computer use across many application areas.
3. Control of development, where management recognizes the advantages of using computers and tries to ensure that their prolific use does not lead to duplication and excessive resource use. This leads to the introduction of formal project management methods and design methodologies. Any new applications are now required to directly address the organization's goals. Coordination of future development becomes the responsibility of the information systems department.
4. Maturity, where there is better understanding of how computers can be effectively used, and users participate in system development. Information systems departments and users now work together in building systems rather than the department maintaining control of the systems.

Although Nolan's work first reached prominence in 1974, it is found that most organizations still go through the above stages when they introduce computers into their everyday operations. This framework gives planners a way of seeing how computer-based information systems evolve in an organization.

ANALYSIS OF STRENGTHS AND WEAKNESSES

Another common planning technique is to list the organization's strengths and weaknesses. By examining the internal resources of the organization, we can recognize areas where it may have developed special skills or is in a very good position to produce some product. Also we can recognize areas where the organization lacks a competitive advantage. Planning will then determine if the organization's strengths can be developed or used to do something from which it will benefit. Alternatively we may look at the weaknesses and determine what needs to be urgently improved. This can mean buying new machines, training or hiring people with new skills, or simply altering procedures.

IDENTIFICATION OF CRITICAL FACTORS AND PROCESSES

Core business
The main business function of an organization.

Following the analysis of strengths and weaknesses, it is often common to list the critical factors that must be developed for the organization to reach its planned objectives. One of these is to identify the **core business** and the critical business processes of the organization. The core business defines what the organization does. For a power company, this may be to provide electric power; for a telephone company, it may be communication. Strategic planning, therefore, should concentrate on the core business rather than on other activities within the company. Information systems are not perceived as being the core business of most organizations; they only support the core business. Some organizations now think that activities other than the core business should be viewed only as service functions, which could be obtained outside the organization.

Once the core business is identified, the next step is to identify the key business processes of the core business and concentrate on them in the allocation of resources.

TEXT CASE C: Universal Electronics—Looking to the Future

Universal Electronics has reaffirmed that its strength lies in its highly recognized set of products and is looking at improving its share of the market. It can do so in a number of ways. These include:

- enlarging its range of products, although this requires considerable investment in manufacturing facilities;
- increasing its marketing effort and improving client relations;
- improving its delivery services; and
- extending its information system to include its customers and allowing them to place orders electronically.

The company is also considering whether it is possible to subcontract deliveries, thus removing the cost of maintaining a fleet of delivery vans and allowing the company to concentrate on its core business of manufacturing electronic items. In that case, others argue, why not also outsource marketing and follow-up support, two areas that need improving anyway?

Management of the information systems department also wishes to re-engineer its infrastructure, converting the system to totally on-line operations with extension to the World Wide Web and thus eliminating items like delivery dockets. Regional centers are pressing for some decentralization of information systems to allow them to adapt to local client requirements. They claim that the organization is now well into Stage 3 of Nolan's model and has the necessary knowledge to progress to Stage 4. There has also been some talk about reducing the number of regional centers.

Strategic planners must consider all these alternatives, develop scenarios for them, decide what to do and set a long-term timetable to implement the decisions.

This includes such questions: What kind of service are our competitors providing? Are there any new ways of keeping in touch with clients? What do you think the kinds of strategic tradeoffs are? How much can the organization spend on developing and re-engineering information systems? How do these re-engineering plans affect overall operation? If you were the information systems manager, what arguments would you use to obtain funds to further develop information systems?

WHAT DOES AN INFORMATION SYSTEM STRATEGY LOOK LIKE?

There is no such thing as a standard description of an organization's information system strategy. It usually contains many components. There is often a statement of the organization's objectives and how information systems will help to meet these objectives. Some of the components of an information systems plan are described below.

APPLICATION DEVELOPMENT PLAN

This component identifies new applications to be developed over the plan period. It will define the application, the time when development will commence and finish, and the resources needed for the development. The relationship of applications to each other and to the organization's business plan must be clearly defined.

THE TECHNICAL PLAN

The technical plan is made up of a number of components.

Database strategy

One important component of any plan is the redistribution of the organization's data. Databases are now considered a valuable organizational resource. They include its client records, its inventory, and in some organizations it may include important business transactions or arrangements. Loss of such data could lead to severe repercussions within the organization. Important considerations include how to ensure data security and its distribution across the organization's computer network. Many strategic plans now also include a high-level enterprise data model that describes the major system entities and relationships.

Network strategy

The equipment strategy includes both the infrastructure and the specific items needed for specific systems. The infrastructure defines features that are common to all applications—for example, whether on-line is to be supported, whether equipment will be centralized or distributed, how the database is to be distributed, the kinds of terminals to be supported, the operating system needed, and so on. The equipment strategic plan will define any proposed changes to the infrastructure, how they will be supported, their timing, and their effect on existing applications. An increasingly important component of networking is how to provide people with the kinds of networking services that were described in Chapter 2—in particular, electronic mail and access to World Wide Web sites. Conversely, it should show how the organization will enable external clients and potential clients to access its service through networks.

An important part of planning is to coordinate all these component plans. This is usually done through graphs.

The technical infrastructure

Infrastructure
A basic structure for supporting a system.

An **infrastructure** is a major commitment of funds to provide the kind of support needed to develop planned applications. There are several broad considerations in developing an infrastructure strategy. First, we must determine in broad terms how the network will be used in the context of the business plan. Are we to allow individual departments to purchase their own microprocessors and develop minor applications on them, or are all such purchases to be coordinated? Do we have centralized or distributed systems? What information is to be kept in a data warehouse? Should a client-server approach be used? Once we decide on this broad approach, we must ensure that the equipment has sufficient capacity to support our applications.

To satisfy capacity needs, it is necessary to ensure that adequate storage capacity exists to store all the needed data and that there is sufficient computer power to maintain and process this data. We must also have enough terminals to allow access to this data.

Choosing an infrastructure with sufficient capacity places considerable reliance on statements in the strategic plan. We know broadly what we must do from the strategic plan; we now need to get the details. How many users will the inventory system have? Where are the users? What is the expected size of our inventory file? All this information is then put together to estimate the size of equipment.

Once agreement on an infrastructure is reached and the necessary funds are allocated, a search for the new equipment or software to construct the infrastructure begins. Depending on the size of the acquisition, tenders may need to be called and alternative proposals evaluated. Major tasks in realizing the strategy are the selection of equipment or software, its acquisition and final installation. The installation may require new accommodation and a new management structure.

Re-engineering strategy

Most organizations find that their systems eventually reach a stage where major change is needed. Re-engineering applies to both the business process and the information system. The business process may be changed to reduce the cost of running the business or to provide new services to clients. In either case, this often requires a change to be made to the information system.

The simplest way to change the information system is to change a program, or programs, and the database structure. However, eventually a stage is reached when it is no longer possible to change the system simply by adding a module or changing a data record structure. This may occur because a business application has radically changed, or because of changes in technology. There are a number of reasons for changing the technical part of the information system. These include:

- Changing a batch to a transaction and enquiry mode. This is often demanded by users, who wish to have a system with better characteristics though they have no new functional needs.
- Changing the technology to improve flexibility. This is often used as a justification to change to object orientation.
- Changing to a new architecture—as, for example, going to a client-server system.
- Changing to support task-oriented teams through better coordination and workflow technologies.

Figure 21.2 shows the process used to develop a technical re-engineering strategy. Here we start with the organization's legacy systems, or those systems developed in earlier days. We then develop a model for the new systems using a process known as **reverse engineering**, where components of the existing system are included in the model. This is often necessary because the legacy systems were not properly documented, or because incremental changes have made the original documentation obsolete. The model is then further refined to show the changes needed to meet new requirements of redesigned business systems. The model can use any of the techniques described in earlier chapters. Then a process known as **forward engineering** is used to propose how the existing system will be changed to meet the new requirements using the existing systems as much as possible.

As an example, we illustrate a possible plan for one of our case studies.

Reverse engineering
Developing a model for an existing computer-based information system.

Forward engineering
Re-engineering an existing system based on a model.

TEXT CASE C: Universal Electronics—A Plan for the Future

Following consideration during strategic planning, a decision was made that the core business of Universal Electronics is to sell electronic components and that top priority should be given to business processes concerned with the core business. Delivery was identified as an important business process, and a decision was made to re-engineer this process because of delays and losses of sales. The highest priority was then given to the inventory system, and lower priority was given to assisting schedulers. It was felt that very little improvement would result in vehicle scheduling

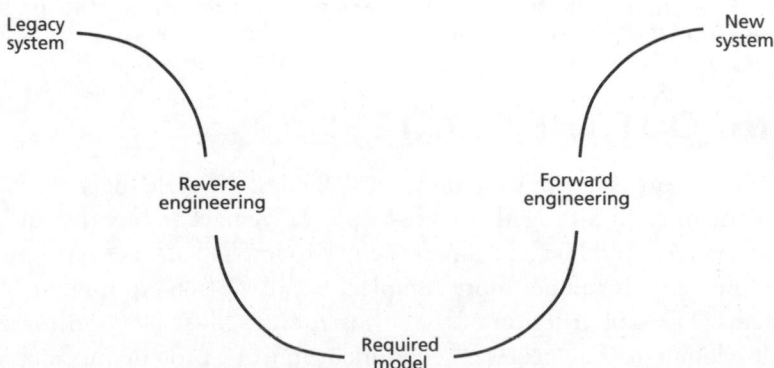

Figure 21.2 *A re-engineering strategy*

and it would become less important as inventory controls improved. The information systems plan was required to give re-engineering of the inventory management function its top priority, with emphasis on decentralizing many of the functions to allow regional centers to adapt them to their local needs. At the same time, facilities are to be provided through the World Wide Web for clients to directly place orders. It was also felt that profit levels could be improved, with increased emphasis on developing sales estimates and tying them directly to production.

The initial applications development plan for Universal Electronics is shown in Figure 21.3. The top priority is to re-engineer the inventory management system to automatically order items from the production department while allowing regional centers to adapt it to their needs. A sales estimates system is then to be developed which will be integrated with inventory management to provide inputs to a production planning decision support system. After this is completed, some decision support for delivery truck scheduling is planned, although this will depend on whether the organization continues to do its own deliveries. At the same time, production will be more closely integrated with the current accounting systems to allow better support for monitoring production costs. Following this, a personnel system is to be developed.

The information system will begin to integrate its databases and develop facilities to support such databases in a distributed environment. This will require establishing a data administrator function to oversee the development and implementation of an enterprise-wide data model. Additional storage, and a large increase of on-line terminals, will also be needed given a decision to move to on-line operation. Some funds were allocated for this purpose given the high profit levels of the organization in the previous year.

Figure 21.3 is a summary of the technical plan and the plan of personnel requirements and their deployment. The equipment must support further decentralization of information systems. Figure 21.3(c) shows estimates of the terminals and disk storage required to support such decentralization. Figure 21.3(b) shows personnel costs for maintaining existing systems and building new ones. There is, of course, close correlation between all the components of the plan; indeed, one of the reasons for making a strategic plan is to ensure that all the components of an information system are available when needed. Thus computer equipment is available in time for new applications, and personnel are available to develop these applications. Personnel are not kept waiting for equipment, nor is equipment kept waiting for personnel to use it.

Finally, a plan for acquiring the skills needed to implement the strategy must be devised. This will include training programs set up for existing staff or plans to hire additional staff with specific skills.

CARRYING OUT THE STRATEGY

Implementing a strategy is like putting the pieces of a jigsaw puzzle together. We know what we want and must put it together piece by piece. We have to buy the equipment, plan individual systems, and hire and allocate people to implement these systems on the computing equipment. It can get more complex, because often equipment is shared between systems. The construction of the infrastructure must be coordinated with application development. The necessary equipment must be provided to support new systems. If such equipment is not available, then the new system cannot be implemented.

(a) Applications plan

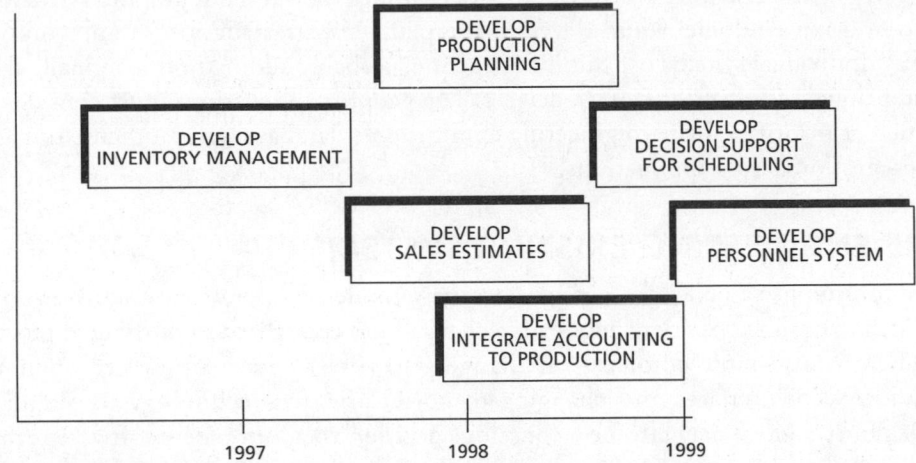

(b) Personnel costs

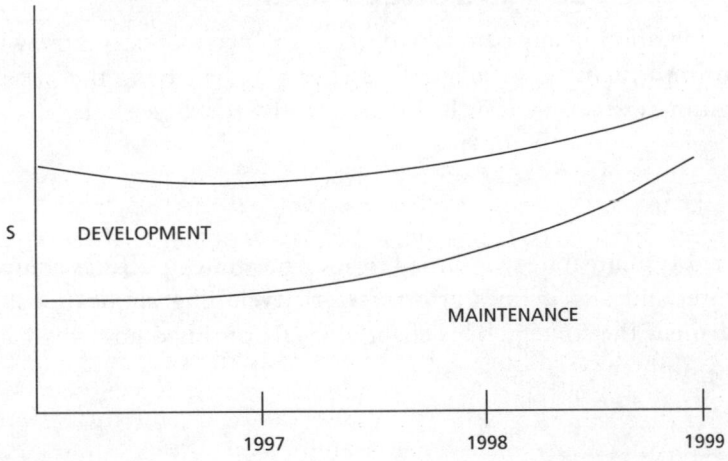

(c) Equipment needs

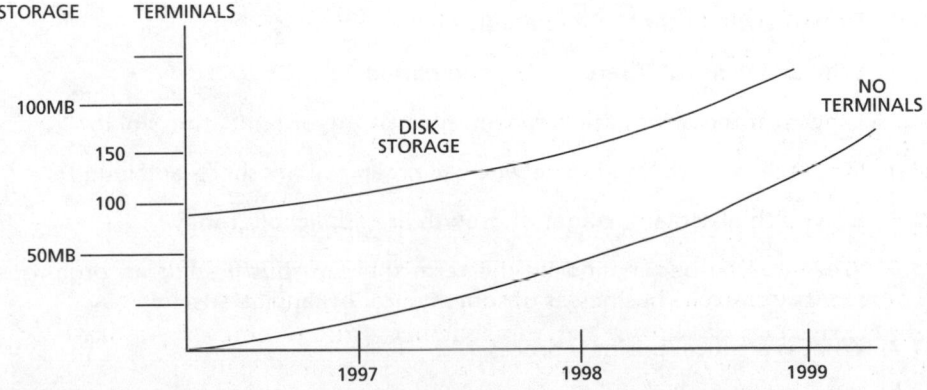

Figure 21.3 *Strategic plan summary for Text Case C*

An equipment acquisition strategy must run in parallel with the system development strategy. The equipment strategy first determines the fundamental infrastructure for computing equipment and develops the planned infrastructure in an evolutionary way. Individual systems use this infrastructure, probably adding to it marginally through additional terminals or storage devices. The plan for applications must consider issues such as priorities for re-engineering applications, database development strategy and integration across applications.

RE-ENGINEERING EXISTING SYSTEMS

A common example of a change to a new mode of operation is conversion from batch to on-line operation; another is a change from centralized to distributed processing. There is also more emphasis on changing to better client support through World Wide Web interfaces and changing to object-oriented technology to obtain more flexibility. There may also be a conscious decision to adopt a new software technique that gives the organization a new capability.

BUILDING UP A PEOPLE RESOURCES BASE

One important consideration in any plan is to develop the necessary expertise within the organization to implement the strategy. This requires identifying the necessary skills and either training existing staff or hiring new staff with these skills.

 ## SUMMARY

This chapter outlined system strategy in broad form. The strategy defines computer needs into the future, and also defines priorities for developing applications. The next step is to implement the strategy. This chapter briefly outlined how to go about implementing the equipment strategy.

 ## DISCUSSION QUESTIONS

21.1 Describe why you need a strategic plan.

21.2 Why do we need different planning periods?

21.3 Why must the information systems plan fit the organization's plan?

21.4 Why is there a relationship between an organization's short- and long-term plans?

21.5 Do you think Nolan's stages of growth are applicable today?

21.6 What do you understand by the term the *core business* of an organization? Identify the core businesses of some typical organizations.

21.7 What is a critical business process?

21.8 What are the main components of an organization's information systems strategy?

21.9   Describe the need for flexibility in computer system acquisition. Why is it difficult to precisely determine computer needs five years into the future?

21.10 Why must the application plan be integrated with equipment acquisition?

21.11 Should a strategic plan be considered as fixed or should it be possible to vary it? Justify your answer.

EXERCISES

21.1   The summary of information systems strategic plan for a wholesale organization which distributes garments to sales outlets is shown in Figure 21.4. This organization experienced difficulties in its invoicing, and its first priority is to develop an accounting system. The accounting system will cost sales orders as they are entered on-line and then generate invoices. This plan was developed the previous year and the development of the accounting system is now in progress. Once the accounting system is completed, it plans to develop both the sales and inventory control systems for its stock.

One sales system objective is to improve sales forecasting through forecasting customer demand and thus improve inventory management by ensuring that items with falling sales are not over-stocked. The inventory control system objective is to improve inventory management by ensuring that item holdings do not drop below safe levels. These systems will be on-line, allowing sales personnel to use its enquiry facilities to provide better customer service.

The cost of developing all these new systems is $340,000. However, due to adverse trading conditions, only $220,000 can be made available for information system development during the year. Rather than starting both sales and inventory control system development concurrently and putting forward their completion date, it is proposed to develop one system only and for it to be completed this year.

Mention some criteria that you would use to choose the system to be commenced this year. Assume that the core business of the organization is to make garments and distribute garments. The fact that it is a wholesale organization

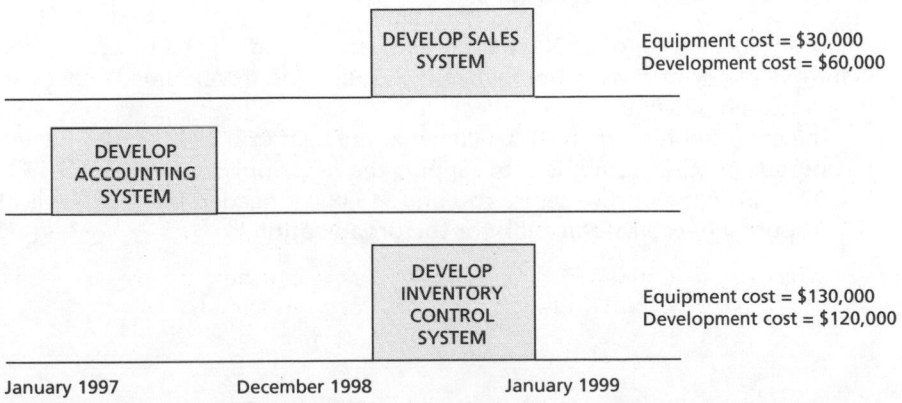

Figure 21.4 *A strategic plan*

and distributes garments to large retail stores makes customer service extremely important.

21.2 An organization is project-oriented and most of its projects are building contracts at a number of locations. So far each project arranges its own material purchases and hires its own contractors and personnel. Invoicing, however, is carried out at a central site. While the organization was small and had only a few projects, it was convenient to leave all decision making to the project sites. Some of these developed their own computer systems with assistance from a small information systems department. The main organization provided support services such as accounting.

However, the growth of project numbers in the last year has led to suggestions that some of the inventory problems and contractor hiring can be centralized to take advantage of the economies of scale. These economies include bulk buying of common parts and replacement of some contract staff by a pool of permanent personnel.

Current strategy

The current strategy is to support decentralized project decision making but to implement centralized systems to assist contractor assignment. The current proposal is to transfer CONTRACT-PAYMENTS into the invoicing system, as shown in Figure 21.5. The proposed equipment configuration is also shown in Figure 21.5. The invoicing system receives invoices from contractors at central office. The invoices are entered into the computer system at central office but are verified at the project site terminals. The results of the verification will be input through terminals and subsequently used to generate cheques using the CONTRACTORS-PAYMENTS system.

New strategy

The information systems strategic plan must now be extended to include additional systems. The following priorities have been established:

- A new inventory control system is needed to eliminate current inventory delays. The expected benefits here are $20,000 per annum with a development cost of $60,000.
- A new personnel system is needed to support a database of external contractors and internal personnel. The expected benefits are $15,000 per annum with a development cost of $60,000.

An additional saving of $5000 per annum can be made if the inventory control system is integrated with the invoicing system. The development cost for this integration is $25,000.

The expected funding is $100,000 per annum. Of this, $50,000 will be needed to upgrade existing equipment to support the new applications. Of this $50,000, $20,000 will be the infrastructure cost and $15,000 is needed for each application.

Propose a new strategic plan for the organization.

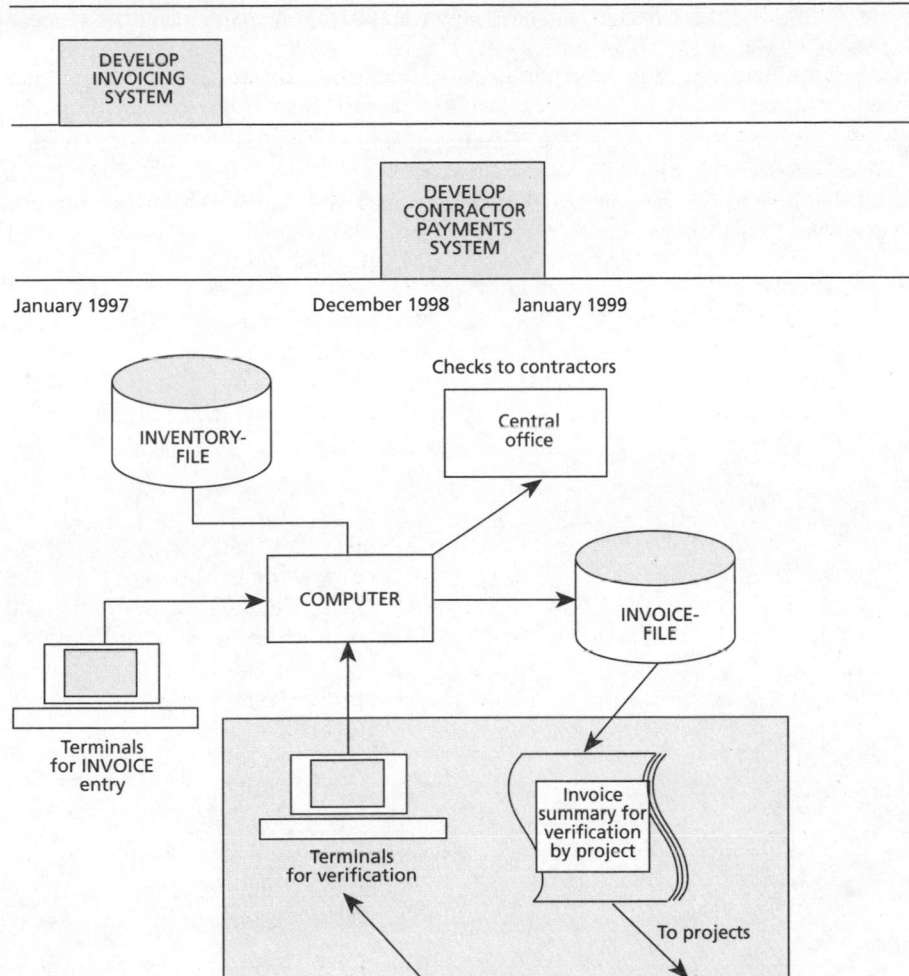

Figure 21.5 *Current system*

BIBLIOGRAPHY

Edwards, C., Ward, J. and Bytheway, A. (1991), *The Essence of Information Systems*, Prentice-Hall, New York.

Espejo, R. (January 1993), 'Strategy, structure and information management', *Journal of Information Systems*, Vol. 3, No.1, pp. 17–31.

McFarlan, F.W. (September–October 1981), 'Portfolio approach to information systems', *Harvard Business Review*, pp. 192–250.

McKeen, J.D. and Guinares, T. (1985), 'Selecting MIS projects by steering committee', *Communications of the ACM*, Vol. 28 No. 12, pp. 1344–62.

Nolan, R.L. and Gibson, C.F. (January/February 1974), 'Managing the four stages of EDP growth', *Harvard Business Review*, pp. 76–88.

O'Connor, D. (April 1993), 'Successful strategic information systems planning', *Journal of Information Systems*, Vol. 3, No. 2, pp. 71–83.

Robey, D. (October 1981), 'Computer information systems and organisation structure', *Communications of the ACM*, Vol. 24 No. 10, pp. 679–87.

Somogyyi, E.K. and Galliers, R.D. (1987), *Towards Strategic Information Systems*, Abacus Press, Tunbridge Wells, Kent.

Sprague, R.H. and McNurlin, B.C. (1993), *Information Systems Management in Practice*, Prentice-Hall, Englewood Cliffs, New Jersey.

Tibbets, J. and Bernstein, B. (December 1996), 'Legacy applications on the Web', *American Programmer*, Vol. 9, No. 12, pp. 18–24.

Quality assurance:
Reviews, walkthroughs and inspections

CONTENTS

KEY LEARNING OBJECTIVES

Quality assurance within the development process
The different kinds of quality assurance checks
When are inspections used?
What is a walkthrough?
How a walkthrough fits into the system development cycle
The structure of the walkthrough team
The process followed in a walkthrough

INTRODUCTION

Greater emphasis on quality in organizations requires quality assurance to be an integral part of information system development. It is important to keep in mind that quality assurance is not something that goes on separate to the development process. On the contrary, the development process must include checks throughout the process to ensure that the final product meets the original user requirements. Quality assurance thus becomes an important component of the development process. It is included in industry standards (IEEE 1993) on the development process. Chapter 7 described how a quality assurance process is integrated into the linear development cycle through validation and verification performed at crucial system development steps. The goal of the management process is to institute and monitor a quality assurance program within the development process. It is an important co-ordination in the process maturity levels described in Chapter 20, where level 3 requires quality assurance activities to be in place. A quality assurance program includes:

- *validation of the system against requirements;*
- *checking for errors in design documents and in the system itself;*
- *checking for qualitative features such as portability and flexibility; and*
- *checking for usability.*

Each of these objectives may be met by a different kind of quality assurance activity. This chapter will describe the reviews, walkthroughs and inspections that often make up the quality assurance program. The definitions and objectives of reviews, walkthroughs and inspections are not yet standardized and may mean different things in different environments. One general view is that reviews are usually made to check whether project management goals have been achieved, walkthroughs are usually made to detect errors in the system, and inspections are made to evaluate its qualitative features. It is also usual to distinguish between reviews made about project resource use, and checks as to whether a system model or technical proposal is correct. These are two different processes with different objectives, one to achieve correctness and the other to ensure effective utilization of resources.

Most organizations now require that proper quality assurance be defined by a set of well-defined steps in the development process rather than being an ad hoc *activity. Quality assurance thus requires special preparation. Since the goal of quality assurance is to look at earlier work, designers are required to prepare for a review, inspection or walkthrough, and be ready to carry out any checks or follow-up work needed. This chapter describes some of the methods used in quality assurance.*

There is also an important distinction between the quality control procedures needed in critical and non-critical systems. Critical systems are those where a fault or error can have dire consequences—as, for example, a nuclear plant failure or failure on an aeroplane. Special techniques are used to prove the correctness of such systems, including using formal proofs of correctness using mathematical techniques.

This is usually not the case with non-critical systems, where a less stringent approach is used usually based on inspections of code, verification of models through discussion and evaluation, and testing using test cases derived from user specifications. In these systems, quality assurance is usually carried out through reviews and inspections of products, in addition to the testing that takes place prior to product delivery.

IMPLEMENTING QUALITY ASSURANCE

So far, when we have discussed tasks it has been assumed that a person responsible for a task receives a request as an input and produces an output. This is as simple as that, when quality assurance is included into a process. Any task has additional requirements—in particular, a review requirement followed by an approval before it can be used to initiate the next task. Reviews are carried out by team members not directly associated with a task to check that task outputs match requirements, as well as satisfying best practice criteria.

The approval is usually part of the management process and is included to ensure that all the necessary reviews have been completed. Reviews can take a number of forms—the most common are inspections and walkthroughs.

Two things are often considered important in achieving quality products. One is a precise set of user requirements, against which general quality is measured. The second is documentation. In a large project, documentation is the central source of all the information needed by the team members. If it is incorrect or out of date, then team members are working toward the wrong goals or using wrong inputs to their work. This is again where management comes in. Not only must it develop and monitor reviews of task outputs, but it must also ensure that any documents used in the tasks are the correct documents. This is often achieved by providing support based on a configuration management system and ensuring that all team members place their latest outputs into the configuration management system.

INSPECTIONS

Perhaps the simplest checks to describe are **inspections**, which is what is done in most reviews. It is usual to allocate roles to people involved in an inspection and outline a procedure for them to follow. Some common roles are the **producer**, whose product is under review, the **inspector**, who evaluates the product, and the **moderator** who controls the review process. There is also a **reader**, who may guide inspectors through the product. It is important in such reviews that the people doing the inspection are not those that produced the product. Apart from their desire to ensure that their product passes the test, people who have worked on a product may not be aware of some of its shortfalls.

Some software engineers suggest that there be a phased program of inspections running parallel with system development, with an objective for each phase and an evaluation made against the objective for that phase. Inspections themselves would be formal, with reports made at defined life-cycle phases. Each of the roles in an inspection team would have well-defined responsibilities within the inspection team. Fagan (1986) suggests a procedure made up of five steps, namely:

1. *Overview*, where the producers of the work explain their work to inspectors.
2. *Preparation*, where the inspectors prepare the work and the associated documentation for inspection.
3. *Inspection*, which is a meeting moderated by the moderator and guided by a reader who goes through the work with the inspectors.

Inspection
An examination of a product to assure quality.

Producer
A person who produced a product.

Inspector
A person who examines a product to assure quality.

Moderator
A person who controls the progress of a review.

Reader
A person who guides the way a system model is examined.

4. *Rework*, which is any work required by the producers to correct any deficiencies.
5. *Follow-up*, where a check is made to ensure that any deficiencies have been corrected.

The important thing here is that the inspections are formal and have a report that must be acted on. It is also important that any recommendations made during inspections be acted upon and followed up to ensure that any deficiencies are corrected.

 # WALKTHROUGHS

Walkthrough
A quality assurance
activity to detect errors.

The **walkthrough** is a procedure that is commonly used to check the correctness of models produced by structured systems analysis, although its techniques are applicable to other design methodologies. Such checking has always been necessary in systems analysis and design. Walkthroughs differ from earlier methods in that they recommend a specific checking procedure and walkthrough team structure. Furthermore, they allocate specific tasks to various members of the walkthrough team and require documentation to be produced during and after the walkthrough.

The team must check that the model:

- meets system objectives;
- is a correct representation of the system;
- has no omissions or ambiguities;
- will do the job it is supposed to do; and
- is easy to understand.

How these checks are made depends on the kind of model, but whatever the model, it is important for the checks to proceed in an orderly way. Walkthroughs are one important method used in quality assurance. Another important feature of the walkthrough is that no actual design or system alteration takes place during the walkthrough; problems are only noted for further action. The responsibility of following up these problems is assigned to the walkthrough team members. The problems are documented in an action list, which also specifies which members of the team are to be responsible for following up these problems.

WHEN ARE WALKTHROUGHS CARRIED OUT?

Walkthroughs can take place throughout system development. In structured systems analysis, they begin when the physical and logical models of the existing system have been completed. The first walkthrough checks the existing system models to detect omissions and inaccuracies in them.

Walkthroughs should also be carried out on the new logical design to detect flaws, weaknesses, errors and omissions in the proposed design. The walkthroughs should be made first on the new logical model and later the new physical model.

There may be more than one walkthrough in each project phase, and there are no set times for doing them. It is time for a walkthrough when you reach a point where you have done all you can on a model and you need to be sure that this correctly represents the system. It is necessary to discuss what you have done with others to verify it.

HOW ARE WALKTHROUGHS CARRIED OUT?

The procedure followed in a walkthrough is shown in Figure 22.1. Before the walkthrough begins, the producers should ensure that obvious problems have been eliminated from the models. It is no good bringing together a walkthrough team to detect obvious and simple problems the model producers should already be aware of. A walkthrough team is brought together to apply the benefit of its combined knowledge to the whole system and to detect the less obvious system problems. It is not there to find simple modeling faults. Some people suggest that you should use a checklist on a structured model before you submit your documents to a walkthrough. The checklist includes the common kinds of errors that often occur in modeling and serves as a guide for detecting such errors.

Once the producers are satisfied with the model, it is time for a walkthrough. Two outcomes are possible from the walkthrough. One is that no errors are found in the model and it is accepted. In that case, review documents are prepared for a subsequent project review. The other outcome is where errors are detected in the model. In that case, an action list is produced. The model is then amended and later submitted to another walkthrough.

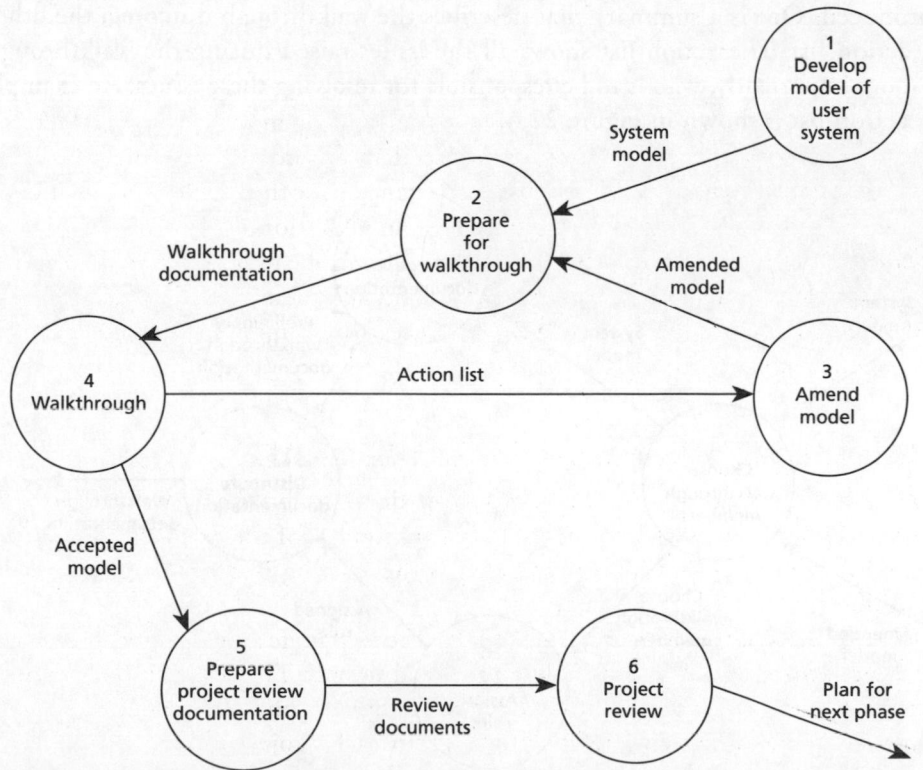

Figure 22.1 *Walkthroughs and reviews*

PREPARING FOR THE WALKTHROUGH

You must ensure that any model you have produced, and its associated documentation, is correct prior to carrying out a walkthrough. The last thing you want to happen is to have the review find trivial errors in your system. Hence models developed during system analysis must be reviewed by the design team before they are submitted to a formal project review. As shown in Figure 22.2, the first preparation step is to assemble the walkthrough team and assign roles to each team member. The next step is to distribute relevant documentation to all team members. The distribution must be made early to give team members sufficient time to become familiar with the documentation. When this has been done, the team members can be called together for the walkthrough.

THE WALKTHROUGH

The procedure used during the walkthrough is shown in Figure 22.3. The person who developed the model actually tracks through the documentation. This may involve following the data flows in a DFD, describing data stores, or going through the logic of each process. Any omissions, ambiguities or inaccuracies are noted in an action list during the walkthrough and followed up later.

WALKTHROUGH DOCUMENTATION

The outcome of the walkthrough is always documented. Usually only two documents are produced. One is a summary that describes the walkthrough outcome; the other is an action list. The action list shows all the issues raised during the walkthrough and, more importantly, who is to be responsible for resolving these issues. An example of an action list is shown in Figure 22.4.

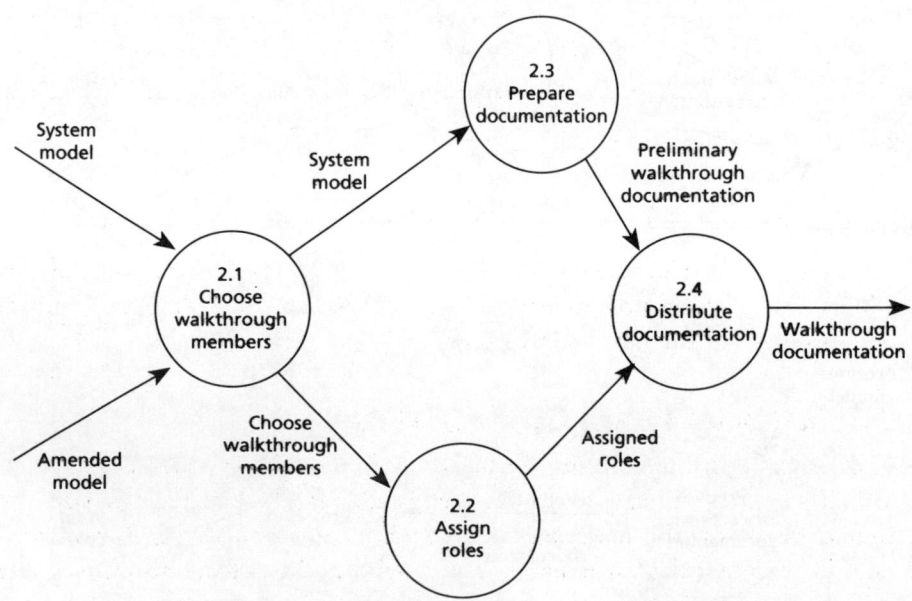

Figure 22.2 *Preparing for the walkthrough*

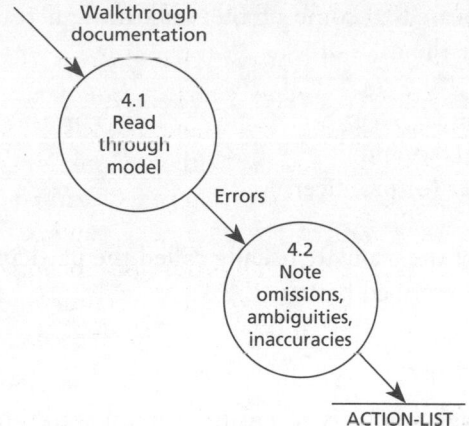

Figure 22.3 *The walkthrough*

WALKTHROUGH ACTION LIST System Description: System Producer:	Walkthrough Action List: Walkthrough Date: Walkthrough Leader:		
ISSUES RAISED	Diagram Reference	Assigned To	Amendment Completed

Walkthrough Secretary:

Figure 22.4 *Action list*

FOLLOW-UP

The follow-up is based on the action list. The members who have been assigned responsibility for correcting errors amend the model. When this amendment is completed, the model is ready for the next walkthrough.

WALKTHROUGH TEAM COMPOSITION

There is no fixed optimum size for a walkthrough team. Team members should be selected in a way that will ensure the material is adequately covered. The size of the team thus depends on the material to be covered and upon the skills and review experience of the potential participants. People with no knowledge about the system under review should not be in the walkthrough team. The number of participants will be somewhere between three and seven.

Specific tasks are allocated to some of the walkthrough team members. They are usually selected to take the roles of:

*   the walkthrough leader;
*   the walkthrough secretary; and
*   the walkthrough reader (or producer).

The remaining members of the team are usually called the participants. Specific roles of the team members are described below.

The walkthrough leader

The job of the walkthrough leader is to ensure a good walkthrough, or to report the reasons why a good walkthrough was not achieved. A good walkthrough produces an accurate assessment of the product as it now stands. One reason for failing to achieve a good walkthrough may be that one or more members of the team were unprepared.

The leader, who should be technically competent to understand points raised in the walkthrough, has a number of functions to perform before, during and after the walkthrough. When told by the producers that some work is ready for review, the walkthrough leader begins by collecting all the relevant materials, selects the people who are to attend the walkthrough, and distributes copies of the relevant materials to these people to ensure that they are well prepared. The leader must then set the meeting time, place and length of the walkthrough. Finally, one of the team members must be appointed as the walkthrough secretary.

During the walkthrough, the leader must make sure that the meeting keeps to the relevant topics and that everybody contributes to the meeting. Finally, the leader must get agreement on the outcome of the walkthrough and make certain that the agreement is truly understood by all the participants.

After the walkthrough, the leader sees that accurate reports are produced promptly and checks that the producer has a reasonable basis for clearing up any issues requiring attention. All relevant people must receive the walkthrough report.

The secretary

Normally, the walkthrough leader chooses one of the participants to take on the role of secretary, whose function is to record the result of the walkthrough.

Before the walkthrough, the secretary should meet all the other walkthrough participants and be able to identify them by name. The secretary must also collect all the available materials necessary for keeping accurate records of the walkthrough.

During the walkthrough, the secretary must record all issues accurately and state each outcome explicitly, unambiguously and neutrally.

After the walkthrough, the secretary prepares all reports promptly and gets all the participants to sign them. When this is done, the secretary distributes copies of the reports to all the relevant people.

The reader (or producer)

The producer's job is to describe the product under review. For structured systems analysis, this is usually a DFD together with any process description, data flow and data models. It is the producer who called the meeting, so every effort should be made to get the most out of the people at the meeting.

It is the producer's responsibility to go through the documentation and bring out any points that caused difficulty or uncertainty during the development of the documentation. The general procedure here is to follow data flows through the DFD. As each process is encountered, it may be elaborated (or leveled if necessary) to explain what it does. Any contentious issues about processes or flows should be raised in order to resolve them as soon as possible.

The walkthrough participant

Each member of the walkthrough team is a reviewer of the product being walked through and has personal responsibility for the outcome. Experience has shown that there are a number of rules each participant should follow to help make the walkthrough a success. First, the participant must be well prepared. If you do not know what is going on, you will contribute little or, more seriously, waste the time of the meeting.

The participant should take a neutral and constructive stand on all issues raised in the walkthrough. Thus discussions of style should be avoided, and participants should not become aggressive or criticize or evaluate the producers.

Each participant should make at least one positive and one negative point. This guarantees that each participant will have an input. Participants should raise issues, rather than resolve them, and attempt to learn about unfamiliar parts of the system rather than unnecessarily criticize them.

SUMMARY

This chapter gave a brief introduction to the kinds of activities that make up quality assurance. It stressed the importance of processes that are objective in order to find modeling errors in an organized way. This chapter outlined one such process, walkthroughs.

DISCUSSION QUESTIONS

22.1   Why is it necessary for quality assurance checks to be separated from system development?

22.2   Why is there a difference between checks carried out to detect errors and those to evaluate some of the more qualitative system features?

22.3   Why is it important for people to take formal roles during quality assurance?

22.4   Define some common roles used in inspections.

22.5   What are the roles used in walkthroughs?

 **EXERCISES**

22.1 Take a DFD that you have developed for one of the cases at the back of the text and walk through this diagram. The walkthrough should include a number of persons, each taking a walkthrough role. An action list should be created during the walkthrough.

22.2 Did you find that the walkthrough you just carried out was useful? Did any problems arise because you did not follow the walkthrough rules?

22.3 Why is a formal review of DFDs preferred to non-formal discussion?

22.4 Review once again the role of walkthrough team members in the light of your experience of a walkthrough.

22.5 Go through the walkthrough action list and, in retrospect, see if you missed anything important in the walkthrough. If so, what do you think was the cause of such an omission?

BIBLIOGRAPHY

Bach, T. (1995), 'The Challenge of "Good Enough" Software', American Programmer, Vol. 8, No, 10, October 1995, pp. 2–11.

Card, D. and Glass, R. (1990), *Measuring Software Design Quality*, Prentice Hall, Englewood Cliffs, New Jersey.

Fagan, M.E. (July 1986), 'Advances in software inspections', *IEEE Transactionson Software Engineering*, Vol. 12, No. 7.

IEEE (1993), *Software Engineering, IEEE Standards Collection*, The Institute of Electrical Engineers, Inc., New York.

Kaplan, C. and Clark, R. (1995), 'Secrets of Software Quality' McGraw-Hill, New York, 1995.

Knight, J.C. and Myers, E.A. (November 1993), 'An improved inspection technique', *Communications of the ACM*, Vol. 36, No. 11, pp. 51–68

Martin, J. and Tsai, W.T. (February 1990), 'N-Fold inspection: a requirements analysis technique', *Communications of the ACM*, Vol. 33, No. 2, pp. 225–32.

Sanders, J. and Curran, E. (1994), *Software quality: A framework for success in software development and support*, Addison-Wesley, Reading, Massachusetts.

Seigel, S. (January 1992), 'Why we need checks and balances to assure quality', *IEEE Software*, pp. 102–3.

Wesselius, J. and Ververs, F. (1990), 'Some elementary questions on software quality control', *Software Engineering Journal*, Vol. 5, No. 6.

Cases

CASE 1—SALES/ORDER SYSTEM

GENERAL DESCRIPTION

A distribution organization sells its wares through personal contact. Its salespersons visit prospective customers either with sample wares or with brochures and other descriptive material. Any customer orders are forwarded by the salespersons to either branch offices or the main office (depending on the salesperson's location). The orders may be forwarded by mail or by telephone. Each order contains the information shown in Table C1.1.

Table C1.1 *An order register*

Order no	Customer	Salesperson	Location	Status	Comment
075	K. Bloggs	Vicki	Store 7	Ordered	
092	B. Jog	Stan	In manufacture	Waiting	Expected August

Table C1.2 *Information in an order*

Sequence	Information
1	Customer name
2	Customer address
3	Date order taken
4	Salesperson
5	Any number of lines containing: • an item code (if the salesperson remembers it) and an item description; • the quantity of item; • the negotiated price.
6	Any special requirements

461

Branch offices and the main office have an order-processing clerk who receives orders from salespersons. The order-processing clerk keeps a register of all the orders. A typical register is shown in Table C1.2. Part of the registration process is to ɡ.ve the order a unique number, identify any items not completely described and allocate the appropriate item codes to items in the order. Any errors or inconsistencies detected by the order-processing clerk are often checked with the salesperson before final registration. The whole order is held over by the order-processing clerk until all inconsistencies have been resolved.

COMMISSIONS

The order-processing clerk is also responsible for computing salespersons' commissions. Salespersons send in their commission invoices at the end of every month, with the commission for each individual order itemized on the invoice. The order-processing clerk must check these invoices to determine their correctness and verify any detected discrepancies with the salesperson. The order-processing clerk then subtracts any commission for orders cancelled or lost through delivery delays. Usually a cancelled or lost order results in only 5 percent of the normal commission, with a limit of $5. The normal is 12.5 percent for sales generating up to $2500 sales revenue for the month and 15 percent for amounts that exceed $2500. When the commission amount is adjusted (if this is necessary), a commission check is ordered and a payment advice is sent to the salesperson. Records of commissions paid to salespersons are kept by the order-processing clerk.

CANCELLATIONS

Occasionally customers cancel orders. These cancellations are telephoned through to the order-processing clerk by the salesperson. The order-processing clerk changes the order register to reflect the cancellation and also sends a cancellation advice to the expeditor.

ORDERS AND ORDER REGISTERS

Orders are normally kept by the order-processing clerk, whereas the order register is the responsibility of the expeditor. The order-processing clerk, however, has access to the register to make the initial order entry. The order is also sometimes removed from the order-processing area and sent to other areas if needed.

HOW ORDERS ARE FILLED

Orders can be filled in one of three ways:

- by obtaining the required items from a store (owned by the organization);
- by ordering the items from a manufacturer (or wholesaler); and
- by manufacturing it.

It is the job of the order expeditor to choose one of these ways. The preferred way is to obtain the item directly from store. If the item is not available in store, the next preference is to order it from a wholesaler. The last resort is to manufacture it internally (if it is one of the items produced by the organization). If none of these methods is possible, the order must be rejected.

Each line of the order can be treated separately. Thus items in one order line can be obtained from the store and those from another line by ordering from a manufacturer. In fact, it is also possible to split an order line so that part of it is obtained from one source and part from another.

OBTAINING AN ITEM FROM STORE

The usual approach here is to select one or more orders for processing and formulate an item request to store for all items in these orders. One copy of the item request is sent to store and another retained by the expeditor. Each item has a unique identifier.

The staff at the store will check whether the requested items are in store and uncommitted. If so, the store advises the expeditor accordingly by an availability note. A copy of the availability note is kept in the store. This commits the store to hold the item for a specified period. The availability note includes a commitment number and length of commitment. A subsequent order must quote the commitment number.

If the expeditor requires the items requested in the availability note, a store order is sent. The store checks each received order against its record of availability notes and, if the order quotes a current commitment number, that order is met. If there is no current commitment number for the order, then the store file is checked for item availability. If the item is available, then it is issued; otherwise, the order is rejected.

PLACING WHOLESALER PURCHASE ORDERS

If the expeditor cannot get an item from store, then the expeditor will attempt to buy the item from a wholesaler. The expeditor will search a wholesaler file and then negotiate a price and delivery date with a selected wholesaler. Once the wholesaler is selected, a wholesaler order request form is prepared. A copy of this request form is stored by the expeditor in a purchase order request register.

Purchase order processing is done centrally. The wholesaler order request form (prepared by the expeditor) is sent to the main office for processing. At the main office, the purchase order request form is first keypunched and then read into the machine. The machine then generates the actual purchase orders, which are then sent to the wholesaler.

The wholesaler supplies the goods, together with a delivery advice. The delivery advice is checked against the purchase orders. If the delivery matches the purchase order, it is accepted; otherwise, a query is sent back to the wholesaler.

Advices about accepted orders are sent back to the expeditor from the main office, together with the delivered goods.

A computer system is currently available to keep track of orders sent to wholesalers. The system consists of a suite of programs made up of:

- INPUT—reads cards containing details of the wholesaler order as prepared by the expeditor (see Table C1.3). Edits the cards and creates an ORDER INPUT file.

- PURCHASE-ORDER-GENERATE (POGEN)—generates purchase orders. Purchase orders are generated once a week to take advantage of grouping lines from different customer orders into larger purchase orders to obtain volume discounts. A file of generated purchase orders is also created.
- DELIVERY—receives delivery advices from suppliers and correlates them against generated purchase orders.
- READY—prepares advices about customer order lines that have been fulfilled by a delivery.

INVOICES FROM WHOLESALERS

Wholesalers send invoices for provided goods. These invoices are received by the accounts department. They are checked against the purchase orders and, if correct, a check is issued. Any discrepancies between the invoice, purchase order and delivery advice must be resolved before a check can be issued to the wholesaler.

DELIVERY TO THE CUSTOMER

The expeditor forwards the goods to the customer as soon as they are received from the store or wholesaler. The goods are sent, together with a goods provided advice. At the same time, the expeditor checks the status of the orders. If the receipt of some goods completes the order, then a completed order advice, together with this order, is sent to the invoice clerk.

Table C1.3 *An expeditor order input to input 1*

Manufacturer/ wholesaler	Date	Item-code	Qty-needed	Customer-order-no	Order-line

OTHER ACTIVITIES

Customers may ring to enquire about the status of their orders. The enquiry is usually made to the salesperson, who then refers it to the order-processing clerk. The order-processing clerk attempts to answer the query by referring to the orders register and then locating the order together with any attachments.

Invoices are sent to a customer as soon as an order is filled. The invoice is prepared by the invoice clerk, who receives the complete order from the expeditor.

The store has a computer-based ordering system. This keeps track of standard lines and automatically generates orders for them (as soon as a reorder point is reached). Updates to the store database are made in batch. Cards are punched for any orders from the expeditor and these are used to generate stores issues. An on-line terminal is used to look up the current stock quantities. The order-processing clerks are responsible for compiling monthly reports on sales volumes by item and area.

QUANTITY OF DATA

The quantity of data for this case is given in Table C1.4

Table C1.4 *Quantitative data*

Data	Quantity
Number of orders	100/day
Average lines/order	3
Average value of an order	$250
Percentage of request met by the store	70%
Average time to get item from manufacturer	14 days
Average number of lost orders	15%
Average time from registration to store issues	2–5 days
Delivery time (expeditor to customer)	(sometimes longer)
Time to issue items from store to expeditor	2 days
Average duration for order registration and other processing	1–2 days
Number of order-processing points	15
Number of salespersons	200

CASE 2—TRAVEL ARRANGEMENTS

GENERAL DESCRIPTION

Customers come to a travel agency to arrange a variety of trips. A sales consultant deals with each customer for a particular trip. At the initial interview the sales consultant records all the customer's requirements.

The sales consultant will then advise the customer on possible trip alternatives and make any bookings on the customer's behalf. To do this, the sales consultant may refer to a variety of timetables, hotel locations or tour brochures.

If the travel arrangements cannot be completed at the first visit, the sales consultant will follow up the first visit with further bookings on the customer's behalf and confirm these with either a phone call or during a subsequent visit.

Once an itinerary is completed, an itinerary schedule is prepared and sent to the customer.

As soon as the itinerary is agreed, the invoicing can begin. The method of invoicing is explained below.

INVOICING

A copy of the invoice sent to customers is illustrated in Table C2.1. It contains the REF-NO of each trip and details of any bookings made on the trip. The invoice is a multi-purpose one in which each invoice line is applicable to all kinds of bookings made by the agency. For this reason, the DESCRIPTION field is used to store some of the details associated with each booking. If only a deposit is required, then the amount of the deposit is included on the invoice.

Once a customer returns the invoice with the payment, the accounts clerk reconciles the payment with the invoice. First the TOTAL-PAYMENT-AMOUNT and DATE-RECEIVED of the payment are recorded and a receipt is prepared for the customer.

Table C2.1 *Invoices*

CUSTOMER-ACCOUNT

NAME: JOE CAPONE ADDRESS:				INVOICE-NO: 369 DATE-SENT: 20 JULY 98	
REF-NO	HOTEL/AIRLINE/ TOUR AGENCY	HELD- UNTIL	DESCRIPTION	AMOUNT	DEPOSIT
3	QANTAS	3 Aug	Flight 203 to Melbourne	$230	$40
3	WINDSOR	6 Aug	4 night stay	$135	$40
5	VIVA	4 July	Hong Kong Tour B66	$950	$950
5	—	4 July	Extra China Trip	$143	$143
			Total owing	$1458	$1173

Then each line of the invoice is checked against the payment. If some invoice lines are not paid for, the payment is called a part-payment; otherwise, the payment is in full. If the payment is in full, then all bookings are confirmed and are recorded as paid for. If a part-payment is made, then those bookings that are fully paid for, or for which a deposit has been paid, are confirmed and the amount of payment (BOOKING PAYMENT) is recorded against each booking.

Another action also takes place when a payment is returned. After the payment is received, recorded and a receipt prepared for the customer, the accounts clerk prepares a payment advice (identified by PAYMENT-NO), together with a check (if necessary) to the hotel, airline or tour agency. This payment advice includes the commission. Sometimes early payments are held over for a few days and combined with those received from other customers to be sent to the same provider. The payment advice is shown in Table C2.2.

Any confirmations received from providers following a payment are sent on to the customer. A record of the confirmation is also made at the travel agency, including any relevant provider reference (PROVIDER-REF).

Cancellations of bookings and packaged trips can be made. Unconfirmed and unpaid bookings are simply deleted. Where some payment has already been made to the provider, the refund is determined. If a refund applies, then the booking clerk advises the provider of the cancellation and forwards a cancellation advice. This, together with any travel agency commission, is returned to the customer. Each cancellation is for one booking only, or one packaged trip only.

DATA USED IN MAKING TRAVEL ARRANGEMENTS

The following facts are known about travel arrangements made by the travel agency:

1. A travel agency keeps a record of each customer. CUSTOMER-NAME is a unique identifier of the customer, and each customer has a CUSTOMER-ADDRESS and PHONE-CONTACT-NO.

Table C2.2 *Payments*

PAYMENT ADVICE

TO: WINDSOR ADDRESS:		PAYMENT-NO: DATE-SENT:		
OUR REF-NO	DESCRIPTION	AMOUNT	COMMISSION	ENCLOSED
3	4 night stay for JOE CAPONE from 6 Aug (deposit only, balance to be paid by customer)	40	13.50	26.50
11	3 night stay for MARY BLUM from 11 Sep	90	9.00	81.00
		130	22.50	107.50

2. Each trip is identified by a unique REF-NO. Each customer can make any number of trips, but each trip is for one customer only. The DATE-ARRANGED and COST are stored for each trip.

3. Trips may either be PACKAGED-TRIPS or SPECIALLY-ARRANGED TRIPS.

4. A packaged trip is for one of the packaged tours that are regularly organized by tour agencies. The travel agency maintains the following information about each packaged tour: the ORGANIZATION-NAME of the tour agency, the TOUR-NAME, the START-DATE and the BASIC-COST. The TOUR-NAME is the unique identifier of the packaged tour within an ORGANIZATION-NAME and the same packaged tour may be available at more than one time. (Thus there may be a Hong Kong tour organized by both Agency A and Agency B. The Hong Kong tour by Agency A may in fact take place twice, with one tour starting on 6 December 1998 and the other on 9 January 1998.)

5. Each packaged trip is for one packaged tour. A field called EXTRAS is provided for each packaged trip to record any special needs of the CUSTOMER. There may be any number of packaged trips taking the same packaged tour.

6. A specially arranged trip is one where the travel agency constructs a trip out of a number of bookings. The booking can be either a hotel booking or an airline booking. Each booking is given a unique LEG-NO within a trip REF-NO. A special description is stored for each specially arranged trip. Each booking has a DATE-MADE associated with it.

7. A hotel reservation is made with one hotel. The travel agency keeps a list of a number of hotels. Each hotel is identified by a unique HOTEL-NAME and has an ADDRESS and FAX-NO. Each hotel booking is made with one hotel. The data stored with a hotel booking includes FIRST-DAY, LAST-DAY, ROOM-TYPE and DAILY-RATE.

8. An airline reservation is made with one airline. The travel agency keeps a list of airlines. Each airline is identified by a unique AIRLINE-NAME and has a PHONE-CONTACT-NO. Each airline reservation is made with one airline and is identified by a RESERVATION-NO. The reservation includes the STARTING-AIRPORT and DEPARTURE-TIME. The reservation also includes details of all the stopovers in the reservation. Each stopover includes the ARRIVAL-TIME, DEPARTURE-TIME and the STOPOVER-AIRPORT.

 ## CASE 3—STANDING ORDERS SUPPORT

The following activities have been identified in an organization.

STANDING ORDER CREATION

An organization receives standing orders from customers (identified by CUSTOMER-ID). The standing order is made for items (identified by ITEM-NO) that are supplied to customers on a regular basis, in this case daily. It is ascertained by a detailed examination of this activity that:

*   Items are identified by ITEM-NO, and information about the weight of items is kept.
*   The address of customers is kept. Both the one MAIN-OFFICE-ADDRESS and any number of DELIVERY-ADDRESSES are stored for each customer. A manager is associated with each DELIVERY-ADDRESS.
*   Standing orders are identified by S-ID. There is a separate standard order for each ITEM-NO to be supplied to each customer and an agreed ITEM-PRICE for that standing order. The standing order contains the ITEM-QTY required for each DAY-OF-WEEK. The DATE-INITIATED and the TERMINATION-DATE are stored for each order.

ITEM DELIVERY

Deliveries are made on each day to satisfy standing orders for that day. Each uniquely identifiable delivery is to one DELIVERY-ADDRESS of one customer and can include items in more than one standing order for the one customer. Detailed analysis shows that:

*   a delivery docket (identifiable by DELIVERY-NO) is made out at each delivery; and
*   the delivery docket contains the DELIVERY-DATE, DAY-OF-WEEK and the QTY-DELIVERED of each ITEM-NO together with S-ID for that item.

INVOICING

Every week an invoice is prepared and sent to the organization's customers. The invoice consists of all the deliveries made up to Friday of the previous week to one customer.

The invoice is shown in Table C3.1.

PAYMENT RECEIPT

Customers return their payments with the copies of one or more invoices. The payment is recorded against the invoice. Full or part-payments may be made for each invoice. The record consists of AMOUNT-PAID and DATE-RECEIVED. Each payment is allocated a unique number. This unique number is the same as the RECEIPT-NO of the receipt that is returned to the customer.

Note that one invoice may be paid up in more than one payment.

Table C3.1 *Invoices*

	DELIVERY-NO	ITEM-NO	S-ID	TOTAL-QTY	AGREED-PRICE	COST
INVOICE-NO: 63	6	23	70	6	1.20	$7.20
CUSTOMER-ID: John	17	37	10	30	.70	$21.00
WEEK-ENDING: 17 June 1996	33	87	16	10	2.30	$23.00
					TOTAL	$51.20

CASE 4—INSURANCE CLAIMS SYSTEM

GENERAL DESCRIPTION

The system is to be developed to support business processes for proving insurance for income protection. Such policies enable clients to receive payments when they suffer an illness or disability which prevents them from continuing full-time employment. The system is to maintain client policies and manage claims made on those policies, and any payments made on accepted claims to replace income.

The main processes supported are the establishment of policies and collection of premiums on the policies and the management of claims on these policies.

A number of use cases have been analyzed.

USE CASES

Set up insurance policy:
- Client approaches salesperson with requirements.
- Salesperson looks up benefit tables and advises client.
- Client decides to set up policy.

Client pays premiums:
- A premium is computed on acceptance of a policy and the client is notified of the amount.
- Client makes regular payments.
- A reminder notice is sent out when a premium is overdue.

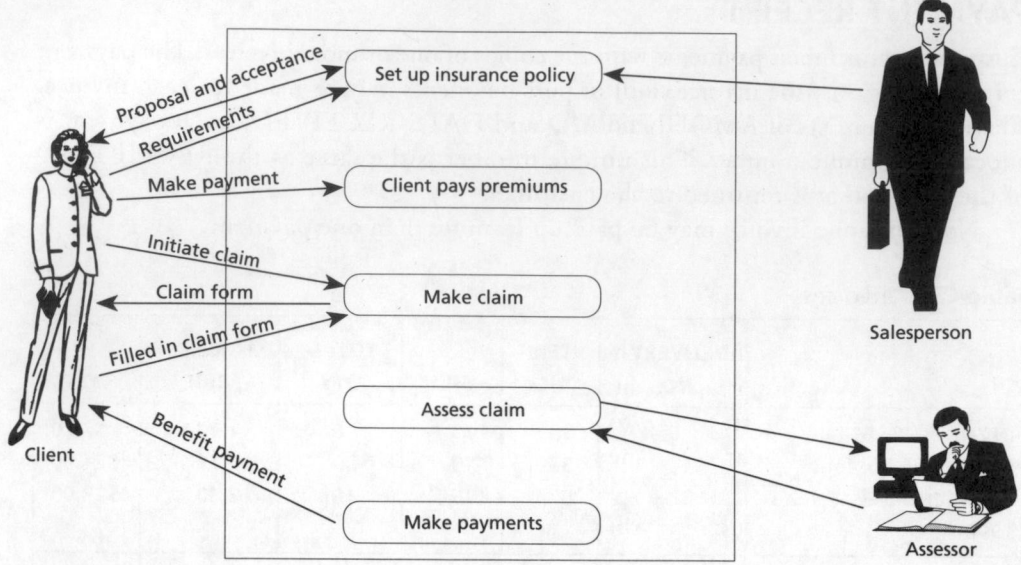

Figure C4.1 *Use case model*

Make and assess a claim:

- A client notifies the company of their intention to make a claim.
- A claim form is sent to the client and returned to the client once it is filled in.
- The claim is recorded and sent to the assessors.
- The assessment is recorded and the client informed of the benefits.
- A payments record is set up to make the payments.

Draw an event flow diagram for each of these uses cases, then suggest an initial class diagram for the system, showing attributes and methods. Figure C4.1 is an example of a use case model.

SOME ADDITIONAL INFORMATION

Making a claim

A claim must include information about:

- the disability type and whether caused by sickness or accident;
- income prior to disability;
- any worker's compensation payments;
- third party insurance claims; and
- other legislative amounts.

Claims are then assessed and a decision is made on whether a benefit is to be paid. In making the assessment, the claims assessor can refer to the client's policy and benefit tables and conditions.

Once a claim is accepted then regular payment claims must be made to the claimant.

Making benefit payments

Payments can be manual or automatic. The check system issues the check and informs the policyholder of the actual amount paid.

A manual check is issued whenever fast payment is needed. In that case, a letter to the client is also produced together with a check requisition form. Details from the requisition are used to issue the check.

Policy details

New policies include details of the client, including address and date of birth. The policy also includes the name of the agent who sold the policy, the waiting period and expiry date, together with a surrender value, if any. The start and expiry dates are included with each premium, together with the amount paid. New benefits can be added to the policy at any time, or refunds made on existing benefits, should the client so desire.

Policies can also include the following information:

- a waiting period;
- an expiry date;
- benefit type;
- any rehabilitation expense;
- minimum benefit for a specific condition; and
- benefit during the waiting period.

There are different conditions to be met for all of these benefits.

Policies also have no-claim bonuses which increase by a percentage over the first few years of a policy. Once a no-claim bonus period is completed, an escalating claim benefit is applied. Benefits increase with the consumer price index.

Glossary

Access requirements. Defining how databases are accessed.

Accounts payable. The subsystem that keeps track of the moneys owed by the organization.

Accounts receivable. The subsystem that keeps track of moneys owed to the organization.

Analysis model. A description of the way in which a system works.

Argumentation structure. A set of arguments used in making a decision.

Artifact. An object processed by a computer.

Asynchronous cooperation. Cooperation where the participants refer to shared information at different times.

Attribute in a relational model. A column of the table or list of values.

Attribute in an E–R diagram. A property of a set in an E–R model.

Autonomous agent. A person or system that makes its decisions independently of other systems.

Batch system. A system that groups a number of transactions for later processing.

Binary relationship. A relationship that contains entities from at most two entity sets.

Brainstorming. Coming up with new ideas.

Bulletin board. A space that stores messages accessible to all members by a cooperating group.

Business analyst. A person analyzing a business at the subject level.

Business process. A set of steps used to achieve a business goal.

Business process re-engineering. Changing an existing business process.

Business unit. A part of a business responsible for a well-defined business operation.

Cardinality. The number of relationships in which one entity can appear.

CASE tool horizontal integration. CASE tools from adjacent life-cycle stages integrated.

CASE tool integration. The ability of one CASE tool to accept the input from another.

CASE tool vertical integration. CASE tools integrated at the same life-cycle stage.

CASE tools. Computer Assisted Software Engineering tools used to keep track of system models.

Class. An object that describes a set of objects with the same features.

Class instance. An object that belongs to the class.

Client relations subsystem. That part of the system that interacts directly with the organization's clients.

Client-server process. A process that describes how a server provides a service to a client.

Clients. People from outside an organization that deal with the organization.

Closed question. A question that requires a direct answer.

Collaboration. Two or more people deciding together on their future activities.

Communication. Interchange of information between people and/or machines.

Computer network. A set of computers connected by communication lines.

Computer node. A computer in a computer network.

Computer operator. A person who operates computers.

Computer-based information system. An information system that uses computers.

Conceptual solution. A broad description of how a system will work.

Configuration. A set of documents used in a system development project.

Configuration management. Managing a configuration.

Context diagram. A diagram that shows the inputs and outputs of a system.

Controls. Checks to ensure that system inputs are correct and do not destroy system integrity.

Conversation. A sequence of speech acts.

Conversion technique. A method used to convert one system model to another system model that uses a different set of modeling constructs.

Cooperative design. Creating new artifacts by joint agreement between a number of participants.

Core business. The main business function of an organization.

Creativity. Coming up with new and innovative ideas.

Critical business process. A business process that is crucial to the survival of a business and supports the core business of the organization.

CSCW (Computer Supported Cooperative Work). Systems that support groups of people working toward a common goal.

Customization. Adapting an object for use in an application.

Data dictionary. A document that contains the DFD and a description of all its components.

Data entry. Transaction input for later batch processing.

Data flow. Data flowing between processes, data stores and external entities.

Data flow diagram (DFD). A method to illustrate how data flows in a system.

Data mining. Looking for patterns in databases.

Data store. A component of a DFD that describes the repositories of data in a system.

Data warehousing. The storage of large volumes of data for organizational use.

Database. An organized store of data.

Database definition. A definition of a database used as an input to a DBMS.

Decision support system. A system that supports decision making.

Dependent entity set. A set of entities whose existence depends on other entities.

Design. Creation of an artifact.

Design methodology. A collection of modeling methods and conversion techniques that start with a model of the user system and produce a computer system.

Design model. A description of the required system using system terms.

Design rationale. The reasoning behind making a decision.

Development process. A set of steps used to build a system.

Development world. The context in which technical development takes place.

Dialog. An interaction sequence between a user and a computer.

Direct access. Retrieval of records based on keywords.

Document configuration. The structure of documents within a project dictionary.

Domain of change. That part of a logical DFD of an existing system that will be changed in the new system.

E-mail. A way of using computers to exchange messages between people.

Economic feasibility. An evaluation to determine whether a system is economically acceptable.

Emic. An inside view of a system.

Empowerment. Giving people additional authority within an organization.

Encapsulation. Inclusion of many features in the one object.

Entity. A distinct object in a system.

Entity set. A component in an E–R diagram that represents a set of entities with the same properties.

Entity-relationship (E–R) model. A model that represents system data by entity and relationship sets.

Ethnography. Gathering information by observation.

Etic. An outside view of a system.

Event flow diagram. A diagram that shows the sequence of information flows between objects.

Event trace diagram. A diagram showing dynamic relationships between objects.

Evolutionary design. An experimental way of gradually building a system.

External entity. An object outside the scope of the system.

Feasibility analysis. An evaluation of whether it is worthwhile to proceed with a project.

Features. A characteristic of a class.

Federated database system. A set of databases managed independently but accessible in a unified way.

Feedback. Using variations from a system goal to change system behavior.

Fifth normal form. A set of relations that have no multivalued redundancy.

Financial services system. A system that keeps track of an organization's financial resources.

Formal interaction. A set of rules that define how people must interact.

Forward engineering. Re-engineering an existing system based on a model.

Function. A part that produces well defined outputs from given inputs.

Functional dependency. Where one value of an attribute determines a single value of another attribute.

General accounts. A system that keeps track of funds within an organization.

Groupware. Software that assists workgroups.

Heterogeneous network. A computer network made up of different computers and software.

Homogeneous network. A computer network made up of the same computers and network.

Human resources subsystem. The part of a business that maintains personnel policy.

Identifier. A set of properties whose values identify a unique object in an object set.

Illocutionary act. The intention of a speech act.

Informal interaction. Working together without a set of prearranged rules.

Information system. A system that provides information to people in an organization.

Infrastructure. A basic structure for supporting a system.

Inheritance. Using the same features as another object.

Inspection. An examination of a product to assure quality.

Inspector. A person who examines a product to assure quality.

Instance. A unique occurrence of a type of object.

Integrated databases. A set of databases managed by a single controlling system.

Interaction. The way people work together to achieve a goal.

Internet. A world wide public network allowing global exchange of information.

Interviewing. Gathering information by asking questions.

Intranet. A network supporting information exchange within an organization.

Inventory. The business function that manages an organization's parts.

Legacy system. An existing working computer system that is to be used in a new business process.

Leveling. Expanding a process into more detailed processes.

Library. A collection of objects that can be reused in many applications.

Linear cycle. A set of predefined steps for building a system.

Logical DFD. Describes the flow of logical data components between logical processes in a system.

Logical process. Describes any changes of values made by the processes on logical data.

Logical record structure. A way of describing records at the system level.

Management. People responsible for organizing and allocating resources.

Management process. The tasks required to manage a development process.

Market research. Determining how to make products acceptable to customers.

Marketing subsystem. A system that determines what an organization is to produce and then publicizes its products.

Materials subsystem. The part of the business that keeps track of its material resources.

Mental model. The way a user sees a problem.

Menu. A set of alternative selections presented to a user in a window.

Merged subset. A collection of objects from more than one entity set.

Methods. A feature that describes programs within an object.

Middleware. Software that connects network services.

Mission. A reason for the existence of an organization.

Modeling construct. A representation that can be used to represent a system component in a system model.

Modeling method. A method used to construct a model of a system.

Modeling procedure. A set of steps provided by a modeling method to create a system model.

Moderator. A person who controls the progress of a review.

Monitoring a system. Checks made to see if a system is meeting its goal.

Multimedia. Integrated storage of information in different media such as graphs, voice, video or alphanumeric data.

Multiple relationship set. A relationship set where the same two entities can appear in more than one relationship.

Multivalued dependency. Where one value of an attribute determines a set of values of another attribute.

N-ary relationship. A relationship that includes entities from more than two entity sets.

Network service. A technical system to support interaction between people.

Normal form relations. A set of relations that describes the data in a system, but where each data component is a simple value.

Object set. A generic term that includes entity sets, relationship sets, subsets and dependent entity sets.

Occurrence diagram. A diagram that represents entities and relationships.

On-line transaction. A transaction made through a terminal.

Open question. A question that requires the responder to express a viewpoint.

Operational feasibility. An evaluation to determine whether a system is operationally acceptable.

Optimal normal form. Set of relations that have no single-valued redundancy.

Organization chart. A chart that shows the business units of the organization.

Outsourcing. Arranging for computer processing to be done outside the organization.

Patterns. A collection of objects that can be adapted to an application.

Payroll subsystem. A business system for paying the organization's personnel.

Perlocutionary act. The effect of a speech act on a hearer.

Personnel development subsystem. A business system for maintaining people's skills.

Personnel subsystem. A business system for keeping information about people.

Phase. A step in the development process.

Physical DFD. Describes the flow of physical data components between physical operations in a system.

Physical process. Usually a physical device used to transform data—for example, computer, person, and so on.

Planned work. Work where the sequence of tasks can be predefined.

Platform. A collection of computer services.

Polymorphism. Selecting the method appropriate for the class of object called.

Presentation. The layout of information on a computer screen.

Privacy. Ensuring that information remains accessible to one or a selected number of people.

Probe. A question that follows up an earlier answer.

Problem-solving cycle. A set of steps that start with a set of user requirements and produces a system that satisfies these requirements.

Process. A component of a DFD that describes how input data is converted to output data.

Process. A set of steps that define how things are done.

Producer. A person who produced a product.

Production subsystem. An organizational function that produces physical goods.

Productivity tools. Software systems that assist analysts and designers to build computer-based information systems.

Programmer. A person who writes computer programs.

Project dictionary. A record of all documents produced during system design.

Properties. A feature that describes values stored within an object.

Prototyping. A method used to test or illustrate an idea and build a system in an explorative way.

Quality assurance. A process to ensure the development of quality products.

Quality service. A service that meets all client needs in a mutually satisfactory way.

Questionnaire. Gathering information by filling in a form.

Re-engineering. Changing an existing system.

Reader. A person who guides the way a system model is examined.

Relation. A table or list of values.

Relation key. A set of attributes whose values identify a unique row in a relation.

Relational model. A set of tables that describes the data in a system.

Relationship. One interaction between one or more entities.

Relationship set. A component in an E–R diagram that represents a set of relationships with the same properties.

Requirements model. A description of what users require the system to do.

Reuse. Using an existing system or module for a new task.

Reverse engineering. Developing a model for an existing computer-based information system.

Rich picture. A pictorial representation of a system.

Robustness. Ability to prevent interface errors from corrupting the system.

Role. The responsibility undertaken by a person.

Scenario. A description of a process in the usage world.

Screen. All the information presented to a user by a computer.

Script. A description of a process.

Seamless platform. A platform whose services are closely integrated.

Search procedure. The process followed to gather information about a system.

Search strategy. A selection of sources and methods to be used to gather information about a system.

Security. Ensuring that computer system faults do not destroy the information stored about a system.

Situated work. Work where the next task is determined from the current situation.

Skeleton object. An object that can be customized for more than one application.

Soft system methodology. A development process centering on the user and subject worlds.

Software configuration. The documents used in a development process.

Software process. Another term for system life cycle but concentrating on software development.

Specialization. Taking on features in addition to those inherited from another object.

Speech act. An interaction between two people based on a single utterance.

Staged development. Building a system by parts.

State diagram. A diagram showing how objects evolve.

Statement of user requirements. A formal definition of what the new system must do.

Storyboard. A sequence of screens that illustrates how a system will work.

Storyboarding. A sequence of computer screens to describe how a system will be used.

Strategic planning. Determining the broad objectives for an organization.

Strategy. The broad objective for an organization.

Structure chart. Program modules and their interconnection.

Subject world. A system seen and described in well-defined business terms.

Subset. Some of the objects from one entity set.

Subsystem. A part of a system.

Supporting process. A process to provide facilities needed by development teams.

Synchronous cooperation. Cooperation where the participants refer to shared information at the same time.

Synthesis. Building a system from existing modules.

System. A collection of components that work together to realize an objective.

System analyst. A person who analyzes the way the system works and its problems.

System boundary. The set of system components that can be changed during system design.

System component. An identifiable part of a system. Examples are computers, persons, documents, data records, and so on.

System development cycle. Another term for the problem-solving cycle.

System development methodology. A predefined set of steps, together with a collection of tools used to design a system.

System directory. Another term for project dictionary.

System environment. Things outside the system study that can affect system behavior.

System life cycle. Another term for the problem-solving cycle.

System model. A model of a system created by using a modeling method.

System procedure. Defines actions to be taken to accomplish a system task.

System specification. A precise description of what the system must do.

System world. A system seen and defined using general system terms.

Systems analysis. Finding out what a system does and what its needs are.

Technical feasibility. An evaluation to determine whether a system can be technically built.

Terms. Words with specific meaning used to describe systems.

Testing. Checking to see if a system does what it is supposed to do.

Transaction. A simple interaction with a computer database.

Transaction processing system. A computer system that manages transactions.

Transparent access. Accessing data from a network independently of its location in the network.

Tuple. A row in the relation.

Usability. A term that defines how easy it is to use an interface.

Usability metrics. The things that can be measured to describe usability.

Usage world. A system seen and described using everyday terms.

Use case. A description of work in usage world terms.

User-friendly. A helpful interface.

User requirements. What users expect the system to do for them.

Validation. Checking whether a particular product satisfies user requirements.

Verification. Checks to ensure that a particular input has been converted correctly to an output.

Version. A variation of the same document.

Walkthrough. A quality assurance activity to detect errors.

Waterfall cycle. The same as a linear cycle.

Weak entity set. Another term for a dependent entity set.

Window. An enclosed area on a screen.

WISIWIG. 'What I see is what I get' interface.

WISIWYS. 'What I see is what you see' interface.

Workflow. An instance of a workflow process.

Workflow process. A process made up of a predefined set of steps.

Workgroup. A group of people working to a common goal.

Workspace. The space and facilities provided for a user on a screen.

World Wide Web (WWW). A service supported on the Internet for the exchange of multimedia information.

Index